Heavens & Hells of the Mind

IMRE VALLYON

Heavens & Hells of the Mind

Volume IV

LEXICON

Sounding-Light Publishing

Heavens and Hells of the Mind, by Imre Vallyon
First edition: October 2007

Sounding-Light Publishing Ltd.
PO Box 771, Hamilton 2015, New Zealand
www.soundinglight.com

Four volume boxed set:
ISBN 978-0-909038-30-4

Individual volumes:
ISBN 978-0-909038-31-1 Volume I: Knowledge
ISBN 978-0-909038-32-8 Volume II: Tradition
ISBN 978-0-909038-33-5 Volume III: Transformation
ISBN 978-0-909038-34-2 Volume IV: Lexicon

Printed in Hong Kong by Regal Printing Ltd.

Source: A selection of the author's handwritten manuscripts dating from 1982 to 2006.

Photo Credits: All photographic images Gérard Stampfli with the following exceptions:
Page 159: NASA, ESA and Jesús Maíz Apellániz (Instituto de astrofísica de Andalucía, Spain).
Acknowledgment: Davide De Martin (ESA/Hubble). Source: ESA
Page 1103: NASA Goddard Space Flight Center, by Reto Stöckli and Robert Simmon
Page 1483: NASA, ESA, S. Beckwith (STScI), and The Hubble Heritage Team (STScI/AURA). Source: ESA
Page 1585: SOHO (Solar and Heliospheric Observatory) (ESA and NASA)
Page 141, 467, 1657: Hamish Cattell
Page 205, 717, 1363, 1411, 1555, 1643: Manu Vallyon
Page 1491: Yaël Pochon

I dedicate this book to the aspiring Soul of Humanity across the planet.
We are One Planet, One Humanity, One Life, One God, One Reality.

May this book help you to recover your own lost Wisdom,
the knowledge of your real Self, and the knowledge of the Real God,
the Bright Eternal SELF that is the Truth, the Love and your own Cosmic Life.

Imre Vallyon

Volume IV: Lexicon

Contents

Overview x
Contents I xi
Contents II xii
Contents III xiii
Charts and Diagrams I xiv
Charts and Diagrams II xvi
Charts and Diagrams III xvii

Appendix A **Detailed Contents** 1731

Appendix B **Lexicon of the Wisdom Language** 1759

Appendix C **Index** 1941

Appendix D **The Foundation for Higher Learning** 2077

OVERVIEW

Heavens and Hells of the Mind

Volume I
KNOWLEDGE

Part 1	Cosmology Unveiled	9
Part 2	Earth Life	267

Volume II
TRADITION

Part 3	Yoga: The Science of Union	517
Part 4	Pure Christianity: The Religion of Love	607
Part 5	Zen: The Path to Enlightenment	749
Part 6	Sūfī Meditation: The Way of the Holy Fire	825
Part 7	Tantra: The Path of Relationship	903
Part 8	The Warrior School: The Way of the Noble Warrior	967

Volume III
TRANSFORMATION

Part 9	The Path of Return	1115
Part 10	The Way of the Heart	1249
Part 11	The Way of Spiritual Psychology	1361
Part 12	The Worship of the Goddess	1481
Part 13	The Yoga of the Sun	1583
Part 14	The Path of Service	1677

Volume IV
LEXICON

Appendix A	Detailed Contents	1731
Appendix B	Lexicon of the Wisdom Language	1759
Appendix C	Index	1941
Appendix D	The Foundation for Higher Learning	2077

Volume I: Knowledge

Contents

Foreword . . . xii
Notes on Sacred Language Usage . . . xvi
The word 'Mind' . . . xvi
The Power of Language . . . xvii
The word 'Man' . . . xvii
Prologue . . . xviii
Acknowledgments . . . xix

Introduction I: Knowledge and Ignorance . . . 1

Part 1 Cosmology Unveiled

1 Planes of Being . . . 11
2 The Human Constitution . . . 31
3 Kāmaloka: The Astral Plane . . . 57
4 Devāchan: The Mental Plane . . . 73
5 Buddhi: The Realm of Unities . . . 83
6 Nirvāṇa: The World of Glories . . . 93
7 The Divine Being . . . 103
8 Kuṇḍalinī and the Goddess . . . 141
9 Creation and Evolution . . . 159
10 The Creative Hierarchies . . . 187
11 Origins of Evil . . . 205
12 Karma and Reincarnation . . . 231

Part 2 Earth Life

13 Atlantis Revisited . . . 269
14 Psychic Phenomena . . . 289
15 Channelling and Mediumship . . . 317
16 Telepathy . . . 345
17 Magical Manifestation . . . 355
18 Human Consciousness . . . 373
19 Death and Liberation . . . 397
20 The Mystery of the Heart . . . 425
21 The Call of the World Mother . . . 467
22 Awakening the Human Glory . . . 489

CONTENTS I

CONTENTS II

Volume II: Tradition

Contents

Introduction II: By Whichever Path . . . 511

Part 3 Yoga: The Science of Union

23 The Goal of Yoga . . . 519
24 Gems from Patañjali's Yoga Sūtras . . . 531
25 Aṣṭāṅga Yoga . . . 559
26 The Yoga of Miraculous Powers . . . 577

Part 4 Pure Christianity: The Religion of Love

27 Teachings of the Saints . . . 609
28 The Heart of Christianity . . . 623
29 Christian History . . . 641
30 Jesus the Christed One . . . 659
31 Christian Fundamentalism . . . 675
32 Christian Prayer . . . 689
33 The Christian Path . . . 717
34 The Greek Mystery Language . . . 731

Part 5 Zen: The Path to Enlightenment

35 The Spirit of Zen . . . 751
36 The Eternal Tao . . . 771
37 Zen Meditation . . . 785
38 The Path of Zen . . . 805

Part 6 Sūfī Meditation: The Way of the Holy Fire

39 The Sūfī . . . 827
40 The Sūfī Heart . . . 843
41 Sūfī Prayer . . . 863
42 Sūfī Mind . . . 885

Part 7 Tantra: The Path of Relationship

43 The Circle of Love . . . 905
44 The One-Hundred-and-Twelve . . . 945

Part 8 The Warrior School: The Way of the Noble Warrior

45 The Spiritual Warrior . . . 969
46 Warrior Training . . . 1001
47 The Primordial Sound Language . . . 1025
48 The Warrior Code . . . 1077

Volume III: Transformation

Contents

Introduction III: The New Spirituality 1103

Part 9 The Path of Return

49 The Aquarian Way 1117
50 The Aquarian Group-Consciousness 1145
51 The Science of Meditation 1173
52 Meditation Practice 1201
53 The Heart and Spontaneous Meditation 1227

Part 10 The Way of the Heart

54 The Heart and the Lost Art of Prayer 1251
55 Hṛdayaṁ: Meditations in the Heart Centre 1279
56 The Heart and the Future Evolution of Man 1309
57 The Way of Holiness 1335

Part 11 The Way of Spiritual Psychology

58 The Psychology of Consciousness 1363
59 Time and Eternity: Action and Destiny 1399
60 Metanoia: The Renaissance of the Mind 1411
61 Mahāvākya: Great Truth Statements 1469

Part 12 The Worship of the Goddess

62 The Great Goddess 1483
63 The Heart of the Divine Mother 1491
64 Śrī-Vidyā: The Holy Science 1515
65 The One-Hundred Names of Lalitā 1555

Part 13 The Yoga of the Sun

66 The Mystery of the Sun 1585
67 The Gāyatrī-Mantra 1601
68 Works of Silence 1643
69 Salutations to the Sun 1657

Part 14 The Path of Service

70 Buddhi Yoga: Liberation by Wisdom 1679
71 The Call to Service 1705
72 In Service to the Spiritual Hierarchy 1719

CHARTS & DIAGRAMS I

Volume I: Knowledge

Charts & Diagrams

Cosmology Unveiled

The Seven Great Planes of Being . . . 15
The Seven Subplanes of the Physical Plane . . . 16
Cosmological Systems Compared . . . 18
Walls of Time and Space . . . 21
Polarities of Forces between the Planes . . . 25
The Seven Elementary Qualities . . . 28
The Planes and the Elementary Attributes . . . 29
The Threefold Structure of Man . . . 33
The Triad reflected in the Human Soul . . . 35
The Human Soul and Personality Complex . . . 37
The Sign of Man . . . 41
The Golden Womb . . . 42
The Human Constitution . . . 43
The Major Cakras and the Glands . . . 44
Symbols of the Seven Major Cakras . . . 45
The Creative Centre . . . 48
The Psychic Centre . . . 49
The Descent of the Spirit . . . 51
The Functioning of the Cakras . . . 52
Ray-Energies in the Human Cakras . . . 54
The Rays and the Planes . . . 55
The Seven Subplanes of the Astral Plane . . . 67
The Seven Subplanes of the Mental Plane . . . 75
The Seven Subplanes of the Buddhic Plane . . . 90
The Seven Subplanes of the Nirvāṇic Plane . . . 99
The Limitless God . . . 110
The Descent of the Word . . . 118
The Light of the Logos . . . 119
The Kingdom of God . . . 123
The Constitution of the Solar Logos . . . 124
The Cycle of Manifestation . . . 134
Dimensions of the Cosmic Fire . . . 137
Attributes of the Guṇas . . . 139
Interaction of a Polarized Pair . . . 164
The Action of the Primordial Sound . . . 165
The Period of the Mahāmanvantara . . . 168
The Sevenfold Evolutionary Scheme . . . 169
Human Evolution and the Awakened Cakras . . . 171
Evolutionary States of Human Consciousness . . . 172

Past and Present Evolutionary Development of the Cakras 178
Variations of the Cross 179
The Future Evolution of Humanity 182
The Far-Future Evolution of Humanity 183
Evolutionary Leaps in Consciousness 184
The Twelve Creative Hierarchies 191
Christian Classification of the Hierarchies 192
Involutionary and Evolutionary Kingdoms 194
Angelic Rulers of the Planes 199
The Wheel of the Law 247

Earth Life

Consciousness and Phenomena 323
Types of Telepathy 346
The Planes and the Kabbalistic Tree of Life 359
The Magical Process in the Four Worlds 360
Tarot Key 1: *The Magician* 362
Centres of Magic 364
Powers of Consciousness 374
Human Types 377
The Brotherhood of Light 395
The Descent of the Plan 396
Tarot Key 13: *Death* 398
From Bondage to Liberation 422
Head and Heart 429
The Heart Path 446
Madonna and Child 469
The Human Bipolarity 475
Qualities of Yin, Yang and Tao 477
Realms of the One Mind 493
The Seven States of Consciousness 495
Development of the Seven States of Consciousness 496
Evolution of the Senses 506
Human Perception on the Subplanes 507

CHARTS & DIAGRAMS I

CHARTS & DIAGRAMS II

Volume II: Tradition

Charts & Diagrams

Symbols of the Religions 515

Yoga: The Science of Union

The Goal of Yoga 521
Perception through Mind 543
Tarot Key 5: The Hierophant 558
Tabulations of the General Powers 580

Pure Christianity: The Religion of Love

The Many Mansions 611
The Tree of Christianity 651
The Breath-Rhythm of the Name 708
The Divine Message of the New Testament 719
The Burning Heart 730

Zen: The Path to Enlightenment

The Goal of Zen 761

Sūfī Meditation: The Way of the Holy Fire

The Equation of History 834
The Thread of the Heart 844
The Mantram of Unification in the Heart Centre 866
Worlds of the Sūfī 890

Tantra: The Path of Relationship

Polarities within the Human Aura 921

The Warrior School: The Way of the Noble Warrior

The Descent of the Light 980
The Unity-Field of Being 1009
The Pure and Combined Vowel Sounds 1030
IAO and the Perfected Man-Species 1035
Powers of the Awakened Centres 1037
The Pure Vowels for Mental Training 1039
Forces and Qualities of the Vowels 1040
Internalizing the Pure and Combined Vowels 1041
Powers of the Semi-Vowel Sounds 1043
The Internalized Semi-Vowels 1044
Internalizing the Semi-Vowels in the Energy Centres 1045
The Semi-Vowels with the Pure Vowels and the M, Ṁ and Ṅ 1046
The Consonants combined with the Pure Vowels 1048
The Consonants with the Vowels and the M, Ṁ and Ṅ 1049
Sounds for Identification with Pure Being 1057
RŪ-HĀ Breathing in the Base and Crown Centres 1063
The Warrior of the Heart 1074

Volume III: Transformation

Charts & Diagrams

Male and Female Systems of Spirituality 1112

The Path of Return

Some Symbols relating to the Path 1131
Leaps in Consciousness 1137
A Comparison of Systems 1183
Sounding the Perfect Chord of Being 1186
The Illumination and Deification of Man 1190
The Threefold Human Constitution 1193
Integration of the Human Consciousness 1195
Steps on the Meditational Path 1197
The Suspending of the Mind 1209
The Way to Bliss-Consciousness 1246

The Way of the Heart

Great Incarnations of Divinity 1270
Personality Integration Chart 1333

The Way of Spiritual Psychology

The Cycle of Desire 1377
Pronunciation of IHVH 1460
Hebrew Divine Names Meditation 1461
Hebrew Angelic Names Meditation 1462

The Worship of the Goddess

Sāvitrī Maṇḍala 1497
The Spiritual Heart Complex 1505
Kwan Yin Maṇḍala 1508
The Immaculate Heart 1513

The Yoga of the Sun

Dimensions of the Solar Logos in Cosmic Space 1591
The Incarnation of the Sun 1593
The Brahma-Gāyatrī in the Cakras 1639
Solar Meditation in the Cakras 1640

The Path of Service

Penetrating into the Kingdom 1707
The Bridge of Consciousness 1713
Hierarchies of Life 1721
The Mystery of the Christ 1724

∞

APPENDIX A

Detailed Contents

VOLUME I

Introduction I: Knowledge and Ignorance
Who are We? 2–3
Māyā: definition 2
The Real Nature 3
Lack of Knowledge 4–5
Mind-Created Heavens and Hells 6–7
Hell: derivation 6
Truth and Mythology 7

Part One
Cosmology Unveiled

1 Planes of Being
The Divine Milieu 12
The Seven Great Planes 13
Perceiving the One Space 13
Planes and Subplanes 14–15
The Seven Great Planes of Being (graph) 15
The Planes in Brief 16–17
The Seven Subplanes of the Physical Plane (graph) 16
Our true Home or Origin 17
The Universal Cosmology 18
Cosmological Systems Compared (graph) 18
The Christian Cosmo-Conception 19
The physical body is your greatest prison 19
Ascending the Planes of Consciousness 20
The Populated Cosmos 20
Walls of Time and Space (graph) 21
The Sense of Time 22–23
Some Esoteric Teachings on Time 22
The Fullness of the Void 23
Nirvāṇa and Śūnyatā defined 23
Primordial Atoms 24
The Monad 24
Love is the Law 25
Polarities of Forces between the Planes (graph) 25
The Cosmic Elements 26–29
  The Cosmic Elements 26
  Applications of the Elements 27
  Attributes of the Elements 28–29
  The Seven Elementary Qualities (graph) 28
  The Planes and the Elementary Attributes (graph) 29

2 The Human Constitution
The Compound Human Being 32–33
Reincarnation is a fact of Nature 32
The Threefold Structure of Man (graph) 33
The Individuality (Ātma-Buddhi-Manas) 34
Jīva: the Human Soul 35
The Triad reflected in the Human Soul (graph) 35
The Personality Complex 36–37
Where are YOU? 36
The Human Soul and Personality Complex (graph) 37
The Kośas: Coverings over the Self 38
Persona: the Mask 38
The Astral Body 39
The Human Constitution (Greek) 39
Terms of Mind (variations) 39
The Light Bodies 40–41
Physical Regeneration 40
The Sign of Man (graph) 41
The Human Aura 42–43
The Golden Womb (graph) 42
The Human Constitution (graph) 43
The Human Cakras 44–53
  The Major Cakras and the Glands (graph) 44
  Symbols of the Seven Major Cakras (graph) 45
  Minor and higher Cakras 45
  Base Centre: Mūlādhāra Cakra 46
  Sex Centre: Svādhiṣṭhāna Cakra 46
  Solar Plexus Centre: Maṇipūra Cakra 47
  Heart Centre: Anāhata Cakra 47
  Throat Centre: Viśuddha Cakra 48
  The Creative Centre (Sex and Throat) 48
  Third-Eye Centre: Ājñā Cakra 49
  The Psychic Centre (Third-Eye and Solar Plexus) 49
  Crown Centre: Sahasrāra Cakra 50
  The Functioning of the Cakras (graph) 52
  Malfunctioning Cakras 53
Health and Fire 50
Created out of the Void 51
The Descent of the Spirit (graph) 51

The Seven Rays 54–56
Ray-Energies in the Human Cakras (graph) 54
The Three Rays in the Human System 54
The Rays and the Planes (graph) 55
Manifestations of the Seven Rays in Humanity 56

3 Kāmaloka: The Astral Plane
The Realm of Desires 58–59
Kill out Desire? 58
Beyond the Astral World 59
The Underworld (terminology) 60
Seven Conditions in One Astral World 61
The Astral Subplanes 62–67
7th Astral Subplane 62–63
Mind-Created Hells 62
The Eighth Sphere (Avītci) 63
5th and 6th Astral Subplanes 64
Earthbound 64
4th Astral Subplane 65
3rd Astral Subplane 65
2nd Astral Subplane 66
1st Astral Subplane 66–67
The Grand Illusion 66
The Seven Subplanes of the Astral Plane (graph) 67
"Eternal" Heavens and Hells? 68
Rearrangement of the Astral Body after Death 69
Life in the Astral World 70–71
Sex on the Astral Plane 70

4 Devāchan: The Mental Plane
Mind Realms 74–75
The Seven Subplanes of the Mental Plane (graph) 75
The Seven Heavens (terminology) 76
Sukhāvatī: the place of happiness 76
Denizens of the Heaven Worlds 77
The Mental Body 78
Manas: definition and description 78
Mind and Brain 79
True Thought 79
Impressions from the Mental Plane 80
Paths to Devāchan 81
Astral Shells 81
To Experience Heaven 82

5 Buddhi: The Realm of Unities
The Ocean of Wisdom (descriptions) 84
The Discovery of Truth 85
Buddhi is characterized by Emptiness 85
Buddhic Consciousness 86
Your Original Face 87
Surrender to the Self 87
Experiencing Pure Consciousness 88
Buddhi is a subtle veil over Ātman 88
The Path of Light 89
To Rediscover Buddhi 90
The Seven Subplanes of the Buddhic Plane (graph) 90
The Mystics 91
Śrī Ramana Mahāṛṣi 91
The Prayer of Saint Francis of Assisi 92

6 Nirvāṇa: The World of Glories
Nirvāṇa! (derivation and description) 94–95
Gnostic terms for Nirvāṇa 95
The Light Body of our Solar Logos 95
Touch Ultimate Emptiness 96
The Two Realities (physical and Nirvāṇic) 97
Nirvāṇa is… 98–101
The Seven Subplanes of the Nirvāṇic Plane (graph) 99
The Truth about Nirvāṇa 102

7 The Divine Being
Mythical Concepts of God 104–105
In the Image and Likeness 104
Why Myths? 105
Can God be Angry? 106
Qualities of the Divine Being 107
God Is… 107
What is "God"? 108
The Form of God is Space 109
The One God of All Religions 110
God is Omnipotent, Omnipresent, Omniscient 110
God Immanent and Transcendent 111
The Intelligent Universe 111
The Transcendental Godhead 112
The Three-Faced God 113
The Christian Trinity 113
The Logos: the Word of God 114–115

The Threefold Christ 115
The Doctrine of the Logoi 116–117
The Threefold Logos 116
Logos, Śabda-Brahman, Daiviprākṛtī: translations 117
Vāk: the Divine Speech 118
The Descent of the Word (graph) 118
The Primordial Light 119
The Light of the Logos (graph) 119
The Elohīm 120
The Lord? 121
Mikrokosmos, Makrokosmos, Chiliokosmos 121
The Constitution of God-Immanent 122–126
The Kingdom of God (graph) 123
The Constitution of the Solar Logos (graph) 124
Inconceivable Divine Realities 126
God is a Sublime Mystery 127
Who are the "Elect"? 128
Humility for Earthlings 129
The Cosmic Fire 130–137
Dimensions of Fire 131
The Kuṇḍalinī Fire 132
The One Force 133
Living Matter 134–135
The Cycle of Manifestation (graph) 134
Words from the Greek Mystery School 135
Some Biblical References to the Cosmic Fire 136
The Holy Spirit (ancient languages) 136
Dimensions of the Cosmic Fire (graph) 137
Ideas and Archetypes 138
The Guṇas 139–140
Understand these Sanskrit Words 140

8 Kuṇḍalinī and the Goddess

The Breath of the Divine Mother 142
The Serpent 142
The Evolutionary Energy 143
The Virgin and the Mother 144
Her Transcendental Form 145
The World Mother of Compassionate Heart 145
Tao: the Great Mother 146
Sophia: the Boundless Feminine Intelligence 146
The Mother of the World 147
Kuṇḍalinī-Fohat 148–149
Śakti: the One Energy 150
The Three Gates to God 151
The Ascent of Kuṇḍalinī 152
Kuṇḍalinī and Alchemy 153
Sex is not Love 153
Signs of the Awakening Kuṇḍalinī 154–156
When Kuṇḍalinī Awakens 157–158
Kuṇḍalinī has to be understood correctly 157

9 Creation and Evolution

Creation and Evolution are One 160
The Plan is in the Divine Mind 161
Mahat: the Divine Mind 161
The Cosmic Creator-Gods 162–163
The Solar Dharma 163
The Law of Polarity 164
Interaction of a Polarized Pair (graph) 164
The Creation Process 165
The Action of the Primordial Sound (graph) 165
The Creation of the Universe 166–167
Let us Understand these Sanskrit Words 167
The Action of the Cosmic Mind 167
Ruach-Elohīm: the Breath of the Creator-Gods 167
The Period of the Mahāmanvantara 168
The Sevenfold Earth-Evolution 169
The Sevenfold Evolutionary Scheme (graph) 169
Human Involution and Evolution 170–172
Human Evolution and the Awakened Cakras (graph) 171
Evolutionary States of Human Consciousness (graph) 172
From Subjective to Objective 173
Existence is Purposeful 173
Vertical Evolution and the Path 174

The Purpose of Christianity 174
The Law of Radiation 175
Human Evolutionary Epochs 176–178
The Sin of the Mindless 176
Past and Present Evolutionary Development of the Cakras (graph) 178
Who are the Āryans? 179
Evolutionary Symbolism of the Cross 179
Manifestation of the Sons of God 180
The Mystery of the Pleiades 181
Planetary Stimulation 181
The Future Evolution of Humanity (graph) 182
The Far-Future Evolution of Humanity (graph) 183
Evolutionary Leaps in Consciousness (graph) 184
Evolutionary Leaps in Consciousness 185
The Great Day of Be With Us 185
Towards Group-Consciousness 186

10 The Creative Hierarchies
The Populated Universe 188–189
Hierarchy (defined) 190
Children of the Cosmic Creators 190
The Twelve Creative Hierarchies (graph) 191
Christian Classification of the Hierarchies 192
Angels and Demons 193
Involutionary and Evolutionary Kingdoms 194
The Elementals 195
The Angels 196–197
Crowned with Glory 197
Some Facts about the Devas 198
The Devas according to the Rays 199
Angelic Rulers of the Planes (graph) 199
The Gandharvas 200
Language of the Gods 200
The Creative and Destructive Power of Sound 201
Sun-Sounds 201
The Makara and Asuras 202
The Biblical "Angels of God" 203

11 Origins of Evil
Roots of Evil 206–207
Wickedness in High Places 207
The Paradox of Evil 208–209
Evil defined 208
Satan and the Fall 210–211
Evil: Human and Cosmic 212–217
  Human Evil 212–213
  The Mind Divine or Demonic 212
  The Body-Elementals 213
  Planetary Evil 214–216
  Solar-Systemic and Cosmic Evil 217
The Mind-Created Devil 218
Shadowland 219
The Dark Side of the Force 219
Appeasing the Gods? 220
The Seed of Evil 221
Animal Suffering 222
The Sufferings of Man 223
Seven things that the Lord despises 223
The Evil Mind 224–225
Brothers of the Shadow 226–227
Brotherhoods of Light and Darkness 228
From Hate to Love 229

12 Karma and Reincarnation
The Power of Thought 232
The Universal Intelligence 232
Thinking and Being 233
Fear of the Lord? 234
Mind and Desire 235
Subconscious Forces 236–237
The Astral Body is the Subconscious Mind 236
The Power of Suggestion 237
In Bondage to the Mind 238
Senses or the Self? 239
Karma: the Law of Action or Adjustment 240–241
Karma is the equilibrating force 240
Karma in the Afterlife 241
The Akashic Records 241
Creating Karma 242
Working out Karma 242
Types of Karma 243

Group Karma 243
Dharma: the Law of Being 244–245
Dharma translated 244
Torah and Dharma 245
Your Fate is Before your Eyes 246
The Wheel of the Law 247
The Chain of Dharma 247
The Wheel of the Law (graph) 247
The Law of Cyclic Activity 248
The Three Kinds of Activity of Matter 248
Punarjanma: Reincarnation 249
Destiny and the Permanent Atoms 250
Children are born innocent? 250
Saṁskāra and Vāsanā 251
Tanhā and Triśnā 251
Karma and Reincarnation Misconceived 252–253
The Law of Effort 254
There is no inequality, injustice or unfairness 254
Karma and your Spiritual Development 255
Freedom from Karma 255
Success is Born of Action 256–257
To Become a True Renunciate 257
You Alone are Responsible 258
Reincarnation and Karma understood by early church 258
To Become a Jīvanmukta in this Lifetime 259
The causes of Reincarnation 259
Destined by the Stars? 260–261
Terms of Destiny 261
The Good Law 262–263
The Three Great Laws of Life 262
Why Life is Suffering 263
The Supreme Act of Karma 264–265

Part Two
Earth Life

13 Atlantis Revisited
Atlantis 270
Wars in Heaven 271
The Land of Atlantis 271
The Great Flood 272–275
Myths are imaginative facts 273
Roots of Modern Shamanism 276
The Power of Conscious Dreaming 277
Magicians of Atlantis and India 277
New Age Phenomena 278
Cosmic Forces influencing the New Age 278
The Action of the Cosmic Fire 279
The New Atlantis 280
The Coming of the Spirit-Guides 281
Cosmic Intervention 282
Vimāna People and Human Destiny 283
The Enduring Vimānas 284
Intervention and Interference 285
Human Response to Cosmic Intervention 286
Religious Reactionaries 287–288
The fundamental note of the Aquarian Age 288

14 Psychic Phenomena
Psychic Humanity 290
Psychology: Science of the Soul? 291
Clairvoyance 292–293
Pure Seeing? 293
Prophecy and Destiny 294–296
Biblical Prophecies? 296
Intelligent Use of Free Will 297
The Physical Projection 297
Dreams 298–299
The Yoga of the Dream State 299
Interpreting Dreams 300
Dreams and Out-of-Body Experiences 300
Astral Projection 301
Types of Astral Projection 302–304
The Etheric Web 304
Objective Experience 305
Hallucinations and out-of-body experiences 305

Experiences on the Astral Plane 306–307
If you visit the Hell Worlds 307
Fasting and Psychic Experience 308
Mediumship (overview) 309
Involuntary Possession 310–311
Who are the Infesting Spirits? 310
Memory of Past Lives 312
Hypnotism 312
Speaking in Tongues 312–313
Ouija Board, Planchette, Automatic Writing 313
Materializations 314
Poltergeist phenomena 314–315
Spontaneous Human Combustion 316

15 Channelling and Mediumship
Roots of Modern Mediumship 318
Degeneration of the word "Spirit" 319
What is "Channelling"? 320–324
  Mediumship (various forms of) 321
  Automatism 322
  Psychic Sensitivity 322
  Mental Telepathy 322
  Personal Transformation 322
  Intuition, Insight, Inspiration 323
  Mysticism 324
Consciousness and Phenomena (graph) 323
"Channelling" the Soul 325
Masters and Mediums 326
Channelling or Soul-Wisdom? 327
What is Intuition? 328
The Way to Higher Consciousness 329
Exalted Sources? 330
Subconscious Sources 331
Higher Consciousness has no Name 331
The Changing Faces of the Spirit-Guides 332–333
Ascended Masters? 332
Who are the "Spirit-Guides"? 334–335
"Miracles" performed by spirits 335
Beyond Spirit-Guides 336
Test the spirits! 336
Humility of the Great Ones 337
H.P. Blavatsky and A.A. Bailey were not mediums 338
Living Guidance 339
Edgar Cayce: Medium or Mystic? 339
Why Channelling is Dangerous 340–343
Already Enlightened? 341
You Must Choose 344

16 Telepathy
Mind to Mind 346
Types of telepathy (graph) 346
The Universal Language 348–349
Thought and Energy 349
Impressions from the Soul 350
Telepathic Communion is a State of Love 350
Communicating by Light 351
Levels of Communication (summary) 351
Mental Telepathy and Psychism 352
To be taught Wisdom... 353

17 Magical Manifestation
The Magician 356
Magos, Magus, Magi, Maga: definitions 356
Supernatural Forces 357
Foundations of Magic (Kabbalistic) 358–362
  The Planes and the Kabbalistic Tree of Life (graph) 359
  The Four Kabbalistic Worlds 360
  The Magical Process in the Four Worlds (graph) 360
  Stages of Manifestation 361
  Symbols of the Cosmic Elements 362
  The Tarot 362
  Tarot Key 1: The Magician 362
Objectives of Magic 363
Energy Materializes 363
Magic: White and Black 364
Magical Prayer 365
The Magic of Ritual Worship 366–371
  Yajña: Ritual Magic 366
  Ritual Degenerated 368
  The Spirit-Helpers 369
  The Temple Not Made By Hands 369
  Invoking the Invisible Helpers 370–371
  Descent of the Teachers 370
  Communication with the Invisible 371
Magical Healing 372
Future Therapy 372

18 Human Consciousness

19 Death and Liberation

20 The Mystery of the Heart

Wisdom and Understanding 439
Heaven and Earth (Biblical translations) 439
The Universal Christ 440
The Christ in the Heart 441
The Religion of Christ 441
The Christ is the Light of the World 442–443
Christ-Consciousness 443
Death in the Heart 444
Dissolving the Knot in the Heart 445
Knots of Consciousness 445
The Lotus of the Heart 446
The Heart Path (graph) 446
Pure Consciousness in the Heart 447
Kohaṁ, Sohaṁ, Ahaṁ 447
The Eastern Heart 448
Sanskrit terms for the Heart Centre 448
Devotion to Kṛṣṇa 449
Kūṭastha: the Highest State to be in 449
Christian Mysticism 450–451
The Way of the Radiant Heart 452–455
Monology 453
The Spiritual Warrior 455
Some Western Heart Mantras 456
Some Eastern Heart Mantras 457
More Mantras for Awakening the Heart 458–461
Techniques for the Expansion of the Heart 461
Physical Symptoms in the Heart 462
Experiencing the Awakening Heart 463–465
The Three Regions of the Heart 463
The Lover and the Beloved (poem) 466

21 The Call of the World Mother
The Feminine Virtues 468–469
Feminine or Feminist? 468
The Eternal Feminine 469
Madonna and Child (graph) 469
Madonna 470
Art and the Follies of Man 470
The Divine Bipolarity 471
Mūlaprākṛtī: the Root of Nature 471
The Human Bipolarity 472
The Breakdown of Family 473
The Gift of Parenthood 474
Mother and Father 475
The Human Bipolarity (graph) 475
Yin, Yang, Tao 476–477
Qualities of Yin, Yang and Tao (graph) 477
The Masculinization of Children 478–479
Primary Relationship 479
The Education System 480–481
Education and Fundamentalism 480
What is Education? 482–483
Education for Life 484–485
Fear of being "conditioned" 485
Violence and War (effects on children) 486
Nourishing the Goal of Life 487
Essential Knowledge 487
Education in the Future 488

22 Awakening the Human Glory
Perceptions of the One Mind 490
The Thread of the Self 491
Realms of the One Mind 492–493
Keys of the Mind (Tarot Keys 0,1,2) 492
The Seven States of Consciousness 494–496
Pure Intelligence 494
The Seven States of Consciousness (graph) 495
Development of the Seven States of Consciousness (graph) 496
Samādhi: the State of Inner Purity 497
Turīya: Pure Consciousness 498
The Fourth State 499
The Fifth State 500
Cosmic Consciousness and God-Consciousness 500
The Sixth State 501
Glimpses of Illumination 501
The Seventh State 502
Kaivalya: Being Alone with the Absolute 502
Śūnyatā: the Void 503
God-Consciousness is the Wholeness of Life 504–505
Balance in Spiritual Life 505
Awakening the Inner Senses 506–507
Evolution of the Senses (graph) 506
Human Perception on the Subplanes (graph) 507
The Law of Mystic Experience 508–509
Descriptions of the Mystic Experience 508

VOLUME II

Introduction II: By Whichever Path

The Eternal is One 512–514
Religion and Politics 513
The One Transcendental Reality 515
Symbols of the Religions (graph) 515
The New and Eternal Way 516

Part Three

Yoga: The Science of Union

23 The Goal of Yoga

Yoga-Mārga: the Path to Union 520
The Activities of Yoga-Mārga 520
Spiritual Evolution for all Humanity is the Goal of Yoga 521
The Goal of Yoga (graph) 521
The Dividing of Yoga 522–523
The One Yoga 522
Haṭha Yoga and Rāja Yoga 524–525
Meanings of the word Haṭha 524
Yoga Vasiṣṭha: the Most Excellent Yoga 525
The Ultimate Reality is the Meaning of Life 526–527
Yoga and Religion defined 527
The Three Stages of Yoga 528–529
To Attain the State of Yoga 530

24 Gems from Patañjali's Yoga Sūtras

The Yoga Sūtras 532–533
Models for Higher Consciousness 532
The Sage Patañjali 534
The Father of Yoga? 534
Pāda II Sūtra 1 535
Kriyā Yoga: Union through Action 535
Pāda I Sūtra 2 536
Pāda I Sūtra 3 536–537
Pāda I Sūtra 4 538–539
Pāda IV Sūtra 17 540
Pāda IV Sūtra 18 541
Pāda II Sūtra 20 542–543
The Process of Seeing or Perceiving 542
Perception through Mind (graph) 543
Pāda II Sūtra 21 544
The Upaniṣads: Illuminating the Nature of the Self 545
The Upaniṣadic Mantrams 546–547
Pāda I Sūtra 23 548
Pāda I Sūtra 27 549
To meditate on the Sūtras 549
Āuṁ, Ōṁ, Nāda 550–551
The Esoteric Mantram 551
The Path of Seeing 552
The Path of Hearing 553
Building the Bridge of Light 554–555
Pāda I Sūtra 30 556–557
Overstimulation on the Path 557
The Attitude for Yoga 558
Tarot Key 5: The Hierophant 558

25 Aṣṭāṅga Yoga

Yoga by Eight Steps (background) 560
Śiva Yoga of the Liṅga Purāṇa 561
Pāda II Sūtra 29 562
Pāda II Sūtra 30 563
Pāda II Sūtra 32 564
Pāda II Sūtra 31 565
Stage One of Aṣṭāṅga Yoga: Yama 566–567
  Ahiṁsā: Non-violence 566
  Satyam (Satya): Truthfulness 566
  Asteya: Non-Stealing 566
  Brahmacarya: Orientation to the Divine 566–567
  Aparigrahā: Non-attachment 567
  Interpretations of Brahmacarya 567
Stage Two of Aṣṭāṅga Yoga: Niyama 568–569
  Śauca: Purification 568
  Santoṣa: Contentment 568
  Tapasya (Tapas): Mental Discipline 568–569
  Svādhyāya: Spiritual Study and Practice 569
  Īśvara-Praṇidhāna: Devotion to God 569
Śauca: Purity 570
Tapas: Spiritual Purification 571
Purification by Diet? 571
Stage Three of Aṣṭāṅga Yoga: Yoga 572
Beyond Āsana and Prāṇāyāma 573
Samādhi: the Goal of Yoga 574–575
The Seven States of Consciousness 575
Modern Yoga Practice 576

26 The Yoga of Miraculous Powers

Pāda IV Sūtra 1 578
Powers by Drugs? 578
Categories of Powers 579
Yogic Powers and Psychism 579
The General Powers 580–581
Tabulations of the General Powers (graph) 580
Seek not Powers 581
Saṁyama 582
Saṁyama and Parapsychology 582
Pāda III Sūtras 16-56 (Saṁyama on…) 583–597
  the three transformations of Nature 583
  a word 584
  the Saṁskāra 584
  the minds of others 584
  the body's form 584
  the quickly and slowly manifesting karmas 584
  the signs of nearing death 584
  friendliness, love, compassion 584
  the strength of an elephant 584
  the Inner Light 585
  the Sun 585
  the Moon 585
  the Pole Star 586
  the Solar Plexus Centre 586
  the Throat Centre 586
  the Kūrmanāḍī 586
  the Third-Eye Centre 587
  the Crown Centre 587
  the Heart Centre 587
  the difference between the Intelligent-Mind and the Self 587
  the causes of Bondage of Consciousness to the body 588
  the upward-moving Life-force 589
  the Samāna Vāyu 589
  the organ of hearing 590
  the relationship between the body and Ākāśa 590
  the Disembodied State 591
  thought-waves that are external 591
  the thought-waves not related to the body 591
  the five states of the Elements 592
  the senses 595
  the difference between Pure Consciousness and Spiritual Consciousness 595
  being in the Moment 596
The Life-Force 589
To Taste the Elixir of Life 593
Further Powers 598
Powers of Divine Descent 599
Powers of the Dream State 600
Knowledge of Past Lives 601
Cosmic Powers 602–603
Know Yourself 604
The Great Way (Conclusion) 605

Part Four
Pure Christianity: The Religion of Love

27 Teachings of the Saints

The Many Mansions (graph) 611
Thus have I heard... 612–622

28 The Heart of Christianity

The Dual Nature of Christianity 624–625
Hesychast: definition and description 624
Theologia, Theologian: definitions 625
The Way of the Christian Mystic 626–628
The Dichotomy of the Mystic 629
Christian Mysticism and Zen 630
The Burning Heart 631
The Christian Heart-Path 632
The Meaning of Life is Love 633
God in the Heart 634–635
The Cave of the Heart 634
The Experience of Mysticism 636
To See and Hear God 637
Be Still and Know 638–639
The Temple of God 639
To Partake of God's Nature 640

29 Christian History

Christian Beginnings 642
The Early Christians 643–644
The Pilgrims 645
The Gnostics 645
Who are the Christians? 646
The Prophets 647
The Hasidim 648–649
Torah: the Law 648
The Masculine God 649
Christianity was One 650
The Tree of Christianity (graph) 651
Twilight of the Christian Truth 652–653
Orthodoxos: correct belief? 653
The Saints 654
What is a Saint? 654
The Heretics 655
Idol-Worship 655
Persecution of the Knowers 656–658
Rulers in High Places 657

30 Jesus the Christed One

The Jewish Messiah 660
Names of the Great Master Jesus 661
The Cosmic Christ 662–663
The Threefold Logos 662
The Threefold Christ 663
The Mystery of Jesus the Christ 664
The Mystery of Jesus and Mary 665
The Messiah Jesus 666
The Mysticism of Saint Paul 666
The Lord of Glory 667
Jesus Christ, Son of Man 668
Jesus was without "sin" 668
The Only Son of God? 669
The Crime of Fundamentalism 669
The Way, the Truth and the Life 670
The Source of Miracles 671
The Virgin Mother 671
The Last Words of Jesus 672
The Sacred Heart of Jesus 673
A Summary of Saint Margaret Mary's Teachings on the Sacred Heart of Jesus 673

31 Christian Fundamentalism

Belief and Experience 676–677
The Hidden Wisdom 677
Jesus the Personal Saviour? 678–679
To Call upon Jesus 679
The Sacrificial Lamb 680
To Worship Jesus... 680
Prayer Spiritual and Material 681
The Truth shall make you Free 682–683
Televangelism 682
Sin and Repentance 683
What is "the Devil"? 684
Tested by God and the Devil? 685
Beyond Phantasia 686–687
Greek classifications of Humanity 687
The Chosen Ones 688

32 Christian Prayer
What is Prayer? 690
Interior Prayer (Eastern Christian) 691–692
The Philokalia: the Love of the Good 691
Stages of Prayer 692
Stages of Interior Prayer 693–695
Concentration 693
Meditation 694
Contemplation (Theoria) 694
Illumination 695
Deification (Theosis) 695
Passion and Dispassion 695
The Path to Ecstasy 696–697
Terms of Prayer (variations) 696
Mystical States of the Medieval Catholic Mystics 698
Wounds of Love 699
Rapture 699
To Develop Perfect Stillness 700
Alone with God 700
Purify the Heart 701
The Radiant Heart Prayer 702–703
Clouds of Unknowing 704–705
Divine Unknowing 705
Mystical Theology 706–707
Have mercy on me, a sinner? 707
The Great Greek Mantra to Jesus 708–710
Some Western Heart Prayers 710
Practising the Presence of God 711
Latin Mantras of the Rosicrucians 712
The Evolution of Christian Prayer 713–716
Meditation on Theos 714

33 The Christian Path
The Unfoldment of the Light 718–721
Baptism 718–720
Transfiguration 721
Crucifixion 721
Resurrection 721
Ascension 721
The Divine Message of the New Testament (graph) 719
The Language of the Bible 720
Baptism and Rebirth 722–723
Subtle Energy Currents 723
The Coming of the Christ 724–725
The Anti-Christ 724
The Divine Incarnation 726
The Coming of Christ in the Heart 727
Jesus Speaks 728–729
Pure Christianity 729
Visualization of the Christ in the Heart 730
The Burning Heart (graph) 730

34 The Greek Mystery Language
Learn the Things that Are 732
Words from the Greek Mystery Schools 733–735
Words from Gnostic Christianity 736–738
Words used by the Christian Hesychasts 739–747

Part Five
Zen: The Path to Enlightenment

35 The Spirit of Zen

Origins of Zen 752
What is Zen? 753
A "Godless" Religion? 754–755
Religion and Spirituality 754
False Zen 756–757
Zen is not Psychism 757
Zen and the World 758–759
The Goal of Zen 760
From Matter to Light 761
The Goal of Zen (graph) 761
The Path of Non-Duality 762
No-Mind and the One Mind 763
Messengers of the One Mind 764
Zen and Christian Science 764
Christian Zen 765
Enlightenment 766
Terms of Awakening 766
The Thought of Enlightenment 767
The Self-Mind 767
When the Mind is Still 768
The Great Wisdom of the Other Shore 769
The Christ in you, your hope of Glory 769
The Enlightenment of Teh Shan 770

36 The Eternal Tao

What is Tao? 772–773
Tao cannot be found in books or scriptures 773
Tao: the Great I AM 774
Tao: the Universal Mind 775
Tao: the Supreme Way 776–778
Tao is Silent 779
An experience of Tao 779
The Zen Master according to Lao Tzu 780–781
The Zen Master 782
Mountains, Clouds and Water 783

37 Zen Meditation

The Attitude of Zen 786
Chi: the Vital Force of Tao 786
Quietly Seeing 786
Zen Listening 787–793
- Listening to a Mantra 788
- Listening to Ōṁ 788
- Listening to the Sound of the Dharma 789
- Zen Silence 790
- The Experience of Silence 791
- Listen to the Silence 792–793

Mindfulness of Breathing 794
Salutation to the Buddha 795
Meditating on Kōans and Hua-Tous 796–797
Zazen: Zen Sitting 798
Sayings of Lao Tzu on Zen Meditation 799
Shikantaza 800–801
Meditating on the Void 801
A Summary of Zen Meditation 802–803
Action Zen 802
The Masters on Meditation 804

38 The Path of Zen

Life as a Zen Monk 806
Spirituality and Renunciation 806
The Japanese Zen Retreat (terminology) 807
- Sesshin: a Zen spiritual intensive 808
- Blind Tradition 808
- Kyōsaku: the big stick 809
- Zazen: the central purpose of a Sesshin 809

Balanced Practice 810–811
Zen Work 810
Rules for a modern Zen Retreat 811
Return to Duty 812
The Steps to the Experience of Zen 813
The Seven Qualities to enter Paradise 813
The Four Vows of the Bodhisattva 814
The Ten Mahāyāna Precepts 814
The Noble Eightfold Path of the Buddha 815
The Governor and the Bird Nest 815
Satori: the Experience of Illumination 816–817
The Way of the Zen Masters 818–819
A Summary of Zen 820–823

Part Six
Sūfī Meditation: The Way of the Holy Fire

39 The Sūfī
Mystics of Islām 828–829
Sūfī: derivations and definition 828
Languages of Islām 829
The Radiant Way 830–832
Sūfī Terminology (variations) 830
The Sūfī Master 832
Esoteric History of the Piscean Religions 833
Zodiacal History 833
The Influence of the Seven Rays 834–835
The Equation of History (graph) 834
Mystics of Pisces and Aquarius 836
From Pisces to Aquarius 837
The Sūfī God 838
The One and Only 839
A Sūfī is... 840–841

40 The Sūfī Heart
The Thread of the Heart 844
The Ancient Heart-Path 845
The Universal Heart Practice 846
Mystical Union 846
Dimensions of the Heart (Arabic) 847
Nūr: the Light of God 847
Qalb: the Sūfī Heart 848
The Purification of the Heart 849
Faith and Wisdom 849
Some Arabic Prayers to the Deity 850–851
The Truth in the Heart 851
Tauḥīd: the Divine Unity 852
The Lover of God 853
The Revelation of God 854
The Journey of the Heart 855–857
The Rose of Divine Love 858–861

41 Sūfī Prayer
The Voice of God 864–865
The Mantram of Unification in the Heart Centre 866–867
Variations of the Mantram of Unification 868
Zikr, Dhikr: the repetition of a prayer 868
The One God of All 869
Breathing God 870–871
Meditation on the Exalted Name of God 871
Let the Sunshine in (mantras) 872
The Dance of Life 873
True Dancing 873
Sūfī Mantras for Meditation 874–877
Allāh Hu Akbar: the Greatness of God 875
The 99 Arabic Divine Names of God 878–884

42 Sūfī Mind
Worlds of the Sūfī 886–889
Worlds within Worlds 886
Worlds of the Sūfī (graph) 890
Dimensions of the Mind 891
Understand your Predicament 892–893
The Human Constitution (Arabic) 892
Beyond the Veils 894
The Five Stages of Certainty 895
The Ordinary Mind 896
Linking the Head with the Heart 897
Transformation of the Ordinary Mind 898–899
Taming the Mind 899
The Sūfī View of Mental Disorders 900
The Seven Stages of Sūfī Silence 901
Murāqabaī: Sūfī Meditation 901

Part Seven
Tantra: The Path of Relationship

43 The Circle of Love

Relational Consciousness 906–907
Periods of Life in Vedic India 907
Warrior Jesus 908
Tantra is for the Living 909
The Feminine Suppressed 910
The Work of the Devil? 910
The Way of Love 911
To Reach Unqualified Existence 911
The Energies of Sex and Love 912
Sexuality and the Life-Force 912
The Many Hues of Love 913–916
- Sexual Love 913
- Emotional Love 914
- Terms of Love 914
- Heart Love 915
- Mental Love 915
- Divine Love in the Head 916

To Understand Sex 917
Natural Sexual Dynamism 918
Natural Attraction 918
The Healing Power of Touch 919
Natural Law 919
Polarities Male and Female 920–921
The Sexless Soul 920
Polarities within the Human Aura (graph) 921
Falling in Love 922
The Circle of Love 923
The Female Dominant 924–925
The Feminine Heart 925
Sex Natural and Divine 926–927
Cultivate the Fires of Love 928–929
Through Sex which is Love 929
When Sex is Love 930
The Meaning of Love 931
The Meaning of Life 931
Freedom is Boundless Love 932
Tantra Mind 933–935
- Stand in your own Centre 934
- Develop a Bird's Eye View 934
- Return to your Root 935
- Surrender to the Limitless 935

Love Lost 936–937
The Tragedy of Human Relationships 936
Mother, Father and Baby 938–939
You are Alone on this Way 939
Live and Let Live 940
You can only Love Now 941
The Path of Tantra 942–943
The Way of Feminine Consciousness 944

44 The One-Hundred-and-Twelve

That the Other One might Live 946
- Space 947
- Consciousness 947–948
- The Self 948–949
- The Light 950
- The Word 951–952
- Centring 952–953
- The Breath 954–955
- Omnipresence 955–956
- Attention 957
- Desire 958
- The Embrace 959
- Other Moments 960–964

The Original Calm 965

Part Eight

The Warrior School: The Way of the Noble Warrior

45 The Spiritual Warrior

Qualities of the Spiritual Warrior 970
Development of the Spiritual Warrior 971
The Warrior, the Sage, the Ruler 972–973
The Eternal Triangle 972
The Sage 973
Your choice of Greatness is of three kinds 973
Mind-Only 974–975
What do you Seek out of Life? 975
The Law of your Being 976–977
Light 978–979
The Invisible Government 980–981
The Descent of the Light (graph) 980
From Darkness into Light 982–983
Surpassing your own Limitations 983
The Warrior of the Light 984
True War 985
Acting from the Centre: Spontaneous Benevolence 985
The Warrior seeks Peace not War 986
No Anger, No Enemies 986
Be Tranquil 987
Mind in Body 988
Skill in Action 989
Overactive Mind 990
The "No-Mind" 990
Monks and Disciples 991
Our task is the Spiritual Regeneration of the world 991
The Law of Action 992–993
Fight Evil with Good 993
Action and the Spiritual Warrior 994
Primordial Balance 995
The Three Forces of the Warrior 996–997
Family and Duty 998–999
Reincarnation and Freedom 998
Is there a Plan in your Life? 1000

46 Warrior Training

The Warrior Path 1002–1003
The Four Degrees of Knowledge 1003
To Enter the Way of the Warrior 1004
Look out for the One 1004
Integrity and Perfection 1005
The Practice of Grounding 1005
The Structure of the Warrior School 1006–1007
What is Initiation? 1007
The Silence of the Warrior 1008
Connecting to the Silent Source of Creation 1008
Cosmic Sensitivity 1009
The Unity-Field of Being (graph) 1009
Getting in Touch with your Inner Feminine 1010–1011
The Active and Passive Way 1011
Meditation and the Joy of Living 1012–1013
How to find Peace and Joy through Meditation 1013
Resting in the No-Mind State of the Absolute 1014–1015
From Action into Stillness, from Stillness into Action 1016
Mindfulness: The Warrior Within 1017
Open-Eyes Meditations for the Warrior 1018
Meditation in Action 1019
Warrior Breathing 1020
Movement and the Life-force 1020
Warrior Calming Breathings 1021
Breathing Techniques to develop Internal Strength 1022
The Significance of Warrior Greetings 1023
Understanding your Work in Silence 1024
The Liberating and Transforming Power of Sound 1024

47 The Primordial Sound Language

The Ancient Primordial Language of Sound-Vibrations 1026–1027
The Primordial Sound Alphabet 1028
The Source of the Primordial Sound Language 1029
The Pure Vowels and Combined Vowels 1030
Pronouncing the Pure Vowels 1030
The Seven Mystic Vowel Sounds 1031
Modern Vowels 1031
Remembrance of the Five Pure Vowels in some Ancient Languages 1032
The Name of the Deity is Sound Itself 1032
Sounding the Vowels 1033
Powers of the Pure Vowels 1033
IAO 1034–1035
Silence Seals 1034
IAO and the Perfected Man-Species (graph) 1035
The Vowels in the Energy Centres 1036
Awakening the Higher Centres 1037–1038
Powers of the Awakened Centres (graph) 1037
Awakening the Serpent-Fire 1038
The Development of the Mind through the Five Pure Vowel Sounds 1039
The Pure Vowels for Mental Training (graph) 1039
The Prolonged Vowels 1039
Personal Development through the Five Pure Vowel Sounds 1040
Forces and Qualities of the Vowels (graph) 1040
The Two Directions of Sound 1041
Internalizing the Pure Vowels and Combined Vowels (graph) 1041
Sounding the Ṁ 1041
Powers of the Primordial Sound Alphabet 1042
The Semi-Vowels or Semi-Consonants 1043
Powers of the Semi-Vowel Sounds (graph) 1043
Internalizing the Semi-Vowels 1044–1045
The Elementary Qualities 1044
Internalizing the Semi-Vowels in the Energy Centres (graph) 1045
The Semi-Vowels combined with the Pure Vowels 1046–1047
The Consonants combined with the Vowels 1048
The Consonants with the Vowels and the Final M and Nasal Sounds 1049
The Sibilants 1050–1051
Centring and Deepening: SHĪ and SHŪ 1052
Shining from Within: MĀ RA MA 1053
Sound-Words 1054
Meditation on KRĪM 1055
Pure Being: IĒNG (YING-YENG) 1056–1057
Sounds for Identification with Pure Being (graph) 1057
Tremendous Sound-Structures for the Development of Humanity 1058
Controlling the Mind through Breathing: SŌ-HĀNG, HŌNG-SAU, HA-SA 1059
Warrior Energizing Breathings 1060–1061
A Connecting Breathing: RŪ-HĀ 1062–1063
RŪ-HĀ Breathing in the Base and Crown Centres (graph) 1063
Healing Sound-Vibration Formula 1064–1067
The Art of Warriorship 1067
RĀM: the Warrior Power 1068–1071
Meditations on Aspects of RĀM (Sanskrit) 1072–1073
The Ten Cosmic Powers of the RĀM Primordial Sound-Vibration 1072
The Warrior of the Heart: ŌM RĀM KLĪM 1074
The Warrior of the Heart (graph) 1074
The Creative Power of the Primordial Language of Sound 1075

48 The Warrior Code

A Guide for Living 1078
Aphorisms of the Spiritual Warrior 1079–1099
Action in the Transcendent 1080
Action and Stillness: the Supreme Way 1083
Conditioned Thinking 1084
Facing the Evil Mind 1087
The Power of Yielding 1088
Stand in the Void 1091
The Righteous Fight 1092
Stillness before Battle 1095
Beyond War 1098
Between the Two Extremes, Find the Middle Point 1100
Persevering to the End until Final Liberation 1101
The Code of the Spiritual Warrior 1101
Farewell 1102

VOLUME III

Introduction III: The New Spirituality

Spirituality Past and Future 1104
Psychology and the New Age Religion 1105–1109
Orthodox Psychology 1105
Transpersonal Psychology 1106–1107
The Omnipresent God 1108–1109
The Gnostic Teachings 1108
Female Buddhas 1110
The Path of Self-Actualization 1110
Unnecessary Practices 1111
The New Age Impulse 1111
The Two Paths 1112
Male and Female Systems of Spirituality (graph) 1112
Inspiration by the Mind of Light 1113
Spiritual Reading 1113

Part Nine
The Path of Return

49 The Aquarian Way

Spiritual Life and Material Life 1118
Is Renunciation Necessary? 1119
Non-Action Misinterpreted 1120
Paths to the Transcendent and Immanent God 1120
Three Schools of Spirituality 1121
Avoid the Errors of East and West 1122–1123
The Science of Cosmic Consciousness 1124
Developing Cosmic Consciousness 1125
Yoga in Cosmic Consciousness 1125
Rāja Yoga: Divine Union by Meditation 1126–1127
Bhakti Yoga: Divine Union by Devotion 1128
The Eastern Christian Way 1128
On the Wings of Devotion 1129
The Catholic Mystical Path 1129
Uniting Head and Heart 1130–1131
Some Symbols relating to the Path (graph) 1131
Karma Yoga: Divine Union by Action 1132–1133
The Law of the Higher Life 1134–1135
Saints of Action 1134
Stages on the Path 1136–1137
Leaps in Consciousness (graph) 1137
The Law of Surrender or Sacrifice 1138
Love and Sacrifice 1139
On Love and Meditation 1140–1143
Heart Union and Sexual Union 1140
The Vision of your own Eternity 1144

50 The Aquarian Group-Consciousness

Group Work 1146
Personal Salvation? 1146
The Aquarian Teachers 1147
The Mystery Schools and Āśramas 1148
Qualifications for Discipleship (Sanskrit) 1149
The Path to Discipleship 1149
The Sacrifice of the Teachers 1150–1151
Responsibility towards the Teacher and the Group 1150
The Approach to Truth 1152
The Group Heart 1152
Sādhanā: the Spiritual Life 1153
Do the Work yourself 1153
Causes of Group Disruption 1154–1155
Psychic Disruption 1155
The Evil of Criticism 1156–1157
You have two families 1156
The Testing of the Soul 1158
Scenes of Battle (Kurukṣetra, Armageddon) 1158
The Tests of the Elements 1159
The Four Stages of Spiritual Life (Arabic) 1160–1161
Crises on the Path 1162–1165
What you must not do (in group work) 1164
The Fields of Life (the Great Breath) 1165
Notes on the Spiritual Path in the New Age 1166–1167
Overstimulation 1166
Difficulties which can arise when Practising the Path 1167
Diseases caused by walking upon the Spiritual Path 1168
Disease and Karma 1169
Solitude and Loneliness 1170–1171
Going Back to the Marketplace 1172

51 The Science of Meditation

In Search of Reality 1174
What is Reality? 1175
Entering the Lost Kingdom 1176–1177
The Lost Radiance 1176
To Achieve Liberation 1177
Quest for Reality 1178
Return to Primeval Happiness 1179
Ēgō: "I am" (levels of meaning) 1179
Meditation Degenerated 1180
The Method of Relaxation-Response 1180
What Meditation is not 1181
The Double Stress of Meditational Life 1181
Maharishi and Transcendental Meditation 1182–1183
A Comparison of Systems (graph) 1183
Types of Meditation 1184–1185
  Reflective Meditation 1184
  Creative (Active) Meditation 1184
  Contemplative (Passive) Meditation 1185
Stages of the Silent Meditation Process 1186–1187
  Meditation with a Seed 1186
  Contemplation 1186
  Sounding the Perfect Chord of Being (graph) 1186
  Illumination 1187
  Deification 1187
  To Contemplate... 1187
Contemplation 1188
Examples of Supernatural Contemplation 1189
Illumination and Deification 1190
The Illumination and Deification of Man (graph) 1190
The Muslim Deification Process 1191
Our Goal is nothing less than God 1191
Some Facts about Meditation (Dhyāna) 1192
Meditation is Integration 1193
The Threefold Human Constitution (graph) 1193
Building the Antaḥkaraṇa 1194
Integration of the Human Consciousness (graph) 1195
Steps on the Meditational Path 1196–1198
Steps on the Meditational Path (graph) 1197
Benefits of Meditation 1199
A Nirvāṇic Visualization 1200

52 Meditation Practice

The Art of Alignment 1202
Some Hints for Meditation Practice 1203
If you Wish to Meditate... 1204
Common Obstacles on the Path of Meditation 1205
Expect Nothing 1205
How to Succeed in Meditation 1206–1207
Your Mind is the Key 1208
The Buddha-Mind 1208
Suspended Mind 1209
The Suspending of the Mind (graph) 1209
Natural Meditation 1210–1211
Meditation with Nature 1210
To Silence the Mind 1212–1214
  The Watcher 1212
  Listen to Nāda 1212
  Rest your Mind in the Heart 1213
  Watching the Breath 1213
  Mantra 1214
  Upaniṣadic Mantras 1214
Listening 1215
Meditation on the Sacred Word 1216–1217
The Science of Bīja-Mantra 1218–1219
Esoteric Knowledge 1218
The Two Applications of Mantra 1219
Three Kinds of Breathing Meditation 1220
Vipassana 1221
Unstructured Meditation 1221
Vipaśyanā Yoga: Internal Observation 1222–1223
Sati-Prajñā: Truth-Discerning Awareness 1223
Meditation in the Third-Eye 1224–1225
Brahma-Nirvāṇa: Dissolution in God 1224
Meditation on the Form of the Guru 1225
Worship only the Divine Self 1226
Rely on your Inner Self 1226

53 The Heart and Spontaneous Meditation

Mental Activity 1228
The Purpose of Spontaneous Meditation 1229
The Way of Spontaneous Meditation 1229–1232
  Preliminary Steps 1229
  Awareness 1230
  Unlearning 1230
  Observing Nature 1230
  Observing Invisible Nature 1231
  Adeptship 1232
  The State of Being 1232
Your mind is attracted to physical things 1231
Liberation from Worldly Consciousness 1233
Attach your Mind to the Eternal 1234–1235
Beyond Heaven 1234
The Mind is Dissolved in the Heart 1235
The Threefold Way (Hṛdaya-Mārga) 1236
Subconscious Renewal 1236
A Summary of the Practice 1237
The Way of the Mind 1238
Cultivate Silence of the Mind 1239
Mind-Waves 1239
Trapped Spirits 1240
Let Go of the Past 1241
Transformations of the Mind 1242–1243
Super-Knowing 1242
How to have a Peaceful Mind in a Troubled World 1244
Being-in-the-Moment Meditation in the Head 1245
The Way to Bliss-Consciousness 1246–1247
The Way of the Mind (mantra) 1247

Part Ten
The Way of the Heart

54 The Heart and the Lost Art of Prayer

The Divine Mood 1252
The Stages of Prayer 1253–1257
  Oral Prayer or Verbal Prayer 1253
  Mental Prayer 1254
  Mental Prayer in the Heart 1254–1255
  Heart-Prayer or Spiritual Prayer 1256
  God-State 1257
The Fire of Love 1255
Balance on the Physical Plane 1257
The Name and the Names 1258
What is the Name? 1259
How to begin Mental Prayer in the Heart 1260
The Names and Mental Prayer in the Heart 1261
Hebrew Divine Names to be Invoked in the Heart 1262–1263
The Hebrew Heart 1263
The Beautiful Names (Arabic) 1264–1265
The same God resides in every Heart 1265
Christian Divine Names 1266–1267
Some Christian Prayers to the Deity 1266
Visualizing the Divinity within the Heart 1268
Some Sanskrit Divine Names for Meditation in the Heart 1269
Īṣta-Devatā: your Chosen Deity 1269
To Worship the Divine Incarnations 1270–1272
Great Incarnations of Divinity (graph) 1270
Astral Disinformation 1271
To Worship the Divine Incarnations in the Heart 1272
Understand the word "Goddess" 1272
Rām: the Universal Name 1273
Conscious Breathing in the Heart 1274–1275
Breath-Prayer in the Heart 1274
To Practice Conscious Breathing 1275
Abba 1275
Yeshua: the Secret Hebrew Name 1276–1277
Yesu-Breathing in the Heart 1276

55 Hṛdayaṁ: Meditations in the Heart Centre

The Experience of the Heart 1280–1281
The Secret of the Heart 1280
The Heart (Hṛdayaṁ) 1282–1283
To pray ceaselessly 1283
What is True Faith? 1284
The Holy Path 1285
Heart Knowing 1286
Develop a pure Heart and a refined Mind 1286
The Fire in the Heart 1287
Sanskrit Mantras to Invoke the Divine Self 1288
Paramātman can be found in your Heart 1288
Signs of Progress in the Heart 1289
My Beloved Lives in my Heart 1290–1291
The Image of God in your Heart Centre 1291
Three Meditations in the Heart 1292
The Bright Eternal Self 1292
To Invoke God in your Heart 1293
Meditations in the Heart Centre 1294–1302
The Saviour in the Heart 1296
The Pure Heart 1300
The Vowels in the Heart 1303
Peace on Earth 1304–1305
The Soul-Power 1305
The State of Innocence 1306
Let the Light Shine 1307
The River of Light 1308

56 The Heart and the Future Evolution of Man

Mysterious Knowledge of the Siddhas 1310–1311
Mysterious Grace 1311
Beyond Natural Evolution 1312
Further Light Bodies 1313
Every form is a Form of God 1313
Twelve Keys to the Heart 1314–1326
The Mystery within the Heart 1315
Quest for the Self 1317
The Avatāras 1320
The Thirteenth Key 1327
The Heart of the Solar Logos 1327
Guard your Heart 1328
The Qualities of the Spiritual-Heart-Consciousness 1329
To Succeed in your Quest 1330
Heart Action 1331
Action while in Samādhi 1331
The Heart and the Energy Centres 1332
Transformation of the Centres 1333
Personality Integration Chart (graph) 1333
The Body of Fire 1334

57 The Way of Holiness

Stages on the Way of Holiness 1336–1339
- The Path of Purification 1337
- The Path of Illumination 1338
- The Path of Union 1339

The Holy Breath 1340
Surrender to the Holy Breath 1341
The Holy Trinity 1342
The Holy Spirit 1343
Spirit (sacred language terms) 1343
Meditation on the Holy Spirit 1344
Holy Spirit (sacred language terms) 1344
Christian Meditation: the Way of Holiness 1345
- Circular Breathing in the Heart 1345
- Memory Breathing (the Rū-Hā) 1345
- Aspects of the Way of Holiness 1345

Christian Meditation on the Holy Breath 1346–1353
Baptism by Fire and the Spirit 1348
Degrees of Union with the Holy Breath 1349
Light (sacred language terms) 1350
Earth (sacred language terms) 1351
Heaven (sacred language terms) 1352
To Safely Perform Miracles 1353
Wisdom: the Light Path 1354
Wisdom (sacred language terms) 1354
The Silence of the Deep 1355
The Jesus Mantra and the Sacred Heart Initiation 1356
Variations of the Name of Jesus 1356
The Rose of Love and the Cross of Light 1357
Meditation in the Cave of the Heart 1358
The Divine Unity Mantra 1359

Part Eleven
The Way of Spiritual Psychology

58 The Psychology of Consciousness

Psychology Ancient and Modern 1364
Cultivate the Positive 1365
Cultivate Knowledge 1366
Education from the Spirit 1366
Transformational Psychology 1367
What is Consciousness? 1368–1369
All Hail to the Brain! 1368
The Three Identifications 1369
Consciousness (aphorisms) 1370–1371
The Basic Enlightened State 1372
Formless Worlds 1372
Formless Consciousness 1373
Mind and Body 1374–1375
The functioning of the lower centres 1374–1375
Mind and Thought 1376
Desire-Streams 1377
The Cycle of Desire (graph) 1377
The Experience of the Transcendent 1378
Manas-Taijasi: Radiant Mind 1378
Spiritual Healing 1379
Karmic Adjustment 1379
The Principle of Choice 1380–1381
Happiness Exist Within 1381
Self-Worth 1382–1383
The State of Unity of the Psyche 1383
The Laws of Group Psychology 1384
The Stages of the Work 1385
The Seven Centres of Force in the Human Species 1385
Silence, Solitude, Peace 1386
How do you Know who You really Are? 1387
The Silent Watcher Meditation 1388
Your personal sense of self is a mystery 1388
Know Thyself 1389
You Are the World 1390–1391
The Infinite Supply 1390
The Purpose of Meditation 1391
To Love God and the World 1392–1393
God's Fools 1392
Holiness to the Lord 1393
The Lighted Way 1394–1395
Brahmājyoti: God's Light 1394
Look for the Light 1395
The Presence of God 1396–1397
To Realize the Presence of God 1398

59 Time and Eternity: Action and Destiny

Past, Present and Future 1400–1401
Why do people cling to the Past? 1401
Action (Karma) 1402–1406
Karma and the Guṇas 1406
Destiny (Dharma) 1407–1409
Be who you are Now 1408

60 Metanoia: The Renaissance of the Mind

What is Metanoia? 1412
Metanoia: derivation and definition 1412
Aspects of Metanoia 1413
The Work of Metanoia 1414
There are two kinds of thinking 1414
Being and Becoming 1415
Reality (Metanoia) 1416–1417
Who is "I AM"? 1418
Activating I AM: the Secret Name of God 1419
Action and Destiny (Metanoia) 1420–1421
The First Circle of Life 1422
The First Circle of Life (Metanoia) 1423
Obstacles to Higher Consciousness 1424
Karma and Death (Metanoia) 1425
Reactive-Emotional Consciousness 1426
Signs of Reactive-Emotional Consciousness 1426
Illumined-Mind Consciousness 1427
Temporary Relief 1427
From Personal to Cosmic Life 1428
Emotional Problems 1429–1431
  Stress 1429–1430
  Anxiety 1430–1431
  Irritability 1431
God, the Healer of Broken Hearts 1432–1433
Attach yourself to Being 1433
Fear and Stress (Metanoia) 1434
How to Deal with Crisis situations in your Life 1435
Crisis (Metanoia) 1436–1437

The Second Circle of Life 1438
The Second Circle of Life (Metanoia) 1439
The Work of Meditation 1440–1441
Meditation (Metanoia) 1442
The Practice of Silence 1443–1447
Stages of Silence 1444
How to Enter Silence 1445
Silence and Activity 1446
Silence (Metanoia) 1447
Four Ways to Enter Silence 1447
The Third Circle of Life 1448
The Third Circle of Life (Metanoia) 1449
The three degrees of Self-Realization 1448
Oneness and Love 1450
Oneness and Love (Metanoia) 1451
Cosmic Renewal 1452
The Kingdom is at Hand 1453
Meditation on the Divine Names 1454–1462
The Inner Healer 1454
The Word (Metanoia) 1455
Hebrew Divine Words for Healing 1456
IOEL: The Healing Mind 1457
Yekhidah: The Hebrew I AM 1458
El Allāh Hū: The Arabic I AM 1459
IHVH: I AM 1460
Sounding the Hebrew Divine Names 1461
Sounding the Hebrew Angelic Names 1462
Healing (Metanoia) 1463
Inner Guidance (Metanoia) 1464
The Path (Metanoia) 1465–1467
The Twofold Way: Via Positiva and Via Negativa 1465
Summary of the Process 1468

61 Mahāvākya: Great Truth Statements
Words of Truth 1470
Mahāvākya Practice 1470
Great Truth Statements (Sanskrit) 1471–1479

Part Twelve
The Worship of the Goddess

62 The Great Goddess
Lalitā: the Eternal Feminine 1484–1485
The Divine Energy 1484
Śakti: the Energy of the Goddess 1486–1488
The Life-Force in Humanity 1486
Some Energy-Forms of the Goddess 1489
The Path of Mantra and the Goddess 1490

63 The Heart of the Divine Mother
The Temple of the Goddess 1492
The Blissful Mother: Mother of Immortal Bliss 1493
Sanskrit words for "Mother" 1493
Amṛteśvarī: the Supreme Spirit-Mother 1494
She is Nirmala-Sundarī: Spotless Beauty 1494
Kālimā: the Mother Beyond Time 1495
Sāvitrī: the Spiritual Sun as Mother 1496–1497
To Meditate on Sāvitrī 1497
Śrī Jagadambā: the Mother of the World 1498–1499
Paraśakti: the Supreme Power 1500
Āuṁ: the Holy Spirit as Cosmic Mother 1501
To Meditate on Ōṁ and Āuṁ 1501
The Role of the Divine Female in the Salvation/Liberation Process 1502–1503
Tranquil Mind 1503
Desire for the Real 1503
Fertilizing the Heart of the Divine Mother for the Conception of the Divine Child within you 1504
Hṛt-Padma: the Heart-Lotus 1505
The Spiritual Heart Complex (graph) 1505
General Children's Initiation Mantra into the Energy of the Goddess 1506
Quan Yin: the Mother of Compassion 1507
To Meditate on Quan Yin 1508
The Melodious Voice of Quan Yin 1509
Latin Mantras to Our Lady 1510–1511
The Sacred Heart of Our Lady (Divine Names) 1510
Mantras to Connect to Our Lady 1512
Visualization of the Immaculate Heart of Our Lady 1513
The Immaculate Heart (graph) 1513
To Approach the Goddess 1513

64 Śrī-Vidyā: The Holy Science

The True Feminine 1516
The two Aspects of Devī, the Goddess 1516
Holy Knowledge 1517
The materialization of Subtle Vibrations 1517
Vibration and Mantra 1518–1519
Important Seed-Sounds of Śrī-Vidyā 1519
Līlā: the Play of the Goddess 1520
Ōṁ Śrī: the Holy Vibration 1520
Śiva-Śakti 1521
Śivo'haṁ: I am Śiva 1521
The Living Form of the Goddess in the Light 1522–1523
Dhāraṇā and Dhyāna 1523
Treasures of the Goddess 1524
The Wisdom of the Goddess 1525
Śrī-Vidyā is a very refined Energy 1525
Garments of Light 1526–1527
The Śoḍaṣī Energy 1527
The Sound-Vibrations 1528
The Sound-Sequences 1529
The Śrī-Vidyā-Mantra 1530
The Śrī-Vidyā-Vajra-Mantra 1531
The Bālā-Mantra 1532
The Saptaḍaṣī-Mantras 1533
The Mother Light 1533
The Secret Heart-Mantra 1534
The Mātangī-Mantra 1535
The Kamalā-Mantra 1536
Kamalā Vibration 1537
The Strī-Mantra 1538
The Rati-Mantra 1539
The Bhairavī-Mantra 1539
The Cāmuṇḍā-Mantra 1540
The Mṛtyuṁjaya-Mantra 1540
The Rāmā-Mantra 1541
The Kālī-Mantra 1541
Potent Vibrations: Bīja-Mantra 1542–1551
  Ōṁ (Ōng) 1542-1543
  Lāṁ 1544
  Vāṁ 1544
  Rāṁ (Rāng) 1544-1545
  Yāṁ 1546
  Hāṁ 1546
  Hūṁ 1546
  Hrī 1546
  Hrīṁ (Hrīng) 1547
  Śrī 1548
  Śrīṁ (Śrīng) 1548
  Strī 1548
  Strīṁ 1548
  Krīṁ (Krīng) 1549
  Klīṁ (Klīng) 1549-1550
  Aiṁ (Aing) 1550
  Īṁ 1550
  Trīṁ 1550
  Trāṁ 1551
  Krāṁ 1551
  Āṁ 1551
  Māṁ 1551
  Śāṁ 1551
  Ha 1551
  Sa 1551
  Ahaṁ 1551
  Svāhā 1551
Bīja-Mantra Practice 1552
Bīja-Mantra and Psychology 1552
Gāyatrī (Sun) Breathing 1553
Prāṇāyāma-Vidyā is the Science of the Breath 1553
The Silent State 1554

65 The One-Hundred Names of Lalitā

Lalitā: the Ultimate Goddess 1556
Meditation on the Names of Lalitā 1557
The One-Hundred Names of Lalitā 1558–1581

Part Thirteen
The Yoga of the Sun

66 The Mystery of the Sun
To Worship the Sun 1586
The Circle of the Sun Teachings 1586
The Solar Constitution 1587
The Universal Creator-God 1588
The Field of Activity of our Solar Logos 1588
The Manifested-God 1589
Children of the Sun 1590
Dimensions of the Solar Logos in Cosmic Space (graph) 1591
The Solar and Human Heart 1592
Hṛdayākāśa: the Heart-Space 1592
Incarnations of the Sun 1593
The Incarnation of the Sun (graph) 1593
The Self-Generating Light 1594
The Shining Lights 1595
Peace of Heart 1595
The Light of the World 1596
Rules of Light 1597
The Mystery of the Sun is the Power of Love 1597
Divine Name Solar Vibrations 1598
The Healing Sun Mantra 1599

67 The Gāyatrī-Mantra
The Savitā-Mantra 1602
The Basic Hymn 1603
Sūrya-Sādhanā 1604
Viśva-Yoga: Cosmic Union 1604
Preliminary Meditation 1605
How to Meditate on the Sun 1606–1607
The Root Gāyatrī-Mantra of Sūrya-Devatā 1608
Meanings of the Root Gāyatrī-Mantra 1609
Detailed Meanings of the Root Gāyatrī-Mantra 1610–1611
The Gāyatrī-Mantra (variations) 1612–1640
The Brahman-State is Brahma-Loka 1613
The Living-Voice is Śabda-Brahman 1615
Hṛdaya-Cakra: the Heart Centre 1616
The difference between Svaha and Svāhā 1617
Warriors of the Sun 1618
The World Priest 1619
Sūrya is Prajāpati, the Lord-of-the-People 1622
Īśvara: levels of meaning 1623
Our Sun is a gigantic Knot of Power 1625
Rāma is the Sun incarnated in a Perfected Spiritual Warrior 1629
Ātman, Ātmā, is the Spiritual Self 1632
The Boundless-Circle-of-Infinite-Light 1633
Paramātman is the Transcendental-Spiritual-Sun 1634
The Shaft of Light from the Sun 1635
Brahma-Gāyatrī-Mantra 1638–1639
The Brahma-Gāyatrī in the Cakras (graph) 1639
Solar Meditation in the Cakras (graph) 1640
Duty and Spirituality 1641

68 Works of Silence
The Eternal 1644
Sūtrātma: description and meditation 1645
The Word, Logos, Voice, Name 1646–1648
God's Cosmic Symphony 1649
God has three Persons or Aspects 1649
See the Light of the Logos 1650
Hear the Sound within the Silence 1651
The Sounds of Nāda 1651
Cosmic Tuning-In: the "I" Sound 1652
Remember the Presence 1653
Rest in the Great Breath 1654–1655
Awareness Meditation 1656

69 Salutations to the Sun
More Mantras to Sūrya, the Sun 1658–1674
The Activity of the Divine Heart 1675

Part Fourteen
The Path of Service

70 Buddhi Yoga: Liberation by Wisdom
The Essence of Wisdom 1680–1684
The self and the Self 1680
The Great Mantram of Buddhi Yoga 1682
To Experience Spiritual Ecstasy 1683
How I write is a Process 1684
What is Wisdom? 1685
The One 1686–1687
Evolution, the Plan, the Path 1688–1692
The Creative Soul 1692
Paths of Spiritual Evolution 1693
The Three Forces at work in Nature and Humanity 1693
The True Teachers 1694–1695
Philosophia: the Love of Wisdom 1694
Mythology and Materialism 1695
Right Practice 1696–1697
Planetary Disturbance 1697
The Sevenfold Practice 1698
The Secret of Meditation 1698
The Wisdom of Not-doing 1699
Inner Absorption by Listening 1699
Practice for Wisdom 1700–1701
The Path to Wisdom 1702–1704
The Enlightened 1702
Nāmaste: the personal greeting of old India 1703

71 The Call to Service
Piscean Spirituality and New Age Spirituality 1706
Penetrating into the Kingdom 1707
Penetrating into the Kingdom (graph) 1707
The New Age and You 1708
The Future 1709
The Cosmic-Sense 1709
Revelation is Continuous 1710
Crisis and Revelation 1711
The Initiation of the World 1712–1713
Dwell on the Positive 1712
The Bridge of Consciousness (graph) 1713
What is True Service? 1714
To Feed the Poor? 1714
The Kingdom of God 1715
To Manifest the Kingdom of God 1716
Universal Service 1717

72 In Service to the Spiritual Hierarchy
The Function of the Spiritual Hierarchy 1720
Let Thy Will Be Done 1720
Hierarchies of Life (graph) 1721
The Buddha and the Christ 1722
Buddha Initiation Mantra 1723
Christ Initiation Mantra 1723
How to become a Buddha or a Christ 1723
Pure Devotion: Initiation Mantram 1724
The Mystery of the Christ (graph) 1724
Jesus: the Fire of Love 1725
The Jesus Mantra 1725
The Hierarchical Mantrams 1726–1727
Postscript 1728–1729

∞

APPENDIX B

Lexicon of the Wisdom Language

The Wisdom Language

The Spiritual Science is taught by words, just as car mechanics is taught by words. If you want to be a car mechanic you need to learn the words for the different parts of a car; then you can read books about it, converse intelligently with other car mechanics and do the practical work of fixing cars, because you know what is what. Yet, when it comes to Spiritual Science, people are short of words because such truths are not taught to them by their parents, nor by schools or universities, nor by the religions. So people are spiritually asleep.

Know the things that are.
Hermes Trismegistus (Thoth)

Know the Truth, and the Truth shall make you free.
John 8:32

Be ye transformed by the renewing of your minds.
Romans 12:2

Words are important because they convey ideas, and correct ideas convey the Truth. "Know the things that are," said the wise old Tehuti (Thoth) of ancient Egypt. By this He did not mean the modern idea of "knowledge": naming various animals, bugs, plants and physical things, dissecting them and naming the parts, and memorizing dates and "facts and figures" of all sorts. No, for the students of old, Knowledge was about invisible realities, forces, energies, realms, entities, and so on, and they *named* these things. Hence the importance of learning the ancient words in Sanskrit, Hebrew, Greek, Latin and Arabic.

When I define the ancient words, I use modern terminology so you may comprehend that they are telling of real things. In ancient times, spiritual words were *realities* to those who spoke them, and today they must be used and interpreted likewise. Dry, scholarly, intellectual translations are too abstract to be of any practical use. Words are *things*. The words I am teaching you represent aspects of the Limitless Truth. They tell you how things really are.

Even if you just know and understand the spiritual words, they alone will transform your mind, even before you do any practical meditational work. Just knowing the Wisdom Language of the past will free you inside yourself. You will begin to look at life differently. Each true spiritual word transforms your mind, renews your mind, puts forth a truth into your mind which was not there before, and hence *expands* your mind.

Even just a knowledge of the "things that are" will change your mind, and hence your life.

God's Writing

Sanskrit is the most frequently used sacred language in this book. It is SAṄSKṚTA, which means "well-made, perfectly polished". It is also called DEVANĀGARĪ, "God's writing". It is the most ancient sacerdotal (priestly) language of India, used for writing the scriptures, mythologies and sciences of the ancient Indian Subcontinent.

Sanskrit is a multi-layered language. It is a language which has the highest number of esoteric, spiritual and religious words, terms and expressions. There is no other language like it on Earth. The spiritual and esoteric terms run into thousands and thousands.

There is no other language like it on Earth

From it have been derived the modern languages of India, which are *corrupted* Sanskrit, in the same way as you could say that French, Spanish, Italian, Romanian and Portuguese are corrupted forms of the Latin language.

We are dealing here with the pure form of Sanskrit, along with its esoteric and spiritual meanings. Most of these meanings are not known to Western scholars, who mostly deal with myths and mythology. Not many of them know the esoteric meanings. The Sanskrit we speak of is the Language of the Initiates.

Standards and Variations

The lower mind, the rational mind, likes to simplify things, to make things "easy" to comprehend, thereby limiting the Truth.

Ultimately we cannot have a completely "standardized" enumeration of Spiritual Truth because things change according to how you look at them: for instance, from the "planes" point of view; from the "consciousness" point of view; from the "practice" point of view. And they are all correct!

Similarly with Sanskrit words and their variations and alternative spellings: there are reasons for these. The same for the Hebrew language: a word can be *sounded* differently, necessitating different vowels and different lengths of vowels.

Further, there is the exoteric view of things and the esoteric (deeper) view. The esoteric is known only to the more advanced on the Path. Most of the time I am using the esoteric view, but sometimes the other also.

Language of the Gods 200
Our Sacred Music and Language 2081

A

Abba, Aba
Hebrew-Aramaic: "God, Father, Source". The First in Creation, the Creator-God, God as the Divine Father in All. Jesus used this Name to invoke the Divine Father in His Heart. Jesus never asked that people should worship Him; on the contrary, He continually pointed towards Abba, the Father, who dwelt in "Heaven".

Abbas
Greek: An elder. A saintly old man of the desert, usually addressed as "father". From this came the English word *abbot,* which in later centuries was the name given to the head of a monastery.

Abhyāsa-Yoga
Sanskrit: Repeated effort in your meditations and devotions. Patient perseverance. This is the key to success in the Spiritual Life.

Abstract Mind
The Higher Mind. The Higher Manas, functioning on the formless subplanes of the Mental Plane. Pure Intellect, "Pure-Reason". In Latin, Intellectus. In Sanskrit, Kāraṇa-Manas (Causal Mind).

Abūdiyat
Arabic: Service to the Teacher and Worship of God. Faithfulness to the Path. This is the fourth stage of the Journey of the Heart. At this stage the Heart impulses are very strong and you express your Devotion by doing things for the Teacher, your Group and the Teaching. This Arabic word is derived from the Persian and Arabic word Abū, "father". (Note also the Hebrew word Abba.) In the spiritual sense, the Spiritual Teacher is a "father" to the devotee-disciple.

Acala
Sanskrit: Tranquil.

Ācārya
Sanskrit: A teacher, a tutor, a pedagogue, a leader, a school master, a religious instructor. An ordinary spiritual teacher who teaches spiritual truths but who is not involved in the pupil's life-stream (in contrast to a Guru, a spiritually magnetic personality who not only teaches, but who by his very existence changes those around him). [See Guru]

Actualize
From the Latin: To make real, to make something a fact, to accomplish a task.

Adhi
Sanskrit: Superior or virtuous.

Adhi-Daivatam
Sanskrit: "The Supreme-Self-Shining". The Intelligence behind all forms; the Substratum of all Cosmic Energies. It shines within you also, unimpeded.

Adhi-Jyoti
Sanskrit: The Inner Light. The Inner Beatific Vision.

Adhipam
Sanskrit: Superior species.

Adhiṣṭhātṛtvaṁ
Sanskrit: Lordship over all. Mastery over the lower five Planes of Being of our System.

Ādi
Sanskrit: The First, the Origin, the Source, the Beginning, the Primeval, the Primordial. Before all things, superior to all things. Also, "the First Plane", Mahāparanirvāṇa, the Logoic Plane, Satya-Loka (the Realm of Truth). Also, "the First Element", the Divine Essence, the Cosmic Element corresponding to the substance of the Mahāparanirvāṇic Plane.

Ādi
Arabic: The very Ancient, the Primeval, the Primordial State.

Ādi-Ānanda
Sanskrit: "Primeval Happiness". The Innermost Self, your true Nature, is inherently Blissful (Ānanda). Therefore, as you go deeper and deeper in your meditations, you will spontaneously experience more and more joy, happiness, felicity and elation in your life. The Way of Meditation is a return to Primeval Happiness (Ādi-Ānanda).

Ādi-Anta-Sakalā
Sanskrit: "The Beginning, the End, the All". The First, the Last, the Complete. A Name of Lalitā, the Goddess. Lalitā was there at the Beginning of all things. She is there at the End. She is the Eternal Continuum.

Ādi-Bhūta
Sanskrit: The substance or matter aspect of the first Cosmic Element, Ādi.

Ādibuddha (Ādi-Buddha)
Sanskrit: "The First Living Being". The Primeval Buddha. A term used by the Mahāyāna Buddhists for the Godhead.

Ādipuruṣa (Ādi-Puruṣa)
Sanskrit: "The First Being, the Original Person, the Primeval Spirit". The Original Spirit, the Primeval Lord. The Godhead within the Universe. The Logos.

Ādi-Śakti
Sanskrit: The Primordial Energy of the Universe, which is part of Fohat, the Cosmic-Electric Force.

Ādi Śaṅkarācārya
Sanskrit: The first Shankaracharya, who lived five hundred years before Christ.

Ādi Śeṣa
Sanskrit: The Primordial Serpent of Wisdom.

Ādi-Tanmātra
Sanskrit: The vibration or force aspect of the first Cosmic Element, Ādi.

Āditattva
Sanskrit: The essential or subtle aspect of the first Cosmic Element, Ādi.

Āditya, Ādita
Sanskrit: The Primordial Solar Logos, the Original-Creative-Force. Also, the Solar Logos, the Golden Being who resides in the Sun and in our Solar System. The Cosmic Soul-Entity whose body is the visible and invisible parts of our Sun and Solar System. Also, the Sun-Light. This is the Dazzling Inner Radiance you can see in meditation in your Third-Eye Centre, in the Crown Centre, in the Heart, in the Solar Plexus Centre and in the Base Centre. The *form* of the Sun (the Sunshine) will be perceived differently in each centre, however.

Āditya-Śabda
Sanskrit: "Sun-Sound". The Vibrations emanated by the Solar Logos in the form of Sounding-Light waves.

Adonai
Hebrew: God. Lord God. The Personal God.

Advaita, Ādvaita
Sanskrit: "Not two". Non-duality, Oneness, Unity. The All-Oneness.

Advaita Vedānta
Sanskrit: Non-Dual Consciousness. Consciousness of Unity, being One with the All, Union with the All. The state of Buddhi.

Aeon, Aion
Greek: Time, an Age, a cycle of Manifestation, a duration, a period or cycle within Time. Also:
- Eternity, Everlastingness.
- Space (All-Space).
- A world, a realm.
- A Creative God, a Ruler or Power that emanated from the Supreme Godhead.
- A Ruler of a realm of Space or of a cycle of Time, or of a realm, a world or a plane.

Thus Aeon can mean Eternity, an Age, Space, a Power emanated from the All-Oneness, a realm or a being.

Aeonian, Aionios
Greek: The Eternal One, the Timeless, the Everlasting, the Transcendental Reality. God the Unmanifest (beyond Creation).

Aeons, Archons
Greek: According to the Gnostics, the reflection-sphere (the Astral World) was ruled by the Aeons, who held all powers in this world and in the next. The Gospel writers avoided the well known Greek words Aeons and Archons, which represented the "rulers of this world" and of the reflection-sphere. They used the Latin words *principalities* and *potentates* and the expression "rulers in high places" (in the Astral World). It is against these "rulers" that we have to struggle to liberate ourselves. [See Archon]

Aequilībrium
Latin: Equilibrium. The old Roman word for the Law of Karma.

Aether
Greek: "Space". Space in its boundless extension, including the visible space known to science, and all the Inner Spaces of the higher dimensions. Aether, or Space, is the *Body of the Absolute*. Aether means the same as the Sanskrit Ākāśa. Space (Aether, Ākāśa) is the container of all. It contains within itself the Seven Great Dimensions and everything within them. It is the Physical Body of God. God is in it, totally, even as you are in your physical body. [See Ākāśa]

Afflatus
Latin: "Inspiration by God". The breathing-in of God's Power, Wisdom and Knowledge at the Soul level. A Divine imparting of Gnosis (Wisdom and Power). The experience of the Divine as an overmastering impulse or energy within the Soul, as the Guide, Teacher or Guru of the Soul, or the perception of the guiding Force of the Divine Presence in the *intimate depths* of the Soul.

Agape
Greek: Universal Love. Spiritual Love. Divine Love. Platonic Love. Transcendental, almost impersonal Love. The Love of God. Universal Love for all Mankind. Similar to the Sanskrit Prema.

Agneya-Astra
Sanskrit: "A weapon that causes all-consuming fire or heat." Atomic bombs or something similar. These used the powers of the atom, electricity, sound, light, colour, mind-force, cosmic energies, and so forth. The ancient Hindu writings are full of descriptions of these awesome weapons.

Agni, Agniḥ
Sanskrit: The Lord of Fire. God in the aspect of Fire. The Fire of the Spirit. Cosmic Fire. The Sacred-Fire within the Sun, or Solar Logos, and within the Universe. Agni is also the Light of Knowledge or Enlightenment produced by the Sun.

Agni-Bhū
Sanskrit: "Reborn of Fire". As your meditation progresses, the Fire of Mind burns more brightly until it burns through the etheric web guarding the Crown Cakra, thus admitting the Fire of the Spirit, Agni. This is the true Second Birth, or being "born again".

Agni-Rūpa
Sanskrit: "Fire-Body". The Body of Fire. When the Fire of the Monad (the Spirit) has transmuted the Heart, the seven cakras are slowly transformed by Fire and become Fire. The Fire within Matter blends with the Fire of the Mind and the two are dissolved in the Fire of Spirit. A Supernatural Transformation takes place, a new body is created which is pure Fire, and the seven cakras are but vortices of Living Fire within the Fire-Body. Such is the future possibility for all Humanity.

Agniṣvātta
The Sixth Manifest Hierarchy, a Creative Order having bodies. (From Agni and Sattva.)

Agnitattva
Sanskrit: The essential or subtle aspect of the Fire Element, Agni or Tejas, the Cosmic Element corresponding to the substance of the Mental Plane. Also called Taijasatattva.

Agnosia, Agnosis
Greek: Nescience, spiritual darkness, spiritual blindness or ignorance, worldly consciousness. The opposite of Gnosis (A-Gnosis). Similar to the Sanskrit terms Māyā (delusion, material illusion, materiality) and Avidyā (nescience, spiritual blindness). There is, however, a higher meaning of the word Agnosia: a *Spiritual Unknowing*. Saint Damascius says that at a very high stage of Mystical Union we perceive the Unknowable Darkness, beyond all mind and thought actions, a Darkness which is, in fact, a super-abundant Light of God, too dazzling for even the eyes of the Soul to contemplate. This is *Contemplation by Unknowing*.

Agnōstikos, Agnostos
Greek: Unwise, unenlightened, ignorant. Hence the English word *agnostic*. Nowadays there are people who are proud to be agnostics, to be spiritually ignorant. It is seen as a virtue! The materialistic mind thinks, "I do not believe it, therefore it does not exist." The Gnōstikos (the Gnostics) were the Wise, the Enlightened, Illumined, Initiated people in touch with Spiritual Realities. [See Physis and Gnōstikos]

Aḥad
Arabic: The One and Only. The One, the Unique, the Singular, the Oneness, the Divine Unity, the One without a Second (without parts, attributes or divisions). The Absolute State of Unity. The same as Waḥīd and Tauḥīd: the indescribable Singularity or Oneness of the Eternal Reality, or Union with God. This is the highest possible experience of God, which includes both God-Immanent and God-Transcendent. This is not speculative philosophy, theological belief or metaphysical guesswork, but the *experience* of the Mystic in the highest states of Ecstasy or Inner Union, beyond the comprehension of the body and the mind, in the Transcendental Vision of the Heart.

Ahaṁ
Sanskrit: "I Am". The Spontaneous-Free-State. Spontaneous Living in the Eternal, which is Karma-less. The state of Ahaṁ is true renunciation, and in this state one becomes an Avadhūta, a renunciate. To become a true "renunciate", however, does not mean to cease to act! It means to *renounce the rewards* of action. To act with a desire for results is Ahaṁkāra, "I am the doer", which produces Karma. In the Sanskrit language, 'A' is the first letter of the alphabet and 'Ha' is the last, while 'Ṁ' is the unifier, the dissolver. Thus, Ahaṁ signifies the alpha and omega, the first and the last, the beginning and the end, the All in One, in the Eternal Now.

Ahaṁ-Ātman
Sanskrit: "I am Pure Spirit, I am the Eternal Self, I am the Breath of God, I am the Being of Light, I am the Inner God, I am the Spiritual Soul, I am Pure Being, I am Pure Existence, I am a Spark of the Eternal Flame". If you realize this in your Heart, you will attain Self-Realization (Enlightenment) in this lifetime.

Ahaṁkāra
Sanskrit: "I am the doer, the performer, the actor, the causer". The Reincarnating Ego, the Individualized Soul (Jīva), working through the personalized self, the personality. Your personal ego-sense in the body, the self-centred "I" sense, the sense of "personal importance". The illusionary sense of the personality being separated from the Spirit. When Divine Consciousness is attained, the Ahaṁkāra simply becomes Ahaṁ, "I am".

Ahiṁsā
Sanskrit: Harmlessness, non-violence, non-killing. Ahiṁsā is the first observance (Yama) of Aṣṭāṅga Yoga, as set down by Patañjali. We begin the Path by learning to be non-violent in thought, word and deed. We must have no desire to hurt anyone or to destroy anyone or anything. A person who is always hateful, violently angry, or planning or doing harm to others, is locked up in a hellish world in his or her mind and therefore cannot rise to Mystical Union.

Ahl Al-Ḥaqq
Arabic: The Followers of the Real (God) or the Absolute Truth. A name given to the Sūfī Saints.

Ahriman
Persian: "A Great Being of Light". The same meaning as the Latin Lūcifer.

Aiṁ (Aing)
Sanskrit: The Bīja-Mantra for Sarasvatī (the flowing river), the Goddess as the River of Light. She is the River of Knowledge, Enlightenment, Illumination. She is the Goddess of learning, culture, skills, crafts and the arts. She gives creative powers to the mind and thoughts, the ability to learn, education, cheerfulness, happiness, joy, Inner Knowledge, Wisdom, Esoteric Knowledge, the powers of speech, music and Mantras. She gives purity of body, mind, emotions and Soul. She removes all ignorance from the mind. Aiṁ (Aing) is also the Guru, the Spiritual Teacher, the Master, and all teaching abilities. [See Sarasvatī]

Ain
Hebrew and Chaldean: The Self-Existent One. The Eternal, beyond Time and Space. The Nameless Unmanifest Godhead. The Absolute in the Absolute Condition, out of which is emanated the Limitless Light which contains the Universal Mind and all the Creator-Gods. Ain is beyond Causation and beyond the Law of Cause and Effect. In Sanskrit, Parabrahman.

Ain Soph
Hebrew: The Endless, the Boundless.

Ain Soph Aur
Hebrew: The Unmanifest, Limitless Light-Being. The Mind of Light of the Absolute. The pre-Genesis God-Self. The great Hebrew Names Ain, Ain Soph, Ain Soph Aur, refer to the Nameless, the Boundless and the Limitless Light, which are above Nirvāṇa, above the Tree of Life. Only such great Prophets as Melchizedek, Enoch, Moses and Jesus knew about those exalted realms of the Divine Mind.

Aion
[See Aeon]

Aionia Zoe
Greek: Eternal Life. Eternity, the true Being. God as God is.

Aionios
[See Aeonian]

Aisthesis
Greek: Perception. To receive impressions through the mind and the senses.

Ajapa
Sanskrit: The non-repetitive or spontaneous method of working with a Mantra, by which you gradually reduce the vibration of the Mantra and allow it to swing upwards or inwards, thus ascending the realms of mind to arrive at the Soul-Realm, or Self-Realization.

Ajapa-Japa
Sanskrit: "The Unrepeated Sound". A meditational technique used in India which is similar to the Japanese Zen and Chinese Chān technique of Hua-Tou (watching the mind before a thought arises). In this method, the student yogī watches the breath in the Heart as it enters and leaves.

Ājñā
Sanskrit: The Divine Command. She is the Voice of Light in the Third-Eye. A Name of Lalitā, the Goddess.

Ājñā Cakra
Sanskrit: The Command Centre. The Third-Eye Centre, situated between the eyes in the forehead. In the unregenerated human the Third-Eye is the seat of the ordinary mind. As this centre is awakened it becomes the seat of higher psychism and spiritual vision. Ājñā means "command, control". From this centre the Soul can control the personality. Also called the *Eye of Śiva*, the *All-Seeing Eye* or the *Single-Eye*.

Ajñāna
Sanskrit: The Spiritual Darkness of Ignorance (A-Jñāna). Similar to another Sanskrit word, Avidyā.

Ajñāta, Ajñātam
Sanskrit: Unknown (A-Jñāta).

Akāla
Sanskrit: "Outside of Time" (A-Kāla). The Timeless, the Eternal, the Everlasting, that which is forever beyond change. Akāla, the Eternal, is *outside* of Time (Kāla). This is the Mystery of the Heart. Notice the difference between Akāla (outside of Time) and Sakala (without Time).

Akarma
Sanskrit: "No action" (A-Karma). Actionless. Non-activity. Also, not accumulating karmas. Similar to another Sanskrit word, Niṣkarmayam.

Ākāśa
Sanskrit: Space. Heaven. The All-Light of Reality. Space in its totality as the physical body of God. "Space" does not mean some kind of emptiness in which particles of matter float. Ākāśa does not mean there is "nothing there"; on the contrary, Ākāśa means that *all* is there—total Fullness. To the ancients, the word *Heaven* (Space) did not mean just the physical sky, but the inner, invisible worlds and spaces as well. While Space is seven-layered, only the outermost layer is visible to the physical eyes; thus, what is seen of Space is but a fragment of its totality. What is more, the ancients understood Heaven to be One, though layered or enfolded. Ākāśa is the One Universal Aether or Element permeating all the seven planes of our Solar System. In this sense, Ākāśa is equivalent to the Greek Plerōma and another Sanskrit word, Pūrṇa. Specifically, Ākāśa is the Cosmic Element corresponding to the substance of the Nirvāṇic Plane (this is an esoteric meaning which reveals how the Sages used the word Ākāśa). [See Aether and *Heaven*]

Ākāśa-Bhūta
Sanskrit: The substance or matter aspect of the Space Element, Ākāśa.

Ākāśa-Smṛti
Sanskrit: "Luminous memory". The Akashic Records, or the *Book of Life* as it is poetically named in the Bible. This is not a book, of course; rather, it is like a photographic film imprinted on Ākāśa, the Luminous Aether that is pervading all dimensions of Space.

Ākāśa-Tanmātra
Sanskrit: The vibration or force aspect of the Space Element, Ākāśa.

Ākāśatattva
Sanskrit: The essential or subtle aspect of the Space Element, Ākāśa.

Ākāśa-Vāṇī
Sanskrit: "The Voice of Heaven". The Sounding-Light, the Celestial Music, the Eternal Word, the Logos. The Voice of the Silence, the Spiritual-Sound which emanates from the Monadic Plane, Paranirvāṇa. Also called Deva-Vāṇī (the Divine Voice), Śabda-Brahman (Sounding-God) and Nāda (the Inner Sound-Current of the Universe).

Ākāśī
Sanskrit: The All-Pervading Goddess.

Akashic Records
The history of every living being, planet or star is written in the Divine Substance (Ākāśa). The astral Akashic Records are an *emotional* record of the past, impressed into the Astral Light. True and accurate Akashic Records are to be found on the Buddhic Plane. Called Ākāśa-Smṛti (Luminous Memory) in Sanskrit, Spēculum Justīciae (the Mirror of Justice) in Latin.

Akbar
Arabic: Great, omnipotent, powerful, very big. Also, a Name of God. [See Allahū Akbar]

Akhanda
Sanskrit: Continuous.

Akṣara
Sanskrit: Immutable, Imperishable, Indestructible, Immobile, Everlasting, Unchanging. A description of the One Reality, Parabrahman, the Godhead.

Alabdha-Bhūmikatva
Sanskrit: Missing the important issues, disappointment for not succeeding fast enough. One of the Antarāyāḥ (obstacles, impediments, problems on the Path to Higher Consciousness).

'Ālam
Arabic: A world, a realm, a kingdom, a sphere or plane of Being. The same as the Hebrew Olam and the Sanskrit Loka.

'Ālam-i-Hāhūt
Arabic: "The World of Divine Essence". This is the Origin, the Source of All Things. Nowadays we call it Mahāparanirvāṇa, the plane of Ādi, the Logoic Plane, the world of the Logos or Deity. In this state you *become* the Logos, and the Way opens up for you to the Door of Cosmic Life, Cosmic Perception.

'Ālam-i-Jabarūt
Arabic: "The World of Omnipotence". Nowadays we call this realm Nirvāṇa or the Ātmic World. The Arabic word Jabarūt means "Omnipotence, all-consuming Power, exceedingly high spiritual state, exalted condition". Very high Mystics or Enlightened Beings go to this realm of Being.

'Ālam-i-Lāhūt
Arabic: "The World of Divine Nature". The Arabic word Lāhūt means "the Godhead, Divine Beingness, Divinity". Nowadays we call this realm the Monadic World, the Divine World, the world of Paramātman, or the sphere of Absolute Glory, Paranirvāṇa. This is an extremely high state of Liberation. In this world abide species of Divine Evolutions.

'Ālam-i-Malakūt
Arabic: "The World of the Kingdom" (the Kingdom of God). Nowadays we call this realm the Buddhic World or Buddhic Plane, the World of Unity or At-One-Ment, the characteristics of which are Love, Bliss, Unity and Luminous Intelligence. The Arabic word Malakūt means "an empire or kingdom", but it also means the Kingdom of God. To this world go the Mystics who have united themselves, to a certain degree, with God. On this plane you are already Liberated.

'Ālam-i-Ma'nā
Arabic: "The World of Immediate Appearance". This is the Mental Plane, the true home of the "mind". Here your thoughts become immediately visible to yourself and to others, and the thoughts of others are clear and shining to you. Nothing that is in your "mind", or in the minds of others, can be concealed or hidden. The seven subdivisions of this plane are the true "Heaven Worlds". In Sanskrit it is called Devasthāna (the Realm of the Shining Ones).

'Ālam-i-Mithāl
Arabic: "The World of Subtle Imagination". In today's language we would call it the world of imaginative consciousness, or dream-consciousness, or reflection. This is the Astral Plane, the afterlife state or the subtle worlds. In Sanskrit it is called Kāmaloka (the Realm of Desires).

'Ālam-i-Nāsūt
Arabic: "The World of Humanity" (embodied Humanity). Nāsūt means Humanity, or pertaining to Mankind in physical bodies. This is the seventh world or realm, the Physical Plane.

'Ālam-i-Ṣūrat
Arabic: "The World of the Soul" (after death). The Arabic word Ṣūrat means an image, a form or appearance, but to the Sūfīs it also meant the "Soul" in the disembodied state. This is the sixth world, the Astral Plane. It is to the Astral World that you go after you exit your physical body.

'Ālam-i-Ṭabi'at
Arabic: "The World of Results" (having been sealed). Ṭabi'at has the sense of having been published or sealed, because it is the last world, the final result of the Creative Effort of Divinity. This is the seventh world or realm, the Physical Plane.

Ālasya
Sanskrit: Laziness, idleness, taking it easy. One of the Antarāyāḥ (obstacles, impediments, problems on the Path to Higher Consciousness).

Alaya
Sanskrit: The Universal Soul. Paramātman.

Alaya-Vijñāna
Sanskrit: "Universal Soul-Consciousness". The Soul of the World. An ancient Sanskrit term for the Soul within all visible Nature, the Feminine Divine Essence, Substance or Matter which pervades and animates all things, and out of which all things manifest by condensation or precipitation as the vibrations are lowered into visible physical shapes and forms. The term can be understood on several levels. At the highest level it is the Archetypal Mind of God, the Cosmic Mind. It is Ātmā-Buddhi, the Spiritual Soul within Creation. It is also the Collective Subconscious Mind or Subjective Mind, the All-Conserving Mind. The Buddhists understood it as the Storehouse Consciousness, the Storehouse of Wisdom, the Universal Treasurehouse—the Infinite Supply which gives you all experience according to your mind. It is the Ocean where the Vijñānas (relative knowledge gathered through the senses) revolve like waves stirred by the winds of objectivity (the senses). The material universe, and everything in it, is the manifestation of the Alaya-Vijñāna or Universal Subconscious Mind. Also called Saundarya-Lahirī (the Ocean Of Beauty). The ancient Egyptians knew it as the Goddess Isis. In Latin it is called Anima Mundi (the World Soul).

Aletheia
Greek: The Law, the Truth, the Original Divine Plan.

Alhamdulillāh
Arabic: "All praise be to God!" Surrendering to God. One of the virtues which must be cultivated on the Shining Path of the Sūfī is the Realization that all praise, glory and fame belongs to God only. In the state of Cosmic Consciousness one forever experiences the Divine Presence and one continually glorifies God, in a most natural and spontaneous way, in everything one thinks, does and feels. Similar to the Sanskrit Prema (the Love of God) and Bhakti (Devotion).

Al-Ḥaqq
Arabic: The One Reality, the Absolute, the Supreme Being. The Truth, Justice, Rightness. The Law.

Allah, Allāh
Arabic: "The God" (Al-Ilāh). The Effulgent One, the Shining One, the Radiant One, the Resplendent One. God as the overpowering Effulgence, the Eternally Shining, the Radiance of Glory, the White Brilliance. The Essence, the Essential Reality, the Ultimate, the Self-Subsisting, the Eternal. That which is beyond naming, comparison, description, images or definitions. Allah is *not* a person. Allah is the Total Reality that is God. Allāh is the Name of God, the greatest Name of God, the exalted Name of God.

Allahā, Alāhā
Aramaic: The Breath of the Eternal. The Universal Sun, the Radiant One. God as Radiant Energy, Fire. The Light of all things and within all things. El and Eloāh in Hebrew, Allāh in Arabic.

Allahū Akbar (Allāh Hu Akbar)
Arabic: "The Greatness of God" or "God is Omnipotent", commonly translated as "God is Great". How misunderstood is the Greatness of God! How tragic that this Name be used for human political ends! God is Great because God is Infinite Glory, Infinite Power, Infinite Majesty. God is the Ruler of all the Worlds, the Fathomless Abyss of Space, the countless stars and galaxies, and a World Everlasting. Who can stand in His Presence?

Allāhu Ta'ālā
Arabic: "The Most Exalted God".

Allegoria
Greek: "Speaking otherwise". Symbolic speech, much used in the Old and New Testaments (such as the story of Adam and Eve and the serpent, or Noah and the flood) and, unfortunately, usually interpreted by the ignorant as *literal events*. From this came the English word *allegory*. Jesus tells many allegories in the New Testament: the pearl of great price, the prodigal son, and so on.

Alta Centre
The Causal Cakra above the head. In Sanskrit, Kāraṇa Cakra.

Amalam
Sanskrit: Immaculately-Pure-in-Being.

Amanaska
Sanskrit: No-mind. The State of Pure Consciousness.

Ambā
Sanskrit: Mother, the Divine Mother.

Ambrosia
Greek: The Food of the Gods. What Jesus called the *Waters of Life* and the *Bread from Heaven*. These are pure and divine Substances of the Higher Worlds. In Sanskrit, Sañjivani (the Elixir of Life) and Amṛta (the Nectar of Immortality).

Amenti
Egyptian: "Underground, the underworld". The Shadowland. The lowest regions of the Astral World, created by the lowest human minds and carried in our physical bodies by our most primitive drives and instincts. The same as the Hebrew Sheol and the Greek Hades.

Amida-Butsu
Japanese: The Infinite Buddha. The Christ in the Heart. In Sanskrit, Amitābha-Buddha.

Amīn
Arabic: God as the Witness to all. The Indweller. A Name of God.

Āmīn
Arabic: The Word, the Logos, the Sound. The Arabic form of Amen.

Amitābha
Sanskrit: "Light-Limitless, Light-Endless, Boundless Light, measureless Ocean of Light". This is the Ain Soph Aur (Hebrew: Boundless Light) of the Jewish Kabbalists, the *Face of God*. In the East this Limitless Ocean of Light has been symbolized as a Buddha because it is not just an impersonal light, like a candle or a torch flame; it is a Living Intelligence, a Cosmic Mind, a Cosmic Person. In Japanese it is known as Amida, which means "Endless Light".

Amitābha-Buddha
Sanskrit: The Infinite Light-Being. The Buddha of Infinite Light. This Buddha of Infinite Light shines in your Heart as a Boundless Ocean of Reality, an Endless Vision of Pure Illumination and Knowing. It is the complete flowering of the Enlightenment Consciousness (Bodhi-Citta). It is the Ineffable Godhead. Amida-Butsu in Japanese.

Ammā, Ambā
Sanskrit: The Mother. The Divine Mother.

Amṛta
Sanskrit: Immortality. The Nectar of Immortality, the Spiritual Nectar, Ambrosia (Greek: the Food of the Gods), a pure and divine Substance of the Higher Worlds. The God of Immortality, the Supreme Spirit, Splendour, Light, Divinity, the Rays of the Spiritual Sun.

Amṛtā
Sanskrit: The Goddess of Immortality. She who is beyond Death. The Immortal One. The Splendid Light-Being. Splendour, Light, Beauty. The Nectar of Immortality. Sweet Nectar, or the Honey Taste of Spirit. The Eternal Spirit, the Inner Spiritual Sun. A Name of Lalitā, the Goddess.

Amṛtam
Sanskrit: Immortal, Undying.

Amṛteśvarī (Amṛta-Īśvarī)
Sanskrit: The Supreme Spirit-Mother. The Immortal Goddess, the Eternal Reality, the Ambrosia of Spirit, the Light of Eternity. She who is Unlimited, the Infinite Goddess. Amṛteśvarī is the Mother of Immortal Bliss, the Inner Mother who reveals Herself in the Heart of the Devotee and in the Heart of the Universe as the All-Compassionate Mother-Self of all beings, the Universal Mother-Power—caring, nurturing, loving, giving, forgiving. This All-Loving-Serving Mother-Power is also Pure Unobstructed Consciousness or Awareness, Eternal Stillness and Cosmic Activity. A Name of Lalitā, the Goddess.

Aṁsa-Avatāra
Sanskrit: A Divine Incarnation who manifests the Divine Nature only partially. These are the Saints and Masters, those who have descended from the Nirvāṇic Plane, the Buddhic Plane or the formless Mental Plane to teach. [See Avatāra and Mahā-Avatāra]

Anāgata
Sanskrit: What is coming. The Future. [See Atīta and Atha]

Anāhata Cakra
Sanskrit: "The silent or inner-music centre". The Heart Cakra, situated near the physical heart, slightly to the right side of the chest. The Heart Cakra is the balancing point between the Personality and the Individuality. This is the centre in Man, the Microcosm. In the unevolved human being the Heart Cakra is turned downwards towards the solar plexus. When the human being becomes an Initiate the Heart Cakra turns *upwards* towards the Throat Cakra. When unawakened, the Heart Cakra is the seat of higher emotions, self-worth, self-esteem, a sense of belonging. When awakened, it is the seat of Selfless Love, Spiritual Love, living for others, surrender to the Divine. The Hindu Mystics also call the Heart Cakra Hṛdayaṁ or Hṛdaya, meaning "I am the Heart". Kardia in Greek, Qalb in Arabic. [See *Heart*]

Anāhata-Nāda
Sanskrit: "The Unproduced Sound", meaning "not produced by external means", heard in the Heart Centre.

Anāhata-Śabda
Sanskrit: "The Uncreated Music". The Uncreated Music of the Eternal Word, the Logos, which plays sweet melodies in your Heart. The True Word of God, the Unutterable Name of God, can be *heard* in the Heart.

Ānanda
Sanskrit: Bliss, Joy, Happiness, Ecstasy. The highest pleasure or enjoyment. Bliss is the very nature of Spirit (the Monad), and of You as a Soul. If you undergo the Transformation, you partake in ever-greater measures of Bliss experience. This Bliss is innate within your Innermost Heart and does not depend on outer circumstances or conditions. You may experience this Bliss within you while the outside world is in turmoil and pain. Ānanda is the discovery of the basic purpose of Existence within you, which is Ineffable Joy.

Ānanda-Kanda
Sanskrit: "The Blissful Realm". The Awakened Heart. The Spiritual Heart.

Ānandamāyākośa
Sanskrit: "Blissful-Veil Body". The Bliss Body, the Christ Body, the Resurrection Body. The vehicle of true Intuition or Buddhi. This Light Body is created when the etheric-physical body and the causal body fuse through the activity of Soul-Light and become exteriorized in the inner worlds, producing the "new creature". The Soul begins to use this Light Body when it ascends out of the causal realms to the Buddhic realms. Also called Ānandamayakośa (the full-of-Bliss Body).

Ānanda-Rūpiṇī-Devī
Sanskrit: "Blissful-Form-Goddess". The Goddess whose Form or Essential Nature is Pure Bliss. She is Śrī Jagadambā, the Holy World Mother.

Ānāpānasati
Pali: "Mindfulness of breathing" or "being aware of breathing". Prāṇāyāma (breath-control) was a favourite method of Yogic meditation in old India before and during Buddha's time and is still so today. There are over a hundred different techniques of Prāṇāyāma, of which Ānāpānasati is one.

Anāpāna Sāti Sūtra
Sanskrit: "The incomparable gift scripture". In Pali, Ānāpānasati Sutta.

Anastasis
Greek: Resurrection into the New Life.

Anathema
Greek: "Curses". The Christian ecclesiastical authorities *anathematized* most spiritual teachings, and for centuries they excommunicated, persecuted or killed those who still believed in them, until now there is no memory of these teachings in the church.

Anavacchināḥ
Sanskrit: Not limited to, not bound by.

Anava-Sthitatvāni
Sanskrit: Slipping down from the state already achieved. Giving up. One of the Antarāyāḥ (obstacles, impediments, problems on the Path to Higher Consciousness).

Andro-Gynē
Greek: Male-female.

Aṅgāni
Sanskrit: Parts, divisions, limbs, members, means, ways, constituents.

Angelos
Greek: Literally, "a messenger, a representative, a spokesperson". A spiritual being *attendant* on God. A being acting as God's messenger. A spiritual or non-human being. One of the gods, or a guardian spirit. An invisible being who can become visible for particular purposes. Hence the English word *angel*. The angels are "spirits", but *not* human spirits. They are of another kind, of many grades, orders and classes. The "spirits" that haunt the seances and channelling sessions of mediums and psychics are *not* angels. They are human spirits, and sometimes not even that. True angels are superior to humans in powers and intelligence, but inferior to God. The angels are called Malachīm in Hebrew, Genii in Latin, Devas in Sanskrit. [See Devatā]

Aṇimā, Animan
Sanskrit: A type of spiritual vision in which your inner gaze can perceive even the most extremely minute things, such as the structure of an atom, and you have the sensation that you become small, like an atom, or like a wave or particle in the Ocean of the Universe. This is one of the nine "general" powers (Siddhis) which can manifest in advanced Humanity.

Animā
Latin: The Soul, which is within the body and beyond the mind.

Anima Mundi
Latin: The Soul of Nature, the Soul within the World, the World Soul. The World Mother, the Feminine Divine Essence, Substance or Matter that pervades and animates all things. In Sanskrit, Alaya-Vijñāna.

Annamāyākośa
Sanskrit: "The illusionary food-body". The gross physical body. Also called Annamayakośa (the consisting-of-food body).

Annamaya-Śakti
Sanskrit: The energy in food, sustenance, nourishment.

Annoia
Greek: Delusion, ignorance, glamour, illusion, unreality. Mundane consciousness. Also, the Divine Unknowing or Unmanifest. The same as the Sanskrit Māyā.

Anta
Sanskrit: Final. The end, the last, that which survives all things.

Antaḥkaraṇa (Antaskaraṇa)
Sanskrit: "Inner cause, inner action, interior frequency, inner sense, inner organ of vision". The channel of Light between the Soul and the self-consciousness, built through meditation. It links the lower mind to the Abstract Mind, and the personality to the Soul. This bridge in Consciousness has been called the *Rainbow Bridge* or the *Bridge of Light*. In the Western Mystical System it is called *Jacob's Ladder* or the *Ladder of Light* or the *Ladder between Heaven and Earth*.

Antar, Antas, Antaḥ
Sanskrit: Inner, within.

Antar-Ātman
Sanskrit: The Inner Self, which is *beyond* your body, emotions and mind. The Inner God. The Spirit of God who dwells in the Innermost part of the Soul. Your God-Self.

Antarātma Sādhanā
Sanskrit: The Quest for the Inner Self.

Antarāyāḥ
Sanskrit: Obstacles, impediments or problems on the Path to Inner Union. From Antar (inner) and Ayāh (iron; something rigid, unbending, strong, blocking). According to Patañjali, these obstacles are as follows:
- Vyādhi: diseases.
- Styāna: dullness, lack of perseverance, stupidity.
- Saṁśaya: doubts, indecision about the Path.
- Pramāda: carelessness, intoxication, drunkenness.
- Ālasya: laziness, idleness, taking it easy.
- Avirati: sensuality, lack of moderation and control.
- Bhrānti-Darśana: false perceptions, illusions, self-delusions, glamour, mistaken ideas.
- Alabdha-Bhūmikatva: missing the important issues, disappointment for not succeeding fast enough.
- Anava-Sthitatvāni: slipping down from the state already achieved, giving up.
- Citta-Vikṣepaḥ (Vikṣepās): mental distractions, confusion, losing your way on many sidetracks.

Antardhāna Siddhi
Sanskrit: The power (Siddhi) to become visible or invisible at will.

Antarikṣa
Sanskrit: The Inner World. The Astral Plane. Also called Antarikṣa-Loka and Kāma-Loka.

Antarjyoti (Antar-Jyoti)
Sanskrit: The Inner Light.

Antar-Jyotī
Sanskrit: "Inner Light". A Name of Lalitā, the Goddess. The Light of the Inner Sun seen in deep meditation. The Light of Intelligence. The Light of the Soul.

Antar-Mukha
Sanskrit: "Inward-facing". By focusing inward into your Heart (Antar-Mukha), through the gross and subtle dimensions, you will discover the Antar-Yāmin (Inner Ruler) of your Heart, the Antar-Ātman (Inner Self).

Antar-Yajña
Sanskrit: "Inner Worship". The direct approach to the Presence of God within the Heart, through meditation and chanting in the Heart.

Antar-Yāmin
Sanskrit: The "Inner Ruler" of your Heart. The Antar-Ātman (Inner Self).

Anthropos
Greek: Man. Mankind. The Human Creative Hierarchy.

Anti-Christ
The Dark Forces, the Brothers of the Shadow. Also, the *Great Deception*. This Great Deception will be a *staging* of the Christ, as in a great cosmic play, with "miracles" and with signs and wonders in the sky. And the millions will be deceived, for it will not, as yet, be the *real* Manifestation. [See *Dark Forces*]

Anu
Sanskrit: A follower, a disciple.

Ānu
Sanskrit: A living being, a human being.

Aṇu
Sanskrit: Very small, minute, subtle, divine. A Monad or Atom. The ancient Sanskrit word Aṇu does not mean the same as the modern scientific understanding of the word *atom*. To the Sages, Aṇu meant:

- Tiny, invisible *lives* (such as an "atom" of modern science, which, to the ancients, is a living, intelligent creature), or creatures so small they are not perceived by physical eyes or instruments.
- Something very minute, or very subtle or ethereal in composition (which, of course, would be invisible to the physical eyes).
- The Original Primordial Homogeneous Substance as a *single undivided entity*, out of which the manifold Creation evolved.
- God, Divinity, the Original State of all things, the subtlest state of Being.
- Man. The complete individual Man, as One. The personality, the Soul, the Triune Self and the Monad, as *one entity*.
- Atomic matter. A plane is a state or condition of Prākṛtī (matter), and the first subplane of any plane is the highest, subtlest matter (Aṇu, atomic matter) of that plane. Each plane or world is different to all others because of the differences in density of the primordial atoms (Aṇu). [See Monad]

Aṇupādaka
Sanskrit: "The Parentless Realm". Paranirvāṇa, the Monadic World. Also, the Cosmic Element corresponding to the substance of the Paranirvāṇic Plane.

Aṇupādaka-Bhūta
Sanskrit: The substance or matter aspect of the Cosmic Element Aṇupādaka.

Aṇupādaka-Tanmātra
Sanskrit: The vibration or force aspect of the Cosmic Element Aṇupādaka.

Aṇupādakatattva
Sanskrit: The essential or subtle aspect of the Cosmic Element Aṇupādaka.

Anupaśyaḥ
Sanskrit: Sees, perceives, cognizes. Appears as if seeing. Goes along with what is perceived. The Self has the power of Pure Seeing, but it goes along with what is presented to it by the mind (Anupaśyaḥ).

Aṇusvāra
Sanskrit: "Small sound, subtle sound". The Ṁ or ṄG sound. The nasal resonance. The "after-sound". Candra-Bindu, the nasal "hum" at the root of the nose, at the Third-Eye.

Anvaya
Sanskrit: "All-pervasive". The Cosmic Elements are all-pervasive (Anvaya) on the Buddhic Plane.

Apāna Vāyu
Sanskrit: That aspect of the Life-force (Prāṇa, Vāyu) which moves in the Base and Sex Cakra regions of the embodied human being.

Aparigrahā
Sanskrit: Non-grasping, non-attachment, not being greedy. Being free from the insatiable desire for wealth. Being free from excessive desires for name, fame and materiality. Aparigrahā is the fifth observance (Yama) of Aṣṭāṅga Yoga, as set down by Patañjali. It has been translated as having nothing to do with money, not accepting gifts, having no possessions, not earning a living, but literally it means "not receiving anything to oneself". It means not being bound by anything—not by any person, nor any object, event or circumstance. It also means that we do not bind others! We do not try to enslave anybody or anything. We give to all the same freedom of thought, speech and action that we would want for ourselves.

Āp, Āpa, Āpas
Sanskrit: The *Water* Element. The Cosmic Element corresponding to the substance of the Astral Plane. The "watery" substance of the radiant-energy of the astral layers of the Universe and throughout Creation. The Living-Waters-of-Light.

Āpas-Bhūta
Sanskrit: The substance or matter aspect of the Water Element, Āpas.

Āpas-Tanmātra
Sanskrit: The vibration or force aspect of the Water Element, Āpas.

Āpastattva
Sanskrit: The essential or subtle aspect of the Water Element, Āpas.

Apatheia
Greek: Dispassion. Spiritual freedom. Liberation from human nature. "Walking like an angel" or "being continually in the Light of God". The opposite of Pathos (passion). From this was derived the English word *apathy,* which means "being without feelings, indifferent, passionless or disinterested". To the classical Greeks and Christian Saints, however, Apatheia was a sought-after spiritual quality; there was nothing morbid in it. Apatheia meant the successful overcoming of the "deadly passions": gluttony, avarice, pride, bitterness, anger, unchastity, laziness and spiritual darkness. It is a state of detachment from the world, but *not* an indifference to things. [See Pathos]

Apekṣitvāt
Sanskrit: Needing, desiring, wanting, expecting, hoping.

Aphtarsia
Greek: The Indestructible, the Imperishable.

Apokryphos
Greek: The many esoteric, occult and Gnostic Christian manuscripts that were in circulation during the first three centuries of Christianity. The esoteric or deeper sayings of Jesus, banned by the church. From the Greek Apokriptein, "to hide, to conceal". All of the Apocryphal gospels, epistles and letters are profound; hence they were excluded from the Bible by the selectors and were declared "heretical" by the ignorant church authorities. Only one of these got into the New Testament: the *Apocalypse*. There is no rational reason why that one alone was permitted to stay in the Bible after it was heavily "edited" during the first four centuries.

Apotheosis
Greek: Union with God, becoming One with God. The Divinization of the Human Soul. God-Consciousness, God-Realization. The goal of Christian meditational practice. [See Theosis]

Aquarian Age
As our Solar System moves through different parts of Space it is subjected to different kinds of energies from the Universal Radiation-Field of the Holy Spirit. It takes our Solar Logos (the Sun) approximately 2,150 years to travel through each sign of the Zodiac. Currently the Piscean Age is ending and the Aquarian radiations are beginning to be felt throughout our Solar System, changing, renewing, re-creating all things. This is why this New Age is often called the *Aquarian Age*. The fundamental note of the Aquarian Age, so far as human reactions on this planet are concerned, incorporates the following principles: sharing, justice, the Unity of Humanity, the Oneness of God, freedom, cooperation, goodwill to all, Love. The ending of an Age and the beginning of a New Age is always *traumatic* for Humanity. [See *Zodiac*]

Arā
Aramaic: Earth. [See *Earth*]

Archetipon
Greek: The first model of things in the Cosmic Mind. From Arche (original, first, archaic) and Tipon (mode, pattern). Hence the English word *archetype*. Archetypes are the *subtlest* forms of things—in modern language, *causal* forms—out of which all denser forms are manifested or created. [See Idea]

Archetypal World
The Causal World (the higher mental subplanes), which is a world of *Ideas* and *Archetypes*. Note that the higher mental subplanes are formless from *our* point of view. [See *Four Worlds*]

Archon
Greek: A ruler of the various planes, realms, layers and worlds of the total Universal Manifestation. A lesser ruler or spiritual intelligence. Similar to the Greek Aeon (Aion). [See Aeons, Archons]

Arhat, Arha, Arhan, Arhant, Arahant
Sanskrit: Worthy of praise and reverence. Peaceful, gentle, kind. A Realized One, a Perfected One, a Venerable One, a God-Man, a Saint. A highly enlightened Seer. One who has developed Buddhic Consciousness. One who has glimpsed Nirvāṇa and is learning to establish himself in it. You become an Arhat by your own interior Realization that "the Kingdom of God is within you". This is done by following the Path of Service and Meditation.

'Ārif
Arabic: The Knowers of God. The Gnostics, the meditators, those who have esoteric knowledge about Man, God and the Universe. [See 'Āshiq]

Arka
Sanskrit: The Fire of Creation. Also, the remover of afflictions.

Armageddon
Hebrew: "Battlefield". From the Hebrew Harmegiddon (Har, "mountain", and Megiddon, "the Valley of Megiddo"). In ancient Palestine there was a great battle fought in a mountain district called Megiddo, in Northern Palestine. In spiritual literature, the word Armageddon refers to the Battle between the personality and the Soul—the Spiritual Crisis. Similar to the Sanskrit word Kurukṣetra.

Ārtha
Sanskrit: Purpose, cause, objective, goal, ways, means, pursuits, meaning, reward, wealth, fulfilment.

Ārthavatva
Sanskrit: "Purpose revealed". The Cosmic Elements reveal their purpose (Ārthavatva) on the Nirvāṇic Plane.

Arūpa
Sanskrit: "Without form" (A-Rūpa). Shapeless, formless, without embodiment. Worlds or beings which have no bodies or forms, not even subtle embodiments. In the context of the Deity, A-Rūpa refers to God-Transcendent. [See Sa-Rūpa]

Arūpa-Deva
Sanskrit: "Formless angel". Incorporeal Angelic Hosts which have no "bodies" (not even subtle bodies).

Arūpa-Loka
Sanskrit: "Formless world". A description of the higher planes, the higher Mental Plane and above, which are without forms and shapes but are characterized by pure Energy and Consciousness. [See Rūpa-Loka]

Arūpa-Manas
Sanskrit: "Formless mind". The Abstract Mind. The Causal Mind, Kāraṇa-Manas, which functions by formless thought-waves and intelligences, or Pure Thought, Pure Consciousness and Transcendental Consciousness.

Ārya, Āryan
Sanskrit: "The Noble Ones, the Sages, the Saintly Ones". Honoured, respected, spiritual, excellent. A noble race, who have attained self-mastery. The word Āryan originally referred to the early civilization of India. Hitler, of course, misused the word Āryan, as well as their symbol, the Svastika, 卍.

Āryan Epoch
The fifth great epoch, or Root-Race, of human evolution upon this planet. This present period of development commenced many thousands of years ago and emphasizes the development of the mental body, the mind structure, the ability to think, to reason, to be logical. This has led to science, philosophy, theology, metaphysics, and so forth.

During this epoch, Humanity is meant to concentrate on the cakras *above* the solar plexus. At this time the emphasis is on the Mental Plane—the evolution of the mental body and the Throat Cakra. What is more, the great Teachers of the past have already indicated the *future* of Humanity by implying the need to meditate in the Heart Cakra, the Third-Eye and the Crown Cakra. Races of Āryan descent include the Europeans, Jews, Arabs and East Indians.

Ārya-Mārga
Sanskrit: "The Noble Path". The Path to Divine Consciousness. The Spiritual Path. Specifically, the re-integration of Nirvāṇa into the four states below. Rather than giving up all activities in all the worlds, one is fully active and benevolent, doing good works, while always retaining the state of Nirvāṇa within oneself. This condition of a Perfected Man is called *God-Consciousness*. This is the Path of Compassion of the Bodhisattva, "one whose very essence is Wisdom and Love". A Bodhisattva is a Buddha, an Enlightened Being, a practical Mystic who sacrifices his or her own Enlightenment for the welfare of Mankind. He or she is the sacrificial victim. This is the better Way.

Asamprajñāta Samādhi
Sanskrit: A state of Samādhi in which you are not aware of anything outside, and all internal activities have quietened down. There is no awareness of mind, thoughts or self. You are free of all differentiation between the experiencer and what is experienced. There is only internal tranquillity, or Śāntiḥ (peace, tranquillity, calmness, silence, poise). From A-Sam-Prajñāta, "not with mind and ego". [See Samprajñāta Samādhi]

Āsana
Sanskrit: Poise, balance, posture. Steady bodily posture. Correct position and attitude. The right physical posture for meditation. The Haṭha Yogīs have made a complete set of physical exercises out of the word Āsana. For a Rāja Yogī, however, Āsana means any comfortable posture you can assume for long periods of meditation. The emphasis is on meditation, *not* on the posture.

Asat
Sanskrit: "Unreality" (A-Sat). Illusion, deception, non-being, non-entity. The phenomenal universe, the temporary Creation. Asat refers to our false perception of ourselves, God and Creation. It is spiritual darkness and ignorance. Similar to the Sanskrit words Māyā and Avidyā. [See Sat]

Ascension
Latin: In the symbolism of the New Testament, *Ascension* is the Union of body, mind and Soul with God. It is the entry into Nirvāṇa, the Kingdom of God.

Asekha, Aseka
Sanskrit: A Spiritual Master. An Adept. One who can enter Nirvāṇa at will or who is in Nirvāṇa all the time. There are Saints (Arhats) and Masters (Asekhas) on the Causal, Buddhic and Nirvāṇic Planes. They comprise the Fifth Kingdom on this planet, the *Spiritual Hierarchy.* [See Saṅgha]

'Āshiq
Arabic: The Lovers of God. Those Saints who are in Love with God, those who have abandoned themselves (annihilated the self) in the Fiery Love of God. [See 'Ārif]

Asketikos
Greek: A hermit, a recluse, one who is retired from the world. One who undergoes severe self-denials. One who is engaged in severe self-discipline, spiritual exercises, austerities, mortifications, and so forth. Also, Askesis, "training yourself". Hence the English words *asceticism* and *ascetic.*

Asmi
Sanskrit: Am.

Asmitā
Sanskrit: The sense of self in the physical body. The sense of "I-am-ness" or individual existence.

Aśokā
Sanskrit: Without sorrow, suffering or death. A description of the Godhead, Parabrahman.

Āśrama
Sanskrit: Stages of development in life. In the ancient Vedic days of India, human life was divided into four periods or Āśrama:

- Brahmacarya: the religious-student life.
- Gṛhastha or Gārhastya: the householder, or married with children.
- Vānaprastha: being in the world but becoming non-attached.
- Bhaikṣya or Sannyāsin: an ascetic or mendicant, one who has completely renounced the world in old age and spends all his time in meditation and spiritual experiences.

Āśrama also means a hermitage, a monastery or a spiritual centre. In the West we call them the *Mystery Schools*, with the Hierophant, or Perfect Master, as head of the School. In the East we have the Guru. The Work of the Mystery Schools and Āśramas is the expansion of Consciousness, alignment with one's own Higher Self, Spiritual Illumination, and service toward the Group Soul and the world, under the guidance of the Guru, the Hierophant, the Spiritual Master. [See *Mystery Schools*]

Aṣṭāṅga Yoga
Sanskrit: "The eight steps to Union". From Aṣṭa (eight) and Aṅgāni (parts, divisions, limbs, members, means, ways, constituents). Patañjali's recorded system of Aṣṭāṅga Yoga (he did not invent it) was divided into three major stages and eight steps:

1. The first stage, *Preparation*, consisted of five Observances or Commandments, Yama, traditionally understood as non-violence, truthfulness, non-covetousness, celibacy, and non-stealing.
2. The second stage, *Dedication*, consisted of five Rules, Niyama, traditionally understood as purification, contentment with one's lot, austerities, spiritual studies, and Devotion to God.
3. The third stage, *Yoga, Union, Mysticism*, consisted of the six remaining steps: Āsana (posture), Prāṇāyāma (breath-control), Pratyāhāra (withdrawal of the senses), Dhāraṇā (concentration), Dhyāna (meditation), and Samādhi (trance, ecstasy, Union).

Aśtara-Vidyā
Sanskrit: The Science of Magic. The highest magical knowledge.

Aṣṭāvakra
Sanskrit: "Eight beads" (short prayer-beads). Also, the name of a great Sage in ancient India.

Aṣṭāvakra-Gītā
Sanskrit: "The Song of the Supreme".

Asteya
Sanskrit: "Non-stealing". Not stealing from others, not misappropriating the property of others. This means that we do not take what does not belong to us, *on any level*—emotional, mental or physical. We do not covet what is not rightfully ours. Asteya is the third Yama (observance) of Aṣṭāṅga Yoga, as set down by Patañjali.

Astral Body
A form or vehicle made up of astral matter, existing on the Astral Plane. Every single entity—a human being, a bird, a tree, an animal—has an astral body. The astral body is a luminous form which interpenetrates the physical form. It is the more real part of your nature, for the physical form is only an extension of this luminous body. The astral body *was* before birth, *is* during the life of the physical form, and continues naturally after the death of the physical form. In Sanskrit it is called Sūkṣma-Śarīra (subtle body) and Kāma-Rūpa (desire-body). Your astral body is your *dream-body,* in which you dream. In modern terminology it is known as your *subconscious mind.*

Astral Plane
"The starry realm". The sixth of the seven great Planes of Being. The Astral Plane is the world of the dead, where people go after they die. In the East it is known as Kāma-Loka, "the realm of desires". It is the realm of emotion and feelings, of psychic energies and forces, of the *subconscious mind*. The seven astral subplanes, or seven states of astral matter, correspond with the various heavens, hells and purgatories of the world religions. [See Kāmaloka]

Astral Projection

The projection of the astral body from the physical body. In reality, it is the other way around: the physical body is projected out (disconnected) from the astral body. The astral body is the more *real* body. You are more "real" in your astral body than in your physical body. In this experience you become aware that you are *outside* your physical body and you can see the body as being separate from you. Out-of-body experiences, or astral projections, are real, objective, valid experiences.

Astral Shell

The astral corpse of a person who has gone on to DEVĀCHAN, the Mental Plane. Ordinary mediums and channellers, who "communicate with the dead", very often get in touch with a shell rather than the real person. The astral corpse can be vivified by the thoughts and psychic vitality of the medium or psychic, the sitters in the circle, and the relatives or friends who eagerly await some words from the departed. Also called a *shade*.

ASTROLOGOS, ASTROLOGIA

Greek: "The science of the stars". The study of cosmic rays, energies and influences. The study of the motions of the planets in relationship to our Sun and how they affect Humanity collectively and individually. The science of the influence of the subtle radiations of the heavenly bodies (planets and stars) upon our Earth and upon Man. Hence the English word *astrology*. Astrology can be used as a genuine tool in understanding human nature and to predict how the future might unfold for an individual, family, tribe, nation, or the planetary Humanity. Astrology has been abused by the ignorant, the uninitiated, the superstitious. But the true science of astrology is a fact, and is just as real as chemistry or biology.

Astronomy

The science of the *material universe* beyond Earth's atmosphere.

ASURA

Sanskrit: "Dynamic god" (ASU-RA). In the very early Āryan Civilization the word ASURA referred to incorporeal Divine Entities in the Cosmos. Because some of these entities "rebelled" and went into opposition to the Devas, in later generations ASURA came to mean evil spirits or demons, the fallen angels, the fallen spiritual or celestial beings. These are the self-assertive, intellectually active gods, the rebellious beings, the positive, active poles of Creation, having self-consciousness and being aware of an ego or "I" structure. The ASURAS are at war with the DHYĀNI-CHOHANS (the meditative gods), the feminine, receptive, group-conscious, selfless Angelic Hierarchies. Note the two meanings: ASU-RA, "the Breath of God", and A-SURA, "not a Solar Angel". [See MAKARA]

ATĪTA

Sanskrit: What has been. The Past. [See ANĀGATA]

ATHA

Sanskrit: The Present Moment. The Here and Now. The Flow of Eternity is always through Now. To identify with the Past is a basic delusion and bondage. Mind creates Time, then becomes entrapped by it. You are reborn every Instant, so why hang on to the Past?

ATHĀ

Sanskrit: The Eternal Now, the Present Moment. A Name of LALITĀ, the Goddess. ĀKĀŚA (Eternal Space) is always Here and Now. ĀKĀŚĪ is the All-Pervading Goddess. The Eternal Present and Space are synonymous. When you relax into the Now you will sense Timeless Being.

Atlantean Epoch

The fourth great epoch of human evolution upon this planet, following the Lemurian civilization and preceding the present Āryan Epoch. In Atlantean days the evolutionary emphasis was on the Astral Plane—the development of the astral body, the Solar Plexus Cakra and the emotional nature. In Atlantean times the Astral World was very close to this physical dimension and we could all function naturally on the Astral, though people could not "think" as we do today.

Atlantis

Atlantean civilization extended over a vast area encompassing parts of the Atlantic Ocean, North America and Europe. Ancient legends and mythologies refer to that once-glorious civilization, but it was too long ago for people to remember accurately. What happened in Atlantis was not merely physical, but encompassed the astral dimensions as well. In Atlantean days the solar plexus was the highest centre to be conquered; consequently there was a strong development of the physical and psychic qualities, but mental and spiritual development were neglected. This led to many forms of psychism: the control of subhuman or elemental lives, shamanism, spirit-worship, ancestor-worship, mediumship, channelling and psychic powers. As a result, the old Atlantean civilization reached a crisis and was destroyed.

Ātmā, Ātma, Ātman

Sanskrit: The Life-Breath of God the Absolute. The Self-Luminous Being, the Light of the Eternal, the Bright Eternal Self, the Spiritual Self, the Universal Spirit or Self within All. Ātman is the Universal Divine I AM, of which Man is a part. It is the Innermost Spirit in Man, the true Man dwelling on the Nirvāṇic Plane, also known as Puruṣa (the Cosmic Man). Ātman is *not* an individualized Spirit or Soul; Ātman is the Universal Soul in *all* men, women and children, the many Selves as One. It is the One Divine Self in the human species, the Universal Principle that gives the sensation of "Selfhood" to the Divine in Man. It is the Timeless-Eternal-Self of all beings, the One, the Universal Formless-Form of Pure Consciousness, beyond body, emotions and mind. It is the true I AM sense within all Creation and within all beings, and within you also. The multiplicity of egos is an illusion caused by separative minds. When we give up our false sense of "I" (Ahaṁ-Kāra: I am the doer), the true "I" (Ahaṁ) shines by its own Light. Ātman is formless, dimensionless, timeless, causeless. It is also called the *Being*, the *Being of Light*, the *Personalized God-Consciousness* and the *Eternal*. Ātmā (Ātman) is the Imperishable Reality, no matter what it is called: Goddess (Ātmā) or God (Ātman). The Goddess is present within us all as Ātmā. It is before Creation and after Creation, and during Creation It pervades the All. The Universe is born out of Ātmā, the Universe is maintained by Ātmā, and the Universe will be reabsorbed again into Ātmā at the last days. Ātmā (Ātman) is the Seer, the Witness to All.

Ātma Bala Siddhi

Sanskrit: The power which flows from the Ātman within you. This enables you to perform many *healings* and other "miracles".

Ātmabodha (Ātmā-Bodha)

Sanskrit: Self-Realization. The Realization of yourself as the Self or Immortal Spirit. This is the purpose of meditation. The Self is Pure Consciousness. It can be found in the Third-Eye or in the Heart. The activities of the Self (Ātma, Ātmā) are very subtle. The mind cannot think of It. That is why the mind (Manas) has to be brought to a standstill, and Prāṇa (the Life-force) tranquillized, before Self-Realization becomes possible.

Ātma-Buddhi

Sanskrit: The Spiritual Soul. The Spiritualized Soul. The Higher Self.

Compounds of Ātma and Ātmā

Ātma, Ātmā and Ātman are all correct in compound words, depending upon the aspect of the One Self being emphasized: the masculine (Ātma, Ātman) or the feminine (Ātmā).

Most authors usually use Ātma in compounds, a few always use Ātmā, and some use a mixture of both, for various grammatical reasons. The use of Ātmā in compounds emphasizes the Self. For instance, if we say Ātma-Bodha the emphasis is on Bodha or Enlightenment, but if we say Ātmā-Bodha the emphasis is on Ātmā, the Universal Self.

Ātma-Buddhi-Manas
Sanskrit: The Triune Self, the Spiritual Triad. The Monadic Spark of the Human Soul. The Spirit (Ātma), the Spiritual Soul (Buddhi) and the Higher Mind (Kāraṇa-Manas), which constitute the Individuality, the real You. The Trimūrti, or God-Trinity, reflected in Jīva, the Living Soul, the Reincarnating Ego. [See Triad]

Ātmadarśana (Ātmā-Darśana)
Sanskrit: The Vision of the Soul in the Heart.

Ātmā-Cetanā
Sanskrit: Consciousness of the Self (not the ego!).

Ātmajñāna (Ātmā-Jñāna)
Sanskrit: "Self-Knowledge". Self-Realization, Self-Discovery. Similar to Ātmā-Vidyā and Ātmā-Bodha.

Ātmajyoti (Ātmā-Jyoti)
Sanskrit: "Self-Light". The Light of the Spirit. The Light of the Soul, which meditation calls down into your conscious mind, producing Illumination.

Ātma-Jyoti-Rūpa
Sanskrit: "Soul-Light-Form". A supernatural Light Body which is developed over a period of time by the Light of the Soul. It is concentrated in the Head Centres and slowly becomes externalized until it appears as a separate body within the natural bodies. The Adept who shifts his or her Awareness into this body becomes Consciously Immortal. This is preceded by a series of inner, supernatural transformations (but each quite natural on its own plane).

Ātmānanda (Ātma-Ānanda)
Sanskrit: "The Self is Bliss". The Bliss of Reality. This means that when you *transcend* your mind, or rise above your mind in your meditations, you *experience* Yourself as Pure-Bliss-Consciousness, Cidānanda. This is not a philosophy but a fact. Your True Form or True Nature (Svarūpa) is Bliss (Ānanda). Bliss is not just a sensation; it is a Realm, a Plane of Being, a World in which you, as Spirit, already dwell. Peace of mind you will not find until you have dissolved your mind in the Bliss of Reality (Ātmānanda).

Ātmā-Rāj
Sanskrit: "Self-rule". True Self-rule is the rule of your Soul (Ātma-Buddhi-Manas) over your personality impulses and desires. This is true Self-control. This is possible only when your Heart becomes awakened to the Light of God within.

Ātmā-Rāma
Sanskrit: The Rule of Spirit. Being ruled by the Spirit.

Ātma-Rūpa
Sanskrit: "The Form of the Self". Brahman, the Godhead, shines in the Form of Ātman (Ātma-Rūpa) with the Immediate Light within the Innermost Sanctuary of the Heart (Hṛdayaṁ) as your true "I" or "I AM-ness" (Ahaṁ).

Ātma-Vicāra
Sanskrit: "Spirit-Search". The Quest for the Self. The Path to Supernatural Evolution. The Way of Light.

Ātma-Vidyā, Ātmā-Vidyā
Sanskrit: "Realizing the Self". Self-Realization. Self-Knowledge. This is not "knowing yourself" on the bodily or personality level, nor learning about your behavioural psychology. This Self is the Boundless, Eternal, Imperishable Divinity *in* you, which is the *real* You. Ātma-Vidyā is the experience of Pure Consciousness, the Transcendental State. This is easiest to attain in the Heart Centre.

Ātma Yoga
Sanskrit: The Way of the Will. Those who follow this Way believe in total impersonality. They believe in strong self-discipline, an iron will, personal power, self-direction, self-motivation, non-dependence on others, being always in control, not giving in to others, not following any other person or Teacher, and all their relationships (their relating to humans, animals or Nature) are *coldly impersonal*. They may be motivated by service for the common good, but they *lack the Warmth of the Heart*, the Fire of the Heart, because they have not developed the Heart within themselves. Such people, especially, should do Heart meditations and awaken the Radiant Love in their Hearts, so that

they can feel truly human. When first you become a Master of Compassion, *then it is safe* for you to become a Master of Will and Power, if you so wish. If you use Will and Power without the Heart, you are doomed, like so many who have gone that way before. Be warned!

Ātmikā
Sanskrit: Embodies, ensouls.

Atomos
Greek: The smallest Universe. Undivided. An atom. To the ancients, an *atom* was a system or self-contained unit. It can be the smallest unit of matter, or the largest, such as a galaxy. An atom is an entity, with a structure. Similar to the Sanskrit Aṇu.

Augoeides
Greek: "Star-like body". The causal body, within which the Living Soul dwells upon the upper regions of the Mental Plane. More generally, a radiating or heavenly body, whether human, angelic, planetary or cosmic.

Āuṁ
Sanskrit: The Divine Word for Involution, Creation, Manifestation, the materialization of the Universe, the descent into Matter. Āuṁ is the Sacred Word, the Logos, the Primordial Vibration that "moves upon the waters of Space". Āuṁ is the Cosmic Creative Sound (the "Word" of the New Testament), the Mother spinning the Web of Creation. Āuṁ is the Holy Spirit as Cosmic Mother, the Great Creative Force and Sounding-Light Vibration of the Third Aspect of the Deity in active, intelligent Matter of the Cosmos and in Man (in the physical, etheric-physical, astral and mental bodies of Man). Āuṁ is the Mystery of Creation, the hidden Force behind Creation which gives objects their shapes—from the tiny atom and cell to the planet, star or galaxy. Āuṁ reverberates throughout the vast Inner Spaces as Sounding-Light Vibration ordering all things into shapes and forms. Āuṁ is the Word or Vibratory Power behind all the worlds, galaxies and universes, behind all the Planes of Being, behind all forces and energies, behind all atoms composed of physical and subtle matter. Āuṁ represents the manifest God and the manifest Universe. It is the Universal Reality, the whole Universe or Cosmos in its totality. Āuṁ is the "Witness" to all Creation. It is the past, present and future of the World, A.U.M. The Force of Āuṁ the Hindu Mantra Yogīs call Śakti (Divine Energy). This Force is inaudible to the physical ears, but It can be heard by the faculties of clairaudience and spiritual hearing. The Sanskrit word Āuṁ has been pronounced as Amun and Amon in old Egyptian, Amen in Hebrew and Amin in Arabic. Āuṁ is the Word of the Personality. [See Ōṁ and Nāda]

Āuṁ-Sai
Sanskrit: Inexhaustible Divine Wealth. The Divine Mother-Light as the Brightness of Inner Space. The Substance of all universes (visible and invisible), all worlds, all planes of Being, all creatures, all hierarchies. The Cosmic Sea, the Cosmic Ocean of Matter.

Aur (Ōr, Ūr)
Hebrew: "Light". Illumination, Radiance, Glory, Enlightenment, Pure Consciousness, Superior Intelligence, Brightness, Illuminative Substance. Also, Aurh (Ōrah, Ūrah).

Aur-Ganuz
Hebrew: The Hidden-Light (AVR-GNVZ). The Name, the Word, which the Mystics found *within* themselves.

Aura (Aurora)
Greek: The invisible emanations, influences and atmosphere emanating from a person or an object. Esoterically, the movement or radiation of Prāṇas (life-forces) from a person, the subtle currents around a person. The Aura is the combined energies emanating from the etheric, astral, mental and causal bodies.

Aureola
Greek: A halo or radiance around a body, whether of a human being, an angel, a planet or the Sun. A radiant glory surrounding a Saint.

Auṣadhi
Sanskrit: A drug, herb, medicinal plant, elixir, chemical preparation.

Autogenes, Autogenetos
Greek: "Born out of oneself, self-produced". From Auto (self) and Genes (born, produced). Autogenes refers to the "Father", the Unmanifest Godhead, the First Aspect of the Deity, which has no parents, which is not a product of previous causes.

Autogenes-Christos
Greek: The self-born Universal Light of the Christ, the "Son", the Second Aspect of the Deity, produced by the Union of the Father and Mother Principles. [See Monogenes]

Avadhūta
Sanskrit: One who has renounced the world. One who has loosened or shaken off his or her attachment to the world. A renunciate, an ascetic, a monk or nun who has left worldly life. Esoterically, this is not an outer, physical renunciation, but the ability to function in Buddhic Consciousness or in Transcendental Unity with the One Self in All, the Ātman. To become a true "renunciate of the world" does not mean to cease to act! It means to *renounce the rewards of action.* For, to act with a desire for results produces Karma. The Mastānaḥ and Avadhūta of India are called "God's fools". They have totally rejected the world and the Path of Service, and spend their time in Inner Intoxication with Bliss-Consciousness. A *true* Avadhūta is a Liberated Soul (liberated from the necessity to be reborn in the Three Worlds). [See Mastānaḥ]

Avadhūta-Gītā
Sanskrit: "The song of the renunciate".

Avalokiteśvara
Sanskrit: "The downward-looking Lord" (Ava-Lokita-Īśvara). The Lord who looks down from on High. The Watchful Lord. The Saving Grace. The Compassionate Power of Divinity.

Avalokiteśvarī
Sanskrit: "The down-descending Goddess" (Ava-Lokita-Īśvarī). The Female Saviour.

Avasthā
Sanskrit: A State or Condition of Consciousness.

Avasthānam
Sanskrit: Dwells in, resides in, abides in, rests in, remains in, is established in.

Avaṣyam
Sanskrit: Controlling, organizing. The Lord God (Īśa) is the Controlling Power (Avaṣyam) of the Universe.

Avatāra
Sanskrit: A Divine Incarnation. One who has descended from the Light Realms. From Ava (down) and Tāra (to pass, to go), or Ava-Trī (to come down, to descend). There are Cosmic Avatāras, Solar-Systemic Avatāras, Planetary Avatāras and Human Avatāras—those who appear to Humanity and the Devas for the purpose of speeding up their evolution and aiding the Divinization of the planet. Human Avatāras are of two broad types:

- A Mahā-Avatāra is an entity descending from the Monadic Plane, or the Divine Power or Potency stepped down to the lower planes, even to our Physical Plane of planet Earth. A Mahā-Avatāra is a Messiah, a Saviour, an Advent of the Divine, an Incarnation of God on Earth in a human form, also called a Pūrṇa-Avatāra (Perfect Incarnation of God). Christ Jesus was such an Avatāra.
- An Aṁsa-Avatāra manifests the Divine Nature only partially. These are the Saints and Masters, those who have descended from the Nirvāṇic Plane, the Buddhic Plane or the formless Mental Plane to teach.

An Avatāra incarnates for a specific purpose. All the pre-Christian religions taught about the existence of Avatāras, or Incarnations of Divinity. (The corrupted anglicized form is *Avatar.*) [See Mashiah and Mahā-Avatāra]

Avatāra Siddhi
Sanskrit: "Divine-Descent power". When the perfected Man completes his or her Journey of Yoga (Union), he or she lives in the Buddhic World or the Ātmic World or the Monadic World in companionship with the Communion of the Saints, the Devas, the Siddhas, and the Gods and Goddesses. Such a Yogī (United One, Integrated One) no longer has a personality mechanism by which to appear in the lower dimensions (the Mental, Astral and Physical Worlds). He or she must therefore create a temporary form in order to appear in the lower worlds. This is one form of the Avatāra Siddhi, called Māyāvi-Rūpa Siddhi (illusionary-form-making power).

Avidyā
Sanskrit: Spiritual ignorance (A-Vidyā). Materialistic blindness. Agnosticism. The lack of true spiritual understanding. [See Agnōstikos]

Avirati
Sanskrit: Sensuality, lack of moderation and control. One of the Antarāyāḥ (obstacles, impediments, problems on the Path to Higher Consciousness).

Avītci
Sanskrit: Hellish conditions of mind. Any hellish condition of the mind, whether human, subhuman or demonic. Also, any place, world or realm created by such minds. The Eighth Sphere, the Outer Darkness, the Nether Darkness. In terms of vibration, this condition is not astral but sub-physical. No matter how inconceivable it might appear, there is a realm *below* this Physical Plane. [See *Eighth Sphere*]

Avyakta, Avyaktam
Sanskrit: The Unmanifest (A-Vyakta). The Invisible, the Imperceptible, the Immutable. The Primordial State from whence issues forth Manifestation or Creation. The Unmanifest Godhead before Creation and above Creation. The Universal Spirit.

Awakening
A Zen expression for awakening to Buddhic Consciousness. It is called Bodhi in Sanskrit, Wu or Lung-Tan in Chinese, and Satori in Japanese Zen traditions. A modern term for it is *Enlightenment*.

Awliyā-Yekhodā
Arabic: "People of Holiness". The Sūfī ascetics or Saints.

Āyustejas
Sanskrit: The Energy of Life. To be healthy you need Āyustejas.

B

Baal Shem
Hebrew: "A Master of the Divine Name". One who has been initiated or baptized into the Divine Power, the Name of God, Shema.

Bāl-Shem-Tau
Hebrew: A Master of the Good Name, the Infinite Power. One who can bring forth a Name (or Names) and unite it to God, the NAME. In the East this Science was called Mantra Yoga, and one who succeeded was a Mantra Yogī.

Bagalā, Bagalāmukhī
Sanskrit: She who restrains, She who controls, She who prevents. She who has the controlling or commanding face. A Name of Lalitā, the Goddess. Bagalā means "a bridle, rope or goad by which someone or something is guided and controlled", and Mukhi means "a face or countenance". Bagalā is powerful. In this aspect, Lalitā is full of Power and in total control of circumstances. A more esoteric meaning is that Bagalā is the Divine Effulgence of Brilliant Light which is irresistible and unconquerable. It is the Decisive Power of the Absolute, the Self-Motivating Power of Reality.

Bahā-u-llāh
Arabic: The Splendour of God. From Bahā, "Splendour, Glory, Beauty, Radiance".

Bahīr
Hebrew: The Illumination. The Brilliance of God. The Cosmic Christ.

Bahirjyotiḥ (Bahir-Jyoti)
Sanskrit: "Outer-Light". The Outer Radiance.

Bala
Sanskrit: Power, strength, energy, force, virtue (masculine).

Balā
Sanskrit: Power, force, energy, strength (feminine). The raw force, energy and strength of matter and material conditions, the atoms and subtle particles, and the strength within forms, bodies, shapes and embodiments.

Bāla
Sanskrit: A boy, young, pure, simple, new, the Sun (masculine).

Bālā
Sanskrit: A girl, a child, young, new, the jasmine flower (feminine). She who is the little girl or girl-child. A Name of Lalitā, the Goddess.

Bālā-Mantra
Sanskrit: The Divine-Child Mantra. Also called Sundarī, the Child-Goddess Mantra.

Bāṇa Liṅga
Sanskrit: An access-way to extra-physical reality, located at the Anāhata Cakra (Heart Centre). From Bāṇa (arrow-shaped) and Liṅga (a Sign for Śiva, the Transcendent). [See Itarā Liṅga and Svāyaṁbhū Liṅga]

Bandha
Sanskrit: A body lock. A system of practices within Haṭha Yoga.

Bāṇi
Sanskrit: Speech, voice, oratorical skill, eloquence. [See Vāṇī]

Baptism
In the symbolism of the New Testament, *Baptism* is the Birth of the Light in the Heart. The Baptism of Jesus is with the Holy Spirit and Fire. Jesus the Christ, or the Holy Light, is *conceived* in our Hearts by the Holy Spirit. This is not symbolic but actual. You feel inside you the Holy Spirit like a mighty Breath (air or wind), and you are burning with the Fiery Energy of Regeneration.

Baptizein
Greek: Baptism. To immerse a person in water is symbolic of purification and regeneration, a common concept in all the old "pagan" pre-Christian religions. In the Mysteries, however, they had Baptism by the Holy Spirit, or Fire.

Barbelo
Greek: The Divine Mother. The Virgin of Light. What the Jews used to call Shekinah (the Feminine Divine Presence). What in the East is called Śakti.

Bardo
Tibetan: An after-death state (the stage of *hallucination)* where you experience all the thoughtforms you have created while in the physical body, and they appear to be very real indeed! Furthermore, every passing emotion you feel at that time will instantaneously produce all kinds of shapes and forms which you will see and feel and experience.

Barhiṣad Pitṛis
Sanskrit: The Lunar Ancestors. The Seventh Manifest Hierarchy, a Creative Order having bodies.

Base Centre
The Energy Centre (cakra) located at the base of the spine. This centre is responsible for your physical life and well-being. It is your point of balance on the dense Physical Plane. The Kuṇḍalinī-Śakti (Serpent-Power) resides coiled up in the Base Centre, and Her normal activity is the perpetuation and

maintenance of the organism. At a certain point of human evolution, however, She will awaken to do Her Liberating Work of transforming a human being into a god or a goddess. [See Mūlādhāra Cakra]

Beatitude
From the Latin: Blessed Unity, Peace, Tranquillity (Hesychia), discovered in the Heart.

Being of Light
Every "dead" person is taken into the presence of the "Being of Light". This Being of Light has been given many names, by many people: *God's Love for us*, the *Holy Guardian Angel*, the *Higher Self*, the *Christ* or *Jesus Christ*, the *Buddha*, *Śrī Kṛṣṇa*. The pre-Christian Greeks and Romans called it the *Virgin of Light*. Female-oriented religions have known it as *Isis*, the *Virgin Mary* or *Shekinah*. Among the Sikhs of Northern India it is known as the *Radiant Form of the Master*. The Mother-oriented religions called it "She", while the Father-oriented religions called it "He", but in fact it is neither. It is the *Light personified*. The Mystic or Adept attaches himself or herself to this Inner Light—what the Tibetans call the *Clear Light*. This Light shines from Nirvāṇa and hence takes one beyond the Astral and Mental Planes of Being. Thus the boundaries of Death are transcended.

Ben Adam
Hebrew: "Son of Man". A title given to the Prophets, Divine Kings and High Priests during Old Testament times. In the pre-Christian centuries of the Jewish world, the Messiah was regularly called Mashiah Ben Adam and Mashiah Ben David. These were titles, not names of people, and have been translated as "Son of Man", meaning that the Messiah will be from the Man-species, that He will be human with divine qualities. Unfortunately the early Christians considered the Son of Man to be *one person only* (Jesus), but this is not so. The title Ben Adam, "Son of Man", was applied to *all* the Prophets, Divine Kings and High Priests. Adam means Humankind, the *species* of beings called Man, as distinct from the other species in the Universe. Each great Prophet was a Ben Adam—a Son of Man, a Child of Humanity. [See Yeshua Ben Adam]

Ben Eloah
Hebrew: "Son of God". A title given to the triumphant Messiah (Jesus) after he conquered human nature and resurrected the Christ, the Immortal Self within (Yeshua Ben Eloah in Hebrew, Yeshuā Bar Alahā in Aramaic). During Old Testament times the expressions "Son of Man" and "Son of God" were titles of respect and distinction, much like what we have in English: "Sir", "your Lordship", "your Excellency". Nowadays, Bibles are translated to mean that Jesus (the historical personality) is the *only* Son of God, and thus they *deny Divinity* to all God's Children. [See Monogenes]

Beni-Elohīm
Hebrew: "Children of the Creator-Gods". The lesser Gods, below the Elohīm. The Angelic Hierarchies (Devas, in Sanskrit).

Bhagavad-Gītā
Sanskrit: "God's Singing, the Song of the Lord". The Eternal Word, the Logos. Also, a great scripture of India, the Hindu masterwork of Karma Yoga.

Bhagavan
Sanskrit: "Fortune-having" (Bhaga-van). The giver of Glory, Splendour, Knowledge, Wealth, Virtue and Power.

Bhagavāna
Sanskrit: Lord, God, the Universal Self, the Glorious One. Divine, adorable, holy.

Bhāgavata
Sanskrit: The Glorious One. The Christ in the Heart.

Bhāgavata-Avasthā
Sanskrit: The Glorified State. Nirvāṇic Consciousness (Ātmā-Vidyā).

Bhāgavata-Bhāva
Sanskrit: Divine-Mood. Intense feeling towards the Divine. Also, Deva-Bhāva. To succeed in prayer (meditation), you must have the Divine-Mood, Bhāgavata-Bhāva or Deva-Bhāva. That is, you have to be "in the mood" to pray, to meditate.

Bhagavatī
Sanskrit: The Glorious Goddess. Illustrious, divine, holy, adorable, blissful. The Divine Mistress of the Universe, full of Fortune and Wealth, Creatrix of the Cosmos. An esoteric meaning is that Lalitā is Universal-Nature (Prākṛtī), the original Primary Substance or Matter, infused with the Universal Spirit (Paramātman), with the Bright Glorious Light of Prakāśa-Āditya (the Universal Sun or Cosmic Solar Logos).

Bhaikṣya
Sanskrit: An ascetic or mendicant, one who has completely renounced the world in old age and spends all his time in meditation and spiritual experiences. Also called Sannyāsin. The fourth period of life (Āśrama) in the ancient Vedic days of India.

Bhairavī
Sanskrit: "She who is terrifying, awesome, powerful, energetic". The Fiery Goddess. Bhairavī is Lalitā as the Essence of Fire. She is the Fire which is within all things, which fuels all actions. She is Tejas (the Radiant One, the Luminous One). This Fire is the Third Logos, Brahmā (the Holy Spirit of Christianity). This is the Fire of Matter, or the Fire *within* Matter (Prākṛtī), and hence within your body. She is also the Fire of Mind, or Cosmic Fire (Agni). The secret of Spiritual Transformation is Fire-Consciousness, or Bhairavī. Fire is transforming. Bhairavī is the Warrior-Goddess who guides, protects, transforms, and overcomes negative forces. [See Tapas]

Bhajan
Sanskrit: Inner worship. Heart chant. Deeply devotional, meditative, contemplative, invocative singing and chanting.

Bhakta
Sanskrit: A Devotee. One who practises Bhakti, or Devotion to God. The supreme Goal of the Bhakta is God.

Bhakti
Sanskrit: Love, Devotion, feeling, emotion. Longing for the Real, for the Eternal. Devotion to God.

Bhakti-Priyā
Sanskrit: She who is fond of Devotion. A Name of Lalitā, the Goddess.

Bhakti Yoga
Sanskrit: The Path of Devotion and Love. The awakening of the dynamic Love Energy of the Heart Centre. Pure, selfless Devotion in the Heart to the God within you (Īśvara) and the Universal Absolute (Brahman) outside of you. Bhakti Yoga is called the "emotional yoga" because it trains the subtle body in pure Devotion and self-surrender. This involves the *purifying* of the astral body (feelings, desires, moods and emotions) through chanting, kirtans, bhajans, religious rituals and meditation in the Heart.

Bhānava
Sanskrit: The giver of Light.

Bhānu
Sanskrit: The Glorious Light of the Inner-Sun.

Bhargo, Bharga, Bhargaha
Sanskrit: Splendour, Divine Glory, Effulgence, Light, Radiance, the Glorious Energy of the Sun (the God-within-the-Sun), God's Glorious Lustre. The Destroyer of darkness and unhappiness, the Purifier, the Remover of sins.

Bhāskara, Bhāskaram
Sanskrit: "Light-producer, Light-maker" (Bhās-Kara). Shining. The Radiating Source of Light. The Radiant Spirit within the Sun.

Bhaumā
Sanskrit: Of the Earth, of the planet.

Bhāva
Sanskrit: Mood, feeling, attitude, emotion. Being, Existence, sensing. The feeling for finer things. The love of the good, the beautiful and the true. To succeed in prayer (meditation), you must have the Divine-Mood, Bhāgavata-Bhāva.

Bhāvana
Sanskrit: "The power that can move mountains". The power of intense belief and thought. The power of Faith. The power to manifest things.

Bhrānti
Sanskrit: Being confused, unsteady in consciousness, spiritually ignorant, subject to glamour. Being deluded by phenomena (Māyā), whether physical, astral or mental. Worldly consciousness, erroneous thinking.

Bhrānti-Darśana
Sanskrit: "Erroneous vision". False perceptions, illusions, self-delusions, glamour, mistaken ideas. One of the Antarāyāḥ (obstacles, impediments, problems on the Path to Higher Consciousness).

Bhū
Sanskrit: Born. Existent.

Bhūr, Bhūḥ, Bhūr-Loka, Bhūh-Loka
Sanskrit: The World of Becoming. The Physical Plane, the Physical Universe, the Earth, the World. Also called Pṛthivī-Loka, "the Physical World". The Basis of the Universe is God.

Bhūta
Sanskrit: "Substance" or "Matter". The manifest aspect of a thing or entity; its tangible or form aspect. The Bhūtas are the Cosmic Elements that constitute the gross Creation and the Inner Worlds. The Elements are qualities, forces or expressions of Nature (Prākṛtī). [See *Elements*]

Bhūtatathatā
Sanskrit: "Suchness, Reality". The Suchness or Thatness of living beings. The fundamental Divinity of All. The essential, unchanging, immutable Original Reality or Buddha-Nature beyond temporary forms, phenomenal limitations, or the cycles of birth and death. The experience of Buddhic Consciousness beyond the personal ego. From Bhūta (Essential Substance) and Tathatā (That which is eternal and unchanging). Similar to the Hindu term Tat (Being, Eternal Reality, That). In the theistic religious language, Bhūtatathatā is "God".

Bhuvaḥ, Bhuvaha
Sanskrit: The Subtle World, the Astral Plane, Antarikṣa (the Inner World), the Desire-World. Also, the Self-Existent God, the Creator-God.

Bhuvah-Loka
Sanskrit: The Astral Plane, the Astral World. Also called Kāma-Loka (Desire-Realm).

Bhuvana
Sanskrit: The World, the Cosmos, the Universe. All that Became (was created).

Bhuvaneśvarī (Bhuvana-Īśvarī)
Sanskrit: The Goddess of all the worlds. The World Mother. A Name of Lalitā, the Goddess. She is the Great Queen of the Universe and the Queen of Heaven. From Bhuvana (the World, the Cosmos, the Universe) and Īśvarī (the Ruler, the Sovereign Goddess, the Mistress of the Cosmos). She is the Supreme Being incarnate.

Biblos
Greek: A book. Also, Biblion, "a little book". Hence the English word *Bible,* the collection of sacred texts used by the Saints.

Bīja-Mantra
Sanskrit: "Seed-Mantra, Seed-Syllable, Seed-Sound-Vibration". A seed vibration that develops into Transcendental Realization. A key frequency-vibration from which Mantras are formed. Bīja means "a seed, an embryo, a source, a beginning, a germ that develops into something greater". A Bīja-Mantra is a seed-thought or sound-frequency with specific results, by which we make contact with deeper and deeper layers of our minds, until even the subtlest layer is transcended and we reach *Self-Realization.* A Bīja-Mantra introduces an harmonious vibration into the mind. It works by focusing and pacifying the mind, by naturally reducing the mind's activities. The Bīja-Mantras help you to transcend the mind and come to the state of no-thought, the Mystical State.The different Bīja-Mantras produce different effects to bring about any desired condition.

Bilocation

Being in two places at the same time: your physical body in one location and your astral body in another. The term was used by the Saints of old.

Binah

Hebrew: "Understanding". Insight or Spiritual Intuition. On the Kabbalistic Tree of Life, Binah is the feminine aspect of Buddhic Consciousness. Chockmah (Wisdom) is the male aspect. The words *Wisdom* and *Understanding* do not mean being smart or clever or worldly-wise. Rather, they refer to what in the East is called Bodhi, the acquiring of which makes one a Buddha (an Enlightened One). One acquires this through meditation and spiritual discipline.

Bindu

Sanskrit: A dot, a spot, an atom, a seed, a drop. The Light in the Third-Eye Cakra. Also, the Seed-Sound of Ōṁ.

Bismillāh

Arabic: "In the Name of God, in the Divine Name". The Divine Name of God is the Omnipresent Light-Vibration of the Ineffable Godhead. To be in the Name is to be Universally Illumined, Cosmic-Conscious, having within one's Heart the Light of Gnosis.

Bodha

Sanskrit: Knowledge, Awakening, Intelligence, Wisdom.

Bodhi

Sanskrit: "Having acquired the Wisdom-Nature". Awakening, Enlightenment, Perfect Wisdom, Illumination. Realizing your own Essential Perfection, the Bodhi-Mind, the Enlightened State or Condition. From the Sanskrit Budh, "to blossom, to awake, to know". When the ordinary mind (the lower mind, the mental body) is quietened of its activity of endlessly producing thoughts, then the Higher Mind (the Causal Mind in the causal body) will manifest. By a further movement inward you awaken to the plane of Buddhi, the Wisdom-Mind (Bodhi). The same as the Japanese Satori.

Bodhī

Sanskrit: Wise. Enlightening. A Sage.

Bodhicitta

Sanskrit: "Enlightenment-Consciousness". The Spiritual Mind. Also, an Energy that works *towards* Enlightenment, and the Energy that comes *from* Enlightenment. Also, an enlightened motive for living.

Bodhicittā

Sanskrit: Wisdom-Mind, the Enlightenment-Consciousness, the Realizing-Intellect, the Buddha-Mind. A Name of Lalitā, the Goddess. Lalitā leads Her devotees to Perfect-Knowledge, Spiritual Enlightenment and complete Self-Realization. She is the Mind (Citta) of Light (Bodhi).

Bodhi-Citta-Śakti

Sanskrit: The Energy you generate in your quest for Enlightenment, Wisdom, Self-Realization. Also, the Energy of the Buddha (the Enlightened, Awakened, Realized Being) *after* his or her Enlightenment.

Bodhisattva

Sanskrit: "One whose very essence is Wisdom and Love". From Bodhi (Love-Wisdom) and Sattva (essence, being, quality). An enlightened Seer or Sage. A Nirmānakāya whose essence is Love-Wisdom. An Enlightened Being who does not merge into Nirvāṇa but remains on the Buddhic and Causal Planes. A Buddha who sacrifices his or her own Enlightenment for the welfare of Mankind.

Bodhisattva-Mahāsattva

Sanskrit: A great Enlightened Being.

Bōn

Tibetan: The true state of Meditation, when you realize the *Self-Mind,* the root of your mind before thoughts have arisen in it. In Chinese Zen it is Chān. In Korean Mysticism it is Zōn.

Borean Epoch
The first great epoch, or Root-Race, of human evolution upon this planet. The Borean and Hyperborean epochs involved the development of the etheric-physical body. During these earliest periods of human evolution, Man had no dense physical body. (This period has also been described as "The Imperishable Sacred Land" and the "Adamic" Epoch.)

Brahma
Sanskrit: God. Divinity.

Brahmā (Bramhā)
Sanskrit: "Expansion into Life". To expand, to scatter in all directions of Space. From the root Brih, "to expand, to scatter, to create". God-into-substance, God-into-matter, God-Incarnate, God-in-Manifestation, God-Immanent. The Creator-God, the Creator of the Universe (of all the star-systems and galaxies). The Origin and Source of Creation—whether the whole Cosmos or our Solar-Systemic Creation. The Creator as the Cosmic Logos or as a Solar Logos (locally, in our Solar System, Brahmā is our Solar Logos, the Sun). Brahmā is the Third Aspect of the Trimūrti or Holy Trinity (Brahmā-Viṣṇu-Śiva), the "Holy Spirit" in Christianity. Brahmā is the Power that makes Creation, Growth and Evolution possible.

Brahmā-Avasthā
Sanskrit: The God-State. Union with God. Monadic Consciousness. The state beyond Nirvāṇa. God-Consciousness (Brahmā-Vidyā).

Brahmacarya
Sanskrit: "Orientation towards God" (Brahma-Carya). Being firmly fixed on God. Self-control for the sake of God. A continuous religious attitude. Godly conduct, good conduct, continually being involved in discipline. This embraces *all* of one's life. Brahmacarya is the fourth Yama (observance) of Aṣṭāṅga Yoga, as set down by Patañjali. The word Brahmacarya has been wrongly translated by the monks and scholars to mean non-involvement in sexual life, chastity, non-marriage, celibacy. But Patañjali clearly does not mean that, for there is no sexual reference in the word at all!

Brahmācārya
Sanskrit: "Being a teacher of God" or "being taught by God" (Brahmā-Ācārya). A religious teacher, a religious person or student, one belonging to a religious institution, or one who has taken a religious vocation. It has been wrongly translated as sexual continence or celibacy, but the word has only a religious meaning.

Brahmacārī
Sanskrit: One who is oriented towards God (Brahma-Carya). The word could be translated as "a missionary for God". It does *not* mean a celibate or a monk. When you are a true Brahmacārī, then you organize all your energies to serve God. A monk or a nun may do it one way, a married person another way. A married person with children and responsibilities, living in the world while remaining centred in his or her Heart, truly *living* the God-Life, is a true Brahmacārī.

Brahmajñāna (Brahma-Jñāna)
Sanskrit: "God-Knowledge". God-Realization. The direct Knowledge of God. Also, Brahmavidyā.

Brahmājyoti (Brahmā-Jyoti)
Sanskrit: "God's Light". The Divine Light, the Divine Effulgence, the Brightness of the Divine Glory, the Ocean of Ineffable Light, the Brightness and Splendour of God's Mind. The Light of God is a Dazzling Brightness, most brilliant, most beautiful, eternal, not subject to change. Whereas all forms in Creation, visible and invisible, will perish, dissolve, be transformed, the Light of God is eternal in its Existence. Nothing exists that is superior to God. The Yogī, Mystic or Saint who beholds this Vision becomes Deified. [See *Light*]

Brahmamayam
Sanskrit: "Made out of God". From Brahma (God, Divinity) and Mayam (made out of, consisting of).

Brahman
Sanskrit: The Godhead. The Universal Being.
The Transcendental Divinity. Universal Radiance, Inconceivable Glory, Immeasurable Consciousness. The Universal Absolute, which includes both the Manifest and Unmanifest Aspects of the Godhead. The God in the Universal Manifestation of All. The final Reality, beyond name, form and qualities, beyond Time and Space, Infinite, Eternal, All-Pervading. Brahman is the Godhead beyond which you cannot go.

Brahmāgranthi (Brahmā-Granthi)
Sanskrit: The knot (Granthi) in the Base Cakra (Mūlādhāra Cakra) at the base of the spine.

Brāhmana
Sanskrit: The Brahmins. The priestly and religious class (caste, Varṇa) of India. Literally, "Knowers of God".

Brahmā-Loka
Sanskrit: The Kingdom of God. The World of Glories. Nirvāṇa.

Brahmanirvāṇam (Brahma-Nirvāṇa)
Sanskrit: "God-Absorption, Dissolution in God". The inner condition of the Enlightened Sage. This was the original Teaching of the Lord Buddha, the Gautama Buddha, who was a Brahmin (the Hindu priest-caste). Centuries later, His Teachings were completely altered by dropping the words Brahman (God) and Ātman, Ātmā (the Immortal Spirit in Man and in the Cosmos). Thus, later on, Buddhism made out that there is no God, no Final, Absolute, Transcendental Godhead or Reality, and no Immortal Spirit (Ātman), and the Goal is to be dissolved (Nirvāṇa) into an Emptiness!

Brahma-Prakāśa
Sanskrit: Divine Light. Divine Grace.

Brahmārandhra
Sanskrit: "The Door to God". The Sahasrāra Cakra at the top of the head (the Thousand-Petalled Lotus, or Crown Cakra). From Brahmā (God) and Randhra (door, gate). In the West it is called the *halo* or *nimbus*.

Brahma-Rūpa
Sanskrit: "God-Form". The Shape or Form of God, the Body of God. She is Śrī Jagadambā, the Holy World Mother.

Brahmātmane
Sanskrit: The Essential Nature of God. From Brahma (God) and Ātmā (the Essential Nature of God).

Brahma-Vidyā, Brahmā-Vidyā
Sanskrit: God-Realization. The direct Knowledge of God. God-Consciousness or Universal Consciousness. Union with God.

Brahmā-Viṣṇu-Śiva
Sanskrit: The Trimūrti (three-faced God) or Holy Trinity. By the Divine Plan, all things in Creation go through these three stages or movements in the Cosmic Mind.
- Brahmā: "To expand, to scatter in all directions of Space". The Creator (the Holy Spirit). Involution.
- Viṣṇu: "To enter into all things, to pervade all things". The Preserver (the Son). Evolution.
- Śiva: "He who sleeps in the atoms". The Transformer. The Destroyer (the Father). Dissolution.

Śiva resides on the plane of Ādi, Viṣṇu on the plane of Aṇupādaka, and Brahmā on the plane of Nirvāṇa. It is from here that the rest of Creation is emanated. [See *Holy Trinity*]

Brāhmī
Sanskrit: The Creatrix of the Universe. She-Who-Creates. The Original Source of all things. Brāhmī also means "That which is Holy". The Feminine Goddess Energy. A Name of Lalitā, the Goddess.

Brahmī-Sthiti
Sanskrit: "In-God-Established". To Rest in God. God-Realization.

Brahmī-Sthiti Samādhi
Sanskrit: "In-God-Living-Ecstasy". The Seventh State of Consciousness. The Absolute-Consciousness State. Also called Brahmā-Avasthā (the God-State).

Bṛhad-Ambā
Sanskrit: The Great Mother of the Universe.

Brotherhood of Light
The Holy Brotherhood, the Holy Communion of the Saints, the Brotherhood of "Just Men made Perfect", the Union of Souls (Jīvas) that are Perfect (Siddha)—Adepts, Masters, Yogīs, Sages. The Spiritual (Invisible) Hierarchy of Enlightened Souls who guide the Evolution of this planet. Also called the *Fifth Kingdom*, the *Spiritual Kingdom*, the *Spiritual Hierarchy* or the *Christ-Hierarchy*. In Sanskrit, Saṅgha or Sata-Saṅgha. [See *Spiritual Hierarchy*]

Buddha
Sanskrit: "Inwardly wide awake". One who is awake within himself. From Budh, "to blossom, to bloom, to wake up, to know". This does not mean someone who is awake on the Physical Plane in the physical body. It means One who has awakened from the Sleep of Ignorance, who is awake on a very high plane of our Solar System, who is in a very high state of Consciousness. In fact, for One who is a Buddha, the Physical Plane "awake state" is a state of complete sleep! A Buddha is Awake (fully Conscious) on the Nirvāṇic Plane. Buddha also means "One who is filled with the Light, One who is Enlightened". A Sage, a Seer, a Wise One, an Enlightened One.

Buddha, Dharma, Saṅgha
Sanskrit: The three aspects of the Spiritual Life according to Buddhism: an Enlightened Being, a Spiritual Teaching, and a group of seekers after Truth.

Buddha-Mānasa
Sanskrit: The Buddha-Mind. The Buddha-Nature or Self-Nature, the *Original Mind* of the Zen Masters, and the Self (Ātman) of the Yogīs of old. This is the "Christ in you, your hope of Glory", spoken of by Saint Paul in the New Testament. It is as if there were two of you: the *you* as you know yourself on the personality level and the *You* that needs to be discovered, the Eternal and Timeless Spirit that you are.

Buddhi
Sanskrit: Pure Consciousness, Spiritual Consciousness, Transcendental Consciousness. Buddhi is the Spiritual Soul, one with Ātman, yet slightly differentiated from Ātman. Ātman is what gives the sensation of "Self" to the Divine in Man, but it is a *universal* principle. Buddhi is a thin "veil" over Ātman. It is the principle of Spiritual Love and Wisdom, Spiritual Intuition, Spiritual Consciousness. It is profound Wisdom and Understanding. Buddhi is the true Mystical Consciousness of the Mystics of Judaism, Christianity, Islam and Hinduism. (Note that, in some schools, the terms Buddhi, Buddhi-Manas and Buddhi-Citta refer also to the Higher Mind in Man, the Causal Mind.)

Buddhic Plane
The fourth of the seven great Planes of Being. The Buddhic Plane has been called the *Realm of Unities* or the *Intuitional World*. It is a formless Light World characterized by Divine Unity, Love and Wisdom. The state of Buddhi is Unitive Consciousness, Transcendental Consciousness or Pure Consciousness, wherein the Mystic experiences Oneness with the Universe and with God. The Sūfī Mystics called this realm 'Ālam-i-Malakūt, "the World of the Kingdom" (the Kingdom of God). In Christianity it is known as the *Christ Realm* or *Paradise*. In Sanskrit, Mahah-Loka. On this plane you are already Liberated.

Buddhi-Manas
Sanskrit: "Wisdom-Mind". The Spiritualized Mind. The mind (Manas, higher and lower) infused with the Light of Buddhi. The mind irradiated by the Light of the Spirit within (Ātma-Jyoti). When the mind (Manas) becomes still, empty of ideas and thoughts, the Soul-Light can be reflected into it. Then arises the faculty of Buddhi, which is the true Intuition, the Revelation-Consciousness whereby the hidden Mysteries are shown to the mind: Bliss-Consciousness, Light-Consciousness, the Christ-Consciousness, Pure Consciousness, Clear-Light and Unity-Consciousness. All of this is Buddhi. It is the Consciousness of the Mystics. This Superknowing-Faculty can be developed by quieting the thoughtform-making faculty of the mind (Citta-Vṛtti-Nirodha).

Bythus
Greek: The Primordial Deep, the Root, the Unmanifest Condition before Creation.

C

Caduceus
Latin: The Serpent Power. Kuṇḍalinī. It was symbolized in Greece and Rome by a staff (the spinal column) entwined by two serpents and bearing a pair of wings at the top. Karukeion in Greek.

Caelum
Latin: "Heaven". The multi-dimensionality of Space, as a Unity or Oneness, as a Continuum between the within (the above) and the without (the below). Shemayā in Aramaic, Shamayīm in Hebrew, Ouranos in Greek, Ākāśa in Sanskrit. [See *Heaven*]

Caitanya
Sanskrit: Divine Consciousness, Pure Consciousness, Pure Awareness, which is the nature of Ātman, the Self-Existent Eternal Being that you are, above your personality level.

Caitanya-Rūpiṇī-Devī
Sanskrit: "Consciousness-Form-Goddess". The Goddess whose Form is Pure Consciousness Itself. She is Śrī Jagadambā, the Holy World Mother.

Cakra
Sanskrit: A circle, a wheel, a sphere, an orb, a revolving disk, a whirlpool of energy, a rotating centre, a wheel of fire. The term can refer to an atom, a planet, a solar system, a galaxy, a planetary vortex, or an Energy Centre in a human being. The Solar System is a large Cakra, and each of the planets is a Cakra within the Solar System. In a human being, the Cakras are subtle Energy Centres in the etheric, astral, mental and causal bodies.

Cāmuṇḍā-Mantra
Sanskrit: The Mantra of Liberation through the destruction of both Rajas and Tamas and thus attaining Sattva. From Caṇḍa, "fierce, violent, passionate (Rajas)", and Muṇḍa, "dull, stupid, blunt (Tamas)". [See Guṇa]

Candra
Sanskrit: The Moon. The Cool Moonlight. The Moonshine you can see in the Head, in the Heart and in the Solar Plexus Centre. Thus you can see that the Inner Light, the Inner Beatific Vision, Adhi-Jyoti, manifests in several places. [See Prakāśa, Āditya]

Candra-Bindu
Sanskrit: The nasal "hum" at the root of the nose, at the Third-Eye. [See Aṇusvāra]

Cannibalis
Latin: One who eats the flesh of another human being. Cannibalism was widespread in Africa and Polynesia and among the jungle tribes descending from Lemurian races. Its origins are the worst forms of Black Magic which deal with entrapping the Souls of the dead.

Catharsis
Greek: Intense physical, emotional and mental purification. The violent purging of the mind and emotions, freeing oneself of images, ideas and thoughts.

Causal Body
The causal body (Kāraṇa-Śarīra in Sanskrit) is made up of matter of the three highest subplanes of the Mental Plane—the Arūpa or formless levels. This is your Higher Manas or Abstract Mind. Your causal body is the lowest part of your imperishable Individuality (Ātma-Buddhi-Manas), beyond your personality complex. Your Reincarnating Ego (Jīva, you as a Human Soul) dwells in your causal body. Your karmas are stored up in your causal body, thus giving you the continuity of existence, life after life.

Causal Mind
The Abstract Mind or Higher Mind (Higher MANAS). The Causal Mind functions by formless thought-waves and intelligences. Nowadays, very few people use this mind. In the Roman Mystery Schools it was called INTELLECTUS (Latin: Inner Knowing). The Greeks called it NOUS, the Spiritual Mind. In Sanskrit it is known as ARŪPA-MANAS or KĀRAṆA-MANAS. The spiritual literature sometimes calls this mind BUDDHI-MANAS or the Superconscious Mind. More precisely, however, BUDDHI-MANAS (the Wisdom-Mind or Superconscious Mind) is the mind (higher and lower) infused with the Light of BUDDHI.

Causal World
The three higher subplanes of the Mental Plane, which are formless (ARŪPA). Also known as the *Archetypal World*. The Causal Worlds are realms of formless Ideas and Archetypes, which are the "cause" of all that manifests in the Three Worlds. (Note that the Causal Worlds are formless from *our* point of view.)

Cave of the Heart
The later Christian Mystics called the Heart "the Cave of the Heart" and "Bethlehem, where the Christ is born". Even as a child is born in the mother's womb, God is born in the human Heart, which is often symbolized as a *cave*. According to the Mystics, Christ was born in a cave in Bethlehem. The cave in Bethlehem is the Heart.

CELĀ
Sanskrit: A Disciple.

CENOBITE
Greek: "Living together". In the early centuries of Christianity there were renunciates who lived by themselves, totally alone in the desert, and others who lived in loosely connected groups. The *Cenobites* were anchorites, hermits and recluses living together in loose communities in the deserts of Syria, Egypt and Palestine.

CHĀN
Chinese: "Meditation". Derived from CHĀNNA, which was in turn derived from the Sanskrit DHYĀNA. In the Japanese language, CHĀN became ZEN. CHĀN (meditation) is the sowing and Buddhahood is the reaping or the reward.

Channelling
From the Latin CANAL: "A waterway". Used nowadays to mean *mediumship*—receiving messages from the dead or from discarnate entities. Usually the medium speaks from her or his own subconscious mind. In rarer cases, an outside entity temporarily possesses the medium, psychic or sensitive and gives messages. Sometimes the term refers to the "channelling" of one's own Soul Wisdom, which has no relation to mediumship. [See *Mediumship, Mediator*]

CHAOS (KAOS)
Greek: Primordial Matter. The *Mother Deep,* or Infinite Space, filled with the Original Homogeneous Matter, *before* the Creation of the Universe. Universal Matter in its unordered state. (Sound shapes this Primordial Matter into the forms you see in Creation.) CHAOS also means "disorder, confusion, no-system"; hence the English words *chaos* and *chaotic*. [See KOSMOS]

CHARIS
Greek: Divine Grace. Later, it also came to mean "charity" and "good-will towards others".

CHARISMA
Greek: Divine Grace, Divine Power or Gift. The power of producing miracles, miraculous powers. Hence the English words *charisma* and *charismatic*. [See KHARISMA, SIDDHI]

CHESED
Hebrew: "Mercy, Love". A Kabbalistic term for the Law of Forgiveness or Love. On the Kabbalistic Tree of Life, CHESED is the feminine aspect of the Higher Mind. The male aspect is GEBURAH (Strength).

Chi (Khi)
Chinese: Breath, Wind, Life-breath, Life-force, Energy (gross or subtle), Force (visible or not), Vitality, Fire. The same as the Latin Spiritus, the Hebrew Ruach, the Sanskrit Prāṇa, the Greek Pneuma. Chi is the Vital Force of Tao, the *Energy* of the Universe which flows through all things. It is a spiritual and psychic energy which becomes the five Elements and gives *substance* to all objects. It is the Soul or Essence behind a body or form. By controlling Chi, the Life-force, one achieves Conscious Immortality. This control of the Life-force is called Chi-Kung. [See Prāṇa]

Chiim
Hebrew: Life. The Life-principle.

Chiliokosmos
Greek: Chiliocosm. The All. The vast Cosmos. The Cosmic Order, the Universal Order, the Cosmic Mind. The Fullness-of-the-Mind. The multi-layered, multi-dimensional, Universal Reality. The Plerōma. Chiliocosm may also refer to the galaxies, or groups of many Soul-Suns or solar systems. Sometimes it is called Kosmos. In Latin it is called Universe, which means, so beautifully, "that which is turning into Oneness". The billions of stars and galaxies around you are *turning into Oneness*. In Latin it is sometimes called the Omnirevelation, which means "that which unveils everything"—another beautiful truth, for the Universe *unveils* the workings of God. And, when you *receive internally* the Omnirevelation, you will *see* the mysterious workings of the Universe, which is seeing into the workings of the Mind of God. [See Makrokosmos, Mikrokosmos]

Chinnamastā
Sanskrit: The Goddess beyond the Mind. The Headless Goddess. The No-Mind state (Unmana), totally beyond reason, logic and the thinking-process. The Power of Infinite Vision which destroys the sense of "I", or ego, and the limited mind-function. Suspended mental functioning. The highest Samādhi. A Name of Lalitā, the Goddess.

Chockmah
Hebrew: "Wisdom". Pure Consciousness. On the Kabbalistic Tree of Life, Chockmah is the male aspect of Buddhic Consciousness. Binah (Understanding, Spiritual Intuition) is the female aspect. A man strives for perfection, a woman for completeness. Men and women both will reach these goals when they attain Wisdom (male) and Understanding (female) in the state of Buddhi or Pure Consciousness.

Chohan
Tibetan: A very highly developed spiritual entity, human or angelic. These beings do not exist in the lower worlds. [See Dhyāni-Chohan]

Chosen Ones
The Elect. Those of any faith who have responded to the Inner Call and stepped upon the Path of Liberation and Enlightenment. [See Ekklesia]

Chozeh
Hebrew: A seer, a clairvoyant.

Chrēsterios
Greek: One who is a Servant of God.

Chrēstēs
Greek: The Purifier. A Prophet.

Chrēstos
Greek: One who inspires you to follow the Truth. The Hierophant of the Inner Mysteries of the Kingdom of God. Chrēstos also means "the Anointed One, the Pure One". Chrēstos was another term for the Greek Sōtēr, "Saviour, Deliverer, the Saving Power of God". So was it used in the ancient Mysteries of Greece. This was the original Greek word for the Christ.

Christ
From the Latin KRISTUS, which came from the Greek CHRISTOS, which meant "the Anointed One, the Sacred One, the Holy One", one who has attained the grade of Supreme Hierophant of the Mysteries, after the custom in the Greek Mystery Schools of anointing an Initiate with precious oils and perfumes after he or she had passed all the tests and triumphed, or risen to Higher Consciousness. The Christ is threefold:

- Christ is the Great Being called MAITREYA, who is the Heart of our Spiritual Hierarchy, the Teacher of Angels and Man, who overshadows all the True Teachers, Masters and Saints of all the religions, of all times. *The Christ is beyond all traditions.*
- Christ is also the Spirit-Spark-Atom in your Heart which responds to the Call from the Christ of the Spiritual Hierarchy (the Communion of the Saints of all religions). Saint Paul called this "the Christ in you, your hope of Glory" *(Colossians 1:27)*.
- Christ is also the Splendour of God, the Cosmic Christ, the Cosmic Logos, the Original Word, through which and by which all things are made.

These three are one. This is the Mystery of the Christ.

Christ-Consciousness
Christ-Consciousness is Light-Consciousness. The Light of Christ, the Light of the World, dwells on the Buddhic Plane and descends onto the Astral Plane and hence into the Heart of the Mystic-Disciple. Christ-Consciousness is Intelligent Love, the human element combined with the Divine. This is the Mystery of the Christ.

Christ-Hierarchy
[See *Spiritual Hierarchy*]

CHRISTOS
Greek: "The Anointed One, the Sacred One, the Holy One". A High Priest of the Mysteries, a Teacher of Teachers, One who has been anointed with the sacred oil of the Mysteries. From the Greek CHRIEIN, "to anoint with holy oils, to make sacred or holy". In the old "pagan" Mystery Schools, a CHRISTOS was one who had passed the highest degrees of the Divine Mysteries, who had attained the highest state of Union with God possible for a human being. In those days they rubbed perfumed oil on important people as a mark of respect. It is not the oil that is important, however, but the attainment of the Christ-State, the Christ-Consciousness! On a still deeper level, the CHRISTOS was the Saviour, Grace, the Christ-Light, the Universal Christ-Principle (the Second Logos), the "Judge of the living and the dead" (those in physical bodies and those in the afterlife conditions). The early Christians obviously borrowed the term from them. From this we have the words *Christ* and *Christian*.

CIDĀKĀŚA, CITTA-ĀKĀŚA, CIDGHANA
Sanskrit: "The Self-Luminous Sky of Consciousness". The Infinite Space or Field of Universal Consciousness. The Boundless Ocean of Intelligence. The Wisdom-Mind which sees all things from *above*, from the point of view of the Transcendental Reality. CIDĀKĀŚA is ŚRĪ JAGADAMBĀ, the Holy World Mother. From this Pure Consciousness come forth all things, and all things dwell in Her and are maintained by Her.

CIDĀNANDA
Sanskrit: Pure-Bliss-Consciousness. [See ĀTMĀNANDA]

CIDRŪPIṆĪ-ŚAKTI
Sanskrit: "The Universal Power whose Form is Pure Consciousness Itself". One of the qualities of the Ultimate Reality (PARABRAHMAN).

CINMAYĪ
Sanskrit: "She who is in the Form of Consciousness Itself". She who is Pure Consciousness. She who is Formless Awareness. The Radiant Consciousness of the Divine Mother, which is Pure Intelligence, Supreme Spirit. She is Omnipresent, Omniscient, Omnipotent, and She is present in you as your own Divine Self. A Name of LALITĀ, the Goddess.

CIT
Sanskrit: Boundless, Universal Consciousness. Also known as CIDRŪPIṆĪ-ŚAKTI (the Universal Power whose Form is Pure Consciousness Itself). This is a Consciousness not related to any form, body, world, period, time, entity or manifestation; that is, it has

no conceivable limitations of any kind whatsoever. It is Universal and Eternal. It is called non-relational Consciousness or Unlimited-Consciousness. It has the quality of VIMARŚA, "Self-Knowing, Self-Awareness, Universal Self-Consciousness, the Cosmic I AM-ness".

CIT-GĀYATRĪ
Sanskrit: Absolute Knowledge. The ŚRĪ-VIDYĀ-VAJRA-MANTRA.

CITI-ŚAKTI
Sanskrit: Universal Awareness, Transcendental Consciousness. According to the Tantra literature, the Yogī enters into SAMĀDHI (Divine Consciousness) by a thought-free, non-relational Awareness, by dissolving the personality-sense in CITI-ŚAKTI.

CIT-JAḌA-GRANTHI
Sanskrit: The connection between your consciousness and your physical body. This Mystery can be solved only in the Heart Cakra. Then you attain MOKṢA (Freedom) and MUKTI (Liberation).

CIT-MĀTĀ
Sanskrit: The Mother of Consciousness.

CIT-ŚAKTI
Sanskrit: "Consciousness-Power". The Source and Consciousness behind all things. Also, the ŚRĪ-VIDYĀ-VAJRA-MANTRA.

CITTA
Sanskrit: Mind, Consciousness, Intelligence. The mind-essence, mind-stuff or mind-substance. The Reality in which all experience of Time (KĀLA), Space (ĀKĀŚA) and Form (RŪPA) takes place.

CITTA-MĀRGA
Sanskrit: "The Way of Intelligence". Also known as RĀJA YOGA (the Royal Way) and MĀNASA-MĀRGA (the Way of the Mind). This Way is centred in your Head. It consists of cultivating Awareness, Consciousness, being in the Moment through total Awareness, using the *total* Mind. This Way is *not* about thinking or theorising, using your ordinary, rational mind.

CITTAMĀYĀKOŚA
Sanskrit: "An illusionary (MĀYĀ) vehicle (KOŚA) of Consciousness (CITTA)". Also called CITTAMAYAKOŚA (consisting-of-Consciousness body). This term can refer to a variety of realities, including the Buddhic Vehicle.

CITTAMAYAKOŚA SAMĀDHI
Sanskrit: "Full-of-Consciousness-body-Ecstasy". The Glorified State of Consciousness. Glory.

CITTASYA
Sanskrit: Of the mind-stuff; by the mind; by Consciousness.

CITTA-VIKṢEPĀS (VIKṢEPAḤ)
Sanskrit: Mental distractions, confusion, losing your way on many sidetracks. One of the ANTARĀYĀḤ (obstacles, impediments, problems on the Path to Higher Consciousness).

CITTA-VṚTTAYAS (VṚTTAYAḤ)
Sanskrit: Mind-fluctuations, mind-modifications, changes in the mind-stuff or in Consciousness. CITTA-VṚTTI.

CITTAVṚTTI (CITTA-VṚTTI)
Sanskrit: Mind-waves. The thought-processes, which generally go on out of control. The endless transformations of the mind-substance resulting from "thinking" and "mind chatter" (verbalizing, speaking, whether silently or aloud). The immense thought-producing activity of the mind (the mental body), which never stops producing thoughts, day or night.

CITTA-VṚTTI-NIRODHA
Sanskrit: "Mental-transformations-suspending". Thought-process-suspension. The suspension of the movements of the mind in deep Silence. This is the immediate goal of meditation because, when this is achieved, the mind can reflect the God-Being (ĀTMAN) within you and attain Self-Realization (ĀTMA-VIDYĀ). When your mind is completely still, this is called SAMĀDHI (SAMĀ-DHI: equilibrated-mind).

Clairvoyance

From the French: "The ability to see clearly". The full usage of the astral and etheric sight and, in its higher aspects, the faculty of Spiritual Sight. True clairvoyance is extremely rare. True clairvoyance is the opening of the Third-Eye Cakra, the Śivanetra, the Eye of Śiva, the All-Seeing Eye, the Eye of Wisdom. The true clairvoyance of the Third-Eye is direct vision, as clear and unimpeded as physical vision. When the Third-Eye Cakra opens, you might initially see visions of people and places, landscapes of other worlds, or clouds of colours. When fully developed, you can see into a person's aura with total accuracy and distinguish every thoughtform in it, in the same way as you can see the lines on the face of the person before you. What is more, you can distinguish between thoughtforms in the aura of the person and astral presences in the Astral World, clearly and accurately, whereas the average clairvoyant cannot. The Egyptians called the visionary faculties *The Eye of Horus*. Clairvoyance has seven levels, the last of them being the Absolute or Beatific Vision.

Communion

Latin: In the terminology of the Catholic Mystics of the Middle Ages, *Communion* is to commune consciously with the Divine Presence.

Concentration

From the Latin Concentrare: "To bring the mind to a centre, to a point of focus, convergence, union" (from Con, "together, toward", and Centrum, "centre, heart, the kernel of a thing"). *Concentration* is the exclusive attention to one object, focusing the mind, the action of the will directing all of one's energies towards a single point, goal, object, person or idea. This is the first stage of the Eastern Orthodox Christian method of *Interior Prayer.* For the Eastern Christian Mystic, Concentration begins by learning to "think in the Heart". It is easier, at first, to concentrate on an "object" such as a Statement of Truth, a Mantra, a Word of Power or a Divine Name. The mind is consciously brought down *into* the Heart by the process of repeating a Divine Name in the Heart, or a sentence or formula such as the Name of Jesus. Concentration, to bring the mind into the Heart, is the first stage on the Path of Mysticism.

Contemplation

From the Latin Contemplātionis: "Being within the temple". To behold, to observe, to gaze upon, to have in view, to study thoughtfully, to look or view with continued attention, to be deeply absorbed in the object of your thought. Contemplation is an intent, sustained gazing at something. In Contemplation you *become* what you behold. The Mystics divide Contemplation into two major divisions: *Natural* Contemplation and *Supernatural* Contemplation. Natural Contemplation can be *sensitive* (through the senses), *imaginative,* or *intellectual*. In Supernatural Contemplation, however, we simply gaze upon Truth, without discursive reasoning, without any emotional, imaginative or intellectual elements involved. According to the pre-Christian Romans and the later Mystics of the Roman Catholic Church, Contemplation is the concentration of the mind upon God or the Soul by drawing your attention inward and beholding the Light. This has been defined by the Mystics as "a simple and affectionate gaze upon God" or "a simple gaze upon Truth". At this stage of your Mystic Path you are nearing your goal of Union with God and you have glimpses of Higher Consciousness or Buddhic Unitive-Consciousness. God is *felt* within the Soul, embraced, touched and seen—not with the physical senses, not even with the senses of the astral body, but with the spiritual senses of the Spiritual Self.

Contemplātionis

Latin: "Being within the temple". Contemplation. From Con (together, with, jointly) and Templum (a temple, church, sacred building). The temple is the Heart Centre.

Conversion

From the Latin: "Turning around". Reversing one's energies from the material world to that of the Soul and Higher Consciousness. Turning away from outer objective consciousness to inner subjective consciousness.

Cosmic Consciousness

The term *Cosmic Consciousness* can be understood in two ways:

- The condition of absorption into the exalted Consciousness of NIRVĀṆA, the Kingdom of God (ĀTMĀ-VIDYĀ).
- The integration of the Buddhic Consciousness (Pure Consciousness, TURĪYA) into the states below. In this exalted condition, therefore, the objective consciousness, the subjective mind (dream states) and the dreamless-sleep state have fused perfectly into the Transcendental State of Pure Consciousness. One is simultaneously aware of the four states of Consciousness, from BUDDHI downwards, while functioning in the waking state in the physical body. This state is known as TURĪYĀTĪTA-AVASTHĀ, "beyond the Fourth State".

Cosmic Fire

The Cosmic Fire is the One Force in the Universe, which acts in all things. The Greeks called this One Force MAGNĒS or DYNAMIS, while in Tibetan it is called FOHAT. The Romans called this One Force the PERPETUUM MOBILE UNIVERSUM, "that which continually moves the Universe". Cosmic Fire is what we call *Life*. It exists within every inch of Space, both visible and invisible. Fire is what animates men and angels and all living things. Fire is the restless Energy of Creation, the evolutionary Force, the motive Energy and Power behind the evolutionary impulse of a man, an animal, a star or a planet. The ancient Jews knew this Power as SHEKINAH (God's Manifest Presence). In Sanskrit there are many terms for the Fire, such as AGNI, TEJAS and KUṆḌALINĪ. The Cosmic Fire has three vast realms:

- The Fires of the Spirit (First-Logos Fire).
- The Fires of Mind (Second-Logos Fire).
- The Fires inherent in Matter (Third-Logos Fire).

Creation

The Universe is a periodic, or cyclic, manifestation. During each period of manifestation, God creates in seven great Cosmic Days, seven vast periods of Cosmic Time, seven great Ages. Notice, God *creates*, because natural and supernatural Evolution are still going on and will go on for myriads of years of Earth-time. Thus: Science has to understand what Evolution really is, and religion has to understand what Creation really is, for they are the *same*. [See *Evolution*]

Creative Hierarchies

The human prototype is but one of twelve Creative Hierarchies of intelligent entities which inhabit appropriate planets, realms and planes of our Solar System. Each of these Hierarchies consists of countless entities. The Hierarchies are groups of lives, at various stages of unfoldment and growth, who use vehicles of expression (forms or vestures), the vehicles varying according to the spiritual development reached. The twelve Creative Hierarchies within our Solar System are together part of the Creative Effort of the Creator, the Cosmic Creative-Intelligence we call "God". Three of the Hierarchies have already been Liberated (released from the Cosmic Physical Plane).

Note that the Creative Hierarchies do not include the great Cosmic Creators, the ELOHĪM (Hebrew). The planets themselves (the Planetary Logoi) and the suns and stars (the Solar Logoi) are beyond even the level of the "gods". They are KOSMOKRATORES (Greek), Beings who *embody* the Plan of the Cosmic Mind.

Creative World

According to the Kabbalistic description, the lower Mental Plane, which is a world of *thoughts*. [See *Four Worlds*]

Crown Centre

The Energy Centre at the top of the head, also called the *Thousand-Petalled Lotus*. The Crown Centre is wholly spiritual. It will put you in touch with the spiritual dimensions and, ultimately, with Nirvāṇa. [See SAHASRĀRA CAKRA]

CRUCIFIXION

Latin: In the symbolism of the New Testament, CRUCIFIXION is the battle between the Personality and the Soul. It is the *Test of the Spirit*, the Soul's final battle with the world, the struggle between the Nirvāṇic Light and the dark matter and material powers of this world.

Cūḍāmaṇī, Cūḍāmaṇīm
Sanskrit: "The greatest jewel". Most excellent, the best, perfect. From Cūḍā (crest, peak, top, most significant) and Maṇi (a jewel, an ornament, something precious). The esoteric meaning is "the Crest Jewel of Wisdom", or Self-Realization.

D

Dabar
Hebrew: The Word, the Logos. God's Creative Speech or Power.

Daemōn, Daimōn
Greek: A spiritual being, an invisible entity, an angel, a spirit, a god or goddess, one's own guardian angel, a Deity. To the initiated Greeks such as Plato, Aristotle and Socrates: one's own Higher Self (Ātman), or God within. In ancient Greece, Daimōn simply meant an invisible spirit or entity, something divine or angelic. Even a human Soul was considered a Daimōn—that is, a *spiritual being*. The Christians changed this to mean an *evil* spirit (a demon or devil). But not all spirits in the invisible worlds are evil, just as not all humans are totally good. Nowadays, the word *demon* refers *only* to evil spirits. How words become corrupted over the centuries!

Daiviprākṛtī
Sanskrit: "The Divine Nature, the Divine Mother-Substance". From Daivi (divine, shining, luminous) and Prākṛtī (substance, matter, energy, nature, source, originating matter or substance). Daiviprākṛtī is the Original Source, the Divine Original Evolver, the Divine Original Substance, the Primordial Light, the Divine Light, the Light of God, the Cosmic Light, the Light of the Logos, the Universal Vital Force. Similar to Śabda-Brahman (Sanskrit) and Logos (Greek).

Daivi-Śakti
Sanskrit: Holy Vibration, Divine Energy.

Daivi-Śakti-Kuṇḍalinī
Sanskrit: The moving, changing, evolving forms in Creation, on all the Planes and Realms of Being. The Immanent Aspect of the Goddess. [See Paramitā]

Dama
Sanskrit: Control of the senses, actions and conduct. One of the Six Mental Qualifications for Discipleship (Śat-Sampatti).

Dark Forces
For hundreds of thousands of years a continuous battle has been fought on the Physical, Astral and Mental Planes, in and above the Earth, between the Forces of Light and the Forces of Darkness, both sides consisting of angelic beings and human types of evolution. The Dark Forces are essentially responsible for the forces of matter and materialism, as opposed to the Christ Forces which are of the Spirit and the Light. On the Physical Plane, the Dark Forces are ruled by six oriental and six occidental leaders, or *negative Masters,* and they have a semi-organized structure called the *Black Lodge*. These Dark Forces have opposed every Mystic, Saint, Guru, Saviour, Master, since the beginning of time. They try to prevent the inflow of Higher Consciousness and Revelation, to hold back the forces of evolution and progress. They stimulate fear and hatred, lies and deceits, glamour and illusion. Their aim is the retardation and crystallization of consciousness. Also called the *Dark Brothers,* the *Brothers of the Shadow* or, collectively, the *Anti-Christ.*

Darśana
Sanskrit: Vision, sight, beholding, seeing, observing. A point of view, a philosophy, a system of thought, a doctrine. Receiving Divine Grace and Blessings. Initiatory Mantra, conveying the Śaktipāta or Divine Energy. (*Darshan* is the anglicized form.) In Darshan session (a special group-meditation) the Guru radiates this Energy out to the group. The Guru conveys his Energy through the medium of a Mantra. This is Śaktipāta, or Divine Grace, through the *agency* of the Mantra. Darshan sessions are very special and very powerful; during these sessions you experience Energy, Light, visions, and so forth.

Darvesh
Persian: A mendicant, a renunciate, an ascetic. One who is wholly devoted to God. Darvesh became Dervis in Turkish, which means "a poor man, a holy man, a wandering ascetic, one who has renounced the world". In English it became *Dervish.*

Deha
Sanskrit: The physical body.

Dehabhrānti
Sanskrit: Identification with the physical body, therefore being deluded by the body. From Deha (the body) and Bhrānti (worldly consciousness, erroneous thinking).

Dehagranthi
Sanskrit: Conditioned by the body and its environment. Identification with the physical body, which limits the Free Flow of Pure Consciousness. From Deha (the body) and Granthi (a knot, a barrier, a conditioning).

Dehātma (Deha-Ātma)
Sanskrit: The personal sense of self in the physical body. Identification with the physical body.

Deification
Latin: God entering into Man. The Monad, the "Father in Heaven", fusing with the Soul. At that moment, the physical body, the personality and the Soul vibrate in unison and harmony, and a channel opens up for the downflow of the Spirit, the Monadic Force. Then the whole Man vibrates to the Note or Sound of the Monad. Then Man becomes God-Man.

The doctrine of Theosis (the Deification of created beings by the Light of Grace) is the essence of the Christian Eastern Orthodox Church's Mysticism. A human being advances towards Union with God to the extent that he or she allows the Divine Grace-Light to flood into his or her Consciousness. [See Theosis]

Deipara
Greek: The Mother of God.

Demiurgos
Greek: The Creator, or a Creator-God of a high order.

Dervish
From the Turkish Dervis: "A poor man, a holy man, a wandering ascetic, one who has renounced the world". [See Darvesh]

Deśa
Sanskrit: Place, country, locality, nation.

Deva
Sanskrit: Shining, Splendid, Divine, Godly, Bright, Immortal, Radiating Light, Shining Substance. God or Divinity. Also, a Shining One, a Being of Light, a Resplendent Being, a Spiritual Being or Angel. Devas are non-human Spiritual Intelligences on another evolutionary line. They are called Malachīm (messengers) in the Jewish tradition, Angelos in Greek and Genii in Latin.

Deva-Bhāva
Sanskrit: "Longing for the Divine". The desire, feeling, emotion, for Union with God. When your Heart, Hṛda, is on Fire with Divine-Longing, you shall *find* God. [See Bhāgavata-Bhāva]

Devāchan
Tibetan: "The abode of the Shining Ones". The Shining Worlds. The *Seven Heavens,* the seven subplanes of the Mental Plane. The word sometimes refers to just the Causal Worlds, the three higher (formless) subplanes of the Mental Plane. In Sanskrit, Devasthāna.

Deva-Loka
Sanskrit: "The Shining World". The place of the Shining Ones. The Heavens. The Mental Plane. Devāchan.

Deva-Manuṣya-Deham
Sanskrit: Angelic-human bodies, derived from the Angelic Kingdom. Our present physical bodies are not human; they were derived from the Animal Kingdom. In the far future, when the Human and Angelic Kingdoms merge, we shall no longer have to struggle with an uncooperative animal body, for we will have bodies on the Physical Plane that will express perfectly the Divine Consciousness within us.

Deva-Mārga
Sanskrit: "The Shining Path". The Spiritual Path, which consists of meditation and selfless Heart-Service.

Devanāgarī
Sanskrit: "God's writing". The Sanskrit Language (Saṁskṛta).

Deva-Netra
Sanskrit: The All-Seeing-Eye. There are great Siddhas, Master Beings, who have the simultaneous Vision of both the Immanent and Transcendent aspects of God, whereby they can scan the Infinite Horizons and discover the Ultimate Mysteries.

Deva-Śakti
Sanskrit: Divine Energy which you touch upon in higher meditation.

Devasthāna (Deva-Sthāna)
Sanskrit: "The abode of the gods". The Angelic Realms. The Heaven Worlds. The seven subplanes of the Mental Plane. In Tibetan, Devāchan.

Devasya
Sanskrit: Divine. Of God, of the Shining One. Spiritual Light, the Light-of-Lights, the Light of the Effulgent God. The Divine One, the Giver of Happiness.

Devatā
Sanskrit: The Shining Divinity, Fiery-Light, the Shining Fire-God, the Spiritual-Sun. Also, a god or goddess. Non-human evolutionary orders or hierarchies. The Angelic Kingdoms. Angelic species everywhere, as distinct from the humanoid species (Manuṣya).

Devavāṇī (Deva-Vāṇī)
Sanskrit: "The Divine Voice". The Voice of the Silence, the Spiritual-Sound which emanates from the Monadic Plane. The Eternal Word, the Logos, the Creative-Energy. [See Ākāśa-Vāṇī]

Deva-Vidyā
Sanskrit: "Shining-Realization". Knowing the Truth directly, above and beyond your mind faculty, with the most spiritual part of your Soul. Then you will understand your Path of Transfiguration or Celestial Evolution. The great Mysteries will be revealed to your Soul's inward Gaze.

Devī
Sanskrit: The Holy Goddess, the Divine, Divinity. The Personal Goddess. The Universal Goddess or Śakti in Her immanence or immediacy in Creation. The Divine Feminine Principle inside you and inside all matter. The Mother Principle out of which, and by which, all things have been made. Devī is the Holy Ghost, the Father's Creative Power. She is the Power responsible for the Creation of the Universe. Although Devī is responsible for Creation, Her Transcendental Nature is Absolute Bliss-Consciousness and Existence. She is also known as Śrī-Lalitā-Devī. Worship of Her is worship of the Supreme Being in Its aspect of Śakti, or Creative Energy.

Devil
Symbolically, the personality, which opposes the Spirit or Individuality. From the Greek Diabolos (an enemy, an accuser, a slanderer). It is true that there are evil spirits in the Universe, fallen angels and fallen human spirits in and around our planet. But no being is equal to God, so there cannot be an entity (called "the Devil") equal and opposite to God. The "devils" (fallen spirits) came *after* the Fall. (Note that there is no such thing as the horned and hoofed monster, so popular with some Christians.) [See Diabolos and Satanas]

Dhāraṇā
Sanskrit: Inner Concentration. Concentrated attention upon the Goal. Being fixed upon the Goal. Focusing the mind at one point. Spiritual exercises. Dhāraṇā is the sixth step of Aṣṭāṅga Yoga, as set down by Patañjali.

DHARMA

Sanskrit: "That which upholds all things". The Force of Destiny. From the Sanskrit root DHRI, "to support, uphold, maintain, carry on, preserve, bear, nourish, foster". DHARMA is all of the following:

- Truth, the Ultimate Reality.
- Justice, results, phenomena.
- Cosmic Law, Cosmic Order, the Law of Life.
- Religious law or doctrine.
- Virtue, morality, righteousness, duty, standard, ideal.
- The TATHATĀ, or "Suchness", of things. The Law of Being inherent in a thing.
- The Path that any entity has to follow in the Cosmos, whether it be an atom, a human being, a galaxy or a Logos. The correct course of conduct for any man, angel, god, plant or animal. The ideal goal or objective in life. The Path of Self-Actualization.

In the old Sanskrit understanding, DHARMA means the Path that you should follow to become what you are *meant* to be. In modern spiritual psychology this process is called *self-actualization*, meaning the development of your personality, the personal ego, the little personal "I". But the word DHARMA means much more than that. It means your total unfoldment as a human entity on your Soul and Spiritual levels as well. It means Self-Realization and also God-Realization.

DHARMAKĀYA

Sanskrit: The "Absolute-Truth Body" of a Buddha. A vesture of Light, or Light Body. The highest body of a Buddha (Enlightened Being). The Body of Glory in which the manifest Son of God, "the Word made Flesh", dwells in NIRVĀṆA, the glorious Worlds of Light. Do not imagine this to be like a physical, emotional or mental body. It is a Buddha's Mind merged in Universal Consciousness. The Human Soul assumes the DHARMAKĀYA if and when he/she chooses to pass out of the Human Kingdom. Once this glorious Light Body is assumed, there is a complete severance from all human evolution and all the lower worlds. Once a DHARMAKĀYA, the Adept or Buddha leaves behind every possible relation with, or thought for, this earth-plane. [See NIRMĀNAKĀYA]

DHARMA-KṢETRA

Sanskrit: The Absolute-Field. The Eternal Reality.

DHARMAMEGHA

Sanskrit: The Absolute Truth (DHARMA) Cloud or Veil (MEGHA).

DHARMAMEGHA SAMĀDHI

Sanskrit: "Cloud-of-Absolute-Truth-Ecstasy". The Sixth State of Consciousness. The first stage of Union with God. BHĀGAVATA-AVASTHĀ.

DHARMĀTMA

Sanskrit: The Essential Nature or Root Condition of all things as Absolute or Original Reality.

DHAT

Hebrew: Gnosis, Illumination, Knowledge.

DHATU

Sanskrit: An Element, a Principle, an essential factor.

DHĪ, DHĪYĀḤ, DHIYO, DHIYAHA

Sanskrit: Mind, Consciousness, Heart. Intellect, Intelligence, Wisdom, Intuition, Spiritual Understanding, Meditation. Inner Vision, Spiritual Vision, Spiritual Faculties, Spiritual Perception. The Buddhi Principle, the Seership Faculty, the Mind of Light. DHĪ is:

- Cosmic-Vision or Absolute-Sight.
- Solar-Systemic-Vision of the Inner Worlds.
- Vision of the Spiritual Self or ĀTMAN.
- Insight or Intuition as manifested through the physical body and brain.

DHIKR (DHIKAR)

Arabic: The repetition of a prayer. [See ZIKR]

DHĪMAHI

Sanskrit: "We meditate, we contemplate". Let us contemplate or recognize or meditate upon. Let us receive and assimilate and realize. Behold the Glorious-Light-Body-of-God.

Dhūmāvatī
Sanskrit: The grey-haired woman. From Dhūmā (smoke, smoke-coloured, grey). The Old Woman, the Wise Woman, the Eldest Woman, the Widow. She who has gone through the Cycle of Life and remained. The Grandmother Goddess, the Primordial Formless Void. A Name of Lalitā, the Goddess.

Dhuna
Sanskrit: "A tune, a passion, an obsession". Inner listening to the Nāda or Inner Sound Current, the Inaudible Word, the Logos, and becoming one with the Śabda-Brahman, Vāk, the Word.

Dhyāna (Dhyān)
Sanskrit: Meditation, Contemplation, Recollection. Intense *internal* meditational practices. Silence, solitude. The spiritual practices that lead to Soul-Consciousness and Union with God as Light. Dhyāna is the seventh step of Aṣṭāṅga Yoga, as set down by Patañjali.

Dhyāna-Mātā
Sanskrit: She who is the Mother (Mātā) of all meditational practices (Dhyāna), all spiritual effort. A Name of Lalitā, the Goddess.

Dhyāna Yoga
Sanskrit: The Path of Meditation and thought-control.

Dhyāni-Buddha
Sanskrit: "Meditative Buddha". A Buddha upon the Nirvāṇic and Paranirvāṇic Planes who is continually in a state of meditation for the salvation of all sentient beings. The meditation of the Dhyāni-Buddhas and the Nirmānakāyas is their act of *Service*. In Tibetan, Dhyān-Chohan or Dhyāni-Chohan.

Dhyāni-Chohan, Dhyān-Chohan
Tibetan: "Meditative Lord". An Archangel or highly evolved Deva. The meditative gods. The feminine, receptive, group-conscious, selfless Angelic Hierarchies. Angelic Orders who are always conscious of the Eternal Unity, who have no separative tendencies, no ego, no self-centredness, no individualistic ambitions and plans. Their lives are always rooted in the Perpetual Light of Original Creation. (Chohan is a Tibetan word and the term Dhyāni-Chohan is used mainly in Tibetan esoteric teachings.)

Diabolos
Greek: An enemy, an accuser, a slanderer. One who throws something at you or who wrongly accuses you. A wicked person or spirit. From this the Christians got the word *devil*. Similar to the Hebrew Sātan and the Greek Satanas.

Diakrisis
Greek: Spiritual Wisdom. The power to discern spirits, the power to discern thoughts, the power to distinguish between what is real and essential and what is unreal and passing. From this was derived the English word *discrimination.* According to the early meaning of the Desert Fathers, however, discrimination was a *spiritual* faculty. It has the same meaning as the Sanskrit Viveka.

Dianoia
Greek: The ordinary lower mind, the reasoning faculty, the objective mind, the conceptualizing mind. The discursive, thinking mind, considered by the early Christian Saints to be an inferior faculty.

Diaspora
Greek: Scattering, dispersion, breaking up. The dispersion of the Jews outside of Palestine/Israel.

Dīkṣā
Sanskrit: Initiation. Even as a candle is lit by another source of fire, so you are ignited within by a Guru at Initiation. This is a *spiritual fact.* This is one of the functions of the Sat Guru (True Teacher).

Dīn
Hebrew: Justice. Divine Justice. The Kabbalistic word for the Law of Karma, known in ancient Israel.

Divākara
Sanskrit: Day-maker, Light-producer (Divā-Kara). The Sun. The Solar Logos.

Divine-Conscious Mind
Absolute Consciousness. BRAHMĀ-VIDYĀ (God-Realization) or BRAHMĀ-AVASTHĀ (the God-State). Monadic Consciousness, on the plane of PARANIRVĀṆA.

DIVYA CITTA
Sanskrit: "Divine Consciousness". Pure Consciousness.

DIVYA DṚIṢTI
Sanskrit: "Divine Eye". The awakened and functioning Third-Eye.

DIVYA-ŚROTA (DIVYAṀ-ŚROTRAM)
Sanskrit: "Divine Hearing". From the Monadic Plane emanates the LOGOS (the "Word" of the Christian Bible), what in Sanskrit is known as ĀKĀŚA-VĀṆĪ, the Sounding-Light, the Voice of Heaven. This Divine Voice, the Name of God, descends through the great planes of our Solar System and manifests as all the sounds, on all the Planes of Being. This is the "Word made Flesh", God-in-Incarnation, God-in-Manifestation. This is the ĀUṀ, the ŌṀ, the *Sound*. By *Inner Listening* to this Sound we return up the planes to our Original Home, the Godhead.

Dogma
A settled or established opinion or belief. From the Greek DOKEIN, "to think, to *seem* good". *Dogma* is a set of *beliefs* authoritatively laid down by the church, usually by popes, bishops or theologians.

DOKUSAN
Japanese: Private instruction and counselling. Private interview with the Zen Master.

DOXA
Greek: "Praise, adoration, an opinion". From DOKEIN, "to think". Also, Divine Glory, Divine Effulgence, Radiance above the Head.

DOXOLOGIA
Greek: Praising and glorifying God through chanting, singing, dancing. From DOXA (praise, adoration) and LOGOS (a word, an idea, a speech).

DRAKŌN
Greek: The Dragon, a symbol of Fire. The Fiery Serpent or Serpent Fire, known in Sanskrit as KUṆḌALINĪ-ŚAKTI. This Fire brings Rebirth, Immortality and Wisdom, the knowledge of all mysteries and all hidden things. It is a mysterious Energy of the Sun, the Solar Logos. This Cosmic Fire, or Dragon, was known to the ancient Chinese, Egyptians, Greeks, Celts, Hindus, and the Nordic Initiates. This Fire is permeating all Space. [See KUṆḌALINĪ and *Serpent-Power*]

DRAṢṬĀ, DRAṢṬUḤ
Sanskrit: The Seer (see-er), Observer, Witness, Perceiver, Onlooker, Spectator. The Self (the Soul) and the SELF (the Spirit). The Visionary, the Sage, the Knower, the Thinker, the True Man. You as the Soul and You in your Divinity, at one with the Spirit. The Seer is ĀTMAN or PURUṢA, the ĀTMĀ, the Spiritual Self in the Heart, the Inner Visionary, the Witness to all that is, the Self who forever abides in His own true Nature. It is Yourself. Also, a JÑĀNI, a Wise One. Some variations are DRAṢṬṚI, DṚṢṬRĀ, DṚṢṬA, DṚṢṬĀ.

DṚIṢTI
Sanskrit: Inner Vision. Opening the Third-Eye and seeing the Universe as it really is—as a Playground of God. Also called DIVYA DṚIṢTI (the Divine Eye).

DṚŚI
Sanskrit: Seeing, perceiving.

DṚŚIMĀTRAḤ
Sanskrit: The power of seeing, perceiving, experiencing. Being aware or conscious of something.

DṚŚYASYA
Sanskrit: What is seen; the observable. Creation, Manifestation, Nature, the World.

DUAD ⊕
Greek: The Two, the Father-Mother, the line, the first Pair or Duality at the beginning of Creation. Mother, ⊖, and Father, ⦶, unite to form the Mother-Father, ⊕. [See MONAD and TRIAD]

Durgā
Sanskrit: The Fearless One. The Deliverer. The Warrior-Goddess. The Inaccessible Goddess. The "difficult-to-please", the "difficult-to-approach". She who is difficult to reach or attain. She who takes you across the Ocean of Saṁsāra (Existence). She who destroys demons and evil powers. Durgā is an aspect of Kālī. She is remote, inaccessible. She is the Reality *behind* visible Nature.

Dvāpara Yuga
Sanskrit: "The Two Parts Only (or half of the Truth and Spirituality) Age". The Bronze Age. An evolutionary period, calculated by the Ṛṣis of ancient India to be equivalent to 864,000 earth-years.

Dvi-Jā
Sanskrit: "Twice-born". Born again. One who has been initiated into the Spiritual Life. The Spiritually Reborn. This is an old pre-Christian concept.

Dynamis
Greek: The One Force. The Cosmic Fire, the One Radiant Energy. Motion, Power, Energy in the Cosmos. The Dynamis of the Universe is an inexhaustible source of Power, Energy and Radiance. Hence the English words *dynamic* and *dynamo*. Equivalent to the Tibetan word Fohat. The Sanskrit Śakti is the feminine aspect of this Power. [See Fohat]

Dzyān
Pre-Sanskrit: The secret knowledge of Atlantis.

E

Earth
Earth is a *key word* in the Mystical Tradition. In the early Semitic languages, *Earth* meant "the physical principle, physical Creation", and the *Heavens* meant "the subtle worlds". Through ignorance, however, the biblical translators translated *Earth* as this planet only and *Heavens* as the stars. *Earth* is called A R Tz (ERETz) in Hebrew, Arā in Aramaic, Gē or Gaia in Greek, Terra in Latin. In all of the ancient tongues, *Earth* means all of the following:

- The basis, the foundation.
- Nature, the Manifestation or Creation, all that is embodied.
- The planet, our globe.
- The shining Sea of Matter, the material universe, the cover over the Real.
- The focus of gravity, or a solid, steady point in Space.
- The energy or quality of solidity, form, stability, fixity.
- The physical body, the Base Centre.

In Sanskrit, the Earth Element is known as Pṛthivī.

Earthbound Spirits
Flatfooted materialists who can sense only this world, whose minds are attached to material objects, to their physical bodies or to the physical bodies of others, become *earthbound spirits* after death, living in the etheric body on the etheric-physical subplanes. In the worst cases they become visible as ghosts, apparitions, phantoms, doubles, due to either their densification or the psychic impression of a sensitive person. These haunting ghosts can be helped by "rescue circles" from this side or by "guides" and "invisible helpers" on the other side. They cannot be released from their condition until they are ready to *re-orient their minds*. The earthbound "dead" sometimes live in their astral bodies on the sixth and fifth subplanes of the Astral World. These people cannot be seen. They live wholly in the Astral World and are often called "the spirits of the ancestors" or "dead relatives". Like the earthbound spirits on the etheric subplanes, they do not know that they are dead or refuse to recognize the fact.

Ecstasy
From the Greek Ekstasis: "Bliss, religious rapture, elation, delight, spiritual exaltation as a result of Mysticism". The Mystics define it as "a mental transport and rapture, an overpowering exaltation from the contemplation of Divine things". In other words, *Union with God* or, in Sanskrit, Samādhi. [See Ekstasis]

Ectoplasma
Greek: "A thing externally formed". From Ectos (outside) and Plasma (a thing formed or moulded).

Ectoplasma is an extremely flexible substance. It looks utterly solid and real, but because it is etheric you can put your hands through it. Ectoplasma can produce such phenomena as rapping noises, spirit-voices, table-turnings, levitation of objects or of the medium, spirit-hands, direct-voice phenomena, and other poltergeist-type phenomena.

Educatio, Educationis

Latin: "To lead out from (ignorance), to draw out (the best from within), to develop (knowledge and skill)". Education was not always materialistic as it is today. True Education is not simply exercising the lower mind, the simple, rational, memory-based, common mind, the analytical, logical, critical mind. The total Heart-Experience and the total Mind-Awakening are true Education, and without the Spiritual Path and commitment to Spiritual Evolution this is impossible.

Effulgentia

Latin: "Radiant Splendour, Brilliant Light, glittering, shining". The shining forth of the Godhead (Deus). Hence the English word *Effulgence*. Effulgentia is the experience of Radiant Light, the White Brilliance, the Supreme Crown, the Supreme Splendour of the Godhead—what is called Nirvāṇa in the East, Allah among the Muslims and Shekinah by the Jews. The Arabic word Allah means "the Effulgent One, God as the Overpowering Effulgence, the Eternally Shining, the Radiant One". The Hebrew word Shekinah (the Divine Presence) means the same: "Radiating Light, Glory (as Light Emanation)". This is the goal and end of the Mystical Path.

Ēgō

Latin: "I" or "I am" (Ego-Sum). The original meaning is the Absolute Spiritual Self or "I AM", the Monad (Greek), the Spiritus (Latin), the Divinity in Man. Later on, it also came to mean the Soul, the Animā (Latin), which is within the body and beyond the mind. Nowadays, the English word *ego* refers to the personal self, the Persona (Latin: the mask), the personality or body-conscious "I", the unreal "I", the false sense of self (the Sanskrit Ahaṁkāra, "I am the doer").

Ehben (A B N)

Hebrew: "The Stone of the Wise". [See *Philosopher's Stone*]

Eheieh (Eheyeh)

Hebrew: This is the most mysterious and holy Name of God of the ancient Hebrew Sages. There is no adequate translation. It means "I AM" in the cosmic sense, the I-AM Consciousness within the Universe, the Soul of the Universe. It is the Paramātman of the Seers of India, the Name of the Transcendental Godhead within Creation. It affirms the Absolute Reality of God as the Indwelling Presence in the Boundless All, and in *you* also, as a human being.

Eheieh Asher Eheieh

Hebrew: "I Am that I Am" or "I Am the I AM" or simply "I AM". This is the great Revelation of the Nature of God given to Moses of Old, the founder of the Jewish religion. This "I AM" is the Universal Christ-Being, the *Alpha and Omega* of the Apocalypse.

Eidolatres

Greek: "A servant who worships an idol". From Eidolon (an image, a form, a representation, a statue, a spectre, an apparition, a ghost, a phantom, an effigy of a god or goddess to be worshipped) and Latris (a servant). A worshipper of forms, images and sense-objects. A materialist. A sensualist. A consciousness whose only experience is through the five senses. The reliance on physical objects, people, forms and conditions for happiness. The lack of awareness of the Great Invisible and of the Power of God in all things. The worship of matter instead of Spirit, of the body instead of the Soul, of the world instead of God. From this came the English words *idolater* and *idolatry*. There are countless humans who are idolaters, worshipping "false gods".

Eidolon

Greek: "A shadow of reality". The shadow, the image, the double, the duplicate. Imagination. The image-making faculty, the mental-creative ability, the ability of the mind to form mental images or pictures. Also, the astral body or "spirit-body".

Eighth Sphere
The *Outer Darkness* or *Nether Darkness*. The lowest, darkest regions of the Astral World. Strictly speaking, this condition is not astral but sub-physical. No matter how inconceivable it might seem, there is a realm of lower vibration than this Physical Plane! Avītci in Sanskrit.

Eikon
Greek: A picture, a maṇḍala, a likeness, a figure, a representation, an image, a resemblance, a symbol, a portrait, an illustration of something (usually of God, Christ, the Holy Trinity, the Virgin Mary or the angels). Hence the English word *icon*. Eikons are usually objects of veneration and worship in the Eastern Orthodox Church, and are equivalent to the pictures, paintings, statues and amulets of the Roman Catholic tradition.

Eirene
Greek: Peace and tranquillity, which are necessary for the Spiritual Life.

Eka
Sanskrit: One, united.

Ekāgratā
Sanskrit: One-pointedness. The breathless, concentrated state when the breath (Prāṇa) and the mind (Manas) are stilled.

Ekāgratā-Pariṇāma
Sanskrit: "Concentrated-transformation of the mind". The ability, developed as a result of meditation and the Spiritual Path, to engage one's mind in action whenever it is necessary and, at the same time, *simultaneously*, always experience the unbroken state of Silence and Stillness.

Ekhfā
Arabic: "The Most Hidden". That part of the Heart (Qalb) which is located in the middle of the chest.

Ekklesia
Greek: "Being called out from among the people." The called-out ones, the elected ones, the selected ones, the chosen ones. From Ek (from) and Klesia (being called). Ekklesia is commonly translated as a spiritual congregation of Christians, but it has a much deeper meaning. This being "called out" or "chosen" is not to be understood in an ordinary religious sense, but in a deeply spiritual sense, as a deep, inward orientation towards God. You are called *out of the world,* into the Soul Kingdom. The "chosen ones" are not just the Jews or the Christians, but those of any faith who have responded to the Inner Call and stepped upon the Path of Liberation and Enlightenment. The Gnostics understood Ekklesia as the Spiritual Hierarchy or the invisible Hierarchies of Spiritual Beings, composed of Angelic and Human Hierarchies. It is identical in meaning to the Sanskrit Satsaṅga (from Sat, "truth", and Saṅga "a gathering, an assembly"). The later Christians degenerated the word to mean the physical, human organization called the "church"—hence the English word *ecclesiastic,* "pertaining to the church". But Salvation is not simply belief in a particular faith. It is a matter of High Attainment. [See Saṅgha]

Ekstasis
Greek: "Going out of oneself". From this came the English word *ecstasy*. Ekstasis is not mediumistic trance. It is not psychic; it is a *spiritual* phenomenon. It is not madness, nor is it a psychological or mental disease. The body of the ecstatic Saint may become temporarily paralysed or immobile, and the normal, objective, wakeful consciousness (the rational faculty) may also be suspended for a while. To the Hesychasts of Eastern Christianity and the Mystics of the Roman Church, Ekstasis (Ecstasy) was a by-product of intense interior meditation or prayer. Ecstasy, according to the Christian Saints, is a sign of being near to God. Saint Diadochos defines Ecstasy as "losing awareness of oneself by a total going out towards the Divine". In other words, you, the personality, is forgotten, and you, the Soul, is remembered. Ecstasy is a condition that is non-verbal, non-intellectual, without thought. It is what the Eastern Yogīs call Samādhi.

El

Hebrew: The Lord God. The Radiant One. God as Radiant Energy, Fire, the Light of all things and within all things. This word is often used in the Old Testament. Al in Palestinian, Alāhā and Allahā in Aramaic, Allāh in Arabic.

Elect

The *Elect* are all those members of the Human Kingdom who have passed beyond the Mental Plane, beyond the Reincarnating Ego, into Buddhi (the Christ Principle, the Being of Light, the Principle of Compassion and Wisdom), and beyond to Ātman (the Spirit, the Cosmic Tongues of Fire), and who have again become Monads (Pillars of Light). This is possible for *all* Humanity, of all races and all religions. The Elect are not simply the Jews or the Christians, the "chosen people". [See Ekklesia]

Elements

The Five Cosmic Elements are the essential substances of all the forms and objects of Creation, both visible and invisible. They are both the physical substances and the subtle, invisible substances forming the Inner Worlds. Each of the Elements also corresponds to the matter or substance of a plane. Using Sanskrit terminology, the Five Elements are as follows:

- Pṛthivī: Earth (Physical Plane).
- Āp, Āpas: Water (Astral Plane).
- Tejas, Taijasa, Agni: Fire (Mental Plane).
- Vāyu: Air (Buddhic Plane).
- Ākāśa: Ether, Aether. (Nirvāṇa, Space).

The ancient Sages understood the Elements as grades of matter and substance extending from the physical universe to the subtlest realms of Divinity. There are in fact *seven* Elements (corresponding to the seven great planes and the seven substates on a plane), but the two highest can be perceived only by the Siddhas. For the Sages, the Elements are *qualities*, *forces* or *expressions* of Nature (Prākṛtī), and Nature is a Living Being. Each Element has a threefold manifestation—three functions, attributes or characteristics:

- Tattva: "That-ness". Its essential or subtle aspect. The Law of it, the inner drive of it, that which is producing it.
- Bhūta: "Substance" or "Matter". Its manifest aspect, its tangible or form aspect.
- Tanmātra: "The Measure of That". Its vibration, motion or force aspect.

Thus, each Element is a Law; it is expressed tangibly in a form; and it is a power, force, energy, vibration, motion.

Elemental Kingdom

The Nature-Spirits of Earth, Water, Fire, Air, and the four etheric subplanes. The elementals are on the *involutionary* arc. They are below the Angelic Kingdom and below the Human Kingdom. The elementals are to the angels what the animals are to us: the Animal Kingdom is one step below the Human Kingdom in evolutionary attainment, and the Elemental Kingdom is one step below the Angelic Kingdom. The normal habitat of the elementals is the Astral World. Some elementals have an etheric body, but they never have a gross physical body. Sometimes they can be seen in their etheric bodies, and folklore has called them by many names according to their species: dryads, naiads, oreads, kelpies, leprechauns, fairies, nature-spirits, brownies, mannikins, fauns, satyrs, centaurs, and so on.

El-Hayyīm (Al-Hayyīm)

Hebrew: "God the Living". The Living God.

Eli, Eloi

Hebrew: "My God".

Elijah

Hebrew: "My God". A compound God-Name, from Eli and Jah, which is another root word for "God".

Elixir of Life

A pure and divine Substance of the Higher Worlds. What the early Christian Mystics called Ambrosia (Greek: the Food of the Gods), and what Jesus called the *Waters of Life* and the *Bread from Heaven*. In Sanskrit, Sañjivani.

Eloāh

Hebrew: "The God". The Supreme Oneness. God as Light. Similar to the Arabic Allāh and the Aramaic Alāhā.

Elohīm
Hebrew: "The Self-Born Gods" (male/female plural). The Kosmokratores (Greek). The Cosmic Creator-Gods, the Spirits who manifest suns, planets and Cosmic Systems of Evolution. The Solar Logoi. Our own Solar Logos, the Sun, is known in Sanskrit as Brahmā, Īśvara or Savitā. The Creator-Gods are not the Angelic Hierarchies, but are far above them. The angels came into being *after* the Creator-Gods had already fashioned the Universe. In *Genesis*, first appear the Elohīm, the male-female Creator-Gods, but the patriarchs did not like this fact because they wanted the work of all Creation to be done by only one Person. In later chapters it becomes Elohīm-Jehovah; then, by the time of Moses, it became Jehovah. The church fathers, and before them the Jewish patriarchs, wanted to *deny* the existence of these great Beings—the Elohīm, the Kosmokratores, the Creators of the Cosmos. But they need not have done so, for there is only one Absolute Reality, one Godhead under which all Beings work—great or small, cosmic or atomic.

El Shaddai
Hebrew: "God Almighty". The Great God. Similar to the Sanskrit term Mahāviṣṇu.

Energia
Greek: The many forces, energies, powers, frequencies and attributes differentiated from the One Energy, Dynamis. Hence the English word *energy*. The same as the Sanskrit Prāṇa and the Chinese Chi.

Enlightenment
"Letting in the Light". Spiritual Illumination. The same as the Latin word Illumination.

Ennoia
Greek: A thought, an idea, a concept, whether in the human mind or in the Divine Mind. Also, the Virgin-Father, the Father before Fatherhood.

Enoch
Hebrew: The esoteric meaning is "Guru, Master, Instructor". Enoch was a giant of Old Testament days in Israel, a most highly attained Esoteric Revealer who attained Nirvāṇa, but His works were suppressed by the Jewish and Christian authorities whose vision of Reality was much less.

Epignosis
Greek: "Spiritual Knowledge". Illumination. According to the Saints, only *Illumination* can bring true peace in the world, as "the sweetness of God destroys the bitterness of quarrel". Thus, Humanity has to become God-centred, Illumined by God's Light, before true peace on Earth becomes possible. Each man and woman must attain this great jewel of Illumination—the *Pearl of Great Price*.

Epinoia
Greek: Thinking upon, magical thinking, creative thinking, directed thinking, purposeful thinking.

Episteme
Greek: Ordinary mental knowledge. Hence the English word *epistemology,* which is the science of mental knowledge.

Episunagoge
Greek: "A gathering together into Oneness". From Sunagoein, "to bring people together". The Greek word Sinagoge means "a meeting" or "a group of people together", while an Episunagoge is a gathering together of "the chosen ones, the elect". Hence the English word *synagogue*. A synagogue is a place where the Jews come together for prayer and worship. It is an assembly or congregation of devoted people. Similar to the Sanskrit Satsaṅga. [See Ekklesia]

Epoptai
Greek: The Higher Seers, the Sages. In the terminology of the Greek Mystery Schools, the Epoptai were those perfected men and women who were initiated into the Greater Mysteries, Gnosis, Nirvāṇa, the Kingdom of God. [See Mystai]

Eretz (A R Tz)
Hebrew: Earth. Arā in Aramaic, Gē or Gaia in Greek, Terra in Latin. [See *Earth*]

Eros
Greek: Sexual attraction and desire. On a deeper level: intense desire, aspiration or longing for Union with God or Ecstasy. To the pre-Christian Greeks, Eros meant Love, and Eros was the god of Love (the Latin name of which was *Cupid)*. From Eros came the English word *erotic,* which nowadays refers to sexual passion. To the classical Greeks, however, and to the early Christian Saints, Eros meant spiritual-passionate Love, or Unitive Love, or Love through inner desire. Saint Evagrios the Solitary interprets Eros as intense Love of God: "Eros transports the mind to the spiritual realms".

Erotikos
Greek: Sexual stimulation or desire. Sexual pleasure. Sexual excitement.

Eshū
Aramaic: Jesus. Yeshua in Hebrew.

Etheric Body
The etheric body exists on the etheric subplanes and is made up of the four states of etheric-physical matter. It is the vehicle of Prāṇa, vitality, the Life-breath. It is also known as the *etheric-physical body*, the *subtle-physical body*, the *vital body* or the *etheric double*. In Sanskrit it is called Liṅga-Śarīra (symbolic body) because it is the prototype and Life-force of your dense physical body. Technically the etheric body is a natural (perishable) Light Body, since it is composed of Light-rays or Light-particles (Prāṇas). At this stage of Human Evolution, however, the ordinary human being is not yet able to use it as a proper Light Body. Also called Prāṇamāyākośa (the illusionary vehicle of Prāṇa).

Etheric Web
An energy-structure within the etheric body which protects a physically embodied being from an influx of energies from the Inner Worlds. A human being has an etheric web, as does a planet and a solar system. At an advanced stage of human evolution the etheric web is burned away by the Kuṇḍalinī Fire, thus leading to Continuity of Consciousness and Cosmic Consciousness. If the etheric web is damaged or artificially breached before the indwelling Consciousness is sufficiently evolved (as by drugs or forced Kuṇḍalinī-Yoga practices), the resulting influx of energies will lead to gross delusion or insanity. During Atlantean times the human etheric web was more tenuous than it is today, leading to general astral awareness and psychic phenomena (along with the associated glamour and delusion).

Eva
Sanskrit: Only, alone, verily. Truthfully or truly I say unto you. I declare this.

Evangelion
Greek: Good news, a good story, a good message. The gospels. Hence the English words *evangelical* and *evangelism*.

Evil
Evil means "physical imperfections and mind-created hell worlds". Evil is the wrong use of the One Force, Power, Energy or Substance (Śakti) by living entities, whether through Ignorance or lack of Intelligence. Evil is caused by separative minds that do not feel and do not know the Unity of all Life. These evil minds can be human, subhuman (elemental) or angelic.

Evocation
Latin: The results of Invocation. A feeling of being pulled from above, of being dragged up by one's Higher Self, the Christ Light, God, or the Guru.

Evolution
Latin: Unfolding, progression, metamorphosis, formation, growth, development, mutation, an unrolling, an opening up, a process of gradual, progressive change. There is a natural evolution (*horizontal* evolution) and there is a supernatural, spiritual evolution (*vertical* evolution). The scientific theory of natural evolution is correct as an idea, but not in its particular details—the details are wrong. And science hasn't even thought about the Supernatural Evolution. [See *Creation*]

Eye of Śiva
The All-Seeing Eye, the Divine Eye (Śiva-Netra) which sees all things in the Eternal Now. The awakened Third-Eye Centre (Ājñā Cakra). [See Śivanetra]

F

Fall
The idea of "the Fall" can be understood on two levels:

- The descent of the Human Monads (Virgin Spirits) from the formless Causal Worlds into the material conditions of the Three Worlds, henceforth losing Awareness of the Immortal Luminous Oneness while cycling endlessly through the material realms (Saṁsāra). The Old Testament story of Adam and Eve being tempted by the serpent is symbolic of this event (the serpent being the Kuṇḍalinī-Śakti, the Evolutionary Force).
- The separation of a vast host of originally-luminous angels from the Primary State of Unity, millions of years ago, thus corrupting certain parts of the Omni-Revelation of the All-Mind. We cannot know whether the "fall" of these angels was by Cosmic Design or an act of free will. When the human family descended onto this planet it became caught up in the Cosmic Evil and has perpetuated it ever since.

Fanā
Arabic: "Passing-away, extinction". Annihilation of the self. The same as the Sanskrit word Nirvāṇa.

Fanā'fi-llāh
Arabic: Annihilation in God, or complete Union with God. In this Fanā (annihilation) the mind and the sense of the personal self, the personal ego, are completely lost, replaced by the Divine Mind and the Divine Ego, or the God-Self. This was the Goal of the Sūfī Mystics during the Piscean Age. The same as the Sanskrit Brahmanirvāṇam (Dissolution in God).

Faqīr
Arabic: A holy man, a dervish, a sādhu, a renunciate (without possessions). A Muslim Saint.

Father ⊙
In Christianity, a symbol for the First Aspect of the Holy Trinity, the Eternal Cosmic Being, the First Logos. On a human level, the term "Father" or "Father in Heaven" symbolizes the Monad, the Divine Spirit in Man (Paramātman, the Transcendental Self, dwelling on the Paranirvāṇic Plane). In the New Testament the Eternal Cosmic Being is called "Father" due to the sexual bias of the old Jewish religious concepts. But God is not a father, not male or masculine. The symbol was used in a Jewish society which was ruled by male politicians and male priests, but at best it is only a symbol, and a bad one at that. [See Abba]

Fiat
Latin: "The Mighty Power of Creation". The Logos, the Word, God's Creative Speech or Power, the Divine Mantram. Also called Verbum.

Fifth Kingdom
The Spiritual Kingdom, consisting of perfected human beings and angels (Devas). The Spiritual Hierarchy of our planet.

Fifth State
The Fifth State of Consciousness (Turīyātīta-Avasthā in Sanskrit) is Cosmic Consciousness, which is the simultaneous functioning of the lower four states of Consciousness. In the state of Awareness of Turīyātīta you experience the Transcendent Condition (the Fourth State) during waking, sleeping and dreaming, at all times and in all conditions. [See *Cosmic Consciousness*]

Fire
[See *Cosmic Fire*]

First Logos ⊙
The First Aspect of the Deity, the Eternal, Infinite Being. The Nameless Transcendental Godhead, above, beyond and before Creation and after Creation. That which always Is. The "Father". In Sanskrit, Śiva, "He who sleeps in the atoms".

Fohat
Tibetan: The Cosmic Fire. The Divine Thought and Energy as it manifests in Creation. Fire is the basic Vital-Force of Creation. It is not merely a combustion process, but an intelligent activity of the Cosmic Mind which pervades all Space. Fohat is Cosmic-Electric-Fire, the Electric Male Force of the Spirit (the same as the Greek Dynamis). In a human being it manifests as the Liquid-Fire, or Kuṇḍalinī-Śakti, the Magnetic Female Force of the Spirit (Magnēs in Greek). Both are Third-Logos Fire, the Third Aspect of the Triune Godhead. The Spirit is both Male and Female, yet the Spirit is One. [See *Cosmic Fire*]

Formative World
According to the Kabbalistic description, the Astral World, which is a world of *forces, energies* and *powers* (all that *motivates* the physical universe). The Physical World is merely the *result,* the end product. [See *Four Worlds*]

Four States
The four lower states of consciousness:
1. Jāgrata-Avasthā: the wakeful state, the self-conscious mind.
2. Svapnā-Avasthā: the dreaming state, the subconscious mind.
3. Suṣūpti-Avasthā: the dreamless-sleep state (when awakened, Causal Consciousness).
4. Turīya-Avasthā: the "fourth state", the Self-Realized State.

Four Worlds
The Jewish Kabbalists described the lower three planes in terms of four worlds: the *Archetypal* (Causal) World; the *Creative* (lower Mental) World; the *Formative* (Astral) World; and the *Physical* World (the result).

Fourth Death
The *Fourth Death* occurs when you leave behind your mental body on the lower Mental Plane and transfer your consciousness to the causal body (the microcosm), and you live as the Living Soul, Jīva, in the Kingdom of Souls (the formless part of Deva-Sthāna).

Fourth Kingdom
The Human Kingdom. Ordinary unregenerated Humanity.

Fourth State
The Fourth State is Pure Consciousness, Transcendental Consciousness, Superconsciousness. It is the Mystical Consciousness of Buddhi. It is Bodiless Consciousness, formless, shapeless, all-inclusive, limitless, beyond the sensations of Time and Space, directionless. It is an unbroken Continuum, indivisible, having no parts or particulars, not consisting of objects. Nothing is or can be outside of It. It is the basis of All, the Centre, the Source, the Root, the Heart of the All. In Sanskrit, Turīya-Avasthā.

G

Gabriel
Hebrew: "The Illuminative Power of God". One of the Hebrew Angelic Names.

Gandharva
Sanskrit: Music-Angel. This Sanskrit word is most esoteric. It refers to the Sound-Angels, the Celestial Angelic Musicians, the non-human (angelic) Intelligences which produce the sounds and colours in the Inner Worlds. The Gandharvas live by creating the most exquisite music, sound, tone, colour and harmony in the Astral World. They like events which include music, singing or dancing and often add their musical skills on the Astral to produce glorious effects.

Garbha
Sanskrit: A womb, source, origin, embryo, primal condition. [See Hiraṇyagarbha]

Garimā, Gariman
Sanskrit: The power to become extremely heavy, fixed, immovable. One of the nine "general" powers (Siddhis) which can manifest in advanced Humanity.

Gaurī
Sanskrit: She who is Fair. She who is Beautiful. The Brilliant One. She who is the caring and nurturing Mother. Gaurī is Lalitā as the Transcendental and Immanent Mother. As the Transcendental Mother She nourishes us with Divine Light, Brightness, Brilliance. She is Jyotirasā (Jyoti-Rasā, the Essence of Light). She is Jyotir-Maya (consisting of Light).

Gāyatrī
Sanskrit: "She who is in the form of a song" (in the form of Mantric Vibration). The Hymn (sound) to the Spiritual Sun behind the Sun. The Daughter of the Spiritual Sun. Lalitā is the Goddess within the Sun, and the Gāyatrī-Mantra is an expression of Her. She is the Face within the Sun. She abides within the Gāyatrī-Mantra as the innermost Truth or Essence. (Note that both the Gāyatrī-Mantra and the Guhya-Gāyatrī-Mantra are Feminine. The Guhya-Gāyatrī is Pure Feminine only, while the Gāyatrī is the Feminine coming through the Masculine Aspect of the Sun.)

Gāyatrī-Mantra
Sanskrit: The most sacred Mantram of India. Also known as the Savitā-Mantra, the Sūrya-Mantra, the Savitṛ-Mantra or Śiva-Sūrya. This Mantra invokes the Male Aspect of the Solar Logos (the Solar Logos is Male-Female-Neuter, all at once). The word Gāyatrī means "a song, a verse of twenty-four syllables, a certain meter or rhythm". The Gāyatrī-Mantra is a Song of God, to God and by God, the Hymn of Glory, Vaidika-Gāyatrī (the Vedic Hymn). This Mantra will invoke the Light. God is Light! This is the Mantra for Enlightenment, Illumination, Transfiguration in Light, moving with the forces of evolution, progress, development. The Gāyatrī is a *wedding ceremony.* It is a Holy Communion, the Union of your Soul with the Divine, the Way to become Divine, God-like. The Gāyatrī is a prayer, not a relaxation technique; it should never be repeated after a Haṭha Yoga class as a relaxation exercise. Do not use the Gāyatrī unless you desire God sincerely. The correct intonation and various uses of the Gāyatrī-Mantram you learn from the Guru directly.

Gāyatrī-Sādhanā
Sanskrit: The Sun-Spiritual-Practice. Also called Sūryamaṇḍala (the Circle of the Sun). The worship of the Sun is the most direct worship of God. It is not the worship of an inanimate object in the sky. The physical Sun is an outer reflection *into* the Physical Plane of the Real-Sun, the Solar Logos (Sūrya, Savitā).

Gē, Gaia
Greek: Earth. Arā in Aramaic, A R Tz (ERETz) in Hebrew, Terra in Latin. [See *Earth*]

Geburah
Hebrew: "Strength, Severity". On the Kabbalistic Tree of Life, Geburah is the male aspect of the Higher Mind. The female aspect is Chesed (Mercy, Love).

Gehinnom
Hebrew: The Valley of Hinnom, the Valley of the Shadow of Death. The Astral World. Gehenna in Greek.

Genii
Latin: Angels. Devas.

Ghost
An earthbound spirit, living on the etheric-physical subplanes after death. [See *Earthbound Spirits*]

Glossolalia
Greek: "The gift of speaking in tongues". From Glossa (tongue, language) and Lalia (gift).

Gnosis
Greek: Direct Divine Knowledge. Inner Revelation through the Heart. From Gnōstiko, "to know directly". The term was used by the Greek Mystery Schools and the Christian Gnostics for the direct experiential Knowledge of Truth or Reality (not only by faith or as a belief-system). Gnosis means all of the following:

- A direct perception of the Mysteries. Direct knowledge of the supersensible worlds. Esoteric Knowledge resulting from a direct, inner vision of Reality. Transcendental Knowledge gained through meditation and inner Revelation.

- Spiritual Knowledge, Spiritual Perception, Inspiration, Illumination, Enlightenment.
- Supernatural Wisdom, the Wisdom of the Soul, Soul-Communion, Self-Realization.
- The Lighted Way or the Way of Light. The Knowledge that comes when the Holy Path is seen within.
- Inner Revelation by the Logos, or the Christos, or the Holy Spirit (Pneuma)—an Omniscient Energy-Radiation of the Godhead, contacted in deep meditation by the Christian Saint.
- The direct, experiential knowledge of the Kingdom of God *within*. A direct Revelation of the Godhead within the Soul. The direct Knowledge of God.

Gnosis is what the Buddhists call *Insight*. It is non-rational Knowledge, from *above* the ordinary mind. It is a non-verbal, non-intellectual, direct perception of the Higher Realities. It means the same as the Hindu Yoga terms Ātmā-Vidyā (Self-Realization) and Brahmā-Vidyā (God-Realization).

Gnosis Theou

Greek: The direct experiential Knowledge of God. Enlightenment by the Divine Light of Christ. The annihilation of the personal self (the personality) and the Deification of the Soul. The supersensual experience of the Presence of God. Spiritual Ecstasy. Union with God. Experiencing degrees of Divine Consciousness through the inner senses.

Gnōstikos

Greek: "One who knows" or "One who is intuitively perceptive". A Knower, a Seer, an Enlightened One. One who knows Spiritual Truth by direct, inner experience. A Gnostic. The Gnostics were early Christian Saints who had a direct vision of the World of Light. The Gnostics upheld the original, true Christianity, the Religion of Light, until they were persecuted and destroyed by the fundamentalists within the early church. They were severely persecuted as "heretics" because they did not always agree with the respected church authorities who had no direct experience of spiritual matters but intellectually *speculated* about the nature of Reality.

Gnosti Seauton

Greek. "Know Thyself". To the Greeks and Romans this meant the process of *inner learning* about yourself—how you are constituted, how you are connected to the Whole, and how you are a Child of the Divine. The true Self is the Presence of God within you. This Union with the Infinite is the goal of all true Spiritual Paths.

God-Consciousness

The term *God-Consciousness* (Brahmā-Vidyā) can refer to the following conditions:

- The State of Union with the Divine Being, the Monad, the "Father in Heaven" (Paramātman). Also called *Divine-Consciousness*.
- The integration and fusing of the Nirvāṇic Consciousness (Ātmā-Vidyā) into the states below.

God-Immanent

God-Inherent. This means that God is *inherent* in all things. God is *remaining within* and *operating* all things. God-Immanent is the "personal" Godhead: Brahmā, Viṣṇu, Śiva, Rāma, Kṛṣṇa, and so on. This is the Guiding Force or Impelling Drive behind all evolutionary unfoldment, large or small, including Man. God is present throughout the Universe; there is not an inch of Space where God is not. Just think of the implications of this, of how it can transform you!

God-Realization

The direct Knowledge of God. Stages of Union with God. God-Consciousness or Universal Consciousness. In Sanskrit, Brahma-Vidyā and Brahma-Jñāna.

God-Transcendent

Transcendent means "surpassing in all degrees of excellence". This means that God is free of all possible limitations. God is superior to and surpasses all things. God comes *before* all things. The Transcendental Godhead, Parabrahman, is above and beyond Creation or Manifestation. It is before, during and after Creation, Eternal, Changeless. The events of Creation have no impact upon It.

Godō

Japanese: The Way of Enlightenment. Also, Daigo.

Gopī
Sanskrit: Cowgirl, herdswoman, milkmaid. A symbol for the Soul.

Gopījana
Sanskrit: The milkmaid folk, cowgirl people, herdswomen folk. The Devotees of God.

Govinda
Sanskrit: The Master of the Heart. The Lord (controller) of the senses, the Kṛṣṇa within the Heart. The keeper of the cows (symbolic of the keeper of Souls). The Lord God within. (In Christianity, the Christ is the Shepherd, or keeper of the Souls, and the Souls are the "sheep".)

Grand Heavenly Man
A Solar Logos. One of the Elohīm or Cosmic-Creators. (A Planetary Logos is known as a *Heavenly Man*.)

Granthi, Grantha
Sanskrit: A knot, a cord, a binding; a book, a script; an entanglement, a conditioning; an obstruction, a barrier, an obstacle, a block; a limitation; identification with unreal things. The Granthis are points where the Self identifies with the ego, the personality and the world, thus causing the sense of *limitation*. These obstacles need to be overcome before the Soul is released and can stand free. On the Path to Higher Consciousness there are two great knots to untie: Hṛdaya-Granthi, the knot in the Heart Cakra; and Śiva-Granthi, the knot in the Head Cakras. When these two great knots are untied in you, the Self shines by its own Light, the Sleeper has awakened and you find yourself in the state of Samādhi, or Transcendental Union with God. In this state, the mind (Manas) is tranquil and the whole of Creation is seen as a play (Līlā). (Granthi is the feminine form, Grantha the masculine.)

Great Day of Be With Us
Ultimately, all of Nature will merge into Nirvāṇa and Paranirvāṇa on *The Great Day of Be With Us*, at the end of Time, when God re-absorbs all things back into Its bosom and the Mind of God returns to Stillness. This expression is used also on an individual level, when an individual Soul achieves final Liberation.

Gṛhastha (Gārhastya)
Sanskrit: A householder. A family person, married with children. The second period of life (Āśrama) in the ancient Vedic days of India.

Guardian Angel
The Spirit or the Spiritual Soul (Buddhi) within you. The Being of Light. In rare cases it can mean a real angel (Deva) who is working with you, in this life, toward a specific goal or purpose. [See *Being of Light*]

Guha
Sanskrit: A cave, a cavern, a concealed place, a secret. Concealed, hidden, occult, esoteric, mysterious.

Guhya, Gudha, Gupta
Sanskrit: Esoteric, secret, occult, hidden.

Guhya (Gudha)-Gāyatrī-Mantra
Sanskrit: The Secret-Gāyatrī-Mantra. The Śoḍaṣī Root Mantra, or the Lalitā Mantra, also known as the Śrī-Vidyā-Vajra-Mantra, the Mahā-Tripurāsundarī. This is the Female line, invoking the Feminine Aspect of the Solar Logos. The Śoḍaṣī Secret Mantra is the Female Sunshine, the Mother-Light of the Universe, of the Solar Logos and of Man. It is the Glorious Radiance of the Goddess.

Guṇa
Sanskrit: "Quality". The Guṇas are properties or types of matter and energy. The three Guṇas are:
- Sattva: that which vibrates to harmony, rhythm, balance, goodness, Truth, Purity, Light. Sattva is the force of *equilibrium*.
- Rajas: that which vibrates with great passion, force, activity, violence or discord. Rajas is the force of *mobility*.
- Tamas: that which vibrates with inertia, ignorance, slowness, stupidity, darkness. Tamas is the force of *passivity, steadiness*.

All actions (Karma), and their after-effects or reactions, are done by the three qualities (Guṇas) of Nature (Prākṛtī).

Gupta-Vidyā (Guhya-Vidyā)

Sanskrit: "Esoteric Knowledge" or "Secret Knowledge". The Science of Spirituality. The legendary powers of the true Magicians of old. This knowledge was widespread in old India, and the Sanskrit language was the guardian of the Esoteric Lore. Within the Sanskrit language we find the knowledge of the ancients: black magic, white magic, science, religion, and so on. The Gupta-Vidyā of old India was but a memory of the Dzyān, or secret knowledge of Atlantis, and the Sanskrit language was a memory of Senzar, the old Atlantean language. Gupta-Vidyā, also known as Guhya-Vidyā, is the secret science of Mantras, or potent formulas to achieve all kinds of purposes, the highest being the Knowledge of God (Brahmā-Vidyā) and Self-Realization (Ātmā-Jñāna).

Guru

Sanskrit: The Illuminator, the Dispeller of Darkness, the Bringer of Light, the Enlightener. The Transcendental Wisdom of God (Brahman), of the Self (Ātman), and of your physical Teacher or Preceptor. Sometimes called Gurudeva (Divine Teacher) or Sat Guru (True Master). He/She who mirrors your mind (the Formless Absolute Self in you and the Formless Absolute Self in your Guru are one and the same). The Master or Spiritual Guide—the Guide of your Soul, not of your personality!

A Guru is an Enlightened Soul with spiritual magnetism, spiritual influence, *who takes disciples.* Not all Self-Realized Souls take pupils; a Guru, however, commits himself or herself to aid in the spiritual unfoldment of his or her pupils. A Guru is a spiritually magnetic personality who not only teaches, but who, by his very existence, changes all those around him. A Guru is connected to Higher Consciousness and has around him a *Radiation Field* of Spiritual Energy. A Guru is a Radiating Field of Power, full of Energy (Śakti) and Sound (Mantra).

Gurus are *not* mediums, nor are their pupils. Gurus teach only their own Inner Wisdom. They communicate and explain their own Inner Realizations and Soul-Knowledge. Their pupils concern themselves with Higher Consciousness, with trying to get *beyond* the lower planes as quickly and efficiently as possible without becoming *entangled* in the Astral World. Thus, they become Liberated after death, attaining Mokṣa or Mukti, the freedom of the Soul from the lower worlds.

Nowadays the word *guru* is commonly used by the ignorant to refer to a mentor or advisor, or any person who gives religious instructions, or an intellectual guide, or any leader or authority in any field. The original Sanskrit word Guru has only a deeply *religious-spiritual* meaning. [See Ācārya]

Gurudeva (Guru-Deva)

Sanskrit: The Divine Teacher, the Sat Guru, the True Master that resides in the Causal Heart Centre. The Soul within, the Inner Guide. At a higher level of Union it is the Monad, the Paramātman. At the highest level it is Īśvara, the Supreme Lord of the Universe.

Guru-Mantra

Sanskrit: An Initiatory Mantra.

Guru-Śakti

Sanskrit: The Energy-Field of the Spiritual Teacher or Master.

H

Ḥabīb

Arabic: "Beloved, sweetheart". A word for God, often used by the Sūfīs. They literally fall in Love with God.

Hades

Greek: The underground, the underworld, the world of shadows. The Shadowland. The lowest regions of the Astral World, created by the lowest human minds and carried in our physical bodies by our most primitive drives and instincts. More generally, the abode of the dead, inhabited by the "departed" Souls. The same as the Hebrew Sheol and the Egyptian Amenti.

Hairesis

Greek: The ability to choose. To have an open mind. From this we have the English word *heresy* (an opinion or doctrine at variance with the orthodox view).

Hairetikos
Greek: "One who has an open mind". A heretic. Throughout its history, the orthodox Christian church has denounced as a "heretic" any person who did not believe in its compulsory "official" doctrine. The "heretics" have been persecuted by the church for two thousand years.

Ḥāj
Arabic: Pilgrimage to the Real. Your Journey upon the Way. Your Quest.

Hāl
Persian: Mystical Rapture, Ecstasy, Superconsciousness, Spiritual Trance, Union. In Sanskrit, Samādhi.

Hālah
Arabic: Glory. The internal shining of the Light and Spiritual Radiance. From this comes the English word *halo*, as seen around Saints.

Hālah
Persian: The complete Rest, Stillness and Equilibrium of the Saint in Trance.

Halleluyāh
Hebrew: Glorify God! (Hallelu-Yāh).

Hall of Ignorance
The first stage on the Path to Discipleship. The Physical Plane.

Hall of Learning
The second stage on the Path to Discipleship. The Astral Plane.

Hall of Wisdom
The third stage on the Path to Discipleship. The Mental Plane. The true Mystery Schools originate in the Hall of Wisdom (the Mental Plane), where they have their seat. [See *Mystery Schools*]

Hāṁ
Sanskrit: The Bīja-Mantra for the Cosmic Element *Aether* or *Space* (the Nirvāṇic Universe).

Hamartia
Greek: "Missing the mark" (as in archery). This is the Greek word the scholars and theologians so morbidly translate as "sin", in the sense of devaluing yourself and destroying your self-esteem. The word *sinner* has acquired, in Christianity, a very unhealthy connotation. But the Greek word actually means "to miss the mark, to miss the point, to go astray, to make a mistake, to falter or fail, to make an error". There is no sense of "eternal hell-fire and damnation" in it, as proclaimed by the evangelicals and fundamentalists of today's Christianity. The correct meaning is that you *try again*. If you failed in some aspect of your nature, you do not thereby become morbid, depressed and negative, but you try again and again. This is how the early Christians looked upon life.

Haṁsa, Hansa, Haṅgsa, Haṁsaḥ
Sanskrit: "I am He (That)" (Ahaṁ-Saḥ). The Swan, a symbol for Pure Spirit. Ha, Haṁ, is the Male Creative Aspect of Consciousness. Sa, Saḥ, is the Female Creative Aspect of Consciousness. Haṁsa is the Sun, the Solar Logos, the Spiritual Sun, who is Male-Female. Haṁsa is the Supreme Spirit, the Divine-Creative-Breath, the Breath of God. Haṁsa is also the individual Immortal Spirit or Soul in Man, the Spiritual Soul, the Spiritual Self within us, a particle of the Sun. Haṁsa is also the Purified Yogī, one who can function in Spiritual Consciousness. [See Sohaṁ]

Haṁsamantra
Sanskrit: The "I Am" principle. The Eternal Word. The Logos. The Creative-Energy.

Hanael
Hebrew: "The Harmony of God". One of the Hebrew Angelic Names.

Ḥaqīqat, Ḥaqqīqat
Arabic: Truth, God. The third stage of the Radiant Way, the Shining Path of the Sūfī (the ninth stage of the Journey of the Heart). This is the state of merging into God, comprising various stages of Perfection, various degrees of Union with God, the Godhead, the Absolute. (This corresponds with the stages within

SAMĀDHI.) These are stages in Spiritual Life where Man turns into Super-Man (above the Man-species), where Man enters streams of Supernatural Evolutions beyond the ken of present Mankind, beyond the wildest dreams of worldly people. ḤAQĪQAT is the experience of the Vision of the Eternal Beauty, the Glorious Light (ALLĀH). It is the enjoyment of the Love of God, the Divine-Bliss-Consciousness, Ecstasy, the Embrace of the Beloved. This is the State of Being of the Messenger, the Prophet. It is the Mystical Flight of Love.

HARA
Japanese: The Solar Plexus Centre, considered to be the centre of gravity for a human being. The early Zen (Dhyāna) Masters of India meditated in the Third-Eye Cakra. Previous to the arrival of Zen, however, the Chinese and Japanese always meditated in the Solar Plexus Cakra; hence the Chinese and Japanese Zen monks and students limit themselves to focusing in the Solar Plexus Centre (HARA), and there they count the breath, or watch the breath, or practise KŌAN or SHIKANTAZA.

HARA
Sanskrit: "The Destroyer, the Seizer". A Name for ŚIVA and for AGNI (the Lord of Fire).

HARAVIRA
Sanskrit: "God's Warrior" (HARA-VIRA). A Warrior of God.

HARE
Sanskrit: The Radiant-Energy of God.

HARI
Sanskrit: God, the Lord and Master of all. Also: yellow, green, tawny colour; a parrot, a peacock, a cuckoo bird, a horse; wind, fire, a ray of light; the Sun, the Moon; the zodiacal sign of Leo.

HARĪ
Sanskrit: The Goddess.

HARIJAN
Sanskrit: In India, a class of person below the Servant Class (ŚŪDRA). The "Untouchables".

HARINĀMA
Sanskrit: "The Name of God". The Eternal Word. The Logos. The Creative-Energy.

HA-SAUḤ
Sanskrit: Male-Female.

HA-SHEM (H-SHM)
Hebrew: The Righteous, the Shining. The Name, the Name of Names. To the ancient Hebrews, and all the initiated inhabitants of the Ancient World, God *was* the Name. The Hebrew Psalms are full of the praising of the Name of God—the real Living-Power of God as it manifests in Sound and Light vibrations throughout the whole Cosmos. This is the Creative Word (Sound), the Creator-God, the Name.

HASIDĪM
Hebrew-Aramaic: The Fervent or Holy Ones. From the Divine Attribute of CHESED on the Tree of Life, which means "Love, compassion, mercy, grace, goodwill, tenderness, fervour". A HASID is an extremely pious, religious or fervent person. Also called "the Silent Ones". The Jewish Mystics. [See TZADDIKĪM]

HAṬHA YOGA
Sanskrit: The best-known branch of Yoga in the West, HAṬHA Yoga consists of ĀSANAS (postures), PRĀṆĀYĀMAS (breath-controls), MUDRĀS (seals), BANDHAS (restraints) and ŚAT-KRIYĀS (purificatory exercises). It is sometimes called the "physical" Yoga, or the Yoga of the body, because it emphasizes the subjugation of the physical vehicle and the balancing of the "Sun" and "Moon" currents in the etheric body. The ancient, esoteric meaning of the word HAṬHA is as follows: HA is the Seer, the Spiritual Self, the Sun, the PURUṢA; and ṬHA is the Consciousness aspect, the Moon, CITTA. A further meaning of the word HAṬHA is "hard, difficult, vigorous, requiring strong will-power, self-discipline and force". Thus, Haṭha Yoga originally

was a method of discovering your Spiritual Self, Ātman, through consciousness-raising exercises or practices. It was an ancient, strenuous form of Yoga to unfold psychic and spiritual powers. Nowadays, Haṭha Yoga is thought to be nothing but keep-fit exercises. By the ancient definition, however, Haṭha Yoga has nothing at all to do with "keeping fit". Haṭha Yoga focuses on the *subjugation* of the physical body. [See Yoga and Yoga-Mārga]

Heart

The Heart is *not* the heart in your physical body. It is a *psychic-spiritual* Heart located near the physical heart, in the subtler dimensions. There are three regions of the Heart:

- The *physical heart*, located in the physical body in this three-dimensional world.
- The *psychic Heart*, connected to your psychic being on the fourth-dimensional level of Space (the astral body).
- The *Spiritual Heart*, the centre of your true Self or Spirit, on the sixth-dimensional level of Space (Buddhi) and above.

The Heart is called Hṛdayaṁ in Sanskrit, Qalb in Arabic, Kardia in Greek. The Mystics of Judaism, Christianity, Islam and Hinduism concentrate in the Heart to discover the Path that leads to "the Kingdom of God within"—the Higher Consciousness.

Heart Centre

The Energy Centre located near the physical heart, on the psychic and spiritual dimensions. The Heart Centre is the most interesting Energy Centre, as it unites Heaven and Earth, the Soul and the personality, God and Man. It puts you in touch with the Buddhic World, wherein are united the above and the below, the spiritual and the material, form and formlessness, the manifest and the unmanifest, the inner and the outer. The Buddhic Plane is the Centre of the Kingdom of God. [See Anāhata Cakra]

Heaven

In the language of the Old and New Testaments there is a shortage of words to describe Spiritual Realities. For instance, the word *Heaven* (or *Heavens)* is used to signify the sky, the starry space above, the after-death worlds, the Kingdom of God, and so on. *Heaven* is called Shemayā in Aramaic, Shamayīm in Hebrew, Ouranos in Greek, Caelum in Latin. In each of these Western languages which relate to original Christianity, *Heaven* means the multi-dimensionality of Space, as a Unity or Oneness, as a Continuum between the within (the above) and the without (the below). Without understanding this sense of Continuum, inwards or up the planes, or from the inner dimensions of the Cosmos downwards into the Physical Plane (the physical universe and the physical body), most of the mysteries hinted at in the Old and New Testaments cannot be comprehended by the modern linear-thinking person. You must understand that the Bible was written in simple language. It is not a philosophical, metaphysical or scientific language. They simply had no words like *Nirvāṇa* or *Cosmic Consciousness.* [See Ākāśa]

Heaven Worlds

The *lower heavens* are the higher, subtler regions of the Astral World. These regions of the Astral World are more rarefied, artistic, intellectual, scientific, creative and religious than the regions below. People in this realm mistakenly call it "Heaven". The true *Heaven Worlds,* however, are the seven subplanes of the Mental Plane, known in the East as Deva-Sthāna, "the abode of the gods" (Devāchan in Tibetan), and in the Christian religion as the *Seven Heavens.*

Heavenly Man

A Planetary Logos. A Cosmic Entity which incarnates into the physical body of a planet. [See *Grand Heavenly Man*]

Heimarmene

Greek: "The compulsion of the stars". Astrology, astrological influences, cosmic rays, the influences of the Zodiac, the impact of the Cosmos on the planet Earth and on the lives of Man. [See Astrologos]

Hela
Arabic: Breathing meditation.

Hell
The English word *hell* comes from the much older Teutonic word Hel or Helan, meaning "underground, a subterranean place, a dark, hidden place, the abode of the dead". This corresponds to the old Jewish idea of Sheol, the Egyptian word Amenti, and the classical Greek word Hades, all of which mean "the place of the dead, underground, the underworld". According to the early Egyptians, Babylonians, Semites, Greeks, Romans and Scandinavians, Hell was not a place of punishment, but the "underworld" where people went after they died. In modern terminology, it is the lower regions of the Astral World.

Hell Worlds
The seventh subplane of the Astral Plane of this Earth-planet. This realm lies in the fourth dimension, partly on the surface of the physical Earth and partly below it, in the solid crust. Hence the traditional concept of Hell being "down" and Heaven being "up". The experience of "Hell", as described by thousands of people and by all world religions, is real. The darkness, the loneliness, the feelings of despair or desolation, as well as the "hellfire" and the "pit", are *real* to those who experience it. Like all seven subplanes of the Astral World, the qualities of the seventh subplane are Man-made. It is a world made by the evil propensities of human beings. The hells are the mental and emotional creations of the sufferer, not a punishment by a vindictive, cruel Deity. "Hell" is quite literally a product of the sufferer's mind, as is the "Heaven" of a more saintly person, because *mind* (whether human or angelic) creates the outer environment in which an entity lives. Hell is not eternal in our time-sense, but it seems eternal to the person experiencing it. In our time-sense a person may spend a few months in the Hell Worlds, or years, or even centuries. But each moment of Hell seems like an eternity to the unfortunate sufferer. The very lowest region of the Hell Worlds is called Avītci in Sanskrit, the *Eighth Sphere* in modern terminology, and the *Outer Darkness* or *Nether Darkness* in the New Testament.

He Of Whom Nought Can Be Said
An ancient term for the Great Architect and Creator of the Universe, whose Name no one can utter.

Heremites
Greek: A recluse. One who has retired from the world and lives in solitude in the desert. From Heremos, "a desert, a desolate and lonely place, a solitary abode". Hence the English words *hermit* and *hermitage*.

Heresy
From the Greek Hairesis: "Choosing another way or opinion".

Heretic
From the Greek Hairetikos. Who were the "heretics"? They were those who had an open mind and did not swallow the ignorant, false doctrines of the church. Throughout its history, the orthodox Christian church has denounced as a "heretic" any person who did not believe in its compulsory "official" doctrine. The "heretics" have been persecuted by the church for two thousand years.

Hērmaphrōdīte
Greek: Both male and female. Hermes is the male prototype, Aphrodite is the female prototype. This is a mystery of ancient human evolution before the separation into male and female sexes took place.

Hermes
Greek: A Wise Teacher, a Master, an Adept. *Hermes Trismegistus* (the thrice-greatest Hermes) was a name ascribed by the Greeks to Thoth (Tehuti), the great Avatāra of Ancient Egypt.

Heros
Greek: A hero. A god or a demi-god. A being distinguished by exceptional virtues or powers, superior or supernatural qualities, great nobility, divine dignity, full of self-sacrifice and great deeds for others.

Hesychast
Greek: "One who practises the silence and stillness of the Heart". A Silent One, a Contemplative, a Mystic. From Hesychia (silence, stillness). A person leading a quiet, contemplative life in the deserts of Egypt, Syria, North Africa or Palestine from the fourth century onwards. A monk or a nun (rare) of the early Christian church. A dweller in the desert, a renunciate, a hermit. One who leads a solitary, isolated life, cut off from Humanity and even from other Hesychasts. A person who has attained the *wordless state of prayer* (who has a still mind and communes with God in silence). The Hesychasts were early Christian Mystics who meditated in the Heart Centre in silence and solitude. The Eastern Christian Hesychast tradition can be clearly traced back as far as the fourth century AD. Before that time it is recognizable as the "orthodox" tradition.

Hesychia, Hesychasm
Greek: Union with God in silence. Solitude, inner tranquillity, stillness. Developing mental stillness and quiet in order to attain Union with God. Living a life of inner calm, quiet, composure, stillness and contemplation. Suspending mental activities. The absence of discursive thinking, being without thoughts. Not only non-talking, but mental equilibrium, equipoise, tranquillity. The complete silence of body, mind and emotions. The state of *Quiet.*

Hexalpha, Hexad ✡
Greek: The union of Spirit and Matter, of Life and Form, of the lower, ▽, and the higher, △, in the Heart of things, whether the human Heart Centre or the Cosmic Heart.

Hidoni
Greek: Pleasure. Delight. The lowest form of pleasure is, of course, sensual. The next is intellectual, as in true knowledge or understanding. But the highest form of delight is in God or Divine Consciousness.

Hierarchia (Hierarkhia)
Greek: Literally, "the rule or power of the High Priest". Very few people nowadays know this original meaning. Hierarchia itself comes from the Greek word Hierarcha, meaning "a High Priest or Guru of a sacred temple, the chief priest of a Mystery School, a chief ruler or authority in religious or spiritual matters, the officer in charge of sacred rites or rituals in a temple". Hence the English word *hierarchy*. In the early sense of the word, *hierarchy* referred to Spiritual Hierarchies—a system of spiritual groups or living entities in the Cosmos, known as the Angelic Hierarchies or Celestial Hierarchies, ranked one above the other in graded orders, increasingly more refined or spiritual. Later on, the Christian church adopted this idea and organized the church, on the material plane, as an "ecclesiastical hierarchy" of pope, cardinals, bishops, priests and lay people. [See *Creative Hierarchies*]

Hierophantēs
Greek: "Revealer of the Sacred Mysteries". From Hieros (sacred, divine, holy, religious, mysterious) and Phainein (to show, to reveal, to expound). The Guru, the Spiritual Master (as depicted in Tarot Key 5). From this we have the English word *hierophant,* "a religious teacher, an expounder of religious rites". Today the word *hierophant* has become degenerated to mean an ordinary religious teacher, such as a pope, a bishop, a priest or a clergyman, but in the Greek Mystery School it had the deeper meaning of the Guru or Master who speaks not just from faith or belief, but from *direct inner experience* of the Truth (Gnosis). At the head of every Mystery School was a Hierophantēs who taught the Mysteries from personal experience. [See *Mystery Schools*]

Hierosgamos
Greek: Mystical Marriage. Mysticism, the Union of the Soul with God. The Union of matter and substance with Spirit and Life.

Higher Mind
The Abstract Mind or Causal Mind, which functions by formless thought-waves. Higher Manas. [See Kāraṇa-Manas and *Abstract Mind*]

Hiraṇya
Sanskrit: Golden, golden Light, radiant, most precious.

Hiraṇyagarbha
Sanskrit: "The Luminous Egg, the Golden Womb". From Hiraṇya (golden, shining, radiant) and Garbha (ovoid, egg-shaped, womb, source, enclosure). The term Hiraṇyagarbha can refer to the following:
- The Auric Being. The entire auric field, encompassing all of the bodies, including the causal body.
- A mysterious golden body which has the shape of a womb or an egg. This is never visible to the physical eyes; it appears only in the Causal World and encloses the Soul of the Adept who has undergone certain alchemical transmutations.
- The Cosmic Sun, the Creator, as the very Self of the Universe and of each one of us.

Hod
Hebrew: "Splendour". On the Kabbalistic Tree of Life, Hod is an aspect of the lower Mental Plane, along with Netzach, "Victory".

Holy Spirit (Holy Ghost)
The Holy Breath, Holy Life-Force, Holy Intelligence, Holy Creative Power. The Radiant Creative Energy, the Fire of Creation. The Cosmic Fiery Energy of the Third Logos, the Third Person of the Trinity. The Holy Spirit is the Immanent Deity (Brahmā, in Sanskrit), that which is concealed in matter, life-forms, bodies. It is God-in-Manifestation, the Embodied God. It is the Organizing and Structurizing Power within the Universe, God's Divine Mind at work, or Cosmic Intelligence. Spiritus-Sanctus in Latin, Pneuma-Hagion in Greek, Ruah-Ha-Qadosh in Hebrew, Ruḥā-Qadash in Aramaic. Also known as Shekinah (the Divine Presence) in Hebrew, and Śakti (the Divine Energy) in Sanskrit.

Holy of Holies
The Cavity of your Heart, the Sanctuary where dwells the Spark of the Eternal. In Latin, Sanctum Sanctorum.

Holy Trinity
The Threefold Logos, the One-in-Three and Three-in-One, consisting of:
- The Father, ☉, the First Logos. The First Aspect of the Triune God is the Nameless Transcendental Godhead, above, beyond and before Creation and after Creation. It is That which always Is. (In Man, this is the Monad.)
- The Son, ⊖, the Second Logos. The Second Aspect of the Triune God is the Christos, the Universal Light of the Christ, the Universal Light Vibration which hovers above the Manifest Condition, the Revealer of the Way to the Unmanifest, to the "Father".
- The Holy Spirit, ⊕, the Third Logos. The Third Aspect of the Triune God is the Immanent Deity, the Holy Breath or Holy Intelligence, that which is concealed in matter, life-forms, bodies. It is the Fire of Creation, God-in-Manifestation, the Embodied God.

It is important to understand that the words *Father* and *Son* do not mean anything like a human "father" and "son". To understand it in such a way would be gross ignorance. The Holy Spirit is the "Mother". The Union of the Father-Mother Principles produces the Autogenes-Christos, the Self-born Universal Light of the Christ, the "Son". [See Trimūrti]

Homopneumata
Greek: "The same spirits". Souls having the same qualities, interests or vibrations. Kindred Souls. The Disciples. From Homo (the same, likeness) and Pneumata (spirits).

Honōma
Greek: The "Name" or "Sound-Vibration". The same as the Sanskrit word Nāma.

Horus
Egyptian: The Progeny or Child Light. The Light of the Christ. [See Isis and Osiris]

Hṛd, Hṛt, Hṛda
Sanskrit: The Heart.

Hṛdaya, Hṛdayaṁ
Sanskrit: "I am the Heart". The Spiritual Heart. A term used by the Hindu Mystics for the Heart Cakra. The Heart is the core of your Being. It is you as the Eternal Self, the Immortal Spirit that you really are. It is the real You who was, is and ever shall be. It is the permanent "I" that is ever the same, whatever your state of consciousness—whether you are alive or dead, asleep or awake, dreaming or in trance.

Hṛdayākāśa
Sanskrit: "Heart-Space" (Hṛdaya-Ākāśa). The Ethereal Space within your Heart Centre. It is also known as Hṛdayaguha (Heart-Cave), the Cave of the Heart where the Christ is found (according to Western Wisdom), and where Ātman, the Self, is found (according to Eastern Wisdom). This is the Spiritual Sun, the Celestial Light which shines brighter than a million physical Suns, your Radiant Spiritual Self.

Everything you perceive is registered as an image in your Heart; thus the Heart-Space (Hṛdayākāśa) is cluttered with images of external forms. The pure empty Space of Pure Consciousness within the Heart is full of external impressions, veiling the Sight of the Kingdom of God within. The Heart (Hṛdaya) has to be *emptied* of these material forms (Rūpa) before you can *see* the Serene Light of the Imperishable Kingdom.

Hṛdaya-Citta
Sanskrit: Spiritual-Heart-Consciousness.

Hṛdaya-Dhyāna-Yoga
Sanskrit: Meditation in the Heart.

Hṛdayagranthi (Hṛdaya-Granthi)
Sanskrit: The knot (Granthi) in the Heart. Hṛdayagranthi is a psychic block which shuts out our awareness of Reality. It is because of this knot in the Heart that we experience only this worldly reality. Before the God-in-the-Heart can be discovered, the knot in the Heart has to be dissolved. According to the Hindu Yoga teachings, we cannot truly love until we return to the Heart. We are not fully human until we dissolve the knot in the Heart and return to our Source. Also called Viṣṇugranthi.

Hṛdayaguha
Sanskrit: "Heart-Cave" (Hṛdaya-Guha). The Cave of the Heart where the Christ is found (according to Western Wisdom), and where Ātman, the Self, is found (according to Eastern Wisdom). The Secret of the Heart. [See Hṛdayākāśa]

Hṛdaya-Mārga
Sanskrit: "The Way of the Heart". Hṛdaya-Mārga consists of a threefold action or practice:
1. Right esoteric and spiritual Knowledge or Realization. This is called Jñāna Yoga.
2. Selfless activity for the benefit of others. All activities that are selfless, for the benefit of others, are Karma Yoga.
3. Pure Devotion in the Heart to the God within you (Īśvara) and the Universal Absolute (Brahman) outside of you. Pure, selfless Devotion in the Heart to the Deity is Bhakti Yoga.

Hṛdaya-Śakti
Sanskrit: The Energy of the Heart. The Prema-Śakti, the Energy of Divine Love, which is the Way of the Saint and Mystic.

Hṛdaya-Śaktipāta
Sanskrit: Heart-Transference. The transference of Spiritual Energies into your Auric Being, or Microcosm, from the Heart Centre of the Guru. These Spiritual Energies are a type of Spiritual Kuṇḍalinī Force, a higher aspect of Cosmic Kuṇḍalinī which will transform your whole inner Self. In Christianity this Force is called the "Holy Spirit". [See Śaktipāta]

Hṛdayasthā
Sanskrit: She who dwells in the Heart. A Name of Lalitā, the Goddess. The Heart is a great Mystery. It is only revealed to the Devotee who has penetrated the Heart Sanctuary. Within the Heart is contained the Universe, and Ātman, the Self.

Hṛdaya-Taijasa
Sanskrit: "Heart-Fire". When your Heart is full of Fire, the Fire of Divine Love, the Fire of Divine Devotion, the Heart-Fire or Heart-Radiance, it will open your Third-Eye (the Eyes of your Soul) and the Crown Centre, the Crown of Glory, and you will become One with the White Brilliance of the Supreme Crown.

Hṛdayāya
Sanskrit: Belonging to the Heart.

Hṛdguhya
Sanskrit: The Secret (Guhya) of the Heart (Hṛt). A Name of Lalitā, the Goddess. Within the Heart is the Secret of the Ahaṁ (I AM), the Mystery of "Who Am I?" Here is revealed Ahaṁ-Brahmāsmi, "I am One with God".

Hrīkārī (Hrī-Kārī)
Sanskrit: She who makes the sound of Hrī, which gives nobility and protection. A Name of Lalitā, the Goddess.

Hrīṁ (Hrīng)
Sanskrit: The Bīja-Mantra for Mahā-Devī, the Great Goddess, who gives Perfection, Wholeness, Fullness, Completeness, Samasti (Unity) and Yoga (Union). Hrīṁ is the Powers of Consciousness, Female Authority, Queenship. Hrīṁ is female grace and dignity, contentment, supreme happiness, healing and harmonizing power, creative imagination. Hrīṁ is the Great Mantra of Lalitā in her form of Bhuvaneśvarī (Bhuvanā-Īśvarī), the Omnipresent Goddess. Within the sound of Hrīṁ there are the three powers or faculties of Creation, Sustenance and Dissolution.

Hrīmatī
Sanskrit: She who is modest in her behaviour: not arrogant, not pushy, not forcing, but gentle. A Name of Lalitā, the Goddess.

Hrīṁkārī (Hrīṁ-Kārī)
Sanskrit: She who is the syllable Hrīṁ. The Hrīṁ-maker.

Hṛllēkhā-Śaktiḥ
Sanskrit: The Energy of Enthusiasm and Inspiration in the Heart. Purifying Power.

Hṛt-Padma
Sanskrit: "Heart-Lotus". The Heart of the Divine Mother. The lotus flower is the symbol for the Feminine Heart. The Spiritual Heart Complex extends to the left side of the chest, the right side of the chest, the centre of the chest, and just below the centre of the chest. Each Cave of the Heart unveils a different quality, a different experience. The Hṛt-Padma is located below the Central Heart Cave. This is the Sacred Heart of the Mother. Here shines in full Jagadambā, the Mother of the Universe.

Hū
Arabic: "He". A Name of God. The Personal God. [See Allahū]

Hua-Tou
Chinese: "A pointer to the Mind-Essence". An ante-word or pre-word. The mind in its state of Pure Consciousness before a thought arises. A form of concentrated self-training.

Hūṁ
Sanskrit: The Bīja-Mantra for dissolving, dissolution, melting away. Also, protection and Fire-Power.

Hyle
Greek: Matter, substance. The One Matter. From this we have the English word *holistic*. The same as the Sanskrit Prākṛtī.

Hyperborean Epoch
The second great epoch, or Root-Race, of human evolution upon this planet. The Borean and Hyperborean epochs concerned themselves with the development of the etheric-physical body. During these earliest periods of human evolution, Man had no dense physical body.

I

Ī, Īṁ, Īkarī, Īṁkarī
Sanskrit: A Name of Lalitā, the Goddess. She is the letter Ī, the Sound of Ī, which is the Sound of Consciousness, the Sound of Light. Ī is also the sound of Kāma (desire), the main motivating power for action in the human being. It is also the power of Rajas (activity). Consciousness is all that Is. Develop the mechanism of perception.

Icchā
Sanskrit: Desire.

Icchā-Śakti
Sanskrit: The Energy of desire and will. The Power generated by will, desire, ambition and purposeful living.

Īḍā and Piṅgalā
Sanskrit: The cold and hot nerve-currents (Nāḍīs) in the human etheric body. Īḍā is the subtle energy current on the left side of the Suṣumna (the subtle spinal chord in the etheric-physical body); Piṅgalā is the subtle energy current on the right hand side. Īḍā is the Moon-current: passive, material energy, the "energy that feeds matter". Piṅgalā is the Sun-current: active, psychic energy, the "energy of psychic unfoldment". The Īḍā and Piṅgalā can be united at two cakras: the Mūlādhāra (Base of Spine) and the Ājñā (Third-Eye).

Idea
Greek: The original form or pattern of a thing. A causal form imbued with energy and power. From the Greek Idein, "to see something". According to the Greek Mystery Schools, an Idea is an Archetype in the Divine Mind, an eternal thought on the higher Mental Planes (the Causal Worlds) which will become manifest as "the things that are". For example, Man, the planets, the stars and the galaxies are Ideas in the Divine Mind which become *manifest* (tangible on this Physical Plane). Creation or Manifestation takes place according to Cosmic Ideas. A human being also creates or manifests his or her life according to his or her Ideas. From this we have the degenerated English word *idea* (a thought, a notion, a thoughtform, a thought-construct, mental force, mental understanding, a conception arising in the human mind). The Sages of ancient Greece said, "Ideas rule the world". [See Archetipon]

Idealogy
Greek: "The Science of the Archetypes". The knowledge of the thoughts in God's Mind. Nowadays, *ideology* refers to the different political, theological, philosophical or metaphysical ideas of Humanity.

Idiology
Greek: "Self-thinking". From the Greek Idios (the concrete mind, reason and logic, *human* thoughts and perceptions from the lower mental worlds). From this we have the English words *idiot, idiotic* and *idiom*. It is a sublime irony that one's own thoughts (when not aligned with the Archetypes in the Divine Mind) are quite idiotic! The disadvantage of the lower mind is that all mental systems are paralysed thoughts by reason of their rigidity and immobility. There is a positive side, however: mental systems put facts into the right sequence and logical order, into their right relationships, thus assisting orientation.

Iesou Evchi
Greek: The Jesus Prayer. The constant invocation of the Divine Name of Jesus in the Heart. Variations are: Jesus; Christ; Jesus Christ; Christ Jesus; Lord Jesus; Lord, Jesus Christ; Lord, Jesus Christ, Son of God; and so on.

Iesous
Greek: The Greek source of the English word *Jesus*. Derived from the Hebrew and Aramaic Yeshua, Yoshua, Yeheshua, Yehoshua or Yeheshuvah.

Iesu, Iesus
Latin: The source of the name *Jesus*. Derived from the older Greek Iesous.

IHVH

Hebrew: The ancient Hebrew Name of God, commonly pronounced as Yahweh or Yehovah. This Name is actually so exalted that it cannot even be translated. The nearest would be "the Eternal One, the Self-Existent One, the Imperishable One, the One Who Always Is, the Living Eternity, the Unknowable Absoluteness, the Ultimate Reality, Existence, Being, the Transcendental Self, the Transcendental Godhead, the Everlasting Light, the Limitless Light". It is the Unpronounceable Name, the Lost Word. Unfortunately, the Bible translators translated this word as "Lord" or "God", meaning a personal God, like the "old man on the throne" or a tribal warrior chief. But this word *cannot* have that meaning. There are Hebrew words that mean "Lord, Master, Sir, Powerful One", but this is not one of them. [See Yehovah, Yahweh]

Illuminati

Latin: "The Enlightened Ones". Those who have *seen* the Light within themselves. Those who have received the Luminous Flux of Divine Grace, Divine Light. To the Roman Mystery Schools the Illuminati were the same as what, in the East, are called the Buddhas.

Illumination (Illuminacion)

Latin: "Letting in the Light". Spiritual Enlightenment. In the old Roman Mystery Schools, Illuminacion was the inner perception and experience of the Unitive State of Buddhi or the Light of Nirvāṇa. There are several kinds of Illumination, several degrees or stages of Mystical Union. Illumination is the experience of Superconsciousness, which begins at the higher (formless) mental subplanes (the Causal Worlds) and includes the seven subplanes of the Buddhic Plane. It begins with the downpour of Light from the Soul into the personality mechanism and the experience of touching upon the Buddhic Plane, bringing about feelings of Oneness, Unity, Ecstasy, Bliss, Joy. When the Soul and the personality vibrate together, there is *Illumination*. When Illumination strikes you while you are embodied in your physical body, then (depending on your level of Union) you are engulfed in a Golden Radiance or a Living Intelligent Light.

Imagination

Latin. The image-making or picture-making faculty of the subconscious mind. There is an esoteric saying: "In the world of imagination, all things are possible".

Imām

Arabic: A king, a leader, a pattern or model to follow. The Spiritual Teacher, the Holy Man, the Guru.

Īmān

Arabic: Having absolute Faith in God.

Immanuel

Hebrew: Commonly translated as "God is with us". The esoteric meaning is "God is *within* us".

Individuality

The Higher Self in Man, consisting of the Spirit (Ātman), the Spiritual Soul (Buddhi) and the Higher Mind (Kāraṇa-Manas). The Spiritual Triad (Ātma-Buddhi-Manas), the Imperishable Self, which clothes itself in a new personality at each incarnation. (Note that this term refers to the individualized Human Soul, not to the "individualism" of the personal ego.) [See Ātma-Buddhi-Manas]

Individualization

The creation of the Human Soul, brought about through the combining of the Fires of Matter and the Fires of Spirit.

Indra

Sanskrit: Powerful, mighty. The Chief of all the Celestial Hosts and Hierarchies. The Angelic Ruler of the Buddhic Plane.

Indrāditya

Sanskrit: The Powerful Sun-God. From Indra (powerful, mighty) and Āditya (the Sun-God, the Light-Being whose outer dense body is the physical Solar System).

Indriya

Sanskrit: Power or capacity. Sense-perception. Also, a sense organ. This involves not only the senses of the physical body, for senses exist in your astral, mental and causal bodies as well. For the Sage, all of your sense-perceptions, whether physical or subtle, relate to your sense of "I-am-ness" or individual existence (Asmitā), and to your sense of ego or self (Ahaṁkāra: I am the doer). The ability to function *without* the sense-organs (that is, above the physical, astral, mental and causal senses) is Buddhic Consciousness, *beyond* your personality, *beyond* your mind.

Infernus
Latin: "The infernal region, the inferno". The lowest regions of the Astral World, called the *Eighth Sphere* in modern terminology and Avītci in Sanskrit. There is a murky fire which casts a macabre glow in some parts of this realm; hence the religious ideas of *hellfire*.

Infidēlis
Latin: "One who has been unfaithful" (such as a husband or wife). The Muslim religious orthodoxies denounced all non-Muslims as "infidels". [See Pāgānus]

Infraversion
Latin: "Turning downwards". The Soul looks down and attends to the personality as a response to meditation or invocation.

Inspiratio
Latin: "Breathing in the Spirit". Inspiration. The blowing of the Holy Spirit into the Soul. This term was used by the old Romans, and later by the Christian Church of Rome, for the Divine Influence that comes through a human being who has touched upon Causal or Buddhic Consciousness. It is through such Inspiration that scriptures are written, great works of art are created, miracles are performed, and superhuman, self-sacrificial deeds are done, most selfless and noble.

Instinctual Telepathy
Instinctual telepathy works through the etheric body and the spleen cakra (near the solar plexus) and was developed as the form of communication in Lemurian times. A remnant of this form of telepathy is seen today when someone in great danger reacts instinctively, irrationally, without thinking, to overcome a difficulty or danger. [See Telepatheia]

Intellectus
Latin: "Knowing inside". Today the word *intellect* refers to the reasoning mind, the book-learned mind, the "educated" mind. The original meaning, however, was the Higher Mind or Abstract Mind, Kāraṇa-Manas (Causal Mind), the mind used by You as a Soul in your causal body. That is why the old Christian Mystics wrote about "Intellectual Visions" as a stage upon the Spiritual Path. The Intellectual Visions are You, as a Soul, perceiving the Universe around you in the formless Causal Worlds.

Introjection
Latin. To internalize your powers, forces, energies.

Introspection
Latin: "Looking within" (as in meditation). Introspection is the process of looking for the Truth within yourself, the observation of your own mental and emotional states, self-examination, soul-searching, looking within yourself for the answers. Similar to the Latin word Introversion.

Introversion
Latin: "Turning within oneself" or "turning into oneself". Usually refers to focusing one's attention within the Heart Cakra.

Intuitionis
Latin: From In-Tuitio, "being taught within" or "learning from within oneself". The spontaneous receiving of Higher Knowledge from the deeper layers of consciousness, without the aid of reason, deduction, method or logic. *Intuition* is nowadays regarded as a subconscious hunch, or an instinct, or a smart guess, or a feeling about something. To the Initiated Romans and the Christian Mystics, however, Intuitionis was a stage of development above Causal Consciousness. In the Roman Mystery Schools it was the faculty of Buddhic Consciousness, direct Spiritual Sight of Reality, spontaneous Knowledge without the use of the reasoning mind. It is what the Buddhist meditators call Insight, Prajñā. There are three degrees of Intuition:

- Receiving knowledge and insight from the Higher Mind, the Abstract Mind, Causal Consciousness.

- A direct flash of Knowledge from the Unitive State of the Spiritual Soul within you, the Buddhi.
- Inner Revelation, the interior experience of the Godhead, being taught inwardly by the Higher Self, the Ātman.

Intuitional World
The Buddhic Plane, the realm of Spiritual Intuition, Insight, Prajñā.

Intuitive Mind
The Wisdom-Mind (Buddhi-Manas). This Mind is infused with Love, Unity and Wisdom (Buddhi). To subjugate your ordinary rational mind (the pride of our civilization) and to awaken the Intuitive Mind, the Non-Dual Mind, is the goal of Zen and all true disciplines of Yoga, Sūfīsm and Mysticism. [See Buddhi-Manas]

Invocation
Latin: Calling down upon oneself, by an act of will, or by a mantram, chant or ritual formula, the Powers and Energies of the Higher Self, God, the Holy Spirit or the Cosmic Christ. [See Evocation]

IO
Egyptian-Polynesian: For the ancient Egyptians, the Māori of New Zealand and the Pacific Islanders, IO was the Ultimate Being, beyond which you cannot go. The Godhead. The Absolute.

Īśa
Sanskrit: "Lord, Master, Ruler, Commander". God, Lord-God, the Lord of the Universe, the Ruler of the Universe and the Solar System and the Heart. The Powerful, the Impeller or Motivator, the Swift, the All-Pervading, the Venerable, the Divine, the Divine Consciousness, the Controller, the Central Authority, the Master Power, the Self within the Heart. Īśa is the Ruling Principle within Man (the Soul), and Īśa is God, the Soul of the Universe. Īśa is God who energizes, impels, directs, and makes Fertile all things. [See Īśvara]

Īśāvaṣyam
Sanskrit: God (Īśa) is the Controller or Ruler (Avaṣyam) of the Universe.

Iṣām-i-A'zam
Arabic: The Highest and Greatest. The Greatest Name.

Īśatva, Īśitva, Īśitritva
Sanskrit: God-like powers. Godliness, Lordship over Nature, Rulership over the All, Supremacy over all beings, absolute Self-Mastery, the ability to manifest or materialize things from the Great Invisible. One of the nine "general" powers (Siddhis) which can manifest in advanced Humanity.

'Ishk
Arabic: Love. This is the fifth stage of the Journey of the Heart. At this stage you become an 'Ishshiq, a Lover. Your Love for God and your Teacher becomes immense. You definitely feel and experience something going on in your Heart—changes, transformations, insights, and the Grace of God working there. You would rather spend all your time in meditation than deal with the world and worldly people. Your Love for God appears to have created in you a conflict with the world. You feel that worldly people are empty and superficial.

Isis
Egyptian: The Mother Light. [See Osiris and Horus]

Islām
Arabic: Surrender or submission to the One God. Surrendering to God's Will.

Israel (Yishrael)
Hebrew: "Ruling with God". The ancient Israelites were given a Revelation of the Nature of God and the Cosmic Law, Torah, the rules of the Universe. When Humanity can understand the spiritual dignity and greatness of Man, we can truly rule, with God, all Nature.

Īṣta
Sanskrit: The Beloved. The Worshipped Deity.

Īṣta-Devatā
Sanskrit: "Chosen Divinity". A representation of Divinity which serves as a focus for meditation in the Heart. The form of the Deity you are most drawn to, such as the form of the Christ, Buddha, Śrī Kṛṣṇa or Rāma. Also known as Upāsanā-Mūrti (spiritual discipline, form or image). Your "Chosen Deity" helps you to focus on the Divine Reality. The human form of the Divine Incarnation serves as an *initial* focal point of your Love, Devotion, Longing, Praise and Worship, knowing full well that the human form of the Incarnation merely veils the glorious Divinity behind it. God has to appear to Humanity in human form until humans possess Śiva-Netra, the Spiritual Eye, by which they will see God everywhere.

Īṣta-Devatā-Rūpa
Sanskrit: "Chosen-Deity-Form". A "Chosen Deity" which has form. Remember, there is only One God! The form itself that you choose to meditate upon in your Heart is but a *representation* of the true Form of the One God, which is vast and cosmic.

Īśvara
Sanskrit: "The Lord-God". The Master, Ruler, Controller, Director. The Supreme Being, the Cosmic Spirit, the Central Intelligence of the Universe, the Highest Authority in the Cosmos. The Lord of All, the Lord of the Universe, the Chief among All, the King of Kings, the Lord of Lords, the Master Power, the Inner-Ruler-Immortal. Īśvara is the Heart Centre, or Centre of Consciousness, in any system, microcosmic or macrocosmic. It is the power of Lordship and independent action, the ruling, guiding or controlling principle within. In particular, Īśvara is:

- The Lord-God, the Universal Sun, the Universal Self, the Supreme Individuality, the Central Authority within the Universe, the Master of the Universe, the Supreme Godhead, the Absolute.
- The Solar Logos, the Creator, the "personal" God, God manifest in this Creation or Emanation, the Spiritual Sun of our Solar System, Sūrya, also known as Brahmā, the Ruler of our Solar Universe. In Hebrew, Adonai (Lord, Lord-God). Or, the Ruler within any solar system in the Universe.
- The Inner-Ruler-Immortal in the Man-species: the Monad, the "Father in Heaven", the God-Within; the Ātman, the Ruler of the Human Heart; the Soul, the Triune Self; the Heart Centre. The Spiritual Sunshine in the Human Microcosm, the Central Organizer of Life.

Īśvara Maitreya
Sanskrit: The Lord Christ, the Heart of the Spiritual Hierarchy. [See Maitreya]

Īśvara-Praṇidhāna
Sanskrit: "Devotion to God". Surrendering yourself to God, the Lord and Master who dwells within the Cave of your Heart. From Īśvara (the Lord God within) and Praṇidhāna (total dedication, total Devotion, total Love). Īśvara-Praṇidhāna is the fifth Niyama (rule) of Aṣṭāṅga Yoga, as set down by Patañjali. It means surrendering yourself completely to the guidance of your Soul, or the Triune Self, or the Monad, or God (the Logos), or Sūrya, the Sun-Being (the Controller of the Solar Universe), or Mahā-Īśvara, the Universal Deity, according to your level of spiritual development.

Īśvarī
Sanskrit: The Goddess, the Ruler, the Mistress of the Cosmos, the Supreme Being. She who rules, guides, protects. A Name of Lalitā, the Goddess.

Itarā Liṅga
Sanskrit: An access-way to extra-physical reality, located at the Ājñā Cakra (Third-Eye Centre) and the Sahasrāra Cakra (Crown Centre). From Itarā, "another one", and Liṅga, a Sign for Śiva, the Transcendent. [See Bāṇa Liṅga and Svāyaṁbhū Liṅga]

J

Jagad
Sanskrit: The World, the Universe.

Jagadambā
Sanskrit: "World Mother". The Mother of the Universe, the Mother of the World. From Jagad (the World, the Universe) and Ambā (Mother, the Divine Mother). There is nothing in this Universe which is not Śrī Jagadambā, the Holy Universal Mother of All. All visible Nature and invisible Nature is the World Mother. Every particle of you is born of the World Mother and is in the World Mother. You *are* the World Mother.

Jaganmātā
Sanskrit: The Mother of the Universe. The Divine Mother.

Jagat, Jagata
Sanskrit: The world, the physical universe. The dense physical subplanes of the Physical Plane. All things moving or alive. People.

Jagatgranthi
Sanskrit: Conditioned by the world, by cosmic processes and events around you. From Jagat (the world) and Granthi (a knot, a barrier, a conditioning).

Jāgrata-Avasthā
Sanskrit: The self-conscious mind. The normal, wakeful state in your physical body. The normal, logical, reasoning, day-to-day mind.

Jā, Jāḥ
Sanskrit: Born.

Jah (Yah)
Hebrew: "God the Living". The Self-Existent or Eternal One. The Creator-God.

Jall, Jallā
Arabic: Splendour, Glory, Radiance, Divine Majesty.

Janah-Loka
Sanskrit: The Spiritual World. The Realm of Nirvāṇa.

Janma
Sanskrit: Birth.

Japa
Sanskrit: "Resounding the sound". From Ja (sound) and Pa (to resound). Also called "taking the Name" or "calling upon God". Mantra Japa is the repeated recitation of a Mantra. It is based on the Law of Vibration or Rhythm.

Jāti
Sanskrit: Class, social status, rank, lineage, race.

Jaya, Jay, Jai
Sanskrit: Victory, Victorious, Conquering, Glorious. Above Death.

Jayamā
Sanskrit: The Divine Mother is beyond Death.

Jehovah (Yehovah)
Hebrew: "The Eternal" or "That which was, is, and ever shall be". This Name refers not to a "personal" God, but to the Absolute Reality. [See Yehovah]

Jesus
The word *Jesus* comes from the Latin Iesus and Iesu, which were derived from the older Greek Iesous and the still older Hebrew and Aramaic Yeshua, Yoshua, Yeheshua, Yehoshua or Yeheshuvah. As a Jewish child He probably would have been known as Yoshua (Joshua). Like the peoples of India, the Jews gave Divine Names to their children. Yeheshua means "the Eternal is my Salvation, in God is Salvation, God is my helper". Yeshua means "Saviour, Deliverer, Salvation, the Power to Save or Liberate, God's downpouring Grace". Hence, *Jesus* means "the Saviour". [See Yeshua and Yeheshua]

Jesus Christ
A compound of Hebrew and Greek words meaning "a Divine Teacher or Guru who has been anointed, or who has been acknowledged as succeeding in the Mysteries of Life and Death". The name "Jesus Christ" is correctly *Jesus the Christed One* (in the original Hebrew, YEHESHUAH HA-MASHIAH).

Jewel in the Lotus
The Spark of the Monad, embedded deeply in the Heart Cakra (the Lotus). This Jewel is the *Sparkling Stone* of the Alchemists. The Gnostics called it the *Spirit-Spark-Atom*. Jesus called it the *Pearl of Great Price*. It is the Supernatural compressed deep within the innermost region of the Heart. This Jewel is the *Innermost*, the Lord-God-Within, the Inner God, the Key to Eternal Life and Everlasting Blessedness. This is the Key to Transfiguration, Resurrection and Ascension into the Everlasting Realms. This is the Key to the Divine Magic of Light. In Sanskrit, MAṆI-PADMA. [See *Spirit-Spark-Atom*]

JISM-I-ALṬAF
Arabic: "Body of Great Subtlety". The mental body or thought-body. Your ordinary mind, by which you think, plan, and so forth.

JISM-I-KASĪF
Arabic: "Body of Denseness". The gross physical body.

JISM-I-LAṬĪF
Arabic: "Body of Delicateness". The subtle body or astral body, through which you sense, feel, have moods, desires, wishes.

JĪVA, JĪVĀTMA, JĪVĀTMĀ, JĪVĀTMAN
Sanskrit: The Living Soul, the Individualized Self. The Human Soul, reflecting the triune nature of the Universal Being as ĀTMA-BUDDHI-MANAS. JĪVA is below the Spiritual Soul (BUDDHI), which is in turn below the Spiritual Self (ĀTMAN). JĪVA is the *individualized* Soul, the recognizable human being which takes on personalities, life after life, until it attains freedom in Nirvāṇa. In the East it is called the *Thinker* and the *Reincarnating Ego* because it takes on a new personality with each new incarnation. Your individualized Human Soul lives in your causal body on the formless subplanes of the Mental Plane and gives you the continuum of existence, life after life. This is the AHAṀKĀRA, the personality's sense of "I am". It is the separated self, as distinct from the One Self. When Divine Consciousness is attained, the AHAṀKĀRA simply becomes AHAṀ (I Am).

JĪVABHRĀNTI
Sanskrit: Identification with an ego (that which we *think* we are), therefore being deluded by the ego. From JĪVA (life, person, Soul, a living being) and BHRĀNTI (worldly consciousness, erroneous thinking, being subject to glamour).

JĪVAGRANTHI
Sanskrit: Conditioned by the ego or sense of "I". Identification with an ego, which limits the Free Flow of Pure Consciousness. From JĪVA (life, person, Soul, a living being) and GRANTHI (a knot, a barrier, a conditioning).

JĪVANMUKTA (JĪVAN-MUKTA)
Sanskrit: "Alive-Liberated". A Liberated Soul. A human being who experiences Liberation, Nirvāṇa, the Kingdom of God, while still in the physical body. An enlightened Seer. From JĪVAN (living) and MUKTA (liberated).

JĪVANMUKTI (JĪVAN-MUKTI)
Sanskrit: "Living Liberation". Enlightenment while still living in the physical body. From JĪVAN (living) and MUKTI (Liberation, Freedom). [See VIDEHĀ-MUKTI]

JÑĀNA
Sanskrit: Knowledge. Self-Conscious Awareness. Mental clarification and understanding. Transcendental Knowledge.

JÑĀNA-JÑEYA-SVARŪPIṆĪ
Sanskrit: She who is both the Knowledge and the Known. A Name of LALITĀ, the Goddess. From SVA-RŪPIṆĪ (whose Self-Form), JÑĀNA (knowledge) and JÑEYA (that which can be known). She is All that Is.

Jñāna-Mātā
Sanskrit: She who is the Mother (Mātā) of Transcendental Consciousness, Transcendental Knowledge, Self-Realization, Enlightenment (Jñāna). A Name of Lalitā, the Goddess.

Jñāna-Śakti
Sanskrit: The Energy that gives Knowledge. The Energy of the Gnostic, the Knower, the Sage, the Seer (Jñāni).

Jñānaśaktī-Icchāśaktī-Kriyāśaktī-Svarūpiṇī
Sanskrit: She whose Self-Form (Sva-Rūpiṇī) is Knowledge (Jñāna), Desire (Icchā) and Action (Kriyā). A Name of the Eternal Feminine, the Goddess. For it is through Knowledge, Desire and Action that all beings live and all things are done in the Universe.

Jñāna Yoga
Sanskrit: Union through Knowledge, Insight, Realization. The Path of Mental Effort and Knowledge. The Yoga of the Mind, utilizing the mental body as a vehicle. This involves mental development, mental clarification, the understanding of truth, science, philosophy and metaphysics, the developing view of our Universe, right esoteric and spiritual Knowledge or Realization, and the awakening of Creative Intelligence. In its higher forms, Jñāna Yoga is the awakening of Buddhi—Insight, Higher Knowledge, the Illumined Understanding.

Jñāni
Sanskrit: Enlightened. A Gnostic, a Knower, a Seer, a Wiseman or Wisewoman. A Sage who follows the Path of Mind for Enlightenment. One whose mind has become Buddhi-Manas (the Wisdom-Mind), who spontaneously knows all things spiritual, all things related to the Soul, the Path and the Godhead within. Also, Gñāni and Gñānin.

Jñāta, Jñātāḥ
Sanskrit: Known.

Jñeya
Sanskrit: That which can be known.

Julāl, Jalāl
Arabic: Shining, radiating, resplendent, glorious.

Jūsticia
Latin: Justice. Rightness, lawfulness, correctness.

Jyoti, Jyotī, Jyotiḥ, Jyotir, Jyotiś, Jyotiṣ
Sanskrit: Light, Fire, Flame, Radiance, Brightness, Brilliance, Glory, Divinity. Also, dawn, lightning. Manifest Light—burning, brilliant, luminous, passionate, sacred, all-consuming. The Light of the Sun. The Light of Īśvara. Light is synonymous with Mind or Intelligence. The Light within you and all around you is God's Intelligence, bathing the Universe in Supernatural Glory. Jyotī is the feminine aspect of the Light. Also, Jyotā (feminine), "Brilliant Light", and Jyotika (masculine), "Flaming, Brilliant". [See *Light*]

Jyotirbhāsin
Sanskrit: Brilliant with Light. A description of the Godhead.

Jyotir-Jyotiḥ (Jyotir-Jyotiś)
Sanskrit: The Light of all Lights.

Jyotir-Mārga
Sanskrit: The Shining Path, the Path of Light.

Jyotir-Maṭha
Sanskrit: The Light Path, or Path of Light, whereby you learn to see the Light in the Third-Eye and Crown Centres and *exit* through them into the Higher Realms.

Jyotir-Maya
Sanskrit: Consisting of Light.

Jyoti-Nirañjanā
Sanskrit: The Unpolluted Light. The Light of Pure Spirit. From Jyoti (Light) and Nirañjanā (without blemish, faultless, perfect). A Name of Lalitā, the Goddess.

Jyotirasā (Jyoti-Rasā)
Sanskrit: The Essence of Light.

Jyotir-Śakti
Sanskrit: The Energy of Light that produces inside you Illumination and Self-Realization.

Jyotiṣa
Sanskrit: The Sun, Light, Fire. Luminous, bright. Astrology.

Jyotiṣa-Śakti
Sanskrit: The energies, forces and powers emanating from planets and stars. This is the proper science of Astrology, when correctly understood.

Jyotiṣmatī
Sanskrit: Luminous Intelligence. Spiritual Light. The Worlds of Light. Brilliant, shining, full of Light, possessing All Light. A Name of Lalitā, the Goddess.

Variations of* Kala *and* Kali *(Sanskrit)

Kalā (feminine): a small point, an atom, a digit of the moon; a part, a fragment, a division, a ray; art, skill, ingenuity; Nature.

Kāla (masculine): Time, Fate, Destiny, Death; black, dark-blue, night, dark; Śiva as the Destroyer; Yama, the God of Death; Saturn. (Kālī is the feminine form.)

Kālī (feminine): dark, black, indigo, night; dark clouds; a bud of a tree; Durgā, the Goddess of Destruction; the Destroyer of Time.

Kali (masculine): sin, vice; the opposer, the negative power, the Devil; the Dark Age, the Age of Ignorance and Materialism. (Kalī is the feminine form.)

Kalī (feminine): the temporary Creation; all things relating to form-life; movement, change; that which passes away; the worlds that are subject to dissolution at the end of Time (the Age).

K

Kabbalah
[See Qabbālāh]

Kaivalya (Kaivalyam)
Sanskrit: "Being Alone with the Infinite, the Absolute". The Aloneness of being above all created things, yet in Absolute Oneness with all things. Detachment, Freedom, Liberation from material conditions. Isolation from the lower states of existence and Union with the higher, the Buddhic and Nirvāṇic Planes and above. The ability to live freely and voluntarily on the Spiritual and Divine Planes (Nirvāṇa and the realms beyond Nirvāṇa), and to work towards the Cosmic Astral Plane. Kaivalya is a form of Liberation or God-Intoxication where the "I" sense is completely annihilated and there is only an awareness of Infinite Joy, Infinite Bliss, Infinite Power and Infinite Love. There is a total sense of Aloneness. There is no consciousness of the Universe, nor of the body, nor of the mind. The Cosmic Sense, or Inner Sense, registers only Unending Bliss and Limitless Life and Boundless Love.

Kāla
Sanskrit: Time, period, age, century. Also, Fate, Destiny, Death. Also, the awareness that every second is simply a surface motion upon Eternity.

Kāla Cakra
Sanskrit: The Wheel of Time.

Kālahaṁsa (Kāla-Haṁsa)
Sanskrit: "Bird of Time". From Kāla (Time) and Haṁsa (a Swan). Eternity, Eternal Duration, the Eternal One, the Everlastingness of the Great Breath of God. Also, one who transcends Time and thus attains Spontaneous Consciousness. Haṁsa is Ātman, the Pure Spirit within you. [See Haṁsa]

Kālī (Kalikā)
Sanskrit: She who is beyond Death. The Destroyer of Fate. The Destroyer of the Time-and-Space sense (the Power that liberates you from the sensation of

Time and Space). The Liberator. The Power of action, activity, active force or energy. The Force of Action in Nature and in Humanity, which can be creative but is very often destructive (unregulated or wrongly expressed). KĀLĪ is an Energy-Form of LALITĀ, the Goddess. [See DURGĀ]

KĀLIMĀ
Sanskrit: The Mother beyond Time. The Divine Mother, KĀLĪ. The Goddess in Her aspect as the Creative Energy, Nourishing Energy and Destructive Energy. She is Nature (PRĀKṚTĪ), the Original Primordial Substance of Space, out of which all things appear (are born), develop and return to the Source (die, perish or undergo transformation). Although all things *appear* to undergo a death or transformation, the Eternal Essence Itself remains above and beyond Time, beyond the endless succession of changes. Nature is a Veil for the Real.

KĀLIMĀTĀ
Sanskrit: The Mother Goddess.

KALI YUGA
Sanskrit: "The Dark Age" (this is not a reference to the Dark Ages of European history). KALI YUGA is the Age of materialism, ignorance and darkness. We live in the Age of KALI YUGA. In this Age materialism prevails, spiritual ignorance and blindness, called MĀYĀ. The peoples of the Earth are blinded by material energies, material powers, material objects. The lives of people are taken up with accumulating material objects for themselves and their families. Material comforts supersede spiritual powers. Name and fame in society supersede the true Kingliness and Majesty of the Perfected Man. [See *Materialism*]

KALĀM-I-LLĀHI
Arabic: The Voice of God, the Word of God, the Heavenly Music, the Divine Name.

KALĀM-U-LLĀH
Arabic: The Word of God, the Divine Vibration of the Name, the Sounding-Light Vibration of God's Name.

KALMA
Arabic: The Word, the Logos, the Speech of God. Also, a prayer, a Mantra, a Word of Power.

KALMA-I-ḤAQQĪQAT
Arabic: Word of Truth. A Word of Power or Mantra.

KALPA
Sanskrit: An Age, a cycle, a period of manifestation or evolution, a period of activity.

KĀMA
Sanskrit: Passion, desire, feeling, emotion, sexual attraction. KĀMA is that which awakens and mobilizes the energies of the Soul towards a given object, person, ideal or goal in life. KĀMA is *feeling energy*. In many Eastern Schools one is taught to "kill out desire". This is an error. One can sublimate some desires and passions, but one cannot attain any goal without a desire for it.

KĀMA-AVASĀYITVA
Sanskrit: Fulfilment of all desires. One of the nine "general" powers (SIDDHIS) which can manifest in advanced Humanity.

KĀMADEVA
Sanskrit: "Desire-angel" (KĀMA-DEVA). An embodied angel or spiritual being, dwelling on the Astral Plane. In the context of the MAKARA (the Fifth Manifest Hierarchy), the KĀMADEVAS are the "angels of desire and lust", those angelic beings who awakened the sexual desire in Man and, to a large degree, keep it going even today. These Devas are focused in the astral and etheric-physical subplanes.

KĀMADEVĪ
Sanskrit: The Energy of desire, attraction, love, passion, wishing, longing, affection, enjoyment, pleasure, worship, devotion, union, at-one-ment, transformation, Divine Love. An Energy-Form of the Goddess.

KĀMA-DHĀRAṆĀ
Sanskrit: "Desire-Concentration". The magical power to fulfil one's passions or desires. A sustained emotional effort to accomplish one's desires.

Kāma-Dhatu
Sanskrit: The Desire-World. The Astral World.

Kāma-Kāya
Sanskrit: The astral body as a vehicle of expression for the Soul on the Astral Plane.

Kāmala
Sanskrit: Erotic, lustful, full of desire.

Kamala
Sanskrit: The lotus flower. The colour red, rose-coloured.

Kamalā
Sanskrit: "Born of the Lotus Flower" (the symbol of absolute Purity, Perfection and Beauty); springtime (which is when all things are reborn and renewed); most excellent; most desirous; full of wealth (the whole Universe is Hers); rose-coloured (which is the Flame of the Pure Spirit-Fire). Kamalā, the Lotus-Born, is the Transcendental-Bliss aspect of Śrī-Vidyā: Pure Consciousness, Cosmic Unity, Divine Oneness with all things, Absolute Peace and Joy and Completeness, Cosmic Beingness.

Kamalā-Ātmikā
Sanskrit: "She whose Nature is the Lotus Flower". To understand this we have to understand the Eastern symbol of the lotus flower. Firstly it represents the Heart Centre, and it also represents all the lotuses or cakras in the human system. The lotus flower is also a symbol for Lakṣmī, that aspect of Lalitā which gives:
- Name, fame, fortune, prosperity, success in all fields of action.
- Beauty, Charm, Grace, Splendour, Lustre, Spiritual Wealth or Powers.

Kamalādevī
Sanskrit: "The Goddess of the Lotus" (Kamalā-Devī). A Name of Lalitā, the Goddess. She is most Beautiful and Desirable. (The lotus is the most beautiful flower of the East.)

Kāmaloka (Kāma-Loka)
Sanskrit: "Desire-Realm". The World of Desires. From Kāma (desires, passions, feelings) and Loka (world, realm, condition). Kāmaloka is the realm of the dead, where people go after they die. In modern terminology we call it the *Astral Plane*. The chief quality of the Astral World is the energies, forces and colours of *feelings, emotions and desires* of all sentient beings. The feelings of humans (Manuṣya) mix with the feelings of the angels (Devas) and those of elementals, animals and plants. The whole Astral World is one big world of feelings and emotions, a thousand times more intense than the "feelings" you experience while in your physical body. Also called Bhuvah-Loka (the Subtle World) and Antarikṣa (the Inner World).

Kāma-Manas
Sanskrit: "Desire-mind". The coupling of your Kāma (astral body) and lower Manas (mental body). The mental body functioning in conjunction with an astral and physical body. In Yoga literature, Kāma-Manas is sometimes called the *versatile psychic nature*. According to the teachings of Yoga, your psychic nature is composed of Kāma (desires, feelings, emotions) and Manas (mind, thinking, thought-patterns, thoughtforms), and while you are alive in your physical body they functions as *one unit*. This is also the mind you use on the Astral Plane after death. Kāma-Manas is the ordinary mind, which is always caught up in desire. Highly emotional temperaments desire first, then think. Others think first and then desire. In this latter case, the coupling of these two personality bodies is called Manas-Kāma. Ideally, Kāma-Rūpa (the desire body, the astral body) should be controlled by Mānasa-Rūpa (the mental body or mind principle).

Kāma-Rāja-Kūṭa
Sanskrit: "The Most Excellent Lord of Desire". The Fulfiller of all Desires. From Kāma (desire, wish, longing, pleasure, affection, Love), Rāja (king, lord, emperor, chief, leader) and Kūṭa (the highest peak, most excellent).

Kāma-Rūpa
Sanskrit: The "desire-body" or "vehicle of passions". On the Astral Plane you have just one body, called Kāma-Rūpa or Sūkṣma-Śarīra (subtle body). This is your astral body, made up of the seven differentiated matters of the Astral World. This is your subjective mind or subconscious mind.

Kāma-Sūtra
Sanskrit: Verses or teachings on sex and desire.

Kāmavṛtti (Kāma-Vṛtti)
Sanskrit: The vibrations of feelings, desires and moods (in the emotional or astral body), which are ever-changing and throwing people constantly into turmoil.

Kāmeśvarī (Kāma-Īśvarī)
Sanskrit: The Goddess in Her Nature as Universal Desire, or the desire-nature of all beings.

Kaṇṭha Kūpa
Sanskrit: "Throat-pit", or pit of the throat. The Throat Centre. Also called the Viṣuddhi (Viśuddha) Cakra.

Kanyākumārī
Sanskrit: The Virgin Goddess, the Eternal Virgin. A Name of Lalitā, the Goddess. [See *Virgin Goddess*]

Kaos
Greek: [See Chaos]

Kāra
Sanskrit: The creative, the causer, the doer, the activator, the maker. Also, a letter of the alphabet (for instance, Rakāra is the letter 'R').

Kāraṇa
Sanskrit: "Cause". The Kāraṇa (Cause) of the Universe is Vāk (the Word, the Logos).

Kāraṇa Cakra
Sanskrit: The Causal Centre, located several feet above the head. At the Causal Centre there is an intense sphere of living Electric-White-Fire, which is Spirit-Light. Also called the *Alta Centre*.

Kāraṇa-Loka
Sanskrit: The Causal World. The Subtlest Realms.

Kāraṇa-Manas
Sanskrit: "Causal Mind". The Higher Mind, the Abstract Mind, functioning on the higher (formless) mental subplanes. The Causal Mind or Abstract Mind is the vehicle of Pure Intellect or Insight. It has the qualities of Pure Intelligence and Activity. The spiritual literature sometimes calls it the Superconscious Mind or Wisdom-Mind (Buddhi-Manas); the true Wisdom-Mind, however, is the mind (higher and lower) infused with the Light of Buddhi.

Kāraṇa-Śarīra
Sanskrit: "Causal body". Your causal body is made up of the matter of the three highest subplanes of the Mental Plane—the Arūpa or formless levels. Your causal body is the lowest part of your imperishable Individuality, beyond your personality complex. This is your Higher Manas or Abstract Mind, sometimes called the Higher Mind or Causal Mind. Your Reincarnating Ego (Jīva or Ahaṁkāra, you as a Human Soul) dwells in your causal body.

Kardia
Greek: The Heart. Hence the English word *cardiac,* referring to the physical heart organ. To the early Greeks and Christians, however, the Heart (Kardia) meant more than just the physical heart organ. A Divine Mystery is concealed in the human Heart. The Heart is the *Spiritual Centre* of the human being, the Sanctuary within the Temple of the physical body, concealing the true Self or God-Being in Man, the Holy of Holies. In the Heart may be found the image of God, a reflection of the Divine Godhead. In the Heart, the human creature and God the Creator meet, commingle and unite. It is the Holy Place where God meets Man, where you become One with God. [See Phylaki Kardias]

Karma
Sanskrit: "Action". Cause and effect, action and reaction, the effect or results of action. From the root Krī, "to do, to act, to perform". Karma is the Law of Cause and Effect, the Universal Law governing all actions: past actions causing present events, and present actions causing future events. Every action has a corresponding reaction; that is, the reaction is *in kind*. In the Jewish, Christian and Muslim religions, karmas are called "sins"—transgressions against the Laws of Nature, which are the Laws of Mind. All actions are caused by some mind; therefore, Karma rules Mind. The Lord Buddha called it "the Good Law".

Karman
Sanskrit: The Creator, the Architect, the Maker, the Doer.

Karmāśaya
Sanskrit: The Reservoir of Karma. Stored-up Karma.

Karmasu
Sanskrit: Actions.

Karma Yoga
Sanskrit: The Path of Action or Service. This involves actions in the Physical World using the physical body. Karma Yoga is action without ego or self. It is Love expressed physically in action. It is physical bodily activity in the form of selfless Service to others—to humans, angels, animals, plants and all life-forms. It is practical Love, not idle theorizing or day-dreaming about future utopias. All activities that are selfless, for the benefit of others, are Karma Yoga.

Kartṛtva-Śakti
Sanskrit: The Power-of-all-Doership. The Omnipotent Power. That which creates, sustains and dissolves the Universe. A quality of Prakāśa, the Eternal Light.

Kauśalam
Sanskrit: Art or skill.

Kavana
Hebrew: A short, concentrated formula or prayer.

Kāya
Sanskrit: A body.

Kāya-Kalpa
Sanskrit: Mysterious and supernatural transformations of Man. Alchemical transfigurations that surpass even the future natural human evolution.

Kenoma
Greek: The Void, the Emptiness, the Unmanifest Condition. The same as the Sanskrit Śūnyatā.

Kenshō
Japanese: "Seeing into one's own true nature." A glimpse into one's own Immortality. Insight, Intuition, seeing into Reality, Inner View. In Western language, this would mean a glimpse of yourself as an Immortal Spirit or Soul on the planes of Eternal Being. The same as the Sanskrit Bodhi and the Japanese Satori.

Kether
Hebrew: "The Supreme Crown, the Crown of Glory, the Supreme Countenance, the Glorious Face, the Royal Throne". The White Brilliance of the Jewish Kabbalists, send forth from Ain, Ain Soph, Ain Soph Aur, the Boundless Light. In Sanskrit, Nirvāṇa.

Khafā
Arabic: "The Hidden". That part of the Heart (Qalb) which is located at the right side of the chest.

Khaga
Sanskrit: Moving through Cosmic Space. The Sun-Lord who moves through Space. From Kha (space, sky) and Ga (moving, going).

Khalvidaṁ
Sanskrit: Wholeness, oneness.

Kharisma (Charisma)
Greek: Grace, favour, powers, talents, supernatural capabilities. The same as the Sanskrit Siddhi. The important factor when you use these faculties is your *intention*. Using these abilities for selfish and revengeful ends is Black Magic. Using these abilities for the

service of others is White Magic. The karmic results in each case are very different. [See CHARISMA, SIDDHI]

KHŌL

Hebrew: "The Voice of God". The Eternal Word, the Logos, the Creative-Energy.

Kingdom

The Biblical authors often used the term *kingdom* to mean the Kingdom of God. But the word *kingdom* also meant the Earth kingdoms, just as *heaven* also meant the sky. They were desperately short of a spiritual vocabulary. When you read the Bible you have to understand these things, and *intuit* when the authors talk of material things and when they refer to real, inner, spiritual happenings.

Kingdom of God

The expression *The Kingdom of God* can represent several things:

- The invisible Spiritual Hierarchy.
- Specifically, the Nirvāṇic Plane.
- Generally, all the invisible planes.

In Reality, however, the Kingdom of God includes everything from ĀDI downwards, including the Physical Plane. The flow of the great Revelation of the Kingdom of God presses downward from Nirvāṇa throughout the ages: down through the Buddhic Plane, the Causal Worlds, the Mental Plane and the Astral Plane, finally manifesting on the Physical Plane, in this Physical World.

Kingdom of the Gods

The Sixth Evolutionary Kingdom of our planet, consisting of great Beings such as Archangels and Dhyāni-Chohans.

KĪRTANA

Sanskrit: Devotional singing and dancing. Devotional chanting, which stirs the ŚABDA, the God-Incarnating Sound. Also, SANKĪRTANA.

KLĪṀ (KLĪNG)

Sanskrit: The BĪJA-Mantra for KĀMA (wish, desire, pleasure, the attractive power of Love as well as physical attraction). KLĪṀ is the famous KĀMA-BĪJA (Desire-Seedpower) which grants all wishes and desires in the form of KĀMEŚVARĪ (the Desire-Goddess). She is the burning desire for God, the desire for another creature or an object, the magnetic attraction to Divinity or worldly things, personal magnetism, wish-fulfilling power. KLĪṀ (KLĪNG) is KĀMADEVA (the Desire-God). She overcomes depression and negative emotional and mental states. She is Devotion to God or to a person or to an ideal. She is the power to fulfil all desires.

KLĪṀKĀRĪ (KLĪṀ-KĀRĪ)

Sanskrit: She who is the Creator of KLĪṀ. A Name of LALITĀ, the Goddess.

KŌAN

Japanese: An unusual expression contrary to all common sense. A riddle which, when meditated upon, penetrates into the heart of Truth. From the Chinese KUNG-AN, "a case which establishes a legal precedent, a formulation pointing towards the Truth". KŌANs are sometimes stories, sometimes just words, all designed to shake up one's normal perception of things. KŌANs are not supposed to be logical; they are not meant to be solved by reason or intellectual thoughts, nor by the discursive intellect. The word, phrase or idea into which a KŌAN is resolved is called WATŌ, from the Chinese HUA-TOU, "a pointer to the Mind-Essence". Some schools of Japanese Zen concentrate heavily on KŌANs as a means of meditation.

KOHAṀ

Sanskrit: "Who am I?" Ramana Mahāṛṣi, the great Sage of Arunāchala, India, asked this in his Heart until he received the answer in the form of Enlightenment.

KOŚA

Sanskrit: A sheath, a covering, an envelope, a case, a close-fitting structure. The KOŚAs are the bodies which are made up of matter of the various planes and which comprise the various layers of the Aura.

Kosmokratores
Greek: "The Cosmic Creators". The Creator-Gods of the Cosmos. In Hebrew, the Elohīm.

Kosmos
Greek: The World, the Universe. Space *after* Creation. The whole Universe as an ordered, structured Reality, as opposed to Kaos (Chaos: unordered). The Cosmos or Created Universe in its totality, including all seven planes of the Cosmic Physical Plane. Matter organized into structures, forms, shapes, by the One Force or Dynamis. The Divine Mind which gives order and system to all things. Kosmos also means order, system, reason, logic, rule by law. This is the *nature* of the Universe. Hence the English words *cosmos* and *cosmic*. [See Chaos]

Krīṁ (Krīng)
Sanskrit: The Bīja-Mantra for Kālī, the Fearless Goddess. She is the Energizer; She gives energy for intense activity and peak performance. She is total fearlessness and overcomes the insecurities of life and fear of death. She is a protecting and liberating power, the power to see beyond death and destruction. She is Force, Power, Energy, the Life-Force in its primitive untamed form, the Primordial Śakti. She is Liberation from form-life and all kinds of limitation. She is the female Warrior-Force. Kālī is the Goddess Durgā in another form. Durgā, or Kālī, gives Self-Knowledge or Self-Understanding, Yoga (Oneness, Union, Uniting), integration of body, mind and Soul, and Union with God (the Goddess). [See Kālī]

Kriyā
Sanskrit: "Action, acting, doing". A psycho-spiritual-physical exercise, a spiritual technique or process, a meditational process, a psycho-physical technique for Spiritual Enlightenment. The secret of Kriyā has to do with the breath (Prāṇa). At the point where breath becomes peaceful (Prāṇāyāma), Eternity can be *realized.* This is Kriyā. Kriyā is movement from Kri (action) into Yā (Eternity).

Kriyamāna Karma
Sanskrit: New Karma, that which you are creating *now* with your present thoughts, feelings and actions, which will precipitate in the future (in this life-cycle or in future life-cycles). This is added to your stored-up Karma. This same principle applies also to your family or group. [See Prārabdha Karma and Sancitta Karma]

Kriyā-Śakti
Sanskrit: The Energy behind all actions. The creative power of the mind. The power to will, to be, to do. Will-power. Also, the power generated by ritual actions, work, activity. Also, advanced Yogic powers.

Kriyā Yoga
Sanskrit: Active Union, practical Yoga, the Yoga of Action, the act of Union with the Divine. Kriyā Yoga is for men and women of *action*, who live *in* the world but are not *of* the world. It is not for the contemplative monks and recluses who are withdrawn from the world. Kriyā Yoga consists of three parts: Rāja Yoga, Bhakti Yoga and Karma Yoga.

Kṛṣṭa, Kṛṣṇa, Krista
Sanskrit: The Christ within your Soul. Kṛṣṭa means "He who attracts the Soul". It is an ancient Sanskrit term for the Christ in the Heart. Later on, it became Kṛṣṇa (the Dark-Blue), the One who carries the Energy of Viṣṇu (the All-Pervading Godhead). When the Christ within your Soul is *born* you enter the *Lighted Way,* or Supernatural Evolution. This was known in India thousands of years before the birth of Jesus, the Christed One. [See *Christ*]

Kṛta Yuga
Sanskrit: "The accomplished, perfect, good Age". The Golden Age, also called Satya Yuga (the Age of Truth). An evolutionary period, calculated by the Ṛṣis of ancient India to be equivalent to 1,728,000 earth-years.

Kṣānika Samādhi
Sanskrit: The momentary glimpse of the Transcendental Consciousness, Turīya, the Fourth State, the level of Pure Consciousness or Buddhi, the Superconscious Mind. Brief periods of Trance.

Kṣatriya
Sanskrit: A Warrior. The Warrior Class (caste, Varṇa) of India. The kings, rulers, soldiers and politicians.

Kṣti
Sanskrit: The Angelic Ruler of the Physical Plane.

Kuang
Chinese: "The Original Tone". The Eternal Word, the Logos, the Creative-Energy.

Kula
Sanskrit: Family, tribe, nation. A group of people.

Kulakumārī
Sanskrit: She who is the Virgin Goddess, the Eternal-Imperishable-Feminine, for those who worship Her.

Kumāra
Sanskrit: On the Physical Plane, a youth or a young man. In the spiritual language, a mighty Immortal Being who never dies. [See Sanat Kumāra]

Kumārī
Sanskrit: A virgin girl, a maiden, a young girl.

Kumārī, Kumārikā
Sanskrit: The Virgin Girl, the Eternal Goddess. The Virgin Goddess, the Goddess in the Youthful Form, the Eternal Female. A Name of Lalitā, the Goddess.

Kumbhaka
Sanskrit: The restraining of the Prāṇa energies in the invisible central nervous system. In Yoga parlance, the holding of the breath. Kumbhaka has innumerable forms and methods. Inhalation and exhalation is stopped in Kumbhaka, but this must not be the forced holding of the breath of the Haṭha Yogī or the holding of the breath under water of the modern rebirther. This suspension of the breath must be attained by the breath-awareness of the Divine Presence in the Heart. The forced methods present innumerable unhealthy side effects and at times even insanity. [See Prāṇāyāma]

Kuṇḍala
Sanskrit: A serpent.

Kuṇḍalī
Sanskrit: Round, circular, coiled.

Kuṇḍalīn
Sanskrit: Sparkling or decorated with jewellery.

Kuṇḍalinī
Sanskrit: "A curl of the hair of the Beloved" or "the coiled Serpent at the Gate". Kuṇḍalinī is an Energy-Form of the Goddess. The Kuṇḍalinī in your etheric body is the *Life-force* of your physical body. This "serpent" is the same serpent as in Genesis. [See *Serpent-Power*]

Kuṇḍalinī-Fohat
Sanskrit-Tibetan: The Spirit is both Male and Female, yet the Spirit is One. The Electric Male Force of the Spirit is called Fohat (Tibetan). The Magnetic Female Force of the Spirit is called Kuṇḍalinī (Sanskrit). Kuṇḍalinī is the Feminine Creative Energy of the Cosmos. Fohat is the Masculine Creative Energy. Both are Third-Logos Fire, the Third Aspect of the Triune Godhead. Kuṇḍalinī-Fohat is Cosmic-Sexual-Desire-in-Action throughout all species, all planes, all worlds. It is Kuṇḍalinī-Fohat that drives human beings relentlessly to sexual expression. It is the Primordial Creative Urge or Power.

Kuṇḍalinī-Śakti
Sanskrit: "The Serpentine Energy, the Energy that moves like a snake". The Supreme Power, the Universal-Life-Principle in all of Nature and within the whole Universe. Kuṇḍalinī-Śakti is the Universal Presence of the Godhead as the Mother-Force. She is the female Nature-Force in Mankind and in all Kingdoms of Nature. The Kuṇḍalinī is the Evolutionary Force of Nature, which is a Veil over the Face of the World Mother. Her normal activity is the perpetuation and maintenance of the organism. At a certain point of human evolution She will awaken to do Her Liberating Work of transforming a human being into a god or a goddess.

Kuṇḍalinī-Śaktī
Sanskrit: "The Serpent-Power." A Name of Lalitā, the Goddess. She is the great Serpent-Power which is coiled up in the Mūlādhāra Cakra at the base of the spine, and the Fire at the Svādhiṣṭhāna Cakra (the Sex Centre). She is a Fiery Energy, the Energy of Subtle Fire.

Kuṇḍalinī Yoga
Sanskrit: The Path of awakening the Kuṇḍalinī-Śakti, the subtle "Serpent-Power" or dynamic psychic energy. Kuṇḍalinī may also open the awareness to the psychic dimension (the Astral World). Kuṇḍalinī also produces many siddhis (occult and psychic powers), for which the yogīs practise Kuṇḍalinī Yoga. These *hinder* you on the Spiritual Path.

Kungan
Chinese: "A case which establishes a legal precedent". A formulation pointing towards the Truth. [See Kōan]

Kūrmanāḍī
Sanskrit: "Tortoise-nerve". A subtle nerve (Nāḍī) within the Throat Cakra.

Kurukṣetra
Sanskrit: The battlefield of the Bhagavad-Gītā. From Kuru-Kṣetra, "the field of the Kurus". A field called Kuru, in ancient India, where a great battle was fought. In spiritual literature, the word Kurukṣetra refers to the battle between the personality and the Soul—the Spiritual Crisis. [See Armageddon]

Kūṭa
Sanskrit: The Highest Peak. Most Excellent.

Kūṭastha
Sanskrit: "The Highest State to be in" (Kūṭa-Stha). The Kṛṣṇa-Consciousness or Christ-Consciousness. The Universal Formless Christ-Light, the Light of the Formless Kṛṣṇa, which can be perceived in the Third-Eye (Ājñā) Cakra *after* the Heart has been awakened. It is the Source of all things, the Supreme Intelligence in Creation. When you can see It with your Third-Eye, you will be guided by It and have Omniscience in the realm of Spiritual Truth. [See Kṛṣṭa]

Kūṭasthā
Sanskrit: The Immovable One. She is fixed in the Third-Eye Centre as the Perpetual Light. A Name of Lalitā, the Goddess.

Kwan Shin Yin
Chinese: The Heavenly Emperor. The Male Saviour. The Christ in the Heart. (Kwan Yin is the feminine form.)

Kwan Yin
Chinese: The Female Saviour. [See Quan Yin]

Kyōsaku
Japanese: The "big stick", a symbol of Manjusri's "delusion-cutting sword". The idea of the "big stick" was to encourage the Zen Buddhist monks to meditate more fanatically in their quest for Enlightenment. This is not part of the Universal Zen tradition, which was originally much softer and more fluidic.

Kyrie
Greek: God, Lord, Master. The God within your Heart Centre.

L

Laghimā, Laghiman
Sanskrit: Weightlessness, overcoming gravity, levitation. The power to become extremely light. One of the nine "general" powers (Siddhis) which can manifest in advanced Humanity.

Laib (LB)
Hebrew: The Heart.

Lakṣmī
Sanskrit: She who bestows good fortune, wealth, prosperity, growth, development, success, beauty, grace, splendour, charm, lustre, fame, glory. She who is the Splendour of the Eternal Light. The Eternal Beauty. The Perfect Feminine. A Name of Lalitā, the Goddess.

Lālelāya
Sanskrit: The seven-tongued Mystic Flame of the Holy Spirit (the God of Fire).

Lalitā
Sanskrit: The lovely, gentle, beautiful Goddess. Lalitā is the Eternal Female Archetypal Force which expresses Herself as Absolute Beauty, Loveliness, Gentleness, Grace, Innocence, Kindness—the most perfect of all female qualities. She is the Force of true Femininity (without the masculine aggressive and intellectual tendencies). She is lovely, attractive, beautiful, perfect, charming, enchanting, wondrous, desirable, magnetic, pleasing, soft, gentle, sweet, graceful, affectionate, caring, playful, youthful, engaging, loving, energetic. Lalitā is the Shining-Goddess, Jyotī, the Divine Light, the Light-of-Beauty-Wisdom-and-Love. Lalitā is the Beauty which is beyond all things, pervading the whole Universe, transcending all the worlds, brilliant with Light rays. Lalitā is immensely blissful (Ānanda), immensely creative, immensely happy. The whole Universe (visible and invisible) is Her Play, Līlā. She plays within the human being as She plays within the Universe. She is full of playfulness, Līlāmayī. She is the Eternal Feminine, the Eternal Beauty, the Goddess.

Lalitāmbikā (Lalitā-Ambikā)
Sanskrit: The lovely, gentle Divine Mother (Ambikā). The Beautiful Mother. A Name of Lalitā, the Goddess.

Lāṁ
Sanskrit: The Bīja-Mantra for the Cosmic Element *Earth* (the Base Cakra, the Physical Universe).

Laya
Sanskrit: The Zero-Condition, the Rest-State, the Neutral State, the Seed-State, the No-Thingness, the Unmanifest, the Uncreated. Reality, *before* Creation began. The God-Being before the manifested Universal-Evolution. The One Mind, the Primordial Mind, the Homogenous or Single Mind of God.

Laya Yoga
Sanskrit: The organization of the cakras (the psychic force-centres in the etheric body) and Prāṇa, the Life-force. Also, "non-action or zero Yoga", that is, surrendering to the Inner Sound, withdrawing, rest, cessation of outer activities, absorption, concentration, awareness.

Lemuria
The third great epoch, or Root-Race, of human evolution upon this planet, preceding Atlantis. The Lemurian epoch concerned itself with the Physical Plane, with the evolution of the gross physical body and the two lowest cakras—the Base Cakra and the Sex Cakra. The physical body of Man has since been slowly evolving over countless millennia. The Lemurian epoch led to gross magic, black magic, earth-control, and so forth. During this epoch, people could not "feel".

Liberation
The Freedom of the Soul from birth and death in the lower worlds (Saṁsāra, wandering). Freeing your consciousness from the pains, delusions and errors of the lower worlds and experiencing the realms of Buddhi and Nirvāṇa. Being able to live freely in the Spirit, unhindered by your physical body, mind and personality structure. Conscious Immortality. In the West this is known as *Salvation* and *Beatitude*. In Sanskrit, Mokṣa (Freedom) and Mukti (Liberation).

Libido
Latin: Desire, sexual energy, psychic energy. In Astrology, the *libido* is the Mars energy, the energy of aggression, the blind impulse to self-affirmation, the expression of aggression without discrimination or concern for consequences or (often) for others. On the Kabbalistic Tree of Life it is called Geburah. The ancient Greeks called it Eros. In Sanskrit it is called Kāma.

Light
Light is not a metaphor or a symbol. It is real. In fact, it is the only Reality! Light is God-in-Manifestation, God-in-Incarnation, God-in-Expression. Light is God's Presence in Creation. Light is living, conscious, substantial Intelligence. Your Soul is made out of It. The physical light of the Sun, Moon and stars is but a fragment of Light. Light is Substance, Matter of a higher order, many invisible grades of Substance and Essence. Light is many-layered, multi-dimensional. It would take a large book just to describe the various aspects of the Light and its various functions and purposes.

Light is called AUR (ŌR, ŪR) in Hebrew, NUHRĀ in Aramaic, NŪR in Arabic, NŪRĀ in Persian, PHŌS or PHŌTISMOS in Greek, LŪX or LŪMEN in Latin. In Sanskrit there are many words for the Light, such as JYOTI, JYOTIR, JYOTIṢ (the Light of the Sun), PRAKĀŚA (Luminosity, Radiance, Splendour, Glory), ĀDITYA (the Sunshine) and CANDRA (the Cool Moonlight). The Light may be found in the Heart Centre, in the Third-Eye Centre and in the Crown Centre. Light is a Field of Energy emanated by God. When you see the Inner Light, you are *close* to God.

Light Body
A vesture composed of non-material Light energies.

LĪLĀ
Sanskrit: "Play, playful, pleasure, amusement". The Play of God. The Play of the Universal ŚAKTI (Energy). In the state of Transcendental Union with God (SAMĀDHI), when the mind (MANAS) is tranquil, the whole of Creation is seen as a Play of the Goddess (LĪLĀ). The whole Universe, visible and invisible, is the Play of the Goddess. She plays within the human being as She plays within the Universe. She plays the Cosmic Drama, LĪLĀ, in miniature within yourself. She is full of playfulness, LĪLĀMAYĪ.

LĪLĀ-VINODINĪ
Sanskrit: A Name of LALITĀ, the Goddess. LĪLĀ means "play", and VINODINĪ means "She who enjoys playing". The whole Creation is LALITĀ's play. LALITĀ is playful. Creation, Evolution and the final Dissolution of all things are LALITĀ's game.

Limbo
The *limbo* states are states in the etheric-physical body on the subtle levels of the Physical Plane. This is the realm of the "ghosts", the earthbound spirits. Sometimes this term refers to the purgatory conditions of the Astral World.

LIṄGA
Sanskrit: A sign or symbol.

LIṄGA PURĀṆA
Sanskrit: An ancient Scripture that points to the Way.

LIṄGA-ŚARĪRA
Sanskrit: "Symbolic body" or "vital-substance body". The etheric-physical body, which is made up of the four states of etheric-physical matter. The etheric-physical body is the Life-force of your dense physical body. It is made wholly out of forces and energies (PRĀṆAS). Also called PRĀṆAMĀYĀKOŚA (the illusionary vehicle of PRĀṆA). It is also known as the *etheric body*, the *vital body* or the *etheric double*.

LIPIKA
Sanskrit: The Lords of Karma. From LIPI, "to write". The LIPIKA are the writers, scribes or recorders of deeds in the sacred Book of Life (the Akashic Records). They are the *Recording Angels* of the Jewish, Christian and Muslim religions. They are the Archangelic Hosts who administer the karmas of human and angelic beings.

Living Soul
Sanskrit: The Human Soul, dwelling on the formless subplanes of the Mental Plane and reflecting the triune nature of the Universal Being as ĀTMA-BUDDHI-MANAS. The Living Soul is below the Spiritual Soul (BUDDHI), which is in turn below the Spiritual Self (ĀTMAN). Called JĪVA or JĪVĀTMAN in Sanskrit, PSYCHE in Greek, NAFS in Arabic. In the East it is called the *Thinker* and the *Reincarnating Ego* because it takes on a new personality with each new incarnation. When functioning through the personality it is known as AHAṀKĀRA, "I am the doer". This is the personality's sense of "I am". [See JĪVA and AHAṀKĀRA]

Locus Dei
Latin: "The Place of God". The Spiritual Heart Centre, where Man meets God and God meets Man.

Logiki-Psyche
Greek: "Logical Soul". A Deified Soul. A spiritualized human being, possessed of spiritual experience.

Logikos
Greek: True Intelligence. Spiritual in perception. Hence the English words *logic* and *logical.* To the classical Greeks and early Christians, however, the word Logikos meant to be intelligent in the *true* sense of that word—not to be merely rational, but rather, to be *spiritual* in perception. One who is Logikos possesses Divine Intelligence.

Logion, Logia, Logoi
Greek: Mantras, sayings, utterances, axioms, words of power, spiritual truths, principles. In the early days of the church the instructions and sayings of Jesus were called Logia. Hundreds of gospels, epistles and writings were circulating, of which just a small fragment now form the New Testament. Some of these Logia, or Logoi (sayings), formed an oral tradition which was never written down, while others were written down and some became part of the gospels. Towards the end of the second century, the four gospels of today's New Testament were declared to be the only authentic gospels and, from then on, all other writings were declared to be heretical.

Logoi
Greek: The plural of Logos. The doctrine of the Logoi was a well established Greek doctrine before Christianity. According to the Christian fathers, the Logoi are "thoughts of God, principles of God, essences of God", the "seeds of things" from which all things come into existence according to their own inherent natures, God's *inner Plan* for them. One can understand the Christian Logoi doctrine only by understanding the previous Greek doctrine of Logoi. For instance, each sun or star is a Logos. Collectively, all the stars, planets, solar systems and universes are Logoi.

Logos
Greek: Literally, "a word, a saying, a discourse, a thought, an idea, a proportion, a ratio, order, reckoning, a science", from the verb Legein, "to choose, to gather, to recount, to tell, to speak". To the Greek Mystery Schools, the Logos was the Creative Word of God, the Universal Creative Intelligence, the Wisdom of God as a *Power,* the Source of Creation, the Cosmic Fatherhood, the Source of all things, the Creative God who created the Universe and in whom the Universe exists (Cosmic Logos), or who created the Solar System (Solar Logos). Logos has the same meaning as the ancient Sanskrit words Vāk, Śabda-Brahman and Daiviprākṛtī: the Creative Potency, the Universal Creative Sounding-Light Vibration, the Universal or Cosmic Christ, Divine Reason, the Fountainhead of All That Is. The Logos is a Force, a Power, a Dynamic Energy, the Kāraṇa (cause) of the Universe. God "uttered" the Universe into being. The Christians borrowed this idea from the Greeks: the Logos is the "Word" of the Christian Bible. The Christian fathers adapted the Logos doctrine to Christianity as follows: the *Father* is the First Logos; the *Son* (or Christ) is the Second Logos; and the *Holy Spirit* is the Third Logos. Yet there is only One God (One Cosmic Logos).

Loka
Sanskrit: A place, a realm, a world, a plane, an abode, a dimension, a kingdom, a sphere.

Lokaika
Sanskrit: Of the World.

Lolitā
Sanskrit: She who is full of activity, agitation, tremor, vibration, passion, action, adventure, excitement. A Name of Lalitā, the Goddess.

Lord
Ruler or Commander. The "personal" God, the Immanent God. Īśa or Īśvara in Sanskrit, El or Adonai in Hebrew. In the Christian Bible the Hebrew words Elohīm, Elohīm-Jehovah and Jehovah are continually mistranslated as "Lord" when, in fact, none of these words suggest a personal God. [See Jehovah]

Lords of Fire
The First Manifest Creative Hierarchy, also called the *Divine Flames* and the *Fiery Lions*.

Lotus Flower
The Eastern symbol for the Heart Centre. The lotus flower also represents all the lotuses (cakras) in the human system. The lotus flower is also a symbol for LAKṢMĪ, that aspect of LALITĀ which gives fortune, prosperity, success in all fields of action. In the Western Mystical Tradition the analogous symbol is the *Rose*. [See PADMA and KAMALA]

Love
Love is an Energy. It is not just a thought or a nice idea. It is a Force, a Power.
- There is personality Love.
- There is Soul Love (Group Love).
- There is Divine Love (Cosmic Love).

Love is not sex. The sexual energy is astral-etheric. In a human being the Energy of Love is found in the Heart Centre.

Lower Mind
The rational mind or concrete mind. In Sanskrit, RŪPA-MANAS (form-mind). It is the activity of the mental body (MĀNASA-RŪPA), functioning on the lower (form) levels of the Mental Plane. This is the common mind, the ordinary intellect, which is connected to the region of the brain between the physical eyes. The brain-mind is cold, abstract, impersonal, analytical, intellectual, heartless, feelingless. It is critical, aggressive, competitive, selective, myopic and limited in its approach. It looks at small segments, never the whole picture. It is slow, methodical and laborious in its approach to Truth. It can become devious, dogmatic and full of errors, and fanatical in defending those errors. It is separative and isolationist. Society is based on such a mind. This is its failure. Most people nowadays are stuck in the brain-mind due to the influence of their upbringing and the worldly education system.

LŪCIFER
Latin: "Light-Bearer". Splendid with Light. Having the Nature of Light. A name commonly attributed to "the Devil". According to medieval Christians, Lucifer was of the angelic order of the Seraphim. According to others, he was of the angelic order of the Archangels, which is one class above the angels.

LUCIS CREATOR
Latin: The Creative Light. The Light of the Universal Christ, the LOGOS.

Lunar Pitṛis
"Lunar Ancestors". The Lunar Angels, or less-evolved spirits, dwelling on the Astral Plane. [See PITṚI]

LUNG-TAN
Chinese: Enlightenment, Awakening, Illumination, Mystical Union. Also called WU. The experience of BUDDHI, or Superconsciousness. The same as the Sanskrit BODHI and the Japanese SATORI.

LŪX, LŪMEN
Latin: "Light". Illumination, Radiance, Glory, Enlightenment, Pure Consciousness, Superior Intelligence, Brightness, Illuminative Substance. [See *Light*]

LŪX AETERNA
Latin: The Eternal Light. The Light of the Universal Christ, the LOGOS.

LYPI
Greek: Sorrow, contrition, repentance. Being sorry for one's imperfections.

M

Macrocosm
[See MAKROKOSMOS]

MADHYAMĀ, MADHYAMĀVĀK, MADHYAMĀVĀCH
Sanskrit: Astral and Causal sound-vibration. Subtle sounds, issuing from the subtle universe. [See VAIKHARĪ and PAŚYANTĪ]

MADONNA
Latin (from the Greek): The Mother Principle of the Great Feminine Intelligence. The World Mother. MADONNA is the *softness* of the true Feminine Principle—gentleness, true Love and Compassion. Madonna is sweet, gentle, kind, caring, innocent, harmless, non-violent, soft. Sometimes you meet young girls born with these qualities, before they are destroyed by the worldly system.

MAGA
Sanskrit: A Priest of the Sun. A Magician.

MAGI
Zoroastrian and Persian: A Magician. A Sage. One who controls the forces of the Cosmos by Will and Knowledge. In the ancient world, the MAGI, or Wisemen, were a superior class, well versed in the *real* Magic, the Laws of Mind.

MAGOS
Greek: A Magician. A Wiseman.

MAGUS
Latin: One who controls the subtle forces of Nature by mental means. A Magician.

MAGNĒS
Greek: The Spirit of Light, the Cosmic Fire, the Living Fire, the Spiritual Fire. The same as the Sanskrit KUṆḌALINĪ (Serpent-Fire). This is the Cosmic Power that attracts the atoms together. Hence the English words *magnet* and *magnetic*.

MAGNUM OPUS
Latin: "The Great Work". The Spiritual Path, Discipleship, Mind Re-Creation, Union with God. The Western term for the Path of YOGA or YOGA-MĀRGA, the Science of Spiritual Regeneration. The term was used widely by the Alchemists of Medieval Europe.

MAHĀ
Sanskrit: Great, mighty, powerful, omnipotent, vast, endless, absolute, limitless.

MAHĀ-AṆIMĀ
Sanskrit: Reaching beyond the experience of the Cosmic Physical Plane (our seven-layered Cosmic Plane). The Cosmic Vision of the Subtlest, or the Glimpse of the Cosmic Astral Plane, which is like a Limitless Subtlety pervading the seven-layered Cosmic Space of our Universe. MAHĀ-AṆIMĀ is one of the "Cosmic Powers".

MAHĀ-AVATĀRA
Sanskrit: "Great-Divine-Incarnation". Also called PŪRṆA-AVATĀRA, "Perfect Incarnation of God". These great Incarnations descend from the Monadic Plane. The four greatest Incarnations of Divinity on Earth in living memory were RĀMA, who gave Mankind Righteousness; KṚṢṆA, who gave Mankind Devotion; BUDDHA, who gave Mankind Wisdom; and the CHRIST (YESHUA HA-MASHIAH), who gave Mankind Love. [See AVATĀRA]

MAHĀ-DEVĪ
Sanskrit: The Absolute Goddess. The Great Goddess, who gives Perfection, Wholeness, Fullness, Completeness, SAMASTI (Unity) and YOGA (Union). The Goddess in Her Cosmic Nature, boundless, measureless. The whole Creation or Manifestation is simply Her Body.

MAHAH-LOKA
Sanskrit: The Realm of BUDDHI. The Buddhic Plane.

MAHĀ-ĪŚATVA
Sanskrit: The ability to rule over all Creation within the sevenfold Cosmic Physical Plane. MAHĀ-ĪŚATVA is one of the "Cosmic Powers".

Mahā-Īśvarī
[See Maheśvarī]

Mahākāla
Sanskrit: The Lord of Time (Śiva).

Mahākālī
Sanskrit: The Goddess Durgā.

Mahā-Kāma-Avasāyitva
Sanskrit: The fulfilment of Cosmic Desire. This is one of the "Cosmic Powers".

Mahā-Laghimā
Sanskrit: Cosmic Weightlessness. That is, not being bound to our Cosmic Physical Plane, but being able to ascend out of even our highest Solar-Systemic Plane, Ādi, into the Boundless Cosmic Astral Realms. One of the "Cosmic Powers".

Mahā-Mahimā
Sanskrit: The experience of the Infinite Vastness of the Universal or Boundless Self, the Vastness of the Cosmic Mind. One of the "Cosmic Powers".

Mahāmantra
Sanskrit: "The Great Sound". The Eternal Word. The Logos. The Creative-Energy.

Mahāmanvantara
Sanskrit: "The Great Age of Creation". A period of Manifestation, which includes the Seven Days of Creation, or seven vast cycles of time, many millions of earth-years each. This includes the stages before the physical manifestation of the Universe, the appearance of the entire Universe, and its total evolutionary unfoldment. [See Manvantara]

Mahāmāyā
Sanskrit: "The Great Illusion" (Mahā-Māyā). The Great Cosmic Illusion of matter and form, substance and energy. The phenomenal worlds (the Physical, Astral and Mental Planes).

Mahāmuni
Sanskrit: The Great Sage, the Superior Self.

Mahāparanirvāṇa
Sanskrit: "The Great Plane beyond or above Nirvāṇa". The Logoic Realm. The Initial Existence on the Cosmic Physical Plane. Also called Ādi (the First Plane) or Satya-Loka (the Realm of Truth). This is the realm of Brahman, the Logos, the Godhead. Any being who experiences this realm has already passed beyond human evolution.

Mahā-Parā-Siddhi
Sanskrit: Going into the Great Transcendent, breaking with the Immanent Aspect of Deity, going beyond the Beyond, leaving the Cosmic Physical Plane, going beyond the boundaries of our Sevenfold Universe altogether, severing one's roots with this Universe, going through one of the Seven Cosmic Gates. Annihilation into the next Cosmic Plane of Being, the Cosmic Astral. Mahā-Parā-Siddhi is one of the "Cosmic Powers".

Mahāprajñāparamitā
Sanskrit: "Great Wisdom-Transcendental" or "the Great Wisdom of the Other Shore reached". The Nirvāṇic Consciousness. The Mind of Light. The Mystic, having attained to "the Great Wisdom of the Other Shore reached", Nirvāṇa, realizes the Original-Mind of the Universe. This is the stage *beyond* Bodhi, one plane above the Buddhic Plane of Being.

Mahā-Prākāmya
Sanskrit: One of the "Cosmic Powers". The Cosmic Astral Plane is perceived as the Universal Desire Nature, the foundation and root upon which the Cosmic Physical Plane (our Sevenfold Universe) exists, and the reason why it came into existence.

Mahāpralaya
Sanskrit: "The Great Dissolution" (Mahā-Pralaya). The Seven Eternities *before* Creation commenced. [See Pralaya]

Mahā-Prāṇa
Sanskrit: The Great Breath. The Breath of God. The Holy Spirit.

Mahā-Prāpti
Sanskrit: The experience of Pervading the whole Cosmos. One of the "Cosmic Powers".

Mahārṣi (Mahā-Ṛṣi)
Sanskrit: "A Great Seer". A Ṛṣi is a See-er, a Sage who has seen the Truth first-hand, by direct experience, beyond the mental faculty. A Mahārṣi is one who has seen the Absolute, Parabrahman.

Mahāśakti (Mahā-Śakti)
Sanskrit: The Cosmic Field that embraces all other fields of force.

Mahāśaktī
Sanskrit: "The Omnipotent Power". A Name of Lalitā, the Goddess.

Mahāśūnyatā
Sanskrit: "The Great Void". The Great Space. Cosmic Space. The Original Divine Nirvāṇa-Space. The Absolute Emptiness of Nirvāṇa. The Source of All.

Mahā-Svastika-Śakti
Sanskrit: The Great-Sign-of-Galaxies, or the Cosmic Power that creates and dissolves Universes. The Miracle is right in front of your eyes when you watch the night sky.

Mahat
Sanskrit: "The Great One, the Great Intelligence". The Divine Mind, the Cosmic Mind, the Cosmic Mental Plane. Mahat is the *operative* Mind, the ordering and disposing Mind, which is the Cause (Kāraṇa) of all things. It is the Cause of the Cosmic Physical Plane. Mahat is God's Infinite Mind, the Universal Mind which animates Creation, the manifested Omniscience of God. It is Mahat, the Cosmic Mind, which creates order and system out of Praḍhāna, the Primordial Matter, during every great Day of Manifestation, called Manvantara.

Mahat-Prākṛtī
Sanskrit: Cosmic-Nature. The Seven Great Planes of Being, and everything within them. Cosmic Prākṛtī.

Mahātma
Sanskrit: "Great Soul". From Mahā (great) and Ātman (Spirit or Self). In classical spirituality the Mahātmas are called the Masters, Elder Brothers and Sisters, Seers, Wisemen, Wisewomen, Perfected Ones or Saints. While in physical bodies they usually have Buddhic Consciousness or Causal Consciousness. The Mahātmas are *Self-Realized.*

Mahā-Tripurā-Sundarī
Sanskrit: "The Great Threefold Beauty". The Beautiful Goddess within the three bodies (physical, astral and mental) and within the Three Worlds (the Physical, Astral and Mental Planes). From Mahā (great, omnipotent, vast), Tri (three), Purā (cities, towns, worlds, realms, bodies) and Sundarī (exquisitely beautiful). A Name of Lalitā, the Goddess. Also, the Śrī-Vidyā-Vajra-Mantra.

Mahāvākya
Sanskrit: "Great Truth Statement" or "Great Word of Power" (Mahā-Vākya). A Word of Truth, a Word of God, an important mantra or affirmation. Vākya (Vāk) means "Divine Speech, the Logos, the Word, or a Word of Power". In the higher sense, Mahāvākya is the pulsation of Truth in the Divine Mind. In our human consciousness it is the Insight into the Mysteries of Being and of the Cosmos. It is the ancient Eastern form of Metanoia.

Mahā-Vaśitva
Sanskrit: Mastery over the whole Cosmic Physical Plane (all the worlds and realms of the seven planes of our Universe). One of the "Cosmic Powers".

Mahāvidehā Siddhi
Sanskrit: "The Great Bodiless State". From Mahā (great) and Videhā (without a body). What is the Great Disembodied State? It is when your consciousness is free of your physical, etheric-physical, astral and mental bodies—that is, when

your consciousness can function above and beyond your personality structure, when you are in Buddhic Consciousness, on the Buddhic Plane. Then the Veil is taken off your Eye and the Light of Ātman shines clear to your Buddhic Vision. This is the *Beatific Vision* of the Christian Mystics.

Mahāvīra
Sanskrit: "Great Hero".

Mahā-Vidyā
Sanskrit: Cosmic Mind, Cosmic Intelligence. A Name of Lalitā, the Goddess.

Mahā-Yuga
Sanskrit: "Great Age". The total period of the Kṛta, Tretā, Dvāpara and Kali Yugas, calculated by the Ṛṣis of ancient India to be equivalent to 4,320,000 earth-years.

Maheśa, Maheśvara
Sanskrit: "The Great God" (Mahā-Īśa or Mahā-Īśvara). A Name for Śiva. Śiva is the Puruṣa (Spirit), and His Śakti is the Female Power or Energy called Prākṛtī (Nature). Śakti is the Energy or Power of Śiva.

Maheśvarī (Mahā-Īśvarī)
Sanskrit: The Great Goddess, the Omnipotent Protector. From Īśvarī (She who rules, guides, protects). Mahā-Īśvarī is the Supreme Being, the Mistress of the Universe. A Name of Lalitā, the Goddess. Also called Mahā-Prākṛtī.

Mahimā, Mahiman
Sanskrit: Glory, Limitlessness, Majesty. Also, a type of spiritual vision through which you perceive extremely large things. This can manifest as planetary vision, solar-systemic vision or, larger still, seeing vast portions of the Universal Manifestation. This is one of the nine "general" powers (Siddhis) which can manifest in advanced Humanity.

Mahī-Mātā
Sanskrit: Mighty Mother, Cosmic Mother.

Maitreya
Sanskrit: "The Compassionate One". Friendly, compassionate, benevolent. It was the Lord Christ, Īśa-Maitreya, who overshadowed that Great Master who was called Joshua (Jesus). Maitreya is the World Teacher, the Teacher of Angels and Man, who is responsible for the spiritual development of the Angelic species and Mankind upon this planet. Maitreya looks after all religious development upon this planet through His agents, the Spiritual Teachers, Saints, Yogīs, Adepts and Mystics, in all religions (Christianity being but one of them). Maitreya is the Heart of the Spiritual Hierarchy of our planet. [See *Christ*]

Makara
Sanskrit: "Sea monsters, crocodiles". (The sea is the Astral Plane.) The Fifth Creative Hierarchy, also known as Asuras. From the Makara came the "fallen angels", the *rebellious angels* of all ancient mythologies, of all great religions of old. They cause chaos and disorder in our Solar System. They are actually great Spiritual Beings who have developed the sense of "I" or independent egos. And it was they, some time in the far-off history of the planet, who gave the sense of individuality to Mankind—the sense of ego, "I am-ness", selfishness, self-will, individualism. Only the Fourth Creative Hierarchy (the Human) and the Fifth (the Makara) have the faculty of Ahaṁkāra (I am the doer), the sense of ego or "I", the freedom of will to choose between right and wrong, good and evil. The Egyptian Mysteries also used the crocodile as a symbol for these beings. [See Asura]

Makrokosmos
Greek: "Large universe". From Makro (large) and Kosmos (a world or universe). A Macrocosm (Makrokosmos) is a solar system, which has a family of planets. Our Sun (the Solar Logos), for instance, is one Living Being, the Soul of our Macrocosm, and the planets are His personality expression. Thus, each solar system is a Cosmic Soul along with His or Her personality complex. Each planet or star is multidimensional, in the same way as is a Microcosm (a human being). A planet or star is a larger Man. [See Mikrokosmos and Chiliokosmos]

Makroposophus
Greek: The Great Face of God. The Sublime Countenance. This word was much used by the Jewish Kabbalists for the Ain Soph Aur (Boundless Light). The Infinite Light is not just an impersonal light, like a candle or a torch flame; it is a *Living Intelligence,* a *Cosmic Mind,* a *Cosmic Person.* In the East this Limitless Ocean of Light has been symbolized as the Amitābha Buddha.

Malachīm
Hebrew: One sent by God. Messengers from God or from Divine Realms. Angels. The *rebellious* angels were called Nephilīm.

Malīk
Arabic: The King, whose Radiance and Glory never dies, from Age to Age, until the end of Time.

Mālikul Mulk
Arabic: The Lord of the World.

Mālikul Raḥīm
Arabic: The King of Mercy.

Malkān Malkā
Arabic: The King of Kings.

Malkuth
Hebrew: "The Kingdom" of the Jewish Kabbalah. The Physical World, which is a projection from the Astral World above it, called Yesod (the Foundation).

Man
Man is an old English (Teutonic) word, synonymous with the Latin Homo and the Hebrew Adam, which means "a human being, a human creature", as distinct from the Animal, Vegetable or Angelic Kingdoms. The word *Man* refers to the human species, the genus of the human race, of both male and female genders. It does not mean only males. *Man* or *Mankind* is "the two-legged species with the thinking brain." Esoterically, *Man* is that Being in the Universe in which the highest Spirit (the Monad) is conjoined to the lowest matter (the physical body) by the Intelligent Principle (the mind). In Sanskrit, Manuṣya or Nara.

Manas
Sanskrit: Mind. The ruling, regulating, creative, ordering principle. The intelligent purpose of some being, working out into active objectivity. In Man, the principle of Manas has two aspects:
- Higher Mind, Kāraṇa-Manas (Causal Mind), which is abstract and formless.
- Lower mind, Rūpa-Manas (form-mind). The lower mind is usually tinged with desire, thus producing Kāma-Manas (desire-mind).

Mānasa
Sanskrit: Pertaining to the mind; of the nature of the mind. Mental powers or intention. Can also refer to the Heart or Soul, or a spiritual centre.

Mānasadeva
Sanskrit: The Radiating Mind, Mind Glorious with Light, a Resplendent Being of the Cosmic Mind, a Mind that is filled with Glory and Might. An Angel of Light. A Mind-Angel. A Man also becomes a Mānasadeva when he/she reaches Perfection in the Spirit (Ātman).

Mānasa-Loka
Sanskrit: "The Realm of Mind". The Mental Plane. The Heaven Worlds, the seven regions where Mind is most creative and expressive. This is Devāchan, the realm of the true Thinker, the Reincarnating Ego.

Mānasa-Mārga
Sanskrit: "The Way of the Mind". Also known as Rāja Yoga (the Royal Way) and Citta-Mārga (the Way of Intelligence). This Way is centred in your Head. It consists of cultivating Awareness, Consciousness, being in the Moment through total Awareness, using the *total* Mind. This Way is *not* about thinking or theorising, using your ordinary, rational mind.

Mānasa-Pūja
Sanskrit: "Mental worship". This means having your mind (Manas) in your Heart (Hṛdayaṁ), and doing your worship there.

Mānasaputra
Sanskrit: A Mind-Born Being (Mānasa-Putra). The Mānasaputras (Sons of the Mind) are the spiritual fathers of Humanity, the Solar Pitṛis or Solar Angels. They are an Angelic Order of high evolution which gave the Principle of Mind (the mental and causal bodies) to Humanity on this planet. Before this, the humans on this planet could not "think" as they do now. They had no mental activity! The angels (Devas) are *Children of the Mind*, as is Man as a species and individually, but Mankind does not know it or realize it.

Mānasa-Rūpa
Sanskrit: "Mind-body". The mental body, when not in conjunction with the astral and physical bodies. The mental body is composed of matter from the four lower subplanes of the Mental Plane—those which have form, Rūpa. This is the lower Manas, the ordinary rational mind. Also, Mano-Rūpa.

Manasi-Jā
Sanskrit: "Things born from the mind". Thoughtforms, existing in the mental body. In your natural condition, you are completely surrounded by your thoughtforms. Although you cannot see them with your physical eyes, your thoughts are objective, real, and you could see them if you had mental clairvoyance. These thoughtforms block your perception of Reality. When you drop your mental activity, you will come to know the *Things that Are*.

Manas-Taijasi
Sanskrit: "Radiant Mind". The Mind of Light. From Manas (mind) and Taijasi (Radiance, Light, Illumination, Splendour). The condition in which, after a long period of meditation, the ordinary mind (Manas) is flooded with the Light of the Divine Immortal Soul (Buddhi), and one *knows* things in terms of Fields of Light rather than as separate objects. This Mind is also known as Buddhi-Manas, or Wisdom-Mind.

Maṇḍala
Sanskrit: A circle, a group; inner space, an enclosure; a world view; a mystic symbol for meditation.

Maṇi
Sanskrit: A jewel, a pearl, a precious stone; an ornament, a magnet, a treasure; something precious.

Maṇi-Padma
Sanskrit: "The Jewelled Lotus". The innermost sanctuary of the Heart Centre wherein dwells the Spirit of God, the Saviour, the Deliverer, the Avalokiteśvara (the downward-looking Lord, the Lord who looks down from on High), the Higher Self in Humanity, the Logos in the Solar System, the Inner Spiritual Guide of the Soul (the Monad). The Maṇi, or Jewel, is the *Spirit-Spark-Atom* of the Imperishable Kingdom of Light, Nirvāṇa, the true Kingdom of God. It is the Pure Light of the Spirit visible in the innermost Cave or Chamber of the Heart, the Spark or Flame of Divinity, a brilliant Electric Fire. The Innermost Temple of the Heart, the Seventh Portal, the Jewel in the Lotus, is where the Triune Self (Ātma-Buddhi-Manas, the Spiritual Trinity in Humanity) finds a focal point of energy and expression. [See *Spirit-Spark-Atom*]

Maṇipūra Cakra
Sanskrit: The Solar Plexus Centre. The cakra in the human system most closely associated with lower feelings and emotions, lower psychism and the Astral World.

Manobhrānti
Sanskrit: Identification with Kāma-Manas, the combined desire-nature and thinking apparatus, therefore being deluded by the mind. From Manas (mind) and Bhrānti (worldly consciousness, erroneous thinking, being subject to glamour).

Mano-Gata
Sanskrit: A concept existing in your mind. While all people have countless thoughts in their mental bodies, some are true but most are not. A *true* thought is a thought that reflects how things *really are* in relation to the Truth of yourself and the Great Invisible. Thoughts which are speculation, theories or hypotheses, blindly acquired by tradition, custom or habit, without substantiation, are *false* thoughts.

People cling to these false thoughts, whether they be religious, political, scientific, psychological, cultural, social or whatever, and they are ready to defend these false thoughts with their lives.

Manogranthi

Sanskrit: Conditioned by the mind and the mental world. Identification with Kāma-Manas, the combined desire-nature and thinking apparatus, which limits the Free Flow of Pure Consciousness. From Manas (mind) and Granthi (a knot, a barrier, a conditioning).

Manohara

Sanskrit: The suspension of the activities of the mind. This is true meditation. People find it difficult to meditate (in the true sense) because this Age is characterized by an intense over-activity of the mind.

Manojavitva Siddhi

Sanskrit: The ability to move or transport one's physical body rapidly anywhere in the world over any distance and to appear anywhere physically. The Yogī or Siddha accomplishes this by focused mental power in combination with Awakened Soul Energy. This is one form of the Avatāra Siddhi (Divine-Descent power). Also called Mano-Java Siddhi.

Mano-Jyoti

Sanskrit: The Light of the Mind.

Manolaya

Sanskrit: The mind which has been neutralized, dissolved.

Manomāyākośa

Sanskrit: "The illusionary mind-sheath". Kāma-Manas. The mental and astral bodies working in conjunction. In the ordinary human being, thoughts (Manas) and desires (Kāma) are mixed, and together they form the principle of Manomāyākośa. Also called Manomayakośa (the consisting-of-mind sheath).

Manomayī

Sanskrit: She who is composed of Mind (Manas). She whose Nature (Mayī) is Mind. A Name of Lalitā, the Goddess. Mind is a manifold reality: Kāma-Manas (the ordinary mind of a human being, full of desires, wishes and longings); Buddhi-Manas (the Enlightened Mind, the Mind of a Sage or Enlightened Being); Mahat (Cosmic Mind, Cosmic Intelligence, Universal Mind, the Mind of a super-advanced Being, the Mind of the Deity).

Manonāśa

Sanskrit: Inactive-mind. When your mind is made all-harmonious and tranquil (Samādhi), Reality appears to your Inner Gaze as the Luminous Light-Being which is within All, and which is your very Self.

Mano-Rūpa

Sanskrit: "Mind-body". The mental body. [See Mānasa-Rūpa]

Mano-Śakti

Sanskrit: The Power generated by thought, thinking and mental activity.

Manovijñāna

Sanskrit: Thought-patterns.

Mantra, Mantram

Sanskrit: "An instrument of the mind, a thinking-tool, an instrument of thought, a mental creation, a thought-vibration". From Manas (mind) and Tra (a tool or instrument). Tra also means "to transcend" and "to protect". Thus, a Mantra is an instrument of your mind, it protects your mind, and it also helps you to transcend the mind. Mantra is most often identified with *sound.* Mantra is Sonic Science, the science of Transformation by sound-vibrations. A Mantra is a magic song, an incantation, a charm, a spell, a sacred scripture text, a purposefully-structured thoughtform or sound-form, a powerful sound-wave, or the key note or vibration of a thing. A Mantra is a vibration, a frequency, a rhythm, a beat, a sound that penetrates deeply into Consciousness. A Mantra is a sound-pattern. It can be physical, astral, mental or causal vibration. The subtle sound-patterns (astral, mental or causal) are just as "real" as the physical sound-patterns and are perceived by the astral, mental and causal bodies. A Mantra produces not only sound, but also colour vibrations and a form, as well as an energy (MANTRA-ŚAKTI). A Mantra is the direct embodiment of the Goddess, literally the incarnation of the Goddess in the form of VĀK, the Divine Speech, the Divine Word or Creative Power. A Mantra is a Divine Name, a Word of Power that connects you to different aspects of Consciousness. Mantra directly affects your Consciousness (CIT) and your Mind (CITTA). There are two basic applications of Mantras:

- For the projection of sound into the environment, as in dynamic singing, chanting and bhajans.
- For inward meditation, to transcend and suspend the mental processes, which is the aim of the silent repetition of Mantras.

A Mantra is a sound-formula outwardly chanted, intoned or sung, or inwardly spoken, sung and *realized*. Mantras, in Sanskrit, Hebrew, Arabic, Greek, Latin and Chinese, are Energy-Units to stimulate your Higher Evolution and your Transformation into the likeness of the God-Being within you.

MANTRA-BĪJA
Sanskrit: A "Seed-Mantra" or "key-note". [See BĪJA-MANTRA]

MANTRA-DEVATĀ
Sanskrit: The Deity of a Mantra.

MANTRA-JAPA
Sanskrit: "Mantra repetition". The repetition of a Mantra wilfully, devotionally, actively, with vigour, liveliness, energy. This will increase those qualities inside you which the Mantra represents. In the AJAPA technique (the non-repetitive or spontaneous method) you gradually reduce the vibration of the Mantra and allow it to swing upwards or inwards, thus ascending the realms of mind to arrive at the Soul-Realm, or Self-Realization. [See AJAPA]

MANTRA ṚṢI
Sanskrit: A Mantra Sage. A Master of the Science of Mantras.

MANTRA-ŚAKTI
Sanskrit: The Power generated by Mantras. The energy of certain types of sound. A Mantra is an energy-field, and outside this energy-field (ŚAKTI) the Mantra is useless. Although a Mantra may be revealed in a book, you must receive the MANTRA-ŚAKTI (MANTRIKĀ-ŚAKTI) from a person *empowered* with the energy of the Mantra—a MANTRA YOGĪ or MANTRA ṚṢI. Such a person has the MANTRA-ŚAKTI inherent in a particular Mantra, which is a real energy-field, a vibration, a sound frequency.

MANTRA-SĀRĀ
Sanskrit: The Essence of all Mantra. A Name of LALITĀ, the Goddess. The Mantric Vibrations of special sound-formulas are Her embodiments or forms—not only the specific female Mantras, but all other Mantras as well. She incarnates in Mantras.

MANTRA ŚĀSTRA
Sanskrit: Books dealing with the Science of Mantras.

MANTRA TANTRA
Sanskrit: The use of Mantras in Tantric (esoteric) works.

MANTRA YOGA
Sanskrit: The Science of the Creative Word. Sound-formulas, frequencies, music. That aspect of Yoga which utilizes Mantras for attainment.

MANTRA YOGA SĀDHANĀ
Sanskrit: The practice of Mantra Yoga.

MANTRA YOGĪ
Sanskrit: A practitioner of the Science of Mantra Yoga.

MANTREŚVARA (MANTRA-ĪŚVARA)
Sanskrit: The ĪŚVARA (Deity) or Force connected with a Mantram.

Mantrikāśakti (Mantrikā-Śakti)
Sanskrit: The Power of Sound. The Power of the Logos. The specific power of a Mantram (Mantra-Śakti).

Manu
Sanskrit: "Thinking Man". The Primordial Mind, the Mind-into-Expression, the Archetypal Mind. The Primordial Man, Primeval Mankind, the first human race of this planet. The same as the Greek Anthropos (from which is derived the word *anthropology*) and the Hebrew Adam-Kadmon (which is male-female, like the words Jehovah, Eloah and Elohīm).

Manuṣya
Sanskrit: The Human Kingdom. The Human Creative Hierarchy. Pertaining to human beings (Man) as distinct from angelic beings (Devas).

Manvantara
Sanskrit: "Day of God". A Day of Creation, a Day of Manifestation, a Creation or Cycle of Evolution. The period or age of the creation and continuation of an object in Space. A period of Evolution, large or small. At the end of Creation, when the Evolutionary processes are completed, all is reabsorbed into Pralaya, which is absolute Rest, the pre-cosmic Divine Darkness, the Night of God.

Māra
Sanskrit: Opposition. Even the Buddha struggled with opposition.

Mārga
Sanskrit: Evolution. The Path, the Way, the Road. The Spiritual Path. The ideal life-model.

Marīa
Latin: The Divine Mother Substance or Essence. Marīa is a Holy Name. The Name is Holy because it carries Her Qualities, Presence and Vibration. The *rose flower* is the symbol of the Heart of the Mother.

- Virgo Marīa (Virgin Mary) refers to the Eternal Feminine's Transcendental Nature, beyond and above the created Universe, spotless, pure, incorruptible, forever shining Bright. [See *Virgin Goddess*]
- Mater Marīa (Mother Mary) refers to the Eternal Feminine as the Mother of all that is, of all Creation, of all created beings. (Therefore She is our Mother also.)
- Marīa (Mary) refers to the Mother of Jesus who was the Christ, She who is the representative of the Great Feminine Intelligence for our planet Earth. [See *Our Lady*]

Marica
Sanskrit: Rays of Light.

Marīcyāditya
Sanskrit: The Radiant Sun. From Marīci (glowing, raying out Light-Waves) and Āditya (the Primordial Solar Logos, the Original-Creative-Force).

Ma'rifat
Arabic: Gnosis, Enlightenment. The seventh stage of the Journey of the Heart, where you have inner insights, revelations from within the Heart, spiritual experiences that transform your life or give a new meaning to your life, profound understandings, glimpses of Self-Realization, glimpses of Divine Unity, deep sympathy with all that lives, and insights into why you need to serve (help) Mankind. The word Ma'rifat can also refer to the final stages of Mysticism, the Height of Mystical Union, Deification, the state where only God's Light exists, in which there is no day or night, no birth or death, no coming or going, no advancement or delay, no Time or Space. It is Conscious Immortality, the Kingdom of God, where everything is *known* as it really *is*. It is the stage of Inner Knowing, called "the Secret of the Messengers".

Mārtaṇḍa
Sanskrit: He who was born from the Cosmic-Egg (Space). The Sun-God, the Solar Logos.

Mashiah, Mashiach

Hebrew: "The Anointed of God" (Mashi-Jah). The Messiah. The word has the same meaning as the Greek Christos. Mashiah also means "the Salvation of the Living God (Jah)" or "only the Living God saves". Mashiah is itself an abbreviation of Mashiah-Jehovah, "the Eternal God's Anointed One, the Eternal God's Salvation, the Eternal is the Saviour". The *Messiah* is the old Hebrew idea of the Divine Incarnation, the Sanskrit Avatāra or Divine Descent, for the redemption of Mankind. [See Avatāra]

Mashiah Adonai

Hebrew: "The Anointed One of the Lord". A Divine King. The ancient peoples rubbed oil, as a token of respect and veneration, upon kings, rulers and admired religious or political figures.

Mashiah Ben Adam

Hebrew: In the pre-Christian Jewish world, the Messiah was regularly called Mashiah Ben Adam or Mashiah Ben David. These were titles (not names) which have been translated as "Son of Man", meaning that the Messiah will be from the Man-species, that He will be human with divine qualities. [See Ben Adam]

Mashiah Nagid

Hebrew: "An Anointed Prince", one who would deliver Israel. The early Christians called Jesus "the Prince of Peace".

Massa

Hebrew: A burden, a message. A prophecy or revealed truth.

Mast-Allah

Arabic: "Fools of God" or "drunks of God". In India these occur by the thousands among the Muslim seekers after God. They exhibit all the signs of madness, infantile regression and senility, and an inability to look after even their own physical bodies. Some people believe they are Saints, but we say that this condition is the result of a wrong approach to the Spiritual Life through a denial of the Physical Plane reality. A balance needs to be developed.

Mastānaḥ

Persian: The God-intoxicated. From the Persian Masti, "being drunk". Those who are continually in a trance, having lost connection with the physical body and the world. Those who have become deranged or spiritually insane, who behave insanely, irrationally, outrageously, with total loss of control over their bodies, emotions and minds. The Mastānaḥ and Avadhūta of India are called "God's fools". They have totally rejected the world and the Path of Service, and spend their time in Inner Intoxication with Bliss-Consciousness. They are but failures on the Spiritual Path. [See Avadhūta]

Mata

Sanskrit: Thought, understanding. Honourable.

Mātā, Mā

Sanskrit: Mother. The Divine Mother. The Mother of the Universe. The Mother of all creatures. Also, Ammā, Ambā, Umā. [See Matṛ]

Mātangī-Mantra

Sanskrit: Mātangī is the Creative Power of Rhythm: outer rhythm and especially Inner Rhythm (Sattva). Also called the Vaikharī-Mantra (the Spoken-Word Power). It is the Dynamic-Creative-Energy (Śakti) of the Goddess.

Materia

Latin: The stuff of which physical objects are composed.

Materialism

The belief in objective matter existing on its own, without the Being of God. The false view that physical matter is all that constitutes the Universe, that mind, Soul and Spirit are but material activities (the brain, nervous system, etc.). Materialists do not have open minds. Their minds are blocked by the false assumption that what they can sense with their physical senses is all that exists. Both orthodox religion and orthodox science are produced by the personality and serve the false, limited sense of ego or "I", the personality sense. They are the limited personality's view of Reality, not Reality as it really is, beyond the five senses.

Material Worlds

The worlds of matter. The *material worlds* include not only this dense Physical World, but also the subtle etheric subplanes, the Astral World, and the Mental and Causal Worlds, since they are all formed from different densities or subtleties of matter (PRĀKṚTĪ).

MATṚ

Sanskrit: Mother, the Goddess, the Divine Mother. The Feminine Qualities, Forces and Energies. Mother Earth. The Cosmic Element *Water*. One with Knowledge (the Feminine Intuition). The ŚAKTI of the masculine Deities. In later centuries, MATṚ became MĀTĀ, and in the past few centuries it became MĀ.

MĀTRA

Sanskrit: A measure, confinement, limitation.

MĀTRIKĀ-MĀYĪ-DEVĪ

Sanskrit: "The letters-full-of-the-Goddess". The Goddess is the Power behind all Mantras and Divine Names. MĀTRIKĀ (the little Mothers) are the letters of the Sanskrit alphabet, which compose all the Sanskrit Mantras as well as all Mantras in all languages.

MAUNA, MAUNAM

Sanskrit: Silence, Peace, Quiet (inner and outer). Silence is a Way of Meditation (DHYĀNA). You must learn to *silence* the activities of the body, emotions and mind-stuff (the lower mind). At first, Silence appears to be empty, meaningless. Later on, we recognize it to be very creative and transforming in our lives. First there is Silence (MAUNA); then you feel the Power of Silence (MAUNA-ŚAKTI); then you hear the Supreme Word, uttered in Silence (MAUNA-PARĀ-VĀK); then there is Ecstasy (MAUNA-SAMĀDHI). To bring your ordinary mind to Peace and Quiet (MAUNA), just sit still and watch your mind. Watch your thoughts come and go, rise and fall, and do nothing about them.

MAUNA-PARĀ-VĀK

Sanskrit: The Silent Supreme Speech. She who speaks in Silence. The Supreme Word. A Name of LALITĀ, the Goddess.

MAUNA-ŚAKTĪ

Sanskrit: The Power of Silence. The Silent Wave of Bliss, the Power that can alter all things, the Miraculous Power. She who dwells in Silence. She who Is Silence. A Name of LALITĀ, the Goddess.

MAUNA-SAMĀDHI

Sanskrit: The Silent Ecstasy. She who unites the Seeker in Silence. A Name of LALITĀ, the Goddess.

MAYA, MAYAM

Sanskrit: Full of, consisting of, made out of.

MAYĀ

Sanskrit: Unreal, impermanent. An architect, a builder.

MĀYĀ

Sanskrit: "Illusion, deception, limitation". The Power that veils or hides the Real, the Truth and the Life. The Creative Power that veils the Absolute. The Self-Limiting Power of the LOGOS (the Creator, BRAHMĀ) by which all forms are produced in Space: the physical forms, the subtle astral forms and the subtlest causal or mental shapes. God sacrificed His/Her Infinite Beingness in order to manifest the Universe, which is a kind of limitation on God's Absoluteness. The Hindus call this Great Sacrifice MĀYĀ. It is by MĀYĀ that this whole Universe was created. Before Creation, God is an Illimitable Circle of Living Light. By MĀYĀ, the Magical Creative Power, God brings about the Universe as a *willing limitation on Beingness*. Thus the Universe becomes a veil (MĀYĀ) over the Absolute and Unconditioned Reality. All the works of MĀYĀ are temporary, not eternal or permanent.

On a human level, MĀYĀ is the delusive power of spiritual darkness and ignorance, the deception of the senses, the power of matter over Spirit, the delusion of materialism. The erroneous way we look at ourselves and the world around us. Our false perception of ourselves, God and Creation. False self-worth, self-image or self-validity. Objective conceptualization or self-conception. The perception of the Universe as only three-dimensional. Ignorance of the vast inner spaces and the Spiritual Law (DHARMA) which rules *all* dimensions of Space. Perceiving only material forms and believing in only material values. The belief that physical, astral and mental phenomena are real. The limited belief structures by which we are bound. Bondage, illusion, delusion. Thus, MĀYĀ is:

- That which is not real.
- The Power that produces illusions.
- The Divine Creative Energy.
- The limiting powers of shapes, forms and material structures and bodies.

Māyā Siddhi
Sanskrit: Powers (SIDDHIs) which give the *advanced* human being power over MĀYĀ, the illusionary Three Worlds (the Physical, Astral and Mental Worlds), the three lowest realms of our planet and solar system, the normal worlds of SAṀSĀRA where ordinary Humanity circulates between birth and death, beyond death and back into incarnation again. [See SVARŪPA SIDDHI]

Māyāvi-Rūpa
Sanskrit: "Illusory form" or "unreal body". The mental body, when not in conjunction with the physical and astral bodies. (On the lower Mental Plane, everything is but thoughtforms which, though illusory, appear very real to the perceiver.) Also, a mental construct which can be projected by an Adept or Magician in order to become visible on the Astral or Physical Planes. This illusory body can be created and destroyed at will through KRIYĀ-ŚAKTI (advanced Yogic powers) when the Adept wants to appear or disappear in the Three Worlds.

Māyāvi-Rūpa Siddhi
Sanskrit: "Illusory-form-making power". The power by which the Yogī or Siddha can make a temporary vehicle of appearance in the lower Three Worlds, on any plane or on any planet, as he or she wills. That MĀYĀVI-RŪPA form will last as long as the Yogī focuses Will-power and Imagination-power upon it. This is one form of the AVATĀRA SIDDHI (Divine-Descent power).

Mā-Yoga-Śakti
Sanskrit: "The Mother-Force of Union". As the KUṆḌALINĪ-ŚAKTI, the Goddess breaks down the barriers between the various states of Consciousness, between the various planes or levels of Being, and between the sensations of inner and outer experiences, thus producing the State of Unity within and without, At-One-Ment, YOGA.

Mediator
From the Latin MEDIATUS: "To come between two things, two realms or two conditions". Using Sanskrit terminology, there are four types of Mediator: the MAHĀTMA, the GURU, the BUDDHA and the AVATĀRA. The Mediators are *not* mediums. If we call them "channels", then they "channel" true Soul-Wisdom, the Wisdom of God within themselves. They simply teach what they *are* and the Wisdom *of their own experience* of the Higher Worlds. The Mediators come between the human and the Divine. This is why Jesus was called the "Son of God" and the "Son of Man": He mediated between God and Man. In His Consciousness He bridged the Higher Worlds and the Physical Plane.

Meditation
Latin: Originally, the Latin word MEDITATION meant "to contemplate Reality, to focus on Reality". This original meaning is radically different from the current usage of the word; only in later times has it come to mean "to think, to reflect, to ponder over a problem". Meditation is a search for Reality. Because Reality is not understood, however, meditation is not understood. This New Age of Aquarius is an extremely materialistic age; therefore, even meditation has been twisted into a quest for material progress. As defined in Mysticism, meditation is "a quiescent, prolonged, spiritual introspection; a devout religious exercise". Meditation is a quest for the Real, the Imperishable, the Eternal One. Reality has been called Divinity, the Self-Existent One, the Godhead, the Immutable, or PURUṢOTTAMA (the Highest Being). The Way is found by going *within* ourselves, transcending the physical body, the ordinary mind and the emotions. The Eternal Reality is beyond thought; therefore, in your meditation you must reach the

thought-less state (UNMANI), beyond the mind. Your mind must by neutralized, dissolved (MANOLAYA) and made inactive (MANONĀŚA). Your mind must be made all harmonious and tranquil (SAMĀDHI). It is only then that Reality appears to your Inner Gaze as the Luminous Light-Being which is within All, and which is your very Self. DHYĀNA in Sanskrit.

MEDIUM

Latin: In the middle. That which connects two things or two worlds. That through which light or energy is transmitted. An agency that communicates information from one world to the next, or between states and conditions, or between the "dead" and the "living". A go-between, an intermediary, a channel between this world and the world of spirits (the Astral Plane).

Mediumship

Contacting the dead or one's "spirit-guides", the so-called "angelic beings", "masters" or "space brothers". Ordinary mediums (nowadays called "channellers") receive their messages from their own subconscious minds, or by allowing a spook on the Astral Plane to speak through them or use their etheric voice-box mechanism, which requires that energy (ectoplasma) be drawn from the etheric body of the medium and those in the seance or circle. In mediumship there is no true spiritual development, no Soul growth. Spiritual development occurs when you touch upon your own Soul-Consciousness through a *proper meditation process*. And mediumship is *not* a meditation process. Mediumship destroys your Soul's evolution because it locks your consciousness into the Astral World.

MELCHIZEDEK

Hebrew: "King of Light". Melchizedek was a Priest-King of ancient Israel, a King of Light, a Magician of the Light, one of the great survivors from the Atlantean line of Divine-Light Magicians of Nirvāṇa. The *Order of Melchizedek* is the Divine Order, the Communion of the Holy Ones, which the church *tries* to be, but of which it is only a faint shadow.

MENAHEM

Hebrew: The Comforter. A Name given to the Messiah.

Mental

From the Latin MENTALIS. The word *mental* refers to the lower mind, the reasoning mind (in Sanskrit, RŪPA-MANAS). [See *Lower Mind*]

Mental Body

The vehicle of the lower mind, the concrete mind, the lower MANAS, existing on the lower four subplanes of the Mental Plane (those with form). In Sanskrit, MĀNASA-RŪPA or MANO-RŪPA (mind-form). The mental body is also called the MĀYĀVI-RŪPA (illusory form), because in those dimensions everything is but thoughtforms which, though illusory, appear very real to the perceiver.

Mentalism

The Law of the Mind. The Law of the Mental Origination of all things, stated as: "All things have a mental origin, and all things have a Destiny according to the mind within them". In the East it is known as the Law of DHARMA. (Note that Behaviouristic Psychology misuses the term *mentalism* to mean illogical or circular functioning of the mind.)

Mental Plane

The fifth of the seven great Planes of Being (counting from above). As the name implies, the Mental Plane is a world of *mind*. The lower four mental subplanes are the realm of the *concrete* mind or *rational* mind, which shapes mental matter into *thoughtforms*. The higher three subplanes (the Causal Worlds) are *formless* and correspond with the *Higher Mind* or *Abstract Mind*. The Human Soul (JĪVA) dwells on the formless levels of the Mental Plane. The seven subplanes of the Mental Plane are the true *Heaven Worlds*. DEVĀCHAN in Tibetan. SVARGA, SUVAH-LOKA and DEVASTHĀNA in Sanskrit.

Mental Telepathy
Mind-to-mind communication, using the mental body and the medium of the Throat Cakra. This is vastly different from any form of psychism. While in the physical body, the transmitting station for mental telepathy should be the Throat Cakra and the receiving stations should be the Third-Eye Cakra and the Crown Cakra. At this stage of human evolution very few people are mental telepaths; the majority of Humanity still focus in the Solar Plexus Centre and pick up the feelings, moods, emotions and psychic atmospheres of people and places. [See TELEPATHEIA]

MERKAVAH
Hebrew: The Throne of God; the Chariot of God. The Throne of Glory (NIRVĀṆA). The direct Vision of God in Mystical Ecstasy. Also, vehicles of Light that traverse Space and which are used inter-dimensionally by some Hierarchies to manifest on this Earth. This word was used by the ancient Jewish Mystics and the later Kabbalists of the DIASPORA (the dispersion of the Jews from Palestine/Israel).

Messiah
From the Hebrew MASHIAH, "God's Anointed One". The *Messiah* is the old Hebrew idea of the Divine Incarnation, the Sanskrit AVATĀRA or Divine Descent, for the redemption of Mankind. [See MASHIAH]

METANOIA
Greek: "Transforming the mind, renewing what is in your mind". Growth in mental understanding. Mental transformation. From META (in, on, of, upon, with, among, after, later, transference, transformation, a change or a process leading to change) and NOUS (mind, understanding, Heart, Spirit, Consciousness). META also means "above and beyond" or "transcendental". Thus, METANOIA can also mean "beyond the mind, above the mind, Transcendental Consciousness (or that which leads to it)". It can also mean "being with the Spirit, being in your Heart" and "the Renaissance of the Soul, a new Birth". METANOIA is the principle of becoming *new* by invoking the Soul-Power, the Being of Light, by the right mind-set or attitude. The New Testament translators interpret METANOIA to mean *repentance,* which means to feel sorrow, regret or sadness for one's sins, but METANOIA does *not* mean repentance. To the early Christians this word was not associated with sin, but rather, with changing one's mind, one's thoughts—to have a new mind, a new way of thinking about things, a rebirth into a Higher Consciousness, acquiring Wisdom, Insight, meditational experience. There is no sense of sin or morbidity in the original Greek word. To the Saints it means "to renew one's mind in God".

METANOIS
Greek: A change of perception, a changing of the mind, a renewing of Consciousness, a change of perspective, attaining a different viewpoint, the transformation of the mind, a mental revolution. To be reborn into a new Consciousness.

METATRON
Hebrew: "The Light of God". One of the Hebrew Angelic Names.

METEMPSYKHOUSTHAI
Greek: Metempsychosis. The wandering of the Soul (PSYCHE) in all life-forms. Metempsychosis is a popular superstition in the East (as it was among the Greeks, Romans and Egyptians) that, after death, the Human Soul will reincarnate as an animal, an insect, a fish, a bird, a tree, or whatever. This is utter nonsense, based on a lack of understanding of reincarnation or *re-embodiment.* A human being cannot reincarnate below the Human Kingdom. No human being can reincarnate as a worm, a snake, a dog, a fish, an insect or a bird. It is an evolutionary impossibility. No matter what a human does, he or she cannot step backward on such a grand scale.

MICHAEL
Hebrew: "The Protective Power of God". One of the Hebrew Angelic Names.

Mikrokosmos

Greek: "Little universe". From Mikro (small, tiny) and Kosmos (a world or universe). A Microcosm (Mikrokosmos) is the small universe of a human being—the whole Man, the Soul-personality complex, the complete Auric Being. It is the Soul-Nature, within which the personality (the "mask") resides. Microcosm refers to you in your incarnation, as a Soul, *living in* the physical, etheric, astral, mental and causal bodies. All of that makes up your "little universe". The ancient Romans call this the Minitum Mundum (little world). [See Makrokosmos and Chiliokosmos]

Mind

From the Latin Mens, Mentis. The word *mental* comes from the Latin Mentalis. The ordinary human mind is *above* the physical body experience and *above* the astral, which is psychic and emotional, having to do with feelings. Your normal "thinking mind" is your mental body, which exists on the Mental Plane separately from your physical body. It is an organism *independent* of the physical body and brain. Thus, when you are not in the physical body, you can use your "mind" as a body in order to function independently in the Mental World. In the Esoteric Teachings, however, the word *mind* does not refer to just the little mind of a member of the human species, but the minds of angels, gods and demigods, as well as Cosmic Intelligences and the Great Cosmic Mind of the Creator-God Him/Herself. [See Manas and Mahat]

Mindfulness

The moment-by-moment Awareness of your mental, emotional and physical states of being. [See Vipaśyanā]

Mind of Light

The descriptive expression *Mind of Light* can have a variety of meanings, depending on the context:

- The Cosmic Mind, the Mind of God (Mahat).
- The Nirvāṇic Consciousness (Ātma-Vidyā).
- The Wisdom-Mind (Buddhi-Manas), which is the mind (higher and lower) infused with the Light of Buddhi.

Mind-Only

An ancient expression describing the Cosmic Mind, the One Mind, the Mind of God, also called the Universal Mind, the Mind of Light, the Divine Mind, the Radiant Light of Reality, the Name, the Cosmic Christ, the Buddha-Nature, the Self-Nature, your Original Nature, Tao, the One Life, the Life-Force of the Universe, the Spirit of God, the Breath of God, the Great Breath, the One Force, the Universal Radiant Energy, the Cosmic Sea of Life. There is Mind-Only. Nothing can exist outside of or separate from this One Mind. All things are built up by this Universal Mind: the planets, the stars, the suns, the galaxies, the Cosmos, and the bodies of all sentient beings, subtle or dense, including your own physical body. [See Tao]

Minitum Mundum

Latin: "Little world". The Microcosm. The Auric Being of a human being. [See Mikrokosmos]

Mirāculum

Latin: A miracle. An event attributed to a supernatural cause, to powers, energies and entities of the Great Invisible World around us. There are really no "miracles", only the scientific application of the laws, forces and entities of the Invisible Worlds. This was the Magic of old. [See Siddhi]

Mitra

Sanskrit: Friend and companion. A friend or benefactor to all.

Mnimi Theou

Greek: "Remembrance of God". This has several layers of meaning. The simplest, of course, is prayer or meditation on God in the Heart. As you progress, however, this *Remembrance of God* acquires greater and greater reality. It is the cornerstone of the Jewish, Christian and Muslim religions.

Mohinī

Sanskrit: She who enchants the Universe. The Enchanter, the Enchanting-One. A Name of Lalitā, the Goddess. She enchants all beings by Her Transcendental Beauty and Dazzling Brightness.

Mokṣa
Sanskrit: Freedom, Liberation, Salvation. The Freedom of the Soul from birth and death in the lower worlds. The State of Everlasting Bliss above the Heaven Worlds. Also called Mukti (Liberation).

Monad ⊙
Greek: "The Indivisible One". The Whole, the All, the Complete, the One. The Original Atom, the Divine Self, the Divine Father-Power, the Seed of the Universe. Also, a Virgin Spirit. The Greek word Monad means the same as the Latin Atom (primordial unit) and the ancient classical Sanskrit Aṇu. A Monad, Atom, Aṇu, can be the little world known by science as the "atom" or it can be a human being, a planet, a solar system or a galaxy; they are all atoms of various sizes. Even a galaxy is just a gigantic Atom or Monad in Omnispace, in the Plerōma, in the Universal Fullness or Reality.

In relation to Humanity, the Monad is the Transcendental Spirit in Man, your "Father in Heaven", the I AM Presence in the innermost depths of the Soul (Paramātman, in Sanskrit). It is the God-Self, the highest point of Spirit within Man, dwelling on the Paranirvāṇic Plane. It is the image of Perfection, "the image and likeness of God". The Monad projects into being the Spiritual Soul (Ātma-Buddhi), who in turn projects into being the personality in the Three Worlds. The Monad is God *individualized* in each human being. It is the individualized God-Being in your Soul, *not* in your personality. It is not your personal Saviour! The Monad, "your Father in Heaven", redeems your *Soul.* The Monad is the Image of God in the human being, while the Christos is the intermediary Light between the Father and your Soul. The Monad cannot be perceived on the personality level of experience, for "no man has seen the Father at any time" *(John 1:18)*. [See Aṇu and Paramātman]

Monogenēs
Greek: "The first-born, the first-produced, born from the One, the product of Divine Oneness" (Mono-Genesis). In the pre-Christian Greek Mystery Schools this term referred to the Second Logos, the Cosmic Word, the Universal Christ-Principle. In his Gospel, Saint John refers to the Messiah as Monogenes. Uninitiated Christians translated this expression as "only-begotten" (which is quite meaningless), and then as "the only Son of God". The later Christians made the *personality* of Jesus, the Messiah, to be the Universal Christ Being and erroneously declared Jesus to be the *only* Son of God. Nowadays, Bibles are translated to mean that Jesus (the historical personality) is the *only* Son of God, and thus they *deny Divinity* to all God's Children.

Monology
Greek: The constant repetition of a mantra or prayer. This is the same concept as the Eastern Mantra Japa. A Monology can be the repetition of any of the Divine Names, such as *Jesus,* or *Jesus Christ,* or *Lord, Jesus Christ,* repeated over and over in the Heart, and contemplated upon.

Monos
Greek: "The Oneness" or "the One". The Second Aspect of the Godhead, also known as the Christos. Also, one who lives alone, one who is alone in the desert, a solitary one, an ascetic living by himself or herself in isolation, an anchorite. Hence the English words *monastery* and *monk.*

Morphe
Greek: Form, body, vehicle.

Mṛtyu
Sanskrit: Lalitā as the Goddess of Death, for all things must die that are born. But She also delivers you from Death (Mṛtyu, Yama) by giving you Conscious Immortality (the Amṛta, the Nectar of Immortality) beyond the physical body. (Yama is the God of Death.)

Mṛtyuṁjaya-Mantra
Sanskrit: The Mantra to Overcome the Fear of Death. From Mṛtyu (death) and Jaya (victory).

Mu
Japanese: "Not-doing". [See Wu]

Mudrā
Sanskrit: Seal. A gesture, a posture, a sign or a symbol.

Muḥammad
Arabic: The Praised One, the Prophet, the giver of the Religion of Islām.

Mukti
Sanskrit: Liberation, Freedom, Beatitude, Conscious Immortality. The Freedom of the Soul from birth and death in the lower worlds. Freeing your consciousness from the pains, delusions and errors of the lower worlds and experiencing the realms of Buddhi and Nirvāṇa. Being able to live freely in the Spirit, unhindered by your physical body, mind and personality structure. Jīvan-Mukti is when you liberate yourself while still living in your physical body. Videhā-Mukti is when you liberate yourself after the death of your physical body, in the after-death condition. This is not possible if you have not commenced the process while still alive in your body. Also called Mokṣa (Freedom).

Mūla
Sanskrit: Root, Basis, Foundation, Original Cause.

Mūlādhāra Cakra
Sanskrit: The Base Centre, located at the base of the human spinal column in the etheric and astral bodies. From Mūla (root, basis) and Ādhāra (support). The Mūlādhāra Cakra is responsible for materiality, attraction to money, objects, matter, worldliness, worldly powers and domination, worldly authority, competition sport, physical endurance, adventure seeking, the Physical Plane. The Kuṇḍalinī-Śakti naturally resides, coiled up like a snake, in the Mūlādhāra Cakra, where She is responsible for the maintenance and perpetuation of the physical body. Confined to Her quarters in the Mūlādhāra Cakra, the Kuṇḍalinī-Śakti makes a person thoroughly "worldly".

Mūlamantra (Mūla-Mantra)
Sanskrit: Root-Vibration. The Primordial or Original Sound of the Universe and of Humanity. Also, the Root or Foundation Mantra, also known as the Śrī-Vidyā-Mantra or the Pañcadaṣa-Ākśarī-Mantra (Fifteen-Syllabled Mantra).

Mūla-Mantra-Ātmikā
Sanskrit: She is the Spirit or Life of the Root Mantra upon which the whole system of Śrī-Vidyā is based. The Pañcadaṣī or Mūla-Mantra is the Subtle Body or Subtle Form of Lalitā. This Subtle Form consists of Sounding-Light Vibrations.

Mūlaprākṛtī
Sanskrit: The Root of Nature; the Primordial Substance; the Primordial Cause of all Nature. From Mūla (Root, Basis, Original Cause) and Prākṛtī (Pra-Kṛti: before Creation, towards activity). Prākṛtī is active Nature or Creation, including both the visible and invisible worlds. Prākṛtī is feminine. There is a Feminine Consciousness within Nature which can be felt by those who have the sensitivity to sense Her. Nature is a Veil over Her true form, Mūlaprākṛtī, the Root-Nature or Primordial Substance, Unmanifested Spiritual Matter, the Eternal Essence, from which comes all Manifestation, all Creation, all phenomena. Mūlaprākṛtī is the Luminous Mother-Light-Substance and Pure Feminine Consciousness beneath, behind and above manifest Nature. Mūlaprākṛtī is the Veil which the Unmanifest Godhead (Parabrahman) forms upon Itself when in Creation, which conceals It from the sight of all created beings.

Mullā
Persian: The learned man. The scholar, doctor, theologian.

Mumukṣatva
Sanskrit: Desire for Liberation or Freedom from reincarnation. The longing for Nirvāṇa. The Fourth Qualification for Discipleship.

Muṇḍa
Sanskrit: Dull, stupid, blunt (Tamas). [See Guṇa]

Muni
Sanskrit: A Sage, Saint, a Seer, an Ascetic, a Silent One, a Yogī. One who is Inspired, an Enlightened One. Being in the State of Ecstasy.

Murāqabah
Arabic: Hope. Confidence in God.

Murāqabaī
Arabic: Meditation. Contemplation of God. A state of awareness or alertness in which you are a *witness* to everything, but without becoming psychologically disturbed by what is being witnessed. This state of meditation is *not* a running-away from the world. It is a condition of "being in the world but not of the world". This can happen only when you become Soul-dependent, when you obey the Master within. It comes as a result of fine inner attunement. Murāqabaī is also the observation of the movement of the mind, moment by moment, and non-reaction to it. Murāqabaī has been described by the Sūfīs as *a state of being in which the ego ceases to be.*

Mūrdha Jyotiṣi
Sanskrit: "Head-Light", or Light in the Head. A term for the Ājñā Cakra (Third-Eye), because the Supernatural Light streaming down from the Crown Centre can be focused out through the Third-Eye. This Light can be thrown upon all hidden things, and all things can be known by it. Also, by this Light in the Third-Eye Centre, the Siddhas can be seen.

Murīd
Arabic: A disciple, a follower, a student, one who is inclined towards or desirous of the Realization of the Truth. This is the second stage of the Journey of the Heart. Your Heart impulses become stronger and more steady towards the Spiritual Life. You become more serious about meditation and other spiritual practices, and you try out many things.

Murshid
Arabic: A leader, a teacher, a guide. The Spiritual Teacher, the Spiritual Master, the Guru. Also, Pīr-o-Murshid (Persian).

Mu-Shin
Japanese: No-mind, no-thinking, no-thought-in-the-mind. The emptiness of the mind in which the One Mind can reveal Itself. It is a mind *not attached* to any forms or objects. Wu-Hsin in Chinese Zen. [See *No-Mind*]

Muslim
Arabic: "A believer". One who believes in the One God.

Mystai
Greek: The Lower Seers. In the terminology of the Greek Mystery Schools, the *Mystics* were those who were initiated into the Lesser Mysteries of the higher Mental Plane (the formless mind-realms beyond thoughts) and into Buddhi, the Unified-Field Consciousness. [See Epoptai]

Mystērion, Mystēria
Greek: A Mystery. The Great Invisible Universe, the Divine Mysteries, the Esoteric Knowledge learned in Mystery Schools. A Mystery is something *hidden* from the uninitiated, but *seen* by the Knower. It is something that is inexplicable and difficult to comprehend by the ordinary mind, but which can be understood by the Super-Mind, or Cosmic Consciousness. From the verb Myein, "to close your eyes and ears", as was the custom in the old pre-Christian Mystery Schools: "Close your eyes and ears to this world so that you might see and hear the Invisible." This has been the basis of all meditational processes, Eastern and Western, orthodox and unorthodox, Christian and non-Christian. The Greek word Mystērion was used several centuries before Christianity, and the early Christian fathers adapted it to their new faith. "God is a Mystery", they said, meaning that God is hidden from the view of mortal eyes and inaudible to mortal ears. "For no one has *seen* the Father at any time" (that is, no mortal!).

Mystery Schools
The Mystery Schools were created in ancient Egypt, Greece and Rome to link up the lower to the higher, the visible to the invisible worlds. In the Mystery Schools one learnt about the invisible worlds surrounding us and penetrating us, and the meditational practices or Path by which one climbs up the worlds into the purely spiritual dimensions, Buddhi and Nirvāṇa, the Kingdom of God. The Work of the Mystery Schools is the expansion of Consciousness, alignment with one's own Higher Self, Spiritual Illumination, and service toward the Group Soul and the world, under the guidance of the Hierophant, the Spiritual Master. The Mystery Schools are the doors to the Temples of Initiation. They possess the Keys to Heaven and Hell—the knowledge of the Higher Worlds. [See Āśrama]

Mystēs
Greek: One who has been initiated into the interior Mysteries of Spiritual Life. In the old Mystery Schools this was done through ritual initiations (the lower Mysteries) or through direct inner meditations (the higher Mysteries). The church rituals were imitations of the old Mystery School rituals.

Mystical Ascent
A stage of the Radiant Heart Way when at least some of the sexual energy has been transmuted into the Heart, and there is a real and intimate relationship established in the Heart between the Mystic and God. This stage is very often likened to sexual embrace or sexual communion. In fact, it is orgasm on a divine scale. The Mystics always likened this stage to a sexual embrace in the Heart, the intensity of which leaves the Mystic wordless—quite literally.

Mystical Contemplation
Mystical Contemplation occurs when you subdue the thoughts in your ordinary, discursive, reasoning mind, leave behind all attachments to worldly things and, in *absolute detachment* from all things (including yourself!), raise yourself into the Stream of Divine Light.

Mystical Trance
In Mystical Trance or Ecstasy you are wholly interiorized in your consciousness, while your body, mind and emotions are in a cataleptic state—immobile, suspended. This is similar to the trance of a medium, but not the same in effect. In the trance of a medium, a spook or "guide" (an astral entity) takes control. In the trance of a Mystic, God (the Supreme Reality) takes control. The trance of a medium is an astral phenomenon, whereas the trance of a Mystic is a truly spiritual phenomenon where God takes possession of the Soul. [See Ekstasis]

Mystical Union
In Mystical Union God's Presence is felt deeply and profoundly. Imaginative activities cease and distractions from the body and mind do not intervene, but the actions of the bodily senses are not entirely suspended. That is, although your awareness is wholly interiorized within your body and shut off from the outside world, you can, at will, still return to normal bodily brain-mind or waking consciousness.

Mysticism
The fervour of the Heart. The fiery aspiration of the Heart towards God. Mysticism is *not* an idea, not a philosophy, not a thought process. It is an approach to Reality via the Heart. In the Old Testament it is called "Holiness to the Lord" because, in the state of Mystical Consciousness, all things appear Holy, Sacred, Whole, One. Mysticism is the Unitive State of the Spiritual Soul.

Mystikos
Greek: A Mystic. One who has been initiated into the Divine Mysteries (Mystērion) by direct experience, not by speculation, theology, metaphysics or philosophy, nor by rituals. One who experiences God inwardly, first hand. The word Mystikos has been applied to the Christian Saints (since the time of Christ), those who have united their Souls with God and the Saving-Light Force of the Cosmos, the Christos.

N

Naba
Hebrew: To prophesy.

Nābhi Cakra
Sanskrit: The Solar Plexus Centre. Also called the Maṇipūraka (Maṇipūra) Cakra.

Nabi
Hebrew: A Prophet. A revealer of the Divine Mysteries.

Nāda
Sanskrit: "The Soundless Sound". The Inner Sound. The Voice of the Silence. The Divine Word on the highest Spiritual Planes. The Pure Transcendental Sound of Absolute Reality. Nāda is the Word of the Spirit, the First Aspect of the Deity. It is the Originating-Sounding-Light-Vibration, the Source, Silence. Nāda (Śabda-Brahman) issues forth from Parabrahman, the Absolute, the Transcendental Reality, the One. Nāda is Eternal and is the vibratory pattern for all things. Listening to the internal sounds (Nāda) was a favourite practice of the Sages of old India. The various sounds of Nāda (the subtle inner sounds) or Śabda-Brahman (the Divine Word, the Logos) that you hear with the Ears of your Soul are various Vibrations of the Cosmic Ōṁ Sound, and they can *resemble* certain physical sounds. This Inner Music can be listened to through the right Inner Ear or the Heart Centre. If you listen to it in the Heart, it is called Anāhata-Nāda or Anāhata-Śabda (the Unproduced Sound, meaning "not produced by external means"). Listening to Nāda will lead you first to Self-Realization (Ātmājñāna) and then to God-Realization (Brahmajñāna). This is called Surat-Śabda Yoga (putting your attention on the Sound). [See Ōṁ and Āuṁ]

Nāda-Bindu
Sanskrit: The Sounding-Light, the Word, which can be seen in the Third-Eye. It acts as a connecting link (Yoga) with your Soul, and between your Soul and God.

Nāda-Brahman
Sanskrit: The Voice of God. The Voice of the Silence which you hear in deep Contemplation. It reveals the Mysteries.

Nāda-Liṅga
Sanskrit: The Sound-Sign. The symbol for the Inner Music heard within the Universe.

Nāda-Rūpā
Sanskrit: "She who is in the Form of Inner Sound". A Name of Lalitā, the Goddess. From Rūpa (body, form, embodiment) and Nāda, the Voice of the Silence, the Soundless Sound, the Sound not heard by physical ears, the continuous Sound-Vibration of Praṇava (the Universal Ōṁ Sound), the Creative Speech, Logos or Word which is listened to by the Yogī and Mystic in the Heart or through the Inner Ear, which will lead to Infinite Consciousness.

Nāda Yoga
Sanskrit: Union with God (Yoga) through the Living-Word (Nāda). Inner Mantra Yoga. An aspect of Mantra Yoga which involves the *hearing* of the inner sounds of the Word, or God-Incarnate. This Yoga is also called Surat-Śabda Yoga and Laya Yoga.

Nāḍī
Sanskrit: Psychic nerve. The Nāḍīs are invisible etheric-psychic nerve currents or energy currents of Prāṇa in the subtle bodies. (These are *not* the dense physical nerves.)

Nafs
Arabic: The Living Soul. The same as the Greek Psyche and the Sanskrit Jīva.

Nairañjanā
Sanskrit: The River of Enlightenment. The Goddess. [See Nirañjanā]

Nāma, Nāman
Sanskrit: Name, identity, identification. A form, a mark. Famous, renowned.

Nāma
Sanskrit: The Name of God. The Divine Name, Vibration, Sound. Śabda, the Sound-Current. The Word, the Logos. God Incarnating within you and in the Cosmos. The Creative Power of God by which all gets done. The Celestial Music or Divine Harmony by which God has created, and is creating, and will be creating in the future, the whole Universe. The Name of God is a Vibration which can be *felt* within the physical body. It is characterized by Music, by Harmonious Vibrations. The whole Universe is made out of the Name of God, made out of Divine Music.

Namah, Namaḥ, Namaha, Namahā
Sanskrit: To the Divine Being; to God or the Goddess; to the Divine Name or Vibration. Veneration, worship, adoration, offering, homage, surrender, obeisance, reverence, bowing down to, salutation to. Invocation.

Nāmaste (Nāmastute)
Sanskrit: "I worship the Divinity within you" or "I worship the Divine Name (Nāma) within you." The personal greeting of old India. How beautiful is this ancient greeting! When you truly serve your relatives, your friends, your colleagues and the world from your Heart, remember: Nāmaste!

Name
The *Name* is the Power emanated from *within* God, from Universal Consciousness. The Greek Mystics and Mystery Schools called this Power the Logos (the Word). The ancient Persians called it Sraosha (the Word or Name-Power). In ancient India is was called Śabda (the Living Word or Sound-Current) and Nāma (the Name of God). It is as real as electricity, magnetism or atomic power—in fact, infinitely more so! It is invisible to physical eyes and permeates all of infinite Space and all the worlds, visible and invisible. The Name can be heard within the Heart as sweet Heavenly Music, and in the Head as the Cosmic-Ocean of Creative-Rumbling Word or Power, the Ocean-Tide of Life. Since very ancient times, the Mystics of all religions have called it by many Names, or expressions in human languages. These are known as the *Names of God* or *Divine Names*.

Namo
Sanskrit: Greetings to; salutations to; reverence for. Praising, invoking, tuning into.

Namo Namaḥ
Sanskrit: "We salute; we invoke; we give praise to; we honour; we bow down to".

Nār
Arabic: The mind. Literally, this word means "fire, hell, mind, intellect, advice, counsel". This practically sums up the true meaning of your "mind"!

Nara
Sanskrit: The species of Man; Mankind; humanoids. Also, a leader. Also, the One-Self or Ātman. Nārī means "woman".

Nāra
Sanskrit: Water.

Nārā
Sanskrit: "The Waters of Life", or Primordial Space, which was void or formless before Brahmā, the Creator, organized Matter into form-structures.

Narakā
Sanskrit: Hell. Hellish conditions of consciousness and mind. The Hell Worlds. Realms of suffering. Nara is Man. Narakā is a product of Human Consciousness.

Narādhipam
Sanskrit: Superior or virtuous species (humanoid and the gods). From Nara (the species of Man, humanoids) and Adhipam (superior species).

Nārāyaṇa
Sanskrit: "The Mover upon the Waters of Space". The Spirit moving over the Waters of Space, the Great Deep, the Boundless Universe. From Nārā (the Waters of Life) and Ayaṇa (moving). "The Waters of Life" represents Primordial Space, which was void or formless before Brahmā, the Creator, organized Matter into form-structures. This same idea was later expressed in the Chaldean, Assyrian, Babylonian, Hebrew and Greek stories of Creation. In Hebrew, Ruach-Elohīm, "the Breath of the Creator-Gods". Nārāyaṇa is the Primordial All-Pervading Spirit, the Supreme-Self, the Vivifying Spirit of God, the Universal Sunshine of the Spirit, the Universal Sun. It is also the abode of the Self (Man and the Universe). It gives Universal Love, Compassion and Wisdom, infinite Power, Majesty, Glory and Radiance. It brings into us Happiness and Joy. It confers upon us total Liberation and Freedom, and includes and balances out all opposites.

Nārāyaṇī
Sanskrit: The All-Pervading Holy Spirit. The Spirit resting upon the Waters of Space. Nārāyaṇī means "She who dwells in the Waters" (in Cosmic Space, in Matter). She is the Indwelling Spirit in all things, the Vivifying, Enlivening Spirit, the Vehicle for Ātman (the Breath of God). A Name of Lalitā, the Goddess.

Nātha
Sanskrit: Lord, God.

Nature
The word "Nature" does not just refer to what you behold with your physical eyes, for that is but an infinitesimal portion of the real Nature, the real Universe in which you "live, move and have your being". In Sanskrit, Nature is known as Prākṛtī, the matter or substance of all seven Planes of Being.

Nehira
Hebrew: The Divine Light.

Nemesis
Greek: The Goddess of retribution, vengeance, punishment. Karma, the Law of Cause and Effect. The spiritual and psychic forces and entities involved in working out individual, group, national or planetary Destiny.

Nepenthe
Greek: The condition of being sedated or drugged into unconsciousness by this material world, material life and materialistic thinking.

Nephilīm
Hebrew: The "fallen angels" of the Old Testament. Those who rebelled against the Rule of the Cosmos. The individualistic angels. [See Malachīm and Makara]

Netzach
Hebrew: "Victory". On the Kabbalistic Tree of Life, Netzach is an aspect of the lower Mental Plane, along with Hod (Splendour).

New Age
[See *Aquarian Age*]

Nidā
Persian-Arabic: The Voice, the Call to Prayer, the Proclamation of God, the Voice of God calling in the Heart. Note that the Persian-Arabic word Nidā has the same meaning as the Sanskrit word Nāda: "the Voice of God, the Inner Sound-Current, the audible Life-Stream that emanates from God, the Infinite Hum of the Creative Power of God".

Nidrā
Sanskrit: Sleep.

Nipsis, Prosochi
Greek: Alertness, sobriety, watchfulness, wakefulness in the Heart Centre. [See Phylaki Kardias and Tirisis Kardias]

Nirākāra
Sanskrit: Formless and Measureless. A description of the Godhead.

Nirākārā
Sanskrit: She who is Formless. With pure Spiritual Vision we behold Her Formless-Form stretching through Infinitude. A Name of Lalitā, the Goddess.

Nirañjana, Nirañjanā
Sanskrit: Purity, Spotlessness, Perfection. Fully Bright. Passionless. Without any imperfections or faults. From Nir-Añjana, "not polluted". Also, the Full Moon. Nirañjana is a Name of God. Nirañjanā (feminine) is the Goddess.

Nirantarā
Sanskrit: She who is present everywhere. The All-Pervading Continuum. She is One. A Name of Lalitā, the Goddess.

Nirbīja Samādhi
Sanskrit: A state of Samādhi without a seed, support or form (no mantras, signs or symbols). [See Sabīja Samādhi]

Nirguṇa (Nir-Guṇa)
Sanskrit: Without forms, qualities or attributes. [See Saguṇa]

Nirguṇā
Sanskrit: She who is beyond the three qualities (Guṇas) of Nature. A Name of Lalitā, the Goddess.

Nirguṇa-Brahman
Sanskrit: "God without attributes". Brahman. The Logos. [See Saguṇa-Brahman]

Nirmalā
Sanskrit: She who is without any form of impurity, not tainted by Matter or the World. Although all actions (Karma) are done by Her Energy (Śakti), She is not tainted by the results of Action. A Name of Lalitā, the Goddess.

Nirmala-Sundarī
Sanskrit: "Spotless Beauty, Shining Grace". The Goddess, who shines within you like a thousand Suns. Pure Consciousness (Nirmala-Sundarī) is ever the same, before Creation, during Creation and after Creation. You were That before your birth, you are That now, and you will be That after you die.

Nirmānakāya
Sanskrit: The "Transformation Body" of a Buddha. A Buddha or Enlightened Being who remains in the Inner Worlds helping human evolution on all levels. These are the Saints, Yogīs and Masters of all religions who have attained Nirvāṇa but chose not to become absorbed in It (Nirvāṇa-Kāya). The Nirmānakāyas are also known as Bodhisattvas (those whose Essence is Love-Wisdom). Their Consciousness is focused in the Buddhic Plane, below Nirvāṇa. The Nirmānakāyas have renounced Nirvāṇa in order to serve Humanity in the Inner Worlds, as far down as the Astral World. They are undying and Consciously Immortal, just like the Nirvāṇīs. [See Dharmakāya]

Nirodha
Sanskrit: Quieting, restraining, suppressing, controlling, suspending, ceasing movement or activities, settling down. Nirodha can also mean "binding", which is the state of your normal thought-producing mind, because it binds You, the Self, to your thoughts.

Nirodha-Pariṇāma
Sanskrit: "Bondage-transformation". When your Consciousness or Attention moves away from the continuous mind-chatter of thoughts and mental activities into Silence, your mind becomes Free to experience Boundless Consciousness.

Nirodha-Pariṇāma Siddhi
Sanskrit: The power (Siddhi) resulting from the control of the transformation of the mind, the control of thoughts and ideas, mental control, conscious mind control (what, in the West, used to be called Metanoia).

Nirvāṇa
Sanskrit: Literally, "blown out, extinguished", from Nir (out, away from) and Vāṇa (to blow, to move). Commonly translated as "annihilation, destruction, dissolution". Nirvāṇa is the blowing away of nescience, ignorance, darkness (Māyā). Nirvāṇa is Unconditioned Being, the annihilation of the personality in a Superior Consciousness, the cessation of Time, Space, form, matter and energy as we know them. In Nirvāṇa one becomes One with the Universal "I AM", the Bright Self of the Universe. Nirvāṇa is the Heart of the Universe, the Beatific Vision, the Experience of the Supreme Glory, the Infinitely Bright, the White Brilliance of the Godhead. Nirvāṇa is the Source of the Great Breath, the Universal Life-Force and Energy from which the Universe is out-breathed at the Dawn of Time, and into which the Universe is in-breathed and dissolved by the Great Breath, or Spirit, at the end of Eternity. (Note that the Sanskrit word Nirvāṇa can sometimes refer to the three highest planes of the Cosmic Physical Plane, the realms of Absolute Light, what Jesus called "the House of the Father". Specifically, however, the Nirvāṇic Plane is the lowest of the three planes of Absolute Light.)

Nirvāṇī
Sanskrit: A Buddha who has entered Nirvāṇa, whose personality (the body-mind-ego complex) has been dissolved, blown away, discarded. An emancipated Dhyāni-Buddha who has crossed the stream of matter of the lower planes, entered Nirvāṇa, and is no longer in touch with the lower worlds. So far as the lower worlds are concerned, a Nirvāṇī has ceased to exist. Such a being retains his Individuality, but even that is absorbed in the Light of Ātman (Nirvāṇa). Also called a Pratyeka Buddha, "a Buddha who walks alone".

Nirvikalpa Samādhi
Sanskrit: A state of Samādhi without imaginings or distinctions. The experiencer is detached from all. In Nirvikalpa Samādhi there are no thoughts or mental activity whatsoever. From Nir-Vikalpa, "without thoughts, imaginings, form". [See Savikalpa Samādhi]

Nirvikārā
Sanskrit: She who is Changeless. A Name of Lalitā, the Goddess. Vikāra (change) does not affect Her. The Universe always changes, but Lalitā is unaffected.

Nirvitarka Samādhi
Sanskrit: A state of Samādhi "without an Idea" (such as "God"), but just the *experience* of It. [See Savitarka Samādhi]

Niṣkalā
Sanskrit: She who is not in parts. A Name of Lalitā, the Goddess. Kalā means "parts, fractions, divisions, segments, fragments". Although the Universe may appear to be composed of parts or separated objects, Lalitā always remains one, whole, unbroken Formless-Form.

Niṣkāma-Karma
Sanskrit: "No-desire-action". Desireless action. Acting without desire for rewards or results. True spiritual action is always selfless, always for the good of others.

Niṣkarmayam
Sanskrit: "Non-action" (Niṣ-Karmayam). Actionless. Non-activity. The concept of non-action has been misinterpreted by the yogīs, sādhus, sannyāsins and holy men for the past six thousand years. They explained non-action as non-attachment to your body, the world and your environment. Such indifference to life was taught to be a virtue: by "killing out desires" (suppressing emotion) and "controlling the mind" (trying to *stop* the thinking process) one attained Mukti (Liberation, Nirvāṇa). The idea was to absorb oneself into Samādhi (Pure Consciousness, the Transcendental State) and to care not for the world, nor for one's body, nor for the environment. But in fact, attaining Samādhi is only half of the Spiritual Journey.

Niṣspanda
Sanskrit: "No-vibration". There will come a stage in your mind-transformation when your mind will be totally disengaged or suspended (Niṣ-Spanda, no-vibration), when you will look and see and hear and taste and smell without a thought in your

mind, without *verbalization* of what you see, hear or experience, without mind chatter, without any mental waves or vibrations. Then you will see and hear and taste and smell and *know* how things *really* are.

Niṣpāra
Sanskrit: Boundless, Limitless. A description of Parabrahman, the Godhead.

Nitya *(masculine)*
Sanskrit: Eternal, everlasting, perpetual. A sea or ocean.

Nityā *(feminine)*
Sanskrit: She who is timeless. She who is eternal. She who is constant. The Goddess Durgā.

Nitya Samādhi
Sanskrit: In this form of Samādhi, one is permanently established in Transcendental Consciousness.

Ni-Vṛtti
Sanskrit: Evolution. Movement forward in the dense lower worlds, and out of them back to Nirvāṇa, the Original Cause. [See Pra-Vṛtti]

Niyama
Sanskrit: "What to do". Rules, regulations, order, precepts, guidelines, practices, spiritual actions, obeying the Law. In Aṣṭāṅga Yoga, as set down by Patañjali, the Niyama (Rules) are fivefold:

- Śauca (purification, cleanliness, purity).
- Santoṣa (contentment with one's lot).
- Tapas (fiery aspiration, spiritual purification).
- Svādhyāya (spiritual studies, understanding yourself).
- Īśvara-Praṇidhāna (Devotion to God).

Noisis
Greek: Abstract thinking. Pure intellection (in the classical sense), where spiritual realities are comprehended intuitively. [See Intellectus]

Noitos
Greek: Intuitive, direct perception by the mind.

No-Mind
The "no-mind" of the Zen Masters is not a mindlessness. It is not a zombie-like condition or unintelligence. It is simply the transcending of your ordinary mind, the Kāma-Manas, the desire-filled mind. "No-mind" actually means "no thoughts". You cannot *not* have a "mind", for your consciousness, awareness and reasoning faculty are all "mind". Thus, when the Masters say that you must have "no-mind" when you perform an action, they mean that your mind must be simple, focused, clear, bright, alert, concentrated, fully in the Here and Now, on the subject of your action. "No-mind" is the stopping of the endless chattering, criticizing commentary of your ordinary mind and the awakening into a silent, non-judgmental, holistic, super-rational Mind: first the formless Causal Mind on the causal subplanes, then the Buddhi-Mind (Wisdom-Mind) on the Buddhic Plane, and finally the Supreme Intelligence on the Ātmic or Nirvāṇic Plane.

Note-of-Withdrawal
The Natural Death Process begins when the Soul sounds the *Note-of-Withdrawal,* a mantram which comes down through the mental, astral and etheric-physical bodies. When the Soul-Note-of-Withdrawal sounds strongly, you *know* that you are going to die.

Noumenon
Greek: "What is thought". The invisible Universe around us and in us. Hence the English word *noumena.*

Nous
Greek: Spirit, Consciousness, Heart, Mind, Intelligence, Intuition, Higher Mind. The Mind of Light, the Divine Intelligence, the Divine Mind (Mahat in Sanskrit). Also, the Spiritual Mind in Man (the Intellect, in the *classical* sense). In the old sense, Nous, or Intellect, had a *spiritual* meaning. To the classical Greeks and early Christians, Intellect was "the eye of the Soul, the depth of the Soul", what in modern terminology is called the *Higher Mind*, the *Abstract Mind* or *Causal Consciousness.* From Nous was derived the English word *noetic,* which means "intellectual", in the *original* sense. Nowadays, an intellectual is someone who is full of ideas and thoughts. [See Mahat and Intellectus]

Nuhrā
Aramaic: "Light". Illumination, Radiance, Glory, Enlightenment, Pure Consciousness, Superior Intelligence, Brightness, Illuminative Substance. [See *Light*]

Nūr
Arabic: "Light". Illumination, Radiance, Illuminative Substance. The Light of God, the Splendour of God, the Glory of God (which is Omnipotence Itself). The Muslim Mystics also call this Light Yaqīn, "the Light of Intuitive Certainty".

Nūr
Persian: The Light; the Moonlight (in the Heart).

Nūrā
Persian: "Light". Illumination, Radiance, Glory, Enlightenment, Pure Consciousness, Superior Intelligence, Brightness, Illuminative Substance.

Nūr 'Alī
Arabic: "Light Most Exalted". The Grand Revealer of the Mysteries of the Heart and the Secrets of the Universe.

Nūrānī
Arabic: The serene, clear Light in the Heart.

Nūrjahān
Persian: The Light of the World (that is, the Light *within* the World).

Nūrul-'Irfān
Arabic: The Light of Gnosis. Direct Realization of the Truth.

Nūrullāh
Arabic: "God's Light". It is God's Light that performs all deeds, all miracles, and gives all powers to the Saints (Sūfīs).

O

Obsession
Latin: From Obsessio, "a blockade, a siege". It also means "being bewitched". *Obsession* has two different meanings:

- The domination of one's thoughts and feelings by a persistent idea, desire, person, goal, image or object.
- An hostile action by an evil spirit (a dead human or an elemental or a non-human spirit).

Oikonomia
Greek: The Divine Plan.

Ojas
Sanskrit: Virility, strength, energy, drive, power, the warrior spirit, the male drive, the supreme masculine force.

Ojas-Śakti
Sanskrit: Mental energy.

Okeanos
Greek: "The Waters of Space". The Mother Substance, the First Matter. Primordial Space. Hence the English word *ocean*. In Latin, the "Mother Substance" was called Prima Materia. In Sanskrit, Nārā.

Olam
Hebrew: A world, a realm, a kingdom, a sphere or plane of Being. The same as the Arabic word 'Ālam and the Sanskrit Loka.

Ōṁ
Sanskrit: The Word of Glory, the Praṇava (Fundamental-Sound-Vibration of the Universe), Śabda (the Universal Sound), the Boundless Light, the Solar Logos, the Sun, the Absolute-Consciousness, Parabrahman (the Transcendental Absolute), Eternal Oneness. Ōṁ is the Divine Word for Evolution, moving upwards and forwards and out of the Three Realms. Ōṁ is the Cosmic Word, the Logos, in the process of *ascending*, moving out of the Sphere of Creation-Activity. Ōṁ is the Sound of Purification

and Union, Liberation and Resurrection, the Second Aspect of the Deity, the Christ Aspect or Power, the Sounding-Light Vibration which releases you from bondage to your forms and bodies. Ōṁ is the Formless-Self, the Sea of Pure Consciousness, Formless Awareness. Ōṁ is the Word of the Soul. [See Āuṁ and Nāda]

Oṁkāra
Sanskrit: The Creative Energy. The God-into-Incarnation Power. The Sounding-Light. The Eternal Word. The Divine Word or Vibration. The Logos, Śabda-Brahman, the Universal Reverberation of God.

Ōṁ Maṇi Padme Hūṁ
Sanskrit: The Jewel in the Lotus. From Maṇi (jewel) and Padma (lotus, the Heart Centre). [See Maṇi-Padma]

Ōṁ-Sai (Āuṁ-Sai)
Sanskrit: The Substance of all things, the Universal Nature, the One Undivided Mother. [See Āuṁ-Sai]

Ōṁ Śrī
Sanskrit: Holy Vibration, Divine Energy (Daivi-Śakti). Śrī is the Energy of the Sacred, the Holy, the Divine. There is material energy and there is Spiritual Energy. Śrī is Pure Spiritual Energy or Vibration. Ōṁ Śrī is the Brightness of the Eternal Glory, the Goddess at Her highest State, the Transcendental Self of All. The Goddess is the Total Energy of the Universe. She is *Everywhere*. But Her highest Form is *Pure Creative Intelligence*, Ōṁ Śrī, the Vibration of Holiness, the Self-Radiant Power. [See Śrī]

Omnipotent
From the Latin Omni and Potens: Infinite in power, unlimited in authority. All-powerful, mighty, supreme. A description of the Godhead.

Omnipresent
From the Latin Omni and Praesens: Being present everywhere at the same time. Ubiquitous. A description of the Godhead. God is the all-enveloping Divine Law and Reality.

Omniscient
From the Latin Omni and Sciens: Having unlimited knowledge and understanding. The power to perceive and comprehend all things at once. A description of the Godhead.

Onomatopoeia
Greek: "A sound which stands for Revelation". The Greek equivalent of the Sanskrit word Mantra. Derived from the Greek Hōnoma (Hōnyma), "a name, a sound, a word" or "the Name or Sound-Vibration" (the same as the Sanskrit Nāma), and Poiein, "to produce, to make, to become". Thus, Onomatopoeia means "a word or sound-vibration which was created to reveal itself" (its hidden meaning, which imitates or reveals something).

Ōr, Ūr
Hebrew: Light. [See Aur]

Ōrāculum
Latin: An Oracle. A person who goes into a "trance" and receives answers to questions asked of them. The famous *Oracles* of ancient Greece and Rome were usually young, mediumistic women or girls, or trained priests and priestesses, who left their bodies in astral projections and sought out answers or information requested of them.

Orthodoxos
Greek: "Correct belief" or "Having acquired the right understanding of Life and Reality". From Orthos (right, correct, true) and Doxa (thought, idea, opinion, belief). From this we have the degenerated English word *orthodox:* conforming to a philosophy or ideology; beliefs or attitudes approved by the church in ignorance, or with immobilized thought-patterns (which usually do not conform to Truth at all!).

Osiris
Egyptian: The Father Light. [See Isis and Horus]

Ouranos
Greek: "Heaven". The multi-dimensionality of Space, as a Unity or Oneness, as a Continuum between the within (the above) and the without (the below). Shemayā in Aramaic, Shamayīm in Hebrew, Caelum in Latin, Ākāśa in Sanskrit. [See *Heaven*]

Our Lady
The great Being who, two thousand years ago, voluntarily became the Mother of Jesus. That great Being was, and still is, an Avatāra (Divine Embodiment) of the Great Feminine Intelligence. She is also known as *The World Mother of Compassionate Heart*. In China She incarnated as *Quan Yin*. We are talking about a real Being, not a mythology. She is neither human nor angelic, but beyond both. Our Lady, Mary, is truly a Queen in the Spiritual Realms, a Queen of Angels and of Mankind, a Queen of vast Powers and Consciousness, yet of extreme *simplicity* and *humility*. She was a human Adept and Master, and went over to the Angelic Kingdom and became an Adept and Master there. Then She rose above all to become the Queen who embodies all the *feminine powers and virtues* of the Logos, the Lord of all. She is the embodiment of the Cosmic Heart-Love, for the Heart of the Deity is Love. She embodies an infinite Love and a tender Mother-Compassion for all beings of all species. She embodies all that is best and noble in Love, Compassion, self-sacrifice, forgiveness, understanding, pity, working for the happiness of others, caring for others, fulfilling the needs of all beings of all types, and leading them to the Path of Liberation through the Power of Love. Her mission is Universal Love. To follow Her is to follow the Heart and the intense Joy of the Spirit, for She is intensely Joyful, Blissful and inwardly Serene. [See Marīa and Quan Yin]

P

Pada
Sanskrit: A footstep, a step, a pace, a place, a trace of something, a concept, a viewpoint, a word.

Pāda
Sanskrit: A quarter, a chapter, a part, a foot, a section, a stage, a path.

Padam
Sanskrit: Station. A state of Being.

Padma
Sanskrit: The lotus flower. The Heart Centre.

Padmapāṇi
Sanskrit: "Lotus-born". Born out of the Spiritual Lotus, the Universal Heart. The Saviour born in the Heart Centre. The Goddess, whose very Substance is the Energy of Love and Primeval Wisdom.

Padma-Siddhi
Sanskrit: The Heart's Power.

Pāgānus
Latin: "A country person or villager". The Christian religionists declared anybody who did not believe in their orthodox beliefs (beliefs sanctioned by their "authorities") as "pagan". [See Infidēlis]

Palingenesia
Greek: Spiritual Regeneration. The freeing of the Soul from the limitations of the body, mind and emotions whereby one attains Union with God. This is the true Mystery Tradition of the Greeks, Romans and Egyptians, and is the same as the Yogic idea of Samādhi.

Pañcaḍaṣa-Ākśarī-Mantra
Sanskrit: "Fifteen-Syllabled Mantra". The Pañcaḍaṣī-Mantra.

Pañcadaṣī
Sanskrit: "Fifteen years old". A Name of Lalitā, the Goddess.

Pañcadaṣī-Mantra
Sanskrit: The Fifteen-Syllabled Mantra. Also called the Mūla-Mantra (Root or Foundation Mantra) or the Śrī-Vidyā-Mantra. The Pañcadaṣī or Mūla-Mantra is the Subtle Body or Subtle Form of Lalitā. This Subtle Form consists of Sounding-Light Vibrations.

Para, Param, Parama
Sanskrit: Beyond, above, supreme, transcendental, infinite, absolute. Far, remote. Proceeding from. Another, of others.

Parā, Paramā
Sanskrit: Going to a distance, going away, going forth. The Supreme, the Highest, the Transcendent. The Supreme Sound-Vibration.

Pāra
Sanskrit: Beyond, above, fulfilling, completing.

Para-Bhakti
Sanskrit: Supreme-Devotion, Supreme-Faith. Intense Devotion, which is a characteristic of the Heart. The condition when your Heart is completely opened up, when your Heart *sees* God in everything and in everyone—angels, humans, animals, plants—and you *experience* the Divine Presence everywhere.

Parabola
Greek: A story, an allegory. A symbolic speech by Jesus in the New Testament, with hidden, spiritual values. From Para (beside, alongside, beyond, past) and Balein (to throw, to cast). Hence the English word *parable*. An enigmatic narrative, similar to the Zen Kōan.

Parabrahman
Sanskrit: "Beyond Brahman". The Supreme Creative Intelligence. The One God. The Transcendental Reality. The Supreme Godhead. The Supremely Transcendent. The Unutterable Truth. The Absolute Beingness. The Godhead beyond and above the Creator (Brahmā). The Unknowable Absolute, which is limitless and which spreads Itself through endless Space. The Hebrews used to call this Ain, the pre-Genesis God-Self. Parabrahman and Ain (Hebrew) refer to the Absolute in the Absolute Condition, out of which is emanated the Limitless Light which contains the Universal Mind and all the Creator-Gods. It is also called Tat (That), because no words can describe It, no thought can approach It. It is the One Universal Existence, which includes within Itself all that is Manifest (Vyakta) and all that is Unmanifest (Avyakta), the Past, Present and Future, Time and Space, and also Eternity. When in Creation, this Unmanifest Godhood forms a Veil upon Itself (Mūlaprākṛtī) which conceals It from the sight of all created beings.

Parabuddhi
Sanskrit: Superconsciousness. The Transcendental State.

Para-Devatā
Sanskrit: The Supreme Divinity.

Paradise
The exalted conditions of the Buddhic Plane, the Plane of Illumination.

Parakāya-Praveṣa-Siddhi
Sanskrit: "Another's-body-entering-power". The ability to enter into other bodies at will, fully conscious, *when it serves a higher purpose*. (This is *not* the same process as mediumship.) Also called Paraśarīra-Āveśaḥ-Siddhi.

Paralipomena
Greek: The esoteric and secret sayings of Jesus that survived the enthusiastic spree of destruction by the church authorities of the first four centuries after Christ.

Paramā
Sanskrit: She who is beyond all things. The Transcendental One. The Supreme or Original Divine Female Archetype. A Name of Lalitā, the Goddess.

Paramahaṁsa
Sanskrit: The Transcendental or Supreme Soul or Spirit within the Universe. The Supreme Self, the Glorious Spiritual Sun. The Omnipresent Spirit of God. Haṁsa is Ātman, the Pure Spirit within you. Paramahaṁsa is Paramātman, the Transcendental Godhead. Paramahaṁsa also means "the Transcendental Breath Process". When your human breath (Prāṇa) is tranquillized, then you begin to breathe *in* the Spirit, the Supreme Breath, Paramahaṁsa, and you begin to breathe *out* the Spirit, the Paramātman, over the world for the benefit of all beings. Paramahaṁsa also means "a Realized person". [See Haṁsa]

Paramānanda
Sanskrit: Absolute Bliss.

Paramānandā (Paramā-Ānandā)
Sanskrit: She who is Transcendental-Bliss-Consciousness. From Ānanda (bliss, joy, happiness) and Paramā (the Transcendent). A Name of Lalitā, the Goddess. In this State there is no more sorrow.

Paramāṅganā
Sanskrit: The most beautiful Female in the Universe. The Super-Woman. The perfect expression of Womanhood. A Name of Lalitā, the Goddess.

Para-Mantra
Sanskrit: The Transcendental Power. The Śrī-Vidyā-Mantra.

Paramapadātmava
Sanskrit: The Transcendent. The Absolute. The one Buddha-Nature in the Universe.

Paramāpūrva-Nirvāṇa-Śakti
Sanskrit: "The Supreme-Ancient-Nirvāṇic-Energy". Nirvāṇa, the plane of Ātman, is the Source of all Creation, including the lower, intermediate and highest realms. And unto Nirvāṇa, or Ātman (the Soul of the Universe), we shall all Return. That is our Goal.

Paramātman
Sanskrit: "The Supreme Being above the Universe." The Supreme Self, the Universal Self, the Eternal Self, the Transcendental Self, the Transcendental Spirit. The Universal Soul, the Over-Soul of the Universe. The Ancient of the Ancients, the Universal Godhead, the Light of Lights. The Absolute Being, the Absolute Existence, Universal Life. The Monad, the "Father in Heaven". Paramātman can be found and experienced in your Heart Centre. Within your Heart, the One Self, Paramātman, can be seen. This One Self is within all forms, large or small, atomic or solar-systemic. When found in meditation, in deep Mystical Experience, Paramātman will become your Inner Teacher and Guide, the Sat Guru.

Paramātmikā (Param-Ātmikā)
Sanskrit: The Supreme Soul, the Highest Spirit, the Greatest Self. The Supreme Intelligence within and beyond the Cosmos. Paramātman.

Paramātmikā (Paramā-Ātmikā)
Sanskrit: The Transcendental Soul of the Universe. The Supreme Being, the Highest Existence. A Name of Lalitā, the Goddess.

Parameśvara (Param-Īśvara)
Sanskrit: The Supreme Lord of the Universe.

Parameśvarī (Paramā-Īśvarī)
Sanskrit: The Supreme Goddess, the Transcendental Goddess. The Goddess beyond all Creation, forms, manifestation and phenomena. The Sovereign Goddess, the Exalted. The Highest (Paramā) Protector (Īśvarī). Lalitā is the best Guide and Protector. Parameśvarī, the Supreme Goddess, lives in the Heart.

Paramitā
Sanskrit: The Transcendental, Immoveable, Unchangeable, Eternal Form, *beyond* all the Realms and Worlds of Being. The Transcendental Aspect of the Goddess. Transcendental Virtue and Knowledge. [See Prajñāparamitā]

Param-Jyotī
Sanskrit: The Supreme Light. The Highest (Param) Radiance (Jyotī). The Transcendental (Param) Brightness (Jyotī). A Name of Lalitā, the Goddess.

Paranirvāṇa
Sanskrit: "Beyond Nirvāṇa". The Paranirvāṇic Plane is the realm of Paramātman, the Monad, the "Father in Heaven", the Universal Divine Spirit in Man. Also called Aṇupādaka (the Monadic World) and Tapah-Loka (the Fiery Realm).

Paraśakti
Sanskrit: "The Supreme Power". The Cosmic Energy, the Primordial Consciousness, the Cosmic Mother Force, the Universal Power of Reality. Paraśakti and Kuṇḍalinī-Śakti are the same thing: an all-pervading Field of Cosmic Energy. Kuṇḍalinī-Śakti is the Supreme Power. It is the Universal-Life-Principle in all of Nature and within the whole Universe. It exists within Man, the plant, the stone, the tree, the angel, the god, planet, sun, star or galaxy, and in interstellar space. Paraśakti is the Dynamic Manifesting Power of Divinity, the Active Principle of the Cosmos, the Substratum of all Creation, the Absolute Consciousness, the Creatrix of the Universe, the Potency and Power within the atoms on all planes: physical atoms, astral atoms, mental atoms, Buddhic atoms and Nirvāṇic atoms. Atoms are simply units of Energy (Śakti) on the Seven Great Planes of Being of Cosmic-Nature, Mahat-Prākṛtī. Whatever exists is made up of Energy units of Kuṇḍalinī. But the Energy is One. All activities in the Cosmos are done by the One Force, Kuṇḍalinī. This Force is also the *substance* out of which all forms (bodies) are made, whether human, angelic, animal, vegetable, planetary or solar-systemic. One Force equals One Substance.

Parā-Śaktī
Sanskrit: The Supreme Power. A Name of Lalitā, the Goddess. She is the Power that transcends all Creation, and She is the Power that is the Energy in all Matter, forms, bodies and substances.

Para-Śakti-Maya
Sanskrit: "Supreme-Energy-full-of". The Goddess is full of the Ultimate Energy of the Universe. She *is* the Ultimate Energy.

Paraśāma
Sanskrit: The Absolute Tranquillity. Divine Peace.

Parāsaṁvit
Sanskrit: The Omniscient. The Supreme Intelligence. A quality of Prakāśa, the Eternal Light.

Para-Śiva
Sanskrit: The Supreme Consciousness.

Parātparaḥ (Parāt-Para)
Sanskrit: Higher than the Highest. The Supreme, the Transcendental.

Parā-Vāk (Parāvāch)
Sanskrit: The Supreme (Parā) Speech (Vāk). The Transcendental (Parā) Logos (Vāk). The Supreme Speech of the Logos, the Creative Word, the Original Sound-Vibration, issuing from the Formless Universe. A Name of Lalitā, the Goddess.

Pariṇāma
Sanskrit: Transformation, change. The transformation of Consciousness.

Parousia
Greek: "The Second Coming". Revelation. The experiencing of the Pure Consciousness of the Christ Being, the Christ Light, the Being of Light, the Buddhi, the "Christ in you, your hope of Glory" of Saint Paul, the "Buddha-Nature" of the Buddhists. The word Parousia has been interpreted as the physical coming of the Christ. For the Mystic, however, Parousia is the coming of the Christ into the Soul, the Divinization of the human being, the *direct experience* of the outpouring of the Universal Christ Light.

Parrisia
Greek: "Talking to God". Inner Communion with God. This is not the same as the way some of the fundamentalist and evangelical Christians "talk to God"—talking verbally or mentally to God as an old man sitting on a throne in heaven (which is usually talking to themselves). This Inner Communion with God is possible for the Saints only after years of meditation and inner development. They have to be in the condition known in the East as Buddhi—Enlightened, Intuitive—which is *not* a verbal-mental consciousness.

Pārvatī
Sanskrit: The Daughter of the Mountains. She is the Great Yoginī forever meditating in the Sacred Mountains (the Spiritual Planes) in Ecstatic Contemplation of Reality. She is the Force which channels your energies towards the higher planes, transcends the mind, leads you out of the lower realms. A Name of Lalitā, the Goddess.

Paśyantī, Paśyantīvāk, Paśyantīvāch
Sanskrit: Transcendental Sound-Vibration. The Voice of the Silence, issuing from the Buddhic Realms and above. [See Vaikharī and Madhyamā]

Patañjali
Sanskrit: "One who should be worshipped". A holy man, a Seer. Patañjali was a great Sage who lived in India before the time of Christ. His full name was Mahā-Ṛṣi Patañjali, the Great Sage Patañjali. He was also known as Yogindra, the King or Chief of Yogīs. Patañjali is considered by the schools of Rāja Yoga to be "the father of Yoga", but there was Yoga in India thousands of years before Patañjali. It so happened that Patañjali wrote down a few notes of what he had learned from his teachers, known as the Yoga Sūtras. Patañjali's Yoga Sūtras are also known as Patañjala Yoga Sūtra and Yoga Darśanam (the Teachings on Yoga). The work consists of 196 Sūtras (verses or aphorisms) on Yoga-Vidyā (the Science of Union).

Pathos
Greek: Passions, strong emotions, vehement feelings. Hence the English words *pathology, pathos* and *pathetic*. Pathology is the study of physical diseases and illnesses, whereas the original Greek word refers not to the physical body, but to passions, feelings, desires and emotional states. How words are changed by later generations! The desert fathers listed several "passions" that were deadly harmful for Spiritual Life and Illumination: gluttony, avarice, pride, bitterness, anger, unchastity, laziness, spiritual ignorance. [See Apatheia]

Pāvana
Sanskrit: The Angelic Ruler of the Nirvāṇic Plane.

Peirasmos
Greek: Tests, trials, that by which the genuineness of anything may be determined. Commonly translated by scholars as "temptations". The Old Testament Jewish idea was that sometimes God sends tests or trials to Man, even tempts a person to see how genuine is his or her fidelity to God. This is an incorrect understanding. It is more the other way around: men and women test themselves by mismatching themselves to the Radiant Glory of God. When we understand the Law of Cause and Effect (Karma in the East, and "as you sow, so shall you reap" in the Bible), then we realize that most evils which come to us are the results of our own wrongdoings—conscious or unconscious.

Pentad, Pentagram ☆
Greek: The five-pointed star. The mind, the ordinary mental faculty, the personal mind, the seeking mind, the power-driven mind. (This is not the Divine Mind, Nous.)

Permanent Atoms
You, the Living Soul (Jīva), dwelling in your Augoeides (Greek: causal body), possess *Permanent Atoms* in your auric-field which belong to the Physical, Astral and lower Mental Planes. You carry these Permanent Atoms with you; they register your evolutionary qualities and enable you to build new physical, astral and mental bodies, life after life. These Permanent

Atoms register both good and evil qualities; thus your character is already predestined before your birth. You can change or improve yourself only while in physical incarnation, and the Permanent Atoms will then take on these new impressions.

Persephone

Greek: The Queen of Hades, the Underworld, "the abode of the dead" (the Astral World).

Personality

The lower self. From the Latin Persona. In the old Roman days, a Persona was a mask an actor wore for a particular act or play. Thus, the personality is but a mask over the Soul. The Soul is immortal, the personality is not. At death the Soul gradually removes the personality or mask it has worn for that lifetime (the physical, etheric, astral and mental bodies). Personality means acting, pretending, role-playing, which people do so seriously! [See Tetrakti]

Phainomenon

Greek: "What is seen". The physical universe, or the universe of sense-perception. From this we have the English word *phenomenon.*

Phantasia

Greek: "A non-physical appearance, a phantom". The origin of the English word *fantasy* (an illusion, a fancy, something unreal, a delusion, an hallucination). To the contemplative Christian fathers, however, Phantasia specifically meant the image-producing faculty of the Soul—the power of *imagination.* When through prayer, meditation or contemplation you break through the ordinary mind, you will *perceive* Phantasia, the realm of the subconscious mind, with all its images, symbols, pictures and archetypes. In modern terminology it is called the *Astral World.* The whole land of Phantasia is intensely active today; millions of people are in the grip of it, including many fundamentalist and evangelical Christians. The Christian Saints warned their disciples not to pay attention to the land of Phantasia, but to go beyond it, above it, to the pure, formless contemplation of the Divine Essence, the Essential Light.

Philadelpheia

Greek: The love of one's particular group.

Philiā

Greek: The love between family members, brothers, sisters, children and close friends. Friendship.

Philokalia

Greek: "The Love of the Good" (God was often called "the Good" by the Ancients). The striving for Perfection. The Philokalia is the voluminous writings of the Eastern Saints of early Christianity. It lists dozens of Saints representing the hundreds of thousands of Christians of the Eastern Orthodox Church who meditated upon God's Name in the Heart. Some of it has been preserved in Russian and Slavonic, and it has been translated into English. It is the greatest book on this Earth on the subject of Prayer in the Heart. "Walk in the Spirit and you will not walk in the ways of the flesh."

Philosopher's Stone

The legendary treasure sought after by the medieval Alchemists. The Philosopher's Stone is manufactured in the Head with the fusion of the pituitary and pineal glands. When the Third-Eye Centre and the Crown Centre become one, the Great Enlightenment occurs and the Alchemist or true Philosopher becomes a Buddha and attains Immortality. The ancient Jewish Sages called this A B N (Ehben), "the Stone of the Wise".

Philosophia

Greek: "The Love of Wisdom" (Philo-Sophia). From this came the English word *philosophy,* but in ancient Greece the word did *not* mean what it means today—merely intellectual verbiage! To the Initiated Greek Sages of old, Philosophy was a detached Contemplation of Reality. It had to do with Contemplation rather than speculation and analysing the meaning of words. This Contemplation is an inner process of Understanding. Wisdom (Sophia) is on the Buddhic Plane, perceived by the Spiritual Soul.

Philosophos
Greek: "A Seeker of Wisdom". A Philosopher. Originally, a *Philosopher* was a Wiseman or Wisewoman, an Initiate who had Buddhic Consciousness.

Phōs, Phōtismos
Greek: "Light". Illumination, Radiance, Glory, Enlightenment, Pure Consciousness, Superior Intelligence, Brightness, Illuminative Substance.

Phronesis
Greek: Wisdom, prudence. A regulated life.

Phylaki Kardias
Greek: "The guarding of the Heart". Having your attention in the Heart. Centring in the Heart. Constantly invoking a Divine Name in the Heart. The practice of keeping the Heart free from worldly thoughts and influences, and praying to God in the Heart for help and mercy. This is the most important practice of the Christian Saints of the Eastern Tradition. [See Kardia]

Phylaki Nou
Greek: "The guarding of the mind". This, after *the guarding of the Heart,* is the next most important practice: watching over our thoughts, day and night, being constantly *aware* of all that goes on in our minds, and consciously resisting any evil impulses in our minds. This is similar to the Buddhist practice of *mindfulness.*

Physical Body
On the Physical Plane you have two bodies:

- Your gross physical body (Sthūla-Śarīra) exists on the lower part of the Physical Plane and consists of solids, liquids and gases. Also called Annamāyākośa (the illusionary food-body).
- Your subtle physical or etheric-physical body (Liṅga-Śarīra) exists on the etheric subplanes and is made up of the four states of etheric-physical matter. Also called Prāṇamāyākośa (the illusionary vehicle of Prāṇa).

Your dense physical body is the least-real part of you. It is an inert mass, vitalized by your etheric body, which is in turn vitalized by your astral body.

Physical Plane
The seventh and last of the seven great Planes of Being. In Sanskrit, Pṛthivī-Loka or Bhūr-Loka. The lower three subplanes of the Physical Plane are called the *dense* or *gross* physical subplanes, corresponding to the three states of matter that we observe with our physical senses: solids, liquids and gases. The higher four subplanes are called the *etheric* or *etheric-physical* dimensions. Science is beginning to explore the etheric dimensions, without understanding them as such.

Physis
Greek: Matter, substance, the gross Creation. Nature on the Physical Plane. Hence the English words *physical* and *physics.* The same as the Latin Natura (Nature).

Physis, Physikos
Greek: In the terminology of the ancient Greek Sages, the Physis and Physikos were the materialistic, ignorant, blind people. These were the worldly-minded masses, ordinary Humanity: body-oriented, materialistic, unbelieving, agnostic, ignorant, sarcastic about the possibility of non-physical realities. These were the people who believed that the Cosmos grinds on aimlessly, from nothing to nothing, having no rhyme or reason at all. They were also called Agnōstikos and Agnostos (the ignorant), from Agnosia (nescience, spiritual darkness, spiritual blindness or ignorance, worldly consciousness). The Gnōstikos (Gnostics) were the Wise Ones, the Knowers, the Enlightened Ones. [See *Materialism*]

Pilgrim
The pilgrims were Christian ascetics of the early centuries who, like the sādhus and sannyāsins of India, lived nowhere and everywhere. There were many of them in Russia, Asia Minor and Greece. They never settled down anywhere, but travelled on foot visiting holy places or shrines.

Piṅgalā
Sanskrit: The subtle energy current on the right side of the Suṣumna or subtle spinal chord in the etheric-physical body. The Sun-current. The energy of psychic unfoldment. Active psychic energy. [See Īḍā]

Pīr
Persian: The Spiritual Teacher, the Spiritual Master, the Guru.

Pīr-o-Murshid
Persian: A venerable Teacher or Guru. Ancient, wise. A Sage.

Piscean Age
The zodiacal period of approximately 2150 years, preceding the Aquarian Age. The Piscean Age is presently drawing to a close. The Stream of Energy that was predominant during the Piscean Age (the Sixth Ray) produced in Human Consciousness the phenomenon of intense *idealism*. The orientation of the Piscean Age was towards the Soul and the invisible worlds and Realities, towards "God" (howsoever people understood that word). The Piscean Age became a Dark Age because people rejected Jesus' new Teachings, the new Energy, the new activity of the Holy Spirit. They rejected Jesus while He was still alive, and after His death they quickly reverted to their old ways of thinking. They pretended that Jesus merely taught old Judaism.

Pisces
Latin: The fishes, an early symbol of the Christ-Energy. In many early Christian churches and gathering places, the Christ was symbolized as a fish or two fishes, drawn or painted on the walls.

Pistis
Greek: Faith, belief, ordinary religion. The power of faith in the Divine. Hope for Glory in the Godhead. Also, those people who have faith and belief. The religious fundamentalists and orthodoxies. To the early Christian Masters, however, faith was not only a matter of *belief* in God or in Jesus, but a total transformation or reorientation of one's life towards God.

Pītha
Sanskrit: A Knot of Power. A swirling centre of Force, Energy, Radiation.

Pitṛi
Sanskrit: Forefather, progenitor, ancestor. The Pitṛis are non-human, divine and semi-divine types of Angelic Hosts, the angelic progenitors of Humanity. Some of the Pitṛis were originally Arūpa (bodiless).

Pitṛi-Devas
Sanskrit: The non-human or angelic progenitors of Mankind.

Pitṛi-Loka
Sanskrit: The place of the departed ancestors. The Astral World.

Planes of Being
The seven great Planes of Being are seven states of Mahat-Prākṛtī (Cosmic Nature, the Cosmic Physical Plane). The Planes of Being are realms, worlds or conditions of existence. Each plane (Loka) is associated with:

- Certain densities of matter.
- A state of consciousness.
- Particular senses of perception associated with that consciousness.
- Actions of particular forces.
- Certain beings or entities which inhabit that realm.
- Forms or "bodies" through which entities can interact with the matter and energies of that realm.

Each of the seven great Planes of Being, the seven dimensions of our Universe, occupies the one Space. The Space is the same, but the *dimensions* are different, the *densities of matter* are different, and the *consciousness* is different in each of the strata of Creation. The matter or substance of each plane *interpenetrates* the one below it, which is of lower vibration and greater density.

Planetary Hierarchy
Humanity's spiritual unfoldment is taken care of by the Planetary Hierarchy, the Spiritual Hierarchy, the Great White Brotherhood, the Inner Government of the World, the Brotherhood of Light. It is called by many names. [See *Spiritual Hierarchy*]

Planetary Logos
A "Heavenly Man" which incarnates through the vehicle of a planet. One of the Cosmic Creators.

Plani
Greek: Illusion, delusion, material bondage, spiritual ignorance, worldly consciousness. Being bonded to materialistic, physical consciousness, and not being aware of one's Soul-Nature. The same as the Sanskrit Māyā.

Plerōma
Greek: The All-Containing Reality. That which contains the All. The Divine Fullness, the Absolute, the All-in-All. The Fullness of Space, the Fullness of Light. Total Space as the Living Body of the Absolute Reality. The Fullness of the All-Mind, the Universal or Divine Mind, in which all things exist. The totality of all that is, visible and invisible. The limitless dimension, the Manifest and the Unmanifest. The Universal Soul of all Existence, from Matter to Spirit. The Cosmic Fullness in which the myriads of galaxies and star systems and planets move and function. The Great Mother, the Mother of the Universe, including all seven Planes of Being and all that is within them. Each of the seven great Planes of Being of the Solar System is a state of Plerōma. The Mental Plane, for instance, is the fifth state of Plerōma (counting downwards), while the Physical Plane (the objective, physical universe) is the seventh state of Plerōma. The Plerōma is the All-Pervading Spiritual Existence. In Latin, Omnirevelation, Omniverse. Equivalent to the Upaniṣadic Pūrṇa (Perfection, Completeness).

Pneuma
Greek: "Spirit, breath, air, wind, life". The Life-Breath, the Spirit of God, the Breath of God. God's Power of Manifestation. The Soul or Essence behind a body or form. Used in the Greek Mystery Schools for the Third Aspect of the Deity, the Holy Spirit, the Virgin-Spirit of the Universe, the Universal Soul. Similar to the Latin Spiritus, the Hebrew Ruach, the Sanskrit Prāṇa, the Chinese Chi.

Pneuma-Hagion
Greek: "Breath-Holy". The Holy Spirit, Holy Breath, Holy Life-Force, Holy Creative Power. The Organizing and Structurizing Power within the Universe. God's Divine Mind at work, or Cosmic Intelligence. Ruḥā-Qadash in Aramaic, Ruah-Ha-Qadosh in Hebrew, Spiritus-Sanctus in Latin.

Pneumata
Greek: Spirits or Souls. Those people who are spiritually awake. The practised meditators. The Knowers (Gnostics). Those who have Mystical Awareness. Those who have attained Salvation and Liberation.

Poltergeist
From the German: "Noisy spirit". Poltergeist phenomena are characterized by the moving and breaking of physical objects. While poltergeist phenomena are generally caused by chaotic astral-etheric-sexual energies, sometimes elementals, elementaries (thoughtforms) in the atmosphere, and genuine human and non-human agencies on the Astral can be involved.

Poseidonis
Greek: An island, remembered by the ancient Greeks, which sank beneath the waves of the Atlantic Ocean thousands of years earlier. Poseidon was the last remnant of the old Atlantis which was destroyed in four great cataclysms over a vast period of time.

Prabhākara
Sanskrit: Light-maker. The Solar Logos.

Prabhu
Sanskrit: Lord, Master, God.

Pracodayāt
Sanskrit: He who unfolds, invigorates, stimulates, unveils. May He unfold, transform, enliven, enlighten, guide, empower, impel, propel, inspire, motivate, quicken and energize, stir up and vitalize, sharpen understanding, lead towards Illumination, direct body, mind and Soul to improvement and growth on all levels.

Prada
Sanskrit: The Giver, the Bestower.

Praḍhāna
Sanskrit: Original Cause. Primordial Matter. The Primordial Substance which is given order and system during each Manvantara or Day of Manifestation. The same as Mūla-Prākṛtī (the Root of Nature). This is Nirvāṇa, the plane of Ātmā, from which the Descent of Creation begins. Nirvāṇa is not only the *end* of the evolutionary process, but its *source* or *beginning* also. Nirvāṇa is the Alpha and the Omega, the Beginning and the End, the First and the Last.

Praḍhāna Jaya Siddhi
Sanskrit: The power over the evolutionary forces of Nature. Here you must not limit yourself to the limited scientific theory of evolution, for Evolution is multi-dimensional. The forward movement of all things in the Physical World is the result of a downward push from the Astral Universe, which itself reacts to forces pushing downwards from the Mental Plane, which itself adapts to the Plan in the Buddhic World, which itself tries to manifest the Seed or Germ of things which have been planted in Śamballa.

Praḍhāna-Loka
Sanskrit: The Formless Unity-Field. Buddhi and Nirvāṇa.

Prajāpati
Sanskrit: "Lord of Creatures (of the born)". From Pati (Lord, Master, God) and Prajā (propagation, birth, offspring). The Creator-Lord, the Creator-God. An emanation of Brahmā, the Creator. [See Elohīm]

Prajñā
Sanskrit: The Ocean of Wisdom. The Wisdom-Mind. This is not the worldly wisdom, but the inner vision and experience of the Higher Realities. This is the mind-transcending, Truth-discerning Awareness of Pure Consciousness, the Buddhic Consciousness. It is pure Knowing, without words, without thoughts, without the mind. It is the Wisdom of seeing into one's Self-Nature. This Self-Nature contains within itself all the universes, all the stars and galaxies, all the worlds, all the angels and human beings, all heavens and hells. This is the Transcendental Wisdom of the Buddhic and Nirvāṇic Planes. It is the state of Inward Oneness with all things. In Prajñā there is no birth and no death.

Prajñā-Jyoti
Sanskrit: "Wisdom-Light". When you have sufficiently purified your mind, then the Light of Wisdom spontaneously arises in your mind.

Prajñānam
Sanskrit: The Awakened Consciousness.

Prajñāparamitā
Sanskrit: "Transcendental Wisdom". The realization of the Self-Nature, the Buddha-Mind—Samādhi, Zen, Satori, Bodhi. This is "the Christ in you, your hope of Glory", as expressed by Saint Paul.

Prākāmya
Sanskrit: To have irresistible will-power. The power to pervade all things, to become visible or invisible, to have all wishes fulfilled. This is one of the nine "general" powers (Siddhis) which can manifest in advanced Humanity.

Prakāśa
Sanskrit: Light, Radiance, Glory. The Eternal Light, the Shining Luminosity of Everlasting Splendour, the Light of Revelation. The Brightness, the Shining Forth, the Lustre of Divine Manifestation. This is the Self-Luminous Self, Paramātman. It is the awesome Grandeur, Power, Beauty and Majesty that truly befits the name "God". This Eternal Light

is Omnipresent. You must not imagine this Light in the sense of a candlelight, or an electric light, or sunlight or moonlight. It is not a lifeless "dead-matter" light. This Light is Supreme Intelligence, PARĀSAṀVIT, the Omniscient. Further, this Universal Light is not only Self-Conscious, and not only Omnipresent and Omniscient, but it is also the Omnipotent Power, KARTṚTVA-ŚAKTI, the Power-of-all-Doership, that which creates, sustains and dissolves the Universe (the All). Such is the experience of the Innermost Heart.

PRAKĀŚA-ĀDITYA
Sanskrit: The Universal Sun. The Cosmic Solar Logos.

PRĀKṚTĪ
Sanskrit: Matter, Nature, Substance. The original Primary Substance of the Universe. The Substance of the All. The Goddess, the Feminine Nature, the First or Original Creation, the Archetype of all existing things. The Cosmic Womb or Mother from which All proceeds. From PRA-KṚTI (before Creation). PRĀKṚTĪ refers also to the Physical Plane, and to all seven Planes of Being (MAHAT-PRĀKṚTĪ, Cosmic Nature).

PRĀKṚTĪ-ŚAKTI
Sanskrit: The energies of Nature.

PRAKTIKI
Greek: Purificatory disciplines. Self-discipline. Practising *consciously* the virtues as aids to the spiritual life. The English derivation, *practical,* no longer refers to the spiritual life; nowadays it pertains to action, worldliness, practising something physical, being "a man of the world", and so forth.

PRALAYA
Sanskrit: "The Night of Dissolution". A period of rest or non-manifestation. Death. The end of a cycle of existence, whether for an atom, a man, a planet, a star or a Universe. On a cosmic scale it is the "Night of God", the Divine Condition of absolute rest after the dissolution of Creation, the pre-cosmic Divine Darkness into which Creation returns after evolutionary processes are completed at the end of the MANVANTARA, or Day of God.

PRAMĀDA
Sanskrit: Carelessness, intoxication, drunkenness. One of the ANTARĀYĀḤ (obstacles, impediments, problems on the Path to Higher Consciousness).

PRĀṆA
Sanskrit: "Breath, Life-breath, Life-force, Vitality, Energy, Fire". PRĀṆA is the Universal Life-Force Fire, the Energy of the Universe which flows through all things. It is a spiritual and psychic Energy which becomes the five Elements and gives *substance* to all objects. PRĀṆA, the invisible Life-Force, permeates all the seven great planes of the Solar System from *within*. PRĀṆA is the Breath of Life, the Breath of God, the Universal Life-Force that energizes Creation. Without PRĀṆA, nothing can live, move or have any being in any part of the Universe, on any plane of Being. Life (PRĀṆA) simply Is. It is by PRĀṆA (the One Life) that all beings live and move upon and in all the worlds, visible and invisible. PRĀṆA is planetary, solar-systemic, and universal or cosmic. The lowest physical expression is VĀYU (air, breath). Similar to the Greek PNEUMA, the Hebrew RUACH, the Chinese CHI and the Latin SPIRITUS. All these words mean "breath, air, Life, Vitality, Spirit, Soul, God's Radiant Life-Energy, Cosmic Life".

PRĀṆA-MANTRA
Sanskrit: Breath-Prayer, using breathing with a Divine Name. This is similar to the Christian *Radiant Heart* practice. The early Christians were taught, or discovered, the same technique as that used before them in ancient India.

PRĀṆAMĀYĀKOŚA
Sanskrit: "The illusionary vehicle of PRĀṆA". The etheric-physical body. Also called PRĀṆAMAYAKOŚA (the consisting-of-Prāṇa vehicle).

PRAṆAVA
Sanskrit: The Essence of Life (PRĀṆA-VA). The Creative Word. The Sound of ŌṀ reverberating throughout all Creation. The ŌṀKĀRA (ĀUṀKĀRA), the Sacred Sound, the Sacred Word, VĀK (the Divine Speech), ŚABDA-BRAHMAN (Sounding-God). PRAṆAVA is the Symbol for

the Infinite, the Logos, the Sound-Current, the Path of Return to the Source. PRAṆAVA means the exaltation and praising of God, singing to God, the ĪŚVARA. It also means the Glorious Voice of God, the Sounding-Light Current that brings the Universe into existence, keeps it going, and will dissolve it at the end of the great Cycle of Time (A.U.M). [See ĀUṀ and ŌṀ]

PRAṆAVA-DEHAM
Sanskrit: A Body of Light, made out of PRAṆAVA, the Creative Word or Logos.

PRAṆAVA-VADA
Sanskrit: "The Science of the Sacred Word". The science of ĀUṀ and ŌṀ.

PRĀṆAVĀYU
Sanskrit: The tranquil state of breath which produces the tranquil mind, SAMĀDHI.

PRĀṆĀYĀMA
Sanskrit: "Control of the Life-breath". From PRĀṆA (the Life-force, the Life-breath) and YĀMA (to regulate, to control, to guide). Conscious breathing. Regulation of the vital-force or PRĀṆA, the Breath of Life. PRĀṆĀYĀMA also means PRĀṆA-AYĀMA (no-control, spontaneous, natural). Thus, esoterically, PRĀṆĀYĀMA means breath which is natural, not forced, in balance, equilibrated. Breathing naturally and easily. In the Haṭha Yoga of ancient India there were several dozen PRĀṆĀYĀMA exercises to master, nine of them being the major techniques. To completely master all the proper breathing exercises was the work of many years. In Rāja Yoga, however, you *don't* do all these breathing exercises. For a Rāja Yogī, PRĀṆĀYĀMA means that the breath should flow evenly, simply, naturally, so that it *does not disturb* the meditation process. True PRĀṆĀYĀMA occurs when the in-breathing and the out-breathing are naturally suspended (transcended) and one attains the tranquil state of breath (PRĀṆAVĀYU), which produces the tranquil mind, SAMĀDHI. When your breathing is calm and steady, your mind is calm and steady. When your mind is calm and steady, your breathing is calm and steady. [See KUMBHAKA]

PRAṆIDHĀNA
Sanskrit: Complete Devotion. Surrender to the Divine. Prayer, meditation, contemplation of the Divine. Worship and selfless service to God (ĪŚVARA).

PRĀPTI
Sanskrit: The ability to go to, or manifest on, any of the worlds, planes or realms one wishes. The ability to travel anywhere in Consciousness, to expand in Awareness at will. This is one of the nine "general" powers (SIDDHIS) which can manifest in advanced Humanity.

PRĀRABDHA KARMA
Sanskrit: That Karma which you were born to work out in *this* lifetime, which has to happen by Cosmic Decree, which is precipitating, manifesting, driving or propelling this life of yours now. It is also called DHARMA (fate, destiny). This holds true also for your family, group, country, race or religion. [See SANCITTA KARMA and KRIYAMĀNA KARMA]

PRASĀDA
Sanskrit: Divine Grace. God's Gift. Although there may be a reason or logical explanation for "Grace" which, in the future, Humanity will know how to invoke purposefully, at this stage its workings appear to be mysterious.

PRAŚĀNTA
Sanskrit: Serene, tranquil, calm, peaceful.

PRASŪTĪ
Sanskrit: The Primordial Essence. The Appearance of All. Having come forth from the Unmanifest. Offspring, child, flower.

PRĀTIBHA (PRĀTIBHĀT)
Sanskrit: The Supreme Faculty of Spiritual Awareness of the awakened Crown Cakra. PRĀTIBHA is the Brilliant Light in the Crown Centre, the Effulgent Light of Deity which shines upon all things from *inside* the Universe.

Prātibhā Siddhi
Sanskrit: The power of Divination. This is the true power of *Prophecy*, which has nothing to do with fortune-telling or prediction of the future by any psychic, physical or astrological means. The Seer is bathed in the Fundamental Light of the Universe, on the Buddhic Plane, and from there the prophetic utterances gush forth in mantric rhythms and sentences.

Pratyag-Jyoti
Sanskrit: The Inner Light, the Profound Light. Inwardly-Radiant. This is the Light within the auric-field of the Saints, which gives them a luminous quality.

Pratyāhāra
Sanskrit: "Turning inwards". Withdrawal of the senses (Indriyas) from occupation with outer objects. Ceasing to look at things and hear things. Regular retirement and abstraction from the world. Withdrawing the senses from the outside world and concentrating the attention within oneself, in the Heart or in the Third-Eye. Pratyāhāra is the fifth step of Aṣṭāṅga Yoga, as set down by Patañjali.

Pratyaya
Sanskrit: Cognition, reliance, faith, confidence, trust, means, device.

Pratyeka Buddha
Sanskrit: "An Enlightened One who walks alone". From Buddha (Enlightened One) and Pratyeka (alone). A Solitary Buddha. A fully enlightened Buddha who, having attained Nirvāṇic Consciousness, merges into Nirvāṇa, never to return to the lower realms. The Pratyeka Buddha has moved out of the human evolutionary field altogether and is therefore no longer accessible to Humanity on this planet. [See Nirvāṇī]

Pra-Vṛtti
Sanskrit: Involution. The movement of Spirit into Matter, from the Nirvāṇic Plane down into the dense realms. [See Ni-Vṛtti]

Precognition
The ability to see the future or have foreknowledge of an event. From the Latin Cognitiō (knowledge). *Precognition* is the modern parapsychological term for pre-vision, premonition, second sight, forewarning. This would include also "hunches" and feelings about something that is going to happen.

Prema
Sanskrit: Love. The Love of God. The Universal Love Principle of the Heart. This is not a solar-plexus feeling, affection or emotion. It is not sexual attraction or magnetic energy between opposites. It is not a poetic or idealistic sentiment. It is not an idea or thought wrought by the mind. It is a Fiery Radiance of the Soul coming through the inner chamber of the Heart complex. It is a Love without the feeling of barriers or separation. It is an identification with the All—all life, all creatures. It is not selective, but completely inclusive. It is an immense sense of Unity.

Prema-Īśvara
Sanskrit: The God of universal, infinite and uninterrupted Love. The Universal Heart, which is awakened by meditation in the Heart Centre.

Prema-Rūpā
Sanskrit: She whose Nature is Love. She who is the Embodiment (Rūpa) of Love (Prema). A Name of Lalitā, the Goddess. Devī Lalitā is Incarnate Love. Her Essence is the Energy of Devotion.

Prema-Śakti
Sanskrit: The Energy of Love.

Presbyterion
Greek: A presbyter. A priest. In the early pre-Christian and Christian religions, the priests acted as mediators between Man and God. They had the Guru function, providing spiritual teaching and guidance to those aspiring to the Mysteries of God and the Soul. In today's climate of ignorance, many priests are social workers with no direct knowledge of God, nor of the Soul. [See *Mediator*]

Preta
Sanskrit: A ghost or disembodied spirit. A person on the Astral Plane or on the etheric subplanes of the Physical Plane.

Preta-Loka
Sanskrit: "The Ghost World". The realm of ghosts or disembodied spirits. The lower astral realms and etheric-physical subplanes.

Pṛthivī
Sanskrit: The *Earth* Element. The Cosmic Element corresponding to the substance of the Physical Plane. The *gross* elements throughout the Universal Creation, and also the solid substance of all the matter of the physical universe.

Pṛthivī-Bhūta
Sanskrit: The substance or matter aspect of the Earth Element, Pṛthivī.

Pṛthivī-Tanmātra
Sanskrit: The vibration or force aspect of the Earth Element, Pṛthivī.

Pṛthivītattva
Sanskrit: The essential or subtle aspect of the Earth Element, Pṛthivī.

Prognosis
Greek: Knowing in advance, foreknowledge, insight into the future, knowing the Divine Plan. From Pro (before) and Gnosis (knowledge).

Pronoia
Greek: Thinking ahead, planning for the future, looking ahead of things. Divine Providence (the Divine as *providing* for the Universe). From Pro (before) and Noia (thought).

Prophetes
Greek: Someone who knows the Will of God, the *Plan,* through an interior revelation, by direct experience. One who speaks for God, the Deity. An inspired *revealer* or *interpreter* of the Divine Will, the Divine Plan. From the Greek Prophecein, "to give religious instruction". From this came the English word *prophet.* A Prophet, in the Old Testament sense, and to the early Christians, was one who could speak on behalf of the Deity. Prophets were not confined to Israel only. Before Christianity, the Greeks and the ancient nations had many "prophets". The word, as used by them, had many distinct meanings.

Propheteia
Greek: The gift of prophecy. From the root Prophero, "to bring forth, to foretell". The origin of the English words *prophecy* and *prophesy.* To *prophesy,* in the Old Testament sense, and to the Eastern Christians, the Byzantine Church, meant "to speak by Divine Inspiration, to be moved to speak by the Holy Spirit, to utter Divine Mysteries as moved by the Spirit, to interpret by Inspiration the inner meanings of the scriptures, to preach the Gospel by the power of the Holy Ghost, to reveal the hidden Mysteries of the Kingdom of God *within*".

Prunikos
Greek: The All-Mother, *after* the Conception of the Universe.

Pseudoprophetes
Greek: A false prophet. A false clairvoyant or seer. From Pseudo (false, artificial, pretentious, not genuine, trickster) and Prophetes (a seer, a clairvoyant).

Psyche
Greek: Soul, Spirit, Consciousness, Life. The Inner Being in Man. That part of you which *indwells* the physical body and is *above* your mind. That which does not die at "death". The immortal principle in Man, what is called the Reincarnating Ego, in the causal body on the Causal Plane, above the personality complex. This is the *original* meaning of the word. Nowadays we have the English word *psychic,* which pertains to the astral sphere.

Psychelogia
Greek: "The Science of the Soul" (Psyche-Logia). The study of the attributes of the Soul, the non-material part of Man. From this we have the English word *psychology*. Nowadays psychology is mainly the study of biology, anatomy, animal behaviour, personality reactions, statistics, and so forth, which have nothing to do with the Soul. Transpersonal Psychology is beginning to re-establish psychology as "Soul-Science".

Psyche-Metanoia
Greek: The Soul's transmutational process. Inner Transformation.

Psychic Telepathy
Feeling people's moods, emotions and psychological states through the Solar Plexus Cakra, and also (often unconsciously) sending out "vibes" from the Solar Plexus which can heal or distress or upset another person. Only the astral bodies of the people concerned are involved. This is "animal telepathy"; the animals use this form of communication most frequently. It may also be called astral telepathy or psychism. Today this is the most common form of telepathy. [See Telepatheia]

Psychikos
Greek: The psychics. In the terminology of the Greek Mystery Schools, the *psychics* were the intellectuals, the mental people, the scholars, the pundits, who viewed everything only as "ideas". (Nowadays the word *psychic* is used for people who are sensitive to the Astral World.)

Psychostasia
Greek: "The weighing of the Soul" (putting the Soul on a scale). Karma, Justice, the Law of Cause and Effect.

Psychotherapy
From the Greek: "The healing of the Soul". Nowadays this word has come to mean "fixing up the personality". How things degenerate!

Pūja
Sanskrit: Ritual.

Punar-Bhavin
Sanskrit: "Becoming again". The Soul's new form or body in the after-death state.

Punar-Janma (Punarjanma)
Sanskrit: "Repeated births". Re-embodiment, reincarnation, rebirth. Punar (Punaḥ) means "again and again" and Janma means "taking birth". Reincarnation is being born again and again in a physical body.

Punar-Janman
Sanskrit: Being born again, in a spiritual sense. Being renewed.

Punar-Janma-Jaya
Sanskrit: Victory (Jaya) over the whole cycle of birth and death.

Punar-Janma-Smṛti
Sanskrit: "Again-and-again-births-recollection". Memory (Smṛti) of past lives. [See Pūrva-Jāti-Jñānam Siddhi]

Purā
Sanskrit: Cities, towns, worlds, realms, bodies.

Purāṇa
Sanskrit: "Ancient". Sacred scriptures.

Pure Consciousness
Buddhic Consciousness, Superconsciousness, Mystical Consciousness. In the state of Pure Consciousness, the consciousness of the experiencer is left without an object to experience and without a process of experiencing. Only *Consciousness* remains. This is the first and lowest state of the Transcendental Field of Being. In Sanskrit, Turīya-Avasthā (the Fourth State).

Purgatory
The third, fourth and fifth subplanes of the Astral Plane, which appear to its denizens as very similar to the physical Earth. This is where ordinary people live after death. These people could be considered "earthbound" because their lives are a reflection of Physical Plane conditions and habits. For this reason these realms are sometimes called the *Reflection Sphere*.

Pūrṇa, Pūrṇaṁ
Sanskrit: Fullness, Wholeness, Completeness, Abundance, Perfection. The Divine Fullness. The Absolute Godhead. The All. From Pūr-Nāma, "the complete All-Vibration of the Name". Equivalent to the Greek Plerōma.

Pūrṇā
Sanskrit: The Whole, the All. Without parts, always complete. Entire, full, abundant, rich, strong, capable, auspicious, contented, perfect. A Name of Lalitā, the Goddess. She is Wholeness, Completeness, Fullness, Oneness. Nothing can be added to or taken away from this Cosmic-Wholeness.

Pūrṇa-Avatāra
Sanskrit: A Perfect Incarnation of God. These great Incarnations descend from the Monadic Plane. [See Mahā-Avatāra]

Pūrṇa-Avatāra-Rūpa
Sanskrit: The Complete Divinity. When you have ascended the Heights of Glory, you will mount the Cosmic Heart, the Heart of Infinity, in the Shining Sea of Everlasting Life. This is the Path of the Avatāra (Divine Incarnation), the Incarnation not of a human being, nor of an angel, but of a god.

Pūrṇa Mano Bala Siddhi
Sanskrit: The power which comes from the use of your *total* Mind, which includes your ordinary mind (mental body), your Higher Mind (causal body), and your Wisdom-Mind (Buddhi-Manas, the mind illumined by the Buddhic Light).

Puruṣa
Sanskrit: The Divine Man, the Divine Person, the Cosmic Man, the Universal Spirit, the Supreme Being, the Ultimate Person of the Universe, the Conscious Principle of All That Is. Also known as Paramātman (Parama-Ātman) and Paramātmikā (Parama-Ātmikā), the Supreme Soul, the Highest Spirit, the Greatest Self, the Supreme Intelligence within and beyond the Cosmos. It is also known as Puruṣottama (Puruṣa-Uttama), the Supreme, Highest, Most Excellent (Uttama) Being or Person (Puruṣa). Puruṣa is the Spirit in Man and the Universal Spirit in the Cosmos. Puruṣa is also the Soul in Man as distinct from the body and mind. It dwells in the human Heart and in the Hearts of all Beings.

Puruṣa-Śakti
Sanskrit: The Energies of Spirit.

Puruṣa-Svāmī
Sanskrit: The Supreme Witness of all Creation, the God Transcendent. Śiva.

Puruṣasya
Sanskrit: Of the Soul or Spirit. Of God.

Puruṣottama (Puruṣa-Uttama)
Sanskrit: The Supreme, Most Excellent (Uttama) Being or Person (Puruṣa). The Highest Being in the Universe. Divinity, the Self-Existent One, the Godhead, the Immutable, the Imperishable, the Eternal One.

Pūrva-Jāti
Sanskrit: Previous births.

Pūrva-Jāti-Jñānam Siddhi
Sanskrit: "Knowledge-of-previous-lives power". Pūrva-Jāti-Jñānam (previous-birth-knowledge) or Pūrva-Jāti-Smarana (previous-birth-remembrance) is a Siddhi which arises when you can function in Causal Consciousness. Also called Punar-Janma-Smṛti (again-and-again-births-recollection), it is the power to recall to memory your past lives. This power has *nothing* to do with the "hypnotic regression" or "past-life therapies" which are popular today in the West.

Pusā
Chinese: A Buddha.

Pūṣan
Sanskrit: Nourisher and Protector. The Sun-God who nourishes and sustains all Life.

Q

Qabbālāh (Kabbalah)
Hebrew: Tradition. From Qābal, "to receive". An esoteric, secret and mystical oral tradition of the Jews. Some of it has been written down during the past two thousand years.

Qalb
Arabic: The Spiritual Heart. The Heart Centre. Although it is connected to the physical heart, this is not the heart of flesh and blood. It is located in the chest area—the left side, the right side, the centre, and the innermost part. The innermost part of Qalb is the Spirit, the Essence, the Innermost Self, the Centre within Man and the Universe. Qalb also means "the middle point, the centre, the core of one's Being, the Essence, the Mind, Soul and Spirit". All these have to do with the Mysteries of the Heart. Qalb (the Heart) is the great Intermediary between God and Humanity, the secret of inner spiritual guidance and the Mystery of Being. The Sūfīs call it "the Divine Subtlety" and "the Human Necessity". Kālb or Qālb in Turkish. In Sanskrit, Hṛdayaṁ.

Qalb-i-Vukuf
Arabic: A Heart set on God. Heart-Consciousness. Heart-Consciousness means turning away from mental activities, gazing into the Heart, and "waiting for the Divine Secret to manifest".

Qalb-Salīm
Arabic: "Pure Heart". A Heart that is Perfect. A peaceful Heart. Enlightenment. The direct Inner Vision of the Divine Face in the Spiritual Heart. God is visible to the inward sight of the Pure Heart. The Light by which the Heart sees God is God's own Light. This the Sūfīs call Ru'yat Al-Qalb (the Vision of the Heart). In the State of Perfection you perceive nothing else but God in all things and the Divine becomes the Centre of your life, the Heart throb of your Being. Your personal ego is dissolved in God, Fanā'fi-llāh.

Qitub, Qutub, Quṭb
Arabic: The hub or axis around which things revolve. Leader, prince, commander, chief. The Guru or Spiritual Master. A special Being who takes care of Souls.

Quan Yin
Chinese: The Female Saviour. Our Heavenly Queen has appeared to Humanity in many lands and at many times. She appeared in China as Quan Yin (Kwan Yin). Quan Yin is the Virgin of Light, the Mother of Compassion, the Ideal Beauty, the Eternal Woman, the Messenger of Divine Grace. Quan Yin is a Bodhisattva, whose very Self-Nature is Love-Wisdom, that is, whose Self-Being is of the Buddhic Plane where Consciousness is of Love, Wisdom, Unity and Bliss, fused into the Perpetual Light. She made a vow, a long time ago, to help alleviate the sufferings of all creatures, not only human but the animals as well, and all other Kingdoms of Life. Quan Yin is the Mother of Mercy who tends to the sufferings of this world. In Sanskrit She is known as Avalokiteśvarī. [See *Our Lady*]

Quaternary □
From the Latin: The Lower Four. The fourfold personality, consisting of the mental, astral, etheric and gross physical bodies. Tetrakti in Greek. [See *Personality*]

Quintessence
From the Latin: The Fifth Element. Aether in Greek, Ākāśa in Sanskrit.

Qūl
Arabic: The Voice.

Qur'ān
Arabic: Revelation.

Qurbiyat
Arabic: The Proximity of Reality. The sixth stage of the Radiant Way, the Shining Path of the Sūfī, corresponding to the Realization of Paranirvāṇa.

Quṭb
Arabic: Perfection. This occurs when the Mystic abandons his human nature altogether and passes away completely from Human Evolution. This takes one out of the human evolutionary system altogether and is the beginning of a new Superhuman development process in the Nirvāṇic Universe. [See Nirvāṇī and Pratyeka Buddha]

Quṭbīyat
Arabic: The Central Axis of Reality. The fifth stage of the Radiant Way, the Shining Path of the Sūfī, corresponding to the Realization of Nirvāṇa.

R

Rabbi
Hebrew: A Man of God. A Saint who is established in God-Consciousness.

Rādhā
Sanskrit: The giver of Fortune, Success and intense Devotion. She who is All-Success. She who is the Power of Devotion. A Name of Lalitā, the Goddess.

Radiare
Latin: To shine, to emit rays, to move like rays from a centre, to project a glow, to emit energy in waves. Hence the English words *radiate* and *radiation.* Radiation is inner energy shining through matter or form. When a human being reaches a certain stage of evolution, he or she also begins to shine. This is the meaning of the symbolic auras and halos around the heads of Saints in all religions. This shining of Man comes about after *Regeneration,* meaning "spiritual rebirth" or "the restoration of an organism to its ideal condition". The radiatory body, in all forms, is the etheric body. Physical bodies, by themselves, are inert. The radiatory substance is the etheric matter or energy.

Rāga
Sanskrit: Colours, colouring, desire, enjoyment. A mood of music (there are different Rāgas in music). Also, attachment to worldly things, which brings only temporary happiness, as all objects and situations are perishable and come to an end. Peace of mind you will not find until you have dissolved your mind in the Bliss of Reality (Ātmānanda).

Rāja Yoga
Sanskrit: "Royal Union". The Way of Kings, the Kingly Science, the Royal Way, the Noble Path. The Kingly Yoga of mind control. Suspending the modifications and activities of the mind by the Path of mental control. The exploration of Consciousness through meditation. Rāja Yoga is a Path of mental effort and knowledge, combined with intense, systematic meditation, which focuses on the mastery of the mental body, Manas (mind), and Citta (the field of Consciousness). This involves the control of your mental body; meditation in the head; the opening of the Third-Eye, the Crown Centre and the centre at the back of the head; the intelligent use of the will; plan, consciousness, purpose. Similar to Jñāna Yoga.

Rajas
Sanskrit: Activity, mobility, force, change. That which vibrates with great passion, force, activity, violence or discord. Rajas is the force of *mobility.* [See Guṇa]

Rāṁ (Rāng)
Sanskrit: The Blissful God-Vibration. The All-Pervading God, the All-embracing Life-Impulse of God. Rāṁ is God in *action.* Rāṁ is Divine Organizing Power, Divinity, Majesty, Kingship, the Supreme Hero, the Solar Dynasty, the Power of the Sun, the Solar Logos and the Spiritual Sun, Cosmic Intelligence, the Ruler of the Universe. Rāṁ is the Bīja-Mantra for the Cosmic Element *Fire* (the Mental Universe).

Rāma
Sanskrit: Delight. The Incarnation of Solar Radiance, the Solar Logos. God the King, the Ruler over Creation. The King of Kings, the Lord of Lords, the Perfect Administrator of the Universe. Divine Majesty, Kingship, Authority, Divine Positivity, Divine Power, Evolutionary Force, Life-enhancing Divine Strength, the Goodwill of God. Rāma is enchanting, beautiful, restful, all-pervading, blissful, delightful. Rāma is healing, unifying, harmonizing, nourishing. Rāma is positive activity, the ability to act correctly in all circumstances.

Ramā, Rāmā, Ramādevī, Ramaṇā, Ramaṇī, Ramaṇikā
Sanskrit: The Delightful One. She who gives Delight. Enchanting, beautiful, charming, splendid, opulent, pleasing, lovely, beloved, joyful, peaceful. She who gives Light, Radiance, Pure Consciousness. She who protects and sustains. A Name of Lalitā, the Goddess.

Rāma-Rāj
Sanskrit: The Kingdom of God.

Rāṁ-Nām (Rāma-Nāma)
Sanskrit: "The Divine Name". The all-pervading Sound-Current, the Logos, the Name (Active Power) of God.

Raphael
Hebrew: "The Healing Power of God". One of the Hebrew Angelic Names.

Rapture
From the Latin Rapturus: "Having been carried away in your Consciousness to a state or condition beyond the normal states". The Christian Mystics describe *Rapture* as the experience of God in the Secret Chamber of your Heart. The Mystics also call this "Ravishment" by the Spirit of God within you, when you receive the Hṛdaya-Śaktipāta, the Transference of Spiritual Energies into your Auric Being or Microcosm. This is a type of Spiritual Kuṇḍalinī Force, a higher aspect of Cosmic Kuṇḍalinī which will transform your whole inner Self. (In Christianity this Force is called the "Holy Spirit".) Rapturus (Rapture) has the same meaning as the Greek Ekstasis (Ecstasy) and the Sanskrit Samādhi.

Rasā
Sanskrit: Essence, Quintessence, Nectar, Juice. Water, milk, quicksilver (mercury), a chemical, a grape, wine. A taste, or the tongue. Spiritual Taste (honey-sweet). Passion, sentiment, charm, attraction, delight. The Earth. The Divine Nature. Immortality. The Ṛg Veda. Rasā is the *essence* of a thing.

Rāsa
Sanskrit: Sport, play, enjoyment, fun, dance. Sentimental, full of feeling, noisy. The Dance of Kṛṣṇa and the Gopī girls.

Rati
Sanskrit: Pleasure, enjoyment, desire, sensation, passion, love, delight, satisfaction, joy, intoxication. Lalitā is all this. It can be understood in the physical sense as well as in the spiritual sense. Rati can be physical sensations, but also the Joy and Ecstasy to be found in Samādhi (Self-Realization, Union with Ātman) or Union with Brahman (God).

Ratziel
Hebrew: "The Unveiling Power of God". One of the Hebrew Angelic Names.

Ravi
Sanskrit: The Self of the Sun who absorbs all within Himself. The Sun in totality on all Planes.

Rays
[See *Seven Rays*]

Reactive-Emotional Consciousness
The human astral-psychic nature. The emotional body of the Astral Plane. The astral body is always reactive and it is always emotional—it cannot be anything else! Peace of mind is not possible while you are in the state of Reactive-Emotional Consciousness. Most people are usually in Reactive-Emotional Consciousness; thus there is no peace in the individual; thus there is no peace on Earth.

Reason
The activity of the lower mind. Systematic "thinking" in the left brain hemisphere. Logic, analysis, criticism, taking apart, separating, dissecting the whole into parts, focusing on the parts rather than on the whole. [See *Lower Mind*]

Reflection Sphere
The middle regions of the Astral Plane, which are a close reflection of Physical Plane life. Also known as *Purgatory*. Also, the entire Astral Plane has been called the *Reflection Sphere* by some modern writers because there you see things reflected, as in a mirror.

Reincarnating Ego
The individualized Human Soul, which forms a new personality for itself at each incarnation, life after life. In Sanskrit, JĪVA (the Living Soul) or AHAṀKĀRA (I am the doer). [See JĪVA]

Religion
From the Latin RE-LIGARE: "To tie, to fasten, to re-unite, to bind, to bring back". In the classical days of Rome, religion was an experience of Unity with the Divine, with the Godhead. Since the fourth century AD the word *religion* has been changed by the church to mean "a set of beliefs concerning the nature of the Universe and God; a set of fundamental (fundamentalist) beliefs and practices agreed upon by the church authorities; the practice of religious beliefs (dogmas), rituals and observances; faith, devotion, ritual, religious conviction".

RESURRECTION
Latin: In the symbolism of the New Testament, *Resurrection* is the control of the personality by the Soul. At this stage of the Spiritual Journey the disciple is established firmly in the Light. There is no turning back. The Spirit has conquered this Creation.

Resurrection Body
The *Resurrection Body* is created when the etheric body and the causal body fuse through the activity of Soul-Light and become exteriorized in the inner worlds, thus producing the "new creature". In the West this Light Body is also called the *Christ Body*. In the East it is called the *Buddhic Body* or, technically, ĀNANDAMĀYĀKOŚA. This is an imperishable Light Body, a body made of higher octaves of Light than can be perceived by the current physical eyes. The Soul begins to use this Light Body when it ascends out of the causal realms into the Buddhic realms. [See ĀNANDAMĀYĀKOŚA]

REVELATION
Latin: In the terminology of the Medieval Catholic Mystics, *Revelation* is the direct experience of Insight, on the Soul level, about God, the Universe, Humanity, the Angelic Hierarchies, and so forth.

Root-Race
According to the Esoteric Doctrine, Human Evolution proceeds through seven great evolutionary epochs, or *Root-Races,* as follows:
1. Borean Epoch
2. Hyperborean Epoch
3. Lemurian Epoch
4. Atlantean Epoch
5. Āryan Epoch (the current epoch)
6. The Future Epoch
7. The Far-Future Epoch

Each of the Root-Races is divided into seven *Sub-Races*.

Rosicrucian
Derived from *Rosy-Crucian*, "the Rose and the Cross". The Fraternity of the Rosy Cross, like the original Freemasons, attempted to keep alive in the West, during the Dark Ages of European History, the old Mystery School Teachings regarding the true nature of Man, God and the Universe. In the West the rose represents the Heart Centre, just as the lotus flower represents the Heart in the East. According to the Rosicrucians, there is the Rose in the Heart (the Spirit, the Divine Christ-Being) which needs to be *awakened,* and there is the Cross in the Heart (the Soul crucified in the flesh, in the body, in material consciousness). This Cross the Hindu Yogīs call HṚDAYA-GRANTHI (the knot in the Heart). This Cross, or knot, is the material consciousness. A true *Rosicrucian* is one in whom the Heart Centre is completely *awake*, who has experienced the Indwelling Christ in the Heart.

Roshi
Japanese: The Spiritual Teacher, the Master, the Guru.

Ṛṣi
Sanskrit: A Sage, a Saint, a Seer of Truth, a Gnostic, a Knower of Reality, a Wise One, an Enlightened Being.

Ṛtaṁbharā-Prajñā
Sanskrit: Truth-bearing Wisdom or Consciousness. The Truth must be actively "thought after", either by listening or reading. The Yoga Masters said that the scriptures are not meant to entertain you or cause intellectual discussion, but rather, by the observance of the rules that are given out in the scriptures, you can conquer your internal enemies (the temptations, the "devils") and become a master of the senses (a Yogī).

Ruah (Ruach)
Hebrew: "Spirit, Breath, Wind, Life-breath, Life-force, Vitality, Fire". The Breath of Life. The Life-Force. The Soul or Essence behind a body or form. God's Power of Manifestation. Spiritus in Latin, Pneuma in Greek, Prāṇa in Sanskrit, Chi in Chinese.

Ruah-Elohīm (Ruach-Elohīm)
Hebrew: "The Breath of God". The Spirit, or Breath, of the Creator-Gods which moved upon the Waters of Space (as written in *Genesis*). The Energy or Force of the Creative Hierarchies. The subtle forces within atoms and beyond, on the etheric and astral dimensions. In Latin it was called Motion. The combined influence of these forces is called the Great Breath or Wind or Spirit (in Sanskrit, Nārāyaṇa).

Ruah-Ha-Qadosh (Ruach-Ha-Kadosh)
Hebrew: "Spirit-the-Holy". The Holy Breath, Holy Life-Force, Holy Creative Power. The Organizing and Structurizing Power within the Universe. God's Divine Mind at work, or Cosmic Intelligence. The Holy Spirit. Also called Shekinah (Hebrew: Radiating Light, Glory as Light Emanation). Ruḥā-Qadash in Aramaic, Pneuma-Hagion in Greek, Spiritus-Sanctus in Latin.

Rūbān (Rūhān)
Persian: "Spirit, Breath, Wind, Life-breath, Life-force, Vitality, Fire". The Breath of Life. The Life-Force. The same as the Hebrew Ruah (Ruach) and the Aramaic Ruḥā.

Rudrāmbā (Rudra-Āmbā)
Sanskrit: "The angry mother". A Name of Lalitā, the Goddess. In this aspect She represents the angry, bellowing, howling, discordant sounds of Nature and of Life. The unrestrained emotions and vibrations.

Rudrāṇī
Sanskrit: The angry goddess. The same as Rudrāmbā (the angry mother).

Rūḥ (Ruha)
Arabic: Soul, Spirit, Life, Revelation, Prophecy. The Spiritual Soul, located in the inner dimensions of the Heart (Qalb). The Spirit that you are (the Ātman, in the Eastern system).

Ruḥā
Aramaic: "Spirit, Breath, Wind, Life-breath, Life-force, Vitality, Fire". The Breath of Life. The Life-Force. The same as the Hebrew Ruah (Ruach).

Ruḥā-Qadash
Aramaic: "Spirit-Holy". The Holy Spirit, Holy Breath, Holy Life-Force, Holy Creative Power. God's Divine Mind at work, or Cosmic Intelligence. Ruah-Ha-Qadosh in Hebrew, Pneuma-Hagion in Greek, Spiritus-Sanctus in Latin.

Rūḥ-u-llāh
Arabic: The Spirit of God (the Paramātman of the East).

Rūpa
Sanskrit: Form, body, embodiment. With forms and shapes. A form, body or vehicle in which an entity lives in a world and in which that entity experiences a certain kind of consciousness or awareness. Also, entities with forms or bodies (including subtle bodies).

Rūpa-Deva
Sanskrit: "Form-angel". Embodied angels, dwelling on the lower mental subplanes. [See Arūpa-Deva]

Rūpa-Kāya
Sanskrit: "Form-body". The physical body.

Rūpa-Loka
Sanskrit: "Form-world". A description of the Physical, Astral and lower Mental Worlds, which contain forms and shapes. [See Arūpa-Loka]

Rūpa-Manas
Sanskrit: "Form-mind". Lower Manas, the lower mind or concrete mind. The mental body, also called Mānasa-Rūpa or Mano-Rūpa.

Ru'yat Al-Qalb
Arabic: "The Vision of the Heart". According to the Muslim Mystics (the Sūfīs), Man cannot know God by the physical senses of the body, for God is immaterial; not by the intellect, for God is unthinkable; not by reason and logic, because logic never goes beyond things that are finite. God is known by Inspiration, Revelation and Illumination, the three spiritual activities of the Heart Cakra. The Heart (Qalb) can know the Essence of God when it is illumined by the Divine Light. Allāh's speech is Light, His works are Light, He moves as Light, and He is seen as Light in the Heart. [See Qalb-Salīm]

S

Sābāhyābhyāntara
Sanskrit: Inner and outer.

Śabda
Sanskrit: The Living Word or Sound-Current. The Voice of God, the Cosmic Word, the Logoic Sound or Reverberation. Nāma, the Name. Śabda is God Incarnating within you and in the Cosmos. It is the Celestial Music or Divine Harmony by which God has created, and is creating, and will be creating in the future, the whole Universe. Śabda is the Life-impulse within all beings, the Creative and Controlling Power of the Second Logos, Immanent in All. All the visible and invisible Universes are made by It. By listening to the Word within yourself, your mind becomes still, your sorrows vanish, and Peace descends into your Heart.

Śabda-Abhyāsa
Sanskrit: The practice of Communion with the Living Word, the Creator-God. Meditation upon the Name of God. This was not a theology or belief system, but a practice (Abhyāsa). This Power is not simply an article of "faith", but a real Living-God. In old India this practice was also called Nāda Yoga.

Śabdabrahman (Śabda-Brahman)
Sanskrit: "The Sounding-God". The Sounding-Absolute. God Incarnate as the Eternal Word or Sound-Vibration. God as the Logos, Daiviprākṛtī, heard in deep meditation. The Immortal Creator-Power that ceaselessly emanates from the Supreme Being, creating and maintaining the World. Vāk, the Voice of God, the Creative Word, Sound-Power, Sounding-Light, Creative Energy. The Incarnating Sound from which crystallizes the lower realms and worlds of Creation. All differentiations are caused by Śabda-Brahman. In each world, realm or region of the Universe, Śabda creates a different Vibration. Thus, on each plane of the Solar System, Śabda (Sounding-Light-Consciousness) arranges things differently. All forms, no matter how gross or subtle, are constructed by Sound-Vibration.

Sabīja Samādhi
Sanskrit: A state of Samādhi with a seed, support or form (such as a mantra, a symbol, a sign, a maṇḍala).

Ṣabūr
Arabic: Patient, gentle, mild, kind. The virtue of Patience, which must be cultivated on the Shining Path of the Sūfī. Also, a Name of God.

Sadā
Sanskrit: Eternal, always, forever.

Sādana
Sanskrit: The room or place of spiritual practice.

Sadguru (Sat Guru)
Sanskrit: "True Guru". Holy Teacher. The same as Gurudeva (Divine Teacher). In the Esoteric Science this refers to one's Divine Self (Ātman) and to God (Brahman). [See Guru]

Sādhaka
Sanskrit: A seeker of the Light. A devotee, disciple, aspirant, spiritual practitioner. A follower of the Way, a practitioner of the Science of Union with God. One who has moved out of worldly consciousness. An Elect. Understand that when you become a Sādhaka your life will become more difficult, not easier. [See *Elect*]

Sādhanā
Sanskrit: The Spiritual Life. Spiritual practice, spiritual discipline, quest. A Way or Path of Meditation consisting of the purification of the mind and the Heart, which results in the Union of the personal self with the Universal Self or Ātman. It is said by the Wise that Sādhanā, or spiritual discipline and spiritual exercises (Kriyā), should not be practised for any benefits or motives. One should also abandon all expectations of results. And, when results appear, one should not cling to them. For the Self is beyond all this.

Sādhu
Sanskrit: A good man, a virtuous man. A virtuous Saint who is a renunciate. A peculiarity of the sādhus and sannyāsins of India, and many yogīs, is their total lack of concern for their physical bodies and surroundings. This is caused by the shifting of the attention from personality-life into the Soul-life. Many of them exhibit abnormalities which Western psychology would classify as mental illness or psychotic behaviour. The aim of spiritual development, however, is to integrate or *synthesize* the human being so that he or she will become physical, imaginative, mental, intuitive and spiritual at the same time. [See Mastānaḥ]

Saguṇa
Sanskrit: With forms, qualities and attributes (Sa-Guṇa). [See Nirguṇa]

Saguṇā
Sanskrit: The Goddess with qualities or attributes.

Saguṇa-Brahman
Sanskrit: God with qualities. Paramātman, the Monad.

Sah (Sat)
Sanskrit: The Real. The Eternal Life and Being. [See Sat]

Sahaja
Sanskrit: Simple, innate, original, natural, easily achieved, inherited.

Sahaja-Avasthā
Sanskrit: The Natural State (that is, the Original State of a human being).

Sahaja-Dhyāna
Sanskrit: Spontaneous or natural meditation.

Sahaja-Mārga
Sanskrit: The spontaneous or natural Path. This is for the Few who are Spontaneous Mystics and who seem to Attain with little effort.

Sahaja Samādhi
Sanskrit: Spontaneous or natural Spiritual Trance. Spontaneous Enlightenment (not sought after). This can happen only *after* you have undergone an Inner Transformation, a Fundamental Change, when you have established yourself in your Inner Reality *permanently*.

Sahasrāra Cakra
Sanskrit: The Crown Centre at the top of the head. Also called the Thousand-Petalled Lotus and the Brahmārandhra (door to God). The awakening of the Crown Cakra gives you the experience of Unbroken-Consciousness. Your waking state, deep-sleep and dreaming states become one in the Fourth State, Turīya. In the Crown Cakra you hear the *Word* and see the *Light*. Here the Light of Reality can be seen.

Sāi
Sanskrit: Full of (Sā) the Divine Mother (Ayi).

Sāi Rāṁ
Sanskrit: Divine Light.

Saint
A true Saint is one who has attained Buddhic Consciousness or Nirvāṇic Consciousness. While a few of the Christian Saints were true Saints who entered the Kingdom of God, many were merely religious fanatics who converted people to the church, either by persuasion or by the sword. They were canonized by the popes because they converted people to the church, but they had no Higher Consciousness of any type. Furthermore, many *true* Saints were never recognized by the church. The church has always been totally confused about the true nature of a Saint.

Sa-Jyoti
Sanskrit: With Light.

Sakala
Sanskrit: The All, the Whole, the Everything. Includes the All, the entire Universe. Complete, full, unified, perfect. Complete with all parts. Not conscious of any parts, not conscious of any separation. Without Time. The untying of the knot in the Crown Cakra. When this happens, the Spirit (Ātman) reveals the Truth (Satyam). Notice the difference between Sakala (without Time) and Akāla (Eternity, *outside* of Time).

Sakalā (Sakalām)
Sanskrit: The All, the Whole, the Everything, the Totality, the Fullness, the Completeness, Perfection, the Totality of the Universe (Sa-Ka-La). A Name of Lalitā, the Goddess. She is Śrī Jagadambā, the Holy World Mother. She is That which includes all things, all the parts as One. This is Her secret: She is everything. Sakalā also means "She who is with Rays of Light, with Beams of Light, with Waves of Radiances, Dazzling, Bright". Out of Her Light-Radiations (Sounding-Light) comes the whole Universe, including the entire human being—body, mind and Soul. She is complete, full, entire, perfect, total Unity or Oneness.

Sakkāyadiṭṭhi
Sanskrit: Identification with the *illusion* that we are separate entities, separate from each other and from the Higher Consciousness, God, Truth, the Divine Mind. The false belief that we are the physical body or the personality. From Sat (Being), Kāya (body) and Diṭṭhi (belief). Similar to the Sanskrit Māyā (believing physical, astral or mental phenomena to be real). All the works of Māyā are temporary, not eternal or permanent. [See Māyā]

Sākṣātkāraṇa
Sanskrit: To see directly with one's Mind's-Eye. The Witnessing principle, the Silent Watcher of phenomena, the Inner Consciousness of Ātman, the Seer looking inside the contents of the Mind and Heart. The basis of Vipaśyanā meditation.

Sākṣātkāra-Yoga
Sanskrit: Beholding Reality directly. The Sākṣī (Witness) is the Ātman.

Sākṣī
Sanskrit: The Witness. The Watcher. The Ātman. The Watcher, the Observer, is the Pure Self beyond your personal ego. Become the Watcher, the Observer, which is the Ahaṁ (I AM). This is different from your personal ego-sense in the body, Ahaṁkāra (I am the doer, the performer, the actor, the causer). In Pure Consciousness you know that your Conscious-Self is not your brain, not your ordinary "mind", but is the Witness (Sākṣī) which is aware, by Itself, of what is going on. Your sense of personality (your personal "I") is dissolved and you are aware of Boundless Being, of Boundless Life and Immortality and Bliss.

Śākyamuni
Sanskrit: One who is within reach of Enlightenment, for whom Enlightenment is possible. Also, a name of Gautama Buddha, or Prince Siddhārtha, the "founder" of Buddhism.

Śakti
Sanskrit: "Energy, force, power, strength, might, ability, skill". The Divine Energy. God's Dynamic Energy. The Holy Spirit. Śakti is the Feminine side of the Deity. Śakti is the totality of the *real* Energy and Forces of this Universe, on all layers and levels, on all planes of Existence. She is the Doer of all things, the Energy behind all activities: subatomic, atomic, planetary, solar-systemic and cosmic. She is the One Energy, the One Force of the Universe, visible and invisible, doing, producing, causing all things natural and "supernatural" (miraculous). She is the Goddess in all Her many forms, aspects and manifestations, and She is the Universal Mother, both as all forms and as the Life *within* forms. All the powers of the various Goddesses are but expressions of Śakti. All that Is is Energy (Śakti).

Śakti-Kūṭa
Sanskrit: "The Peak of Power". From Śakti (the Divine Power and Energy) and Kūṭa (the highest peak, most excellent).

Śaktipāta (Śakti-Pāta)
Sanskrit: Energy-Transference. The descent of Grace. The conveying of the Divine Energy, the Word, from the Guru to the disciple. The aura of the Guru vibrates with Śakti; when he initiates you into a Mantra, or chants some sacred Mantras with you, the Power will go out from his aura and communicate the Śakti to you. In such a way you can more quickly find the Centre of your Being and experience the Bliss and Peace of the Eternal.

Sālik
Arabic: A pilgrim, a traveller (in the spiritual sense). A devotee. This is the third stage of the Journey of the Heart. At this stage you have found a Teacher and you are serious in following out the spiritual instructions, meditations and practices that the Teacher gives. You have great Devotion (Sulūk) towards God, and your Heart is burning with desire to realize God in this lifetime.

Salvationis
Latin: Salvation, rescue, deliverance from troubles. Being saved from destruction. The deliverance of the Soul from the death of immersion in matter (the lower worlds). Deliverance from the effects and power of sins (karmas). Liberation from ignorance and illusion (Avidyā and Māyā). Liberation from the necessity of cyclic rebirth in the Three Worlds (the Physical, Astral and Mental Planes), and awakening to the Worlds of Light, the Buddhic Plane and above. The realization of God, the Infinite Mind.

Sama *(masculine)*
Sanskrit: Equal, even, smooth, flat; balanced, peaceful, together; just.

Samā *(feminine)*
Sanskrit: Peaceful, tranquil, equilibrated, poised, settled; a year.

Śama *(masculine)*
Sanskrit: Tranquillity, calmness, equanimity, quietude.

Śamā *(feminine)*
Sanskrit: Tranquil, peaceful, calm; a lamp.

Śāma *(masculine)*
Sanskrit: Equanimity. Inner Calmness. Control of the mind and thoughts. One of the Six Mental Qualifications for Discipleship (Śat-Sampatti).

Ṣamad
Arabic: The Eternal, the Everlasting, the Never-Ending; beyond Time, Space, Causation.

Samādhāna
Sanskrit: Peace, mental equilibrium, poise, contentment. One of the Six Mental Qualifications for Discipleship (Śat-Sampatti).

Samādhijāḥ
Sanskrit: Powers born out of Samādhi, as a result of Samādhi.

Samādhi
Sanskrit: "The collecting together of the Intuitive or Direct Awareness of Reality", from Sama (together) and Dhī (the faculty of Intuition, the inner realizing principle). Equilibrated-mind (Samā-Dhi). The state of equilibrium, tranquil knowing, intuitive perception, passive awareness. That stage of Dhyāna (meditation) wherein the mind is no longer disturbed by anything. Quietness, softness, tranquillity, poise, balance, evenness. Mystical Consciousness, Yogic Absorption, also described as *Emptiness* or *Void*. The mystical trance-state, the suspended animation of your ordinary mind. The no-mind state wherein the ordinary mind of reason and logic does not function and you experience Causal Consciousness and Pure Consciousness.

Samādhi also means "Ecstasy, Union with the One", from Sam (with, together) and Ādhi (the Primeval Lord, the First One). Stages of Union with the Soul, the Spiritual Triad and God. Total absorption in a thought, idea, quality, power or attribute of God. Complete Knowing, perfect Intuition, Revelation, Self-Realization, Ecstatic Trance, Superconsciousness, Transcendental Consciousness, Cosmic Consciousness.

Samādhi also means Sam-ā-dhā, "to fix together, to gather together, to revert to the Origin, to bind back to the Source". This is similar to the Latin word Religare (religion), which also means "to bind back to the Source". In Samādhi you live by Śakti (Divine Energy) and Caitanya (Divine Consciousness) alone.

Generally, the word Samādhi might be defined as "a State beyond and above the three ordinary states" (beyond the wakeful state, the dreaming state and the deep-sleep state). Samādhi is the Experience of the Transcendent, or aspects of the Transcendent, or Higher Consciousness. It may be esoterically defined as "a State of Absorption of Consciousness or Attention". In this State, various types of experience are possible, depending upon what interior perception is taking place, and what interior mechanism is being used, and on what Plane of Experience or Being. The terms for the various *types* of Samādhi describe the *mechanisms* by which the Higher States of Consciousness are experienced. Hence, the word Samādhi *cannot* have a rigid or final definition. The word is used *variously* by different Yoga and esoteric schools.

Samādhi-Pariṇāma
Sanskrit: "The tranquil-mind transformation state". The ability to *alternate at will* between focusing on a necessary mental activity and on Boundless Consciousness.

Samāna Vāyu
Sanskrit: That aspect of the Life-force (Prāṇa, Vāyu) that moves in the Solar Plexus and Heart Cakra regions of the embodied human being.

Samasti
Sanskrit: Unity.

Śamatha
Sanskrit: Mental quiescence. The mind's natural state of clear perception, crystalline peace and pure awareness.

Samaya
Sanskrit: Condition, circumstance, situation.

Śamballa
Sanskrit: The Divine Kingdom, the Original Kingdom, the Imperishable Realm, which exists on the Nirvāṇic Plane and the planes above. The Work of the Śamballa-Hierarchy is Solar-Systemic and Cosmic in relation to our planet Earth. Their concern is not only Humanity, but all the evolving Life-forms on and around the planet. Our Planetary Hierarchy, the Christ-Hierarchy, implements the Plan from Śamballa as it relates to our evolving Humanity.

Sambhogakāya
Sanskrit: A particular type of Light Body, or mode of functioning, of a Nirmānakāya. The Nirmānakāya Body "with the additional lustre of three perfections, one of which is the entire obliteration of earthly concerns".

Saṁkalpa
Sanskrit: Thoughts, thinking, thought-constructs (when used to describe the activities of the mind). [See Sankalpa and Vikalpa]

Samprajñāta Samādhi
Sanskrit: A type of Samādhi where you no longer cognize the outer world through the five senses, but there is still an intense internal activity, with awareness of mind, thoughts and self. From Sam-Prajñāta, "with mind and ego". [See Asamprajñāta Samādhi]

Saṁsakāra
Sanskrit: Habits acquired by the *current* repetition of an act. [See Saṁskāra]

Saṁsāra
Sanskrit: "Wandering" in the Three Worlds. Conditioned existence. Going around the Wheel of Birth and Death in the Three Worlds (the Physical, Astral and Mental Planes). Saṁsāra, our material Creation, essentially represents a realm of woe and unsatisfactory existence.

Saṁsāra-Mokṣana
Sanskrit: Liberation from the Wheel of Birth and Death. Saṁsāra is the endless wandering (circulating) between the Physical, Astral and Mental Worlds through the process of Reincarnation. Mokṣana is Freedom from the need for further rebirth. This is achieved when you have reached the Buddhic and Nirvāṇic Planes.

Saṁśaya
Sanskrit: Doubts, indecision about the Path. One of the Antarāyāḥ (obstacles, impediments, problems on the Path to Higher Consciousness).

Saṁskāra (Saṅskāra)
Sanskrit: Previous subliminal (subconscious) impressions, or psychic imprints left over from previous embodiments. Mental behaviour resulting from past-life experiences and from previous experiences in this lifetime. Conditioning factors which give you your present moral and behavioural tendencies. Unconscious attachments to past habit patterns. The force of habits from the past. The karmic consequences of your past behavioural tendencies. Saṁskāra are accumulations of latent impressions from the past which will work out now or in the future. From Saṁs (together) and Kara (acting, putting, doing). Impressions or grooves in the mental and astral bodies are "put together" from past thoughts, feelings and actions, which are the seeds for future Karma and Dharma. Saṁskāra are produced by external circumstances, and by thoughts, feelings and physical actions, which form seeds for actions, propensities or impulses in this or future lifetimes. [See Vāsanā and Saṁsakāra]

Saṁskāra-Kṣaya
Sanskrit: The dissolution or obliteration (Kṣaya) of old habit-patterns and subconscious memories (Saṁskāra). Without dissolving them, you cannot attain your Goal of Liberation. [See Vāsanā-Kṣaya]

Saṁskṛta (Saṅskṛta)
Sanskrit: "Consecrated, well-made, perfectly polished". The perfected, polished language. The Sanskrit Language. Also called Devanāgarī (God's writing). Saṁskṛta also means "All becoming One", or uniting with the Eternally Silent Self, in the Crown Cakra.

Samyaksaṁ Buddha
Sanskrit: Perfectly-completely-Enlightened (Samyak-Saṁ-Buddha). A fully realized Buddha (above the ordinary Buddhas). A Buddha who has passed out of Human Evolution and who dwells in exalted conditions on the plane of Mahāparanirvāṇa.

Saṁyama (Saṅyama)
Sanskrit: "Holding together". Profound concentration. Mental action with purpose in the state of Superconscious Ecstasy. This is beyond concentration or contemplation. It is the ability to *act* from Samādhi, the Superconscious State. Saṁyama is a very peculiar internal state of Consciousness, a superior state of Knowing. While you are in the state of Superconsciousness (Samādhi), you concentrate on a topic (Dhāraṇā) and contemplate it (Dhyāna) from within yourself. When Saṁyama is applied to a focal point of endeavour, what appear to be "supernatural" or "miraculous" powers are attained, called Siddhis or Vibhūtis. When such a power is perfected, the Yogī

has fully conscious use of it, at any time, anywhere, at will. While these accomplishments may appear to be "supernatural" or "miraculous" to the materialist (the ignorant), they are understood by Those who Know (the Wise) to be simply a result of intense inner work, self-discipline and effort.

Saṁyama Yoga
Sanskrit: The Yoga of Miraculous Powers.

Sanātanaḥ
Sanskrit: Eternally.

Sanātana-Dharma
Sanskrit: "The Eternal Truth". The Ancient Wisdom Religion. The original, pure Vedic Religion of India.

Sanat Kumāra
Sanskrit: The Lord of the World, the Ancient of Days, the King of Kings, the Lord of Lords, the Master of Masters on this planet. Sanat Kumāra is the Undying Seed of Eternal Life, the Youth of Endless Summers, the Eternally Undying One.

Sancitta Karma
Sanskrit: The massive reservoir of Karma that you have stored up on the Causal Plane, which is still to be worked out, which is waiting for release, transformation or neutralization, which will be precipitated, transformed and neutralized in future lives or periods of your manifestation. This is true also for your family, group, race, country or religious grouping. [See Prārabdha Karma and Kriyamāna Karma]

Sanctum Sanctorum
Latin: The Holy of Holies. The Adytum or Inner Shrine of the Temple of the Universe. Nirvāṇa.

Sandalphon
Hebrew: "The Immediate Presence of God". One of the Hebrew Angelic Names.

Sandhyā
Sanskrit: An interval between two Epochs or Ages.

Saṅgha (Sata-Saṅgha)
Sanskrit: "Going together into Liberation or Fulfilment". The Spiritual Hierarchy. The Communion of the Saints—those great Souls who have attained some perception of Infinite Being (Sat) and have linked into a Communion, forming a Spiritual Kingdom. It has been said since ancient times that all Workers and Knowers of God, whether they be in or out of physical bodies, in whatsoever field of the Divine Manifestation they are working, form part of the Spiritual Hierarchy, the Saṅgha. This Living-Hierarchy of Light is composed of elements from the Human Kingdom (Manuṣya) and the Angelic Kingdom (Devatā). Also known as Sata-Saṅgha (the Brotherhood of Truth), the *Christ-Hierarchy* and the *Fifth Kingdom*.

Sañjivani
Sanskrit: The Elixir of Life. A pure and divine Substance of the Higher Worlds.

Sanjivāni
Sanskrit: A drug used in Ancient India to induce the "self" back into the body following an astral projection.

Sankalpa (Saṅkalpa)
Sanskrit: Will, desire, imagination, purpose, determination, commitment (when used to describe the activities of the mind). [See Saṁkalpa and Vikalpa]

Śaṅkarācārya
Sanskrit: A good Teacher (Śaṅkara-Ācārya). An excellent religious Preceptor.

Sankīrtana
Sanskrit: Devotional singing and dancing. Lively group singing or chanting. [See Kīrtana]

Sannyāsa
Sanskrit: Renunciation.

Sannyāsī, Sannyāsin
Sanskrit: One who has renounced the world. An ascetic, a renunciate, a hermit. This was a common practice during the Piscean Age and was misunderstood to be the only form of true Spirituality.

Saṅskṛta
Sanskrit: [See Saṁskṛta]

Sant
Sanskrit: A Saint. One with Buddhic Consciousness.

Śāntiḥ
Sanskrit: Peace, tranquillity, calmness, silence, poise.

Śāntī, Śānti-Devī
Sanskrit: The Goddess of Tranquillity, Peace, Harmony, Quiet. A Name of Lalitā, the Goddess.

Santoṣa (Saṁtoṣa)
Sanskrit: Contentment with one's lot. Satisfaction with your life as it is. Santoṣa is the second Niyama (rule) of Aṣṭāṅga Yoga, as set down by Patañjali. It means being happy in your life, living a relaxed and balanced life free of stress and violence. It also means the virtue of *patience*. Here, most disciples fail. The life of our whole society is based on *discontent*, ever seeking and struggling for the so-called "better". Contentment manifests when your mind is at *rest*, when the endless seeking and searching and battling and struggling with the world comes to a stop. The Spiritual Life is only possible when you live in the Here and Now, not in an imagined better future. When you are content with your life, there is no more stress.

Sapientia
Latin: Wisdom. The same as the Greek Sophia and the Hebrew-Aramaic Chockmah. In ancient times, these words did not mean being "worldly-wise", intellectual or learned in our present sense, but the Inner Wisdom that revealed the Path of Light.

Saptaḍaṣī
Sanskrit: The Seventeen-Years-Goddess (the Saptaḍaṣī-Mantra is given at the age of seventeen).

Saptaḍaṣī-Mantra
Sanskrit: The Seventeen-Syllabled Mantra.

Saptaparna
Sanskrit: "The seven-leafed plant". Man, because a human being has seven principles or coverings over the Spirit or the Absolute. Also, the seven-leafed lotus flower (the Heart Centre). The Spiritual Heart, which has seven layers or dimensions.

Sāra, Sāram
Sanskrit: Substance, essence, basis. The essence or substance of a thing. An essential quality or knowledge.

Sarasvatī
Sanskrit: The River of Knowledge. She who is in the Form of the Ocean of Knowledge. From Saras (a lake, an ocean, a river) and Vati (She who has). Sarasvatī is an Energy-Form of the Goddess. She is the Energy that gives the ability for learning, intelligence, knowledge, understanding, speech, eloquence, music, singing, dancing, acting, art, calligraphy, visual arts, performing arts, creative expression. She is the Form of all Mantras, speech, sound, music and art. She is the Mother Goddess in the form of the Sanskrit Language (Mantra-Śakti). She is also the Goddess of tranquil creativity, joy in expression, and silent power. She is also the Goddess of geometry, mathematics and architecture. The esoteric meaning is that She is the River of Nectar (Amṛta), the River of Light which flows from the Crown Centre into the Third-Eye. This gives the devotee Esoteric Knowledge, True Knowledge.

Sa-Rūpa
Sanskrit: "With form". In the context of the Deity, Sa-Rūpa refers to God Immanent in Creation. [See A-Rūpa]

Sārūpya
Sanskrit: Resembles, similar to, in the likeness of, assumes the character of.

Sarva, Sarvaṁ
Sanskrit: All, everything, everybody, everywhere, universally.

Sarvagā (Sarva-Gā)
Sanskrit: She who Pervades All. She who is Omnipresent. A Name of Lalitā, the Goddess.

Sarvajña
Sanskrit: All-Knowledge. The Omniscience of a Buddha (Omniscience in a certain sense, pertaining to certain worlds and conditions).

Sarva-Jñāna
Sanskrit: All-Knowing, Omniscient.

Sarvajñātṛtvaṁ
Sanskrit: Omniscience. This occurs when Buddhic Consciousness has been stabilized and Nirvāṇic Consciousness has been attained.

Sarva-Mantra-Sva-Rūpiṇī
Sanskrit: "She who is in the Form of all Mantras". A Name of Lalitā, the Goddess. From Sarva (all), Sva (own) and Rūpiṇī (form). All Mantras are Sound-Forms. Lalitā incarnates into these Sound-Forms and becomes the Consciousness behind them.

Sarva-Yantra-Ātmikā
Sanskrit: "She who ensouls all Images and Symbols of the Deity". A Name of Lalitā, the Goddess. Sarva means "all, everything". A Yantra is an image, symbol or picture, a representation or diagram of the gods and goddesses (which are but tools to remember aspects of the Absolute). Ātmikā means "embodies, ensouls".

Sarveṣa (Sarva-Īśa)
Sanskrit: The Lord of the Universe, the All-Lord, the Logos, the Lord of the Solar System.

Sarx
Greek: The flesh or gross physical body of the human being.

Śāstra
Sanskrit: A sacred scripture or text.

Sat, Sata
Sanskrit: "The Real". Truth, Reality, Existence, Being, God. The Ultimate Reality, Perfect Being, Pure Existence, the Absolute Condition, the Ultimate Godhead, the Eternal. *He Of Whom Nought Can Be Said.* Parabrahman. You may call it He, She or It; these are but human limitations you would put on something which is limitless in every way. [See Tat]

Sata-Nāma
Sanskrit: "True Name". God as the True Name (or Vibration) of all things.

Sātan
Hebrew: A tempter. One who plots against you or tempts you to do wrong, to bring about your ruin or downfall. An enemy, an adversary, an opposition. A bad person or spirit. Satanas in Greek. Hence the English word *Satan,* nowadays called "the Devil". The word *Satan* has innumerable significances. You could say that anything or anyone (including yourself!) who opposes you on the Path to re-integration with Divinity is Satan. Thus, Satan could be simply matter; it could be your physical body; it could be your mind; it could be a spirit on the psychic dimensions; it could be your attitude towards or understanding of Reality, or many other things. By this broad definition, the word *Satan* may be translated simply as "the enemy". [See *Devil*]

Satanas
Greek: The same as the Hebrew Sātan, "an enemy, an adversary, an opposition, one who plots against you, a tempter".

Satcidānanda (Sat-Cit-Ānanda)

Sanskrit: "Being-Intelligence-Bliss". A term used In the Ādvaita School of old India to describe the Godhead.

- Sat: Absolute Beingness. Sat means that God eternally exists or eternally *is*.
- Cit: Absolute Consciousness. Cit means that God is the Creative Intelligence behind the Universe on all levels and in all states.
- Ānanda: Absolute Blissfulness. Ānanda means that God experiences Being or Existence in terms of unending Bliss and eternal Ecstasy.

God is the Infinite Intelligence of All-Space, visible and invisible, of all the worlds and realms of Being. As we ascend in Consciousness we become increasingly aware of God's Presence and Being. We have an increasingly dynamic awareness of God's threefold Being: Sat-Cit-Ānanda, "Being-Intelligence-Bliss".

Sat-Cid-Ānanda-Rūpiṇī

Sanskrit: "She whose Nature is Existence, Consciousness, Bliss". A Name of Lalitā, the Goddess. Rūpiṇī means "Her essential Nature or Form". She is the Supreme Sat: Being, Existence, the Immutable Everpresent Godhead (Parabrahm), the Eternal One. She is Cit: ever Conscious, Pure Intelligence and Knowing. She is Ānanda: forever Joyful, forever Blissful.

Sat Guru (Sadguru)

Sanskrit: "True Teacher". A spiritual Guru who is on the true Spiritual Path and not the psychic path. Also, the Ātman within you, the Spirit. On the highest level, Brahman, the Godhead. [See Guru and Gurudeva]

Sati-Prajñā

Sanskrit: "Truth-Discerning Awareness". This dawns upon you when you inwardly *realize* that behind and beneath all transitory and changing outer events and phenomena (the world-process, your breathing, your thoughts, feelings or moods, successes or failures, sicknesses or health, and changing fortunes of life and circumstances) is the Abiding Reality, the Unborn, Unmade, Unbecome, Unchanging Eternal Reality, the Transcendental Awareness, the Realm of Absolute Life and Being.

Śat-Kriyā

Sanskrit: "Six actions". From Śat (six) and Kriyā (action, activity). In Haṭha Yoga, the Śat-Kriyās are six techniques for internally cleansing the physical body. [See Haṭha Yoga]

Satori

Japanese: Enlightenment, Awakening, Illumination, Mystical Union. The experience of Buddhi, or Superconsciousness. The experience of the seven subplanes of the Buddhic Plane and, later on, the seven subplanes of the Nirvāṇic Plane. Satori is a mass of Brightness and a resurgence of the sense of the Real within you. The same as the Sanskrit Bodhi. In Chinese, Wu or Lung-Tan.

Sat-Puruṣa

Sanskrit: The Everlasting Lord.

Śat-Sampatti

Sanskrit: The Six Virtues, Six Treasures, or Six Mental Qualifications for Discipleship:

- Śāma: control of the mind and thoughts.
- Dama: control of the senses, actions and conduct.
- Uparati: tolerance, patience, abstinence.
- Titikṣa: endurance, perseverance.
- Śraddhā: faith, hope in success.
- Samādhāna: peace, mental equilibrium, poise, contentment.

Satsaṅga

Sanskrit: "The Brotherhood of Truth". A group of disciples or seekers after Truth. From Sat (truth) and Saṅga (a gathering, an assembly). Nowadays, Satsang means a gathering of people for a religious occasion, such as chanting, worship, or hearing a spiritual discourse. In olden days it meant much more. The full Sanskrit word is Sata-Saṅgha. Sata is the Primordial Truth-Vibration, or the Realm of Infinite Being (Sat), and Saṅgha refers to those great Souls who have attained some perception of It and have linked into a Communion, forming a Spiritual Kingdom. Sata-Saṅgha is the Holy Communion of the Saints, the Brotherhood of "Just Men made Perfect", the Union of Souls (Jīvas) who are Perfect (Siddha)—Adepts,

Masters, Yogīs, Sages. It is the Spiritual Hierarchy of Enlightened Souls who guide the Evolution of this planet. [See SAṄGHA]

SATTVA (SATTVA-GUṆA)
Sanskrit: The quality (GUṆA) of Harmony, Peace, Spirit, Consciousness, Life. That which vibrates with rhythm, balance, poise, goodness, Truth, Purity, Light. The quality of Purity, or high vibration, which is necessary for Inner Contact and Union (YOGA). SATTVA is the force of *equilibrium*. [See GUṆA]

SATTVA-BUDDHI
Sanskrit: Pure Intelligence, Pure Consciousness, Pure Reason. This is your Mind when you are in Transcendental Consciousness, Superconsciousness (SAMĀDHI).

SATTVAM-UTTAMAM
Sanskrit: "The Highest Truth". This is experienced in God-Consciousness.

SATYA, SATYAM, SATYAṀ
Sanskrit: "The Truth". SATYA (SATYAM) is the second YAMA (observance) of AṢṬĀṄGA YOGA, as set down by Patañjali. It means truthfulness, sincerity, honesty, being virtuous, genuine, non-devious. This not only means that we cease telling lies and deceiving others, but also that we carry in our minds the *Truth Principle,* a certain amount of true Spiritual Knowledge, a certain amount of *discrimination* between what is real and what is false, between that which pertains to the Eternal and that which is transitory and ephemeral.

SATYA-LOKA
Sanskrit: "The Realm of Truth". The Universe of ĀDI (the First Plane). The Divine World. MAHĀPARANIRVĀṆA.

SATYA YUGA
Sanskrit: "The Age of Truth". The Age of Enlightenment and Spirituality. Also called KṚTA YUGA (the accomplished, perfect Age). An evolutionary period, calculated by the Ṛṣis of ancient India to be equivalent to 1,728,000 earth-years.

ŚAUCA
Sanskrit: "Purification, cleanliness, purity". ŚAUCA is the first NIYAMA (rule) of AṢṬĀṄGA YOGA, as set down by Patañjali. It means internal *and* external cleansing, raising the vibrations of the physical, etheric, astral and mental bodies. It does not mean abstaining from sex, as some religionists would believe. It literally means bodily hygiene and cleanliness, and cleanliness and tidiness of your environment. It also means the purification of your emotions and thoughts by elevating them from the gross, the morbid, the material, the dense, into vibrations of Light, Love, Bliss and Joy. Purification is necessary to increase the vibrations of the personality before Higher Consciousness can be experienced.

SAUNDARYA-LAHIRĪ
Sanskrit: "The Ocean Of Beauty". The Beautiful Ocean, the Lovely Waves of the Celestial Sea. The Ocean of universal magnetic-electric energies surrounding you and within you. The Universal Subconscious Mind. Also called ALAYA-VIJÑĀNA (Universal Soul-Consciousness). Your personalized subconscious mind is but a wavelet, a small rivulet, in this great Sea. It is always spoken of as "She".

SAVIKALPA SAMĀDHI
Sanskrit: A state of SAMĀDHI with imaginings and distinctions, in which the experiencer distinguishes between the "I" and the experience. In SAVIKALPA SAMĀDHI, thoughts and mental functions are still possible. From SA-VIKALPA, "with thoughts, imaginings, form". [See NIRVIKALPA SAMĀDHI]

SAVITARKA SAMĀDHI
Sanskrit: A state of SAMĀDHI "with an Idea" (such as "God"), but with no thinking about It. [See NIRVITARKA SAMĀDHI]

Savitā
Sanskrit: The Sun-God, the Solar Logos. The physical Sun, as seen by the physical bodily eyes, is the outermost part of a small organ (the dense-physical Heart) of the Solar Deity (Sūrya, Savitā). Savitā means "the Impeller, the Begetter, He who drives Manifestation". He is also known as Sūrya-Nārāyaṇa (the Sun-Spirit, that is, the Self within the Spiritual Sun). He is also known as Savitṛ-Deva (the Sun-God). He is also known as Īśvara (the Lord or Ruler of the Solar System, the Solar Logos). He is also known as Viṣṇu (He who pervades all Space with His Being) and Agni (the Lord of Fire, Cosmic Fire). Savitā, Īśvara or Savitṛ (Savitri) is the Male Aspect of the One Godhead; Sāvitrī is the Female Aspect.

Savitā-Mantra
Sanskrit: Also known as the Gāyatrī-Mantra. When we intone or meditate silently on the Savitā-Mantra, we are meditating on Divinity as Light, Reality as Light. Sūrya or Savitā is Divine Light—the Vivifier, the Life-Giver, the Energizer-Light, the Fertilizer, Arouser, Stimulator. [See Gāyatrī-Mantra]

Savitur, Savituḥ
Sanskrit: The Universal-Light manifesting through the Solar Logos: Sūrya (the Sun-God, or God-in-the-Sun); Īśvara (the Sovereign-Ruler, the All-Powerful-God); Savitā (the Impeller, Energizer, Vivifier, Life-Giver, Begetter, Creator); Sūryadeva (the Sun-God); Āditya (the Golden-Being residing in the Sun).

Savitṛ
Sanskrit: The Solar-Dynamic-Energy-of-Life. The Male Aspect of the Spiritual Sun.

Sāvitrī (Sāvitrikā)
Sanskrit: The Spiritual Sun as Mother. The Goddess in the Form of Solar Radiance, Solar Power, the Creative Power of the Universe, the Energy of the Sun, Rays of Light, Light-Radiation. She is the Feminine Sun, or the Feminine Aspect within the Sun. She is the All-Producer, the All-Begetter, the Mother of all things, the Cause of all things, the Other-Side-of-the-Sun. Sāvitrī is gentleness and compassion, tolerance, forgiveness, loving kindness, calmness in the face of persecution or opposition. She has no enemies (She does not perceive anybody as an enemy). She receives all equally. She is the Compassionate Heart. She is always poised, balanced, centred. The whole Universe is filled with the presence of Her Radiant Consciousness (Cinmayī), which is Pure Intelligence, Supreme Spirit. She is Omnipresent, Omniscient, Omnipotent, and She is present in you as your own Divine Self.

Scandalum
Latin: A slander, a scandal, false or defamatory words, inflammatory statements. A mind that causes offence, for a religious, political, business, or any other motive.

Scientia
Latin: "Knowledge". A true scientist (seeker of knowledge) is not afraid to know the Truth, whether it is material, psychic or spiritual.

Scientia Intuitiva
Latin: Spiritual Science. Mysticism. The Science of Interior Illumination.

Scientia Materia
Latin: Materialistic science or knowledge.

Seance
Seance is a French word, derived from the Latin Sedere, "to sit down". A seance consists of a group of people sitting in a circle with a medium to contact the "dead".

Second Death
The *Second Death* occurs after the death of the physical body, when you leave behind the etheric-physical body. Then you are completely free of the Physical Plane and begin to live in the Astral World properly.

Second Logos ⊖
The Universal Light of the Christ. Viṣṇu. The "Son". [See Christos]

Seged
Aramaic: To bow down, to surrender oneself, to glorify and adore the Divinity.

Selah
Hebrew: Rest, tranquillity. The state of natural meditation. Also, Shīlōh.

Self-Conscious Mind
Objective Mind. The linear, verbal, conceptual, logical, reasoning mind. The normal wakeful state in your physical body. In most people the lower mind is mixed with desire, thus forming Kāma-Manas (desire-mind). Also known as Jāgrata-Avasthā.

Self-Realization
Realization of the Self (the Soul) and the SELF (the Spirit). In Sanskrit, Ātmā-Vidyā, Ātmā-Jñāna, Ātmā-Bodha.

Senzar
Pre-Sanskrit: A universal language (universal to Initiates) predating even the most ancient Sanskrit of six to eight thousand years ago. The language of Atlantis.

Serpent-Power
Also called the Serpent-Fire, the Fiery Dragon, the Serpent-Force or Dragon-Power. In Sanskrit it is called the Kuṇḍalinī-Śakti. This is the Female Force, the Body of the Universe—that is, the Fiery Energy locked up in the structure of matter itself, in forms or bodies. When mastered, this Force gives miraculous powers. The Fiery Dragon or Serpent-Fire is a devastating Force and it should never be awakened until the Heart has been awakened and, through it, Universal Compassion and Wisdom have been attained. [See Drakōn]

Sesshin
Japanese: A spiritual retreat. To train oneself in seclusion. A Zen intensive, normally composed of Zazen, Teishō, Dokusan and Kyōsaku.

Seva
Sanskrit: Service, Worship, Homage, Reverence, Devotion. To serve your Teacher, your group and the world unselfishly. Goodwill towards all men and women, and prayer and praise towards the Deity.

Seven Heavens
The seven subplanes (regions, vibratory states, dwelling places) of the Mental Plane, or Devāchan. These are the true Heavens, beyond the lower heavens of the Astral World.

Seven Rays
The Seven Rays are the Seven Life-Energies, the Seven Sounds, the Seven Light-Waves, the Sevenfold Holy Spirit, or the Seven-Sided Breath of God. They are seven force-streams or energy-patterns in the Mind of God. They express themselves in Nature, in Man and in all the Kingdoms of Life. The Rays are *qualities* or *types* of energies in the Divine Mind which stir things in certain ways, to which the many intelligent Hierarchies respond. The Rays are seven types of *consciousness* of the One Universal Consciousness.

Ray 1: Will, Power
Ray 2: Love, Wisdom
Ray 3: Activity, Understanding
Ray 4: Beauty, Harmony
Ray 5: Fire, Mind
Ray 6: Devotion, Love
Ray 7: Law, Order

Seventh State
The Seventh State of Consciousness, the God-State, the second stage of Union with God, is an Ineffable Oneness in which you "see" God in All, and All in God. In Sanskrit, Brahmā-Avasthā.

Sex Centre
An Energy Centre located slightly above the base of the spine. The Sex Centre is responsible for the etheric portion of the Physical Plane, your vitality and strength, magnetism and personal radiance. Sex is only one of its functions; it also provides you with physical energy. [See Svādhiṣṭhāna Cakra]

Shade
An astral corpse. The cast-off astral body of a dead person who has moved on to Devāchan, the Mental Plane. Also called a *Shell*. [See *Astral Shell*]

Shaikh
Arabic: A chief, an elder, a patriarch. The Holy Man, the Guru, the Spiritual Teacher or Master, who is the Leader and Guide in life. Also, the Spiritual Teacher's influence.

Shaman
The word *shaman* is a degeneration of the original Sanskrit word Śramana (an ascetic training for spiritual powers). A shaman is a witch-doctor of the American Indians, the Eskimos, the Tibetans and the Mongolians. All are descendents of the old Atlanteans.

Shamayīm, Shemayīn
Hebrew: "Heaven". The multi-dimensionality of Space, as a Unity or Oneness, as a Continuum between the within (the above) and the without (the below). Shemayā in Aramaic, Ouranos in Greek, Caelum in Latin, Ākāśa in Sanskrit. [See *Heaven*]

Shang-Ri-Lah
Tibetan: The abode of the Celestial Beings. Nirvāṇa, the Kingdom of Light.

Sharī'at
Arabic: The Divine Plan, the Spiritual Laws governing Creation. The word Sharī'at also refers to the first stage of the Radiant Way, the Shining Path of the Sūfī. This is the stage of *ordinariness* or *sleep* in which average men and women find themselves. It is full of suffering and dualities such as pleasure and pain, light and dark, good and evil. This is the stage of ordinary religion, where one strives to abide by the Sacred Law, the Holy Qur'ān, the words of the Messengers and the Prophets.

Shekinah
Hebrew: "Radiating Light, Glory as Light Emanation". The Divine Fiery Energy. God's Immanence. The Cloud of Glory or Brightness within Creation. The Glory of God's Presence, illuminating the world from within. The Glorious Hebrew Name Shekinah means the Light of Nirvāṇa sent forth from the Infinite Light, Ain Soph Aur. It is the Divine Presence in the Universe of Light, which is Feminine in nature towards the Boundless Godhead or Everlasting Light. God's Holy Presence vibrates through every part of Creation. Also known as the Ruah-Ha-Qadosh (Spirit-the-Holy), the Holy Breath or Fire of God.

Shell
[See *Astral Shell*]

Shem (Sh M)
Hebrew: Name, renown, fame, vibration.

Shemā (Sh M O)
Hebrew: Fame, glory, repute, inner sound.

Shemayā
Aramaic: "Heaven". The multi-dimensionality of Space, as a Unity or Oneness, as a Continuum between the within (the above) and the without (the below). Shamayīm in Hebrew, Ouranos in Greek, Caelum in Latin, Ākāśa in Sanskrit. [See *Heaven*]

Sheol
Hebrew: A cavern, a cave, a pit. The place of the dead, underground, the underworld. Outer Darkness. The lower regions of the Astral World. The same as the Egyptian Amenti and the Greek Hades.

Sherārā
Aramaic: Harmony, balance, rhythm, liberating force, forceful, vigorous, overcoming.

Shikantaza
Japanese: "Just-sitting" or "to sit fully aware". From Shikan (wholeheartedly) and Taza (to hit the awareness). In any situation, if you can "drop body and mind", you will gain *Insight,* the goal of meditation. This is Shikantaza. You should attempt it only after you can meditate with an object, when your mind is positively concentrated and alert. When practising Shikantaza you must have faith in your own hidden Buddha-Mind and in the Higher Order of Reality (Dharma) which pervades the Universe. One day, sitting like this, persevering, you will *directly perceive* your own Bodhi-Mind, which leads to Enlightenment, Satori.

Shukūr, Shakūr
Arabic: Thankful, grateful. Happiness, peace, contentment. One of the virtues which must be cultivated on the Shining Path of the Sūfī. Also, a Name of God.

Siddha
Sanskrit: An Adept, a Master Yogī, a Perfected Human Being, a highly realized Saint. The Siddhas are Nirmānakāyas. They remain in the lower worlds to become Teachers of Angels and of Man.

Siddhānta
Sanskrit: The Mysterious Knowledge of the Siddhas.

Siddha-Yogī
Sanskrit: A power-seeking Yogī. A Yogī with strange and mysterious powers.

Siddhi
Sanskrit: A magical, psychic or spiritual power. Any power that appears "supernatural" to the ignorant. The word Siddhi refers to all kinds of "miraculous" powers, realizations, perfections, accomplishments, talents, skills, abilities, attainments, fulfilments, mastery or empowerments (material, psychic, occult or spiritual). Specifically, the "miraculous" powers attained through focused meditational and spiritual disciplines by the Siddha-Yogī (power-seeking Yogī) when his trained consciousness (Citta) learns to master the Laws of the Invisible Universe. Similar to the Sanskrit Vibhūti (Divine Graces and Gifts). [See Mirāculum]

Sila
Sanskrit: Virtuous conduct, or the right way to be *for you.* Achieving a harmonious state of being inside yourself.

Silver Cord
The Silver Cord is the lifeline of the body, a stream of Life-energy emanating from the back of the head of the astral body and attached to the solar plexus region of the etheric-physical body and hence to the physical body. This is the lowest manifestation of the Sūtrātma (Sanskrit: the Thread of the Self). So long as this Silver Cord is unbroken, the physical body remains alive. When it is broken, irreversible death ensues and the body starts decomposing. [See Sūtrātma]

Simrān
Sanskrit: Remembrance. Recollection of the Divine Presence. From Smṛti, "that which is remembered".

Sin
[See Hamartia]

Siri
Sanskrit: Great, reverent, wonderful. From Śrī, "radiant, holy, sacred, beautiful, honourable".

Sirr
Arabic: "The Secret". That part of the Heart (Qalb) which is located at the left side of the chest.

Sitā
Sanskrit: She who Shines like Moonlight. Bright, pure, white. A Name of Lalitā, the Goddess.

Śiva
Sanskrit: "He who sleeps in the atoms". The Transformer, the Dissolver, the Destroyer, the Reproducer. From the root Śiv, "to dissolve, to return, to sleep, to go into a state of Laya or quiescence". Śiva is He in whom all things dwell and have their Being. All of Creation moves in Him, the Transcendental Godhead. Śiva is Puruṣa-Svāmī, the Supreme Witness of all Creation, the God Transcendent. The word Śiva has other meanings as well:
- The auspicious, favourable, beneficent, benign, dear, friendly, kind, gracious, benevolent, who grants all wishes and good fortune.
- The Fire of Rebirth and Regeneration, the Immortal Fire, the Fire of Yoga.
- The God-Self, the Tranquil Self, the Transcendental Self in its Eternal Tranquillity.
- The Supreme Consciousness (Para-Śiva).

Śiva is the First Aspect of the Trimūrti or Holy Trinity (Brahmā-Viṣṇu-Śiva), the "Father" in Christianity.

Śivā
Sanskrit: The All-Pervading, All-Knowing, Transcendental Consciousness. The Highest Feminine Consciousness. The Supreme Witness of All Creation. The Supreme Self or Soul (Paramātman) in all things and all beings. The Benefactor. A Name of Lalitā, the Goddess.

Śivagranthi (Śiva-Granthi)
Sanskrit: The knot (Granthi) at the Head Cakras (the Crown and the Third-Eye). [See Granthi]

Śivam
Sanskrit: Pure, auspicious, good.

Śivanetra (Śiva-Netra)
Sanskrit: "The Eye of Śiva". The All-Seeing Eye, the Eye of Wisdom. The fully awakened Third-Eye (Ājñā) Cakra. This is the highest Spiritual Vision attained by the greatest Saints, Mystics, Yogīs and Devotees. This is as different from the "hunches" and psychic impressions of a psychic or "sensitive" as is a candlelight from the blazing Sun.

Śiva-Śakti
Sanskrit: The Union of polar opposites. God united with the Divine Creative Force or Power. Śiva is the Puruṣa (Transcendental Spirit) and Śakti is His female consort or "wife", the Female Power or *Energy,* called Prākṛtī (Nature). Śiva and Śakti are always in the state of Yoga or Union, or "Sexual Bliss". Creation is the result of this constant Sexual Union of Śiva-Śakti (Father-Mother), which is the Radiant-Energy of Cosmic Love. Śiva is Pure *Being:* the Eternal, unchanging, motionless. Śakti is always *Becoming:* moving, energizing, changing, transforming. It is Śakti which awakens the *sleeping* Śiva (God) in the human being.

Śivay
Sanskrit: God as Light. A form of Śiva (used as a Mantric Sound).

Śiva Yoga
Sanskrit: The ancient Hindu system of the Liṅga Purāṇa, the Great Scripture of Śiva, upon which Patañjali's Aṣṭāṅga Yoga was based.

Śivo'haṁ, Śivōhaṁ
Sanskrit: "I Am Śiva" (Śiva-Ahaṁ). The Transcendental I AM. This Ahaṁ (I AM) is the Highest Being, Puruṣottama.

Sixth State
The Sixth State of Consciousness is Bhāgavata-Avasthā (Sanskrit), the Glorious State, the Beatific Vision. This is the first stage of Union with God, the State of Glory, Nirvāṇa, the Kingdom of God. Also called Ātma-Vidyā (Realization of the Self).

Smṛta, Smṛti
Sanskrit: Memory, remembrance, recorded. Laws, scripture, understanding. Traditional teachings.

Smṛtī
Sanskrit: Remembrance. Recollection of the Divine Presence. Remembering God in the Heart Centre. The practice of the Name. Practising the Presence of God.

Sod (SVD)
Hebrew: The Secret of the ancient Jewish Kabbalist Initiates. The Secret of the Heart.

Śoḍaṣākśarī-Mantra
Sanskrit: "The Sixteen-Syllabled Mantra". The Śoḍaṣī-Mantra. Also called the Śrī-Vidyā-Vajra-Mantra.

Śoḍaṣī
Sanskrit: "Sixteen years old". The Perfect Goddess. Śoḍaṣī is the Soft-Feminine-Force. It is a feeling-energy—inward-touching, sensitive-uniting. It is also a non-intellectual *Knowing*, what in the West used to be called *Feminine Intuition*, or Knowing without using the verbalizing-mind. Śoḍaṣī is the Inner-Mind, completely different from the aggressive, male, analytical, separative, "logical" outer-mind, so much used today everywhere. Nowadays most people in the West cannot tune into Śoḍaṣī because they have been brought up in the intellectualized education system. The "uneducated" and people in the East have a better chance to develop Śoḍaṣī. You can still *see* and *feel* Śoḍaṣī Energy in young girls in the West, *before* they have gone through the "education" mill.

Śoḍaṣī-Mantra
Sanskrit: "The Sixteen-Years-Goddess Mantra" (the Mantra is given at sixteen years of age). This Mantra produces Sattva (harmonious vibration) in the Initiate which leads to Self-Realization and Transcendental Knowledge (Śrī-Vidyā) and Unending Bliss (Ānanda).

Sohaṁ, So'haṁ, Sōhaṁ, Sōhan, Sōhaṅg
Sanskrit: "That am I" or "He is I" (So-Ahaṁ). The Supreme Spirit, the Divine Creative-Breath, the Breath of God, the Divine Self. Also, the Human Soul. Also, the Purified Yogī, one who can function in Spiritual Consciousness. The same as Haṁsa. [See Kohaṁ and Haṁsa]

Solar Logos
A Cosmic Creator-God, such as our Sun. The physical body of our Solar Logos is our Solar System, and each planet is one of His cakras or "wheels of force". Many thousands of years ago these Creator-Gods (whose bodies are stars and planets) were called Prajāpatis in India, Demiurgos and Kosmokratores in old Greece, and Elohīm among the Semitic races of the Middle East.

Solar Pitṛis
"Solar Ancestors". The Solar Angels. The Mānasaputras, or Sons of the Mind. The spiritual fathers of Humanity. [See Mānasaputra]

Solar Plexus Centre
The Energy Centre which is responsible for your emotional well-being. All of your emotions, moods, feelings and desires go through it. It puts you in touch with the Astral World. [See Maṇipūra Cakra]

Soma
Greek: A *form* of something. A body. The Universe is the Body of God, in the same way as the human physical body is but the body of the human Soul.

Somā
Sanskrit: A drug employed in Ancient India to produce an astral projection or out-of-body experience. Another drug called Sanjivāni was used to induce the "self" back into the body.

Son ⊖
In Christianity, a symbol for the Universal Light of the Christ, the Second Aspect of the Holy Trinity (the Second Logos), which is an Infinite Field of Intelligence. It is the Universal Light Vibration which hovers above the Manifest Condition, and is the Revealer of the Way to the Unmanifest, to the "Father". In Sanskrit, Viṣṇu. [See Christos]

Sophia
Greek: Wisdom. Spiritual Wisdom. Primordial Wisdom. The Transcendental Consciousness in Man, what in the East is called Buddhi. The Mind of Light experienced in the head (Buddhi-Manas). To the ancient Masters, Wisdom did not mean just being clever, worldly-wise, learned or intellectual. Wisdom is an Energy Stream. Wisdom is the *Breath of the Power of God* and a *Mighty Influence from the Radiance of the Almighty.* Wisdom is the Soul of the Universe, the Divine-Mother-Power. The task of Wisdom is to encourage the mind to be in strict watchfulness of the thought-processes, to establish firmness in mind, tranquillity and spiritual contemplation.

Sophos
Greek: A Wiseman or Wisewoman.

Sōtēr
Greek: "Saviour, Deliverer". The Gnostics called Jesus by this title, which has the same meaning as Yeshua.

Sōtērios
Greek: Salvation, Liberation, Emancipation. Making holy or healthy. Similar to the Sanskrit Mokṣa and Mukti.

Spanda
Sanskrit: Vibrations, Pulsations, Frequencies, Pulses or Rhythms of the Universal Consciousness. All things are Spanda. Everything vibrates. Everything is in motion, all the time. Evolution is a state of vibration or motion, Spanda. Material evolution has its own vibration. Psychic evolution has another. Spiritual Evolution has the highest frequency of Spanda. As you evolve spiritually, your Spanda, or Vibration-

Frequency, increases. The physical body is at the lowest SPANDA, as is the material universe. The Pure Spirit, Pure Consciousness, the Luminous-Bliss, is at the highest range of SPANDA. Each object, each being or entity, whether an animal, a man, an angel or a god, has its own unique SPANDA or Vibration. These unique vibrations constitute the "differences" between entities.

Spēculum Justīciae

Latin: "The Mirror of Justice". This means that every thought, word and deed is reflected in the Divine Substance (ĀKĀŚA). [See *Akashic Records*]

Spirit

The term *spirit* is often erroneously applied to disembodied beings on the Astral World, three planes below the realm of the true Human Spirit, ĀTMAN, the Self, dwelling on the Nirvāṇic Plane. The words *spirit* and *spiritual* come from the Latin SPIRITUS, which refers to both the Transcendent and Immanent aspects of God.

- The Transcendental Spirit is the PURUṢA, the Divine Person, the Divine Self in the Universe and in Man, the First Logos. In Man it is the MONAD, manifesting as the ĀTMAN, the Self, the Divine Being within you. During Roman and classical times, a *Spirit* was the highest apex of a human being, defined as "a bodiless, immortal being having intelligence and will".
- The Holy Spirit (SPIRITUS SANCTUS, the Holy Breath) is the Cosmic Fiery Energy of the Third Logos (in Sanskrit, BRAHMĀ or ŚAKTI). It is the vital Life and Energy, the Creative Intelligence and formless Light of the whole of Creation, the *Fire of Creation.*

Spirit is called RUAH (RUACH) in Hebrew, RŪḤ in Arabic, PNEUMA in Greek. The mediums degenerated the truth about *Spirit* and lowered it to astral phenomena.

Spirit-Spark-Atom

Within the Causal Heart is concealed a Great Mystery. This is symbolized by the Western Adepts as the *Mystical Rose* or the *Rose and the Cross,* and by the Eastern Adepts as the *Lotus Flower* or the *Jewel in the Lotus*, since this Heart does look like a rose or a lotus flower. Within the Lotus or Rose is concealed the Mystery, covered by twelve petals. It is a Mystery because it does not belong to this Creation or even to the Causal World. This Mystery is the Monadic Spark, the Eye of the Monad, the One Self, the Divine Spark, looking down from the Monadic Plane into the lower Creation. It is a bluish-white Electric Fire of tremendous intensity, a brilliant point of Monadic Light, Cosmic Intelligence compressed into a minute atom, resembling a transparent crystal, a precious stone, pearl or jewel. The Gnostics called it the *Spirit-Spark* or the *Spirit-Spark-Atom*. It is the *Sparkling Stone* or the *Stone of the Wise* of the Alchemists and the *Stone that the Builders Rejected* or the *Foundation Stone* of the Ancient Mystery Schools. The initiated Christians of the first three centuries called it the *Captured Sparks of the Spirit* or a *Spark of the Original Imperishable Kingdom of Light* (the Paranirvāṇic Plane, the realm beyond even the boundless Nirvāṇa). According to the Gnostics, this *Spirit-Spark-Atom* is the gateway, first of all, to the "Light of the Soul" and, later on, to the "Greater Mysteries" of Divinity. The Particle of Light in the Heart needs to be awakened and made to *shine*. [See MAṆI-PADMA]

Spiritual Hierarchy

Man's spiritual unfoldment is guided by the Planetary Hierarchy, the Great White Brotherhood, the Inner Government of the World, the Brotherhood of Light. It is also known as the Fifth Kingdom, the Kingdom of God, the Spiritual Kingdom, or the Christ-Hierarchy. It is the next human Hierarchy *above* the Human Hierarchy (the Fourth Kingdom). It is the Hierarchy of Saints, Masters, Yogīs and Teachers who have gone beyond the ordinary Man-type and are now evolving on the Causal, Buddhic and Nirvāṇic Planes. The Christ-Hierarchy also has Devas (Angelic Orders) working for them. This Hierarchy embraces the Nirvāṇic Realms, the Buddhic World and the formless Causal Worlds. It is from these realms that the Hierarchy sends down AVATĀRAS, Divine Incarnations or Divine Messengers, to remind human beings of who they truly are, and to teach Mankind about the Kingdom of God. In Sanskrit, SAṄGHA or SATA-SAṄGHA.

Spiritual Soul
The principle of Spiritual Love and Wisdom in Man, dwelling on the Buddhic Plane. The second aspect of the Human Triad or Individuality. In Sanskrit, ĀTMA-BUDDHI.

SPIRITUS
Latin: "Breath, Wind, Life-breath, Life-force, Vitality, Fire". Energy (gross or subtle). Vitality, Force (visible or not). God's Power of Manifestation. The manifested energy of the Holy Spirit, or ŚAKTI. PNEUMA in Greek, RUACH (RUAH) in Hebrew, PRĀṆA in Sanskrit, CHI in Chinese. Also, the Name of God, the Holy One. SPIRITUS is the Soul or Essence behind a body or form, which includes also the Transcendental Spirit, beyond and above Creation. [See *Spirit*]

SPIRITUS SANCTUS
Latin: "The Breath which is Holy". The Holy Spirit, Holy Breath, Holy Life-Force, Holy Creative Power. The Cosmic Fiery Energy of the Third Logos, the Third Person of the Trinity. The Organizing and Structurizing Power within the Universe. God's Divine Mind at work, or Cosmic Intelligence. RUAH-HA-QADOSH in Hebrew, RUḤĀ-QADASH in Aramaic, PNEUMA-HAGION in Greek.

Spook
An etheric or astral entity which invades the aura of a person in the physical body.

ŚRADDHĀ
Sanskrit: Faith, hope in success. One of the Six Mental Qualifications for Discipleship (ŚAT-SAMPATTI). To succeed in your Quest for Eternal Life you must have Faith (ŚRADDHĀ) that the Heart of God is good, that in the end all things will work out well for you, no matter how hopeless your situation may appear to be.

ŚRAMANA
Sanskrit: An ascetic training for spiritual powers. The source of the word *shaman*.

SRAOSHA
Persian: The Word or Name-Power.

ŚRĪ
Sanskrit: The Sacred, the Holy. Divine Glory, Effulgence, Brightness. ŚRĪ is the Goddess in the form of Divine Beauty, Divine Light, Divine Wealth, Glory, Prosperity, Opulence (abundance of powers, virtues, qualities, charms). ŚRĪ is the Light of Knowledge, the Light of Love: pure, refined, excellent, glittering, beautiful, shining, radiant, illuminating, glorious, perfect, holy, sacred, illustrious, revered, worshipped, honourable, royal, dignified, majestic, noble, grand, exalted, victorious. ŚRĪ is the Goddess as Brightness, Glory, all-Powers, all-Radiance, all-Majesty, the Power of Sacredness, Holiness, Grace, Divinity, the Luminous Ocean of Reality, the Shining Consciousness, the Eternal Beauty, the Imperishable and Incorruptible Power, the Undying Goodness, the Eternal Welfare of All, the Prosperity of the Universe. ŚRĪ is the Unbroken Light that is Solid Bliss.

ŚRĪṀ (ŚRĪNG)
Sanskrit: The BĪJA-Mantra for the Goddess LAKṢMĪ, the Beautiful One, She who gives good fortune, prosperity, wealth, abundance, Divine Wealth, Self-Realization (ĀTMĀ-VIDYĀ), Splendour, Light, Glory. She gives rewards, fortune, good luck, success, happiness, satisfaction, livelihood, RAMĀ (delight, joy, pleasure).

ŚRĪṀKĀRĪ (ŚRĪṀ-KĀRĪ)
Sanskrit: She who is the doer (KĀRĪ) of abundance (ŚRĪṀ). A Name of LALITĀ, the Goddess. LALITĀ is full of richness and abundance on all levels: physical, psychic, emotional, mental and spiritual. She is the maker, doer, producer, creator (KĀRĪ) of all wealth and prosperity (ŚRĪṀ).

ŚRĪ-MAHĀ-RĀJÑĪ
Sanskrit: The Dazzling Queen of the Universe. The Empress of the World. A Name of LALITĀ, the Goddess.

ŚRĪ-MĀTĀ
Sanskrit: The Holy Mother. The Universal Mother. She is the Mother of the Universe, the Cause of all that is. A Name of LALITĀ, the Goddess.

Śrī-Rāṁ
Sanskrit: The Glory of God.

Śrī-Śoḍaṣākśarī-Mantra
Sanskrit: "The Holy Sixteen-Syllabled Mantra". Also called the Śrī-Vidyā-Vajra-Mantra.

Śrī-Śoḍaṣākśarī-Vidyā
Sanskrit: The Realization (Vidyā) of the Holy (Śrī) Sixteen-Syllabled Mantra (Śoḍaṣ-ākśarī).

Śrī-Sūryanārāyaṇa
Sanskrit: The Holy-Spirit-within-the-Sun. [See Nārāyaṇa]

Śrī-Vidyā
Sanskrit: "Holy Knowledge". The Holy Science, the Sacred Knowledge. The Secret Knowledge of the Self. This Holy Knowledge is not only an intellectual idea but a direct Supernatural Experience in Ecstatic Bliss-Consciousness. This Holy Knowledge is the Realization, through profound meditational experience, that She, the Ultimate Goddess, is everything. Although the Ultimate Reality is present everywhere, at all times, in Her form as the Universal Presence (Paraśakti), we can invoke Her more intimately within ourselves, in our auric-field, in our spinal system, in our Soul, in our Spiritual Heart, the Centre and Axis of our Being. Thus can we come to know Her intimately, and She knows us more specifically. This is the purpose of Śrī-Vidyā, Holy Knowledge or Sacred Science. Śrī-Vidyā is not a philosophy, but a Science of Sound and Light, the Science of Vibrations. It is done by *Energy-Transmission.* In fact, Śrī-Vidyā is the Light-Sound Vibrations of Universal Consciousness. Śrī-Vidyā is the Goddess of Ultimate Knowledge, or the Ultimate Knowledge in the Form of the Goddess. The Goddess is the Mantra, the Mantra is the Goddess. Kuṇḍalinī is the Goddess, Śrī-Vidyā, the Holy Science, the World Mother, which is your own Self. This is the Secret.

Śrī-Vidyā-Mantra
Sanskrit: "The Holy-Realization-Mantra". Also called Para-Mantra (the Transcendental Power), Mūla-Mantra (the Basic or Root Mantra), Pañcadaṣī-Mantra (the Fifteen-Syllabled Mantra), Tripurāsundarī (the Threefold Beauty), Vāk-Śakti-Mantra (the Mantra to awaken the Power of the Creative Word in the Form of the Goddess as Sound and Speech).

Śrī-Vidyā-Vajra-Mantra
Sanskrit: "The Holy-Realization-Thunderbolt-Mantra". Also called Śoḍaṣī-Mantra (the Sixteen-Years-Goddess Mantra), Śrī-Śoḍaṣākśarī-Mantra (the Holy Sixteen-Syllabled Mantra), Mahā-Tripurāsundarī (the Great Threefold Beauty), Gudha-Gāyatrī-Mantra (the Secret Gāyatrī-Mantra), Cit-Gāyatrī (Absolute Knowledge), Cit-Śakti (the Consciousness-Power).

Śruti
Sanskrit: "That which is heard". Hearing the Inner Teacher. Revelation, scriptures.

Stella Matutīna
Latin: "The Star of the Morning". The Pure White Light in the Third-Eye.

Sterge
Greek: The love of one's whole community or nation.

Sthirattva
Sanskrit: Tranquillity, steadiness, serenity. To see the Light in the Head and hear the Cosmic Sound in the Crown Centre, you first need Tranquillity of the Heart. That is, you need Śāntiḥ: inner peace, inner calm.

Sthitiḥ
Sanskrit: Peace, tranquillity.

Sthūla
Sanskrit. Gross or physical. Gross physical matter.

Sthūla-Loka
Sanskrit: "Gross-World". The Physical Plane.

Sthūla-Śarīra
Sanskrit: "Gross-substance body". The dense physical body, which exists on the lower part of the Physical Plane and consists of solids, liquids and gases. Also called Annamāyākośa (the illusionary-food-body).

Stigmata
[See Transverberation]

Strī
Sanskrit: A strong Feminine Power which is creative, mothering, nursing, caring, protecting, nourishing, sustaining and transforming. She is Strī (the mature Woman, the Woman concept, the Woman archetype or prototype) and She is Vadhū (the Wife, the Female Partner). She is complete Womanhood, the Feminine Nature, the companion to the male powers. A Name of Lalitā, the Goddess.

Strī-Mantra
Sanskrit: Also called Vadhū-Mantra (the Female-Partner Mantra) and Yoginī-Mantra (the Female-who-has-Realized-the-Truth Mantra). Strī and Vadhū represent Feminine Consciousness, the Feminine Nature. A Yoginī is One who has Realized the Self (Ātman), the Spirit within. Thus, this Mantra helps the Devotee attain the State of Yoga, Union, Oneness with the Goddess, with the Absolute Truth, with Transcendental Consciousness, with the Eternal.

Styāna
Sanskrit: Dullness, lack of perseverance, stupidity. One of the Antarāyāḥ (obstacles, impediments, problems on the Path to Higher Consciousness).

Subconscious Mind
That which is *below* your conscious mind. The subjective mind, the dreaming mind, the symbolic mind. Dreamtime, imagination. The astral-body consciousness. In Sanskrit, Svapnā-Avasthā.

Subplane
Each of the seven great Planes of Being has seven subdivisions or *subplanes*—seven realms, spheres or vibrational states of increasingly finer matter or energy. Thus, there are a total of forty-nine subplanes, or states of matter, within the Cosmic Physical Plane of our Solar System. In the Secret Doctrine, the Primeval Wisdom, these forty-nine states of matter are called the *forty-nine Fires*.

Śuddha, Śuddhā
Sanskrit: Pure, immaculate, holy, sacred, innocent, clean, unsullied, white, bright, blameless, correct. (Śuddhā is the feminine form.)

Śuddha-Caitanya
Sanskrit: "Pure Consciousness". This is the link or connection (Yoga) with your Wisdom-Mind (Buddha-Mānasa). You must still all activities of your mind if you would hear the Voice of the Higher Self, the Voice of God within you.

Śuddha-Deham
Sanskrit: "Pure Body". Purified and perfected physical bodies that vibrate differently than normal bodies.

Śuddha-Manas
Sanskrit: "Pure Mind". The original Pure State of Mind, which gets ruffled and disturbed by the thought-processes.

Śuddha-Mānasā
Sanskrit: "Pure-Minded". Pure Consciousness, Pure Mind. A Name of Lalitā, the Goddess. The one who constantly dwells in Lalitā will experience the Self (Ātman) as Transcendental Bliss. She is Śuddha-Mānasā (Pure-Minded).

Śuddhāmaṇi
Sanskrit: "Pure Jewel". Nectar-Precious. A sparkling jewel, a sacred ornament. Holy Radiance.

Śūdra
Sanskrit: The Servant Class (caste, Varṇa). The labourers, the slaves, the unskilled, the uneducated.

Sufflation
Latin: In the terminology of the Medieval Catholic Mystics, *Sufflation* is the experiencing of oneself as a Spiritual Soul, and the experience *within* the Soul of being overshadowed by the Divine Presence. In the East this is known as the awakening of Buddhi, the Love-Wisdom Principle.

Sūfī
Arabic-Persian: "One who has purified the Heart". One who has attained Mystical Union with God. A Pure One. A Muslim Saint. The Sūfīs are all those great Saints of the Muslim religion who have attained Union with God, or who have merged into the Eternal Light. In the Persian language the word for Wisdom is Sūf, and Sūfī means "a Wise Person, an Enlightened One, an Illumined Mystic who has experienced God first-hand". In Arabic, Sūf means "wool", and a Sūfī was one who wore a coarse woollen garment. It was a monkish outfit, similar to that of the Christian monks, worn by the early Muslim Mystics who renounced the world in order to search for God. A Sūfī is "Pure in Heart" (Qalb-Salīm, a Heart that is Perfect). In the State of Perfection you perceive nothing else but God in all things, and the Divine becomes the Centre of your life, the Heart throb of your Being. Your personal ego is dissolved in God, Fanā'fi-llāh.

Sukhāvatī, Sukhavatī
Sanskrit: "The place of happiness". The Mental Plane. The Heaven Worlds. The Mental Plane is called Sukhāvatī (the place of happiness, joy, pleasure) because it is the highest happiness for many Souls on the incarnatory cycle. Your mental body is composed of the Elemental Essence (matter) of the Mental Plane, which is essentially a sea of colour, light and sound, a living ocean of Joy and Vibrancy. Thus, if you can function in your mind-body in Sukhāvatī, you will be naturally in a state of intense Joy and Happiness, or "Heaven".

Sūkṣma
Sanskrit: "Subtle". The Cosmic Elements exist in subtle states (Sūkṣma) on the Astral and Mental Planes.

Sūkṣma-Loka
Sanskrit: "Subtle World". The Astral and Mental Worlds.

Sūkṣma-Śarīra
Sanskrit: "Subtle body". The astral body, made up of the seven differentiated matters of the Astral World. Also called Kāma-Rūpa (desire-body). This is your subjective mind or subconscious mind.

Sulṭān-ul-Azkār
Arabic: The King of Prayers, the Victorious Power, the Divine Word.

Sulūk
Arabic: Devotion towards God.

Sundara
Sanskrit: Beautiful.

Sundarī
Sanskrit: Exquisitely beautiful.

Śūnyatā (Śūnya)
Sanskrit: "Emptiness". A formless condition. A Buddhist term for the Mystical Consciousness (Buddhi), which is characterized by Formlessness, No-Thingness, Clarity, Light. Nirvāṇa they call Mahāśūnyatā (the Great Emptiness). To confuse the issue, some schools use this word to mean non-existence or unreality. Others use this word to mean the sky or space.

Superconscious Mind
That which is *above* the self-conscious mind. Mystical Union, which begins at the higher, formless mental subplanes (the Causal Worlds) and includes the seven subplanes of the Buddhic Plane. Thus there are several degrees or stages of Superconsciousness. The true Superconscious Mind is Pure Consciousness, Mystical Consciousness, the Transcendental State, the Fourth State (Turīya-Avasthā). This experience is the same as the Sanskrit Bodhi, the Japanese Satori and the Greek Gnosis.

Supernātūralis
Latin: "Beyond physical nature". From Super (above, beyond) and Nātūra (nature, physical matter, physical forces and events). The Romans understood the "Supernatural" to be invisible forces, agencies, entities or realms of being, beyond the range of the five physical senses. It does not mean that the Supernatural does not exist!

Supraversion
Latin: "Turning above". Focusing above the head or above the personality level. Focusing one's energies into the Causal Centre above the head and into the causal body.

Sura
Sanskrit: A Solar Angel. The Suras are Gods, Divine Hierarchies, Archangels, Devas.

Surat
Sanskrit: Attention. From Surata, "tranquil, calm, well-disposed".

Surat-Śabda Yoga
Sanskrit: "Putting your attention on the Sound". Listening to God as the Word within. Listening internally to Śabda (the Sound-Current), Nāda (the Inner Sound), Nāma (the Name), the Logos, the Word. The Yoga of the Sounding-Light. Similar to Nāda Yoga and Laya Yoga.

Sureśam
Sanskrit: The Ruler of all the Spiritual-Hierarchies of Being. From Sura (Divine Hierarchies, Devas) and Īśa (God, Lord, Ruler, Commander).

Sūrya
Sanskrit: The Sun-God, the Solar Logos. Sūrya is also known as Savitā, Savitṛ (Savitri), Īśvara, Sūrya-Nārāyaṇa, Nārāyaṇa, Agni (the Fire-God), Āditya (the Sun) and Ātman (the Self). Sūrya stands for Light: Boundless Light, Limitless Light, Inter-Cosmic Light, Solar-Systemic Light, Light on the various planes of Being, the Light of Love, the Light of Intelligence, the Unmanifest Light and the Light of Evolution. Sūrya, Savitā, means "the Stimulator, Energizer, Life-Giver, Rouser, Impeller, Vivifier, Enlightener, Illuminator, Inspirer, Guide, the Awakener-Light-of-God, the Solar Logos, the Being-within-the-Sun, the Sun-God". The physical Sun, as seen by the physical bodily eyes, is the outermost part of a small organ (the dense-physical Heart) of the Solar Deity (Sūrya, Savitā). [See Savitā]

Sūrya-Jyoti
Sanskrit: The Light of the Solar Logos. Illumination in the human Heart and Head Centres is received directly from the Sun of our Solar System.

Sūrya-Maṇḍala
Sanskrit: The Circle of the Sun. Also called Gāyatrī-Sādhanā (the Sun-Spiritual-Practice).

Sūrya-Maṇḍalā
Sanskrit: "Sun-Circle". The Circle of the Sun, which is the Anāhata Cakra, the Heart Centre. The Heart is the Mystery of Being, of Life, of Consciousness. It is the Mystery of "Who Am I?" Parameśvarī, the Supreme Goddess, lives in the Heart. This Supreme Goddess is Lalitā. The Devī dwells in the Heart of Her devotee.

Sūrya-Sādhanā
Sanskrit: "Sun-Worship". The worship of the Sun is the most direct worship of God. It is not the worship of an inanimate object in the sky. The Work of Rebirth, Regeneration, Spiritual Vitalization, Spiritual Evolution, is carried out by the Energies of the Sun (Śakti) on higher Planes of Being. The New Creature, the New Man, is a Restructured Human Being whose Aura is regenerated, reorganized into a glorious angelic-like Being who is conscious of Immortality, Heavenly Love and Bliss. This is all done by the Power of the Sun, by the Grace of the Solar Deity, who represents for us God-the-Absolute. [See Viśva Yoga]

Sūrya-Vaṁśa
Sanskrit: "The Sun-Race". The Children of the Sun, the Children of the Light. These are men and women who have Realized their Identity with the Sun, their Oneness with the Light.

Sūrya-Vaṁśa-Kṣatriya
Sanskrit: "The Race of the Sun-Warriors". The Warriors of the Sun, the Solar Lords, the Spiritual Warriors. From Sūrya (the Sun, the Solar Logos), Vaṁśa (a race of people) and Kṣatriya (a Warrior). Many ancient Dynasties of kings and emperors and great rulers of nations belonged to this Sun-Race of Warriors. They ruled their kingdoms by the Power of the Sun, that is, their Conscious-Identification with the Solar Deity (being in various degrees of Union with the Sun), and their understanding of the Mystery of the Solar Logos and His significance for Human Evolution on this planet, our Earth.

Suṣumna
Sanskrit: The spiritual current. The central nerve-current. The subtle, invisible spinal column in etheric, astral and mental matter. (This is *not* the physical spinal system.) Suṣumna is the ladder upon which spiritual (non-worldly) Consciousness ascends and descends. It is the Path upward to Heavenly Regions and Spiritual Dimensions. The literal meaning of Suṣumna is "great happiness, extreme well-being". This alone will explain to you a lot about Śrī-Vidyā, the Sacred Knowledge. It produces in your inner Self or Being an "extreme happiness"—nay, Absolute Bliss.

Suṣūpti-Avasthā
Sanskrit: The "dreamless-sleep" state. When awakened, this manifests as Causal Consciousness.

Suṣūpti Yoga
Sanskrit: Yoga practised in the dream state. This Way of Yoga came from India, but the Tibetans made it into a major Path towards Self-Realization.

Sūtra
Sanskrit: "A thread upon which pearls or jewels are strung". A thread, a line, a connection, a link; a verse, a statement, an aphorism; a sacred scripture or holy text.

Sūtrātma
Sanskrit: "The Thread of the Spirit" (Sūtra-Ātma). The Link with the Spirit. The Life-line from the Monad. The Sūtrātma is the Light of the Spirit which works *from above to below*. It is made out of cables or tubes of Light which connect the Monad to the Soul, and the Soul to the personality. It links all your bodies together so that you can function as an integrated human entity. The Sūtrātma descends from the Monad (Paramātman) as a triple conduit of Spiritual Light: Light, Life and Energy. One strand of this Light-Life-Energy reaches the Crown Centre and shines there as Pure Light. The second strand descends into the Heart Centre and shines therein as the Light of the Soul. The third strand descends into the Base Centre and manifests there as the Energy of Matter, Kuṇḍalinī. On a lower level, your etheric-physical body is linked to your physical body by the Silver Cord, which is a lower reflection of Sūtrātma. The Silver Cord is a cable of Ethereal Light. It is called the *Silver Cord* because of its silvery strands of shining Light-substance. Once the cable snaps, your physical body dies.

Suvaḥ, Suvaha, Svaḥ, Svaha
Sanskrit: The Heaven World, Devāchan, the Mental Plane. Svarga (the Heavenly Realms), the Celestial Realms, the Shining World, the Fiery World, God-who-pervades-the-Universe, the Eternal Breath. (Please note the difference between Svaḥ, Svaha, "the Heaven World, the Mental Plane", and Svāhā, the Bīja-Mantra for consecration, offering, sacrifice, oblation, outpouring.)

Suvah-Loka
Sanskrit: The Mental Plane. Devāchan.

Sva
Sanskrit: One's self. One's own.

Svabhāva
Sanskrit: "Self-becoming" (Sva-Bhāva). One's essential being or innate disposition. Desire for manifestation or sentient existence. Self-actualization. [See Svāyaṁbhū]

Svabhavat
Sanskrit: The Primordial Self-Condition of the Absolute Being. The Infinite State from which the Universe comes into being.

Svacitta
Sanskrit: Self-consciousness, self-awareness (Sva-Citta). While the Three Worlds are the manifestation of the Cosmic Mind, your own reality is a manifestation of *your* mind or consciousness (Svacitta).

Svādhiṣṭhāna Cakra
Sanskrit: The Sex Centre, also called the Sacral Centre or the Reproductive Centre. This cakra is responsible for reproduction and the sexual instinct. The energy of sexual attraction is *not* physical. Physical bodies are inert, they cannot attract. It is the etheric energies in the etheric-physical body (which permeate the physical) that attract. When the Sex Centre is awakened, great explosions of sexual energy can occur in the body, or orgasms, or feelings of intense bliss and well-being and release from tension.

Svādhyāya
Sanskrit: "Self-study". Spiritual Studies. Understanding yourself, knowing yourself. Spiritual practices which lead to the Knowledge (direct experience) of the Self. Svādhyāya is the fourth Niyama (rule) of Aṣṭāṅga Yoga, as set down by Patañjali. It refers to many things. Svādhyāya was wrongly interpreted by the monks as the study of scriptures and spiritual books in monasteries and Āśramas. In truth, however, the word Svādhyāya means "studying yourself", understanding the whole gamut of yourself: you as a personality, you as a Living Soul, you as the Spiritual Self, you as the Divine Self, and you as a particle of God. All of this is Self-study. Meditation (Yoga) is the *means* of Self-study.

Svāhā
Sanskrit: "We unite with, we dissolve in, we make offerings to Reality". Offerings of the Heart. Offering oneself to Divinity. Religious worship of Deity or Goddess. The Bīja-Mantra for consecration, offering, sacrifice, oblation, outpouring. Svāhā is the Female Aspect of the Spiritual Fire, the Fire of Purification and self-surrender to Divinity. Svāhā also means "one's own Mantra", from Sva (own) and Aha (speech, word, sound, affirmation). Svāhā is the Mantra best suited to you.

Svāhā-Devī
Sanskrit: The Goddess of Offerings. All rituals, religious ceremonies and rites are, in essence, offered to Her, the One Reality. A Name of Lalitā, the Goddess.

Svāmī
Sanskrit: Lord, Master, God, owner. Also, a monk, a sannyāsin, a renunciate.

Svapnā-Avasthā
Sanskrit: The dreaming state. The subconscious mind or subjective mind. The astral consciousness of dreaming, psychism, hallucination, imagination, day-dreaming, astral projection, and so forth.

Svapnā-Avasthā Siddhi
Sanskrit: "Dream-state power". The power of conscious dreaming. On the Path of Yoga (Union) your normal waking-consciousness and your dreaming-consciousness will be *empowered* by the dynamism, creativity and vitality of Superconsciousness or Transcendental Consciousness (Samādhi). Thus, your actions in the Physical World will have more powerful effects, and what you "dream" will *manifest*. Then your dreaming becomes just another tool for creativity, which you may use while you are awake or while you are "asleep". You can "dream" things consciously into manifestation, and your dreams become physical realities. Furthermore, your Soul will be able to communicate with you in your "dreams", as will, later on, the Spirit or Monad, your "Father in Heaven", your Source of Revelation.

Svarga, Svarga-Loka
Sanskrit: "The Heaven World". The Mental Plane. Devāchan.

Svarṇa-Deham
Sanskrit: "Golden Body". A physical body, talked about by the Siddhas, that glowed like liquid gold or glittered like gold dust. That is, either the natural physical body was transmuted into the Golden Body, or the Golden Body was projected from the Astral Plane into the physical body, thus transmuting the natural body into a luminous golden body.

Svarūpa
Sanskrit: "One's own true form". The real Self-Nature, how one really is, your Formless Self. The Cosmic Elements exist in their true form (Svarūpa) on the etheric subplanes.

Svarūpa Siddhi
Sanskrit: Powers (Siddhi) belonging to one's own intrinsic form (Svarūpa) or true Self-Nature; that is, belonging to the Soul (Jīvātman, the Reincarnating Ego), or to the Triune Self (Ātma-Buddhi-Manas), or to the Divinity in Man (Paramātman, the Monad). These are powers of Pure Consciousness (Divya Citta, Divine Consciousness) which relate to the Buddhic, Nirvāṇic and Paranirvāṇic Planes of Being, and to Ādi, the Divine World of God. [See Māyā Siddhi]

Svastika 卍
Sanskrit: "Well-being, good health, strong life-force". The Whirling Cross. The Svastika represents the Primordial Life-Force of the Universe. This is the Force that sweeps galaxies into a whirling motion. The Christian cross is stationary and is the symbol of the crucifixion of Life in Matter. In the Svastika, that Life is set free. This takes place in the Heart. (Hitler, of course, misused this symbol, which has been used in India for thousands of years.)

Svastika-Śakti
Sanskrit: The Mystic Force or Spiritual Power that can be placed in symbols, emblems, talismans, auspicious objects or signs. [See Mahā-Svastika-Śakti]

Svatantrayaśakti
Sanskrit: "Your-Self-Creative-Power" (Sva-Tantraya-Śakti). Your Innate Creative Intelligence.

Svāyaṁbhū
Sanskrit: "The Self-Existent" (Svāyam-Bhū). Your own Self-Nature, the Self-Existent Being. The Spontaneous State of Being. The State of Living Spontaneously. The Transcendental Awareness, which is eternal and immutable. When the action of Prāṇa inside you is suspended (Prāṇāyāma) and the mind (Manas) stops, then the individual Soul (Jīvātma) and the Over-Soul of God (Paramātma) are experienced to be as One. This is Self-Becoming, Svāyaṁbhū or Svabhāva. Also, Brahmā, Viṣṇu, Śiva, Buddha, Vasudeva (the Lord of all Living Beings). The Buddha-Mind is your own Fundamental Mind, beyond conceptualizing and thinking. It is your Essential Reality.

Svāyaṁbhū Liṅga
Sanskrit: An access-way to extra-physical reality, located at the Mūlādhāra Cakra (Base Centre). From Svāyaṁbhū (the Self-Existent) and Liṅga (a Sign for Śiva, the Transcendent). [See Bāṇa Liṅga and Itarā Liṅga]

Svāyam-Jyoti (Svāyamjyotiḥ)
Sanskrit: The Self-Existing Light. The Self-Effulgent Light.

Śyām
Sanskrit: Dark, black, deep-blue, indigo. Kṛṣṇa.

Synesis
Greek: Insight, Intuition, the direct understanding of the Truth.

Syzygie
Greek: The Female Energy-Power. What in the East would be called Śakti. The companion or opposite to the Male Energy-Powers of the Universe.

T

TACITURNAS
Latin: "Silent Ones". The Mystics.

TAD
Sanskrit: Thus, thereby, from that.

TADARTHAḤ
Sanskrit: For that purpose, for the sake of, for His sake.

TAIJASA-BHŪTA
Sanskrit: The substance or matter aspect of the Fire Element, AGNI or TEJAS.

TALA
Sanskrit: Negative vibration. A negative type of consciousness associated with a world or realm.

ṬALABĀN
Arabic: Seekers of God.

ṬĀLIB
Arabic: A seeker, a neophyte, one who searches for God. This is the first stage of the Journey of the Heart. At this stage of your life upon the Path (ṬARĪQAT), you are seeking, searching for Truth everywhere, motivated by the hidden impulses from your Heart. Occasionally you attempt to meditate or try some practice, but you are very easily distracted.

TAMAS
Sanskrit: That which vibrates with inertia, ignorance, slowness, resistance, stupidity, darkness. TAMAS is the force of *passivity, steadiness*. [See GUṆA]

TANHĀ
Sanskrit: The desire to be born in a physical body. The thirst or desire for sentient existence, on the personality level, in the Three Worlds. Similar to the Sanskrit word TRIŚNĀ. It is this sentient desire (TANHĀ, TRIŚNĀ) that causes reincarnation and consequently karmas.

TANMĀTRA
Sanskrit: "The Measure of That". The vibration, motion or force aspect of a thing or entity.

TANNO
Sanskrit: That.

TANTRA
Sanskrit: The term TANTRA is most difficult to describe. It is abbreviated from TANTRASĀRA. TAN means "to stretch out, to weave" and "the physical body". TRA is "a tool, instrument, equipment" or "that which transcends". SĀRA means "substance, essence, basis; the essence or substance of a thing; an essential quality or knowledge". Thus, TANTRASĀRA is an essential field of knowledge which transcends the limitations of the physical body. The word TANTRA can mean the loom and warp of a weaving machine; something that is important, essential or mystical; esoteric philosophies or systems of teachings; mental and spiritual procedures, processes and techniques; sacred books; rituals, magical formulae; polarity, relationship; female energies of goddesses; Insight, the perception of Reality; being fully Aware in the moment; transformation through Awareness.

TANTRA-PRAṆAVA
Sanskrit: The Esoteric Praise of the Goddess.

TAO
Chinese: "The Great Absolute Ruler, the Heavenly-Master of Creation". TAO has been translated as "the One Truth or Reality underlying all Creation, the Single Principle of the Universe". Everything emerges out of TAO, develops and returns to its Source, which is TAO. TAO is the Essential Simplicity, which is the Source, Root and Origin of things, and at the same time, the Way, the Truth and the Life. It is the Manifest and Unmanifest Godhead all at once, in Oneness. TAO is the *Being* or *Essence* of all things, the *Source of Active Power* within all things, the *Force* or *Energy* behind all forms. According to the ancient Chinese, TAO gave *order* to Primordial Matter, which then became Nature. TAO is transcendental and abstract, but, in its capacity as the Subjective Power within Creation, it is God

Immanent within the Universe *and* within Man. TAO is the ultimate meaning of all things, the *why and how* of all things, since beneath and within all objects is to be found TAO. Thoughts (which are subtle objects) and objects throughout Omnispace are but modifications arising in the Universal Mind, TAO. No object, gross or subtle, is separate from TAO, the One Mind. TAO means the same as the old Hebrew Name of God that Moses received on Mount Sinai: EHEIEH (I AM, Being, Beingness). TAO is the Universal Self of All, the One Beingness of the Universe, the One Living God. For the Christian Mystic this would be the LOGOS, the Universal Christ-Being, the Cosmic Christ. For the Hindu it would be the ĀTMAN, the Universal Self, the One-Selfhood-in-All, or PARABRAHMAN, the Transcendental Reality. Thus, TAO may be described as the Truth-Principle, the Eternal Reality, the Self, or the I AM. The ancient Egyptian word for this was TAU. Not originated by anything, it is the One Principle which is before all else. Thus, TAO cannot be talked about, but It can be *demonstrated* by Silence and Consciousness. Some people call TAO "God". [See *Mind-Only*]

TAO TEH
Chinese: "Silence and Action". The great original religion of China.

TAPAH-LOKA
Sanskrit: The Fiery Realm. The Monadic World. The Realm of PARANIRVĀṆA.

TAPAS, TAPASYA, TAPAḤ
Sanskrit: A burning longing for God or Liberation. Being on Fire for God and in God. Fiery Devotion, fiery effort in spiritual practice, the desire for Perfection, religious fervour, intense self-discipline, fiery aspiration, spiritual purification. Burning away impurities in the body, emotions and mind. Being on fire from the Fire within. TAPAS is the third NIYAMA (rule) of AṢṬĀṄGA YOGA, as set down by Patañjali. Scholars usually translate the word as "austerities". As practised by the common yogīs and ascetics, TAPAS came to mean "austerities, penance, harsh disciplines, punishing the physical body, self-torture", which have nothing at all to do with the original meaning. The word TAPAS literally means "being on fire" or "internal burning", from TĀPA (burning, fiery, heat, zealous). There is no suggestion in the word of torturing your body! TAPAS has to do with the Fire of the Mind; it can be translated as "self-discipline" or "mental discipline". It refers to disciplining one's thoughts, one's mental life, for the key to the Spiritual Path is mental regeneration, mind transformation. TAPAS has to do with interior purification of your whole Psyche or Inner Being by Inner Fire as you progress on the Spiritual Path through pure Devotion towards the Deity.

TĀRĀ
Sanskrit: She who is like a Star. Starlike radiation, silver-like Light, radiant Energy. The Force of goodness or goodwill. A Force which is capable of producing Glory. Saviour, Liberating Force, Active Grace. She who Saves. She who carries you across the Ocean of Existence to the Other Shore. A Name of LALITĀ, the Goddess. The Goddess is not only the Mother, but our Saviour (TĀRĀ) also.

TĀRAKA, TĀRAKAṀ
Sanskrit: Transcendental, shining, clear, bright, exalted. The Deliverer of Knowledge or Realization.

TĀRAKA-MANTRA
Sanskrit: The shining, clear, bright Sound-Vibration.

TĀRINĪ
Sanskrit: Saving-Grace, Saving-Power.

ṬARĪQAT
Arabic: The second stage of the Radiant Way, the Shining Path of the SŪFĪ. This is the beginning of the Mystic Path. Here one *imitates* the lives of the Holy Messengers and the Prophets. Here is true *conversion* to the religious life, true faith in God. This is the stage of discipleship and spiritual practice. One begins to act only according to virtues and perfections, positive qualities such as Faith, Hope, Love, Charity, Kindness, Wisdom and Compassion. One lives a saintly life, resigned to God's Will. More generally, the word ṬARĪQAT can denote the Shining Path itself, the Journey to Spiritual Enlightenment.

Tarot
Derived from Thoth, the old Egyptian word for Enlightened Wisdom or Illumination. The so-called Tarot Cards originated in the eleventh or twelfth century, from an Esoteric Brotherhood in Europe, to preserve the Esoteric Teachings through the Dark Ages of the Piscean Age. This early Tarot symbolism was but a modified symbolism of the old Egyptian Mystery School teachings.

Tat
Sanskrit: "That". The Inconceivable Reality. The One Existence, the Final Truth, the Boundless Absolute, the Eternal Godhead. Parabrahman (the Boundless All, the Absolute Godhead), Parabrahm (the Infinite Invisible Existence). The final, inconceivable, indescribable Absolute Truth or Reality of the Godhead within Man and the Cosmos. The Spiritual Sun. The Unnameable. [See Sat]

Tathāgatā
Sanskrit: "One who has gone to That". From Tathā (Tat, That, the Absolute State) and Gatā (gone to, arrived at). A fully Enlightened Buddha.

Tathatā
Sanskrit: The "Suchness" of things.

Tattva
Sanskrit: "That-ness" (Tat-Tva). Substance, truth, essence, element, reality, basis. The essential nature of a thing, the inherent quality in a thing or entity, whether a human being, an angel, a god, a Logos, a Plane of Being, or the Absolute. The subtle aspect of a thing, the Law of it, the inner drive of it, that which is producing it.

Tau
Egyptian: For the ancient Egyptians, Tau was the Beginning and the End, the Great Mother from which all proceeds and unto which all will one day return. It is Tā, the Outgoing, and Ū, the returning Wave. [See Tao]

Tauḥīd (Tawhīd)
Arabic: The One. The Oneness of God. The Unbroken Sameness of the Godhead. The Indivisible One. The Divine Unity. Also, the State of Unity, Union with God, Union with the All. This is the central teaching of Sūfī-sm, and the Goal of the Mystics of Islām. [See Aḥad]

Tauḥīd-e-Zāti
Arabic: The Unity of God's Essence or God's Being. This is the Goal that the Mystic experiences in the higher stages of the Spiritual Journey (Ṭarīqat).

Tawakkalallāh
Arabic: "Trust in God" (Tawakkal-Allāh). Absolute trust in God is one of the virtues which must be cultivated on the Shining Path of the Sūfī.

Teishō
Japanese: Formal class or lectures by the Zen Master.

Tejas, Taijasa, Agni
Sanskrit: The Cosmic Element *Fire*. The Cosmic Fire (Cosmic Electromagnetic Energy or Radiant Matter) corresponding to the substance of the Mental Plane. The Cosmic Fiery Substances and Energies throughout Creation.

Tejas-Tanmātra
Sanskrit: The vibration or force aspect of the Fire Element, Agni or Tejas.

Telepatheia
Greek: "Being in communion from a distance". From Tele (at a distance) and Patheia (affinity, communion, feeling, sensing, or suffering). Hence the English word *telepathy*. There are many forms of telepathy, such as instinctual telepathy, psychic telepathy, mental telepathy, and Soul-telepathy. In parapsychology, telepathy is defined as "the communication of impressions from one mind to another, independently of the five physical senses". Mental telepathy is mind-to-mind communication, either between two people living in the flesh or between a person who is in the invisible realms and one who is in the physical body. Telepathy is the universal language. Telepathy is *not* mediumship.

Terra
Latin: Earth. [See *Earth*]

Tetrakti □
Greek: The Four. The lower four in Creation and in Man. The Quaternary. Matter, the lower aspects of Creation. In Man, the physical, etheric, astral and mental bodies. Together, the Tetrakti and the Triad constitute the *Sacred Seven*. [See Triad]

Tettei
Japanese: Complete Enlightenment.

Theologia
Greek: "God-Knowledge". The Science of God-Realization. From Theos (God) and Logos (God as the Creative Principle, the Divine Word or Wisdom, the Divine Discourse or Reason). Hence the degenerated English word *theology*. In the early centuries of Christianity, theology was not just a set of intellectual ideas and dogmas as it is today. It was the *direct realization* of Divine Realities, the *inner perception* of the Spiritual Realms and Hierarchies through the processes of prayer, meditation and contemplation, the direct *realization* of God, deep within the Soul. From the first to the fourth centuries, this science was known as Gnosis; henceforth it was usually called Theologia, the Science of God-Realization. Similarly, to *theologize* means to have flashes of inner Insight. Theologia has the same meaning as the Sanskrit Brahma-Vidyā.

Theologian
Greek: "A Knower of God by experience". One who has attained Nirvāṇic Consciousness, the Kingdom of God. To the early Hesychasts of the deserts, a *Theologian* was a saintly person who *experienced* some degree of Divine Consciousness. From this we have the degenerated English word. Nowadays, most theologians do not have a direct knowledge of God and some do not even believe in God!

Theophainesthai
Greek: A manifestation or appearance of God in a mystical Vision, in Ecstasy, or in an interior Revelation.

Theophania
Greek: "God-manifestation". An appearance of God. From Theos (God) and Phania (to appear, to manifest). The fact of Divine Incarnation according to the ancient pre-Christian Greeks. Similar to the Sanskrit Avatāra.

Theoria
Greek: Contemplation. Meditation. Inner spiritual discipline of the mind, or a method of spiritual practice. In a more specific sense, the Saints understood Theoria as "an Inner Vision of the Primeval Light of God; the flooding of the upper regions of the mind (the root of the mind) with Light or Transforming Fire; the contemplation of the Inexpressible Light; the Union of the Soul with God by the Energy of God's Light; deep, inner Spiritual Knowledge". The lowest form of Theoria is the vision of the essences or energies beyond physical Creation, of the subtle worlds, such as the heavens and hells. But the objective of the Hesychast is the contemplation of God Him/Herself. From this came the English word *theory,* which nowadays has a radically different meaning: speculation, guessing, conjecture, hypothesis, a point of view. How things change!

Theos
Greek: God, the Creator. God is the *Centre, Source* and *Origin* of all things. God is the beginning and the end (the Alpha and Omega) of all Creation. God is both Timelessness and the Ever-Living, Eternal, Here-and-Now Moment. This is the Mystery of God. God *is* Creation, yet God is *above* Creation. God is both the ever-changing shadow-play and the Changeless Light.

Theosis
Greek: Union with God. The Deification of created beings by the Light of Grace. The Deification of the Human Soul. Attaining Divine-Likeness. Conscious Immortality. This, of course, is the goal of Yoga, Sūfīsm, Jewish Hasidism, Zen, Taoism and Buddhism. When the mind perceives the Holy Spirit in full consciousness, we realize that Grace is beginning to paint the Divine-Likeness over the Divine Image within us.

Theosophia
Greek: "The Wisdom of God". Divine Wisdom, Divine Illumination. From Theos (God) and Sophia (Wisdom). This is the *direct experience* of Wisdom. The term Theosophia was used by the pre-Christian Greek Mystery Schools to signify Buddhic Consciousness. From this we have the English word *theosophy*. [See Sophia]

Theosophos
Greek: A Sage. One who is wise *in* God. A man or woman of God. One who is filled with the Spirit of God. From Theos (God) and Sophos (a Wiseman or Wisewoman). Hence the English word *theosophist.*

Theotokos
Greek: "One who bringeth forth God". The same as the *Virgin Mary* concept in Western Christianity. From Theos (God) and Tokos (to bring forth, to manifest). [See *Virgin Goddess*]

Therapeia
Greek: "Healing". There were no divisions in the minds of the ancient healers between the visible and the invisible Nature; therefore they used the vast resources of the unseen Universe around us for healing. In ancient Greece, a Therapon was "a healer, a doctor". Today we have the English words *therapy* and *therapist.* Therapy is "curative power or quality" or "the treatment of disease or disorders by some remedial, rehabilitating or curative process". Examples are physiotherapy and psychotherapy. Unlike the ancient practices, today's idea of therapy or healing is extremely limited and *out of tune with total Nature or Reality.*

Third-Eye Centre
The Third-Eye is located between the eyes and is responsible for your ordinary mind, your mental body. It puts you in touch with the lower Mental Plane. When awakened, it becomes the seat of Spiritual Vision. It has been called the Wisdom-Eye, the Eye of Śiva, the All-Seeing Eye, the Single-Eye, the Spiritual Eye, the Clairvoyant Eye, and the Cyclopean Eye. [See Ājñā Cakra]

Third Death
The *Third Death* occurs when you die in your astral body. You then leave the Astral World and go to the Mental Plane (the "Seven Heavens").

Third Logos ⊕
The Fire of Creation. Brahmā. The Holy Spirit. Also called Shekinah in Hebrew and Śakti in Sanskrit. [See *Holy Trinity*]

Thoughtform
A thought-structure existing in the mental body, built from matter of the lower mental subplanes. In Sanskrit, Manasi-Jā, "things born from the mind". In your natural condition you are completely surrounded by your thoughtforms. Although you cannot see them with your physical eyes, your thoughts are objective, real, and you could see them if you had mental clairvoyance. These thoughtforms block your perception of Reality. When you drop your mental activity, you will come to know the Things that Are.

Thousand-Petalled Lotus
The Crown Centre at the top of the head. [See Sahasrāra Cakra]

Three Worlds
The Physical, Astral and Mental Planes, constituting the realm of the personality of Man. The Cycle of Reincarnation takes place within the Three Worlds, the worlds of form. Tripurā in Sanskrit. [See Saṁsāra].

Throat Centre
The Throat Centre is the higher creative centre. A healthy, well-functioning and developed Throat Centre will lead to a creative life. The Throat Centre is responsible for your Abstract Mind (the philosophical mind) and the causal body. When highly developed it becomes the instrument for telepathic transmission and gives you sensitivity to the energies of the higher Mental Plane. [See Viśuddha Cakra]

Tikkun
Hebrew: The giving of one's life for one's fellow human beings. Service to everybody and everything, sharing with people, caring for all of Creation because it is a Veil for Shekinah, the Glory of God. This was a central practice for the Jewish Mystics of old.

Tiphareth
Hebrew: "Beauty". On the Kabbalistic Tree of Life, Tiphareth is the Egoic Plane, at the junction of the lower and higher parts of the Mental Plane.

Tirisis Kardias
Greek: Vigilance in the Heart. [See Phylaki Kardias]

Titan
Greek: A Great One. A god who is very strong and powerful.

Titikṣa
Sanskrit: Endurance, perseverance. One of the Six Mental Qualifications for Discipleship (Śat-Sampatti).

Torah
Hebrew: "The Law". Religion, instruction. Torah is popularly understood as the five Moses books of the Old Testament. (In the Jewish religion, the Torah is a parchment scroll used in the synagogue, upon which is written the Law of Moses.) But in fact, Torah is the Law of the Universal Mind, the Cosmic Mind, the Mind of God, the Mind of Light, which imposes its own Laws on every aspect, layer, condition or state of Creation. It is the Divine Order as it manifests throughout all Creation. There is also the Law (Torah) as it applies to the species of Man. This has been the subject of the Teachings of all the great Teachers of Humanity. The Jewish idea of the Torah teaches that Man is responsible for his Destiny or Fate. The *active* agent of the Law (Karma) the Jews also know well as "the vengeance of the Lord", the retribution aspect of the Law, or Cause and Effect. The Hebrew word Torah has the same significance as the Sanskrit word Dharma. [See Dharma and Karma]

Traditionis
Latin: Tradition. The original Latin word meant "surrender" and "delivery of a teaching". Delivery on the part of the Teacher and surrender (receptivity) on the part of the pupil. When a tradition becomes crystallized and frozen, however, and when the Teacher no longer knows the real Truth behind the tradition, it becomes an enormous handicap for Mankind. There are "traditions" in all present day religions which are not in contact with the Truth, or which no longer serve any useful function for this generation. Yet people cling to these outdated traditions and are ready to defend them with their lives.

Trailokya
Sanskrit: Of the Three (Trai) Worlds (Lokya).

Transfiguration
Latin: In the symbolism of the New Testament, *Transfiguration* is the Illumination of the Head by the Light. In the story of the Transfiguration of Jesus, His Third-Eye and Crown Cakras were bathed with the Nirvāṇic Light.

Transpersonalis
Latin: "Through or across the mask" (Trans-Persona). Beyond the unreal. Knowing the true Self, as opposed to the apparent little self, the personal "I". *Transpersonal Psychology* looks beyond the "personality stuff" which is dealt with in the behavioural, humanistic and psychoanalytic schools of psychology. [See *Personality*]

Transverberation
Latin: The piercing of the Heart by God's Love, called by several Mystics "the Seraph's assault". A fiery Seraph attacks the Heart and pierces it through with a fiery dart, a lance, a sword or a sharp-pointed blade. The Mystic is mortally wounded and is transfixed, transformed by the Love of God into a *new creation.* Even the physical heart can react to this and may bleed. If these "Wounds of Love" appear on the hands and feet they are called the Stigmata.

Tratakam
Sanskrit: "Fixing the gaze inwardly". A technique of meditation in the Third-Eye (Ājñā) Cakra whereby you shut out the world and focus your attention in the middle of the forehead.

Tree of Life
A glyph or symbol of Reality (cosmic and human) known and taught by the Jewish Kabbalists of ancient Israel.

Tretā Yuga
Sanskrit: "The Threefold (three parts of Truth and Spirituality) Age". The Silver Age. An evolutionary period, calculated by the Ṛṣis of ancient India to be equivalent to 1,296,000 earth-years.

Tri, Trai
Sanskrit: Three.

Triad ◬
Greek: The Trinity, the Triangle, Father-Mother-Child. Generation. The Original Perfection of the Universe. The Spirit. The Archetypal World. In Man, the Triad is the Spirit (Ātma), the Spiritual Soul (Buddhi) and the Higher Mind (Kāraṇa-Manas). [See Ātma-Buddhi-Manas]

Triguṇā (Tri-Guṇā)
Sanskrit: She who embodies the three primary qualities of Matter. A Name of Lalitā, the Goddess. From Tri (three) and Guṇa (attributes). The Guṇas are Tamas (inertia), Rajas (activity) and Sattva (rhythm, purity, light). All things in Nature, and all beings and entities, are made out of these three modes of manifestation in different proportions.

Trimūrti
Sanskrit: "The Three-Faced God". The Holy Trinity. A Hindu term for Parabrahman, the Transcendental Godhead, illustrating the aspects of Creation, Evolution and Dissolution (Brahmā-Viṣṇu-Śiva). There is only One God, Parabrahman, the Transcendental Absolute, who always manifests as a threefold Being or Trinity (Trimūrti) in any part of Space or Creation. The One God appears as three "Persons" (Selves, Beings), without a break in Unity. This is a profound Mystery, beyond the comprehension of the human mind. [See Brahmā-Viṣṇu-Śiva]

Trinity
[See *Holy Trinity*]

Tripurā
Sanskrit: The Physical, Astral and Mental Planes, the Three Worlds of human evolution, which include the three bodies in which the Human Soul dwells (the physical, astral and mental bodies). From Tri (three) and Purā (city, realm, plane).

Tripurāsundarī
Sanskrit: The Beautiful Goddess of the Three Worlds. Divine Beauty. From Tri (three), Purā (city, realm, plane) and Sundarī (beautiful). She pervades the three lower worlds and the human personality-self with Divine Beauty, Dazzling Brightness, and She helps you to transcend the Three Worlds and the three bodies.

Triśnā
Sanskrit: The thirst or desire for sentient existence. The desire for embodied existence in the Three Worlds. [See Tanhā]

Turīya, Turyā, Turīya-Avasthā
Sanskrit: "The Fourth State". The Transcendental State, also called Pure Consciousness or Superconsciousness. Transcendental Consciousness (Turīya) is larger than your ordinary consciousness, yet it is Yourself. It is the Mystical Consciousness of Buddhi, the Spiritual Soul above body, mind, emotions and Ego, which leads to Nirvāṇa, or Beatitude. The Fourth State (Turīya) is the first of the trance-states (Samādhi). In itself it is Infinite Consciousness; you begin to sense Infinitude, beyond your personality level. You know that your Conscious-Self is not your brain, not your ordinary "mind", but is the Witness (Sākṣī) which is aware, by Itself, of what is going on. Your sense of personality (your personal "I") is dissolved and you are aware of Boundless Being, Boundless Life, Immortality and Bliss. [See *Pure Consciousness*]

Turīya-Cetanā
Sanskrit: "The Fourth Consciousness". Pure Consciousness. Consciousness without thought, feeling or physical sensory impression. The Transcendental State of Being. Turīya-Avasthā.

Turīyātīta-Avasthā
Sanskrit: "Beyond the Fourth State". The Fifth State of Consciousness. The integration and fusing of the Four States: Jāgrata, Svapnā, Suṣūpti and Turīya. Cosmic Consciousness. In the state of Awareness of Turīyātīta you experience the Transcendent Condition (the Fourth State) during waking, sleeping and dreaming, at all times and in all conditions. You are aware of the Eternal Silence and Tranquillity and Peace behind all phenomena and manifestation, the Great-Unmanifest, while at the same time you are willing, feeling, thinking and acting as "normal" people do. You are living life in *this* world fully, while at the same time—concurrently, simultaneously—you live in the Eternal.

Turyātman
Sanskrit: "The Self that is seen by Buddhic or Mystical Consciousness". From Turīya (the Spiritual Consciousness, the Fourth State, the Buddhi) and Ātman (the Self). This Buddhic Consciousness is the Mystical Consciousness which comes before Nirvāṇa.

Twofold Lives
The Second Manifest Creative Hierarchy, a Creative Order dwelling in the formless realms of our Solar System.

Tyāga
Sanskrit: Renunciation of manifest forms by abiding in the Ātman alone.

Tzadik
Hebrew: One who *lives* his faith. A human being further advanced upon the Path. The Guru or spiritual model, sometimes called the *Elect* or a *Perfected One*.

Tzaddikīm
Hebrew: The Righteous Ones (the plural of Tzadik). The Tzaddikīm and the Hasidīm (the Fervent or Holy Ones) are the Jewish Saints of all times, going back to Old Testament days. They have become Righteous through Union with the Eternal, Yahveh.

Tzaphkiel
Hebrew: "The Understanding Power of God". One of the Hebrew Angelic Names.

U

'Ubūdiyat
Arabic: The Reality. The seventh stage of the Radiant Way, the Shining Path of the Sūfī, corresponding to the Realization of Mahāparanirvāṇa.

Udāna Vāyu
Sanskrit: That aspect of the Life-force (Prāṇa, Vāyu) that moves in the Throat, Third-Eye and Crown Cakra regions of the embodied human being. Also called the "upward-moving Life-force".

Udgitha
Sanskrit: The Primordial Song, the Sound-Current, the Nāda, the Word, the First Hymn of the Universe.

Umā
Sanskrit: The Mother. The Divine Mother. The Universal Mother. Also, Ammā, Ambā.

Unconscious Mind
The "dreamless-sleep" state, the experience of the Causal Mind *before* it has been awakened. Sometimes refers to the abyss, the black hole of consciousness, the Outer Darkness, the nether pole of mind. In reality, there no "unconscious" mind.

Universe
From the Latin: "That which is turning into Oneness". The billions of stars and galaxies around you are *turning into Oneness*.

Unmana, Unmani
Sanskrit: The no-mind state. The thought-less state, beyond the mind, when the mind has been neutralized, dissolved (Manolaya) and made inactive (Manonāśa). [See *No-Mind*]

Upaniṣad
Sanskrit: "Sitting at the feet of the Master, listening". Scriptures. In old India, the Upaniṣads were a type of mystical writings or shorthand notes written by the Sages for students of the Spiritual Life. Basically, they are attempts to describe the Soul and the Spirit, and their relationship to the ego or lower personality and the physically embodied human being.

Uparāga
Sanskrit: Colouring, conditioning, influencing.

Uparati
Sanskrit: Tolerance, patience, abstinence. One of the Six Mental Qualifications for Discipleship (Śat-Sampatti).

Upāsanā-Mūrti
Sanskrit: "Worshipful Image". The form of the Deity you are most drawn to, such as the form of the Christ, Buddha, Śrī Kṛṣṇa or Rāma. Also called Īṣta-Devatā (Chosen Divinity). Meditation on your *Chosen Deity* helps you to focus on the Divine Reality. [See Īṣta-Devatā]

Ūriel
Hebrew: "The Fire of God". One of the Hebrew Angelic Names.

Utkrāntiḥ Siddhi
Sanskrit: "The power of levitation". This means several things. Utkrāntiḥ does mean physical levitation, but it also means going beyond boundaries. To go beyond the boundaries of your body, for instance, would mean out-of-body experience or astral projection. But it also means Ascension out of all bodily limitations (physical, astral and mental) and raising your Awareness up to the Buddhic or Nirvāṇic levels of Consciousness—that is, ascending or levitating beyond the boundaries of the Three Worlds.

V

Vāk (Vāg, Vāch)
Sanskrit: "Speech, voice, utterance". Divine Speech. The Sacred Word, the Logos, the Primordial Vibration. The Creative-Speech of Parabrahman, the Transcendental Reality. God "uttered" the Universe into being. Similar to Nāda (the Sound of the Universe). Vāk is a Force, a Power, a dynamic Energy, the Kāraṇa (Cause) of the Universe. In ancient Vedic days, Vāk was personified as "the Goddess of the Creative Tone", in agreement with the Greek idea of the Logos (although, to the Greeks, the Logos was masculine). The ancient Vedic Hindus also understood Vāk as "thought, reason". The Greek concept of the Logos was simply the ancient Vedic concept of Vāk. Many of the great and true Mystics and philosophers of Greece received their teachings from India. [See Logos]

Vāk-Śakti-Mantra
Sanskrit: The Mantra to awaken the Power of the Creative Word in the Form of the Goddess as Sound and Speech. The Śrī-Vidyā-Mantra.

Vacana
Sanskrit: Speech, language, order, command, instruction, declaration of the Deity. Sacred Language. The Vedas. From Vacā, the feminine form of Vāk (Vāch).

Vadhū
Sanskrit: Wife, or female partner.

Vāg-Bhāva-Kūṭa
Sanskrit: "The Peak of Creative Speech". From Vāg (Vāch, Vāk, the Logos, the Creative Speech), Bhāva (Being, Existence, feeling, sensing) and Kūṭa (the highest peak, most excellent).

Vāgīśvarī (Vāg-Adhīśvarī)
Sanskrit: The Goddess of the Creative-Speech (Vāk, the Divine Word, the Logos). She bestows Wisdom, eloquence, creative abilities, artistic talents. A Name of Lalitā, the Goddess.

Vāhan
Sanskrit: A vehicle, a carriage, a means of transportation in the lower worlds, an instrument for the transmission of one's Soul-Energy and Soul-Life. A body (Rūpa), gross or subtle.

Vāhi, Vāhin
Sanskrit: Carrying, bearing, upholding, driving, bringing to, causing, liberating. Being dissolved in Bliss.

Vaidika-Gāyatrī
Sanskrit: The Vedic Hymn. The Gāyatrī-Mantra.

Vaikharī, Vaikharīvāk, Vaikharīvāch
Sanskrit: Physical sound-vibrations of the physical universe. The gross sounds we can hear with our physical ears and the sounds we produce when we speak. [See Madhyamā and Paśyantī]

Vaikharī-Mantra
Sanskrit: The Spoken-Word Power. The Dynamic-Creative-Energy (Śakti) of the Goddess. The Mātangī-Mantra.

Vairāgya
Sanskrit: Divine Indifference or Dispassion. Indifference to things that are of no real value or concern. Indifference to name and fame, to wealth and poverty, to success and failure, to the fleeting and temporary values of life. Non-attachment to one's possessions. This manifests in day-to-day life as Inner Calmness (Śama) under all circumstances: in sickness or in health; in fortune or misfortune; when people praise you or when they blame you; when things are given to you or taken away; in enjoyment or suffering; in gain and in loss; in life and in death. Vairāgya is the Second Qualification for Discipleship.

Vaiśvānara
Sanskrit: The Fire-God. God as the Divine Fire aspect.

Vaiśya
Sanskrit: The Trading Class (caste, Varṇa). The merchants, business people and financiers.

Vajra
Sanskrit: Lightning. Thunderbolt.

Vajra-Guru
Sanskrit: Indestructible Teacher.

Vallabha
Sanskrit: Beloved, favourite, desired, loved.

Vāṁ
Sanskrit: The Bīja-Mantra for the Cosmic Element *Water* (the Astral Universe).

Vaṁśa
Sanskrit: A race of people.

Vānaprastha
Sanskrit: Being in the world but becoming non-attached. The third period of life (Āśrama) in the ancient Vedic days of India.

Vande
Sanskrit: Worship, adoration.

Vāṇī
Sanskrit: Speech, singing, sound, voice, music, praise, chanting, litany. Also, the Creative Word. Sarasvatī. (Note that, in some parts of India, the svāmīs mispronounce this word as Bāṇi.)

Varadāya
Sanskrit: All-benefits-giver (Vara-Da).

Vareṇyaṁ
Sanskrit: "We bless, we implore, we venerate, we honour, we revere, we glorify, we praise, we exalt, we worship or adore, we aspire to." Adoration to, devotion to. Desirable, adorable, worthy of worship, worthy to strive after. The Supreme God, the Transcendent, the Most Excellent.

VARṆA
Sanskrit: Colour, species, type. A covering or external appearance. A sound, a syllable, a letter of the Sanskrit alphabet. Also, classes or castes, according to which human beings were described during Vedic times, and which exist in India today as the caste system:

- BRĀHMANA: the Brahmins. The priestly and religious class. The priests, the pundits, the scholars, the religious leaders.
- KṢATRIYA: the Warrior Class. The military, police and government officials. The kings, rulers and politicians.
- VAIŚYA: the Trading Class. The merchants, farmers and business people. The industrialists and financiers.
- ŚŪDRA: the Servant Class. The labourers, the slaves, the servants, the unskilled, the uneducated.

This was a basic recognition of certain human *types*. Over the thousands of years since the Vedic civilization, however, this idea of caste became crystallized, rigid, traditional.

VARUṆA
Sanskrit: The Angelic Ruler of the Astral Plane.

VAS
Latin: The Grail or Holy Cup, which is the symbol for Spiritual Regeneration.

VĀSANĀ
Sanskrit: Desires for the future. Longings, unfulfilled hopes, desires, drives, urges and psychic impulses left over from previous lives. Subliminal imprints left over from the scars, seeds, pains, traumas, stresses or desires of previous lives, to be re-enacted in this life or future lives as subconscious drives. Habit-patterns acquired in previous existences which form the character of a child at birth, and which include all the subconscious cravings to which a man or woman is predisposed. [See SAṀSKĀRA]

VĀSANĀ-KṢAYA (SAṀSKĀRA-KṢAYA)
Sanskrit: The dissolution or obliteration (KṢAYA) of old habit-patterns, subconscious memories, past tendencies of behaviour inherited from your previous lives or created during this life, psychological tendencies which *prevent you now*, in this lifetime, from attaining your Goal of Liberation. This includes all your past "traumas" and unhappy experiences (which ignorant people believe they are "victimized" by for the rest of their lives, but it is not so!). These past impressions, habit-patterns, desires, mental tendencies, compulsive drives in the subconscious part of the mind, are called VĀSANĀ or SAṀSKĀRA. Without dissolving them, you cannot succeed in your Work.

VAŚINĪ
Sanskrit: The Mistress, the Controller or Goddess of the Universe, the Ruler of all things.

VASIṢṬHA
Sanskrit: Most excellent. [See YOGA VASIṢṬHA]

VAŚITVA
Sanskrit: Control over the Elements, dominion over all Creation, control of all beings in the Three Worlds. One of the nine "general" powers (SIDDHIS) which can manifest in advanced Humanity.

VASTU
Sanskrit: An object, a thing, anything.

VASU
Sanskrit: Indwelling.

VASUDEVA
Sanskrit: The Indwelling God (VASU-DEVA). The Immanent God, the Omnipresent God, the Indwelling Universal-Energy. God the Liberator.

VĀYU
Sanskrit: The Cosmic Element *Air*, which represents degrees of Light. The Cosmic Element corresponding to the substance of the Buddhic Plane.

VĀYU-BHŪTA
Sanskrit: The substance or matter aspect of the Air Element, VĀYU.

VĀYU-TANMĀTRA
Sanskrit: The vibration or force aspect of the Air Element, VĀYU.

Vāyutattva
Sanskrit: The essential or subtle aspect of the Air Element, Vāyu.

Veda
Sanskrit: "The sounds by which you realize the Self". Knowledge, Gnosis, Illumination, sacred Scripture. The secret books of Ancient India.

Vedānta
Sanskrit: The end of Knowledge. The Final Knowledge. The Final or Great Illumination. From Veda (Gnosis, Illumination) and Anta (final, the end).

Verbum
Latin: "The Word". The Logos. God's Creative Speech or Power, the Divine Mantram. Also called Fiat, "the Mighty Power of Creation".

Via Negativa
Latin: "Way-Passive". The Passive Path, which consists of Silence, Stillness, training yourself to receive Grace and to surrender to the Divine Presence. Being alone, in Solitude. Being Still. This is the *Receptive* Path.

Via Positiva
Latin: "Way-Dynamic". The Active Path, which consists of singing, chanting, movement, structured and formal meditations, meditations with Mantra, Yantra, and so forth. Being with others, and being dynamically active for the *good* of others. This is the *Transformative* Path.

Vibhūti
Sanskrit: Divine Graces and Gifts. Extraordinary powers. The "miraculous" powers attained through focused meditational and spiritual disciplines by the Siddha-Yogī (power-seeking Yogī) when his trained consciousness (Citta) learns to master the Laws of the Invisible Universe. Similar to the Sanskrit Siddhi. Vibhūti Pāda, "Chapter on Miraculous Powers", is the third chapter of Patañjali's Yoga Sūtras in which he lists many powers that can be developed by a process called Saṁyama, which involves concentration (Dhāraṇā), meditation (Dhyāna) and Transcendental Consciousness (Samādhi), all together. [See Saṁyama]

Vicche
Sanskrit: The Slayer, or the slaying of.

Videhā-Mukti
Sanskrit: "Without-the-body-Liberation". From Vi-Deha (without the body) and Mukti (Liberation, Freedom). Liberation after the death of your physical body, in the after-death condition. This is not possible if you have not commenced the process while still alive in your body. [See Jīvan-Mukti]

Vidmahe
Sanskrit: May we Realize; may we Know.

Vidyā
Sanskrit: True Knowledge. Gnosis. Realization. Wisdom.

Vidyā-Śakti
Sanskrit: The Power that comes to you through Knowledge and Insight.

Vihāyasa Siddhi
Sanskrit: The power to move bodies or objects through space.

Vijñāna, Vijñānam, Vigñāna
Sanskrit: True Knowledge, Discrimination, Understanding. Also, the Mental Plane, ordinary mind, intellectual knowledge, ordinary learning.

Vijñānamāyākośa
Sanskrit: "The illusionary Wisdom vehicle". Buddhi mixed with mind. The Wisdom-Mind (Buddhi-Manas). The causal body infused with the Buddhic Consciousness. Also called Vijñānamayakośa (the full-of-Wisdom body).

Vikalpa
Sanskrit: Fancy, imagination, thoughts (when used to describe the activities of the mind). [See Saṁkalpa and Sankalpa]

Vikāra
Sanskrit: Change.

Vikaraṇā Bhāva Siddhi
Sanskrit: The power of bodiless perception, or the power to have knowledge or perception without the physical body at all. It is as if you never had a physical body or personality complex at all, and you are just a Pure Spirit, trans-dimensional, all-knowing, all-wise.

Vimāna
Sanskrit: "A vehicle controlled by the mind". A flying chariot, an airship, a flying machine. From the Atlantean Wiwāna. The power of the Vimānas lies in the etheric and astral dimensions. UFOs are not necessarily dense physical objects, as materialists insist.

Vimāna-Vidyā
Sanskrit: "Flying-ship-knowledge". The science of flying in air-vehicles.

Vimānika
Sanskrit: The science of building airships. In ancient India, six to eight thousand years ago, there were many textbooks on building flying chariots, utilizing magical knowledge, will-power and the secrets of Space (Ākāśa).

Vimarśa
Sanskrit: Self-Knowing, Self-Awareness, Universal Self-Consciousness, the Cosmic "I-AM-ness". One of the qualities of the Ultimate Reality (Parabrahman).

Vimukta
Sanskrit: Ever-liberated.

Vipaśyanā
Sanskrit: Internal Observation. Insight into Reality. Knowing things as they really are. Insight-breathing. Your mind is normally occupied with what is happening outside you, in the world around you. Internal Observation means that you are observing your own consciousness, mind and thought-processes. You are observing yourself, the Experiencer of those experiences, rather than the events outside. Observing from a Quiet Mind is Vipaśyanā (Vipassana in Pali). This is similar to the Christian *Prayer in the Heart.* In the Buddhist Vipaśyanā meditation, however, this *alertness* or *watchfulness* or *mindfulness* is in the Head rather than in the Heart.

Vipaśyinbuddha
Sanskrit: The 998th Buddha of the Glorious (Golden) Age.

Vira-Jyotiṣa
Sanskrit: A Warrior of Light.

Virgin Goddess
According to the pre-Christian Hebrew Tradition, the Mother of the Messiah (Saviour) is the Shekinah (the Light of Glory, the Divine Light, the Radiation from the Infinite Light, Ain Soph Aur). To the Initiated Jews of old, Shekinah was the *Goddess*, the Feminine Divinity, the Feminine or Mother aspect of God, the Eternal Feminine Power. It is what the Greek Sages called the *Virgin Light* or *Virgin Mother.* The ancient Egyptians knew this Reality as the Goddess Isis.
She is that part of the Eternal Feminine which we call the *Soul of Nature*, the *Soul within the World* or the *World Soul* (in Latin, Anima Mundi). In ancient Sanskrit She was called Alaya-Vijñāna, "Universal Soul-Consciousness", or the Soul within all visible Nature, the Feminine Divine Essence, Substance or Matter which pervades and animates all things, and out of which all things manifest by condensation or precipitation as the vibrations are lowered into visible physical shapes and forms. Thus, in fact, all things are composed of the Virgin who becomes the All-Mother.
On the Cosmic Level, the Great Feminine Intelligence manifests as the Eternal Beauty. The Mystic, having reached the highest Purified Vision, sees Her shining through Matter as a Holy Light, a Supernatural Beauty within and beyond the Universe. This is the *Virgin Mary*, the Original, Primordial Mother Sea.
The Christian church confused this Reality with that great Being who, two thousand years ago, voluntarily became the Mother of Jesus. [See *Our Lady*]

Virgin Spirits
The Human Monads on their own plane, the Paranirvāṇic Plane.

Virgo Marīa
Latin: "Virgin Mary". The Transcendental Nature of the Eternal Feminine, beyond and above the created Universe, spotless, pure, incorruptible, forever shining Bright. [See Marīa]

Virgo Potens
Latin: "Virgin All-Powerful". This means that She is the Power or Energy of Divinity.

Virtus
Latin: Virtue, courage, energy, excellence, righteousness. At the time of Jesus, two thousand years ago, *Virtue* meant not only moral goodness, uprightness, morality, bravery and valour, but Spiritual Power emanating from the Soul, or God-Consciousness. It is in this sense that Jesus was *Virtuous*.

Vīrya
Sanskrit: Vigour, energy, strength, virtue, righteousness.

Viṣṇu
Sanskrit: "He who pervades all Space with His Being". To enter into all things, to pervade all things. From the root Viṣ, "to pervade, to uphold, to sustain". The All-Pervading, All-Penetrating God. The *Preserver*. The *Evolver*. Viṣṇu is the Second Aspect of the Trimūrti or Holy Trinity (Brahmā-Viṣṇu-Śiva), the "Son" in Christianity.

Viṣṇugranthi (Viṣṇu-Granthi)
Sanskrit: The knot (Granthi) in the Heart Cakra. Before the God-in-the-Heart can be discovered, the knot in the Heart has to be dissolved. Also called Hṛdayagranthi.

Viṣṇu-Mūrti
Sanskrit: "God-form". An image or representation of God, existing in your Heart Centre. This is truly the Personal God present in your Heart. This is *not* a human invention, not a theory or philosophy, but truly a Seal of God and a proof of your final Redemption. The Yogī, Mystic or Devotee (Bhakta) will discover this God-Presence in his or her Heart through intense prayer, devotion, chanting or meditation in the Heart.

Viśuddha
Sanskrit: "Purity-force" or "high-frequency-whirling-energy".

Viśuddha Cakra
Sanskrit: The Throat Centre. The Viśuddha Cakra is the seat of higher creativity in the human being. In the healthy Throat Cakra resides the Creative Force or Cosmic Creative Intelligence. This Creative Force is sometimes called the Holy Spirit, or Brahmā (the Creator-God), or the Force of Active Intelligence, or the Intelligence of Activity. When the Viśuddha Cakra is functioning correctly it is the expression of the Logos as the Creative Word, or Mantra, or Divine Speech, Vāk. This is its glory or higher Creative Power. From this comes poetry, the art of speaking powerfully, Inspiration, the Words of Power and the Scriptures. Sometimes called Viṣuddhi Cakra or Kantha.

Visualization
From the Latin: The power to see with the "eye of the mind". Visualization is related to the faculty of imagination.

Viśva
Sanskrit: The Universe, the All, the whole of Creation, the World.

Viśvakarman
Sanskrit: The Creator of the Universe, who dwells within our Solar Logos, the Sun. From Viśva (the Universe, the All, the whole of Creation) and Karman (the Creator, the Architect, the Maker, the Doer). Also called Viśvakārya, "the Maker of the Universe"; Viśvakāraka, "the Lord-Who-Made-Everything"; Viśvākaru, "the Creator of All"; and Viśvaka, "the All-Pervading, the All-Containing". He performs all actions through our Sun, as He does through all the countless Suns in the Infinity of Space. Everything upon our planet, within our Solar System, and outside the influence of our Sun, is done by Viśvakarmā. Ultimately, all actions are done (indirectly, through agencies) by the Universal Creator-God.

Viśva-Rūpa
Sanskrit: The Form of God. The Universal Body. The Cosmic Form, beyond the angelic or human forms. The whole Cosmos is the Body of God, within which God resides fully and completely.

Viśva Yoga
Sanskrit: "Cosmic Union". Uniting with the Solar Logos. Cosmic Yoga is Union of the individual Soul (that is, You) with the Cosmos (on all seven Planes of Being) and with the Godhead, the Primordial Reality whose Body is the vast Cosmic Manifestation. It is the perfect balancing-out of the personal and transpersonal aspects of yourself: the body, mind, Soul and Spirit; the material aspects of life with the Transcendental Aspects; Matter and Spirit; energy and force. This is a divinely appointed form of Yoga for the coming generations. It leads to Wisdom, Bliss, Joy and Action. [See Sūrya-Sādhanā]

Vitae Patrum
Latin: "The Lives of the Fathers". A written work describing the Western Christian tradition. (The Philokalia describes the Eastern Christian tradition.)

Vivasvata (Vivasvān)
Sanskrit: Shining forth, giving out Light. The Brilliant Light, the Shining Splendour, the Diffuser-of-Light. The Sun-God, the Solar Logos. The Spiritual Sun shining brilliantly in the Nirvāṇic and other higher Spheres.

Viveka
Sanskrit: Discrimination between the Real and the unreal, between the Self and the non-Self, between the Eternal and the transitory, between that of value and that which is only glamour, between Spirit and matter, between the Soul and the personality. The First Qualification for Discipleship.

Vivekaja Jñāna (Vivekajaṁ Jñānam)
Sanskrit. Exalted Perception, Exalted Consciousness, Pure Discriminative Awareness, Spiritual Consciousness, Total Awareness, Buddhic Consciousness, Pure and True Intuitive Knowledge. The Higher Consciousness which comes when you can *consciously* function in Samādhi, and from that state you *consciously explore* the nature of Man, God and the Universe.

Vratam
Sanskrit: Vow, promise, obligation.

Vṛndāvana
Sanskrit: Paradise. The forest or garden where Śrī Kṛṣṇa and Rādhā spent their time. A Hindu term for the Heart, where Śrī Kṛṣṇa eternally plays His flute. According to this tradition the Kingdom of Heaven is to be found in the Heart. Vṛndāvana is the Paradise Condition of the Heart. (Commonly written as Vrindaban.)

Vṛtti
Sanskrit: Mental waves, movements of the mind, mind-currents, mental activities, thoughts, transformations within the mind-stuff, modifications of the mind, behaviour patterns of the mind, fluctuations of thoughts, thoughtforms.

Vyādhi
Sanskrit: Diseases. One of the Antarāyāḥ (obstacles, impediments, problems on the Path to Higher Consciousness).

Vyakta
Sanskrit: All that is Manifest. The Unmanifest is called Avyakta.

Vyāna Vāyu
Sanskrit: That aspect of the Life-force (Prāṇa, Vāyu) which manifests as interior energies generally permeating the body or form of the embodied human being.

W

Wāqif
Arabic: The charitable workers. Those serving others on the Physical Plane, those skilful in *action* towards others.

Wāṣif
Arabic: Those who praise God continually. The devotees of the active type (singing, dancing, chanting).

Wijd, Wijdān
Arabic: Ecstasy, direct Knowledge, direct Realization of the Truth. Illumination of the Heart by the Light of God, the Light of Gnosis (Nūrul-'Irfān). This is the eighth stage of the Journey of the Heart, also called Hāl (Persian: spiritual ecstasy, spiritual trance, spiritual tranquillity of the mind). Equivalent to the Sanskrit Samādhi of the Yogīs, the Superconscious State.

Will, Will-Power
The determinative energy, the directing force. The force of self-determination, self-direction. In modern psychology, will-power is the "psycho-spiritual energy of self-actualization". The will is not an emotional energy (Kāma); rather, it is a mental energy (Manas). A person possessing a strong will can obtain any goal or objective. There is also the Will-Power of the Soul.

Wisdom
Wisdom is called Prajñā or Bodhi in Sanskrit, Chockmah in Hebrew, Sophia in Greek, Sapientia in Latin. In ancient times, these words did not mean being "worldly-wise", intellectual, or learned in our present sense, but the Knowledge that revealed the Path of Light. This is the mind-transcending, Truth-discerning Awareness of Pure Consciousness. It is pure Knowing, without words, without thoughts, without the mind.

Wisdom-Mind
The mind (higher and lower) infused with the Light of Buddhi. In Sanskrit, Buddhi-Manas. Sometimes called the *Mind of Light*.

Wiwāna
Atlantean: Flying ship. The Atlantean word Wiwāna became, in the later Sanskrit of India, Vimāna.

Word
The Logos (Greek), the Verbum (Latin). The Primordial Creative Vibration, the Sounding-Light. Referred to in the Vedas, Upaniṣads and other sacred books of ancient India as Vāk. The Christian fathers translated the word Logos as "the Word", and later as "the Christ", and still later as the historical *personality* of Jesus, and finally as the *book* called the Bible. [See Logos]

Wu
Chinese: "Not-doing". Wu (Chinese) is Mu in Japanese. That is why, in some old Japanese monasteries, you hear the monks bellowing "Mu!" (Not this, not this!).

Wu-Hsin
Chinese: No-mind, no-thinking, no-thought-in-the-mind. The emptiness of the mind in which the One Mind can reveal Itself. It is a mind *not attached* to any forms or objects. Mu-Shin in Japanese Zen. [See *No-Mind*]

Wuqūf-Qalbī
Arabic: The Awareness of the Heart. Direct knowledge or experience of God in the Heart. When the Heart becomes aware of God, infinite Mysteries are revealed to you.

Wu-Wei
Chinese: "The Not-Doing of the Eternal", or Transcendental Inactivity. The "Undisturbable Throne of Reality" of the Chinese Mystic Masters. The Transcendental Reality. In Sanskrit, Nirvāṇa. "Action in Stillness" or "not-doing" is the condition of true Zen, the state of the Perfectly Enlightened One, where You are doing, yet it is not *you,* the ego, who is doing it. This is the same as the true Karma Yoga of the Indian Sages.

Y

Yah (Jah)
Hebrew: "God the Living". The Self-Existent or Eternal One. The Creator-God.

Yahweh (Yahveh)
Hebrew: The Name of God, the Sound of the Universe. Universal Motion or Sound-Vibration—gross, subtle and subtlest. This is the Spirit of God, the Breath of God. It is the Sound of God's Breath or Spirit. God is the State of Unity, the Eternal Oneness. [See Yehovah and IHVH]

Yajña
Sanskrit: "Sacrifice". A sacrificial activity or offering. A religious rite, ritual or performance. A holy ritual or sacrificial ceremony in which gifts are offered to a presiding Deity. Vedic rites, performed to please the "gods" (angels). The purpose of these rites is to connect Man to the Invisible so that he or she may receive the goodwill, blessings and knowledge of the "gods" and their guidance through the right Path of Life. It should be remembered, however, that Ritual Magic is *not* the same as the Path of Self-Realization, Yoga, Mysticism, Soul-Consciousness or Inward Contemplation. The higher meaning is that when you can perform all actions as spiritual sacrifices (Yajña), those actions will not bind you to this world. Yajña is the act of Service or Sacrifice through Dhyāna (meditation) towards God, and through Karma (action) towards Creation.

Yāṁ
Sanskrit: The Bīja-Mantra for the Cosmic Element *Air* (the Buddhic Universe).

Yama
Sanskrit: "Control" (meaning self-control). Self-restraint, self-regulation, abstention from, abstinence from, following commandments, observances you take upon yourself voluntarily. In Aṣṭāṅga Yoga, as set down by Patañjali, the Yama (Observances) are fivefold:
- Ahiṁsā (harmlessness, non-violence).
- Satya (truthfulness, sincerity, honesty).
- Asteya (not stealing from others).
- Brahmacarya (being firmly focused on God).
- Aparigrahā (not grasping, not being greedy).

Yama is also the God of Death. [See Mṛtyu]

Yāmi
Sanskrit: Ruler.

Yang
Chinese: The masculine qualities. Whether you are a male or a female, you *cannot* approach Tao with the aggressive male mind (Yang). This is the Law of Nature. So, become more Yin (female) in order to receive Tao. [See Yin and Tao]

Yantra
Sanskrit: A geometric form, symbol, image or maṇḍala. A representation or diagram of the gods and goddesses (which are but tools to remember aspects of the Absolute).

Yantra Yoga
Sanskrit: A system of spiritual development using geometric forms, symbols, maṇḍalas.

Yaqīn
Arabic: The Light of Certainty by which the Heart sees God. God is seen by His own Light, which shines in the Heart. There are five *Stages of Certainty* on the Path of the Sūfī:
- 'Ilm-ul-Yaqīn: Knowledge of Knowledge.
- Yaqīn-ul-Yaqīn: Certainty of Knowledge.
- 'Ain-ul-Yaqīn: the Eye of Knowledge.
- Ḥaqq-ul-Yaqīn: True Knowledge.
- 'Urf-ul-Yaqīn: Beatitude-Knowledge.

Yeheshua, Yehoshua, Yeheshuvah
Hebrew: "The Eternal is my Salvation, in God is Salvation, God is my helper". From Yah (the Self-Existent or Eternal One) and Hoshua (who Saves, who is the Saviour). Yeheshuvah is the Saving Grace of God, the Redeeming Power which lifts you out of your personality-consciousness into Soul-Consciousness, into the Awareness of the Kingdom of God. It is a Fiery Energy, burning away your materiality and liberating your Spirit.

Yehovah (Jehovah)
Hebrew: "The Eternal" or "That which was, is, and ever shall be". Yehovah (Jehovah) is an androgynous Name having the characteristics of both sexes: Yah (the male God) and Hovah (the Goddess). The correct pronunciation is Yah-Haveh. Yah (Jah) means "God the Living" and Haveh means "the Breath, the Life". Thus, Yah-Haveh is "the Breath of the Eternal". It means "the Father-Mother God, the Male-Female Potential". In the Christian Bible the word Yehovah is commonly mistranslated as "Lord". This Name refers not to a "personal" God, however, but to the Absolute Reality. [See IHVH]

Yehovah Eloah Ve Daath (Jehovah Aloah Va Daath)
Hebrew: The Eternal God of the Heart. The Everlasting Being of Wisdom (Gnosis). An expression used by the Initiated Jews of Old for the Christ in the Heart.

Yeshua, Yoshua
Hebrew: "Saviour, Deliverer, Salvation". The Power to Save or Liberate. God's downpouring Grace. God who Saves, the Saving Grace of God, the Liberator, the Fire of God. Hence the name *Jesus,* "the Saviour". Jesus was known as Yeshua Ben-Pandira (Pandira being His Jewish family name), or Yeshua Ben-Yoseph (Jesus, son of Joseph), or Yeshua Ben-Myriam (Jesus, son of Mary). He was also known as Yeshua Nazir (Jesus of Nazareth, His place of origin). This is how names were given in those days. As a child he was probably known as Yoshua (Joshua).

Yeshuā Bar Alahā
Aramaic: "Jesus, the Son of God".

Yeshuā Bar Nashā
Aramaic: "Jesus, the Son of Man".

Yeshua Ben Adam
Hebrew: "Jesus, the Son of Man". In the New Testament, Jesus is referred to as the *Son of Man,* which was a common designation used throughout the Old Testament *for* the Prophets and *by* the Prophets, the special messengers from on High. Unfortunately the early Christians considered the Son of Man to be *one person only* (Jesus), but this is not so. Each great Prophet was a Ben Adam—a Son of Man, a Child of Humanity. [See Ben Adam]

Yeshua Ben Eloah
Hebrew: "Jesus, the Son of God". Nowadays, Bibles are translated to mean that Jesus (the historical personality) is the *only* Son of God, and thus they *deny Divinity* to all God's Children. [See Ben Eloah]

Yeshua Ha-Mashiah
Hebrew: "The Saviour, the Anointed One". Jesus the Messiah. This was not His name, but a title. [See Mashiah]

Yeshuā Meshikā
Aramaic: Jesus the Messiah. (The native language spoken by Jesus was Aramaic, which is related to the ancient Hebrew, though there are differences in word endings.)

Yesod
Hebrew: "The Foundation". On the Kabbalistic Tree of Life, Yesod is the Astral Plane, which is the underlying substratum, the support, the basis, the origin of this physical universe. The real power inherent in the physical universe (the atomic, for instance) is of the Astral World. You can think of the astral matter as the foundation or basis out of which everything in this universe is built.

Yin
Chinese: The feminine qualities. To approach Tao, your consciousness must become Yin, female. [See Yang and Tao]

Yo, Yaha
Sanskrit: Which, who.

Yoga
Sanskrit: "Joining together, yoking, aligning, linking, uniting, going into Oneness or Union". From Yugh, "to unite, join, put together, integrate". The State of Union. Union with the Ātman. Union with God. Yoga also means "a method, an application of a principle, a means to an end, an arrangement, meditation, devotion". Yoga requires the control of the mind and the emotions. When the emotions and mind are tranquil, the breath (the Life-force, Prāṇa) is harmonized and the Self (Ātma) is realized. Pure Consciousness can shine only in Tranquillity.

Yoga-Agni-Mayam-Śarīram
Sanskrit: The physical body (Śarīram) transformed (Mayam) by the Fires (Agni) of Yoga (Union with the Higher Self, Union with God). This is an altered natural physical body.

Yoga Darśanam
Sanskrit: "The Teachings on Yoga".

Yoga-Mārga
Sanskrit: "The Path of Union". From Mārga (a path, road, way, track) and Yoga (integration, at-one-ness, Union, Salvation). In the early days of the Science of Yoga, there was only one Yoga. The Way to Cosmic Consciousness known as Yoga-Mārga was a totally integrated, balanced, holistic way of life. Later on, the one integrated Science of Divine Union (Yoga-Mārga) was forgotten and the different *activities* of Yoga became separated. Yoga was split into parts—Haṭha Yoga, Rāja Yoga, Bhakti Yoga, Śakti Yoga, Karma Yoga, and so on—and people began to practise them separately from one another and separately from worldly life.

Yoga-Nidrā
Sanskrit: "The Sleep of the Yogī". This occurs when the Heart is awake and the rest of the human being is asleep. True Yoga-Nidrā is not falling off to sleep during meditation. In Yoga-Nidrā one's body and senses are at rest (asleep), while one's consciousness is wide awake inside.

Yoga-Siddhi-Śakti
Sanskrit: Yogic powers (Yoga-Siddhi). The physical, psychic and spiritual powers attained by the Yogīs.

Yoga Vasiṣṭha
Sanskrit: "The Most Excellent Yoga". The Yoga Vasiṣṭha Mahā Rāmāyāna is a textbook on Yoga written in Sanskrit over two thousand years ago. Its concept of Yoga is based on the mind, not on bodily exercises.

Yoga-Vidyā
Sanskrit: The Science of Realization.

Yogeśvara
Sanskrit: "Lord of Yoga" (Yoga-Īśvara). There are Yogeśvaras who have ascended on the Wings of Devotion, from world to world, to the very Throne of God, the Divine Heart.

Yogī, Yogin, Yoginī
Sanskrit: "One who is united or integrated". A practitioner of the Science of Yoga (Yoga-Mārga). One who has attained the State of Union (Yoga), or Samādhi. Or, one who has attained the highest state of Yoga or Union (Nirvāṇic Consciousness). A Saint of the Hindu and Esoteric Buddhist religions who has attained Union with Ātman (the Universal Spirit) and Brahman (the Ultimate Reality). A true Yogī is a Jīvanmukta (one who is liberated while still in the physical body). A female Yogī or Yogin is called a Yoginī.

Yogindra
Sanskrit: The King or Chief of Yogīs. A name ascribed to the Great Sage Patañjali.

Yoshua
[See Yeshua]

Yoshua Immanuel
Hebrew: "The Saviour, God is with us". A name given to Jesus, who was a disciple of the Christ.

Yuga
Sanskrit: A day, an age, a cycle, a generation, a period of time, a period of evolution.

Yukta
Sanskrit: Divine Unity.

Z

Zazen
Japanese: Intensive meditation practice. Zen-sitting, or sitting down and meditating. In the earliest days of Zen, in both India and China, sitting down and meditating was not the main practice at all. You could realize Enlightenment at any time, by any means, under any circumstances! It is because the human mind became increasingly degenerated by materialism that formal sittings in Chān (Chinese: meditation) became necessary. Some Zen Masters say: "To enter fully into every action with full Consciousness is also Zazen."

Zen
Japanese: Zen originated in India as a method of Tantra, where it was called Dhyāna (or Dhyān), meaning "meditation-contemplation". The word Zen is an abbreviation of Zenna, from the Sanskrit Dhyāna and the Chinese Chānna (which was also abbreviated to Chān).

Zendō
Japanese: The room where Zazen is practised. The meditation hall. Also, Sōdō.

Zenji
Japanese: A Zen Master.

Zikr (Zikar)
Arabic: Prayer, meditation, invocation. Repetition of Divine Names or Mantras (Kalimah) in the Heart. The meaning is the same as the Sanskrit Mantra-Japa, but the Arabic word has another meaning also: *Remembrance*. The prayer helps you to remember the One whom you are calling upon (God). Thus, you pray in your Heart while completely remembering the Oneness of the Divine Nature within you and within All That Is. Also called Dhikr and Dhikar.

Zodiakos
Greek: "A circle of animals". The *Zodiac* is made up of the twelve signs, or *constellations*, known as Aries, Taurus, Gemini, Cancer, Leo, Virgo, Libra, Scorpio, Sagittarius, Capricorn, Aquarius and Pisces. Each sign of the Zodiac is a group of stars located in space in our Milky Way Galaxy.

Zoe
Greek: The Primordial Life-Force. The Prāṇa or Life-Energy in all things.

Zōhar
Hebrew: Splendour, glittering.

Zuhd
Arabic: Intense Devotion to God. Non-worldliness, the intense desire to cut yourself away from the world, to have nothing to do with the world. This is the sixth stage of the Journey of the Heart. You want to live in seclusion, possibly alone, away from everybody. You may develop fanatical ideas about diet and your physical body, and you are sharply aware of the imperfections of the world and of people around you. The pull from within your Heart is tremendous, while the impressions of the world are less significant in your life. You question why you are in the world at all; material life is totally unsatisfactory and meaningless. You sense the Centre within your Heart and you know that that Centre is also your Goal and Beginning.

∞

APPENDIX C

Index

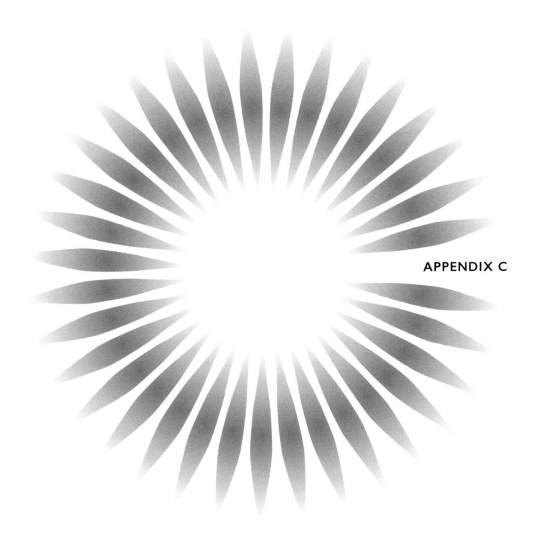

Notes

- Numbered references refer to chapters.
- Major subject headings are followed by one or more chapter references, delineating the central development of that subject or energy-line.
- References are capitalized according to their source. Hence, references to headings retain their Title Capitals, while references to specific text are generally in lower case.

A

Abba
Invoked by the early Christians 680
Meditations in the Heart Centre 1297
The Evolution of Christian Prayer 713
Used by Jesus to invoke the Divine Father 1275

Abbas
Christian Hesychast definition 739

Abhyāsa-Yoga
To Succeed in your Quest 1330

Aborigines
Have a forty-thousand-year genealogy 214
Lived in dreamtime 277

Abortion
Abortion and the Incarnation Process 413–415
An Offence against the Indwelling God 415
Latin definition 413
Reveals a deep sickness 474
The destruction of the mother instinct 479

Abstract Mind. *See also* Higher Mind, Causal Mind, Kāraṇa-Manas
Dimensions of the Mind 891
Kāraṇa-Manas 34
Meditating with the pure Intellect 1188
Realms of the One Mind (graph) 493
The source of abstract Ideas 361
Those polarized in the causal body 376
What is Intuition? 328

Abūdiyat
Service to the Teacher and Worship of God 855

Accidents
There are no "accidents" 243
What are "accidents"? 363

Action. *See also* Karma
12 Karma and Reincarnation 231–266
59 Time and Eternity: Action and Destiny 1399–1410
Action (Karma): aphorisms 1402–1406
Action and Destiny (Metanoia) 1420–1421
Action and Stillness: the Supreme Way 1083
Action and the Spiritual Warrior 994
Action in the Transcendent 1080
Action while in Samādhi 1331
Action Zen 802
Akarma: the doctrine of non-action 504
All action is born out of desire or intention 988
From Action into Stillness, from Stillness into Action 1016
Heart Action 1331
Just Doing 1018
Karma: the Law of Action or Adjustment 240–241
Karma Yoga: Divine Union by Action 1132–1133
Kriyā Yoga: the Yoga of Action 535
Meditation in Action 1019
Mental Activity 1228
Movement and the Life-force 1020
Niṣkarmayam: Non-Action Misinterpreted 1120
Saints of Action 1134
Silence and Activity 1446
Silence and Activity must alternate 1443
Skill in Action 989
Spontaneous-action-awareness 763
Success is Born of Action 256–257
The Active and Passive Way 1011
The Law of Action 992–993
The Power of Action 374–375
The purpose of physical action 1002–1003
The Threefold Way (Hṛdaya-Mārga) 1236
Via Positiva: the Active Path 1465
You Alone are Responsible 258

Adam-Kadmon
Manu: Primeval Mankind 167

Agnosia
Christian Hesychast definition 744
Divine Unknowing 705

Agnosis
Agnōstikos: the ignorant 1105
Source of the word Agnostic 663

Aḥad
The God-State 1257
The One and Only 839, 877

Ahaṁ
Activating I AM: the Secret Name of God 1419
Ahaṁ-Ātman: I am the Self 1213
Definition and description 447
Mahāvākya Practice 1472–1479
Potent Vibrations: Bīja-Mantra 1551
The One I AM 1687
The Spontaneous-Free State 257
The Watcher 1212
Your true "I AM-ness" 1317

Ahaṁkāra
Acting with a desire for results 257
Covers the Formless Divinity in the Heart 1328
Definition 35, 75
Manifested only by Fourth and Fifth Creative Hierarchies 202
The Mind is Dissolved in the Heart 1235
To Achieve Liberation 1177

Ahiṁsā
Definition 563
Harmlessness is not enough 1143
The first Observance of Aṣṭāṅga Yoga 566

Ahriman
A great Being of Light 211

Aiṁ
Potent Vibrations: Bīja-Mantra 1550
The Seed-Sound for Sarasvatī 1489

Ain, Ain Soph, Ain Soph Aur
Ain: the Transcendental Godhead 108, 112
Definitions 101
The Evolution of Christian Prayer 713
The Kabbalistic Tree of Life 358–359

Aionia Zoe
Gnostic Christian definition 737

Air. *See also* Vāyu
The Air Element 26–28
Vāyu Bīja 1546

Aisthesis
Gnostic Christian definition 738

Ajapa
Ajapa-Japa 461
The non-repetitive use of a mantra 1206

Ājñā
A Name of Lalitā, the Goddess 1558

Ājñā Cakra. *See also* Third-Eye Centre
General description 49
The Command Centre 350
The Heart and the Energy Centres 1332

Akarma
The doctrine of non-action 504

Ākāśa. *See also* Space
Ākāśa Bīja 1546
As understood by the Sages 590–591
Definition 13, 30
Eternal Space is always Here and Now 1579
The Form of God is Space 109
The seven-layered Heaven or Space 271
The Space Element 26–28

Ākāśa-Vāṇī
The Voice of Heaven 590

Akashic Records
Description 241
Knowledge of Past Lives 601
Reflection on the Astral Plane 59

Akṣara
The Nature of Parabrahman 1178

Alāhā, Allahā
The Divine Unity Mantra 1359

'Ālam
Worlds of the Sūfī 886–890

Alaya-Vijñāna
The Infinite Supply 1390
The Storehouse of Wisdom 492
Universal Soul-Consciousness 144

Alchemy
Kuṇḍalinī and Alchemy 153
Mysterious Knowledge of the Siddhas 1310–1311
To Taste the Elixir of Life 593

Alcohol
Temporary Relief 1427

Aletheia
Gnostic Christian definition 737

Alhamdulillāh
All Praise be to God 874, 1128

Al-Ḥaqq
Ahl Al-Ḥaqq: the Followers of the Real 836
Muslim term for Nirvāṇa 94, 100
The Absolute-Truth-Being 872
The Muslim Deification Process 1191
The Sūfī God 838

Allāh
Allah, Allāh 871
Conceived of as a personal God 106
Meditation on the Exalted Name of God 871, 1301
Refers to God as Light 94
The Divine Unity 852
The Divine Unity Mantra 1359
The One God of All Religions 110
The Sūfī God 838
The Truth in the Heart 851

Allāhu Akbar
The Arabic Mantram of the Omnipotence of God 851
The Greatness of God 875

Allegoria
Christian Hesychast definition 747

Alta Centre. *See also* Kāraṇa Cakra, Causal Centre
Integration of the Human Consciousness (graph) 1195
The Functioning of the Cakras 52–53

Āṁ
Potent Vibrations: Bīja-Mantra 1551

Amanaska
Formless Consciousness 1373

Ambā
Ambā, Jagadambā: definitions 1493, 1498
A Name of Lalitā, the Goddess 1575

Ambrosia
The Food of the Gods 593

Amen
God's Cosmic Symphony 1649
Hebrew Divine Words for Healing 1456
Pronunciations in ancient languages 1501

Amenti
Lowest regions of the Astral World 218
The Underworld 6

American Indians
Limitations of knowledge 276
The Changing Faces of the Spirit-Guides 332

Amida-Butsu
Meditations in the Heart Centre 1299
The Christ in the Heart 441

Amitābha
Amitābha-Buddha: the Buddha in the Heart 1299
The Christ in the Heart 441
The Limitless Ocean of Light 795

Ammā
A Name of Lalitā, the Goddess 1493, 1575

Amṛta
Definition 1615
The Nectar of Immortality 593

Amṛtā
A Name of Lalitā, the Goddess 1574
Definition 1494

Amṛteśvarī
A Name of Lalitā, the Goddess 1574
The Supreme Spirit-Mother 1494

Aṁsa-Avatāra. *See also* Avatāra
The Saints and Masters 389

Anaesthesia
Astral projection under anaesthesia 303

Anāhata Cakra. *See also* Heart
General description 47
The Heart and the Energy Centres 1332
Translation 448

Anāhata-Śabda
God's Cosmic Symphony 1649
The sounds of Nāda 1651
The Unproduced Sound 1212

Ānanda. *See also* Bliss, Sat-Cit-Ānanda
Ātmānanda: the Self is Bliss 1518
A quality of the Spiritually Awakened Heart 1329
Definition 499
Keys to the Heart 1323
Return to Primeval Happiness 1179
Steps on the Spiritual Path 561
The Experience of the Heart 1281

Ānandamāyākośa
Coverings over the Self 38
Definition 40
Development in the next epoch 177
The Resurrection Body 40
The vehicle of Soul-telepathy 346

Ānanda-Rūpiṇī-Devī
The Blissful-Form-Goddess 1498

Ānāpānasati
Mindfulness of Breathing 794

Anastasis
Gnostic Christian definition 738

Anathema
Teachings enforced by the church 32
The Ecumenical Councils 652–653

Ancient of Days
Mantram to the Lord of Light 1727
Source of the Divine Plan 980
The True Warrior serves the King 984–985, 990

Angelic Hierarchies. *See also* Hierarchies
Christian Classification of the Hierarchies 192
Intervention by 180, 282
Non-human evolutionary units 189
The Devas according to the Rays 199

Angels. *See also* Hierarchies, Devas
Angelic Rulers of the Planes (graph) 199
Angelos: definition 197, 746
Angels and Demons 193
Angels talk by telepathy 348
Denizens of the Heaven Worlds 77
Hebrew Divine Words for Healing 1456
Involutionary and Evolutionary Kingdoms 194
Lipika: the Recording Angels 241
Nephilīm: the fallen angels 211
Some Facts about the Devas 198
Sounding the Hebrew Angelic Names 1462
The Angelic Builders 198, 250, 414
The Angels 196–197
The Biblical "Angels of God" 203
The Gandharvas 200

Anger
Can God be Angry? 106
Emotional Problems 1429–1431
No Anger, No Enemies 986
Reactive-Emotional Consciousness 1426

Aṇimā
The General Powers 580

Animal Kingdom
Animals on the Astral Plane 71
Animals talk by telepathy 348
Animal Suffering 222
Animal telepathy 347
The Sevenfold Earth-Evolution 169
Uniting with animals: Saṁyama and Shamanism 584

Anima Mundi
The World Soul 144

Annamāyākośa
Coverings over the Self 38

Annamaya-Śakti
The Energy of the Goddess 1487

Annoia
Gnostic Christian definition 738

Antaḥkaraṇa
Building the Antaḥkaraṇa 1194
Building the Bridge of Light 554–555

Definition 42
The Bridge to Union 521
To build the Rainbow Bridge 1331

Antar-Ātman
The Inner Self 327
The Inner Self in the Heart 1317

Antarāyāḥ
Obstacles to Union with the Soul 556

Antardhāna Siddhi
Powers of Divine Descent 599

Antar-Jyotī
The Inner Light: a Name of Lalitā, the Goddess 1574

Anthropomorphism
Attributes human characteristics to the Absolute 677
Buddhism denies Jewish-Christian ideas of God 754–755
Can God be Angry? 106
Fear of the Lord? 234
God has no human attributes 107
God is a Sublime Mystery 127
In the Image and Likeness 104
The One Transcendental Reality 515
The Sūfī God 838
Words describing Reality have been humanized 1174

Anthropos
Gnostic Christian definition 737
Manu: Primeval Mankind 167

Anti-Christ
Brothers of the Shadow 226–227
The Great Deception 724

Aṇu
Primordial Atoms 24
The subtlest matter of each plane (graph) 15

Aṇupādaka. *See also* Paranirvāṇa
The Monadic World 17
The Second Element 28–29

Anxiety
Emotional Problems 1429–1431

Apāna
An aspect of the fivefold Life-force 589
That which flows out 1224

Aparigrahā
Definition 563
The fifth Observance of Aṣṭāṅga Yoga 567

Āpas
The Water Element 26–28

Apatheia
Christian Hesychast definition 745
Passion and Dispassion 695

Aphrodite
The Eternal Feminine 469

Aphtarsia
Gnostic Christian definition 736

Apokryphos
Christian Hesychast definition 747

Apotheosis. *See also* Theosis
Christian Hesychast definition 740
The Goal of the early Christians 644

Apuleius
The Golden Ass story and astral projection 303

Aquarian Age
13 Atlantis Revisited 269–288
49 The Aquarian Way 1117–1144
50 The Aquarian Group-Consciousness 1145–1172
Beginning of a New Age is always traumatic 725
Cosmic Intervention 282
From Darkness into Light 982–983
From Pisces to Aquarius 837
Group Work 1146
Human Response to Cosmic Intervention 286
Influenced by energies from the Cosmos 278
Influence of the Zodiac 279
Mystics of Pisces and Aquarius 836
New Age Phenomena 278–281
Penetrating into the Kingdom 1707
Piscean Spirituality and New Age Spirituality 1706
Principles of the Aquarian Age 288
Psychology and the New Age Religion 1105–1109
Religious Reactionaries 287–288
Spirituality Past and Future 1104
The Action of the Cosmic Fire 279
The Aquarian Mystic 638

The Aquarian Teachers 1147
The Influence of the Seven Rays 834–835
The New Age and You 1708
The New Age Impulse 1111
The New and Eternal Way 516
The New Aquarian Energies 426
The New Atlantis 280
The Warrior of the Light 984

Arā
Western words for "Earth" 1351

Arabic
Dimensions of the Heart (Arabic) 847
Languages of Islām 829
Pure Arabic has no E and O vowels 877, 1032
Some Arabic Prayers to the Deity 850–851
Sūfī Mantras for Meditation 874–877
The Beautiful Names 1264–1265
The Four Stages of Spiritual Life (Arabic) 1160–1161
The Human Constitution (Arabic) 892
The Ninety-Nine Arabic Divine Names 878–884

Aramaic
Spoken by Jesus 661
The Last Words of Jesus 672
The native language of Jesus 1341

Archangels
Christian Classification of the Hierarchies 192
The Angels 196

Archetypes
Archetipon: Greek Mystery School definition 735
Archetypes of the Divine Feminine 145
Ideas and Archetypes 138
The Archetypal World 360–361

Architecture
The Creative Soul 1692
The Temple Not Made By Hands 369

Archon
Gnostic Christian definition 737
Rulers in High Places 657

Arhat. *See also* Saints
Arha, Arhan, Arhat, Arhant, Arahant: definition 394
Definition 172, 1196

Aridity
The Desert Condition 1168

'Ārif
The Knowers of God 836–837

Armageddon
Scenes of Battle 1158
The field of battle 726

Art
Action is an Art 995
Art and the Follies of Man 470
Piscean and Aquarian art 835
Ray 4: Beauty, Harmony 56
The Art of Alignment 1202
The Creative Soul 1692

Arūpa. *See also* Rūpa, Formlessness
Arūpa-Deva: formless angels 77
Arūpa-Loka: formless worlds 74
Definition 30, 77
Formless meditation 1268–1269
Formless planes and subplanes 14–15
States of Energy and Consciousness 760

Arūpa-Manas. *See also* Kāraṇa-Manas
The Causal Mind 74

Ārya, Āryan
Definition 177
Mental telepathy developed during Āryan Epoch 347
The Āryan Epoch 177
Thought and speech are Āryan developments 349
Who are the Āryans? 179

Ārya-Mārga
The Noble Path 504

Asamprajñāta Samādhi
Definition 497, 574

Āsana
Applied to Haṭha Yoga and Rāja Yoga 524–525
Beyond Āsana and Prāṇāyāma 573
Definition 562
The third step of Aṣṭāṅga Yoga 572

Asat. *See also* Sat
Non-existence 112

Ascended masters
Invented by channellers 332
Ascension
The Union of body, mind and Soul with God 721
Asekha. *See also* Spiritual Masters
Definition 172, 394
'Āshiq
The Lovers of God 836
Asketikos
Christian Hesychast definition 739
Asmitā
The sense of individual existence 595
The sense of self in the physical body 543, 551
Aśokā
Qualities of the Divine Being 107
Aspiration. *See* Self-Actualization, Self-Determination
Āśrama
Definition 523
Periods of Life in Vedic India 907
The Mystery Schools and Āśramas 1148
Aṣṭāṅga Yoga
25 Aṣṭāṅga Yoga 559–576. *See* Yoga
Aśtara-Vidyā
The Science of Magic 273, 275
Asteya
Definition 563
The third Observance of Aṣṭāṅga Yoga 566
Astral body
Identification with the astral body after death 71
Negative emotions are conditions of the astral body 1432
Polarities Male and Female 920–921
Reactive-Emotional Consciousness 1426
Rearrangement of the astral body after death 69, 407, 411
The Astral Body (general description) 39
The Astral Body is the Subconscious Mind 236
The Personality Complex 36–37
Those polarized in the astral body 376
Astral Light
Aether 27
and the Akashic Records 241
Planetary Stimulation 181
Polluted by wrong thinking 218
The agency of Magic 357, 391
Astral Plane
3 Kāmaloka: The Astral Plane 57–72
Beyond Phantasia 686–687
Beyond the Astral World 59
Brief description 16
Derivation of the term Astral 65
"Eternal" Heavens and Hells? 68
Experiences on the Astral Plane 306–307
Hallucinations in the Afterlife 408–409
Increasing stimulation of the Astral World 278–279
Life in the Astral World 70–71
Mind-Created Hells 62
Planned intrusion into the Physical World 280–282
Seven Conditions in One Astral World 61
Sex on the Astral Plane 70
The Astral Subplanes (in detail) 62–67
The Earthbound 64
The Eighth Sphere 63
The Formative World 360–361
The Grand Illusion 66
The most delusive region in and around our planet 336
The Realm of Desires (general introduction) 58–59
The Seven Subplanes of the Astral Plane (graph) 67
The Sixth World (Arabic) 887
The Underworld (terminology) 60
We all already live in the astral dimension 270
Yesod: the Foundation 358–359
Your character determines your appearance on the Astral 410–411
Astral projection
Astral travel and Samādhi 302
Experiences on the Astral Plane 306–307
General description 301
The Final Astral Projection 401
Types of Astral Projection 302–304
Astral shells
A source of mediumistic communications 330
Materialization of a shade 314
The astral corpse 81

Astral travel. *See* astral projection

Astrology
Astrologos, Astrologia: definition 260
Destined by the Stars? 260–261
Disease and Karma 1169
Precessional Age and Zodiacal Age 725
Zodiacal History 833

Asura
Definition and derivation 211
The Makara and Asuras 202
Wars in Heaven 271

Athā
A Name of Lalitā, the Goddess 1579

Atlantis
13 Atlantis Revisited 269–288
Atlantis (general description) 270
Magicians of Atlantis and India 277
Psychic telepathy developed in Atlantis 347
Roots of Modern Shamanism 276
The Atlantean Evolutionary Epoch 176–177
The Great Flood 272–275
The Land of Atlantis 271
The New Atlantis 280
Vimāna People and Human Destiny 283
Wars in Heaven 271

Ātman, Ātmā. *See also* Self, I AM
and the Spirit-Spark-Atom 926
Ātmā: a Name of Lalitā, the Goddess 1579
Ātmā Bīja 1542
Ātman, Ātmā: general description 34
Incarnations of the Sun 1593
Mahāvākya Practice 1478–1479
Rūḥ (Arabic): the Spirit that you are 890, 892
Senses or the Self? 239
Tao: the Great I AM 774
The Christ in you, your hope of Glory 769
The Cosmic I AM-ness of the Godhead 1132
The Eternal 1727
The Experience of the Heart 1281
The Latin Spiritus 319
The Second Stage of Yoga 529
The Spiritual-Self within us 1632
The three degrees of Self-Realization 1448
The Universal Divine I AM 327
The Upaniṣadic Mantrams 546–547
The Way of the Spirit 381
The World exists for the sake of the Self 544
To achieve Liberation 1177
To be in the Consciousness of Ātman 1235
What is Reality? 1175
You are Ātman even now 1179

Ātma-Ānanda
Return to Primeval Happiness 1179
The Self is Bliss 1518

Ātma Bala Siddhi
The power which flows from the Ātman 598

Ātmā-Bodha
Self-Realization 1304
The purpose of meditation 1179

Ātma-Buddhi. *See also* Spiritual Soul
The second aspect of the Sūtrātma 491

Ātma-Buddhi-Manas. *See also* Triad
Finds a focal point in the Heart 1298
Reflected in the Human Soul 35
The Individuality 34
Who is "I AM"? 1418
Your Triune Self transcends Time and Space 1371

Ātmā-Cetanā
Formless Consciousness 1373

Ātma-Jyoti-Rūpa
A supernatural Light Body 1313

Ātmā-Rāj
The rule of the Soul over the personality 1282

Ātma-Vicāra
Quest for the Self 1317

Ātma-Vidyā, Ātmā-Vidyā
Bhāgavata-Avasthā: the Glorified State 495–496
Definition 5
The Second Stage of Yoga 529

Ātma Yoga
Limitations of the Way of the Will 429

Atom
Aṇu: atomic matter on the planes (graph) 15
Atomic matter: definition 24
Atomos: definition 24
Atoms are units of Energy (Śakti) 1500
Primordial Atoms 24

Attachment. *See also* identification
Aparigrahā: non-attachment 567
Attachment to past sufferings 1401
Attach Yourself to Being 1433
Attach your Mind to the Eternal 1234–1235
Emotional Problems 1429–1431
Expect Nothing from your meditations 1205, 1206
Live and Let Live 940
Reactive-Emotional Consciousness 1426
Your mind becomes attached to physical things 1231

Augoeides. *See also* causal body
The star-like body 40, 738

Āuṁ
All vibrations are within the Āuṁ 788
Āuṁ, Ōṁ, Nāda 550–551
God's Cosmic Symphony 1649
The Holy Spirit as Cosmic Mother 1501

Āuṁ-Sai
Inexhaustible Divine Wealth 1496
The One Undivided Mother 1501

Aur (Ōr, Ūr). *See also* Ain, Ain Soph, Ain Soph Aur
Words for "Light" in Western Mysticism 1350
Aur-Ganuz: the Hidden-Light 1259

Aura
Aura, Aurora: definition 42, 738
Auras of the planets, stars and galaxies 140
Polarities within the Human Aura (graph) 921
The Auric-Field of the Solar Logos 1589–1591
The Human Aura 42

Aureola
A halo or radiance around a body 42

Austerities. *See also* Tapas
Mistranslation of the word Tapas 568–569
Unnecessary Practices 1111

Autogenes
Gnostic Christian definition 736
Autogenes-Christos: the Self-Born Light 137, 662, 736

Automatism
Dangers of automatic writing 313
Leads to possession 322
Often the subconscious mind at work 331

Avadhūta
God's Fools 1392
To Become a True Renunciate 257

Avalokiteśvara
The Christ in the Heart 441
The Saviour in the Heart 1298

Avalokiteśvarī
Quan Yin: the Mother of Compassion 1507

Avasthā
The Seven States of Consciousness 494–496

Avatāra
Avatāra Siddhi: Powers of Divine Descent 599
Derivation and definition 1270
Divine Incarnations mythologized 105
Great Incarnations of Divinity (graph) 1270
Kings of Light 275
Messengers sent by the Spiritual Hierarchy 396
The Avatāra (detailed description) 389
The Avatāras 1320
The Divine Incarnation 726
The Jewish Messiah 660
The Word incarnates through the Avatāras 664
To Worship the Divine Incarnations 1270–1272

Avidyā. *See also* ignorance
Definition 7, 364

Avītci
Definition 30, 218
The Eighth Sphere 63

Avyakta
Definition 118
Qualities of the Divine Being 107

Awakening. *See also* Enlightenment
Awakening the Inner Senses 506–507
Experiencing the Awakening Heart 463–465
Signs of the Awakening Kuṇḍalinī 154–156
Terms of Awakening (Zen) 766
True Death 424

Awareness. *See also* Mindfulness
Awareness Meditation 1656
Meditation is focusing Awareness 1440–1441
Stage Two of Spontaneous Meditation 1230
Tantric meditations on Attention 957

Awliyā-Yekhodā
People of Holiness 873

Āyustejas
The Energy of Life 1488

B

Baal Shem
A Master of the Divine Name 648
Bāl-Shem-Tau: a Master of the Infinite Power 1261

Bagalā, Bagalāmukhī
Names of Lalitā, the Goddess 1581

Bahā-u-llāh
Persecution of the Knowers 658
The Universal Christ 440

Bahīr
The Universal Christ 440

Bailey, Alice A.
Alice Bailey was not a medium 338

Balā
The Energy of the Goddess 1487

Bālā
A Name of Lalitā, the Goddess 1564
The Bālā-Mantra 1532

Balance
Avoid the Errors of East and West 1122–1123
Balanced Practice (Zen) 810–811
Balance in Spiritual Life 505
Balance on the Physical Plane 1257
Between the Two Extremes, Find the Middle Point 1100
Cosmic Sensitivity 1009
Duty and Spirituality 1641
Penetrating into the Kingdom 1707
Primordial Balance 995
Spiritual Life and Material Life 1118
The Active and Passive Way 1011
The Power of Yielding 1088
The Silence of the Warrior 1008
Yin, Yang, Tao 476–477

Bāṇa Liṅga
Access-way at the Heart Centre 151

Baptism
Baptism and Rebirth 722–723
Baptism by Fire and the Spirit 627, 718, 1348
Baptism by Light 1350
Baptizein: definition 722
The Birth of the Light in the Heart 718–720

Barbelo
Gnostic Christian definition 736

Bardo
Hallucinations in the Afterlife 408

Barhiṣad Pitṛis
Did not fall 216
The Seventh Manifest Hierarchy 191

Base Centre. *See also* Mūlādhāra Cakra
General description 46
The Heart and the Energy Centres 1332

Beatific Vision
The Beatific Vision of the Christian Mystics 95, 591
The highest level of clairvoyance 293
The Sixth State 501

Beatitude
In Nirvāṇa there is Beatitude 1720
The attainment of Buddhic Consciousness 422–423

Beatitudes
and the ten Mahāyāna Precepts 814
Similar to Aṣṭāṅga Yoga 560

Beauty
- Natural Attraction 918
- Ray 4: Beauty, Harmony 56
- The Feminine Virtues 468–469

Being
- Attach Yourself to Being 1433
- Being and Becoming 1415–1417
- Be who you are Now 1408
- Dharma: the Law of Being 244
- Pure Being: IĒNG (YING-YENG) 1056–1057
- The Essence of Wisdom 1680–1684
- The Law of your Being 976–977
- The State of Being 1232
- Thinking and Being 233

Being in the Moment. *See also* Mindfulness, Time
- Athā: She who is the Eternal Now 1579
- Being-in-the-Moment Meditation in the Head 1245
- Be who you are Now 1408
- Do the Work yourself 1153
- God dwells in the Moment 1701
- Let Go of the Past 1241
- Liberation from Worldly Consciousness 1233
- Past, Present and Future 1400–1401
- The "No-Mind" 990
- The Enlightened 1702
- The Kingdom is at Hand 1453
- The Principle of Choice 1380–1381
- The purpose of Physical Action (Warrior) 1002–1003
- The Way of Spontaneous Meditation 1229–1232
- You can only Love Now 941

Being of Light
- Ātman, Ātmā 34
- Encountering the Being of Light at death 416–417
- Names for the Being of Light 417
- The Being of Light in Meditation 418–419

Belief. *See also* Faith
- Belief and Experience 676–677
- Pistis: those who have faith and belief 687
- The Truth shall make you Free 682–683

Beni-Elohīm
- Manifestation of the Sons of God 180
- Spiritual Beings who did not fall 211

Ben Adam
- A title given to the Prophets 668

Ben Eloah
- A title given to the triumphant Messiah 669

Bhagavad-Gītā
- God's Singing 1216
- Karma Yoga: Divine Union by Action 1132
- Teaching on the Mind 212
- Use of the term Brahmanirvāṇam 1224–1225

Bhagavan
- The giver of good fortune 1673

Bhāgavata
- Bhāgavata-Avasthā: the Glorified State 495–496
- Bhāgavata-Bhāva: the Divine Mood 1252
- The Christ in the Heart 441

Bhagavatī
- A Name of Lalitā, the Goddess 1569

Bhaikṣya
- Periods of Life in Vedic India 907

Bhairavī
- The Bhairavī-Mantra 1539

Bhakta
- The Goal of the Devotee is God 1129

Bhakti
- Bhakti-Priyā: a Name of Lalitā, the Goddess 1574
- Para-Bhakti: Supreme Devotion 1280

Bhakti Yoga. *See also* Yoga
- Activities of Yoga-Mārga 520
- Bhakti Yoga: Divine Union by Devotion 1128
- Definition 535
- Paths of Spiritual Evolution 1693
- The Science of Cosmic Consciousness 1124
- The Threefold Way 1236
- The Way to the Divine Heart 1505
- Traditional concept of 522–523

Bhargo
- Bhargo, Bharga, Bhargaha: definition 1611

Bhāva
- Mood, feeling, attitude, emotion 1252
- Terms of Love 914

Bhujangī
The Serpent of Wisdom 1516

Bhūr-Loka, Bhūh-Loka. *See also* Physical Plane
and the Goal of Yoga 521
Bhūr, Bhūḥ: definition 1610
Dimensions of the Solar Logos in Cosmic Space 1591
The physical universe: the realm of science 28–29

Bhūta
Attributes of the Elements 28–29

Bhūtatathatā
Definition 86
Derivation and definition 796

Bhuvah-Loka. *See also* Astral Plane
and the Goal of Yoga 521
Bhuvaḥ, Bhuvaha: definition 1610
Dimensions of the Solar Logos in Cosmic Space 1591
Elementary Attributes 29

Bhuvaneśvarī
A Name of Lalitā, the Goddess 1560
Lalitā: the Ultimate Goddess 1556

Bible
Biblical Prophecies? 296
Biblical References to the Cosmic Fire 136
Biblos, Biblion: Christian Hesychast definition 747
Cannot be understood by the male intellect 665
Desecrated by fundamentalist translators 676
Lack of detail on levels of consciousness 39
Limitations of Biblical mythologies 214
Many Biblical stories are UFO stories 282
Mistranslation of "earth" and "heavens" 439
Old Testament stories are remnants of older myths 273
Old Testament teaches the Law of Karma 220
The Bible was not written by God 383
The Biblical "Angels of God" 203
The Divine Message of the New Testament (graph) 719
The Language of the Bible 720
The Logos mistranslated as the Bible 663

Big stick. *See* Kyōsaku

Bīja-Mantra
64 Śrī-Vidyā: the Holy Science 1515–1554
Bīja-Mantra and Psychology 1552
Bīja-Mantra Practice 1552
Important Seed-Sounds of Śrī-Vidyā 1519
Personality Integration Chart (graph) 1333
Some Energy-Forms of the Goddess 1489
Sound-Vibrations of the Śrī-Vidyā Mantra 1528
The Gāyatrī-Mantra (variations) 1608–1640
The Science of Bīja-Mantra 1218–1219
Used by Maharishi 1182
Vibration and Mantra 1518–1519
Potent Vibrations: Bīja-Mantra 1542–1551
Ahaṁ 1551
Aiṁ 1550
Āṁ 1551
Ha 1551
Hāṁ 1546
Hrī 1546
Hrīṁ 1547
Hūṁ 1546
Īṁ 1550
Klīṁ 1549–1550
Krāṁ 1551
Krīṁ 1549
Lāṁ 1544
Māṁ 1551
Ōṁ 1542–1543
Rāṁ 1544–1545
Sa 1551
Śāṁ 1551
Śrī, Śrīṁ 1548
Strī, Strīṁ 1548
Svāhā 1551
Trāṁ 1551
Trīṁ 1550
Vāṁ 1544
Yāṁ 1546

Binah
Spiritual Intuition 498
The Kabbalistic Tree of Life 358–359
Wisdom and Understanding 439

Birth. *See also* Incarnation Process, Rebirth
Baptism and Rebirth 722–723
Continuity of Consciousness 391

Bismillāh
In the Name of God 850

Black Lodge. *See* Dark Forces

Black Magic. *See* Magic

Blavatsky, H.P.
H.P. Blavatsky was not a medium 338
Her Teachings misused by mediums 332
Teachings on Magic 357

Bliss. *See also* Ānanda
Ātmānanda: the Self is Bliss 1518
Meditation and the Joy of Living 1012–1013
Return to Primeval Happiness 1179
The Blissful Mother 1493
The Self is Bliss 1323
The Way to Bliss-Consciousness 1246–1247
Towards Bliss-Consciousness 423

Bodhi
Definition 87, 430
Definition and derivation 753
Terms of Awakening 766
The Experience of Illumination 816–817
What is Wisdom? 1685
Wisdom and Understanding 439

Bodhicitta
Bodhi-Cittā: a Name of Lalitā 1566
Bodhi-Citta-Śakti: the Energy of the Goddess 1487
Definition 30
The Stream of Bodhicitta 789

Bodhidharma
Brought Dhyāna to China 752

Bodhisattva
Definition 172
Definition and derivation 753
God-Consciousness is the Wholeness of Life 504
Hierarchies of Life (graph) 1721
The Christ in the Heart 441
The Four Vows of the Bodhisattva 814
The Nirmānakāya 390
The Path of Zen or Tantra 1121
Those who do not pass away in Nirvāṇa 1191

Bodies. *See* Human Constitution

Body of Glory. *See also* Dharmakāya
Light Bodies 41

Bondage. *See also* identification
Causes of bondage to this earth-life 588
From Personal to Cosmic Life 1428
In Bondage to the Mind 238
Obstacles to Higher Consciousness 1424
The cause of your Bondage to this world 1231
The First Circle of Life 1422
The physical body is your greatest prison 19
The physical senses entrap the mind 1519
Three Great Mysteries to solve in life 1369
To Achieve Liberation 1177
Trapped Spirits 1240
Understand your Predicament 892–893
Your personal sense of self is a mystery 1388

Book of Life. *See* Akashic Records

Borean Epoch
Brief description 176
Past and Present Evolutionary Development of the Cakras (graph) 178

Brahma
Definition 111
Mahāvākya Practice 1471–1472

Brahmā
Brahmā Bīja 1544
Day of Brahmā 168
Definition 111
Expansion into Life (derivation) 113
Locally, Brahmā is our Solar Logos 1615

Brahmā-Avasthā
The God-State 495, 502

Brahmacarya
Brahmacarya, Brahmācārya: definitions 567
Definition 563
Periods of Life in Vedic India 907
The fourth Observance of Aṣṭāṅga Yoga 566–567

Brahmāgranthi
Knots of Consciousness 445
The Knot at the Base Cakra 1424

Brahmājyoti
The Divine Effulgence 1394

Brahmā-Loka
The Kingdom of God 1707

Brahma-Nirvāṇa
Dissolution in God 1224–1225
Paths to the Transcendent and Immanent God 1120
The Brahman-State 1613
The goal of traditional Spiritual Science 1311
The Heart and Head Centres united 1286

Brahma-Rūpa
The Shape or Form of God 1498

Brahmā-Sthiti
The goal of traditional Spiritual Science 1311

Brahma-Vidyā, Brahmā-Vidyā
Brahmā-Avasthā: the God-State 495–496
Is best realized in the Crown Centre 1286
The Third Stage of Yoga 529

Brahmā-Viṣṇu-Śiva. *See also* Trimūrti, Trinity
Dimensions of the Cosmic Fire (graph) 137
The Creation Process 165
The Kingdom of God (graph) 123
The Three-Faced God 113

Brahman
and the Spirit-Spark-Atom 926
Definition 111, 327, 520
Mahāvākya Practice 1475
Shines in the form of Ātman within the Heart 1317
The One God of All Religions 110

Brāhmī
A Name of Lalitā, the Goddess 1570

Brahmī-Sthiti Samādhi
Types of Samādhi 575

Brahmins
Distorted the Vedic religion 368
The Brāhmana 378–379

Brain
All Hail to the Brain! 1368
Connected to lower mind and Higher Mind 429
Mind and Body 1374–1375
Mind and Brain 79
Mind in Body 988
The brain is not the mind 588

Brain-mind. *See* lower mind

Bread from Heaven
To Taste the Elixir of Life 593

Breath. *See also* Holy Breath, Holy Spirit
Baptism and Rebirth 722–723
Movement and the Life-force 1020
Your breath is a wavelet upon the Great Breath 1274

Breathing. *See* Meditational Practices

Bṛhad-Ambā
The Eternal Feminine 1485

Bridge of Light. *See also* Antaḥkaraṇa
Building the Bridge of Light 554–555

Brotherhood of Light. *See* Spiritual Hierarchy

Brothers of the Shadow. *See* Dark Forces

Buddha
Bodies of the Buddhas 392–393
Buddha Initiation Mantra 1723
Definition 30, 343, 420, 752, 755
Female Buddhas 1110
Hierarchies of Life (graph) 1721
How to Become a Buddha or a Christ 1723
Meditational Service of the Buddhas 393
Mediums and Mediators 388
Pratyeka Buddha 504, 906, 1121
Salutation to the Buddha 795
Samyaksaṁ Buddha 1198
The Buddha and the Christ 1722

Gautama Buddha
An Avatāra of Wisdom 1320
A Mahā-Avatāra 389
Corrected the distorted Vedic religion 368
Spoke from Nirvāṇic Consciousness 1448
Gautama Buddha was a Hindu Brahmin 788
His Teachings were altered 1224

Legends of the Buddha 393
The Buddha had Relational Consciousness 906
The Buddha never taught of a personal God 754
To Worship the Divine Incarnations 1270–1272

Buddha-Mind, Buddha-Nature
Man's Original State 753
The Buddha-Mind 1208
The Christ in you, your hope of Glory 768–769
The Discovery of Truth 85
The Universal Saviour-Principle 755
Touch Ultimate Emptiness 96

Buddhi
5 Buddhi: The Realm of Unities 83–92
Buddhic Consciousness 86
Buddhi is a subtle veil over Ātman 88
Discrimination between the Real and the Unreal 1448
Experiencing Pure Consciousness 88
How to develop Buddhic Consciousness 1723
Intuitionis: definition 375
Realms of the One Mind 492–493
Śūnyatā: the "emptiness" 23
Super-Knowing 1242
Surrender to the Self 87
The "I am" is dead! 762
The Buddhic Plane in brief 17
The Buddhic Plane is formless 760–761
The Discovery of Truth 85
The dual characteristic of the Intuitional Plane 753
The Fourth World (Arabic) 888
The Mystics 91
The Ocean of Wisdom 84
The Path of Light 89
The Seven Subplanes of the Buddhic Plane (graph) 90
The Spiritual Soul 34
The Way to Bliss-Consciousness 1246–1247
Towards Bliss-Consciousness 423
To Rediscover Buddhi 90
Your Original Face 87

Buddhic Body. *See also* Ānandamāyākośa
The Resurrection Body 40

Buddhic Consciousness. *See* Pure Consciousness, Mystical Consciousness, Buddhi, Prajñā

Buddhic Plane. *See* Buddhi, Pure Consciousness

Buddhi-Manas
Manas-Taijasi: Radiant Mind 1378
Manomayī: She who is composed of Mind 1577
Realms of the One Mind (graph) 493
The Intelligent-Mind 588
The Mind of Light 891
The Path of Non-Duality 762
The Super-Knowing faculty 1242
Variations in terminology 39
Vijñānamāyākośa: the illusory Wisdom vehicle 38
When mind is combined with Buddhi 235
Your mind irradiated by the Light 353

Buddhism. *See also* Zen
A "Godless" Religion? 754–755
Buddhist Names for the Christ-Principle in the Heart 441
Denies the existence of a real Self in Man 1123
Errors of later Buddhist teachings 1224
The Four Vows of the Bodhisattva 814
The Infinite Light conceived of as a Buddha 795
The Noble Eightfold Path of the Buddha 815
The Ten Mahāyāna Precepts 814

Buddhi Yoga. *See* Yoga

Business
Many business people are magicians 356
Objectives of Magic 363

Bythus
Gnostic Christian definition 736

C

Caduceus
Definition 155

Caelum
Western words for "Heaven" 1352

Caitanya
The Watcher 1212

Caitanya-Rūpiṇī-Devī
The Consciousness-Form-Goddess 1498

Cakras
Cakra: definition 44, 346, 637
Malfunctioning Cakras 53
The 72 Cakras of the Solar Logos 1327
The planets are Cakras of the Solar Logos 1589, 1590
Human Cakras 44–53
Cakras above the head 45
Centres of White Magic and Black Magic 364
Distribute the Life-force in Humanity 1486
Exit-Points from the Physical Body 401
Human Evolution and the Awakened Cakras (graph) 171
Past and Present Evolutionary Development of the Cakras (graph) 178
Primitive and minor cakras 45
Ray-Energies in the Human Cakras 54
Symbols of the Seven Major Cakras (graph) 45
Telepathy and the cakras 346–347
The Creative Centre 48
The Functioning of the Cakras (graph) 52
The Heart and the Energy Centres 1332
The lower centres responsible for the physical body 1375
The Major Cakras and the Glands (graph) 44
The Psychic Centre 49
The Seven Centres of Force in the Human Species 1385
The three lower cakras are most active 242, 1374
Cakra Transformation
Awakening the Higher Centres 1037
Building the Antaḥkaraṇa 1194
Integration of the Human Consciousness (graph) 1195
Internalizing the Semi-Vowels in the Energy Centres 1045
Personality Integration Chart (graph) 1333
Powers of the Awakened Centres (graph) 1037
Solar Meditation in the Cakras (graph) 1640
The Body of Fire 1334
The Brahma-Gāyatrī in the Cakras (graph) 1639
The Vowels in the Energy Centres 1036–1038
Transformation of the Centres 1333

Cāmuṇḍā
The Cāmuṇḍā-Mantra 1540

Candra
Candra Bīja 1551
The Shining Lights 1595

Cannibalism
A form of Black Magic 364

Caste
The Caste System 378–379

Catharsis
Christian Hesychast definition 743

Causal body
An imperishable Light Body 40
Beyond the personality complex 36–37
Explanation of the term "causal" 361
Polarities Male and Female 920–921
The Intellect 891
The Work of Meditation 1440
Those polarized in the causal body 376

Causal Centre. *See also* Alta Centre
The Kāraṇa Cakra above the head 1645

Causal Consciousness
Knowledge of Past Lives 601
Suṣūpti-Avasthā 494, 496
To be taught Wisdom by higher beings 353

Causal Mind. *See also* Abstract Mind, Higher Mind
Intellectus: definition 375
Kāraṇa-Manas 34, 78
Mind Realms 74
The Path for many in the New Age 837
Will manifest when the mind is still 768

Causal World
The Archetypal World 360–361
The Seven Subplanes of the Mental Plane (graph) 75

Cause and Effect. *See* Karma

Cave of the Heart
Hṛdaya-Guha: Heart Cave 1592
Hṛt-Padma: the Heart Lotus 1505
Meditation in the Cave of the Heart 1358
The Cave of the Heart (Christian) 634
The Eastern Heart 448

Cayce, Edgar
Neither a medium nor a mystic 339

Celibacy
Control of only the perishable 927
Mistranslation of the word Brahmacarya 566–567
Promulgated by the religions 917
The most colossal delusion 560

Cenobites
Christian Hesychast definition 739

Centring. *See* Balance, Mindfulness

Certainty
The Five Stages of Certainty (Arabic) 895

Chān
Definition and derivation 752
The aim of Chān 766

Change
Change is the Absolute Law 405
Developing the Cosmic-Sense 1709
The world is changing all the time 1238
Transformations of the Mind 1242–1243
We must change ourselves before death 411

Channelling. *See* Mediumship
15 Channelling and Mediumship 317–344

Chanting
Our Sacred Music and Language 2081
Right Chanting 1697

Chaos (Kaos)
Greek Mystery School definition 733
Primordial Matter 135
Unordered 13

Charis
Gnostic Christian definition 738

Charisma
Christian Hesychast definition 744
Kharisma (Charisma): definition 312

Chastity. *See* celibacy

Cherubim
Christian Classification of the Hierarchies 192

Chesed
Opposite to the Law of Karma 240
The Hasid comes under the Love of God 648–649
The Kabbalistic Tree of Life 358–359

Chi. *See also* Prāṇa
Chi-Kung: control of the Life-force 786
Spirit 1343
The Vital Force of Tao 786

Children
Children born innocent? 250
Education shuts down spiritual faculties 481
General Children's Initiation Mantra into the Energy of the Goddess 1506
Mother, Father and Baby 938–939
Mother and Father 475
Natural Sexual Dynamism 918
Nourishing the Goal of Life 487
The Breakdown of Family 473
The Gift of Parenthood 474
The Masculinization of Children 478–479
Violence and War (effects on children) 486

Children of God
Children of the Sun 1590
Pure Christianity 729
The true Christians 619
The Way, the Truth and the Life 670
We are all Children of God 1178

Children of Light
Levels of meaning 41

Chiliocosm
Chiliokosmos: definition 13, 121

Chinnamastā
A Name of Lalitā, the Goddess 1581

Chockmah
Pure Consciousness 498
The Eternal Feminine 469
The Kabbalistic Tree of Life 358–359
Western words for "Wisdom" 1354
What is Wisdom? 1685
Wisdom and Understanding 439

Chohan
Definition 394

Choice
The Principle of Choice 1380–1381
You Must Choose (mediumship or mysticism) 344

Chosen Ones. *See also* Elect
Ekklesia: definition and description 688
God shows no favouritism 107
Mediums chosen by the White Brothers? 309
The Chosen Ones 688
The Eternal is One 512–514
The Law of the Higher Life 1134–1135
Who are the Elect? 128

Chozeh
The Prophets 647

Christ
20 The Mystery of the Heart 425–466
30 Jesus the Christed One 659–674
72 In Service to the Spiritual Hierarchy 1719–1730

What is the Christ?
Chrēstos: Greek Mystery School definition 734
Christos: definition 115, 420, 734, 741
Greek words for the Christ 664
Kṛṣṭa, Kṛṣṇa, Krista: the Christ within your Soul 1320
Names of the Being of Light 417
Names of the Great Master Jesus 661
The Buddha and the Christ 1722
The Christ in the Heart 441
The Christ is the Light of the World 442–443
The Cosmic Christ 662–663
The Holy Trinity 1342
The Imperishable Seed in the Heart 926–927
The Mystery of Jesus the Christ 664
The Mystery of the Christ (graph) 1724
The Threefold Christ 115, 663
The Universal Christ 440

The Coming of the Christ. *See also* Second Coming
Christ in you, your hope of Glory 768–769, 774, 912
How to Become a Buddha or a Christ 1723
The Birth of the Christ on the mass level 1713
The Christos lives in you 1294
The Coming of the Christ 724–727
The Jewish Messiah 660
The Kingdom is at Hand 1453
The Religion of Christ 441
Universal Service 1717

Meditation on the Christ
Christ Initiation Mantra 1723
Pure Devotion: Initiation Mantram 1724
The Being of Light in Meditation 418–419
The Path of Illumination 1338
To Worship the Divine Incarnations 1270–1272
Visualization of the Christ in the Heart 730

Christ Body. *See also* Ānandamāyākośa
The Resurrection Body 40

Christ-Consciousness
Kūṭastha: the Highest State to be in 449
Tao: the Great I AM 774
What is Christ-Consciousness? 443

Christ-Hierarchy. *See also* Spiritual Hierarchy
72 In Service to the Spiritual Hierarchy 1719–1730
The Christ-Hierarchy and Śamballa 396

Christ Realm
The Christian Cosmo-Conception 19
The Many Mansions (graph) 611

Christianity. *See also* Jesus
27 Teachings of the Saints 609–622
28 The Heart of Christianity 623–640
29 Christian History 641–658
30 Jesus the Christed One 659–674
31 Christian Fundamentalism 675–688
32 Christian Prayer 689–716
33 The Christian Path 717–730
34 The Greek Mystery Language 731–748
57 The Way of Holiness 1335–1360

What is Christianity?
Be Still and Know 638–639
Jesus Speaks… 728–729
Pure Christianity 729
The Dual Nature of Christianity 624–625
The Gnostic Teachings 1108
The Lord of Glory 667
The Mystery of Jesus and Mary 665
The Mystery of Jesus the Christ 664
The Purpose of Christianity 174, 640
To Partake of God's Nature 640
Who are the Christians? 646

The Christian Heart
God in the Heart 634–635
Purify the Heart 701
The Burning Heart 631
The Christian Heart-Path 632
The Coming of Christ in the Heart 727
The Meaning of Life is Love 633
Wounds of Love 699

Christian Mysticism
Christian Mysticism 450–451
Christian Mysticism and Zen 630
Christian Zen 765
Mystical States of the Medieval Catholic Mystics 698
Rapture 699
Teachings of the Saints 612–622
The Dichotomy of the Mystic 629
The Experience of Mysticism 636
The Way of the Christian Mystic 626–628

Christian Cosmology
Christian Classification of the Hierarchies 192
Confuses Jesus with the Cosmic Christ 115, 663, 1453
The Christian Cosmo-Conception 19
The Christian Trinity 113, 611, 662–663
The Many Mansions (graph) 611
The mythical Divine Family 104–105

Christian History
Christianity was One 650
Christian Beginnings 642
Christian Mysticism 450–451
Idol-Worship 655
Persecution of the Knowers 656–658
Records of Early Christianity 642
The Christian Heart-Path 632
The Dual Nature of Christianity 624–625
The Early Christians 643–644
The Gnostics 645
The Heretics 655
The Pilgrims 645
The Prophets 647
The Saints 654
The Tree of Christianity (graph) 651
Twilight of the Christian Truth 652–653

Christian Fundamentalism
Belief and Experience 676–677
Beyond Phantasia 686–687
Biblical Prophecies? 296
Church will be shaken by the Holy Spirit 279
Clinging to Old Testament ideas 220
Fear of the Lord? 234
Fundamentalism is based on duality 1108–1109
Fundamentalists misrepresent Self-Knowledge 324
Jesus the Personal Saviour? 678–679
Prayer Spiritual and Material 681
Protagonists of Ignorance 383
Repentance 683
Speaking in tongues 312–313
Televangelism 682
Tested by God and the Devil? 685
The Chosen Ones 688
The Crime of Fundamentalism 669
The Sacrificial Lamb 680
The Truth shall make you Free 682–683
What is "the Devil"? 684

The Christian Path
Baptism and Rebirth 722–723
Jesus Speaks... 728–729
Stages on the Way of Holiness 1336–1339
  The Path of Illumination 1338
  The Path of Purification 1337
  The Path of Union 1339
The Catholic Mystical Path 1129
The Christian Heart-Path 632
The Coming of Christ in the Heart 727
The Divine Message of the New Testament (graph) 719
The Unfoldment of the Light 718–721

Christian Practice
Alone with God 700
Christian Divine Names 1266–1267
Christian Meditation: The Way of Holiness 1345
Christian Meditation on the Holy Breath 1346–1353
Clouds of Unknowing 704–705
Interior Prayer (Eastern Christian) 691–695
Latin Mantras of the Rosicrucians 712
Latin Mantras to Our Lady 1510–1511
Mantras to Connect to Our Lady (Latin) 1512

Meditation on Theos 714
Meditation on the Holy Spirit 1344
Mystical Theology 706–707
Passion and Dispassion 695
Practising the Presence of God 711
Purify the Heart 701
Some Christian Prayers to the Deity (English) 1266
Stages of Prayer 692
The Evolution of Christian Prayer 713–716
The Great Greek Mantra to Jesus 708–710
The Jesus Mantra and the Sacred Heart Initiation 1356
The Path to Ecstasy 696–697
The Radiant Heart Prayer 702–703
The Rose of Love and the Cross of Light 1357
The Way of the Radiant Heart 452–455
To Call upon Jesus 679
To Develop Perfect Stillness 700
To See and Hear God 637
Visualization of the Christ in the Heart 730
Visualization of the Immaculate Heart of Mary, Our Lady 1513
What is Prayer? 690

Christian Science
Christian Science and Zen 764

Christmas
Esoteric meaning of 720

Cidākāśa, Cidghana
The Infinite Field of Universal Consciousness 1499
The Sky of Consciousness 932

Cidrūpiṇī-Śakti
Experienced at highest stages of Yoga 526

Cinmayī
A Name of Lalitā, the Goddess 1572

Cit. *See also* Sat-Cit-Ānanda
Cit-Śakti: the Energy of the Goddess 1488
Mantra directly affects your Consciousness 1490
One of the qualities of the Ultimate Reality 526
The Experience of the Heart 1281
The Mother Light 1533

Cit-Jaḍa-Granthi
The connection between consciousness and the physical body 1280

Citta
Definition 30, 499, 536, 1242
Meditation and the mind-substance 1203

Citta-Ākāśa
The Boundless Ocean of Intelligence 1499
The Sky of Consciousness 932

Citta-Mārga
The Way of the Mind 1238–1239

Cittamāyākośa
Cittamayakośa Samādhi 575
Coverings over the Self 38

Citta-Vṛtti
Mind-Waves 1239, 1242

Citta-Vṛtti-Nirodha
The cessation of the activities of the mind 536
The immediate goal of meditation 1209
Transformations of the Mind 1242

Clairaudience
An active Throat Cakra allows astral hearing 48
Higher clairaudience uses the inner ear 293, 352
Saṁyama and Parapsychology 582

Clairsentience
Saṁyama and Parapsychology 582
Utilizes the Solar Plexus Centre 352

Clairvoyance
General description 292–293
Heart-Clairvoyance 1300
Saṁyama and Parapsychology 582
The Tao cannot be found by clairvoyance 773
The Third-Eye is the organ of vision 49, 352
Unreliability of most clairvoyants 293, 352

Cleanliness. *See* Purity, Śauca

Cleansing stations
on the Astral Plane 71

Collective Subconscious Mind
The Astral World of our planet 58

Collective Unconscious
Incorrect terminology 58, 236

Communion
Catholic mystical terminology 698

Compassion
First become a Master of Compassion 428
Madonna 470
The Being of Light 416–417
The Eternal Feminine 469
The Mother of the World 147
The Mystics 91
The Path of Zen or Tantra 1121
The same God or Divinity resides in every Heart 1265
The Second Stream of Spiritual Energy 972–973
The Soul-Power 1305
The Three Forces of the Warrior 996–997
The World Mother of Compassionate Heart 145

Concentration
Derivation and definition 697
Dhāraṇā: Inner Concentration 562, 572
Dhāraṇā is the Concentration of the mind 1523
Stages of Interior Prayer 693

Conditioning
Conditioned Thinking 1084
Obstacles to Higher Consciousness 1424
True Thought 79
You are being conditioned all the time 485
You perceive according to your conditioning 540

Consciousness. *See also* Causal Consciousness, Pure Consciousness, Cosmic Consciousness, God-Consciousness
18 Human Consciousness 373–396
22 Awakening the Human Glory 489–510
58 The Psychology of Consciousness 1363–1398

What is Consciousness?
Citta-Ākāśa: the Sky of Consciousness 932
Consciousness (aphorisms) 1370–1371
Consciousness and Phenomena (graph) 323
Energy comes from Consciousness 134–135
Everything is conscious 169
Perceptions of the One Mind 490
What is Consciousness? 1368–1369
Your world is the reflection of your consciousness 633

The Evolution of Consciousness
Ascending the Planes of Consciousness 20
Awakening the Inner Senses 506–507
Beyond the Veils 894
Evolutionary States of Human Consciousness (graph) 172
From Subjective to Objective 173
Human Evolutionary Epochs 176–178
Human Involution and Evolution 170–172
Integration of the Human Consciousness (graph) 1195
The Far-Future Evolution of Humanity (graph) 183
The Future Evolution of Humanity (graph) 182
The Goal of Zen 760–761
The Sevenfold Earth-Evolution 169
Vertical Evolution and the Path 174

States of Consciousness
Being Alone with the Absolute 502
Buddhic Consciousness 86
Christ-Consciousness 443
Evolutionary Leaps in Consciousness 184–185
Formless Consciousness 1373
God-Consciousness is the Wholeness of Life 504–505
Illumined-Mind Consciousness 1427
Liberation from Worldly Consciousness 1233
Reactive-Emotional Consciousness 1426
Realms of the One Mind 492–493
Samādhi: the State of Inner Purity 497
Stages on the Path 1136–1137
Steps on the Meditational Path 1196–1198
The Basic Enlightened State 1372
The Fifth State 500
The Fourth State 498–499
The Seventh State 502
The Seven States of Consciousness 494–496, 575
The Sixth State 501
The State of Being 1232
Turīya: Pure Consciousness 498

Types of Consciousness
Greek classifications of Humanity 687
Human Types (graph) 377
Mediums and Mediators 388–389
Powers of Consciousness 374–375
The Brotherhood of Light (graph) 395
The Caste System 378–379
The Way of the Spirit 381
The Way of the World 380
Types of Conscious Immortality 390–391
Types of Humanity 376

Consciousness (general)
Higher Consciousness has no Name 331
Identification with the bodies 893
Knots of Consciousness 445
Tantric meditations on Consciousness 947–948
The Law of Mystic Experience 508–509
The Way to Higher Consciousness 329

Conscious Immortality
Description of 32
From Bondage to Liberation (graph) 422
Learn to Die before you Die 420–421
The Path of Tantra 942–943
The Path to Immortality 430–431
Types of Conscious Immortality 390–391

Constantine
Made Christianity the religion of Rome 644

Contemplation
Contemplātionis: definition 630
Contemplative (Passive) Meditation 1185
Definition 418, 697
Examples of Supernatural Contemplation 1189
Four Ways to Enter Silence 1447
Natural and Supernatural Contemplation 1188
Stages of Interior Prayer 694
Stages of the Silent Meditation Process 1186
To Contemplate 1187
To Develop Perfect Stillness 700

Continuity of Consciousness
Gaps in Continuity of Consciousness 521
The awakened Crown Centre 50
The death experience for the Enlightened 400
The lowest form of Conscious Immortality 391

Cosmic Consciousness
Developing Cosmic Consciousness 1125
Stages on the Path 1136–1137
Steps on the Meditational Path 1196–1197
The Fifth State 500
The Science of Cosmic Consciousness 1124
Turīyātīta-Avasthā: beyond the Fourth State 495–496
Variations in terminology 500
Yoga in Cosmic Consciousness 1125

Cosmic Elements. *See* Elements

Cosmic Fire 130–137
Biblical References to the Cosmic Fire 136
Dimensions of Fire 131
Dimensions of the Cosmic Fire (graph) 137
Influence on the Aquarian Age 279
Kuṇḍalinī-Fohat 148–149
Lalitā as the Essence of Fire 1539
Living Matter 134–135
Purification by Fire 571
The Cosmic Fire 130–131
The Kuṇḍalinī Fire 132
The One Force (according to Hermes Trismegistus) 133

Cosmic Mind. *See also* Mahat, One Mind, Tao
Mahat: definition 161
Mind-Only 974–975
Tao: the Universal Mind 775
The Action of the Cosmic Mind 167
The Intelligent Universe 111
The One 1686–1687
The Plan is in the Divine Mind 161
The Universal Intelligence 232

Cosmic Planes of Being. *See* Planes

Cosmology
1 Planes of Being 11–30
7 The Divine Being 103–140
9 Creation and Evolution 159–186
10 The Creative Hierarchies 187–204
11 Origins of Evil 205–230
42 Sūfī Mind 885–902
66 The Mystery of the Sun 1585–1600
Cosmological Systems Compared (graph) 18
Dimensions of the Cosmic Fire (graph) 137
Dimensions of the Solar Logos in Cosmic Space 1591
The Christian Cosmo-Conception 19
The Constitution of the Solar Logos (graph) 124
The Creation of the Universe 166–167
The Form of God is Space 109
The Goal of Yoga (graph) 521
The Goal of Zen 760–761
The Kingdom of God (graph) 123
The Many Mansions (graph) 611

The Universal Cosmology 18
Worlds of the Sūfī 886–890

Creation. *See also* Evolution
9 Creation and Evolution 159–186
Created out of the Void 51
Creation and Evolution are One 160
Hierarchies of Manifestation 120
Past, Present and Future 1400
Stages of Manifestation 361
The Action of the Primordial Sound (graph) 165
The Cosmic Creator-Gods 162–163
The Creation Myth 160, 168, 214
The Creation of the Universe 166–167
The Creation Process 165
The Creative and Destructive Power of Sound 201
The Creative Power of the Primordial Language of Sound 1075
The Cycle of Manifestation (graph) 134
The Divine Bipolarity 471
The Law of Cyclic Activity 248
The Law of Polarity 164
The Period of the Mahāmanvantara 168
The Plan is in the Divine Mind 161
The Universal Creator-God 1588
The World exists for the sake of the Self 544

Creative Hierarchies. *See* Hierarchies
10 The Creative Hierarchies 187–204

Creativity. *See also* Mind: Creative Power of the Mind
Creative (Active) Meditation 1184
Creative Intelligence manifests through the Throat Centre 1194
Creativity is the purpose of Tantra 911
Function of the Throat Centre 428
Mind and Thought 1376
Ray 3: Activity, Adaptability 56
Stages of Manifestation 361
The Creative Centre (Throat and Sex Cakras) 48
The Creative Power of the Primordial Language of Sound 1075
The Creative Soul 1692
The new Aquarian energies 1708
The Third Stream of Spiritual Energy 972–973

Creator-Gods. *See also* Elohīm
Children of the Cosmic Creators 190
Ruach-Elohīm: the Breath of the Creator-Gods 167
The Cosmic Creator-Gods 162–163
The Elohīm 120

Crime
Criminals are subject to Shadowland 219
Death-experience of the suicide and the murdered 404–405
In Bondage to the Mind 238
Kuṇḍalinī and sexual offences 153
Resulting from demonic possession 311

Crisis. *See also* tests
Crises on the Path 1162–1165
Crisis (Metanoia) 1436–1437
Crisis and Revelation 1711
How to deal with Crisis situations in your Life 1435
Love Lost 936–937
Persevering to the End until Final Liberation 1101
The Testing of the Soul 1158
The Tests of the Elements 1159

Criticism
The Evil of Criticism 1156–1157
Thought and Energy 349

Cross
Evolutionary Symbolism of the Cross 179
The Cross in the Heart 712
The Rose of Love and the Cross of Light 1357

Crown Centre. *See also* Sahasrāra Cakra
Divine Love in the Head 916
Entry point for the Soul 1194
General description 50
Saṁyama in the Crown Centre 587
The Heart and the Energy Centres 1332

Crucifixion
Evolutionary Symbolism of the Cross 179
The Battle between the Personality and the Soul 721
The Last Words of Jesus 672

Cycles
Past, Present and Future 1400
Reincarnation and Freedom 998
The Circle of Love 923

The Law of Cyclic Activity 248
The Three Kinds of Activity of Matter 248
The Wheel of the Law 247

Cyclops
and the Third-Eye 49

D

Dabar
The Hebrew Logos 664

Daemon, Daimon
Daimon: Christian Hesychast definition 746
Original meanings 193

Daivi-Śakti-Kuṇḍalinī
The two Aspects of the Goddess 1516

Daiviprākṛtī
The Eternal Feminine 469
The Light of the Logos (graph) 119
The Primordial Light 119
The same meaning as the Greek Logos 117

Dama
The Six Mental Qualifications 1149

Dance
Dance and the Kuṇḍalinī 156
Movement and the Life-force 1020
The Creative Soul 1692
The Dance of Life (Sūfī) 873
True Dancing 873

Dangers
Clouds of Unknowing 704–705
Dangers of awakening the Kuṇḍalinī 157–158, 1522
Dangers of Black Magic 364, 371
Dangers of damaging the etheric web 304
Dangers of developing the Head before the Heart 428–429
Dangers of the lower solar-plexus emotions 427
Involuntary Possession 310–311
Meditating on the Void 801
Mediumship often leads to possession 309
Ouija Board, Planchette, Automatic Writing 313
Seek Not Powers 581
To Approach the Goddess 1513
Why Channelling is Dangerous 340–343

Darkness. *See also* Shadow
Brotherhoods of Light and Darkness 228
From Darkness into Light 982–983
The Warrior stands between the Light and the Darkness 984

Dark Forces. *See also* Evil
Avītci: the Eighth Sphere 63
Brotherhoods of Light and Darkness 228
Brothers of the Shadow 226–227
The Dark Side of the Force 219
True War 985
Wars in Heaven 271

Day of God
Mahāmanvantara 168

Death
19 Death and Liberation 397–424

The Death Process
Death-bed visions 403
Exit-Points from the Physical Body 401
Tarot Key 13: Death 398
The breaking of the Silver Cord 401
The Death Experience 400
The Death Process for the Enlightened 401
The Final Astral Projection 401
The Four Deaths 399, 422
The Law of Death 398
The Natural Death Process 399
True Death 424

The After-Death Experience
Becoming earthbound after death 402–403
Change is the Absolute Law 405
Hallucinations in the Afterlife 408–409
Karma in the Afterlife 241
Life in the Astral World 70
Most people don't realize they have died 402
Rearrangement of the Astral Body after Death 69
The After-Death Life 402–405
  Death by Lingering Disease 403
  Sudden Death 402
  The Suicide and the Murdered 404–405

The Being of Light 416–417
The happy and wrathful "deities" 408
The Hell Condition 406–407
The Law of the Afterlife 410–411
Violent death by accident or war 302

Death (general)
Abortion and the Incarnation Process 413–415
Death in the Heart 444
Karma and Death (Metanoia) 1425
Knowledge of the time of one's death 584
Learn the Art of Dying 399
Learn to Die before you Die 420–421
Remembering the Dead 412
The Mantra to Overcome the Fear of Death 1540

Dehagranthi
Obstacles to Higher Consciousness 1424

Dehātma
Identification with the physical body 1177

Deification
Illumination and Deification 1190
Stages of Interior Prayer 695
Stages of the Silent Meditation Process 1187
The Muslim Deification Process 1191

Deipara
Christian Hesychast definition 741

Delusion. *See also* illusion, ignorance, Māyā
Already Enlightened? 341
Astral Disinformation 1271
Dense materialism 384
Happiness Exists Within 1381
Identification with the body 895
Mahā-Māyā: the Ultimate Delusion 1714
Māyā: definition 2
of the Astral World 336
of the physical body 3
Only celibate males can attain Salvation? 560
Self-delusion of mediums 309
The cause of astral delusion 328

Demiurgos
The Cosmic Creator-Gods 162

Demons. *See also* devils
Angels and Demons 193
can possess mediums 330
Daemon, Daimon: original meanings 193
Demonic possession 311
Hallucinations in the Afterlife 408
Invoked through Black Magic 364
In the lower hell worlds 60, 63
The Asuras 211

Dervish
The Dancing Dervishes 156, 873

Desert Condition
Diseases caused by walking the Path 1168

Desert Fathers
The Early Christians 643–644
The Tree of Christianity 651

Desire. *See also* Kāma
Desire-Streams 1377
Desire for the Real 1503
Kāma Bīja: that which stimulates the Astral Nature 1549
Kill out Desire? 58
Mind and Desire 235
Niṣkāma-Karma: desireless action 1331
Tantric meditations on Desire 958
The Cycle of Desire (graph) 1377
The Realm of Desires 58–59
True Death: the cessation of desire 424

Desire-mind. *See* Kāma-Manas

Desire body. *See* astral body

Destiny. *See also* Dharma
12 Karma and Reincarnation 231–266
59 Time and Eternity: Action and Destiny 1399–1410
Action and Destiny (Metanoia) 1420–1421
Destined by the Stars? 260–261
Destiny (Dharma): aphorisms 1407–1409
Destiny and the Permanent Atoms 250
Dharma: the Law of Being 244
Prophecy and Destiny 294–297
Terms of Destiny 261
The Chain of Dharma 247
Vimāna People and Human Destiny 283

Detachment. *See* attachment, identification

Deus
Meditations in the Heart Centre 1301

Deva
A Name for the Solar Logos 1658
Definition 1611
Devasya: definition 1611

Devas. *See also* angels
Denizens of the Heaven Worlds 77
Deva: definition 169, 189
Language of the Gods 200
Some Facts about the Devas 198
The Devas according to the Rays 199
The Gandharvas 200
The Spirit-Helpers 369

Deva-Bhāva
The Divine Mood 1252

Devāchan. *See also* Mental Plane
4 Devāchan: the Mental Plane 73–82
Beyond the Astral World 59
Definitions 76
Devāchanic Rest 413
Enlightenment for the personality-consciousness 76
Hallucinations in the Afterlife 409
Mediumistic communication not possible 330
Mind Realms 74–75
Paths to Devāchan 81
The Seven Subplanes of the Mental Plane (graph) 75
To Experience Heaven 82

Deva-Loka
The Shining World 76

Deva-Manuṣya-Deham
Bodies derived from the Angelic Kingdom 1312

Deva-Netra
The All-Seeing-Eye of the Siddhas 1129

Deva-Śakti
The Energy of the Goddess 1486

Devasthāna
The abode of the gods 76

Devatā
Form part of the Spiritual Hierarchy 394, 396
Non-human evolutionary orders 194, 366

Devī
A Name of Lalitā, the Goddess 1561
Devī Bīja 1548
The Goddess in Her Immanence 1485
The two Aspects of Devī, the Goddess 1516

Devil
Ahriman: a great Being of Light 211
Diabolos: the source of the word "Devil" 209
Lūcifer: the Light-Bearer 210
No such thing as a personal "Devil" 107
Sex the Work of the Devil? 910
Tested by God and the Devil? 685
The Devil is not a person 208
The Mind-Created Devil 218
What is "the Devil"? 684

Devils. *See also* demons
Christian misunderstanding of the elementals 310
In the Eighth Sphere 63

Devotion. *See also* Heart
Awakens the Kuṇḍalinī 152, 157
Bhakti Yoga: Divine Union by Devotion 1128
Destroys the effects of negative karmas 1331
Devotion and miraculous powers 578
Devotion to Kṛṣṇa 449
Īśvara-Praṇidhāna: Devotion to God 548, 564, 569
Kṛṣṇa gave Mankind Devotion 1270
Love and Devotion will purify your Heart 571
My Beloved Lives in my Heart 1290–1291
On the Wings of Devotion 1129
Para-Bhakti: Supreme Devotion 1280
Practising the Presence of God 711
Pure Devotion: Initiation Mantram 1724
Ray 6: Devotion, Sacrificial Love 56
Teachings of the Saints 612–622
The Divine Mood 1252
The Influence of the Seven Rays 834–835
The Lover of God 853
Visualizing the Divinity within the Heart 1268
Waiting upon the Lord 1447

Dhāraṇā
Definition 562
Dhāraṇā is the Concentration of the mind 1523
The sixth step of Aṣṭāṅga Yoga 572

Dharma. *See also* Destiny, Karma
12 Karma and Reincarnation 231–266
59 Time and Eternity: Action and Destiny 1399–1410
Between the Two Extremes, Find the Middle Point 1100
Definition 30
Destiny (Dharma): aphorisms 1407–1409
Dharma: the Law of Being 244–245
It is your Destiny to rebecome a Child of God 1178
Listening to the Sound of the Dharma 789
The Chain of Dharma 247
The Path of Self-Actualization 1110
The Plan is in the Divine Mind 161
The Solar Dharma 163
The Wheel of the Law 247
Your Fate is before your eyes 246

Dharmakāya
Bodies of the Buddhas 392–393
The Body of Glory 41
The Dharmakāya is neither male nor female 1110
Touch Ultimate Emptiness 96

Dharmamegha Samādhi
Types of Samādhi 575

Dhī, Dhiyo
Dhīyāḥ, Dhiyo, Dhiyaha, Dhī: definition 1611

Dhikr. *See* Zikr

Dhīmahi
Definition 1611

Dhūmāvatī
A Name of Lalitā, the Goddess 1581

Dhyāna. *See also* Meditation
Activities of Yoga-Mārga 520
Definition 418, 562
Dhāraṇā and Dhyāna 1523
Origins of Zen 752
Some Facts about Meditation (Dhyāna) 1192
Steps to the Experience of Zen 813
The seventh step of Aṣṭāṅga Yoga 572

Dhyāna-Mātā
A Name of Lalitā, the Goddess 1567

Dhyāni-Buddha
Definitions 390–391
Meditational Service of the Buddhas 393

Dhyāni-Chohan
Definition and description 192
The Sevenfold Evolutionary Scheme 169

Diabolos
Source of the word "Devil" 209

Diakrisis
Christian Hesychast definition 742

Dianoia
Christian Hesychast definition 742

Diet
Balance on the Physical Plane 1257
Diet can raise the vibration of the physical body only 597
Purification by Diet? 571

Dīkṣā
Āryan Initiation process 179
Initiation from a Guru 1225

Dimensions. *See* Planes, Loka

Dīn
Divine Justice 648
Kabbalistic word for Karma 233, 240

Disasters
The Sufferings of Man 223

Discipleship
Monks and Disciples 991
Qualifications for Discipleship (Sanskrit) 1149
Rely on your Inner Self 1226
The Brotherhood of Light (graph) 395
The Path to Discipleship 1149

Disease. *See also* psychosis, health, healing
Death by Lingering Disease 403–404
Diseases caused by walking the Path 1168
Disease and Karma 1169
Disease is the flow of unregulated energies 1454
Disease resulting from emotional problems 1429–1431
Malfunctioning Cakras 53

Malfunction of the spleen 50
Mental diseases and emotional states 1364–1365
Physical Symptoms in the Heart 462
The Soul's disconnection from the personality 1432
The Sūfī view of Mental Disorders 900

Divination
Original meaning 261

Divine Being. *See* God
7 The Divine Being 103–140

Divine Kingdom. *See also* Śamballa
The Sevenfold Earth-Evolution 169

Divine Milieu
Jesus lived in the Divine Milieu 667
The Plerōma 12

Divine Mind. *See* Cosmic Mind, One Mind, Mahat

Divine Mother. *See also* World Mother, Goddess
8 Kuṇḍalinī and the Goddess 141–158
21 The Call of the World Mother 467–488
62 The Great Goddess 1483–1490
63 The Heart of the Divine Mother 1491–1514
The Breath of the Divine Mother 142
The Feminine Suppressed 910
The Mother 1493
The Mother of the World 147
The Virgin and the Mother 144

Divine Name, Names. *See also* Mantra
20 The Mystery of the Heart 425–466
32 Christian Prayer 689–716
41 Sūfī Prayer 863–884
47 The Primordial Sound Language 1025–1076
54 The Heart and the Lost Art of Prayer 1251–1278
65 The One-Hundred Names of Lalitā 1555–1582

The Name and the Names
All true Names of God are the Divine Name 457
Expressed in the Hebrew and Sanskrit Alphabets 1552
God's Cosmic Symphony 1649
Meditation on the Divine Names 1454
The Creative Power of the Primordial Language of Sound 1075
The Evolution of Christian Prayer 713–716
The Names and Mental Prayer in the Heart 1261
The Name and the Names 1258
The Name connects the three Aspects of the Trinity 1342
The Name is the cause of all miraculous powers 1352–1353
The Name of the Deity 1032
The Universal Heart Practice 846
The Voice of God (Sūfī) 864–865
The Way of the Radiant Heart (Christian) 452–453
The Word, Logos, Voice, Name 1646–1648
What is the Name? 1259

Arabic Names
Allāh: the exalted Name of God 871
Breathing God 870–871
El Allāh Hū: the Arabic I AM 1459
Names for Nirvāṇa 100
Some Arabic Prayers to the Deity 850–851
Sūfī Mantras for Meditation 874–877
The Beautiful Names 1264–1265
The Ninety-Nine Arabic Divine Names 878–884

English Names
Christian Divine Names 1266
Divine Names of Our Lady 1510

Greek Names
Meditation on Theos 714
The Evolution of Christian Prayer 714–715

Hebrew Names
Hebrew Divine Names to be Invoked in the Heart 1262–1263
Hebrew Divine Words for Healing 1456
IHVH: I AM 1460
IOEL: the Healing Mind 1457
Sounding the Hebrew Angelic Names 1462
Sounding the Hebrew Divine Names 1461
The Christ-Child-Light in the Heart 718–719
The Evolution of Christian Prayer 713
To Call upon Jesus 679
Yahweh (Yōd-Hey-Vau-Hey) 1346–1351
Yekhidah: the Hebrew I AM 1458
Yeshua: the Secret Hebrew Name 1276–1277

Latin Names
Latin Mantras of the Rosicrucians 712
Latin Mantras to Our Lady 1510–1513
The Evolution of Christian Prayer 714–715

Sanskrit Names
Names of the Divine Mother 1493–1501
Sanskrit Divine Names for Meditation in the Heart 1269
Some Eastern Heart Mantras 457
Some Energy-Forms of the Goddess 1489
The One-Hundred Names of Lalitā 1555–1582
General Languages
Activating I AM: the Secret Name of God 1419
Christian Divine Names 1266–1267
Divine Name Solar Vibrations 1598
IAO 1034–1035
Meditations in the Heart Centre 1294–1302
More Mantras for Awakening the Heart 458–461
Names of the Eternal Feminine 469
Names of the Great Master Jesus 661
Quan Yin (Kwan Yin) 1507–1509
Rām: the Universal Name 1273
Rām: the Warrior Power 1068–1073
Some Western Heart Mantras 456
The Divine Unity Mantra 1359
The Vowels in the Heart 1303
Variations of the Name of Jesus 1356

Divine Plan
Administered by the Christ-Hierarchy and Śamballa 396
Creation and Evolution are One 160
Divine Will is a subtle form of Consciousness 221
Evolution, the Plan, the Path 1688–1692
Let Thy Will Be Done 1720
Oikonomia: the Divine Plan 650
Revelation is Continuous 1710
The Descent of the Plan (graph) 396
The Divine Plan for Humanity 1428
The Function of the Spiritual Hierarchy 1720
The Future 1709
The Goal of Human Evolution 1000
The Great Way 605
The Initiation of the World 1712–1713
The Invisible Government 980–981
The Plan is in the Divine Mind 161
The World was planned by Divine Will 544
To Manifest the Kingdom of God 1716

Divine Presence
Holiness to the Lord 1393
Meditation on the Holy Spirit 1344
Paths to the Transcendent and Immanent God 1120
Practising the Presence of God 711
Remember the Presence 1653
Smṛtī: Recollection of the Divine Presence 723
Tauḥīd: the Divine Unity 852
The Omnipresent God 1108–1109
The One God of All 869
The One God of All Religions 110
The Presence of God 1396–1397
To Love God and the World 1392–1393
To Realize the Presence of God 1398

Divya-Śrota
The power of Divine Hearing 590

Dogma
Derivation and definition 527

Dokusan
Zen definition 807

Dominions (Dominations)
Christian Classification of the Hierarchies 192

Doxa, Doxologia
Christian Hesychast definitions 743

Dragon
Drakōn: symbol of the Cosmic Fire 132
The Three Forces of the Warrior 996–997
True meaning of 142

Draṣṭā, Draṣṭuḥ
Definition and description 536, 542–543
The Spiritual Self in the Heart 551

Dreams
Dreams and Out-of-Body Experiences 300
Experiences on the Astral Plane 306–307
Interpreting dreams 300
In the dream state you create your reality 297
Nightmares 307
Powers of the Dream State 600
Retrospective dreams 300
The dream-world and dream-body 59
The Power of Conscious Dreaming 277

The Yoga of the Dream State 276, 299
Types of dreams 298–299

Dṛiṣti
Steps on the Spiritual Path 561

Drowning
and astral projection 302

Drugs
Astral projection by drugs 304
Danger of damaging the etheric web 304
Misuse for mental and emotional problems 305
Powers by Drugs? 578
Temporary Relief 1427
Used by shamans 276

Duad
The Father-Mother 24, 736

Dumah
The Silence of the Deep 1355

Durgā
A Name of Lalitā, the Goddess 1573
Definition and description 1495

Duty. *See also* Service
Duty and Spirituality 1641
Family and Duty 998–999
Return to Duty 812
Sādhanā: the Spiritual Life 1153
The Warrior seeks Peace not War 986

Dvāpara Yuga
The Period of the Mahāmanvantara 168

Dvi-Jā
Twice born, the spiritually Reborn 722

Dweller on the Threshold
The Mind-Created Devil 218

Dynamis
Definition 135
Gnostic Christian definition 737
Living Matter 134–135
The Cosmic Fire 130–131

E

Earth
A Cosmic Citizen 162–163
A dark planet 228
Mistranslation of "earth" and "heavens" 439
Pṛthivī Bīja 1544
The Earth Element 26–28
Western words and meanings for "Earth" 1351

Earthbound consciousness
On the astral subplanes 64
The earthbound "dead" 403

Earthbound spirits
Becoming earthbound after death 402–403
On the etheric subplanes 64

Easter
The Triumph of the Christ 1722

Ecstasy
Ekstasis: Christian Hesychast definition 744
Ekstasis: definition 697
Ekstasis: the Greek word for Samādhi 574
The Path to Ecstasy 696–697
To Experience Spiritual Ecstasy 1683

Ectoplasma
Definition and description 314

Ecumenical Councils
Twilight of the Christian Truth 652–653

Education
Cultivate Knowledge 1366
Destroys the Śoḍaṣī Energy 1527
Education and Fundamentalism 480
Education conditions you 485
Education for Life 484–485
Education from the Spirit 1366
Education ignores the Higher Mind 481
Education in the Future 488
Essential Knowledge 487
Mental Activity 1228
Nourishing the Goal of Life 487
The Education System 480–481

The function of education 4
The Future 1709
The Masculinization of Children 478–479
What is Education? 482–483

Effort
The Law of Effort 254

Effulgence
Effulgentia: definition 698

Ego, Egotism. *See also* Personality, Reincarnating Ego
Asmitā: your false sense of self 551
Causes of Group Disruption 1154–1155
Dissolving the Knot in the Heart 445
Ēgō: levels of meaning 1179
Egotism of inferior astral spirits 337
Existential and materialistic philosophies 264
Jīvagranthi: conditioned by the sense of "I" 1424
Mystics of Pisces and Aquarius 836
Not being aware that you are the World 1393
Surrender to the Self 87
Tantra Mind 933
The Great Ones did not destroy their egos 906–907
The Mask 38
The self and the Self 1680
Towards Group-Consciousness 186
To Achieve Liberation 1177
Who is "I AM"? 1418
Your personal sense of self is a mystery 1388

Eheieh (Eheyeh)
Activating I AM: the Secret Name of God 1419
Eheieh Asher Eheieh: translation 106, 324
Tao: the Great I AM 774
The Cosmic "I AM" 100
The Evolution of Christian Prayer 713
The Way, the Truth and the Life 670

Eidolatres
Christian Hesychast definition 746

Eidolon
Gnostic Christian definition 738

Eighth Sphere
Avītci: the Outer Darkness 63
Who are the Infesting Spirits? 310

Eikon
Christian Hesychast definition 746

Eirene
Gnostic Christian definition 738

Ekāgratā-Pariṇāma
Transformations of the Mind 1243

Ekhfā
Dimensions of the Heart (Arabic) 847

Ekklesia
Being called out from among the people 688
Christian Hesychast definition 747
Gnostic Christian definition 737
The called-out ones 128

El, Eli
Definitions 672
The Divine Unity Mantra 1359
The Evolution of Christian Prayer 713
The Lord 121

Elect. *See also* Chosen Ones
Pre-Christian term for the Initiates 676–677
The Law of the Higher Life 1134–1135
Who are the "Elect"? 128
Wisdom: the Light Path 1354

Electric
Pre-scientific definition 53

Elementals
As experienced on the Astral Plane 306
Attracted to seances 310
A source of mediumistic communications 330
Involutionary and Evolutionary Kingdoms 194
National and Religious Elementals 385
The Angelic Builders 414
The Body-Elementals 213, 989, 1312
The Elementals 195

Elements 26–29
Applications of the Elements 27
Attributes of the Elements 28–29
Dimensions of the Cosmic Fire (graph) 137
Elements of the West 360, 362
Personal Development through the Vowel Sounds 1040
Saṁyama upon the Elements 592

Symbols of the Cosmic Elements 362
The Cosmic Elements 26
The Elementary Qualities 1044
The five states of the Elements 592
The Seven Elementary Qualities 28
The Seven Subplanes of the Physical Plane (graph) 16
The Tests of the Elements 1159
Use the Powers of the Five Elements 1172

Elixir of Life
Kuṇḍalinī and Alchemy 153
To Taste the Elixir of Life 593

Eloah
Androgynous gods 121
Refers to God as Light 94

Elohīm
Misunderstood by theologians 117
The Cosmic Creator-Gods 162, 190
The Elohīm 120
Translations 474

Emotion
Dangers of negative emotions 427
Emotional Love 914
Emotional Problems 1429–1431
Emotional rape 925
Emotional stability is required for meditation 1202
Emotions and the Magical Process 361
God, the Healer of Broken Hearts 1432–1433
Mind and Body 1374–1375
Mind and emotion are not simply brain-activity 988
Negative emotions are not mental diseases 1364–1365
Negative emotions block higher telepathy 349
Negative emotions block the Soul-Light 1432
Passion and Dispassion 695
Polarities Male and Female 920–921
Reactive-Emotional Consciousness 1426
Temporary Relief 1427
The Initiation of the World 1712–1713
The nature of the Astral World 58
The Sūfī view of Mental Disorders 900
Those polarized in the astral body 376

Emotional body. *See* astral body

Emptiness. *See also* Void, Formlessness, Śūnyatā
Buddhic Consciousness is characterized by Emptiness 85
Formless Worlds 1372
The "emptiness" of Space is an illusion 1589
The Fullness of the Void 23
Touch Ultimate Emptiness (Nirvāṇa) 96

Energy. *See also* Force
Atoms are units of Energy (Śakti) 1500
A human being is an energy system 1441
Energy comes from Consciousness 134–135
Energia: definition and explanation 135
Energy follows thought 349
Energy is just a form of Light 1594
Energy Materializes 363
New Age forces and energies 278
Śakti: the One Energy 150, 1484
Subtle Energy Currents 723
The Energies of Sex and Love 912
The Energy of Śrī-Vidyā 1525
The Evolutionary Energy 143
The Light of the Logos (graph) 119
The Soul sends down three streams of Energy 428

Energy Centres. *See* Cakras

Enlightenment
Already Enlightened? 341
Enlightenment 766
Loneliness of the Enlightened 1171
Several levels of Enlightenment are possible 760
Terms of Awakening 766
There is no instant Enlightenment 573
The Basic Enlightened State 1372
The Death Process for the Enlightened 401
The Enlightened 1702
The Thought of Enlightenment 767
To "See God's Face" 891

Ennoia
Gnostic Christian definition 737

Enoch
Enoch walked with God and was no more 192, 390

Epignosis
Christian Hesychast definition 741

Epinoia
Gnostic Christian definition 738

Episteme
Greek Mystery School definition 735

Episunagoge
Christian Hesychast definition 747

Epoptai
Greek classifications of Humanity 687

Eros
Christian Hesychast definition 744
Terms of Love 914

ESP. *See also* Psychism
Confused with channelling 322
Extrasensory perception defined and explained 291

Eternal Heaven and Hell
Change is the Absolute Law 405
Eternal Heavens and Hells? 68

Eternity
59 Time and Eternity: Action and Destiny 1399–1410
Attach your Mind to the Eternal 1234–1235
The Eternal 1644
The Eternal is One 512–514
The Eternal Reality is beyond thought 1174
The Flow of Eternity is always through Now 1579
The State of Innocence 1306
The Vision of your own Eternity 1144

Ether. *See* Aether

Etheric body. *See* etheric-physical body, Liṅga-Śarīra

Etheric-physical body
A perishable Light Body 40
Becoming earthbound after death 402–403
Health and Fire 50
Mould for the physical body 413
Physical health depends on the etheric body 594
Polarities Male and Female 920–921
Space is the Etheric Body of God 109
The illusory vehicle of Prāṇa 38
The Personality Complex 36–37
The Second Death 399

Etheric-Physical World
The Seven Subplanes of the Physical Plane (graph) 16

Etheric web
Damaged by negative music 201
General description 304

Evangelion
Christian Hesychast definition 747

Evil
11 Origins of Evil 205–230
Animal Suffering 222
Appeasing the Gods? 220
Brotherhoods of Light and Darkness 228
Brothers of the Shadow 226–227
Dangers of the lower solar-plexus emotions 427
Evil: Human and Cosmic 212–217
Human Evil 212–213
Planetary Evil 214–216
Solar-Systemic and Cosmic Evil 217
Facing the Evil Mind 1087
Fight Evil with Good 993
Roots of Evil 206–207
Satan and the Fall 210–211
Separatism and the Law of Love 386
Seven things that the Lord despises 223
Shadowland 219
Some Human Evils 384–385
The Body-Elementals 213
The Dark Side of the Force 219
The Evil Mind 224–225
The Evil of Criticism 1156–1157
The Law of Action 992–993
The Mind-Created Devil 218
The Mind Divine or Demonic 212
The Paradox of Evil 208–209
The Seed of Evil 221
The Sufferings of Man 223
True War 985
Wickedness in High Places 207

Evolution. *See also* Creation
9 Creation and Evolution 159–186
Universal Evolution
Creation and Evolution are One 160
Evolution: Latin definition 160
Existence is Purposeful 173
Fundamentalist paranoia about Evolution 683
Hierarchies of Life (graph) 1721
Involution, Evolution, Dissolution 165
Involutionary and Evolutionary Kingdoms 194
Natural and Supernatural Evolution 160
The Action of the Primordial Sound (graph) 165
The Creation Process 165
The Cycle of Manifestation (graph) 134
The Evolutionary Energy 143
The Law of Polarity 164
The Plan is in the Divine Mind 161
The Sevenfold Earth-Evolution 169
The Solar Dharma 163
Human Evolution 170–186. *See also* Spiritual Path
18 Human Consciousness 373–396
22 Awakening the Human Glory 489–510
56 The Heart and the Future Evolution of Man 1309–1334
Beyond Natural Evolution 1312
Evolution, the Plan, the Path 1688–1692
Evolutionary Leaps in Consciousness 184–185
Evolutionary States of Human Consciousness (graph) 172
Evolutionary Symbolism of the Cross 179
From Subjective to Objective 173
Human Evolutionary Epochs 176–178
Human Evolution and the Awakened Cakras (graph) 171
Human Involution and Evolution 170–172
Manifestation of the Sons of God 180
Evolutionary Development of the Cakras (graph) 178
Paths of Spiritual Evolution 1693
Planetary Stimulation 181
Spiritual Evolution for all Humanity is the Goal of Yoga 521
Spiritual Evolution is movement into higher vibration 1413
The Far-Future Evolution of Humanity (graph) 183
The Future Evolution of Humanity (graph) 182
The Goal of Human Evolution 1000
The Law of Radiation 175
The Mystery of the Pleiades 181
Towards Group-Consciousness 186
Types of Humanity 376–377
Vertical Evolution and the Path 174

Extrasensory perception. *See* ESP, Psychism

Eye of Śiva. *See also* Śiva-Netra
The Ājñā Cakra 49
True clairvoyance 292–293

F

Face
Makroposophus: the Great Face of God 795
To "See God's Face" 891
Your Original Face 87

Faith. *See also* Belief
Faith and Wisdom 849
The Solar and Human Heart 1592
To Succeed in your Quest 1330
What is True Faith? 1284

Fall
of Adam and Eve 132
Satan and the Fall 210–211

Fallen angels
Nephilīm: the fallen angels 211
Not the original source of evil 217
Roots of Evil 206–207
The Makara and Asuras 202

Family
Dysfunctional families 385
Family and Duty 998–999
Family and loneliness 1170
The Breakdown of Family 473
You have two families 1156

Fanā
Sacrificing the personal self 836
Sūfī term for Nirvāṇa 94
The Muslim Deification Process 1191

Fanā'fi-llāh
Annihilation in God 513, 836
To experience the Mantram of Unification 867

Fasting
Fasting and Psychic Experience 308

Fate. *See also* Destiny
Terms of Destiny 261
Your Fate is Before your Eyes 246

Father
Dimensions of the Cosmic Fire (graph) 137
Jewish symbol for the Godhead 112
Mythical Concepts of God 104–105
The Father Force: the White Brilliance 151, 153
The Holy Trinity 1342
The House of the Father 667
The Kingdom of God (graph) 123
The Many Mansions (graph) 611
The Masculine God 649, 671
The Monad: the Father in Heaven 1322
The Threefold Logos 662
Variations in symbolism 113

Fear
Face directly your fears 1433
Fear and Stress (Metanoia) 1434
Fear of the Lord? 234
Overstimulated Solar Plexus Centre 1431
The Hell Condition 406–407

Feelings. *See* Emotion

Feminine Principle. *See also* Women, Goddess
Become feminine in order to meditate 1207
Become Yin to approach Tao 476–477
Cosmic Sensitivity 1009
Female Buddhas 1110
Female energies destroyed by education system 478–479
Female polarity: definition 25
Feminine or Feminist? 468
Getting in Touch with your Inner Feminine 1010–1011
Her Transcendental Form 145
Lalitā: the Eternal Feminine 1484–1485
Madonna: the Mother Principle 470
Male and Female Systems of Spirituality (graph) 1112
Sophia 146
Tantra is the Way of Feminine Consciousness 944
The Divine Bipolarity 471
The Eternal Feminine 469
The Feminine Heart 925
The Feminine Suppressed 910
The Feminine Virtues 468–469
The Human Bipolarity 472
The Mother of the World 147
The Śoḍaṣī Energy 1527
The True Feminine 1516
The Virgin and the Mother 144

Feminism
Confusion about femininity 468, 476
Feminine or Feminist? 468

Fiat
The Cosmic Christ 662–663

Fifth Kingdom. *See* Spiritual Hierarchy

Fifth State
Cosmic Consciousness 500

Fire. *See also* Cosmic Fire
Agni Bīja 1544–1545
Baptism by Fire and the Spirit 627, 718, 1348
Health and Fire 50
Spontaneous Human Combustion 316
Tapas: Purification by Fire 571
The Body of Fire 1334
The Burning Heart 631
The Fire Element 26–28
The Fire in the Heart 1287
The Fire of Love 1255
Wounds of Love 699

Flood
The Great Flood 272–275

Fohat. *See also* Kuṇḍalinī-Fohat
Definition 131
Kuṇḍalinī-Fohat 148
The Cosmic Fire 130–137

Force. *See also* Energy, Life-force
Astral forces and the Magical Process 360–361
Cosmic Forces influencing the New Age 278
Karma is the equilibrating force 240
"May the Force be with you" 132
Polarities of Forces between the Planes (graph) 25
Subconscious Forces 236–237

Supernatural Forces 357
The Dark Side of the Force 219
The One Force 133
The Seven Centres of Force in the Human Species 1385
The Three Forces at work in Nature and Humanity 1693
The Three Forces of the Warrior 996–997

Forgiveness. *See also* Love, Compassion
From Hate to Love 229
Love and Sacrifice 1139
Oneness and Love 1450
Shadowland 219
The greatest healing agent 1379
The Messiah Jesus 666
The Soul-Power 1305
The Supreme Act of Karma 264–265

Form. *See* Rūpa

Formlessness. *See also* Arūpa, Void, Śūnyatā
Arūpa-Loka: formless worlds 74
Formless Worlds, Formless Consciousness 1372–1373
The Fullness of the Void 23
The Goal of Zen 760

Fortune. *See also* Fate, Destiny
Terms of Destiny 261

Fortune-telling. *See also* Prophecy
Intelligent use of Free Will 297

Forty-nine Fires
The forty-nine states of matter 14

Fourth dimension
Time is not the fourth dimension 22
Walls of Time and Space (graph) 21
We already live in the fourth dimension 270

Fourth Kingdom. *See* Human Kingdom

Fourth State. *See also* Turīya, Pure Consciousness
Buddhic Consciousness 86
Formless Consciousness 1373
Turīya: the Fourth State 498–499

Four Deaths. *See also* Death
From Bondage to Liberation (graph) 422
Opportunities for Liberation 420
The Natural Death Process 399

Four Worlds
The Four Kabbalistic Worlds 360

Francis of Assisi
A practical Mystic 91
The Prayer of St Francis of Assisi 92

Freedom. *See also* Liberation, Salvation, Mokṣa, Mukti
Freedom from Karma 255
Freedom is Boundless Love 932
Reincarnation and Freedom 998
The Discovery of Truth 85
The Truth shall make you Free 682–683
To Become a Jīvanmukta in this Lifetime 259

Free Will. *See also* Will, Will-power
Communication with the Invisible 371
Free Will and Destiny 294–295
Free Will is limited by Karma 1169
Intelligent use of Free Will 297
Live and Let Live 940
Your Fate is Before your Eyes 246

Fundamentalism
31 Christian Fundamentalism 675–688
Belief and Experience 676–677
Developing the Cosmic-Sense 1709
Education and Fundamentalism 480
Fundamentalism is based on duality 1108–1109
Protagonists of Ignorance 383
Religious Reactionaries 287–288
The abuse of Divine Magic 365
The Crime of Fundamentalism 669

Future. *See also* Time, Being in the Moment
Cosmic Intervention 282
Education in the Future 488
Human Response to Cosmic Intervention 286
Past, Present and Future 1400–1401
Prophecy and Destiny 294–295
Spirituality Past and Future 1104
The Far-Future Evolution of Humanity (graph) 183
The Future Evolution of Humanity (graph) 182
The Future for Mankind 1709
The New Age and You 1708
The New Atlantis 280

G

Gabriel
Hebrew Angelic Names Meditation 1462
Hebrew Divine Words for Healing 1456

Gaia
Western words for "Earth" 1351

Galactic Lord
A vast Living Being 140
The Form of God is Space 109

Gandharvas
Can assist in devotional worship 369
The Gandharvas 200
Understanding your Work in Silence 1024

Garimā
The General Powers 580

Gaurī
A Name of Lalitā, the Goddess 1580

Gautama Buddha. *See* Buddha

Gāyatrī
67 The Gāyatrī-Mantra 1601–1642
A Name of Lalitā, the Goddess 1561
Brahma-Gāyatrī-Mantra 1638–1639
Detailed Meanings of the Root Gāyatrī-Mantra 1610–1611
Gāyatrī: definition 1603
Gāyatrī-Prāṇāyāma: Sun-Breathing 1553
Gāyatrī-Sādhanā: the Sun-Spiritual-Practice 1586
Guhya-Gāyatrī, Gudha-Gāyatrī 1531, 1602
Meanings of the Root Gāyatrī-Mantra 1609
Solar Meditation in the Cakras 1640
The Basic Hymn 1603
The Gāyatrī-Mantra (variations) 1608–1637
The Savitā-Mantra 1602
The Secret Gāyatrī Mantra 1526–1527, 1531

Geburah
Dīn: Divine Justice 648
The Kabbalistic Tree of Life 358–359
The principle of Karma 240

Gehinnom
The Underworld 60

Genii
The Angels 197

Ghosts. *See* earthbound spirits

Glamour
Channelling is Spiritual Ignorance 342
Difficulties on the Path 1167
Psychic Disruption 1155

Glands
The glands and health 53
The Major Cakras and the Glands (graph) 44

Glory
Crowned with Glory 197
Jesus: the Lord of Glory 667

Glossolalia
Speaking in tongues 312–313

Gnomes
The Elementals 195

Gnosis
Christian Hesychast definition 741
Definition 129, 1108
Gnosis Theou: Christian Hesychast definition 741
Gnostic Christian definition 738
Greek Mystery School definition 733
The Path of Gnosis 1121
The same as Ātmā-Vidyā and Brahmā-Vidyā 95
What is Wisdom? 1685

Gnostics
Gnostic descriptions of the Deity 1594
Gnostic terms for Nirvāṇa 95
Gnōstikos: Gnostic Christian definition 738
Gnōstikos: Greek Mystery School definition 733
Gnōstikos: the Enlightened 1105
Greek words from Gnostic Christianity 736–738
Persecution of the Knowers 656–658
The Gnostics 645
The Gnostic Teachings 656, 1108

Gnosti Seauton
Know Thyself 324, 1389

God
7 The Divine Being 103–140
66 The Mystery of the Sun 1585–1600
The Nature of God
Can God be Angry? 106
Eastern and Western concepts of God 754–755
Fear of the Lord? 234
God Immanent and Transcendent 111
God is a Sublime Mystery 127
In Search of Reality 1174
Mythical Concepts of God 104–105
Qualities of the Divine Being 107
Reality (Metanoia) 1416–1417
The Greatness of God (Arabic) 875
The Lord? 121
The Omnipresent God 1108–1109
The Sūfī God 838
What is "God"? 108
What is Reality? 1175
The One God
Tauḥīd: the Divine Unity 852
The Eternal is One 512–514
The One 1686–1687
The One and Only 839
The One God of All 869
The One God of All Religions 110
The One Transcendental Reality 515
The Three-Faced God 113
God-Immanent. *See also* Brahmā, Īśvara, Divine Presence
Dimensions of the Solar Logos in Cosmic Space 1591
From Matter to Light 761
Immanent: definition 111
The Constitution of God-Immanent 122–126
The Constitution of the Solar Logos (graph) 124
The Doctrine of the Logoi 116–117
The Elohīm 120
The Logos: the Word of God 114–115
The Manifested-God 1589
The Presence of God 1396–1397
The Primordial Light 119
The Universal Creator-God 1588
Vāk: the Divine Speech 118
God-Transcendent. *See also* Parabrahman
Parabrahman: definition 111
The Transcendental Godhead 112
The Universes are not separate from the Absolute Godhead 1589
Transcendent: definition 111
God Male and Female
Dimensions of the Cosmic Fire (graph) 137
Śiva-Śakti 1521
The Divine Bipolarity 471
The Feminine Suppressed 910
The Masculine God of the Old Testament 649
The Temple of the Goddess 1492
God in Humanity. *See also* Heart: God in the Heart
Entering the Lost Kingdom 1176–1177
God in the Heart 634–635
God, the Healer of Broken Hearts 1432–1433
Incarnations of the Sun 1593
Sex Natural and Divine 926–927
The Mystery within the Heart 1315
The One and Only 839
The Revelation of God 854
The Temple of God 639
The Way, the Truth and the Life 670
To Partake of God's Nature 640
Within Man, God Can Rule 1707
God-Consciousness
Brahmā-Avasthā: the God-State 495–496, 502
God-Consciousness is the Wholeness of Life 504–505
Stages on the Path 1136–1137
Step Four of the Meditational Path 1198
The One 1686–1687
The Third Circle of Life 1448
Variations in terminology 500
Goddess. *See also* Divine Mother, World Mother, Kuṇḍalinī
8 Kuṇḍalinī and the Goddess 141–158
21 The Call of the World Mother 467–488
62 The Great Goddess 1483–1490
63 The Heart of the Divine Mother 1491–1514
64 Śrī-Vidyā: the Holy Science 1515–1554
65 The One-Hundred Names of Lalitā 1555–1582

What is the Goddess?

Erroneous concepts of the Goddess 150
Lalitā: the Eternal Feminine 1484–1485
Lalitā: the Ultimate Goddess 1556
Līlā: the Play of the Goddess 1520
Śakti: the Divine Energy 1484
Śakti: the Energy of the Goddess 1486–1488
Śakti: the One Energy 150
Śiva-Śakti 1521
The Breath of the Divine Mother 142
The Divine Bipolarity 471
The Evolutionary Energy 143
The Mother of the World 147
The True Feminine 1516

Aspects of the Goddess

Her Transcendental Form 145
Holy Knowledge 1517
Kuṇḍalinī-Fohat 148–149
Quan Yin: the Mother of Compassion 1507–1509
Tao: the Great Mother 146
The Feminine Virtues 468–469
The Immaculate Heart of Mary, Our Lady 1513
The Mother Light 1533
The Śoḍaṣī Energy 1527
The two Aspects of Devī, the Goddess 1516
The Virgin and the Mother 144
The World Mother of Compassionate Heart 145

The Path to the Goddess

Bīja-Mantra Practice 1552
Gāyatrī (Sun) Breathing 1553
Meditation on the Names of Lalitā, the Goddess 1557
The Living Form of the Goddess in the Light 1522–1523
The Path of Mantra and the Goddess 1490
The Role of the Divine Female in the Salvation/Liberation Process 1502–1503
The Silent State 1554
The Temple of the Goddess 1492
The Way to the Divine Heart 1505
The Wisdom of the Goddess 1525
To Approach the Goddess 1513
To Meditate on Quan Yin 1508
Vibration and Mantra 1518–1519

Names of the Goddess

Divine Names of Our Lady 1510
Madonna: the Mother Principle 470
Mūlaprākṛtī: the Root of Nature 471
Names of the Eternal Feminine 469
Some Energy-Forms of the Goddess 1489
Sophia: the Boundless Feminine Intelligence 146
Śrī Jagadambā: the Mother of the World 1498–1499
The One-Hundred Names of Lalitā 1558–1581

Goddess Mantras

Amṛteśvarī: the Supreme Spirit-Mother 1494
Āuṁ: the Holy Spirit as Cosmic Mother 1501
Fertilizing the Heart of the Divine Mother for the Conception of the Divine Child within you 1504
Garments of Light (Śrī-Vidyā) 1526–1529
General Children's Initiation Mantra into the Energy of the Goddess 1506
Kālimā: the Mother Beyond Time 1495
Latin Mantras to Our Lady 1510
Mantras to Connect to Our Lady (Latin) 1512
Ōṁ Śrī: the Holy Vibration 1520
Paraśakti: the Supreme Power 1500
Potent Vibrations: Bīja-Mantra 1542–1551
Sāvitrī: the Spiritual Sun as Mother 1496–1497
She is Nirmala-Sundarī 1494
The Bālā-Mantra 1532
The Bhairavī-Mantra 1539
The Blissful Mother: Mother of Immortal Bliss 1493
The Cāmuṇḍā-Mantra 1540
The Kālī-Mantra 1541
The Kamalā-Mantra 1536–1537
The Kumārikā-Mantra 1534
The Mātangī-Mantra 1535
The Mṛtyuṁjaya-Mantra 1540
The Rāmā-Mantra 1541
The Rati-Mantra 1539
The Saptaḍaṣī-Mantras 1533
The Śrī-Vidyā-Vajra-Mantra 1531
The Śrī-Vidyā-Mantra 1530
The Strī-Mantra 1538
Treasures of the Goddess 1524

Godō
Zen definition 807

Gods and Goddesses. *See also* Devas
Appeasing the Gods? 220
Denizens of the Heaven Worlds 77
Human beings are gods limited to a human form 1369
Invoking the gods and goddesses 366–371
Unnecessary Practices 1111
Worship only the Divine Self 1226
Ye are gods 1393

Golden City with a Thousand Gates
The lower heavens 65

Gopī
Definition 1319

Govinda
The God within the Heart 1298
The Master of the Heart 1319

Grace
Christian and Jewish understanding of Grace 679
Mysterious Grace 1311

Grail
The symbol for Spiritual Regeneration 1511

Grand Heavenly Men
The Solar Logoi 217

Granthi
Dissolving the Knot in the Heart 445
Knots of Consciousness 445
Obstacles to Higher Consciousness 1424
Two great knots must be untied 497

Gravity
The Guṇas 139–140

Great Day of Be With Us
Returning to our Origin 17
When Nature merges into Nirvāṇa and Paranirvāṇa 185

Great White Brotherhood. *See* Spiritual Hierarchy

Greek
34 The Greek Mystery Language 731–748
Greek classifications of Humanity 687
Living Matter (Greek and Sanskrit terminology) 134–135
The Great Greek Mantra to Jesus 708–709
The Human Constitution (Greek) 39
The Mysticism of Saint Paul 666

Greetings
Nāmaste: the personal greeting of old India 1703
The Significance of Warrior Greetings 1023

Gṛhastha
Periods of Life in Vedic India 907
The best Mantra for the Gṛhastha 1602

Grounding
The importance of being grounded 1167
The Practice of Grounding 1005

Group-Consciousness
50 The Aquarian Group-Consciousness 1145–1172
Causes of Group Disruption 1154–1155
Family and Duty 998–999
From Hate to Love 229
Group Work 1146
Monks and Disciples 991
Piscean Spirituality and New Age Spirituality 1706
Remember Group Unity 1172
Responsibility as a member of a Soul Group 1150, 1164
Separatism and the Law of Love 386
The Fields of Life (the Great Breath) 1165
The Group Heart 1152
The Laws of Group Psychology 1384
The Structure of the Warrior School 1006–1007
The Supreme Act of Karma 264–265
Towards Group-Consciousness 186

Group Karma. *See also* Karma
Types of Karma 243

Guhya-Gāyatrī, Gudha-Gāyatrī
Invokes the Feminine Aspect of the Solar Logos 1602
The Śoḍaṣī-Mantra 1531

Guhya-Vidyā, Gupta-Vidyā
Esoteric Knowledge 1218
The Path of Seeing 552

Guṇa
Karma and the Guṇas 1406
Nirguṇā: a Name of Lalitā, the Goddess 1575
Nir-Guṇa, Sa-Guṇa 1498
Qualities of the mind 1208–1209

The Cāmuṇḍā-Mantra 1540
The Guṇas 139–140
The Three Forces at work in Nature and Humanity 1693
Triguṇā: a Name of Lalitā, the Goddess 1575

Guru. *See also* Sat Guru, Spiritual Teachers, Spiritual Masters
Definition 30
Detailed description 389
Do not "follow" a Master outside yourself 1229
Gurus speak the Wisdom of their own Souls 325–327
Guru Bīja 1550
Guru-Śakti: the Energy of the Goddess 1487
Initiation from a Guru (Dīkṣā) 1225
Inner Guidance (Metanoia) 1464
Meditation on the Form of the Guru 1225
Radiance of the Guru seen in the Third-Eye 916
Rely on your Inner Self 1226
Revelation is Continuous 1710
Sat Guru: definition 343
The Mystery Schools and Āśramas 1148
The personality of the Guru must be imperfect 325
The Sacrifice of the Teachers 1150–1151
The True Teachers 1694–1695
Vajra-Guru: Indestructible Teacher 1302

Gurudeva
Derivation and definition 1473
The God within your Heart Centre 1302

H

Ha
Potent Vibrations: Bīja-Mantra 1551

Ha-Shem
Definition 411
The Name of Names 1259

Ḥabīb
The Sūfīs fall in Love with God 850

Hades
Lowest regions of the Astral World 218
The Golden Ass story 303
The Underworld 6, 60

Hairesis. *See* Heresy

Ḥāj
Pilgrimage to the Real 829, 892, 899

Hāl
The eighth stage of the Journey of the Heart 857
The Revelation of God 854

Hālah
Definitions (Arabic and Persian) 857

Halleluyah
Meditations in the Heart Centre 1297
The Evolution of Christian Prayer 713

Hallucination
Hallucinations and out-of-body experiences 305
Hallucinations in the Afterlife 408–409

Halo
Hālah: the internal shining of the Light 857
The awakened Crown Cakra 431
The Law of Radiation 175

Hāṁ
Potent Vibrations: Bīja-Mantra 1546

Hamartia
Christian Hesychast definition 745
Have mercy on me, a sinner? 707
Wrongly translated as "sin" 683

Haṁsa. *See also* Sohaṁ
Definitions 1655, 1667
Gāyatrī (Sun) Breathing 1553
Haṁsah: breathing in and out of the Heart 461
Pure-Breathing 1328
Rest in the Great Breath 1654
Three Kinds of Breathing Meditation 1220

Hanael
Hebrew Angelic Names Meditation 1462

Happiness. *See also* Bliss, Ānanda
Happiness Exists Within 1381
Meditation and the Joy of Living 1012–1013
Return to Primeval Happiness 1179
The Experience of the Transcendent 1378
Towards Bliss-Consciousness 423

Happy Hunting Ground
The lower heavens 65

Ḥaqīqat
Stage Three of the Radiant Way 831
The fourth stage of Spiritual Life 1161
The ninth stage of the Journey of the Heart 857

Hara. *See also* Solar Plexus Centre
Japanese Zen focuses in the solar plexus 797, 798
Traditional focus of Zen meditation 809
Zen definition 807

Hara (Sanskrit)
An aspect of the Śiva energy 1473

Hare Krishnas
Materialistic heavens 65
Prabhupāda made Kṛṣṇa to be a person 677

Harijan
The Untouchables 379

Harmlessness. *See* Ahiṁsā

Harmony. *See also* Balance, Peace
Ray 4: Beauty, Harmony 56

Ha-Sauḥ
Definition 1534, 1537

Hasidim
Definition and description 512
Hasid: definition 649
The Hasidim 648–649
The Names and Mental Prayer in the Heart 1261
The Silent Ones 1355

Haṭha Yoga. *See also* Yoga
Activities of Yoga-Mārga 520
Haṭha: definition 157
Haṭha: derivation and definition 524
Haṭha Yoga and Rāja Yoga 524–525
Saṁyama on the physical body 594
Traditional concept of 522–525
Unnecessary Practices 1111

Hatred
and the misuse of Prayer 365
A true Warrior has no hostile tendencies 984–987
From Hate to Love 229
Hate does not exist in God 1265
Reactive-Emotional Consciousness 1426
The Hell Condition 406–407
Thought and Energy 349

Head
Being-in-the-Moment Meditation in the Head 1245
Dangers of awakening the Head before the Heart 428
Develop a pure Heart and a refined Mind 1286
Divine Love in the Head 916
From Head to Heart 427
Head and Heart (graph) 429
Heart and Mind 429
Linking the Head with the Heart 897
Qualities of the Head and the Heart 426–433
Taming the Mind 899
The Head-person must descend into the Heart 837
The Two Paths 1112
The Way of Knowledge (Rays) 55
The Way of the Mind 1238–1239
Uniting Head and Heart 1130–1131

Healing
Deva Orders who inspire healers 198
Divine Name Solar Vibrations 1598
Future Therapy 372
God, the Healer of Broken Hearts 1432–1433
Healing (Metanoia) 1463
Healing Sound-Vibration Formula 1064–1067
Hebrew Divine Words for Healing 1456
IOEL: The Healing Mind 1457
Magical Healing 372
Planetary healing 181
Spiritual Healing 1379
Temporary Relief 1427
The Healing Power of Touch 919
The Healing Sun Mantra 1599
The Inner Healer 1454
The Laws of Group Psychology 1384

Health. *See also* disease
Complete health is not possible 1432
Emotional problems and health 1429–1431
Haṭha Yoga: the "health yoga"? 524–525
Health and Fire 50

Malfunctioning Cakras 53
Mind and Body 1374–1375
Physical health depends on the etheric body 594
Sexuality and the Life-force 912
Skill in Action 989
To be healthy you need Āyustejas 1488

Hearing. *See also* Listening, Meditational Practices
Listening 1215
Hear the Sound within the Silence 1651
Just Hearing (Warrior) 1018
The Experience of Mysticism 636–637
The Path of Hearing 553
The power of Divine Hearing 590
The scriptures were heard in deep meditation 1216
Zen Listening 787–793

Heart. *See also* Hṛdaya, Hṛdayaṁ
20 The Mystery of the Heart 425–466
28 The Heart of Christianity 623–640
40 The Sūfī Heart 843–862
43 The Circle of Love 905–944
53 The Heart and Spontaneous Meditation 1227–1248
54 The Heart and the Lost Art of Prayer 1251–1278
55 Hṛdayaṁ: Meditations in the Heart Centre 1279–1308
56 The Heart and the Future Evolution of Man 1309–1334
57 The Way of Holiness 1335–1360
63 The Heart of the Divine Mother 1491–1514

What is the Heart?
Heart and Mind 429
Qalb: the Sūfī Heart 848
The Abode of the Self 434
The Ancient Heart-Path 845
The Heart (Hṛdayaṁ) 1282–1283
The Heart is essentially Consciousness 1595
The Kingdom of God 1715
The Truth in the Heart 851
The Universal Heart 436
What is the Heart? 435

The Universal Heart
Hṛdaya-Cakra: the Heart Centre 1616
Incarnations of the Sun 1593
Mystical Union 846
The Activity of the Divine Heart 1675
The Group Heart 1152
The Heart of the Solar Logos 1327
The Immaculate Heart of Mary, Our Lady 1513
The Mystery of the Christ 1724
The Revelation of God 854
The Sacred Heart of Jesus 673
The Solar and Human Heart 1592
The Universal Heart 436

The Heart Centre
Anāhata Cakra: general description 47
A reflection of our Solar Logos 1593
Dimensions of the Heart (Arabic) 847
Entry point for the Soul 1194
Heart and Mind 429
Hṛdaya-Cakra: the Heart Centre 1616
Hṛt-Padma: the Heart Lotus 1505
Sanskrit terms for the Heart Centre 448
The Feminine Heart 925
The Heart and the Energy Centres 1332
The Hebrew Heart 1263
The Lotus of the Heart 446
The Secret of the Heart 1280
The Spiritual Heart Complex (graph) 1505
The Three Regions of the Heart 463

God in the Heart
Christ-Consciousness 443
God in the Heart 634–635
Incarnations of the Sun 1593
My Beloved Lives in my Heart 1290–1291
Quest for the Self 1317
Sex Natural and Divine 926–927
The Abode of the Self 434
The Christ in the Heart 441
The Eastern Heart 448
The Lover of God 853
The Mystery within the Heart 1315
The Perennial Source of Love 438
The Saviour in the Heart 1296
The Temple of the Goddess 1492
The Truth in the Heart 851
The Universal Christ 440

Experiencing the Heart
Death in the Heart 444
Experiencing the Awakening Heart 463–465
Falling in Love 922
Heart Knowing 1286
Heart Love 915
Heart Union and Sexual Union 1140
Physical Symptoms in the Heart 462
Pure Consciousness in the Heart 447
Qualities of the Spiritual-Heart-Consciousness 1329
Signs of Progress in the Heart 1289
The Experience of the Heart 1280–1281
The Lover and the Beloved 466
Wisdom and Understanding 439

The Fire in the Heart
Cultivate the Fires of Love 928–929
Hṛdaya-Taijasa: the Heart-Fire 432
The Burning Heart 631
The Fire in the Heart 1287
The Fire of Love 1255
Wounds of Love 699

Purifying the Heart
Develop a pure Heart and a refined Mind 1286
Devotion to Kṛṣṇa 449
Dissolving the Knot in the Heart 445
Purify the Heart 701
Tapas: Spiritual Purification 571
The Path of Purification 1337
The Pure Heart 1300
The Purification of the Heart 849
The Secret of the Heart 1280
The State of Inner Purity 497
The State of Innocence 1306
The Way of the Radiant Heart 452–455
To Invoke God in your Heart 1293
To Worship the Divine Incarnations 1270–1272

Guarding the Heart
Do not leave your Heart unguarded 704
Guard your Heart 1328
Phylaki Kardias: the Guarding of the Heart 632
The Way of the Radiant Heart 452

The Heart-Path
Awaken First the Heart 428
Bhakti Yoga: Divine Union by Devotion 1128
Christian Mysticism 450–451
Crisis and Revelation 1711
Family and Duty 998–999
From Head to Heart 427
Heart Action 1331
Hṛdaya-Mārga: the Threefold Way of the Heart 1236
Let the Light Shine 1307
Mysterious Knowledge of the Siddhas 1310–1311
New Aquarian Energies negate the Heart 426
On Love and Meditation 1140–1143
On the Wings of Devotion 1129
Peace on Earth 1304
Search out your Heart 437
Stages on the Way of Holiness 1336–1339
  The Path of Illumination 1338
  The Path of Purification 1337
  The Path of Union 1339
The Ancient Heart-Path 845
The Christian Heart-Path 632
The Heart-Path (graph) 446
The Holy Path 1285
The Importance of the Heart in Approaching God 432–433
The Initiation of the World 1712–1713
The Journey of the Heart (Sūfī) 855–857
The Path to Immortality 430–431
The River of Light 1308
The Thread of the Heart (graph) 844
The Two Ways of the Heart 1347
The Unfoldment of the Light (Christian) 718–721
The Way of Mysticism (Rays) 55
The Way of the Christian Mystic 626–629
Uniting Head and Heart 1130–1131
What is True Service? 1714

Heart Practice. *See* Meditational Practices

Heart Mantras. *See also* Mantra, Divine Name
Christian Divine Names 1266–1267
Hebrew Divine Names to be Invoked in the Heart 1262–1263
Keys to the Heart 1314–1327
Latin Mantras of the Rosicrucians 712

Latin Mantras to Our Lady 1510–1512
Meditate in your Heart (Sanskrit) 1288
Meditations in the Heart Centre 1294–1302
More Mantras for Awakening the Heart 458–461
Some Arabic Prayers to the Deity 850–851
Some Eastern Heart Mantras 457
Some Sanskrit Divine Names for Meditation in the Heart 1269
Some Western Heart Mantras 456
Sūfī Mantras for Meditation (Arabic) 874–877
The 99 Arabic Divine Names of God 878
The Beautiful Names (Arabic) 1264–1265
The Divine Unity Mantra 1359
The Evolution of Christian Prayer 713–716
The Great Greek Mantra to Jesus 708–710
The Mantram of Unification in the Heart Centre 866–868
The Secret Heart-Mantra 1534
The Vowels in the Heart 1303
Three Meditations in the Heart (Sanskrit) 1292
Yeshua: the Secret Hebrew Name 1276–1277

Heart Centre. *See* Heart, Anāhata Cakra, Hṛdaya

Heaven

Beyond Heaven 1234
Denizens of the Heaven Worlds 77
Eternal Heavens and Hells? 68
Form-heavens 65
Intellectual heavens 66–67
Lower heavens 65–67
Mind-Created Heavens and Hells 6–7
Mistranslation of "earth" and "heavens" 439
Sukhāvatī: the place of happiness 76
The Christian Cosmo-Conception 19
The Fifth World (Arabic) 888
The seven-layered Space or Ākāśa 271
The Seven Heavens 76
The state of mind resulting from White Magic 364
To Experience Heaven 82
Traditional concepts of Heaven 6–7
Wars in Heaven 271
Western words and meanings for "Heaven" 1352

Heavenly Men

The Planetary Logoi 217

Hebrew

Hebrew Divine Names to be Invoked in the Heart 1262–1263
Language of the Gods 200
Meditation on the Divine Names 1454-1460
Hebrew Divine Words for Healing 1456
Hebrew Vowels were kept secret 1457
Sounding the Hebrew Divine Names 1461
Sounding the Hebrew Angelic Names 1462
The Divine Name expressed in the Hebrew Alphabet 1552
The Hebrew Heart 1263
Yeshua: the Secret Hebrew Name 1276–1277

Heimarmene

Gnostic Christian definition 737

Hell

Avītci: definition 218
Change is the Absolute Law 405
Derivation of the word "Hell" 6, 60
Eternal Heavens and Hells? 68
Human Evil 212–213
If you visit the Hell Worlds 307
Mind-Created Heavens and Hells 6–7
Narakā: definition 218
Self-Created Hells 407
The Christian Cosmo-Conception 19
The Eighth Sphere 63
The Hell Condition 406–407
The Mind-Created Devil 218
The seventh astral subplane 62–63
The state of mind resulting from Black Magic 364
Traditional concepts of Hell 6–7

Hellfire

Infernus: the Eighth Sphere 63

Heremites

Christian Hesychast definition 739

Heresy

Hairesis: choosing another way or opinion 514
Hairesis: definition 655
Hairesis: Greek Mystery School definition 734
Persecution of the Knowers 656–658
The Heretics 655

Hermaphrodite
Derivation and definition 920
The Law of Polarity 164

Hermes
Gnostic Christian definition 738

Hermes Trismegistus
Teaching on the One Force 133

Hero
Heros: A god or a demi-god 274
The true Hero 1007

Hesychasm
Greek Words used by the Christian Hesychasts 739–747
Hesychasm vs fundamentalist prayer 681
Hesychast: definition and description 450–451, 624
Hesychia, Hesychasm, Hesychast: definitions 739
Interior Prayer 691–695
The Silent Ones 1355

Hexalpha, Hexad
Gnostic Christian definition 736

He Of Whom Nought May Be Said
A description of God 112, 126
Worshipped in Atlantis 270

Hidoni
Christian Hesychast definition 745

Hierarchies. *See also* Spiritual Hierarchy
10 The Creative Hierarchies 187–204
Angelic Rulers of the Planes (graph) 199
Angels and Demons 193
A spiritual definition of the Hierarchies 190
Children of the Cosmic Creators 190
Children of the Sun 1590
Christian Classification of the Hierarchies 192
Hierarchies of Life (graph) 1721
Hierarkhia: derivation and definition 190
Inconceivable Divine Realities 126
Involutionary and Evolutionary Kingdoms 194
Language of the Gods 200
Manifestation of the Sons of God 180
Pseudo-hierarchies on the Astral Plane 66
Saṅgha: the Spiritual Hierarchy 394–396
Some Facts about the Devas 198
The Angels 196–197
The Devas according to the Rays 199
The Elementals 195
The Gandharvas 200
The Hierarchies occupy the same Space 20
The Populated Universe 188–189
The Sevenfold Earth-Evolution 169
The term "Creative Hierarchies" 188
The Twelve Creative Hierarchies (graph) 191
Wickedness in High Places 207

Hierophant
Hierophantēs: definition 325
Hierophantēs: Greek Mystery School definition 734
Tarot Key 5: The Hierophant 558
The Attitude for Yoga 558
The Mystery Schools and Āśramas 1148

Hierosgamos
Gnostic Christian definition 737

Higher Mind. *See also* Abstract Mind, Causal Mind, Kāraṇa-Manas
Education ignores the Higher Mind 481
Intellectus: definition 375
Kāraṇa-Manas 34
Manas: higher and lower 78
Spiritual Reading 1113
The Intellect 891
The means to see God 1177
Those polarized in the causal body 376

Higher Self. *See* Individuality, Triad, Self, Ātman

Hindrances. *See* obstacles

Hiraṇyagarbha
A mysterious golden body 1313
Definition 391
The Human Aura 42–43

History
Esoteric History of the Piscean Religions 833
The Equation of History (graph) 834
The Influence of the Seven Rays 834–835
Zodiacal History 833

Hitler
Misuse of Svastika and the term Āryan 179

Hod
The Kabbalistic Tree of Life 358–359

Holiness
57 The Way of Holiness 1335–1360
Holiness to the Lord 1393
The Four Ways of Holiness 1345
The Holy of Holies 101
The Holy Vibration 1520

Holy Breath. *See also* Breath, Holy Spirit
Christian Meditation on the Holy Breath 1346–1353
Degrees of Union with the Holy Breath 1349
Rest in the Great Breath 1654–1655
Ruach-Elohīm: the Breath of the Creator-Gods 167
Surrender to the Holy Breath 1341
The Breath of the Divine Mother 142
The Fields of Life (the Great Breath) 1165
The Holy Breath 1340
The Path of the Holy Breath 1345

Holy Ghost. *See also* Holy Spirit
Poor translation of Spiritus-Sanctus 1340
The Christian Trinity 113
The Kingdom of God (graph) 123
The Many Mansions (graph) 611

Holy Guardian Angel
The Being of Light in Meditation 418–419

Holy Spirit. *See also* Holy Breath
Appears in two forms 718
Āuṁ: the Holy Spirit as Cosmic Mother 1501
Baptism by Fire and the Spirit 1348
Dethroned by celibate monks 910
Dimensions of the Cosmic Fire (graph) 137
Holiness to the Lord 1393
Influence on the Aquarian Age 279
Kuṇḍalinī-Fohat 148–149
Meditation on the Holy Spirit 1344
Misunderstood by the church 113
Mythical Concepts of God 104–105
Nārāyaṇa: the Mover upon the Waters of Space 167
Spiritus Sanctus: definition 279
Terms and meanings in ancient languages 1344
The Breath of the Divine Mother 142
The Holy Spirit 1343
The Holy Trinity 1342
The Seven Rays 54–55

Holy Trinity. *See also* Trinity, Trimūrti
Christian Divine Names 1266
Dimensions of the Cosmic Fire (graph) 137
Mythical Concepts of God 104–105
The Christian Trinity 113
The Holy Trinity 1342
The Holy Trinity and Jesus 94
The Holy Trinity is found in the Heart 435
The Many Mansions (graph) 611
The Threefold Logos 662

Homopneumata
Gnostic Christian definition 737

Homosexuality. *See also* Polarity, Sex
and the merging of polar opposites 924
An imbalance in Nature 476
Polarities Male and Female 920–921
The "right" to have children 475

Honoma
Greek Mystery School definition 735

Horus
Eye of Horus 293
The Child Light 122–123

House of the Father
As described by Jesus 667
The Many Mansions (graph) 611
The Plerōma 12

Hṛdaya. *See also* Heart
A Name of Lalitā, the Goddess 1562
Hṛdaya-Citta: the Spiritual-Heart-Consciousness 1329
Hṛdaya-Ākāśa: the Heart-Space 1280, 1592
Hṛdaya Bīja 1546
Hṛdaya-Cakra: the Heart Centre 1592, 1616
Hṛdaya-Granthi: the Cross in the Heart 712
Hṛdaya-Granthi: the Knot in the Heart 445, 497, 1424
Hṛdaya-Guha: the Cave of the Heart 1592
Hṛdaya-Mārga: the threefold Heart-Path 1236
Hṛdaya-Śakti: the Energy of the Goddess 1487
Hṛdaya-Śaktipāta: a type of Kuṇḍalinī Force 1256
Hṛdaya-Taijasa: the Heart-Fire 432

Hṛdayaṁ
55 Hṛdayaṁ: Meditations in the Heart Centre 1279–1308
A Name of Lalitā, the Goddess 1562
Hṛdayaṁ: derivations 1281, 1282
Keys to the Heart 1317
Sanskrit term for the Heart 434, 448
The Heart (Hṛdayaṁ) 1282–1283

Hṛdguhyā
A Name of Lalitā, the Goddess 1568

Hrī
Potent Vibrations: Bīja-Mantra 1546
Hrīkārī, Hrīmatī: Names of Lalitā, the Goddess 1563

Hrīṁ
Hrīṁkārī: a Name of Lalitā, the Goddess 1563
Potent Vibrations: Bīja-Mantra 1547
Sound-Vibrations of the Śrī-Vidyā Mantra 1528
The Seed-Sound for Lalitā 1489

Hṛt-Padma
The Heart Lotus 1505

Hua-Tou
Meditating on Kōans and Hua-Tous 796–797
The mind in its state of Pure Consciousness 460

Hūṁ
Potent Vibrations: Bīja-Mantra 1546

Human Consciousness. *See* Consciousness

Human Constitution
2 The Human Constitution 31–56
A human being is a replica of the Solar Logos 1587
Greek terminology 39
Jīva: the Human Soul 35
Kāma-Manas and Buddhi-Manas 39
Malfunctioning Cakras 53
Polarities Male and Female 920–921
Symbols of the Seven Major Cakras (graph) 45
The Astral Body 39
The Compound Human Being 32–33
The Functioning of the Cakras (graph) 52
The Human Aura 42–43
The Human Cakras 44–53
The Human Constitution (Arabic) 890, 892
The Human Constitution (graph) 43
The Individuality 34
The Kośas: Coverings over the Self 38
The Light Bodies 40–41
The Mask (Persona) 38
The Personality Complex 36–37
The Sign of Man (graph) 41
The Threefold Human Constitution (graph) 1193
The Threefold Structure of Man (graph) 33
Trapped Spirits 1240
Understand your Predicament 892–893
Who is "I AM"? 1418

Human Evolution. *See* Evolution, Spiritual Path

Human Kingdom. *See also* Hierarchies
18 Human Consciousness 373–396
Ancient definition of Man 235
Art and the Follies of Man 470
Crowned with Glory 197
Greek classifications of Humanity 687
Human Evil 212–213
Involutionary and Evolutionary Kingdoms 194
In the image and likeness of God 104, 122, 163
Manuṣya: definition 189
Manuṣya: the Fourth Manifest Hierarchy 191
Relationship between Humankind and the Angels 196–197
Some Human Evils 384–385
The Creative and Destructive Power of Sound 201
The Planetary Destructive Hierarchy? 470
The Sevenfold Earth-Evolution 169
The Sign of Man (graph) 41
The Temple of God 639
Trapped Spirits 1240
Types of Humanity 376–377

Human Soul. *See also* Jīva, Jīvātman
"Channelling" the Soul 325
Impressions from the Soul 350
Jīva: the Human Soul 35
Psychology: Science of the Soul? 291
The Creative Soul 1692
The Kingdom of Souls 1688
The Ray of the Soul 54
The Second Circle of Life: Life as a Soul 1438
The Sexless Soul 920

The Soul-Power 1305
The Soul is caught up in the Three Worlds 1422
The Soul sends down three streams of energy 428
The State of Unity of the Psyche 1383
The Testing of the Soul 1158
Who is "I AM"? 1418

Humility
Beyond Phantasia 686–687
Humility for Earthlings 129
Humility of the Great Ones 337
Required to speak with the gods 367
The Approach to Truth 1152
The Attitude for Yoga 558
The Soul-Power 1305
To be a Mystic you must become humble 627

Hyle
The One Matter 135

Hyperborean Epoch
Brief description 176
Past and Present Evolutionary Development of the Cakras (graph) 178

Hypnotism
General description 312
Hypnotic astral projection 303

I

I AM. *See also* Self, Ātman, Paramātman
Activating I AM: the Secret Name of God 1419
Ātman, Ātmā 34
Ēgō: levels of meaning 1179
El Allāh Hū: The Arabic I AM 1459
Experiencing Pure Consciousness 88
IHVH: The Hebrew Name of God 1460
Śivo'haṁ: the Transcendental I AM 1323
Summary of the Process (Metanoia) 1468
Tao: the Great I AM 774
The Fields of Life (the Great Breath) 1165
The One 1686–1687
The Threefold Human Constitution (graph) 1193
The Way, the Truth and the Life 670
Who is "I AM"? 1418
Yekhidah: The Hebrew I AM 1458

IAO
The Name of the Deity 1032
The Pure Vowel sequence IAO 1034–1035
The Vowels in the Heart 1303

Icchā
Icchā-Śakti: the Energy of the Goddess 1486, 1499
Powers of the Eternal Feminine 1485

Ichthus
Symbol of the Jesus Dispensation 458, 709

Icons
Eikon: Christian Hesychast definition 746
Idol-Worship 655

Īḍā and Piṅgalā
Gāyatrī (Sun) Breathing 1553
Subtle Energy Currents 722–723

Ideas
Idea: Greek Mystery School definition 735
Idealogy: Greek Mystery School definition 735
Ideas and Archetypes 138
Ideas and the Magical Process 360–361
Idiology: Greek Mystery School definition 735

Identification. *See also* attachment
Attach your Mind to the Eternal 1234–1235
Death in the Heart 444
Desire for the Real 1503
Ego means identity 933
From Darkness into Light 982–983
Happiness Exists Within 1381
Identification with suffering 1401
Obstacles to Higher Consciousness 1424
The mind identifies with sense-impressions 1519
The Soul's identification with the bodies 1422
The Three Identifications 1369
Three Great Mysteries to solve in life 1369
To identify yourself with the Spirit 1233
Understand your Predicament 892–893
What do you Seek out of Life? 975
Your mind is attracted to physical things 1231
You identify with what goes on in your mind 538–539

Idols
Accusations of idol-worship 515
Idol-Worship 655
Idols of modern generations 387
The One God of All 869

Iesou Evchi
Christian Hesychast definition 744
The Jesus Prayer 437, 715

Ignorance. *See also* Materialism, Māyā
Introduction I: Knowledge and Ignorance 1–8
21 The Call of the World Mother 467–488
Abortion demonstrates total ignorance 415
Astral Disinformation 1271
Avoid the Errors of East and West 1122–1123
Channelling is Spiritual Ignorance 342, 1271
False Zen 756–757
From Darkness into Light 982–983
Fundamentalist fear of Knowledge 682–683
Ignorance is the negative pole of Being 1366
Ignorance of the inner dimensions of Sex 917
Karma and Reincarnation Misconceived 252–253
Mahā-Māyā: the Ultimate Delusion 1714
Māyā: definition 2
Meditation Degenerated 1180–1181
Misuse of spiritual words by the media 319
Orthodox science, medicine and psychology 305
Protagonists of Ignorance 382–383
Ritual Degenerated 368
Some Human Evils 384–385
The abuse of Prayer 365
The Hall of Ignorance 1149
The Way of the World 380
The wrong view of the sexual function 570
Unnecessary Practices 1111
Zen and the World 758

IHVH. *See also* Yehovah, Yahweh
Christian Meditation on the Holy Breath 1346–1353
Definition 98
IHVH: I AM: definition and pronunciation 1460
The Great Name of God 679

Illuminati
The Enlightened Ones 89

Illumination. *See also* Light
Energy for Illumination 978
Glimpses of Illumination 501
Illuminacion: letting in the Light 89
Illumination and Deification 1190
Illumination is our birthright 1178
Illumination through the Way of Purification 597
Illumined-Mind Consciousness 1427
Satori: the Experience of Illumination 816–817
Stages of Interior Prayer 695
Stages of the Silent Meditation Process 1187
The Lighted Way 1394–1395
The Mind of Light 891
The Path of Illumination 1338
The Path of Light 89
The Self-Generating Light 1594

Illusion. *See also* delusion, Māyā
Hallucinations in the Afterlife 408–409
Illusory worlds 97
Mahā-Māyā: the Great Illusion 181
The "emptiness" of Space is an illusion 1589
The Astral World is a grand illusion 66

Īṁ
Īṁkarī: a Name of Lalitā, the Goddess 1563
Potent Vibrations: Bīja-Mantra 1550

Imagination
Is in the Sex Centre and Throat Centre 48
The Power of Imagination 374–375

Imām
Imam Mahdi: the Divine Incarnation 726
The Spiritual Teacher 832

Immaculate Heart
The Immaculate Heart of Mary, Our Lady 1513

Immanuel
Hebrew Divine Words for Healing 1456
Incorrectly translated in the Bible 459
Meditations in the Heart Centre 1297
The Evolution of Christian Prayer 713
The Realization of the Divine Presence in the Heart 719

Immortality. *See* Conscious Immortality

Incarnation Process
Abortion and the Incarnation Process 413–415
Incarnation is a great privilege 474
Influence of the Permanent Atoms 250
The Angelic Builders 198, 250, 414

Incubus
and poltergeist phenomena 315

Individualism
Caused by the lower mind 432
Orthodox Psychology 1105
Piscean Mystics worked alone 1146
Separatism and the Law of Love 386

Individuality. *See also* Triad
Integration of the Individuality and Personality 504
The Imperishable Self 32–35

Individualization
The creation of the Human Soul 130

Indriya. *See also* senses
Awakening the Inner Senses 506–507
Saṁyama upon the senses 595

Infernus
The Eighth Sphere 63

Infidel
Infidēlis: definition and usage 514

Initiation
Dīkṣā: Initiation from a Guru 1225
Initiation into a Mantra 788, 1603
Initiatory Mantrams 2081
The Divine Message of the New Testament 719
The Initiation of the World 1712–1713
The Star of the One Initiator 1727
The Wisdom of the Goddess 1525
What is Initiation? 1007

Innocence
Children are born innocent? 250
The State of Innocence 1306

Insanity. *See also* psychosis
Mast-Allah: fools of God 505
Resulting from Kuṇḍalinī activity 157–158
Resulting from possession 310–311

Insight
The activity of the Higher Mind 323
The difference between learning and Insight 755
Vipassana: the Pali word for Insight 1221

Inspiration
Genuine Inspiration comes from your own Soul 353
Inspiratio: definition 375
Inspiration by the Mind of Light 1113
Intuition, Insight, Inspiration 323
Spiritual Inspiration is required for meditation 1202

Instinct
Instinctual telepathy 346
The lowest manifestation of your Inner Feminine 1010

Integration. *See also* Balance, Union, Yoga
God-Consciousness is the Wholeness of Life 504–505
Integrating everyday life with Spiritual Life 1428
Integration of the Human Consciousness (graph) 1195
Integrity and Perfection 1005
Meditation is Integration 1193
Personality Integration Chart (graph) 1333
The Art of Alignment 1202

Intellect
Dimensions of the Mind 891
Intellectus: definition 375
Meditating with the pure Intellect 1188

Intellectualism. *See also* lower mind
Cannot understand Kuṇḍalinī 152
Destroys sensitivity to Female Consciousness 468, 478
Education from the Spirit 1366
From Darkness into Light 982
Lacks the warmth of the Heart 426–427, 429
Orthodox Psychology 1105
Reality is not a thought or an idea 1280
The Importance of the Heart in Approaching God 432–433
What is Consciousness? 1368–1369
Zen is not a form of intellectualism 753, 756

Intelligence
Action and the Spiritual Warrior 994
Intelligence is not a lower mind function 481
Intelligent Use of Free Will 297
Pure Intelligence 494

Qualities of the Spiritual Warrior 970
Ray 3: Activity, Adaptability 56
The Eternal Feminine Intelligence 468–469
The Intelligent Universe 111
The Third Stream of Spiritual Energy 972
The Universal Intelligence 232

Intervention
Cosmic Intervention 282
Human Response to Cosmic Intervention 286
Intervention and Interference 285
Manifestation of the Sons of God 180
Planetary Evil 214–216
The Mystery of the Pleiades 181
The Spirit-Helpers 369–371

Intuition
Intuitionis: definition 375
Intuition is not mediumship 323
Spiritual Intuition 1011
The Power of Intuition 374–375
What is Intuition? 328

Intuitional World. *See* Buddhi

Involution
Human Involution and Evolution 170–172
Involutionary and Evolutionary Kingdoms 194
The Action of the Primordial Sound (graph) 165
The Cycle of Manifestation (graph) 134

IO
The Godhead 108
The Name of the Deity 1032

Irritability
Emotional problems 1431

Īśa
A Name of the Solar Logos 1658, 1664
Hierarchies of Life (graph) 1721
Īśa Bīja 1546
Mahāvākya Practice 1471, 1474
The Self within the Heart 1316

Iṣām-i-A'zam
The Greatest Name 864

Īśatva
The General Powers 581

'Ishk
The fifth stage of the Journey of the Heart 856

Ishtar
The Eternal Feminine 469

Isis
The Eternal Feminine 469
The Mother Light 122–123
The Soul of Nature 144

Islām. *See also* Sūfīsm
Mystics of Islām 828–829
Surrender to the One God 828

Isolation
Solitude and Loneliness 1170–1171

Israel
Definition 246
Symbolic of all Humanity 616
The Evolution of Christian Prayer 713

Īṣṭa-Devatā
Bhakti Yoga: Divine Union by Devotion 1128
How to have a Peaceful Mind in a Troubled World 1244
The Saviour in the Heart 1296
To discover the Deity in the Heart 445
Visualizing the Divinity within the Heart 1268–1269

Īśvara
A Name of the Sun-God 1608
Definition 120, 564
Īśvarām: derivation and definition 1316
Īśvara: levels of meaning 1623
Our Solar Logos is the Immanent God 122
The ruling principle within 548
The Solar Logos 162

Īśvara-Praṇidhāna
Definition 535, 564
Pāda I Sūtra 23 548
The fifth Rule of Aṣṭāṅga Yoga 569

Īśvarī
A Name of Lalitā, the Goddess 1571
Definition 1494

Itarā Liṅga
Access-way at the Head Centres 151

J

Jacob's Ladder. *See also* Antaḥkaraṇa
Building the Bridge of Light 554
Evolutionary Symbolism of the Cross 179
The Planes of Being 1148

Jagad
Definition 1498
Jagadambā: the Mother of the World 1498–1499

Jagatgranthi
Obstacles to Higher Consciousness 1424

Jāgrata-Avasthā
The self-conscious mind 494–496

Janah-Loka. *See also* Nirvāṇa
and the Goal of Yoga 521
Dimensions of the Solar Logos in Cosmic Space 1591
Elementary Attributes 29

Japa
Derivation and definition 1219
Repetition of a mantra 1206

Jehovah. *See* Yehovah

Jesus
30 Jesus the Christed One 659–674
A Mahā-Avatāra 389
Christian Beginnings 642
Danced with His disciples 873
Declared to be the Logos 115, 663, 1453
His new Teachings rejected 288
Jesus: the Fire of Love 1725
Jesus tried to reinterpret the Law of Moses 234
Jesus Christ, Son of Man 668
Jesus Speaks… 728–729
Jesus the Personal Saviour? 678–679
Jesus was without "sin" 668
Names of the Great Master Jesus 661
One of the Prophets of Old? 258
Saints of Action 1134
Spoke from Nirvāṇic Consciousness 1448
Temptations of Jesus 308
The "sacrifice" of Jesus 220
The "Second Coming" of Jesus 1453
The early Christians did not worship Jesus 680
The Gnostic Teachings 1108
The Great Greek Mantra to Jesus 708–710, 715
The Jesus Mantra 1725
The Jesus Mantra and Sacred Heart Initiation 1356
The language of Jesus 105
The Last Words of Jesus 672
The Lord of Glory 667
The Messiah Jesus 666
The Mystery of Jesus and Mary 665
The Mystery of Jesus the Christ 664
The Only Son of God? 669
The Sacred Heart of Jesus 673
The Sacrificial Lamb 680
The three Magi and the birth of Jesus 356, 666
The Way, the Truth and the Life 670
To Call upon Jesus 679
To Love God and the World 1392–1393
Variations of the Name of Jesus 1356
Warrior Jesus 908

Jewel in the Lotus. *See also* Spirit-Spark-Atom
Maṇi-Padma: the Jewelled Lotus 1298
The Esoteric Mantram 551
The Imperishable Seed in the Heart 926–927
The Mystery within the Heart 1315
The Perennial Source of Love 438
The Spirit within the Heart 1322

Jism
The Human Constitution (Arabic) 892

Jīva, Jīvātman. *See also* Human Soul
Can be found in the Heart 445
Is caught up in the Three Worlds 1422
Jīva: the Human Soul 35
Jīva-Ahaṁ: I am a Living Soul 1325
The focal point for Illumination 1190
The Second Circle of Life: Life as a Soul 1438
The three degrees of Self-Realization 1448

Jīvagranthi
Obstacles to Higher Consciousness 1424

Jīvan-Mukta
Definition 259, 196
To Become a Jīvanmukta in this Lifetime 259

Jīvan-Mukti
Definition 1237
Living Liberation 503
To Achieve Liberation 1177

Jñāna
Activities of Yoga-Mārga 520
Jñāna-Jñeya-Svarūpiṇī: a Name of Lalitā 1577
Jñāna-Mātā: a Name of Lalitā 1567
Jñāna-Śakti: the Energy of the Goddess 1487, 1499
Powers of the Eternal Feminine 1485

Jñānaśaktī-Icchāśaktī-Kriyāśaktī-Svarūpiṇī
The Eternal Feminine 1485
The Mother of the World 1499

Jñāna Yoga. *See also* Yoga
and the Threefold Way 1236
Mahāvākya Practice 1470
The Path of Mental Effort and Knowledge 1124
The Way to the Divine Heart 1505
Traditional concept of 522–523

Jñāni
The Knower, the Gnostic 377
The Super-Knowing faculty 1242

John the Baptist
A prototype for all true Christians 643
The Prophets are not spooked 325

Joy. *See also* Happiness, Bliss, Peace
How to find Peace and Joy through Meditation 1013
Meditation and the Joy of Living 1012

Judaism
Holiness to the Lord 1393
Made Jehovah into a person 104, 106
Persecuted the Prophets 657
Rejected Jesus as the Messiah 649
The Eternal is One 512–514
The Hasidim 648–649
The Jewish Messiah 660
The Masculine God 649
The Sacrificial Lamb 680

Judgment Day
At the end of an Age 725
Period of self-examination after death 408
The Being of Light 416–417
Your own realization of your shortcomings 813

Justice. *See also* Karma
Cannot be escaped after death 411
There is no injustice 254
Western word for Karma 240
You Alone are Responsible 258

Justinian
The Fifth Ecumenical Council 652–653

Jyoti, Jyotir, Jyotiṣ. *See also* Light
Definition 118, 175
Jyoti-Nirañjanā: a Name of Lalitā, the Goddess 1575
Jyotirbhāsin: a quality of the Divine Being 107
Jyotir Maṭha: the Path of Light 1693
Jyotir-Śakti, Jyotiṣa-Śakti: the Energy of the Goddess 1486
Jyotiṣ Mantra 1476
Jyotiṣmatī: a Name of Lalitā, the Goddess 1574
The Self-Generating Light 1594

K

Kabbalah
Chockmah and Binah: Wisdom and Understanding 439, 498
Foundations of Magic 358–362
Hebrew Divine Names to be Invoked in the Heart 1262
Qabbālāh: definition 358
Symbols of the Cosmic Elements 362
The Four Kabbalistic Worlds 360
The Hebrew Heart 1263
The Planes and the Kabbalistic Tree of Life (graph) 359
The Tarot 362
To Call upon Jesus 679

Kaivalya
Being Alone with the Absolute 502
Eternal Liberation 595–597
Loneliness of the Enlightened 1171
Steps on the Spiritual Path 561

Kāla. *See also* Time
Akāla: timeless, eternal, everlasting 1302
Definition 30
Steps on the Spiritual Path 561
The Sense of Time 22–23

Kālahaṁsa
Eternal Duration 1655
To become a Bird of Time 257

Kalām-i-Ilāhi
The Voice of God 864

Kālī
An Energy-Form of the Goddess 1489
Definition and description 1495
Kālī, Kalikā: Names of Lalitā 1573
Kālī Bīja 1549
Kālimā: the Mother Beyond Time 1495
The Kālī-Mantra 1541

Kali Yuga
The current Age of materialism 384
The Period of the Mahāmanvantara 168
We live in the Age of Kali Yuga 605

Kalma
Kalma-i-Ḥaqqīqat: Word of Truth 866
The Speech of God 864

Kalpa
Definition 168

Kāma. *See also* Desire, Emotion
Definition and description 58
Kāma Bīja 1549–1550
Kāma-Devī: an Energy-Form of the Goddess 1489
Kāma-Vṛtti: desire waves 1239
Kāmeśvarī: the Desire-Goddess 1485, 1564
Mind and Desire 235
Terms of Love 914
To attain the First Stage of Yoga 528

Kāma-Avasāyitva
The General Powers 581

Kāma-Deva
Desire-angels dwelling on the Astral Plane 77
The Makara 202

Kamalā
Kamalā, Kamalādevī: Names of Lalitā 1568
The Kamalā-Mantra 1536–1537

Kāma-Loka. *See also* Astral Plane
3 Kāmaloka: the Astral Plane 57–72
Derivation and definition 58
The Realm of Desires 58–59

Kāma-Manas
Experienced after death 408–409
Manomāyākośa 38
Manomayī: She who is composed of Mind 1577
Mind and Desire 235
The Attitude for Yoga 558
The mind in the Astral World 246
The mixing of desires with mind 78
The root problem is your ordinary mind 762–763
The Suspending of the Mind 1208–1209
The versatile psychic nature 528
True Death: control of the psychic nature 424
Variations in terminology 39

Kāma-Rūpa. *See also* astral body
The Personality Complex 36–37

Kanyākumārī
A Name of Lalitā, the Goddess 1564

Kāraṇa Cakra. *See also* Alta Centre
The Causal Centre above the head 1645

Kāraṇa-Loka
The Causal World 1707

Kāraṇa-Manas. *See also* Causal Mind, Abstract Mind
Intellectus: definition 375
The Causal Mind 74, 78
The Higher Mind 34
The Seven Subplanes of the Mental Plane (graph) 75

Kāraṇa-Śarīra. *See also* causal body
Beyond the personality complex 36–37
Can become a permanent Light Body 1313
Definition 75

Kardia
Christian Hesychast definition 743
Christian word for the Heart 632

Karma. *See also* Action, Dharma
12 Karma and Reincarnation 231–266
59 Time and Eternity: Action and Destiny 1399–1410
Action (Karma): aphorisms 1402–1406
Astrology and Karma 260
Cosmic Karma 217
Creating Karma 242
Disease and Karma 1169
Fear of the Lord? 234
Freedom from Karma 255
Karma: derivation and definition 233
Karma: the Law of Action or Adjustment 240–241
Karma and Death (Metanoia) 1425
Karma and Reincarnation banned by the church 652–653
Karma and Reincarnation Misconceived 252–253
Karma and the Guṇas 1406
Karma and your Spiritual Development 255
Karma in the Afterlife 241
Karmic Adjustment 1379
Karmic Difficulties on the Path 1167
Lipika: the Lords of Karma 241
Mind and Desire 235
Operates throughout the Three Worlds 422–423
Primordial Balance 995
Saṁskāra and Vāsanā 251
Subconscious Forces 236–237
Success is Born of Action 256
The First Circle of Life 1422
The Good Law 221, 262
The Law of Action 992–993
The Law of Effort 254
The Supreme Act of Karma 264–265
The Wheel of the Law 247
Thinking and Being 233
Types of Karma 243
Working out Karma 242
You Alone are Responsible 258

Karma Yoga. *See also* Yoga
Activities of Yoga-Mārga 520
Definition 535
Karma Yoga: Divine Union by Action 1132–1133
Success is Born of Action 256–257
The Science of Cosmic Consciousness 1124
The Threefold Way 1236
The Way to the Divine Heart 1505
Traditional concept of 522–523

Kartṛtva-Śakti
The Power of all Doership 527

Karukeion
Definition 155

Kavana
The Names and Mental Prayer in the Heart 1261

Kāya-Kalpa
Supernatural transformations of Man 1310

Kenoma
Gnostic Christian definition 736

Kenshō
Zen definition 807

Kether
Nirvāṇa is Kether 94, 100
The Kabbalistic Tree of Life 358–359

Khafā
Dimensions of the Heart (Arabic) 847

Kharisma. *See* Charisma

King. *See also* Ancient of Days, Sanat Kumāra
Kings of Light 275
Malīk, Mālikul (Arabic) 829
The Warrior serves the King 977, 984–990

Kingdom of God
Entering the Lost Kingdom 1176–1177
Meanings of "The Kingdom of God" 1720
Penetrating into the Kingdom 1707
The Christ-Hierarchy 396
The Christian Cosmo-Conception 19
The Kingdom is at Hand 1453
The Kingdom of God 1715
The Kingdom of God (graph) 123
The planes of Divine Evolution 1688
To Manifest the Kingdom of God 1716

Kingdom of the Gods
The Sevenfold Earth-Evolution 169

Klīṁ
Klīṁkārī: a Name of Lalitā, the Goddess 1564
Potent Vibrations: Bīja-Mantra 1549–1550
The Seed-Sound for Kāmadevī 1489

Knots of Consciousness. *See* Granthi

Knowers. *See also* Gnostics, Jñāni
Persecution of the Knowers 656–658
The Knowers and the Yogīs 377

Knowledge
Introduction I: Knowledge and Ignorance 1–8
Be Still and Know 638–639
Cultivate Knowledge 1366
Esoteric Knowledge 1218
Essential Knowledge 487
Heart Knowing 1286
Holy Knowledge 468–469, 1517
How do you Know who you really Are? 1387
Inspiration by the Mind of Light 1113
Knowledge is Power 991
Knowledge of Past Lives 601
Know Thyself 1389
Lack of Knowledge 4–5
Mysterious Knowledge of the Siddhas 1310–1311
Relative and Absolute Knowledge 1415
Self-Knowledge is not selfishness 324
Spirituality Past and Future 1104
Super-Knowing 1242
The Four Degrees of Knowledge 1003
The Threefold Way 1236
The Truth shall make you Free 682–683
The Way of Knowledge (Rays) 55
To maintain a steady spiritual practice 1708
Tranquil Mind 1503
Wordless Knowledge 1010

Kōan
Meditating on Kōans and Hua-Tous 796–797
Repeated in the Heart 460
The Japanese Zen Retreat 807

Kohaṁ
Experiencing Pure Consciousness 88
Three Meditations in the Heart 1292
Who am I? 447, 459

Kośas
Coverings over the Self 38
The Way to Bliss-Consciousness (graph) 1246

Kosmokratores
The Cosmic Creator-Gods 162–163
The Cosmic Creators 190
The Elohīm 120

Kosmos
Definition 13, 135
Greek Mystery School definition 733
Kosmos-Metanoia: Cosmic Renewal 1452

Krāṁ
Potent Vibrations: Bīja-Mantra 1551

Krīṁ
Potent Vibrations: Bīja-Mantra 1549
The Seed-Sound for Kālī 1489

Krishnamurti
A modern Zen Master 782

Kriyā
Kriyā-Śakti: the Energy of the Goddess 1486, 1499
Powers of the Eternal Feminine 1485

Kriyamāna Karma
Karma which you are creating now 243

Kriyā Yoga
The highest act of Kriyā Yoga 551
The Way of Union through Action 535

Kṛṣṇa
A Mahā-Avatāra 389
Devotion to Kṛṣṇa 449
Had Relational Consciousness 906
Kṛṣṇa Bīja 1544, 1549
Kṛṣṇa and Arjuna 1132
Kṛṣṭa, Kṛṣṇa, Krista: the Christ within your Soul 1320
Pure Devotion: Initiation Mantram 1724
Spoke from Nirvāṇic Consciousness 1448
The Christ in the Heart 441
To Worship the Divine Incarnations 1270–1272

Kṛṣṇa-Consciousness. *See also* Christ-Consciousness
Kūṭastha: definition 449

Kṛta Yuga
The Period of the Mahāmanvantara 168

Kṣānika Samādhi
Types of Samādhi 575

Kṣatriya
Sūrya-Vaṁśa-Kṣatriya: Warriors of the Sun 1618
The Warrior Class (Caste) 378

Kulakumārī, Kulakumārikā
Names of Lalitā, the Goddess 1564

Kumāra
Definition 394
Hierarchies of Life (graph) 1721
The Brotherhood of Light (graph) 395

Kumārī
A Name of Lalitā, the Goddess 1564
The Secret Heart-Mantra 1534

Kumbhaka
The restraining of the Prāṇa energies 723

Kuṇḍalinī. *See also* Goddess, World Mother
8 Kuṇḍalinī and the Goddess 141–158

What is Kuṇḍalinī?
Śakti: the One Energy 150
Dimensions of the Cosmic Fire (graph) 137
Kuṇḍala, Kuṇḍalī, Kuṇḍalīn, Kuṇḍalinī: definitions 143
Kuṇḍalinī-Śaktī: a Name of Lalitā 1562
The Breath of the Divine Mother 142
The Kuṇḍalinī Fire 132
The Mother of the World 147
The Supreme Power (Paraśakti) 1500
The third aspect of the Sūtrātma 491
The True Feminine 1516

Activities of Kuṇḍalinī
Breaks down barriers in Consciousness 1522
Health and Fire 50
Kuṇḍalinī and Alchemy 153
Natural and Supernatural activities of Kuṇḍalinī 148–149
The Cosmic Fire in the human system 44
The Energy of the Goddess 1487
The Evolutionary Energy 143
The letters of Śrī-Vidyā are Kuṇḍalinī Herself 1524–1525
The Path of Mantra and the Goddess 1490

Kuṇḍalinī-Fohat
Both work in matter and through matter 1168
Dimensions of the Cosmic Fire (graph) 137
Kuṇḍalinī-Fohat 148–149
The power behind miracles 132
The Third Aspect of the Godhead 1168

Experiencing Kuṇḍalinī
Diseases caused by walking upon the Path 1168
Signs of the Awakening Kuṇḍalinī-Śakti 154–156
The Ascent of Kuṇḍalinī 152
The Serpent-Fire or Dragon-Force 996–997
The Three Gates to God 151
When Kuṇḍalinī Awakens 157–158

Kuṇḍalinī Yoga
Activities of Yoga-Mārga 520
Dangers of Kuṇḍalinī Yoga 157–158, 1168
Danger of damaging etheric web 304
Paths of Spiritual Evolution 1693

Kung-An. *See* Kōan

Kūrmanāḍī
The tortoise-nerve 586

Kurukṣetra
Scenes of Battle 1158
The Battle-Field is this relative world 1409

Kūṭastha
Definition and description 449
Kūṭasthā: a Name of Lalitā, the Goddess 1558

Kwan-Shin-Yin
The Christ in the Heart 441

Kwan Yin. *See* Quan Yin

Kyōsaku
The "big stick": general description 809
Zen definition 807

L

Laghimā
The General Powers 580

Lakṣmī
An Energy-Form of the Goddess 1489
A Name of Lalitā, the Goddess 1569
Lakṣmī Bīja 1548

Lalitā. *See also* Goddess
65 The One-Hundred Names of Lalitā 1555–1582
An Energy-Form of the Goddess 1489
Lalitā: the Eternal Feminine 1484–1485
Lalitā: the Ultimate Goddess 1556
Lalitā-Ambikā: a Name of the Goddess 1556, 1559
Lalitā Bīja 1547
Lalitā is Śrī-Vidyā 1517
Meanings of the Name Lalitā 1558
The Eternal Feminine 469

Lāṁ
Potent Vibrations: Bīja-Mantra 1544
The Practice of Grounding 1005

Language
34 The Greek Mystery Language 731–748
47 The Primordial Sound Language 1025–1076
Languages of Islām 829
Language of the Gods 200
Our Sacred Music and Language 2081
Senzar: an ancient universal language 272
Standards and Variations 1761
The Language of the Bible 720
The Universal Language 348–349
The Wisdom Language 1760

Lao Tzu
Description of Nirvāṇa (Tao) 96
Description of the Way of Tao 1446
Sayings of Lao Tzu on Zen Meditation 799
The Zen Master according to Lao Tzu 780–781

Latin
Latin Mantras of the Rosicrucians 712
Latin Mantras to Our Lady 1510–1511
Mantras to Connect to Our Lady 1512

Law. *See also* Dharma, Torah
Dharma: the Law of Being 244–247
Existence is Purposeful 173
Karma: the Law of Action or Adjustment 240–241
Love is the Law 25
Natural Law 919
The Good Law 262–263
The Intelligent Universe 111
The Laws of Group Psychology 1384
The Laws of Magic are the Laws of the Mind 356
The Law of Action 992–993
The Law of Cyclic Activity 248
The Law of Death 398
The Law of Effort 254
The Law of Mentalism 244–245, 247
The Law of Motion or Change 405
The Law of Mystic Experience 508–509
The Law of Polarity 164
The Law of Radiation 175
The Law of Surrender or Sacrifice 1138
The Law of the Afterlife 410
The Law of the Higher Life 1134–1135
The Law of your Being 976–977
The Three Great Laws of Life 262
The Universal Intelligence 232
The Wheel of the Law 247
Torah: the Law 648

Laya
Laya Bīja 1546
The Unmanifested State 167

Laya Yoga
Activities of Yoga-Mārga 520
Brief description 157

Learning
The difference between learning and Insight 755
The Hall of Learning 1149
The Tao cannot be found by learning 773
Unlearning 1230

Left-hand path
Avītci: the Eighth Sphere 63

Legends. *See* Mythology

Lemuria
Instinctual telepathy developed in Lemuria 346
Past and Present Evolutionary Development of the Cakras (graph) 178
The Lemurian Epoch 176

Lesbianism. *See also* homosexuality
Lesbos: an island in ancient Greece 475

Levitation
Saṁyama upon the upward-moving Life-force 589
The activity of Kuṇḍalinī 154, 156
The power of levitation 590–591

Liberation. *See also* Salvation, Mukti, Mokṣa
19 Death and Liberation 397–424
22 Awakening the Human Glory 489–510
Definition 32
From Bondage to Liberation (graph) 422
Karma and your Spiritual Development 255
Learn to Die before you Die 420–421
Liberation from the Wheel of Birth and Death 421
Liberation from Worldly Consciousness 1233
Opportunity missed at death 417
Saṁsāra-Mokṣana: definition 1422
Sōtērios: definition 129
The Being of Light in Meditation 418–419
The Role of the Divine Female in the Salvation/Liberation Process 1502–1503
To Achieve Liberation 1177
To Become a Jīvanmukta in this Lifetime 259
True Death 424
You Alone are Responsible 258

Life-force. *See also* Prāṇa
Chi-Kung: control of the Life-force 786
Contained in the etheric-physical body 988
Controlling the Mind through Breathing 1059
Health and Fire 50
Movement and the Life-force 1020
Sexuality and the Life-force 912
The Descent of the Spirit (graph) 51
The Energies of Sex and Love 912
The Life-Force 589
The Life-Force in Humanity 1486
The Three Forces of the Warrior 996–997

Life after Death. *See* Death, Afterlife

Light
Brahmājyoti: God's Light 1394
Jyoti, Jyotir, Jyotiṣ: definition 118, 175
Light 978–979
Nūr: the Light of God 847
Prakāśa: definition 1329
Qualities of the Eternal Light 527
Sūrya or Savitā is Divine Light 1602
The Christ is the Light of the World 442–443
The Descent of the Light (graph) 980
The Infinite Light conceived of as a Buddha 795
The Light of the Logos (graph) 119
The Light of the World 1596
The Mother Light 1533
The Primordial Light 119
The Self-Generating Light 1594
The Shining Lights 1595
Words for "Light" in Western Mysticism 1350

The Light Path
Communicating by Light 351
From Darkness into Light 982–983
From Matter to Light 761
How to let the Light shine inside you 1307
Look for the Light 1395
Rules of Light 1597
Saṁyama upon the Inner Light 585
Satori: the Experience of Illumination 816–817
Tantric meditations on the Light 950
The Being of Light 416–417
The Being of Light in Meditation 418–419
The Jyotiṣ Mantra 1476
The Law of Radiation 175
The Lighted Way 1394–1395
The Path of Illumination 1338
The Path of Light 89
The River of Light 1308
The Shaft of Light from the Sun 1635
The Unfoldment of the Light (Christian) 718–721
The Warrior of the Light 984
What is the Way of Light? 1325

Light Bodies
Bodies of the Buddhas 392–393
Further Light Bodies 1313
Mysterious Knowledge of the Siddhas 1310–1311
The Body of Fire 1334
The Light Bodies 40–41
The Light Body of our Solar Logos 95, 761

Līlā
Lalitā plays within the Universe 1517
Līlā: the Play of the Goddess 1520
Līlā-Vinodinī: a Name of Lalitā 1565
The State of Inner Purity 497

Lily of the Valley
The Lotus of the Heart 446
The Rose of Divine Love 859

Limbo
Aborted children thrown into limbo 414–415
Degrees of non-Love 406
The Christian Cosmo-Conception 19
The Earthbound Spirits 403

Liṅga
Definition 561
Liṅga Bīja 1551
The Three Gates to God 151

Liṅga-Śarīra. *See also* etheric-physical body
Can become a permanent Light Body 1313
The Life-Force in Humanity 1486
The Personality Complex 36–37

Liṅga Purāṇa
and Śiva Yoga 561

Lipika
The Great Four 273, 275
The Lords of Karma 241

Listening. *See also* Hearing, Meditational Practices
Inner Absorption by Listening 1699
Listening 1215
Listen to Nāda 1212
Meditation on the Sacred Word 1216–1217
The Path of Hearing 553
Zen Listening 787–793

Living Soul. *See also* Jīva, Human Soul
Jīva: the Human Soul 35

Locus Dei
The Place of God 716

Logia, Logoi
Instructions and sayings of Jesus 746

Logiki-Psyche
Christian Hesychast definition 742

Logikos
Christian Hesychast definition 742

Logion, Logia
Gnostic Christian definition 738

Logoi. *See also* Solar Logoi, Planetary Logoi
Christian Hesychast definition 746
Dimensions of the Cosmic Fire (graph) 137
The Doctrine of the Logoi 116–117
The Threefold Logos 116, 123, 662
The three stages of manifestation of the Logos 1353
The Universe is run by the Logoi 725

Logos. *See also* Word, Divine Name
Daiviprākṛtī: the Light of the Logos 119
Definition and derivation 114
Emanates from the Monadic Plane 590
Gnostic Christian definition 737
God's Cosmic Symphony 1649
Greek Mystery School definition 734
Meanings of the word Logos 117
Meditation on the Sacred Word 1216–1217
See the Light of the Logos 1650
The Action of the Primordial Sound (graph) 165
The Cosmic Christ 662–663
The Creative Power of the Primordial Language of Sound 1075
The Logos: the Word of God 114–115
The Logos and Tao 772
The Self-Generating Light 1594
The Voice of God (Sūfī) 864–865
The Word, Logos, Voice, Name 1646–1648
The Word (Metanoia) 1455
Vāk: the Divine Speech 118
What is the Name? 1259

Loka. *See also* Planes
Definition 30, 77
Dimensions of the Solar Logos in Cosmic Space 1591
Frequencies or Vibrations of the Solar Light 1594
The Seven Great Planes 13

Lolitā
A Name of Lalitā, the Goddess 1569

Loneliness
Solitude and Loneliness 1170–1171

Lord
IHVH wrongly translated as "Lord" 1460
Jesus: the Lord of Glory 667
Mistranslation of the Hebrew Divine Names 117, 121
Our Solar Logos is Lord 120

Lords of Fire
The First Manifest Hierarchy 191

Lord of the World. *See* Ancient of Days, Sanat Kumāra

Lost Souls
The Eighth Sphere 63

Lotus. *See also* Padma
Hṛt-Padma: the Heart Lotus 1505
Kamalā: the Lotus-Born 1536
Maṇi-Padma: the Jewelled Lotus 1298
Padma: the lotus flower 1322
The Jewel in the Lotus 926–927
The Lotus of the Heart 446
The Mystery within the Heart 1315

Love. *See also* Heart
20 The Mystery of the Heart 425–466
43 The Circle of Love 905–944

What is Love?
Love and Sacrifice 1139
Love is an Energy 436
Oneness and Love 1450–1451
Terms of Love (Sanskrit and Greek) 914
The Energies of Sex and Love 912
The four degrees of Love 633
The Many Hues of Love 913–916
Divine Love in the Head 916
Emotional Love 914
Heart Love 915
Mental Love 915
Sexual Love 913
The Meaning of Life is Love 633
The Meaning of Love 931

Universal Love
Christ gave Mankind Love 1270
Love is the Nature of the Solar Logos 1327
Polarity and the Law of Love 25
The Activity of the Divine Heart 1675
The Being of Light 416–417
The Eternal is One 512–514
The Feminine Virtues 468–469
The Mystery of the Sun is the Power of Love 1597
The Perennial Source of Love 438
The World Mother of Compassionate Heart 145
To Manifest the Kingdom of God 1716

Love-Wisdom
Qualities of the Spiritual Warrior 970
Ray 2: Love, Wisdom 56
The dual characteristic of the Buddhic Plane 753
The Essence of Wisdom 1680–1684
The Second Stream of Spiritual Energy 972–973
The Soul manifesting through the Heart Centre 1194

The Experience of Love
Falling in Love 922
Freedom is Boundless Love 932
Love Lost 936–937
My Beloved Lives in My Heart 1290–1291
Mystics of Pisces and Aquarius 836
Tantra is the Way of Love 911
Telepathic Communion is a State of Love 350
The Fire of Love 1255
The Lover and the Beloved (poem) 466
The Lover of God (Sūfī) 853
The You grows by Knowledge and Love 1389
Wounds of Love 699

The Practice of Love
Cultivate the Fires of Love 928–929
Duty and Spirituality 1641
From Hate to Love 229
Live and Let Live 940
Love is the greatest purifier 571

On Love and Meditation 1140–1143
Separatism and the Law of Love 386
The Rose of Divine Love 858–861
The Supreme Act of Karma 264–265
To Love God and the World 1392–1393
You can only Love Now 941
You may Love God as Father or God as Mother 1492

Lower mind. *See also* Rūpa-Manas, Kāma-Manas
Dimensions of the Mind 891
Education focuses on the lower mind 481
Manas: higher and lower 78
Stimulated by the Fifth Ray 426
The cause of superficial personalities 897
The Knowledge of how the mind works 588
The Ordinary Mind 896
The seat of separative consciousness 426–433
Those polarized in the mental body 376

Lower self. *See* personality, ego

Lucifer
The Light-Bearer 210

Lunar Angels
Gave Man his astral body 176
Lunar and Solar Angels 216
The lesser gods of the Astral Plane 275

Lung-Tan
Terms of Awakening 766

Lūx, Lūmen
Words for "Light" in Western Mysticism 1350

Lypi
Christian Hesychast definition 745

M

Mā
A Name of Lalitā, the Goddess 1493, 1575

Macrocosm
As above, so below 125
Makrokosmos: definition 121, 733

Madhyamāvāk
Astral and causal sound 1577

Madonna
Madonna and Child (graph) 469
The Eternal Feminine 469
The Mother Principle 470

Magic
13 Atlantis Revisited 269–288
17 Magical Manifestation 355–372
Black Magic led to destruction of Atlantis 272–275, 280
Centres of Magic (graph) 364
Dangers of Black Magic 371
Definitions of Magic 356–357
Energy Materializes 363
Foundations of Magic (Kabbalistic) 358–362
Magic: White and Black 364
Magical Healing 372
Magical Prayer 365
Magicians carried a Rod of Power 151
Magicians of Lemuria, Atlantis and India 276–277
Magos, Magi, Magus, Maga: definitions 356
Objectives of Magic 363
Ray 7: Ceremony, Order 56
Stages of Manifestation 361
Supernatural Forces 357
The Magical Process in the Four Worlds (graph) 360
The Magician 356
The Magic of Atlantis 270–278
White Magic and Black Magic 357, 363–365
The Magic of Ritual Worship 366–371
Communication with the Invisible 371
Invoking the Invisible Helpers 370
Ritual Degenerated 368
The Spirit-Helpers 369
The Temple Not Made By Hands 369
Yajña: definition and description 366

Magnēs
Definition 131
Dimensions of the Cosmic Fire (graph) 137

Magnetic
Pre-scientific definition 53

Magnum Opus
Meditation is Integration 1193
The Western term for Yoga-Mārga 529

Mahā-Avatāra. *See also* Avatāra
A Messiah, a Saviour 389

Mahā-Devī
A Name of Lalitā, the Goddess 1571
The Eternal Feminine 1485

Mahah-Loka. *See also* Buddhi
and the Goal of Yoga 521
Dimensions of the Solar Logos in Cosmic Space 1591
Elementary Attributes 29

Mahāmanvantara
The Great Age of Creation 167
The Period of the Mahāmanvantara 168

Mahā-Māyā
The Great Illusion 181
The Great Sleep of Spiritual Ignorance 1714

Mahāmuni
Definition 1504

Mahāparanirvāṇa. *See also* Ādi
in brief 17
The First World (Arabic) 889
The Initial Existence on the Cosmic Physical Plane 166

Mahāprajñāparamitā
The Great Wisdom of the Other Shore 768–769

Mahāpralaya
The Great Dissolution 167

Mahā-Ṛṣi
Definition 534, 1182
Maharishi and Transcendental Meditation 1182–1183

Mahā-Śakti
Mahāśaktī: a Name of Lalitā 1574
The Divine Energy 1484

Mahāśūnyatā
Definition 23
Nirvāṇic Consciousness 85
The Original Divine Nirvāṇa-Space 503

Mahā-Svastika-Śakti
The Energy of the Goddess 1487

Mahat. *See also* Cosmic Mind, One Mind
Definition 111, 161
Manomayī: She who is composed of Mind 1577
Perceptions of the One Mind 490
The Action of the Cosmic Mind 167
The Divine Intelligence 134–135
The Plan is in the Divine Mind 161
The whole Universe is the Mind of God 74

Mahātma
Definition and description 388

Mahā-Tripurā-Sundarī
A Name of Lalitā, the Goddess 1559

Mahāvākya
61 Mahāvākya: Great Truth Statements 1469–1480
Great Truth Statements (Sanskrit) 1471–1479
Keys to the Heart 1314–1315
Mahāvākya Practice 1470
Words of Truth 1470

Mahāvidehā Siddhi
The Great Bodiless State 591

Mahā-Vidyā
A Name of Lalitā, the Goddess 1560

Mahāvīra
Had Relational Consciousness 906

Mahāyāna
The Ten Mahāyāna Precepts 814

Mahā Yuga
The Period of the Mahāmanvantara 168

Maheśvarī
A Name of Lalitā, the Goddess 1571

Mahimā
The General Powers 580

Maitreya
Christ Initiation Mantra 1723
Hierarchies of Life (graph) 1721
The Buddha and the Christ 1722
The Christ in the Heart 441
The Hierarchical Mantrams 1726
The Mystery of Jesus the Christ 664
The Threefold Christ 663

Makara
The Fifth Manifest Hierarchy 191
The Makara and Asuras 202
The rebellious angels 206

Makroposophus
The Great Face of God 795

Malachīm
Messengers sent by God 197

Male-Female. *See* Polarity, Sex

Malīk
The King whose Radiance and Glory never dies 829

Malkuth
The Kabbalistic Tree of Life 358–359

Māṁ
Potent Vibrations: Bīja-Mantra 1551

Man, Mankind. *See* Human Kingdom

Manas. *See also* Rūpa-Manas, Arūpa-Manas, Kāraṇa-Manas, Kāma-Manas, Buddhi-Manas
Definition 30
Manas: higher and lower 78
Mind and Desire 235
Mind and Thought 1376
Super-Knowing 1242
Suspended Mind 1209
Your Mind is the Key 1208

Mānasa-Loka. *See also* Mental Plane
Definition 76
Mind Realms 74–75

Mānasa-Mārga
The Way of the Mind 1238–1239

Mānasa-Pūja
Mental worship 1272

Mānasaputras
Gave Man his mental body 176
The Sons of Mind 216
The Third Manifest Hierarchy 191

Mānasa-Rūpa. *See also* mental body
The mental body 78
The objective-thoughtform mind 74
The Personality Complex 36–37

Manasi-Jā
Things born from your mind 82

Manas-Taijasi
Radiant Mind 1378

Maṇḍala
Kwan Yin Maṇḍala 1508
Madonna and Child 469
Meditation with a Seed 1186
Sāvitrī Maṇḍala 1497
Sūrya-Maṇḍala: the Circle of the Sun 1586
Sūrya-Maṇḍalā: a Name of Lalitā, the Goddess 1563
The Burning Heart 730
The Immaculate Heart 1513

Maṇi
Definition 551
The ancient symbol for the Spirit 1322
The Spirit-Spark-Atom 1298

Maṇipūra Cakra. *See also* Solar Plexus Centre
General description 47
The Heart and the Energy Centres 1332

Mano-Gata
A concept in the mind 79

Manogranthi
Obstacles to Higher Consciousness 1424

Manohara
Suspension of the activities of the mind 1208

Manojavitva Siddhi
Powers of Divine Descent 599

Manomāyākośa
Coverings over the Self 38

Manomayī
A Name of Lalitā, the Goddess 1577

Mano-Śakti
The Energy of the Goddess 1486

Mansions. *See also* Planes, Loka
Realms of Being 12
The Many Mansions (graph) 611

Mantra, Mantram. *See also* Sound, Prayer, Bīja-Mantra, Divine Names

What is Mantra?

Activities of Yoga-Mārga 520
Language of the Gods 200
Mantra: definition and application 457
Mantra-Śakti: the Energy of the Goddess 1486
Mantra-Sārā: a Name of Lalitā, the Goddess 1558
Mantra Yoga is White Magic 365
Miraculous Powers and Mantra 578, 593
Similarity to the Greek word Metanoia 1412
The Creative and Destructive Power of Sound 201
The Living Form of the Goddess in the Light 1522–1523
The Path of Mantra and the Goddess 1490
The Science of Bīja-Mantra 1218–1219
The Temple Not Made By Hands 369
Transcendental Meditation and Mantra Yoga 1182–1183
Vibration and Mantra 1518–1519

Mantra Practice

Four Ways to Enter Silence 1447
Guarding your Heart by Mantram 1328
Listening to a Mantra 788
Mantra-Dhyāna: Mantra-meditation 1328
Mantra-Japa: Mantra-repetition 453, 1219, 1328
Meditation with a Seed 1186
Right Use of Mantra 1697
Stilling the mind by Mantra 1214
The Two Applications of Mantra 1219
The use of Mantra in the Astral World 307
Understanding your Work in Silence 1024
Zikr, Dhikr: Mantra repetition (Arabic) 868

Arabic Mantras

Allāh: the exalted Name of God 871
El Allāh Hū: the Arabic I AM 1459
Let the Sunshine in 872
Some Arabic Prayers to the Deity 850–851
Sūfī Mantras for Meditation 874–877
The Beautiful Names 1264–1265
The Mantram of Unification 866–867
The Ninety-Nine Arabic Divine Names 878–884
Variations of the Mantram of Unification 868, 871

English Mantras

Activating I AM: the Secret Name of God 1419
A Gnostic Christian Heart Mantram 849
Mystical Theology 706–707
Some Christian Prayers to the Deity 1266
Some Western Heart Prayers 710
The Hierarchical Mantrams 1726–1727
The Upaniṣadic Mantrams 546–547
The Way of the Mind 1247

Greek Mantras

The Evolution of Christian Prayer 713–716
The Great Greek Mantra to Jesus 708–709

Hebrew Mantras

Eheieh (Asher Eheieh). *See* Eheieh (Eheyeh)
Fertilizing the Heart of the Divine Mother 1504
Hebrew Divine Names to be Invoked in the Heart 1262–1263
Hebrew Divine Words for Healing 1456
IHVH: I AM 1460
IOEL: the Healing Mind 1457
Sounding the Hebrew Angelic Names 1462
Sounding the Hebrew Divine Names 1461
The Evolution of Christian Prayer 713–716
The Jesus Mantra 1725
The Mantra to the Living Jesus 665
To Call upon Jesus 679
Yahweh (Yōd-Hey-Vau-Hey) 1346–1351
Yekhidah: the Hebrew I AM 1458
Yeshua: the Secret Hebrew Name 1276–1277

Latin Mantras

Latin Mantras of the Rosicrucians 712
Latin Mantras to Our Lady 1510–1511
Mantras to Connect to Our Lady 1512
The Evolution of Christian Prayer 713–716

Sanskrit Mantras

Buddha Initiation Mantra 1723
Children's Initiation Mantra into the Energy of the Goddess 1506
Christ Initiation Mantra 1723
Fertilizing the Heart of the Divine Mother for the Conception of the Divine Child 1504
Gāyatrī (Sun) Breathing 1553
Great Mantrams of Buddhi Yoga 1682

Keys to the Heart 1314–1327
Koham̐, Naham̐, So'ham̐ 1292
Mahāvākya: Great Truth Statements 1469–1479
Mantras to Sūrya, the Sun 1658–1674
Mantras to the Divine Mother 1493–1501
Mantras to the Human and Divine Self 1288
Meditations on Aspects of Rām 1072–1073
Potent Vibrations: Bīja-Mantra 1542–1551
Pure Devotion: Initiation Mantram 1724
Salutation to the Buddha 795
Sanskrit Divine Names for Meditation in the Heart 1269
Some Eastern Heart Mantras 457
The Esoteric Mantram 551
The Gāyatrī-Mantra (variations) 1601–1642
The Healing Sun Mantra 1599
The Śrī-Vidyā-Mantras 1524–1541
The One-Hundred Names of Lalitā 1555–1582
To Meditate on Quan Yin 1508

General Languages

Meditations in the Heart Centre 1294–1302
More Mantras for Awakening the Heart 458–461
Rām: the Universal Name 1273
Some Western Heart Mantras 456
The Divine Unity Mantra 1359
The Vowels in the Heart 1303

Manu

Primeval Mankind 167

Manuṣya. *See also* Human Kingdom

Involutionary and Evolutionary Kingdoms 194
The Fourth Manifest Hierarchy 191
The Human Kingdom 189

Manvantara

Day of Creation 167

Māori

Houses of learning 482
Mākutu (black magic) 274
The Third-Eye touch 1023
Tohungas 276
Whare Whananga 276

Māra

Opposition 219

Margaret Mary

Teachings on the Sacred Heart of Jesus 673, 703

Ma'rifat

Stage Four of the Radiant Way 831
The seventh stage of the Journey of the Heart 856
The third stage of Spiritual Life 1161

Mārtaṇḍa

A Name for the Solar Logos 1658

Martial Arts

Action Zen 802
and the Spiritual Warrior 985
The dynamic-immediacy of Tao 786
The purpose of physical action 1002–1003

Mary. *See also* Our Lady, Virgin Mary

Divine Names of Our Lady 1510
Her Transcendental Form 145
Latin Mantras to Our Lady 1510–1511
Marīa is a Holy Name 1512
The Immaculate Heart of Mary, Our Lady 1513
The Mystery of Jesus and Mary 665

Masculine Principle. *See also* Feminine Principle, Polarity

Male and Female Systems of Spirituality (graph) 1112
Male polarity: definition 25
The Divine Bipolarity 471
The Human Bipolarity 472
The Masculine God 649
The Masculinization of Children 478–479
The Unity-Field of Being (graph) 1009
Yin, Yang, Tao 476–477

Mask

Ēgō: I AM 1179
Persona (Latin): the Mask 38

Masons

The Temple Not Made By Hands 369

Mast-Allah

Fools of God 505

Mastānaḥ

God's Fools 1392
The God-Intoxicated 1164

Masters. *See* Spiritual Masters

Mātā
A Name of Lalitā, the Goddess 1575
The Mother 1493

Mātangī
The Mātangī-Mantra 1535

Materialism. *See also* ignorance, Māyā
All Hail to the Brain! 1368
Avoid the Errors of East and West 1122–1123
Cannot defeat the Human Soul 1177
Degeneration of Haṭha Yoga 524–525
Denial of God 108
Dense Materialism: a human evil 384
Destroys sensitivity towards Female Consciousness 468
Happiness Exists Within 1381
Humility for Earthlings 129
Identification with the body 895
Lack of Knowledge 4–5
Mahā-Māyā: the Ultimate Delusion 1714
Materialism Rules 1368
Materialistic concepts of Heaven 65
Materialistic Consciousness is Primeval Ignorance 1366
Materialistic psychology 291
Materialistic religions of the West 365
Meditation Degenerated 1180
Orthodox science, medicine and psychology 305, 1105
Prayer Spiritual and Material 681
Ray 7: Ceremony, Order 56
Scientific Materialism 382
Stimulated by the Seventh Ray 426
Subtle Eastern vibrations destroyed in the West 1517
The belief in objective matter existing on its own 1367
The Breakdown of Family 473
The Earthbound Spirits 403
The Education System 480–481
The Lost Radiance 1176
The materialist's subconscious motto 383
The orientation of today's Aquarian Age 835
To Feed the Poor? 1714
True War 985
What Meditation is not 1181
Wickedness in High Places 207
Zen and the World 758–759

Materializations
Explanation of 314

Matṛ
The Mother 1493

Mātrikā-Māyī-Devī
The letters-full-of-the-Goddess 1499

Matter. *See also* Prākṛtī
A fragment of Spirit 150
From Matter to Light 761
Living Matter 134–135
Material worlds: definition 26
Matter consists of all the worlds 351
Matter is organized according to a Plan 161
The Invisible World solidified 756
The Three Kinds of Activity of Matter 248

Mauna. *See also* Silence
Mauna-Śakti: the Energy of the Goddess 1487
Names of Lalitā, the Goddess 1578
Silence, Solitude, Peace 1386
Steps on the Spiritual Path 561

Māyā. *See also* ignorance, bondage, illusion, delusion
Definition 2
Illusion of the Astral World 59
Levels of meaning 38
Mahā-Māyā: the Great Illusion 181, 1714
Maya, Māyā: definitions 38
Māyā Siddhi 579
Obstacles to Higher Consciousness 1424
The "emptiness" of Space is an illusion 1589
The Astral Plane is the realm of Māyā 342
The Grand Delusion 3
The Physical Projection 297
The self-limiting Power of the Logos 1138
The Vibration of Hrīṁ 1528, 1547

Māyāvi-Rūpa
Levels of meaning 78
Māyāvi-Rūpa Siddhi 599
The illusionary body 1310

Mediators. *See also* Spiritual Teachers, Spiritual Masters
Mediums and Mediators 388–389
The ancient priests were mediators 367

Medicine
Discarded the idea of a life-force 589
Materialistic view of Man 305
Orthodox Psychology 1105
Temporary Relief 1427

Meditation. *See also* Prayer, Meditational Practices
32 Christian Prayer 689–716
37 Zen Meditation 785–804
41 Sūfī Prayer 863–884
46 Warrior Training 1001–1024
51 The Science of Meditation 1173–1200
52 Meditation Practice 1201–1226
53 The Heart and Spontaneous Meditation 1227–1248
54 The Heart and the Lost Art of Prayer 1251–1278

What is Meditation?
A process to connect with the Soul 1438
Benefits of Meditation 1199
Building the Antaḥkaraṇa 1194
Dhāraṇā and Dhyāna 1523
Dhyāna: the seventh step of Aṣṭāṅga Yoga 562, 572
Entering the Lost Kingdom 1176–1177
In Search of Reality 1174
Meditation: as defined in Mysticism 697
Meditation and the Joy of Living 1012–1013
Meditation Degenerated 1180
Meditation is Integration 1193
Mediumship is not a meditation process 321
On Love and Meditation 1140–1143
Some Facts about Meditation (Dhyāna) 1192
The Purpose of Meditation 1391
The Work of Meditation 1440–1441
What Meditation is not 1181

The Meditation Process
Examples of Supernatural Contemplation 1189
Illumination and Deification 1190
Stages of Interior Prayer 693–695
Stages of the Silent Meditation Process 1186–1187
Steps on the Meditational Path 1196–1198
Suspended Mind 1209
The Muslim Deification Process 1191
Transformations of the Mind 1242–1243
Your Mind is the Key 1208

Types of Meditation
Action Zen 802
Maharishi and Transcendental Meditation 1182–1183
Meditating on the Void 801
Meditation in the Heart and in the Head 898
Natural and Supernatural Contemplation 1188
Natural Meditation 1210–1211
The Science of Bīja-Mantra 1218–1219
The Way of Spontaneous Meditation 1229–1232
The Way of the Mind 1238
Types of Meditation 1184–1185
Unstructured Meditation 1221

Meditation Practice
Attach your Mind to the Eternal 1234–1235
Common Obstacles on the Path of Meditation 1205
Cultivate Silence of the Mind 1239
Expect Nothing 1205
How to find Peace and Joy through Meditation 1013
How to have a Peaceful Mind in a Troubled World 1244
How to Succeed in Meditation 1206–1207
If you Wish to Meditate 1204
Meditate first in the Heart 428, 430–431
Meditation (Metanoia) 1442
Rāja Yoga: Divine Union by Meditation 1126–1127
Rely on your Inner Self 1226
Right Meditation 1696
Some Hints for Meditation Practice 1203
The Art of Alignment 1202
The Being of Light in Meditation 418–419
The Secret of Meditation 1698
To Silence the Mind 1212–1214
Worship only the Divine Self 1226

Meditational Practices

Action
Action Zen 802
Heart Action 1331
Just Doing (Warrior) 1018
Meditation in Action (Warrior) 1019
The "No-Mind" 990
The Wisdom of Not-doing 1699

Meditational Practices (continued)

Breathing

A Connecting Breathing: Rū-Hā 1062–1063
Breathing God (Sūfī) 870–871
Breath-Prayer in the Heart 1274
Christian Meditation on the Holy Breath 1346–1353
Circular Breathing in the Heart 1345
Conscious Breathing in the Heart 1274–1275
Controlling the Mind through Breathing 1059
Gāyatrī (Sun) Breathing 1553
Guarding your Heart by Pure-Breathing 1328
Just Breathing (Warrior) 1018
Memory Breathing (the Rū-Hā) 1345
Mindfulness of Breathing 794
Rest in the Great Breath 1654
Tantric meditations on the Breath 954–955
Three Kinds of Breathing Meditation 1220
Warrior Breathing 1020
Warrior Breathing to Develop Internal Strength 1022
Warrior Calming Breathings 1021
Warrior Energizing Breathings 1060–1061
Watching the Breath 1213
Yesu-Breathing in the Heart 1276–1277

Cakras

Hebrew Divine Names Meditation 1461
Internalizing the Semi-Vowels in the Centres 1044–1045
Rū-Hā Breathing in the Base and Crown Centres 1063
Solar Meditation in the Cakras 1640
The Brahma-Gāyatrī in the Cakras 1639
The Vowels in the Energy Centres 1036–1038
Transformation of the Centres 1333

Divine Names. *See* Divine Name, Names

Goddess. *See* Goddess

Heart. *See also* Heart: Heart Mantras
20 The Mystery of the Heart 425–466
32 Christian Prayer 689–716
41 Sūfī Prayer 863–884
43 The Circle of Love 905–944
54 The Heart and the Lost Art of Prayer 1249–1278
55 Hṛdayaṁ: Meditations in the Heart Centre 1279–1308
56 The Heart and the Future Evolution of Man 1309–1334
57 The Way of Holiness 1335–1360
Christian Meditation on the Holy Breath 1346–1353
Christ Initiation Mantra 1723
Circular Breathing in the Heart 1345
Conscious Breathing in the Heart 1274–1277
Cultivate the Fires of Love 928–929
Devotion to Kṛṣṇa 449
How to begin Mental Prayer in the Heart 1260
Interior Prayer (Eastern Christian) 691–695
Keys to the Heart (Sanskrit) 1314–1327
Let the Sunshine in (Sūfī) 872
Linking the Head with the Heart 897
Mantras to the Human and Divine Self 1288
Meditations in the Heart Centre 1294–1302
Meditation in the Cave of the Heart 1358
Meditation on the Exalted Name of God (Sūfī) 871
Mental Prayer in the Heart 1260–1267
Mystical Theology (Eastern Christian) 706–707
Peace of Heart 1595
Practising the Presence of God 711
Pure Devotion: Initiation Mantram 1724
Rest you Mind in the Heart 1213
Saṁyama in the Heart Centre 587
Sūfī Mantras for Meditation (Arabic) 874–877
Techniques for the Expansion of the Heart 461
The Circle of Love 923
The Divine Mood 1252
The Divine Unity Mantra 1359
The Jesus Mantra 1725
The Jesus Mantra and the Sacred Heart Initiation 1356
The Jesus Prayer (Eastern Christian) 706–710
The Mantram of Unification in the Heart Centre 866–868
The Mind is Dissolved in the Heart 1235
The Ninety-Nine Arabic Divine Names 878–884
The Path to Ecstasy (Christian) 696–697
The Radiant Heart Prayer (Western Christian) 702–703
The Rose of Divine Love 858–861
The Rose of Love and the Cross of Light 1357
The Stages of Prayer 1253–1257
The Universal Heart Practice 846
The Warrior of the Heart 1074
The Way of the Radiant Heart 452–455
Three Meditations in the Heart (Who am I?) 1292
To Develop Perfect Stillness (Christian) 700

To Invoke God in your Heart 1293
To Meditate on Quan Yin 1508–1509
To Worship the Divine Incarnations 1270–1272
Visualization of the Christ in the Heart 730
Visualization of the Immaculate Heart of Mary, Our Lady 1513
Visualizing the Divinity within the Heart 1268–1269
Yeshua: the Secret Hebrew Name 1276–1277

Healing

Healing Sound-Vibration Formula 1064–1067
Hebrew Divine Words for Healing 1456–1457
The Healing Sun Mantra 1599

Listening, Hearing

Four Ways to Enter Silence 1447
Hear the Sound within the Silence 1651
Inner Absorption by Listening 1699
Just Hearing (Warrior) 1018
Listening 1215
Listen to Nāda 1212
Meditation on the Sacred Word 1216–1217
The Path of Hearing 553
Zen Listening 787–793
  Listening to a Mantra 788
  Listening to Ōṁ 788
  Listening to the Sound of the Dharma 789
  Listen to the Silence 792–793
  The Experience of Silence 791
  Zen Silence 790

Mantra. *See* Mantra, Mantram

Mind

60 Metanoia: the Renaissance of the Mind 1411–1468
61 Mahāvākya: Great Truth Statements 1469–1479
Controlling the Mind through Breathing 1059
Linking the Head with the Heart 897
Rāja Yoga: Divine Union by Meditation 1126–1127
Tantra Mind 933–935
The Pure Vowels for Mental Training 1039
The Way of the Mind 1238–1239
The Way of the Mind (mantra) 1247
The Upaniṣadic Mantrams 546–547, 1214
Transformation of the Ordinary Mind 898–899
Uniting Head and Heart 1130–1131

Mindfulness

Awareness Meditation 1656
Being-in-the-Moment Meditation in the Head 1245
Mindfulness: the Warrior Within 1017
Mindfulness in the Heart and in the Head 452
Mindfulness of Breathing 794
Murāqabaī: Sūfī Meditation 901
Tantric meditations on Attention 957
The 112 Methods of Instant Enlightenment 945–966
The "No-Mind" 990
The Silent Watcher Meditation 1388
The Watcher 1212
The Way of Spontaneous Meditation 1229–1232
Vipaśyanā Yoga: Internal Observation 1222–1223
Watching the Breath 1213

Remembrance. *See also* Divine Presence

Christian Meditation on the Holy Breath 1346–1353
Meditation on the Holy Spirit 1344
Practising the Presence of God 711
Remember the Presence 1653
The Path of Seeing 552

Seeing. *See also* Seeing

A Nirvāṇic Visualization 1200
Just Seeing (Warrior) 1018
Look for the Light 1395
Quietly Seeing (Zen) 786
See the Light of the Logos 1650
The Being of Light in Meditation 418–419
The Path of Seeing 552
Visualization of the Christ in the Heart 730
Visualization of the Immaculate Heart of Mary, Our Lady 1513
Visualizing the Divinity within the Heart 1268–1269

Silence. *See also* Silence

68 Works of Silence 1643–1656
Clouds of Unknowing 704–705
Connecting to the Silent Source of Creation 1008
Contemplative (Passive) Meditation 1185
Hear the Sound within the Silence 1651
How to have a Peaceful Mind in a Troubled World 1244
Methods to Silence the Mind 1212–1214
Resting in the No-Mind-State of the Absolute 1014–1015
The Path of Hearing 553

The Practice of Silence 1443–1447
Four Ways to Enter Silence 1447
How to Enter Silence 1445
Silence (Metanoia) 1447
Silence and Activity 1446
Stages of Silence 1444
The Silent State 1554
The Silent Watcher Meditation 1388
The Wisdom of Not-doing 1699
To Silence the Mind 1212–1214
Zen Silence 790–793

Sitting
Just Sitting (Warrior) 1018
Shikantaza: to sit fully aware 800–801
Zazen: Zen Sitting 798

Sound. *See also* Mantra, Divine Name
47 The Primordial Sound Language 1025–1076
Activating I AM: the Secret Name of God 1419
Cosmic Tuning-In: the 'I' Sound 1652
Personality Integration Chart 1333
Potent Vibrations: Bīja-Mantra 1542–1552
The Vowels in the Heart 1303

Sun. See Sun

Third-Eye
Buddha Initiation Mantra 1723
Look for the Light 1395
Meditation in the Third-Eye 1224–1225
Remember the Presence 1653
See the Light of the Logos 1650
The Path of Seeing 552
The Silent Watcher Meditation 1388
Transformation of the Ordinary Mind 898–899

General Practices
Building the Bridge of Light 554–555
Meditating on Kōans and Hua-Tous 796–797
Meditating on the Void 801
Meditation on the Form of the Guru 1225
Meditation on the Sūtrātma 1645
Open-Eyes Meditations for the Warrior 1018
The Hierarchical Mantrams 1726–1727
The Practice of Grounding 1005
The Sevenfold Practice 1698

Mediumship. *See also* Psychism
15 Channelling and Mediumship 317–344
Ascended Masters? 332
Astral Disinformation 1271
Astral projection and mediumship 304
Beyond Spirit-Guides 336
Channelling or Soul-Wisdom? 327
"Channelling" the Soul 325
Consciousness and Phenomena (graph) 323
Exalted Sources? 330
H.P. Blavatsky and A.A. Bailey were not mediums 338
Humility of the Great Ones 337
Masters and Mediums 326
Medium: Latin definition 318
Mediumship: general introduction 309
Mediums and Mediators 388–389
Roots of Modern Mediumship 318
Subconscious Sources 331
Telepathy is not mediumship 80
The Changing Faces of the Spirit-Guides 332–333
The Coming of the Spirit-Guides 281
Types of Mediumship 321
What is "Channelling"? 320–324
Who are the "Spirit-Guides"? 334–335
Why Channelling is Dangerous 340–343
You Must Choose 344

Melchizedek
A Priest-King of ancient Israel 728
The Order of Melchizedek 729

Mentalism
Dharma: the Law of Mentalism 244–245, 247
Mediumship vs the Laws of Mentalism 322

Mental body. *See also* Mānasa-Rūpa
General description 78
Polarities Male and Female 920–921
The Personality Complex 36–37
Those polarized in the mental body 376

Mental Plane. *See also* Devāchan
4 Devāchan: The Mental Plane 73–82
Denizens of the Heaven Worlds 77
Forms and formlessness 760
Impressions from the Mental Plane 80

Mind and Brain 79
Mind Realms 74–75
Paths to Devāchan 81
Sukhāvatī: the place of happiness 76
The Archetypal and Creative Worlds 360–361
The Fifth World (Arabic) 888
The Mental Body 78
The Mental Plane in brief 17
The Seven Heavens 76
The Seven Subplanes of the Mental Plane (graph) 75
To Experience Heaven 82

Mental Prayer
How to begin Mental Prayer in the Heart 1260
The Stages of Prayer 1253–1257

Mental telepathy. *See* Telepathy

Merkavah
The Throne of God 94
Vehicles of Light 283

Messiah
False Messiahs 726
Jewish and Christian expectations of the Messiah 678
Jews rejected Jesus as the Messiah 649
Mashiah, Mashiach: definition 660
The Avatāra 389
The Divine Incarnation 726
The Jewish Messiah 660
The Jewish Messiah recognized by the Magi 356
The Messiah Jesus 666
When will the Messiah come? 619

Metanoia. *See also* Spiritual Psychology
60 Metanoia: the Renaissance of the Mind 1411–1468

What is Metanoia?
Aspects of Metanoia 1413
Christian Hesychast definition 743
From Personal to Cosmic Life 1428
Gnostic Christian definition 738
Metanoia: derivation and definition 1412
Mistranslated as "Repentance" 683
Summary of the Process 1468
The Western form of Mahāvākya 1470
What is Metanoia? 1412

Levels of Metanoia
Being and Becoming 1415
Cosmic Renewal 1452
Illumined-Mind Consciousness 1427
Reactive-Emotional Consciousness 1426
The First Circle of Life 1422–1423
The Second Circle of Life 1438–1439
The Third Circle of Life 1448–1449
Who is "I AM"? 1418

Metanoia Practice
Activating I AM: the Secret Name of God 1419
Attach Yourself to Being 1433
Emotional Problems 1429–1431
God, the Healer of Broken Hearts 1432–1433
How to deal with Crisis situations in your Life 1435
Meditation on the Divine Names 1454–1462
Obstacles to Higher Consciousness 1424
Oneness and Love 1450–1451
The Kingdom is at Hand 1453
The Practice of Silence 1443–1447
The Work of Meditation 1440–1441
The Work of Metanoia 1414

Metanoia Statements
Action and Destiny 1420–1421
Crisis 1436–1437
Fear and Stress 1434
Healing 1463
Inner Guidance 1464
Karma and Death 1425
Meditation 1442
Oneness and Love 1451
Reality 1416–1417
Silence 1447
The First Circle of Life 1423
The Path 1465–1467
The Second Circle of Life 1439
The Third Circle of Life 1449
The Word 1455

Metanois
Christian Hesychast definition 742

Metatron
Hebrew Angelic Names Meditation 1462

Metempsychosis
A popular superstition 252
Michael
Hebrew Angelic Names Meditation 1462
Hebrew Divine Words for Healing 1456
Microcosm
As above, so below 125
Mikrokosmos: definition 121, 733
Milieu
The Divine Milieu 12
Mind. *See also* lower mind, subconscious mind, Higher Mind, Superconscious Mind, Mind of Light, Cosmic Mind, One Mind
What is Mind?
All Hail to the Brain! 1368
Derivation of the word "mind" 74
Do not mistake your mind for your Soul 1370
Heart and Mind 429
Manas: definition 78
Mind and Body 1374–1375
Mind and Brain 79
Mind and Desire 235
Mind and Thought 1376
Mind in Body 988
Ray 5: Fire, Mind 56
The Knowledge of how the mind works 588
The Mental Body 78
The mind is the directive agent 1502–1503
Yogic Teachings on Mind and Self 536–547
Your mind has two functions 350
Dimensions of Mind
Dimensions of the Mind 891
Kāma-Manas and Buddhi-Manas 39
Manomayī: She who is composed of Mind 1577
Mind-Only 974–975
Mind Realms: the Mental Plane 74–75
Mind to Mind (telepathy) 346–347
Powers of Consciousness 374–375
Realms of the One Mind 492–493
Tao: the Universal Mind 775
You Are the World 1390–1391
The Law of the Mind. *See also* Karma, Dharma
Dharma: the Law of Being 244–245
The Good Law 262
The Laws of Magic are the Laws of the Mind 356
The Universal Intelligence 232
The Creative Power of the Mind
Action and Destiny (Metanoia) 1420–1421
Energy Materializes 363
Fear of the Lord? 234
Mind-Created Heavens and Hells 6–7, 62
Mind and Thought 1376
Prophecy and Destiny 294–297
Subconscious Forces 236–237
The Law of the Afterlife 410–411
The Power of Suggestion 237
The Power of Thought 232
The Thought of Enlightenment 767
The world is the product of Mind 1234
Thinking and Being 233
Thought creates even in the Astral World 246
Why Life is Suffering 263
Your Fate is before your eyes 246
The Mind Downturned
A mind used selfishly will lead you to ruin 1503
Human Evil 212–213
In Bondage to the Mind 238
Limitations of the ordinary mind 426–427
Reactive-Emotional Consciousness 1426
Self-Created Hells 407
Senses or the Self? 239
The Evil Mind 224–225
The Mind-Created Devil 218
The Mind Divine or Demonic 212
The physical senses entrap the mind 1519
The Seed of Evil 221
Why Life is Suffering 263
Your mind is attracted to physical things 1231
You identify with what goes on in your mind 538–539
You perceive according to your mind's conditioning 540

The Mind Transformed
Attach your Mind to the Eternal 1234–1235
Bīja disentangles your mind 1519
Develop a pure Heart and a refined Mind 1286
Illumined-Mind Consciousness 1427
Impressions from the Soul 350
Inspiration by the Mind of Light 1113
Manas-Taijasi: Radiant Mind 1378
Perceptions of the One Mind 490
Tantra Mind 933–935
The Mind Divine or Demonic 212
The Mind is Dissolved in the Heart 1235
Tranquil Mind 1503
Transformations of the Mind 1242–1243
Stilling the Mind. *See also* Silence, Stillness
Cultivate Silence of the Mind 1239
Dhāraṇā and Dhyāna 1523
How to have a Peaceful Mind in a Troubled World 1244
Mental Activity 1228
Mind-Waves 1239
No-Mind and the One Mind 763
Overactive Mind 990
Silence, Solitude, Peace 1386
Skill in Action 989
Suspension of the mind by surrender to God 548
The "No-Mind" 990
The Practice of Silence 1443–1447
The Suspending of the Mind (graph) 1209
To Experience Heaven 82
To Silence the Mind 1212–1214
When the Mind is Still 768
Yoga is the cessation of the activities of the mind 536–537
Your Mind is the Key 1208
Zen Silence 790–793
The Way of the Mind
Mystics of Pisces and Aquarius 836–837
Rāja Yoga: Divine Union by Meditation 1126–1127
Taming the Mind 899
The Two Paths 1112
The Way of the Mind 1238–1239
The Way of the Mind (mantra) 1247
Transformation of the Ordinary Mind 898–899
Uniting Head and Heart 1130–1131

Mind-Only. See Mahat, One Mind

Mindfulness. See Meditational Practices

Mind of Light
Buddhi-Manas 891
Inspiration by the Mind of Light 1113
Manas-Taijasi: Radiant Mind 1378
Nirvāṇic Consciousness 492–493
Variations of usage 891

Mineral Kingdom
The Sevenfold Earth-Evolution 169

Minitum Mundum
The Microcosm 121

Miracles, Miraculous Powers. *See also* Magic
26 The Yoga of Miraculous Powers 577–606. See Yoga
Kharisma: definition 312
Magicians of Atlantis and India 277
Miracles performed by spirits and UFO people 335
Mirāculum: definition 277
Mysterious Knowledge of the Siddhas 1310–1311
Pāda III Sūtras 16-56 (Saṁyama on…) 583–597
Powers by Drugs? 578
Saṁyama 582
Seek Not Powers 581
Siddhi, Vibhūti: definitions 277, 578
The General Powers 580–581
The Source of Miracles (Christian) 671
To Safely Perform Miracles 1353
Yogic Powers and Psychism 579

Mirror of Justice
Spēculum Justīciae 1511

Mnimi Theou
Christian Hesychast definition 743

Mohammed. See Muḥammad

Mohinī
A Name of Lalitā, the Goddess 1568

Mokṣa. *See also* Mukti, Freedom, Liberation
Definition 32, 418, 1237
Learn to Die before you Die 420–421
The Discovery of Truth 85
True Death 424

Moment. *See* Time, Being in the Moment

Monad. *See also* Paramātman
- Christian Hesychast definition 741
- Definition 5, 24, 733
- Deification 1190
- Ēgō: variations of meaning 1179
- Gnostic Christian definition 736
- The Father in Heaven 1322
- The last stages of the Great Work 1193
- The Mystery within the Heart 1315
- The Pure Spirit that you are 1233
- The Self as One 1727
- The Spirit, dwelling on the Paranirvāṇic Plane 491
- Who is "I AM"? 1418

Monks
- Internalized the processes of Tantra 909
- Interpreted the scriptures for themselves 565
- Life as a Zen Monk 806
- Monks and Disciples 991
- Only celibate males can attain Salvation? 560
- Spiritual Life and Material Life 1118
- Unnatural views of women and of sex 910
- Unnecessary Practices 1111

Monogenes
- Christian Hesychast definition 741
- Gnostic Christian definition 736
- The Only Son of God? 669

Monology
- Repetition of a mantra or prayer 453, 743

Monos
- Christian Hesychast definition 739
- The Second Aspect of the Godhead 122–123

Moon
- Candra: the Cool Moonlight 1595
- Contacting the Hierarchy during Full Moon 981
- Saṁyama upon the Sun and Moon 585

Morality. *See* Virtue, Righteousness

Morphe
- Gnostic Christian definition 738

Moses
- The great Revelation given to Moses 106, 324
- The Prophets are not spooked 325

Mother. *See also* Divine Mother, World Mother, Goddess
- Dimensions of the Cosmic Fire (graph) 137
- Mater Marīa: Mother Mary 1512
- Sanskrit words for "Mother" 1493
- Tao: the Great Mother 146
- The Blissful Mother: Mother of Immortal Bliss 1493
- The Mother Force: the Force of Nature 150, 151
- The Mother Light 1533
- The Mother of the World 147
- The Threefold Logos 662
- The Virgin and the Mother 144
- The World Mother of Compassionate Heart 145

Motherhood
- Mother, Father and Baby 938
- The Call of the World Mother 468–475
- The Feminine Heart 925

Mother Theresa
- An example of practical Love 1123, 1143
- A practical Mystic 91

Motion. *See* change

Mṛtyu
- Lalitā as the Goddess of Death 1540

Mu. *See also* Wu, Wu-Wei
- Terms of Awakening 766

Mudrā
- Definition 524

Muḥammad
- Had Relational Consciousness 906
- The giver of the Religion of Islām 829, 833
- The Prophets are not spooked 325

Mukti. *See also* Mokṣa, Liberation, Freedom
- Definition 32, 185, 1237
- Learn to Die before you Die 420–421
- The Discovery of Truth 85
- True Death 424

Mūlādhāra Cakra. *See also* Base Centre
Definition 143
General description 46
The Heart and the Energy Centres 1332

Mūlamantra
A Name of Lalitā, the Goddess 1561
The Root Mantra of Śrī-Vidyā 1526, 1530

Mūlaprākṛtī
A Name of Lalitā, the Goddess 1565
The Root of Nature 471
Veil over the Unmanifest Godhead 112

Mullā
The learned man 829

Mumukṣatva
Qualifications for Discipleship 1149

Muni
Definition 30, 1205, 1504

Murāqabaī
Sūfī Meditation 901

Murder
Death-experience of the suicide and the murdered 404–405

Mūrdha Jyotiṣi
The Light in the Head 587

Murīd
The second stage of the Journey of the Heart 855

Murshid
The Spiritual Guide 832

Music
Art and the Follies of Man 470
God's Cosmic Symphony 1649
Our Sacred Music and Language 2081
Sounding the Perfect Chord of Being (graph) 1186
Sounds experienced through Kuṇḍalinī 156
The Creative and Destructive Power of Sound 201
The Music of the Universe 1648
When you listen to music 787

Music-angels. *See* Gandharvas

Muslim. *See also* Sūfīsm
One who believes in the One God 828

Mystai
Greek classifications of Humanity 687

Mystery
God is a Sublime Mystery 127
Mysteria: Greek Mystery School definition 734
Mysterion: Christian Hesychast definition 739
Mysterion: definition 208
Mysterious Grace 1311
Mysterious Knowledge of the Siddhas 1310–1311
The Mystery of Jesus and Mary 665
The Mystery of Jesus the Christ 664
The Mystery of the Sun is the Power of Love 1597
The Mystery of the Trinity 265
The Mystery within the Heart 1315
The Paradox of Evil 208–209
The Path of Mantra and the Goddess 1490
Three Great Mysteries to solve in life 1369
To Achieve Liberation 1177
Truth is more powerful than fiction 285
Why Human Souls have received animal bodies 893
Your personal sense of self is a mystery 1388

Mystery Schools
A New Age Spiritual School 2078
Future Esoteric Schools 1709
The Mystery Schools and Āśramas 1148
The Structure of the Warrior School 1006–1007
Words from the Greek Mystery Schools 733–735

Mystical Consciousness. *See also* Pure Consciousness, Buddhi, Satori
Buddhic Consciousness 86
Descriptions of the Mystic Experience 508
Glimpses of Illumination 501
Mystical Ascent 455
Mystical Marriage 96
Mystical Trance 1189
Mystical Union 85, 466, 639, 816–817, 846, 1189
Pure Consciousness in the Heart 447
Spiritual Marriage 1189
The Law of Mystic Experience 508–509
The Lotus of the Heart 446
Your Original Face 87

Mysticism
27 Teachings of the Saints 609–622
28 The Heart of Christianity 623–640
35 The Spirit of Zen 749–770
40 The Sūfī Heart 843–862
57 The Way of Holiness 1335–1360
A Sūfī is... 840–841
Be Still and Know 638–639
Channelling or Soul-Wisdom? 327
Christian Mysticism 450–451
Christian Mysticism and Zen 630
Contemplative and Practical Mystics 91
Mystes: definition 91
Mysticism is not a philosophy 451
Mysticism is not mediumship 324, 328, 626
Mystics of Islām 828–829
Mystics of Pisces and Aquarius 836–837
Mystikos: definition 91, 512
Natural Meditation 1210–1211
Search out your Heart 437
The Dichotomy of the Mystic 629
The Experience of Mysticism 636–637
The Hasidim 648–649
The Lover of God 853
The Mysticism of Saint Paul 666
The Mystics 377
The Prayer of a Practical Mystic 92
The Two Paths 1112
The Way of Mysticism (Rays) 55
The Way of the Christian Mystic 626–628
Uniting Head and Heart 1130–1131

Mythology
Legends of the Buddha 393
Limitations of Biblical mythologies 214
Mythical Concepts of God 104–105
Mythologies are imaginative facts 273
Mythology is not the Truth 1695
Myths are taken as "reality" 539
Stories of the imagination 1271
The Great Flood 272
Truth and Mythology 7
Why Myths? 105

N

Nabi
The Prophets 647

Nāda
Āuṁ, Ōṁ, Nāda 550–551
Listen to Nāda 1212
Meditation on the Sacred Word 1216–1217
Nāda-Bindu: Sounding-Light 1212
Nāda-Brahman: the Voice of God 311
Nāda-Rūpā: a Name of Lalitā, the Goddess 1570
Recreating yourself by Nāda 1523
The Action of the Primordial Sound (graph) 165
The Divine Substance 1647
The same as the Arabic Nidā 864
The Sounds of Nāda 1651
The Voice of the Silence 1570
What is the Name? 1259

Nāḍī
Psychic nerves depend on the Heart 434
Subtle Energy Currents 723

Nafs
The Living Soul (Arabic) 892

Nahaṁ
Three Meditations in the Heart 1292

Nāma. *See also* Divine Name
God Incarnating in you and in the Cosmos 1212
Nāma, Nāman: definition 30
Nāmaste: the personal greeting of old India 1703
The Name of God 1647

Name, Names. *See* Divine Name

Nār
The Human Constitution (Arabic) 892

Narakā
Hellish conditions of mind 218

Nārāyaṇa
Nārāyaṇī: a Name of Lalitā, the Goddess 1570
Sūrya-Nārāyaṇa: the Sun-Spirit 1608
The Mover upon the Waters of Space 167
The Universal Sunshine of the Spirit 1672

Nationalism
Nationalism and Tribalism 385
Separatism and the Law of Love 386

Natural disasters
The Sufferings of Man 223

Nature
Meditation with Nature 1210
Mountains, Clouds and Water 783
Observing visible and invisible Nature 1230–1231
Prākṛtī: definition 14
Sexuality and Natural Law 918–919
Supernātūralis: beyond physical Nature 357
The Kingdom of Nature 1688
The Real Nature 3
The Three Forces at work in Nature and Humanity 1693

Nature-spirits
The Angelic Builders 414
The Elemental Kingdom 194–195

Nazarenes
Followers of the man from Nazareth 642

Nectar of Immortality
Kuṇḍalinī and Alchemy 153
To Taste the Elixir of Life 593

Nemesis
The Goddess of Retribution 233, 1404

Nepenthe
Being sedated by material life 285

Nephilīm
The fallen angels 211

Netzach
The Kabbalistic Tree of Life 358–359

New Age. *See* Aquarian Age

New-Agers
Already Enlightened? 341
Dangers of Black Magic 364, 371
Don't need Teachers? 339
Fear of being "conditioned" 485
New-agers who treat Kuṇḍalinī lightly 157
Why most new-agers never attain 318, 573

New Jerusalem
The lower heavens 65

Nidā
The Voice of God 864

Nightmares
The seventh astral subplane 62

Nipsis
Wakefulness in the Heart Centre 632

Nirākāra
Nirākārā: a Name of Lalitā, the Goddess 1576
Qualities of the Divine Being 107

Nirañjana
Definition 5
Qualities of the Divine Being 107

Nirantarā
A Name of Lalitā, the Goddess 1576

Nirbīja Samādhi
Types of Samādhi 575

Nirguṇā
A Name of Lalitā, the Goddess 1575

Nirmala
Nirmalā: a Name of Lalitā, the Goddess 1576
Nirmala-Sundarī: Spotless Beauty 1494

Nirmānakāya
Bodies composed of filaments of Light 1313
Bodies of the Buddhas 392–393
Definition 41, 391
General description 390
Meditational Service of the Buddhas 393
Understanding your Work in Silence 1024

Nirodha
Definition 536, 1242
Nirodha-Pariṇāma 1243
Nirodha Pariṇāma Siddhi 598

Nirvāṇa
6 Nirvāṇa: The World of Glories 93–102
A description of Nirvāṇa 329
A Nirvāṇic Visualization 1200
Bhāgavata-Avasthā: the Glorified State 495–496
Cannot be attained by ordinary death-processes 329
Gnostic terms for Nirvāṇa 95
In Nirvāṇa the Will of God is perfectly expressed 1720
Mahāprajñāparamitā 768–769
Mahāśūnyatā: the Great Emptiness 23, 85
Nirvāṇa! (derivation and description) 94–95
Nirvāṇa is… 98–101
Praḍhāna: Original Cause 595
Step Three of the Meditational Path 1198
The Experience of the Heart 1281
The Fullness of the Void 23
The Goal of Evolution 1689
The Nirvāṇic Plane in brief 17
The Seven Subplanes of the Nirvāṇic Plane (graph) 99
The Third Circle of Life 1448
The Third World (Arabic) 889
The Truth about Nirvāṇa 102
The Two Realities (physical and Nirvāṇic) 97
Touch Ultimate Emptiness (Taoism) 96

Nirvāṇī
A Buddha who lives in Nirvāṇa 390

Nirvāṇic Consciousness. *See* Nirvāṇa, God-Consciousness

Nirvāṇic Plane. *See* Nirvāṇa

Nirvikalpa Samādhi
Types of Samādhi 574

Nirvikārā
A Name of Lalitā, the Goddess 1576

Nirvitarka Samādhi
Types of Samādhi 575

Niṣkalā
A Name of Lalitā, the Goddess 1575

Niṣkāma-Karma
Desireless action 1331

Niṣkarmayam
Non-Action Misinterpreted 1120

Niṣpāra
Qualities of the Divine Being 107

Niṣspanda
Transformations of the Mind 1243

Nityā
A Name of Lalitā, the Goddess 1576

Nitya Samādhi
Types of Samādhi 575

Ni-Vṛtti
Evolution 595

Niyama
Definition 562, 564
Stage Two of Aṣṭāṅga Yoga 568–569

No-mind
Clouds of Unknowing 704–705
No-Mind and the One Mind 763
Resting in the No-Mind State of the Absolute 1014–1015
Śūnyatā: the Void 503
The "No-Mind" 990
The Wisdom of Not-doing 1699

Noisis
Christian Hesychast definition 742

Noitos
Christian Hesychast definition 742

Non-violence. *See* Ahiṁsā, violence

Note-of-withdrawal
Begins the Natural Death Process 399

Noumenon
Greek Mystery School definition 735

Nous
Christian Hesychast definition 742
Gnostic Christian definition 737
The Divine Intelligence 134–135
The Human Constitution (Greek) 39

Now. *See* Time, Being in the Moment

Nūr
Nūr, Nūrā, Nuhrā: Light 1350
Nūr 'Alī: Light Most Exalted 829
The Light of God 437, 847

O

OBE. *See* out-of-body experience

Objectivity
- From Subjective to Objective 173
- Objective Experience 305

Observer. *See* Witness, Watcher, Draṣṭā

Obstacles. *See also* tests
- Causes of Group Disruption 1154–1155
- Common Obstacles on the Path of Meditation 1205
- Crises on the Path 1162–1165
- Karmic Adjustment 1379
- Notes on the Spiritual Path in the New Age 1166–1167
- Obstacles to Higher Consciousness 1424
- Overstimulation on the Path 557
- Passion and Dispassion 695
- Persevering to the End until Final Liberation 1101
- Planetary Disturbance 1697
- The Ascent of Kuṇḍalinī 152
- The Double Stress of Meditational Life 1181
- The obstacles to Union with the Soul 556–557
- When Kuṇḍalinī Awakens 157–158

Ojas
- Definition 153

Okeanos
- The Waters of Space 167

Ōṁ
- Āuṁ, Ōṁ, Nāda 550–551
- Āuṁ: the Holy Spirit as Cosmic Mother 1501
- God's Cosmic Symphony 1649
- Listening to Ōṁ 788
- Oṁkāra: Meditations in the Heart Centre 1295
- Ōṁ is the Word of Power for Īśvara 1623
- Potent Vibrations: Bīja-Mantra 1542–1543
- Preliminary Meditation on the Sun 1605
- The Seed-Sound for Tārā 1489
- The Word of Glory 1610

Ōṁ Maṇi Padme Hūṁ
- Description and translations 460
- Keys to the Heart 1322
- Meditations in the Heart Centre 1298
- Sex Natural and Divine 926
- The Esoteric Mantram 551

Ōṁ-Sai. *See* Āuṁ-Sai

Ōṁ Śrī
- The Holy Vibration 1520
- To Meditate on Sāvitrī 1497

Omito-Fu
- Meditations in the Heart Centre 1299

Omnipotence, Omnipresence, Omniscience
- Adhiṣṭhātṛtvaṁ: Lordship over all 596
- Sarvajña: the Omniscience of a Buddha 755
- Sarvajñātṛtvaṁ: Omniscience 596
- Tantric meditations on Omnipresence 955–956
- The Greatness of God (Arabic) 875
- The Limitless God 110
- The Omnipresent God 1108–1109
- The Soul is Omnipotent and Omniscient 1554

Omnirevelation
- Chiliokosmos: definition 121

Oneness. *See* Unity

One Mind. *See also* Mahat, Cosmic Mind, Unity
- Messengers of the One Mind 764
- Mind-Only 974–975
- No-Mind and the One Mind 763
- Perceptions of the One Mind 490
- Realms of the One Mind 492–493
- Tao: the Universal Mind 775
- The Eternal is One 512–514
- The One 1686–1687
- What is Consciousness? 1368
- What is Tao? 772–773
- Your mind is one with the All-Mind 1390–1391

Onomatopoeia
- Greek Mystery School definition 735

Openness
- Remain Flexible and Open 1172
- The Approach to Truth 1152
- The Attitude for Yoga 558

Opposition
All opposition is destroyed by itself 1446
Causes of Group Disruption 1154–1155
Common Obstacles on the Path of Meditation 1205
Facing the Evil Mind 1087
Jesus and Buddha struggled with opposition 219
Notes on the Spiritual Path in the New Age 1166–1167
Opposition from the Astral Plane 1167
Religious Reactionaries 287–288
Rulers in High Places 657
The Power of Yielding 1088
What is "the Devil"? 684

Oracles
Ōrāculum: definition 292

Oral prayer
The Stages of Prayer 1253

Ordinary mind. See lower mind

Orthodoxy
and the New Age Impulse 1111
Developing the Cosmic-Sense 1709
Orthodoxos: correct belief? 653
Orthodoxos: Greek Mystery School definition 735
Orthodox and mystical religion 828–829
Orthodox religion and science are produced by the personality 1367
Religious Reactionaries 287–288

Osiris
The Father Light 122–123

Ouija board
Dangers of 313
Leads to possession 322

Ouranos
Western words for "Heaven" 1352

Our Lady. *See also* Mary, Virgin Mary
Contactee phenomena 333
Divine Names of Our Lady 1510
Her Transcendental Form 145
Latin Mantras to Our Lady 1510–1511
Mantras to Connect to Our Lady 1512
The Call of the World Mother 468–479
The Feminine Avatāra 144
The Feminine Virtues 468–469
The Immaculate Heart of Mary, Our Lady 1513
The Mystery of Jesus and Mary 665
The World Mother of Compassionate Heart 145

Out-of-body experience. *See also* astral projection
Confused with channelling 322
Dreams and out-of-body experiences 300
Hallucinations and out-of-body experiences 305

Outer Darkness
The Eighth Sphere 63

Overactivity
Balance on the Physical Plane 1257
Cultivate Silence of the Mind 1239
Mental Activity 1228
Overactive Mind 990

Overstimulation
Diseases caused by walking upon the Spiritual Path 1168
Notes on the Spiritual Path in the New Age 1166–1167
Overstimulated Sex, Throat and Solar Plexus Centres 1431
Overstimulation of the Sex Centre 153
Overstimulation on the Path 557
The Ascent of Kuṇḍalinī 152

P

Pada, Pāda
Definitions 535

Padma
A symbol for the Heart 1322
Hṛt-Padma: the Heart Lotus 1505
Padmapāṇi: the Lotus-born 1298
The lotus flower 551

Pagan
Pāgānus: definition and usage 514

Palingenesia
Spiritual Regeneration 185

Pañcadaṣī
A Name of Lalitā, the Goddess 1561
The Pañcadaṣī Vibration 1526
The Śrī-Vidyā-Mantra 1530

Para-Bhakti
Supreme Devotion 1280

Parabola
Christian Hesychast definition 747

Parabrahman. *See also* God
Definition 14, 111
Keys to the Heart 1325
Mahāvākya Practice 1473
Only the Godhead is real 1178
The Absolute in the Absolute Condition 358
The Transcendental Godhead 112
The Universes are not separate from the Absolute Godhead 1589

Paradise
The Christian Cosmo-Conception 19

Parakāya-Praveṣa-Siddhi
Another's-body-entering-power 588

Paralipomena
Christian Hesychast definition 746

Parallel Universes
A distortion of Truth 13

Paramā
A Name of Lalitā, the Goddess 1569

Paramahaṁsa
Regain what you have Lost 381
The Omnipresent Spirit of God 1655

Paramānandā
A Name of Lalitā, the Goddess 1572

Paramāṅganā
A Name of Lalitā, the Goddess 1569

Paramapadātmava
The one Buddha-Nature 1208

Paramāpūrva-Nirvāṇa-Śakti
The Mother of the World 1498

Paramārthādharma
Derivation and meaning 1407

Paramātman. *See also* Monad
All actions are performed by the Universal Self 1132–1133
Ātman and Paramātman are one and the same 551
At the level of Paramātman there are no limitations 38
Can be found in your Heart Centre 1288
Eheyeh (Eheieh): the Cosmic I AM 324
Incarnations of the Sun 1593
Paramātman Bīja 1551
Puruṣa: the Supreme Being 1318
Rūḥ-u-llāh: the Spirit of God 890, 892
The Omnipresent God 1109
The One God of All Religions 110
The real You is the Monad 545
The Third Circle of Life 1448
The Third Stage of Yoga 529
The three degrees of Self-Realization 1448
The Transcendental-Spiritual-Sun 1634
The Upaniṣadic Mantrams 546–547
The Way of the Spirit 381

Paramātmikā
A Name of Lalitā, the Goddess 1570

Parameśvarī
A Name of Lalitā, the Goddess 1565
The Supreme Goddess lives in the Heart 1563

Param-Īśvara
Parameśvara: Mahāvākya Practice 1473
The Self within the Heart of the Universe 1603–1604

Paramitā
Definition 769
The two Aspects of the Goddess 1516
The Virgin and the Mother 144

Param-Jyotī
A Name of Lalitā, the Goddess 1567

Paranirvāṇa
Our true Home or Origin 17
The Kingdom of the Father 128
The most boundless Human Consciousness 490
The realm of the Monad, Paramātman 17
The Second World (Arabic) 889

Parapsychology. *See also* Psychism, Psychology, Spiritual Psychology
Errors of 2, 290–291
May be studied from the perspective of Kuṇḍalinī 156
Parapsychological terminology 290–291
Saṁyama and Parapsychology 582

Paraśakti
Parā-Śaktī: A Name of Lalitā, the Goddess 1558
Para-Śakti-Maya: the Mother of the World 1498
The Great Mother of All 592
The Supreme Power 1500

Parāsaṁvit
The Omniscient Light 527

Parā-Vāk
A Name of Lalitā, the Goddess 1568
The Supreme Sound-Vibration 1577

Parenthood. *See also* Polarity, Motherhood
Mother, Father and Baby 938–939
Mother and Father 475
Nourishing the Goal of Life 487
The Gift of Parenthood 474

Pariṇāma
Transformations of the Mind 1242–1243

Parousia
Christian Hesychast definition 741
The experiencing of the Christ Light 500
The Kingdom is at Hand 1453
The Second Coming 727

Parrisia
Christian Hesychast definition 743

Pārvatī
An Energy-Form of the Goddess 1489
A Name of Lalitā, the Goddess 1572
The Eternal Feminine 469

Passion. *See also* Desire, Emotion, Kāma
Passion and Dispassion 695
Vairāgya: dispassion 1149, 1330

Passivity
The Active and Passive Way 1011
The Eternal-Timeless-Self is passive 1229
Via Negativa: the Passive Path 1465

Past. *See also* Time, Being in the Moment
Knowledge of the Past and the Future 583
Let Go of the Past 1241
Past and Present Evolutionary Development of the Cakras (graph) 178
Past, Present and Future 1400–1401
Spirituality Past and Future 1104
The Kingdom is at Hand 1453

Past lives. *See also* Reincarnation
Knowledge of Past Lives 601
Memory of past lives 312

Paśyantīvāk
Transcendental Sound-Vibration 1577

Patañjali. *See also* Yoga
The Father of Yoga? 534
The Sage Patañjali 534

Path. *See* Spiritual Path

Pathos
Christian Hesychast definition 745
Passion and Dispassion 695
When the Soul overcomes the passions 686

Paul
Belief and Experience 676–677
Teaching on Prophecy 294
Teaching on the Opposition 207
The Mysticism of Saint Paul 666

Peace. *See also* Balance
Be who you are Now 1408
How to have a Peaceful Mind in a Troubled World 1244
Illumined-Mind Consciousness 1427
Is it possible to have a peaceful mind? 1245
Meditation and the Joy of Living 1012–1013
Peace of Heart 1595
Peace on Earth 1304–1305
Silence, Solitude, Peace 1386
The Peace of the Buddhic and Nirvāṇic Planes 1240
The Peace of the Heart 1324
The Warrior seeks Peace not War 986
To find peace of mind 1413

Pearl of Great Price
The Jewel in the Lotus 1322

Peirasmos
Christian Hesychast definition 745
Tested by God and the Devil? 685

Pentad, Pentagram
Gnostic Christian definition 736

Perception. *See also* Seeing, Hearing
Awakening the Inner Senses 506
Evil is a limitation of perception 209
Human Perception on the Subplanes (graph) 507
Perceptions of the One Mind 490
Perception and the sense of Reality 97
Perception through Mind (graph) 543
The Process of Seeing or Perceiving 542

Perennial Philosophy
The Buddhic Consciousness 85

Permanent Atoms
Destiny and the Permanent Atoms 250

Persecution
Persecution of the Gnostics and the scientists 682–683
Persecution of the Knowers 656–658
The Gnostics 645
The Heretics 655
The One and Only 839
The Sūfī God 838

Persona
Ēgō: I AM 1179
Persona (Latin): the Mask 38

Personality. *See also* ego, egotism
and the Individuality 32–33
Asmitā: your false sense of "I" 551
From Personal to Cosmic Life 1428
Personality Integration Chart (graph) 1333
Personality types 376
Personal Development through the Five Pure Vowel Sounds 1040
The Body-Elementals 213
The Personality Complex 36–37
The Personality of the Solar Logos 125
The Ray of the Personality 54
The self and the Self 1680
Trapped Spirits 1240
Your personal sense of self is a mystery 1388

Personality problems
Do not bring personal problems to group work 1164
Emotional Problems 1429–1431
Reactive-Emotional Consciousness 1426
Temporary Relief 1427

Personal God. *See also* God-Immanent
Buddha never taught of a personal God 754–755
Can God be Angry? 106
Īśvara: the "personal" God 120
The Lord? 121
The Sun is a Cosmic-Person 1586, 1592

Personal Saviour
Buddha never taught of a personal Saviour 754–755
Do not look for a Saviour outside in the world 1296
Jesus the Personal Saviour? 678–679
Modern Bibles emphasize a Personal Saviour 676
Personal Salvation? 1146
Prayer Spiritual and Material 681

Phantasia. *See also* Astral Plane
Beyond Phantasia 686–687
Christian Hesychast definition 745

Phenomena
14 Psychic Phenomena 289–316. *See* Psychism
Phainomenon: Greek Mystery School definition 735

Philadelpheia
Terms of Love 914

Philia
Christian Hesychast definition 744
Terms of Love 914

Philokalia
Basic proposition of the Philokalia 434, 452
Christian Hesychast definition 745
Definition and description 691
Divine Union by Devotion 1128
Records of Early Christianity 642–643

Philosopher's Stone
Fusion of the pineal and pituitary glands 430
Kuṇḍalinī and Alchemy 153

Philosophy
Modern philosophers have lost the Way 387
Philosophia, Philosophos: definitions 387
Philosophia: Christian Hesychast definition 740
Philosophia: Greek Mystery School definition 734
Philosophia: the Love of Wisdom 1694

Phōs, Phōtismos
Words for "Light" in Western Mysticism 1350

Phronesis
Gnostic Christian definition 738

Phylaki Kardias
Christian Hesychast definition 743
The Guarding of the Heart 632

Phylaki Nou
Christian Hesychast definition 743

Physical body
A great barrier to telepathy 349
A shadow of a shadow of a shadow 545
Balance on the Physical Plane 1257
Belongs to the Animal Kingdom 893, 1312
Drags our attention into this world 865
Identification with 3
Mind and Body 1374–1375
Mind in Body 988
Physical changes caused by Kuṇḍalinī 154
Regeneration by Light 40
Saṁyama on the physical body 594
Skill in Action 989
The Body-Elemental 989
The body is here to serve the Soul 594
The centres responsible for the physical body 1375
The illusory food-body 38
The importance of your physical body 1236
The Personality Complex 36–37
The Ray of the physical body 54
The Temple of the Soul 415
Those polarized in the physical body 376
Transformed physical bodies 1310–1311
Your greatest prison 19

Physical Plane
in brief 16
The Physical Projection 297
The Seventh World (Arabic) 886
The Seven Subplanes of the Physical Plane (graph) 16
The two Realities (physical and Nirvāṇic) 97

Physikos
Greek classifications of Humanity 687

Physis
Gnostic Christian definition 737
Greek classifications of Humanity 687
Greek Mystery School definition 734

Piṅgalā. *See* Īḍā and Piṅgalā

Pilgrim
The Pilgrims 645

Pīr-o-Murshid
The Spiritual Guide (Persian) 832

Piscean Age
Became a Dark Age 287–288
Esoteric History of the Piscean Religions 833
From Pisces to Aquarius 837
Holding onto Piscean Age thinking 384
Ichthus: the sign of the Piscean Age 458, 709
"Judgment" at the end of the Piscean Age 725
Mystics of Pisces and Aquarius 836
Penetrating into the Kingdom 1707
Piscean Mystics became God-intoxicated 1164
Piscean Mystics worked alone 1146
Piscean Spirituality and New Age Spirituality 1706
Piscean Teachers represented a particular tradition 1147
Religions are still of Piscean vibration 516
The Influence of the Seven Rays 834–835
The Piscean Mystic 638

Pisces
The Christ Energy 155

Pistis
Christian Hesychast definition 742
Greek classifications of Humanity 687
Greek Mystery School definition 735

Pītha
Our Sun is a gigantic Knot of Power 1625

Pitṛis. *See also* Barhiṣad Pitṛis
Of particular interest to us 203
The angelic progenitors of Mankind 216, 368

Pitṛi-Loka
Definition 60

Planchette
Dangers of 313

Planes. *See also* Subplanes
1 Planes of Being 11–30
3 Kāmaloka: the Astral Plane 57–72
4 Devāchan: the Mental Plane 73–82
5 Buddhi: the Realm of Unities 83–92
6 Nirvāṇa: the World of Glories 93–102
66 The Mystery of the Sun 1583–1600
What are the Planes?
All the Worlds are in the Sun 1590
Dimensions of the Solar Logos in Cosmic Space 1591
Frequencies or Vibrations of the Solar Light 1594
From Matter to Light 761
Planes and Subplanes 14
The Planes in Brief 16–17
The Seven Great Planes 13
The Seven Great Planes of Being (graph) 15
Worlds within Worlds 886
Tradition and the Planes
The Goal of Yoga (graph) 521
The Goal of Zen (graph) 761
The Kabbalistic Worlds 358–361
The Many Mansions (graph) 611
The Planes and the Kabbalistic Tree of Life (graph) 359
Worlds of the Sūfī 886–889
Worlds of the Sūfī (graph) 890
Cosmic Planes of Being
Cosmic Physical Plane explained 122
Cosmic Powers 602–603
Dimensions of the Solar Logos in Cosmic Space 1591
Explanation of the Cosmic Planes 14
Inconceivable Divine Realities 126
The Constitution of God-Immanent 122–126
The Constitution of the Solar Logos (graph) 124
The Solar Constitution 1587
Planes (general)
Angelic Rulers of the Planes (graph) 199
Ascending the Planes of Consciousness 20
Polarities of Forces between the Planes (graph) 25
Properties associated with the planes 13
The Kingdom of God (graph) 123
The Rays and the Planes (graph) 55

Planetary Hierarchy. *See* Spiritual Hierarchy

Planets, Planetary Logoi
Cakras in the Aura of the Solar Logos 1589, 1590
Children of the Cosmic Creators 190
Destined by the Stars? 260–261
Less evolved than a Solar Logos 1590
Seven sacred planets and the Seven Rays 55
Solar-Systemic and Cosmic Evil 217
The 72 cakras of the Solar Logos 1327
The Cosmic Creator-Gods 162–163
The Doctrine of the Logoi 116
The Elohīm 120
The Planetary Planes 1590

Plani
Christian Hesychast definition 742

Play. *See also* Līlā
Līlā: the Play of the Goddess 1520

Pleiades
The Mystery of the Pleiades 181

Plerōma
Definition 5
Definition and description 12
Greek Mystery School definition 733
Tantra Mind 933
The Plerōma is already full of the Triune God 1453

Pneuma
Christian Hesychast definition 740
Greek Mystery School definition 734
Pneuma-Hagion: Spirit-Holy 1344
Spirit (Greek) 1343
The Third Aspect of the Deity 122–123

Pneumata
Greek classifications of Humanity 687

Polarity. *See also* Sex
Cosmic Sensitivity 1009
Duad: definition 24
Falling in Love 922
Interaction of a Polarized Pair (graph) 164
Mother and Father 475
Polarities between the planes 25
Polarities Male and Female 920–921

Polarities within the Human Aura (graph) 921
Powers of Consciousness 374–375
Śiva-Śakti 1521
Tantra is the Way of Love 911
The Circle of Love 923
The Divine Bipolarity 471
The Gift of Parenthood 474
The Human Bipolarity 472
The Human Bipolarity (graph) 475
The Law of Polarity 164
Yin, Yang, Tao 476

Politics
Religion and politics should not be mixed 513

Poltergeists
Poltergeist phenomena 314–315

Poseidonis
A remnant of Atlantis 271

Positivity
Action and Destiny (Metanoia) 1420–1421
Cultivate the Positive 1365
Dwell on the Positive 1712
God, the Healer of Broken Hearts 1432–1433
Mind and Body 1374–1375
Self-Worth 1382–1383
The Principle of Choice 1380–1381

Possession. *See* spirit-possession

Power. *See also* Will-power
Beyond the Will 429
Paraśakti: the Supreme Power 1500
Ray 1: Will, Power 56
The first aspect of the Sūtrātma 491
The Power of Sound 201, 1024
The Power of Thought 232
The Power of Yielding 1088
The Soul-Power 1305
Through the Head come Power, Will and Purpose 428–431

Powers. *See also* Psychism, Magic, Miracles
26 The Yoga of Miraculous Powers 577–606
Cosmic Powers 602–603
Knowledge of Past Lives 601
Mind to Mind (telepathy) 346–347
Powers arising from meditation in the Heart 445
Powers by Drugs? 578
Powers of Consciousness 374–375
Powers of Divine Descent 599
Powers of the Dream State 600
Seek not Powers 581
The General Powers 580–581
The Māyāvirūpa 78
The Power of Conscious Dreaming 277
To Safely Perform Miracles 1353
Yogic Powers and Psychism 579

Powers (Hierarchy)
Christian Classification of the Hierarchies 192

Pracodayāt
Definition 1611

Practice. *See* Meditational Practices

Pradhāna
The Primordial Matter 167
The same as Mūlaprākṛtī 595
Pradhāna-Loka: the Formless Unity-Field 1707

Pradhāna Jaya Siddhi
The power over the evolutionary forces of Nature 598

Prajāpati
Derivation 366
Sūrya, the Solar Logos 1622
The Cosmic Creator-Gods 162

Prajñā. *See also* Buddhi, Pure Consciousness
A quality of the Spiritually Awakened Heart 1329
Buddhist term for Buddhic Consciousness 84
Intuitionis: definition 375
Mahāvākya Practice 1475
Prajñāparamitā: Transcendental Wisdom 768
Sati-Prajñā: Truth-Discerning Awareness 1223
The Superconscious Mind 492–493
The Wisdom of seeing into one's Self-Nature 769

Prākāmya
The General Powers 581

Prakāśa
A quality of the Spiritually Awakened Heart 1329
Experienced at highest stages of Yoga 527
The Universal Christ 440

Prākṛtī
Cosmic Prākṛtī 122
Definition 14, 30
Dimensions of the Cosmic Fire (graph) 137
Living Matter 134–135
Mūlaprākṛtī: the Root of Nature 471
Prākṛtī-Śakti: the energies of Nature 1484

Praktiki
Christian Hesychast definition 743

Pralaya
Night of Dissolution 167

Prāṇa. *See also* Life-force
All things are made of the Life-force 109
Definition 30, 133
Dimensions of the Cosmic Fire (graph) 137
Kuṇḍalinī-Fohat 148
Mahā-Prāṇa: the Great Breath 1340
Manifests as sexual attraction 912
Prāṇa and Rebirth 722–723
Prāṇa-Mantra: Breath Prayer 453
Spirit 1343
The fivefold Life-force 589
The Life-force in Humanity 1486
To receive Prāṇa from the Sun 1607

Prāṇamāyākośa
Coverings over the Self 38

Praṇava
Definition 520
Definition and description 549
Praṇava Bīja 1542–1543
Praṇava-Deham: a Body of Light 1310
The Fundamental-Sound-Vibration of the Universe 1610

Prāṇāyāma. *See also* Meditational Practices: Breathing
Applied to Haṭha Yoga and Rāja Yoga 524–525
Beyond Āsana and Prāṇāyāma 573
Definition 562
Exoteric and Esoteric derivations 1553
Meditation in the Third-Eye 1224
Mindfulness of Breathing 794
Prāṇāyāma-Vidyā: the Science of Breath 1553
The fourth step of Aṣṭāṅga Yoga 572

Praṇidhāna
Surrender to the Divine 548

Prāpti
The General Powers 581

Prārabdha Karma
Common Obstacles on the Path of Meditation 1205
Karma to be worked out in this lifetime 243

Prasāda
Mysterious Grace 1311
Prasāda Bīja 1551

Prasūtī
The Primordial Essence 1537

Prātibha
Prātibhā Siddhi 598
The Light in the Crown Centre 587

Pratyāhāra
Definition 562
The fifth step of Aṣṭāṅga Yoga 572
Withdrawing the senses 1224

Pratyeka Buddha
A Buddha who walks alone 906
Enlightened for oneself alone 504
The Path of Gnosis 1121

Pra-Vṛtti
Involution 595

Prayer. *See also* Meditation, Meditational Practices
32 Christian Prayer 689–716
41 Sūfī Prayer 863–884
54 The Heart and the Lost Art of Prayer 1251–1278
What is Prayer?
Magical Prayer 365
Prayer Spiritual and Material 681
Pure Prayer (early Christian) 644
Remembering the Dead 412
Stages of Prayer (Christian) 692
Terms of Prayer (Christian) 696
The abuse of Prayer 365
The Divine Mood 1252
The Name and the Names 1258
The Prayer of Quiet 1189
The Source of Miracles 671

The Stages of Prayer 1253–1257
1. Oral Prayer or Verbal Prayer 1253
2. Mental Prayer 1254
3. Mental Prayer in the Heart 1254–1255
4. Heart-Prayer or Spiritual Prayer 1256
5. God-State 1257
The Voice of God 864–865
What is Prayer? 690
What is the Name? 1259

The Practice of Prayer
Alone with God 700
Conscious Breathing in the Heart 1274–1277
Four Ways to Enter Silence 1447
How to begin Mental Prayer in the Heart 1260
Interior Prayer (Eastern Christian) 691–695
Meditation on the Exalted Name of God (Sūfī) 871
Practising the Presence of God 711
Right Prayer 1696
The Evolution of Christian Prayer 713–716
The Great Greek Mantra to Jesus 708–710
The Mantram of Unification in the Heart Centre 866–868
The Names and Mental Prayer in the Heart 1261
The Prayer of a Practical Mystic 92
The Radiant Heart Prayer 702–703
The Way of the Radiant Heart 452–455
To Call upon Jesus 679
To Invoke God in your Heart 1293
To pray ceaselessly 1283
To Worship the Divine Incarnations 1270–1272
Visualizing the Divinity within the Heart 1268

Precognition. *See also* Prophecy
Definition and description 295

Prema
A quality of the Spiritually Awakened Heart 1329
Prema-Rūpā: a Name of Lalitā, the Goddess 1566
Terms of Love 914

Present Moment. *See* Time, Being in the Moment

Preta
A ghost or disembodied spirit 61
Preta-Loka: definition 61

Pride
Causes of Group Disruption 1154–1155

Priests
Interpreted the scriptures for themselves 565
Invented purification rituals 570
Presbyterion: definition and description 367
Priestcraft always resisted the Teachers 368
Priestcraft lose touch with Reality 5
Their Devotion expressed through rituals 1129
The valid way for the Priest 565
The World Priest 1619
Unnecessary Practices 1111
Warped the idea of sexual activity 570
Were mediators between the gods and Mankind 367

Prima Materia
The Mother Substance 167

Primordial Sound Language. *See also* Sound
47 The Primordial Sound Language 1025–1076
Powers of the Primordial Sound Alphabet 1042
Sound-Words 1054
The Ancient Primordial Language of Sound-Vibrations 1026–1027
The Art of Warriorship 1067
The Creative Power of the Primordial Language of Sound 1075
The Name of the Deity 1032
The Primordial Sound Alphabet 1028
The Source of the Primordial Sound Language 1029
The Three Levels of Sound-Practice 1064
The Two Directions of Sound 1041

Vowels. *See also* vowels
Forces and Qualities of the Vowels (graph) 1040
IAO and the Perfected Man-Species (graph) 1035
Internalizing the Pure Vowels and Combined Vowels 1041
Modern Vowels 1031
Personal Development through the Five Pure Vowel Sounds 1040
Powers of the Pure Vowels 1033
Remembrance of the Five Pure Vowels in some Ancient Languages 1032
Sounding the Vowels 1033
The Development of the Mind through the Five Pure Vowel Sounds 1039

The Pure Vowels and Combined Vowels 1030
The Pure Vowel Sequence IAO 1034–1035
The Seven Mystic Vowel Sounds 1031
The Vowels in the Energy Centres 1036–1038

Semi-Vowels
Internalizing the Semi-Vowels 1044–1045
Powers of the Semi-Vowel Sounds 1043
The Semi-Vowels combined with the Pure Vowels 1046–1047
The Semi-Vowels or Semi-Consonants 1043

Consonants
The Consonants with the Vowels 1048
The Consonants with the Vowels and the Final M and Nasal Sounds 1049

Sibilants
Centring and Deepening: SHĪ and SHŪ 1052
The Sibilants 1050–1051

Breathing
A Connecting Breathing: RŪ-HĀ 1062–1063
Controlling the Mind through Breathing 1059
Warrior Energizing Breathings 1060–1061

Specific Sounds
Healing Sound-Vibration Formula 1064–1067
Meditation on Aspects of RĀM 1072–1073
Meditation on KRĪM 1055
Pure Being: IĒNG (YING-YENG) 1056–1057
RĀM: the Warrior Power 1068–1073
Shining from Within: MĀ RA MA 1053
SŌ-HĀNG, HŌNG-SAU, HA-SA 1059
The Warrior of the Heart: ŌM RĀM KLĪM 1074
Tremendous Sound-Structures for the Development of Humanity 1058

Principalities
Christian Classification of the Hierarchies 192
Rulers in High Places 657

Prognosis
Gnostic Christian definition 738

Pronoia
Gnostic Christian definition 738

Prophecy
Biblical Prophecies? 296
"Channelling" the Soul 325
Greek and Hebrew terminology 294
Knowledge of the Past and the Future 583
Prātibhā Siddhi: the true power of Prophecy 598
Prophecy and Destiny 294–297
Propheteia: Christian Hesychast definition 742
Prophetic dreams 299
The real burden of Prophecy 647

Prophets
Greek and Hebrew terminology 294
Persecution of the Knowers 656–658
Prophetes: Christian Hesychast definition 742
Prophetes: derivation and definition 647
Prophets and Gurus are not mediums 325
Pseudoprophetes: false prophets 296
Revelation is Continuous 1710
The Prophets 647

Prosochi
Wakefulness in the Heart Centre 632

Pṛthivī
Pṛthivī Bīja 1544
The Earth Element 26–28

Prunikos
Gnostic Christian definition 736

Pseudo-hierarchies
on the Astral Plane 66

Psyche
Christian Hesychast definition 741
Gnostic Christian definition 737
Psyche-Metanoia: Inner Transformation 1452
The Human Constitution (Greek) 39
The State of Unity of the Psyche 1383

Psychiatry
Temporary Relief 1427
Treats non-physical experience as mental illness 305

Psychikos
Greek classifications of Humanity 687

Psychism. *See also* Mediumship
13 Atlantis Revisited 269–288
14 Psychic Phenomena 289–316
15 Channelling and Mediumship 317–344
Astral Disinformation 1271
Biblical Prophecies? 296
Dangers to the Warrior School 1007
Intelligent Use of Free Will 297
Mental Telepathy and Psychism 352
New Age Teachers have nothing to do with psychism 1147
Objective Experience 305
Prophecy and Destiny 294–296
Psychic Disruption of group work 1155
Psychic Humanity 290
Psychism and Mysticism 319–320, 324
Pure Seeing? 293
Saṁyama and Parapsychology 582
The New Atlantis 280
The Power of Suggestion 237
The Psychic Centre 49
Where are your Wisemen? 387
Yoga is not psychism 530
Yogic Powers and Psychism 579
Zen is not Psychism 757

Psychic Phenomena
Astral Projection 301–304
Clairvoyance 292–293
Consciousness and Phenomena (graph) 323
Contactee phenomena 333
Dreams 298–300
Dreams and out-of-body experiences 300
Experiences on the Astral Plane 306–307
Fasting and Psychic Experience 308
Hallucinations and out-of-body experiences 305
Hypnotism 312
Involuntary Possession 310
Materializations 314
Mediumship (general introduction) 309
Memory of Past Lives 312
New Age Phenomena 278–281
Ouija Board, Planchette, Automatic Writing 313
Poltergeist Phenomena 314–315
Powers resulting from Kuṇḍalinī activity 156
Psychic telepathy 347
Speaking in Tongues 312–313
Spontaneous Human Combustion 316
The Power of Conscious Dreaming 277

Psychology. *See also* Parapsychology, Transpersonal Psychology, Spiritual Psychology
Dwell on the Positive 1712
Errors of materialistic psychology 4–5, 305, 1364
Orthodox Psychology 1105
Psychelogia: Christian Hesychast definition 741
Psychology Ancient and Modern 1364
Psychology and the New Age Religion 1105–1109
Psychology in the Future 1709
Science of the Soul? 291
Western Psychology vs Spiritual Psychology 494

Psychosis. *See also* insanity
and out-of-body experiences 305
Balance in Spiritual Life 505
Emotional Problems 1429–1433
Resulting from Kuṇḍalinī activity 157–158
Temporary Relief 1427
The Sūfī view of Mental Disorders 900
The Testing of the Soul 1158
The Tests of the Elements 1159

Psychostasia
Gnostic Christian definition 737

Pūja
Most ritual is done absent-mindedly 1253

Punarjanma. *See also* Reincarnation
Punar-Bhavin: becoming again (after death) 249
Punar-Janma-Jaya: victory over birth and death 249, 533
Punar-Janma-Smṛti: recollection of past lives 249, 601
Punar-Janma: Reincarnation 32, 249
Punar-Janman: being born again spiritually 249

Purāṇa
Definition 532

Pure Consciousness. *See also* Mystical Consciousness, Turīya, Prajñā, Buddhi
Attach your Mind to the Eternal 1234–1235
Buddhic Consciousness 86
Chockmah and Binah 498
Experiencing Pure Consciousness 88

Formless Consciousness 1373
Learn to Die before you Die 420–421
Nirmala-Sundarī: Spotless Beauty 1494
Pure Consciousness in the Heart 447
Stages on the Path 1136–1137
Steps on the Meditational Path 1196
The Fourth State 499
Turīya: Pure Consciousness 498

Purgatory
Degrees of non-Love 406
Purifying vibrations 887
The Christian Cosmo-Conception 19
The Seven Subplanes of the Astral Plane (graph) 67

Purification. *See also* Heart: Purifying the Heart
Illumination through the Way of Purification 597
Purification by Diet? 571
Purification rituals invented by the priestcraft 570
Purify the Heart 701
Śauca: Purification 568
Tapas: Spiritual Purification 571
Tapas: the third Rule of Aṣṭāṅga Yoga 568–569
The Initiation of the World 1712–1713
The Path of Purification 1337
The Purification of the Heart 849
To Invoke God in your Heart 1293
To purify your psychic-self 870

Purity
Guard your Heart 1328
Samādhi: a State of Inner Purity 497
Śauca: Purity 570
Śauca: the first Rule of Aṣṭāṅga Yoga 568
The Pure Heart 1300
The State of Innocence 1306

Pūrṇa
Definition 5
Equivalent to the Greek Plerōma 12
Pūrṇā: a Name of Lalitā, the Goddess 1562

Pūrṇa-Avatāra-Rūpa
The Complete Divinity 1327

Pūrṇa Mano Bala Siddhi
The power which comes from the total Mind 598

Puruṣa
Also known as Paramātman 1318
Definition 30, 541
Meditations in the Heart Centre 1302
Puruṣa-Śakti: the energies of Spirit 1484
Puruṣa-Svāmī: the God Transcendent 1321
The God-Image is found in the Heart 438

Puruṣottama
Meditation is a quest for the Real 1174
The Supreme Being 1318

Pūrva-Jāti. *See also* Punarjanma
Previous births are a fact of Nature 32
Pūrva-Jāti-Jñānam: knowledge of previous births 601

Pūṣan
The Sun-God 1673

Q

Qalb
Dimensions of the Heart 847
Qalb: the Sūfī Heart 848
The Beautiful Names 1264–1265
The Sūfī seeks out the Heart 437

Qitub
The Spiritual Master 832

Quan Yin
Her Transcendental Form 145
Kwan Yin Maṇḍala (graph) 1508
Quan Yin: the Mother of Compassion 1507
The Eternal Feminine 469
The Melodious Voice of Quan Yin 1509
To Meditate on Quan Yin 1508

Quaternary. *See also* Personality, Tetrakti
The Threefold Structure of Man (graph) 33

Qur'ān
Revelation 828–829

Qurbiyat
Stage Six of the Radiant Way 832

Quṭb
The Muslim Deification Process 1191

Quṭbīyat
Stage Five of the Radiant Way 832

R

Rabbi
A name given to Jesus 661

Rādhā
A Name of Lalitā, the Goddess 1572

Radiant Form of the Master
Names of the Being of Light 417
The Being of Light in Meditation 418–419

Radiation. *See also* Light
Radiare: definition 175
The Law of Radiation 175
The Lost Radiance 1176

Rainbow Bridge. *See also* Antaḥkaraṇa
Building the Bridge of Light 554
How to build the Rainbow Bridge 1331

Rajas
That which produces Fire 1693
The force of mobility 1406
The Guṇas 139–140

Rāja Yoga. *See also* Yoga
Activities of Yoga-Mārga 520
Definition 523, 535
Haṭha Yoga and Rāja Yoga 524–525
Paths of Spiritual Evolution 1693
Rāja Yoga: Divine Union by Meditation 1126–1127
The Science of Cosmic Consciousness 1124
The Way of the Mind 1238–1239
Traditional concept of 522

Rām, Rāṁ
Mahāvākya Practice 1476–1477
Meditations on Aspects of Rām 1072–1073
Potent Vibrations: Bīja-Mantra 1544–1545
Rām: the Universal Name 1273
Rām: the Warrior Power 1068–1071

Rāma
The Sun incarnated in a Perfected Spiritual Warrior 1629
To Worship the Divine Incarnations 1270–1272

Rāmā
Names of Lalitā, the Goddess 1567
Ramā (Rāmā) Bīja 1548
The Rāmā-Mantra 1541

Ramana Mahāṛṣi
A modern Mystic 91, 782
Teachings on the Heart 447

Rape
Physical and emotional rape 925

Raphael
Hebrew Angelic Names Meditation 1462
Hebrew Divine Words for Healing 1456

Rapture
Heart-Prayer or Spiritual Prayer 1256
Rapturus: definition 699
Rapturus: the Latin word for Samādhi 574

Rasā
Definition 1615

Rati
The Rati-Mantra 1539

Rational mind. *See* lower mind

Ratziel
Hebrew Angelic Names Meditation 1462

Ravi
The Self of the Sun 1673

Ravishment
Heart-Prayer or Spiritual Prayer 1256

Rays. *See* Seven Rays

Reactionaries
Religious Reactionaries 287–288

Reactive-Emotional Consciousness
The Principle of Choice 1380–1381
Your astral-psychic nature 1426

Reading
If you "speed-read" this material it will be a waste of time 1413
Spiritual Reading is reading with the Higher Mind 1113

Reality
Beyond the Veils 894
Desire for the Real 1503
In Search of Reality 1174
Meditation is connecting to Reality 1440–1441
Quest for Reality 1178
Reality (Metanoia) 1416–1417
The One 1686–1687
The One Transcendental Reality 515
The Two Realities 97
The Ultimate Reality is the Meaning of Life 526–527
What is Reality? 1175
Your Being in Nirvāṇa 767

Rebirth
Baptism and Rebirth 722–723
Dvi-Jā: twice born 722
Punar-Janman: being born again 249
Sex Natural and Divine 926–927
Sūrya-Sādhanā 1604

Reflection Sphere
The fifth and sixth astral subplanes 64
The Grand Illusion 66

Reincarnating Ego. *See also* Jīva, Human Soul
Ēgō: variations of meaning 1179
Jīva: the Human Soul 35
Residing on the Mental Plane 75
The source of genuine Inspiration 353

Reincarnation 248–253. *See also* Punarjanma
12 Karma and Reincarnation 231–266
Banned by the church 32, 258, 652–653
Caused by Saṁskāra and Vāsanā 251
Causes of Reincarnation 249, 259
Children born innocent? 250
Karma and Reincarnation Misconceived 252–253
Liberation from Reincarnation 32, 421
Memory of past lives 312
Punarjanma: Reincarnation 249
Reincarnation and Freedom 998
Reincarnation of the planets and suns 163, 249
The First Circle of Life 1422
The Law of Cyclic Activity 248
The Soul itself does not reincarnate 35

Relationship. *See also* Tantra
21 The Call of the World Mother 467–488
43 The Circle of Love 905–944
Falling in Love 922
Family and Duty 998–999
Girls brought up as males 478–479
Love Lost 936–937
Mother, Father and Baby 938–939
Primary Relationship 479
Ray 4: Beauty, Harmony 56
Relational Consciousness 906–907
The Divine Bipolarity 471
The Feminine Heart 925
The Human Bipolarity 472
The Path of Tantra 942–943
The Tragedy of Human Relationships 936

Relaxation-Response
Meditation Degenerated 1180

Religion
Introduction II: By Whichever Path 511–516
What is Religion?
Esoteric History of the Piscean Religions 833
Religion and Spirituality 754
Religion has greater scope than science 367
Symbols of the Religions (graph) 515
The original purpose of all true religions 1257
Yoga and Religion defined 527
The Universal Religion
Christian Mysticism and Zen 630
Our Goal is nothing less than God 1191
The Ancient Heart-Path 845
The Eternal is One 512–514
The One God over All 432
The One Transcendental Reality 515
The Thread of the Heart 844
The Universal Heart Practice 846
To Manifest the Kingdom of God 1716
To Partake of God's Nature 640
Zen: a "Godless" Religion? 754

Religion Degenerated
All traditions have been corrupted by ignorance 234
Conditioned Thinking 1084
Evil actions done in the name of God 993
Fundamentalism is based on duality 1108–1109
Only celibate males can attain Salvation? 560
Piscean religions discriminate against women 384
Religion's warped view of sex 570
Religion and Politics 513
Religious Fundamentalism 383
Religious Reactionaries 287–288
Ritual Degenerated 368
The abuse of Prayer 365
The Caste System 378–379
The Feminine Suppressed 910, 1110
The Lost Radiance 1176
The Religious Elementals 385
Traditionis: definition 379
Western Religions inherited false ideas about God 838
Western religions rejected the Goddess 142, 1516
The Future Religion
Female Buddhas 1110
Psychology and the New Age Religion 1105–1109
Religion in the Future 1709
Religious divisions will be broken down 1147
Spirituality Past and Future 1104
The Influence of the Seven Rays 834–835
The New and Eternal Way 516
The Religion of Christ (a prophecy) 441
Remembrance. *See also* Divine Presence
Guard your Heart 1328
Meditation on the Holy Spirit 1344
Practising the Presence of God 711
Remember the Presence 1653
Smṛtī: Remembering God in the Heart 723
To Realize the Presence of God 1398
Zikr, Dhikr (Arabic) 868
Renunciation
Avoid the Errors of East and West 1122–1123
Balance in Spiritual Life 505
Is Renunciation Necessary? 1119
Non-Action Misinterpreted 1120
Not the right human condition 763
Penetrating into the Kingdom 1707
Periods of Life in Vedic India 907
Piscean Spirituality and New Age Spirituality 1706
Practised during the past six thousand years 560
Relational Consciousness 906–907
Spirituality and Renunciation 806
Spiritual Life and Material Life 1118
Tantra is not for renunciates 909
To Become a True Renunciate 257
Repentance
Perverted translation of the Greek Metanoia 683
Resurrection
The Control of the Personality by the Soul 721
The Resurrection Body (Ānandamāyākośa) 40
Retreat
Balanced Practice 810–811
Rules for a modern Zen Retreat 811
The Japanese Zen Retreat 807–809
Revelation
Catholic mystical terminology 698
Crisis and Revelation 1711
Revelation is Continuous 1710
The Revelation of God 854
Reverence
The Approach to Truth 1152
The Attitude for Yoga 558
Righteousness. *See also* Virtue
Dharma (aphorisms) 1408–1409
Rāma gave Mankind Righteousness 1270
Righteousness and the afterlife 411
The Righteous Fight 1092
Ring-pass-not
A boundary of Consciousness 490
The Auric-Field 42
Ritual
Most ritual is done absent-mindedly 1253
Purification rituals invented by the Priestcraft 570
Ray 7: Ceremony, Order 56
The Magic of Ritual Worship 366–371
Communication with the Invisible 371

Invoking the Invisible Helpers 370–371
Ritual Degenerated 368
The Spirit-Helpers 369
The Temple Not Made By Hands 369
Yajña: definition and description 366

Rod of Power
Served to direct the Kuṇḍalinī Force 151

Root-Races
and the separation of the sexes 920
and the Seven Mystic Vowel Sounds 1031
Human Evolutionary Epochs 176–178

Rose
Symbol of the Heart of the Divine Mother 1511
The Fraternity of the Rosy Cross 450
The Lotus of the Heart 446
The Mystery within the Heart 1315
The Rose and the Cross 712
The Rose of Divine Love 858–861
The Rose of Love and the Cross of Light 1357

Roshi
Zen definition 807

Rosicrucians
Kept the Mystery Teachings alive in the West 450
Latin Mantras of the Rosicrucians 712
Rosy-Crucian: the Rose and the Cross 712

Ṛṣi
Definition 30, 394, 1205

RSPK
Poltergeist Phenomena 314–315

Ṛtaṁbharā-Prajñā
Truth-bearing Wisdom or Consciousness 530

Ru'yat Al-Qalb
The Vision of the Heart 437, 848

Ruah, Ruach
Meditations in the Heart Centre 1301
Ruach-Elohīm: the Breath of God 1340
Ruach-Elohīm: the Breath of the Creator-Gods 167
Ruach Elohīm Aur: the Breath of God is Light 713
Ruah-Ha-Qadosh: Spirit-Holy 1344
Spirit 1343

Rūbān, Rūhān
Spirit (Persian) 1343

Rudrāṇī, Rudrāmbā
Names of Lalitā, the Goddess 1580

Rūḥ
Dimensions of the Heart (Arabic) 847
Spirit (Arabic) 1343
The Spirit that you are 892

Ruḥā
Ruḥā-Qadash: Spirit-Holy 1344
Spirit (Aramaic) 1343

Rūmī
The Lover of God 853

Rūpa. *See also* Arūpa
Definition 30, 77
Planes and subplanes with form 14–15
Rūpa-Deva: embodied angels 77
Rūpa-Loka: form-worlds of the Mental Plane 74
Sa-Rūpa: Meditation with Form 1268–1269

Rūpa-Manas. *See also* lower mind
Form mind, lower mind 78
The Personality Complex 37
The Seven Subplanes of the Mental Plane (graph) 75

S

Sa
Potent Vibrations: Bīja-Mantra 1551

Śabda
Listen to Nāda 1212
The Sounding-Principle of the Godhead 1648
What is the Name? 1259

Śabda-Brahman
All differentiations are caused by Śabda-Brahman 1648
God's Cosmic Symphony 1649
Heard in deep meditation 311
The Living Voice 1615
The same meaning as the Greek Logos 117

Sabīja Samādhi
Types of Samādhi 575

Sacred Heart
Concealed instead of revealed 716
The Jesus Mantra and the Sacred Heart Initiation 1356
The Radiant Heart Prayer 702–703
The Sacred Heart of Jesus 673
The Sacred Heart of Our Lady 1510

Sacrifice. *See also* Service
Love and Sacrifice 1139
On Love and Meditation 1140–1143
The Feminine Virtues 468–469
The Gift of Parenthood 474
The Law of Surrender or Sacrifice 1138
The Sacrifice of the Teachers 1150–1151

Sacrifices
Appeasing the Gods? 220
Ritual Degenerated 368
The Sacrificial Lamb 680

Sadguru. *See* Sat Guru, Guru

Sādhanā
Sādhanā: the Spiritual Life 1153
Spiritual Practice or Discipline 569
Sūrya-Sādhanā: Sun-Worship 1604

Sādhu
Balance in Spiritual Life 505
Definition 1205
Non-Action Misinterpreted 1120
Unnecessary Practices 1111

Sage. *See also* Spiritual Teachers, Spiritual Masters, Guru
The Law of the Higher Life 1134–1135
The Warrior, the Sage, the Ruler 972–973

Sahaja-Avasthā
The Natural State (Formless Consciousness) 1373

Sahaja Samādhi
Spontaneous or natural Spiritual Trance 1232
Types of Samādhi 575

Sahasrāra Cakra. *See also* Crown Centre
General description 50
The Heart and the Energy Centres 1332

Saints
General Powers manifesting in the Saints 581
May or may not be known in the world 377
Saints of Action 1134
Teachings of the Saints (Christian) 612–622
The Brotherhood of Light (graph) 395
The Saints 654
Were not mediums or channellers 326–327
Your thoughts can touch the Saints 412

Sakalā
A Name of Lalitā, the Goddess 1562
Lalitā: the Ultimate Goddess 1556
The World Mother is everything 1498, 1506

Sākṣātkāraṇa
The Witnessing Principle 1212

Sākṣī
The Witness 1212
Your Conscious-Self is the Witness 499

Śakti
Activities of Yoga-Mārga 520
Definition 133
Forms of Śakti, the Goddess-Force 1486–1487
Kuṇḍalinī-Śakti: definition and description 143
Śakti: the Divine Energy 150, 1484
Śakti Bīja 1546, 1551
Śakti is the essence of Bīja-Mantra 1519
Śiva-Śakti 1521
The True Feminine 1516

Śākyamuni
Definition 1504

Salamanders
The Elementals 195

Sālik
The third stage of the Journey of the Heart 855

Salvation. *See also* Liberation
Definition 32
Learn to Die before you Die 420–421
Personal Salvation? 1146
Salvationis: definition 421
Sōtērios: definition 129
The Being of Light in Meditation 418–419

The Role of the Divine Female in the Salvation/ Liberation Process 1502–1503
To re-enter the Kingdom of Light 128
Your Day of Salvation is always Now 616

Śāma
Śāma Bīja 1551
The Six Mental Qualifications 1149

Ṣamad
Definition 877

Samādhāna
The Six Mental Qualifications 1149

Samādhi
Action while in Samādhi 1331
Activities of Yoga-Mārga 520
Definition 86, 562
Derivations and definitions 497
Formless Consciousness 1373
In Samādhi you live by Śakti and Caitanya alone 752
Ḥaqīqat (Arabic) 831
Rapture 699
Samādhi and miraculous powers 578, 581
Samādhi is only half the Spiritual Journey 1120
Samādhi: the Goal of Yoga (types of Samādhi) 574–575
The eighth step of Aṣṭāṅga Yoga 572
The Silent State 1554
The State of Inner Purity 497
The Sūfī Journey of the Heart 857
To Experience Spiritual Ecstasy 1683

Samādhi-Pariṇāma
Transformations of the Mind 1243

Samāna
An aspect of the fivefold Life-force 589

Śamatha
Definition 30

Śamballa
The Brotherhood of Light (graph) 395
The Christ-Hierarchy and Śamballa 396
The Divine Kingdom 1715
The Family of Life 1170
The Goal of the Spiritual Path 423
The Purpose of Christianity 174

Sambhogakāya
Bodies of the Buddhas 392

Samprajñāta Samādhi
Definition 497, 574

Saṁsakāra
Definition 251

Saṁsāra
A realm of unsatisfactory existence 185
Definition 239
Phenomenal life in the Three Worlds 766
Saṁsāra is coexistent in Space with Nirvāṇa 1391
Wandering in the Three Worlds 421–422

Saṁsāra-Mokṣana
Liberation from the Wheel of Birth and Death 503, 1422

Saṁskāra. *See also* Vāsanā
Held by the World Mother 1502
Known in the state of Saṁyama 583
Saṁskāra-Kṣaya: subconscious renewal 1236
Saṁskāra and Vāsanā 251
The First Circle of Life 1422
To Achieve Liberation 1177
Your karmic disposition 1330

Saṁskṛta (Saṅskṛta). *See also* Sanskrit
Definition 30, 1761

Samyaksaṁ Buddha
Definition 394, 1198

Saṁyama. *See also* Yoga
A Superior State of Knowing 582
Development of miraculous powers 583–597
Saṁyama and Parapsychology 582

Sanātana-Dharma
Definition 368

Sanat Kumāra. *See also* Kumāra, Ancient of Days
Hierarchies of Life (graph) 1721

Sancitta Karma
Karma stored up on the Causal Plane 243

Sandalphon
Hebrew Angelic Names Meditation 1462

Sandhyā
An interval between Ages 168

Saṅgha. *See also* Spiritual Hierarchy
Definition 30
Saṅgha: the Spiritual Hierarchy 394

Sañjivani
The Elixir of Life 593

Sanjivāni
Drug to induce the self back into the body 304

Śaṅkarācārya
Teachings on the mind and senses 239

Sannyāsin
Balance in Spiritual Life 505
Non-Action Misinterpreted 1120
Periods of Life in Vedic India 907
Sannyāsa, Sannyāsī, Sannyāsin: definitions 1119

Sanskrit. *See also* Mantra, Divine Names, Yoga, Goddess, Sun
God's Writing 1761
Language of the Gods 200
Mahāvākya: Great Truth Statements 1471–1479
Saṁskṛta: definition 30
The Divine Name expressed in the Sanskrit Alphabet 1552
Twelve Keys to the Heart 1314–1326

Śānti, Śāntiḥ
Inner Calm is required to see the Light 1595
Keys to the Heart 1324
Meditations in the Heart Centre 1299
Śāntī, Śānti-Devī: Names of Lalitā 1579
Śānti Bīja 1548

Santoṣa
Definition 564
The second Rule of Aṣṭāṅga Yoga 568

Sapientia
Western words for "Wisdom" 1354

Saptaḍaṣī
The Saptaḍaṣī Vibration 1526
The Saptaḍaṣī-Mantras 1533

Saptaparna
The Lotus of the Heart 446
The seven-leafed plant 448

Sarasvatī
An Energy-Form of the Goddess 1489
A Name of Lalitā, the Goddess 1566
Sarasvatī Bīja 1550
The Divine Consciousness in the aspect of Vāk 200

Sarvagā
A Name of Lalitā, the Goddess 1578

Sarvajña
Sarvajñātṛtvaṁ: Omniscience 596
The Omniscience of a Buddha 755

Sarva-Mantra-Sva-Rūpiṇī
A Name of Lalitā, the Goddess 1571

Sarva-Yantra-Ātmikā
A Name of Lalitā, the Goddess 1571

Sarx
Christian Hesychast definition 746
The Human Constitution (Greek) 39

Śāstra
Definition 532

Sat
Definition 499
The Experience of the Heart 1281
The Ultimate Reality 112

Sat-Cit-Ānanda
A description of God 112
God's threefold Being 499
Mahāvākya Practice 1475
Sat-Cid-Ānanda-Rūpiṇī: a Name of Lalitā 1578
The Experience of the Heart 1281
To reach Unqualified Existence 911

Sat Guru. *See also* Guru
Initiation (Dīkṣā) 1225
The Law of the Higher Life 1134–1135
The True Master 389

Satan. *See also* Devil
Sātan: definition 209
Satanas: Christian Hesychast definition 745
Satan and the Fall 210–211
What is "the Devil"? 684

Sati-Prajñā
Truth-Discerning Awareness 1223

Satori
Definition 87, 430
Satori: the Experience of Illumination 816–817
Several levels of Enlightenment are possible 760
Terms of Awakening 766
The same as the Pali Vipassana 1221
To be anxious for Satori does not work 800

Śat-Sampatti
Qualifications for Discipleship 1149

Satsaṅga
Identical to the Greek Ekklesia 688
Originally referred to the Spiritual Hierarchy 394

Sattva
That which produces Light 1693
The force of equilibrium 1406
The Guṇas 139–140
The quality of Purity necessary for Union 568

Satya (Satyam)
Definition 563
The second Observance of Aṣṭāṅga Yoga 566

Satya-Loka. *See also* Mahāparanirvāṇa, Ādi
and the Goal of Yoga 521
Dimensions of the Solar Logos in Cosmic Space 1591
Elementary Attributes 29

Satya Yuga
The Period of the Mahāmanvantara 168

Śauca
Definition 564
Śauca: Purity 570
The first Rule of Aṣṭāṅga Yoga 568

Sauḥ, Soū
Seed-Sound for Pārvatī 1489

Saundarya Lahirī
The Beautiful Ocean 1496

Sarvārthādharma
Derivation and meanings 1407

Savikalpa Samādhi
Types of Samādhi 574

Saviour. *See also* Messiah, Warrior, Personal Saviour
Inner Guidance (Metanoia) 1464
Relational Consciousness 906–907
The Buddha-Mind 755
The Path of the Warrior is not easy 908
The Saviour in the Heart 1296

Savitā. *See also* Sun, Solar Logos
66 The Mystery of the Sun 1585–1600
Definition 1602, 1608, 1658
Savitur, Savituḥ, Savitā, Savitṛ: definitions 1610
The Savitā-Mantra 1602

Savitarka Samādhi
Types of Samādhi 575

Sāvitrī
A Name of Lalitā, the Goddess 1561
Sāvitrī Maṇḍala (graph) 1497
The Female Aspect of the One Godhead 1610
The Other-Side-of-the-Sun 1488
The Spiritual Sun as Mother 1496–1497

Scandalum
Definition 224

Science
Avoid the Errors of East and West 1122–1123
Fiddling with the forms of life 589
Limits of investigation 129
Materialistic view of Man 4–5, 305
Persecution of the scientists 682
Psychology: Science of the Soul? 291
Religion has greater scope than science 367
Science in the Future 1709
Scientia Materia and Scientia Intuitiva 328
Scientific Materialism 382
Spirituality Past and Future 1104
The Intelligent Universe 111
True Science 382
Unable to ascertain the true causes 361
Uniting Head and Heart 1130–1131

Scripture
How I write is a Process 1684
Observing the scriptures 530
Revelation is Continuous 1710

Sanskrit terms for scriptures 532
Spiritual Reading 1113
The scriptures were heard in deep meditation 1216
This is a Book of God 1728–1729

Seance
Derivation and definition 314

Second Coming
Cosmic Intervention 282
Manifestation of the Sons of God 180
Parousia: the experiencing of the Christ Light 500
The Anti-Christ 724
The Coming of Christ in the Heart 727
The Coming of the Christ 724–725
The Divine Incarnation 726
The Initiation of the World 1712–1713
The Kingdom is at Hand 1453
When will the Messiah come? 619

Second death. *See also* Four Deaths
Death of the etheric-physical body 399, 420

Seed
Meditation with a Seed 1186
The perishable and imperishable seed 926–927
The Seed of Evil 221

Seeing. *See also* Clairvoyance, Meditational Practices
Dṛiṣṭi: definition 561
Inner vision begins in the Third-Eye 431
Just Seeing 1018
Look for the Light 1395
Pure Seeing? 293
Quietly Seeing (Zen) 786
See the Light of the Logos 1650
The Beatific Vision 293
The Being of Light in Meditation 418–419
The Experience of Mysticism 636–637
The Path of Seeing 552
The Process of Seeing or Perceiving 542
The Vision of the Beloved 418–419
True clairvoyance 293

Seer. *See* Witness, Watcher, Draṣṭā, Ṛṣi

Seged
To glorify and adore the Divinity 1341

Self. *See also* Ātman, Paramātman, I AM
Descent into the personality 545
Self-Knowledge is not selfishness 324
Senses or the Self? 239
Surrender to the Self 87
Sūtrātma: the Thread of the Self 491
The Abode of the Self is the Heart 434–435
The Bright Eternal Self 1292
The Essence of Wisdom 1680–1684
The self and the Self 1680
The Self in you is one with Paramātman 529
The Sun is the Self 1603
The true Sun is the Cosmic Self 1596
The Upaniṣads: Illuminating the Nature of the Self 545–547
Who is "I AM"? 1418
Who or what is your true Self? 1324
Yogic Teachings on Mind and Self 536–544

Self-Actualization, Self-Determination
Be who you are Now 1408
Be ye Lamps unto yourselves 780
Channelling takes away self-reliance 343
Dharma (aphorisms) 1408–1409
Do the Work yourself 1153
Inner Guidance (Metanoia) 1464
Intelligent Use of Free Will 297
Is there a Plan in your Life? 1000
Jesus the Personal Saviour? 678–679
Live and Let Live 940
Persevering to the End until Final Liberation 1101
Planetary Disturbance 1697
Rely on your Inner Self 1226
Self-Worth 1382–1383
Success is Born of Action 256–257
Surpassing your own Limitations 983
Tapas: Mental Discipline 568–569
Tapas: Spiritual Purification 571
The important point is not to "follow" a Master 1229
The Law of Effort 254
The Law of your Being 976–977
The Path of Self-Actualization 1110
The Principle of Choice 1380–1381
The Sacrificial Lamb 680
The Vision of your own Eternity 1144

The Way to Higher Consciousness 329
To Enter the Way of the Warrior 1004
To maintain a steady spiritual practice 1708
To Succeed in your Quest 1330
Universal Service 1717
What do you Seek out of Life? 975
Worship only the Divine Self 1226
Your Fate is Before Your Eyes 246
You Alone are Responsible 258

Self-conscious mind. *See also* lower mind, Kāma-Manas
Realms of the One Mind 492–493

Self-Mind
The root of your mind 767

Self-Nature. *See also* Self, Ātman, Buddha-Mind
Manifests when the mind is still 768
Prajñā: seeing into one's Self-Nature 769
Zen is the perception of the Self-Nature 753, 766

Self-Realization. *See also* Ātma-Vidyā
Ahaṁ-Ātman: I am the Self 1213
Beyond the Veils 894
Buddhic Consciousness 86
Cannot happen without aspiration 1237
Development of the Spiritual Warrior 971
How do you Know who You really Are? 1387
Knowing Yourself as you truly are 977
Know Thyself 1389
Know Yourself 604
Pure Being 1056–1057
Quest for Reality 1178
Quest for the Self 1317
Regain what you have Lost 381
Suspended Mind 1209
Tantric meditations on the Self 948–949
The final Goal of Self-Realization 1233
The Path to Wisdom 1702–1704
The Self is Realized in the Heart 434, 1235, 1286
The Silent Watcher Meditation 1388
The three degrees of Self-Realization 1448
The Upaniṣadic Mantrams 546–547
The Way, the Truth and the Life 670
To Love God and the World 1392–1393
You Are the World 1390–1391

Senses
Awakening the Inner Senses 506–507
In Bondage to the Mind 238
Pratyāhāra: withdrawing the senses 562, 572
Saṁyama upon the senses 595
Senses or the Self? 239
Supersensory powers 588
The physical senses entrap the mind 1519
The Sense of Time 22–23

Senzar
An ancient universal language 272
Fragment on the destruction of Atlantis 273

Separatism
Separatism and the Law of Love 386
The sin of separatism 264

Seraphim
Christian Classification of the Hierarchies 192
The Seraph's assault 699

Serpent
Awakening the Serpent-Fire 1038
Bhujangī: the Serpent of Wisdom 1516
The Kuṇḍalinī Fire 132
The Serpent 142
The Three Forces of the Warrior 996–997
When the Serpent is conquered 153

Service
71 The Call to Service 1705–1718
72 In Service to the Spiritual Hierarchy 1719–1730
Duty and Spirituality 1641
Family and Duty 998
Heart Action 1331
How to Become a Buddha or a Christ 1723
Meditational Service of the Buddhas 393
Meditation as Service 1203
Required in the Āryan Epoch 813
Required to overcome the lower mind 897
Return to Duty 812
Service is as important as meditation 1260
Seva 1153
The Dichotomy of the Mystic 629
The Stages of the Work 1385
The Warrior of the Light 984

The World Priest 1619
To Feed the Poor? 1714
To Love God and the World 1392
Universal Service 1717
What is True Service? 1714

Sesshin
General description 808
The Japanese Zen Retreat 807

Seva
Sādhanā: the Spiritual Life 1153
The Energy of the Goddess 1488

Seven Heavens
Terms for the Mental Plane 76
The Christian Cosmo-Conception 19

Seven Rays 54–56
Dimensions of the Cosmic Fire (graph) 137
Manifestations in Humanity 56
Overstimulation of the Base and Sex Centres 1228
Ray-Energies in the Human Cakras (graph) 54
The Devas according to the Rays 199
The Influence of the Seven Rays 834–835
The New Aquarian Energies 426
The Rays and the Planes (graph) 55
The Three Rays in the Human System 54
The Warrior, the Sage, the Ruler 972

Seven sacred planets
and the cakras 438
and the Seven Rays 55

Seventh State
Brahmā-Avasthā: the God-State 502

Sex. *See also* Polarity, Tantra
43 The Circle of Love 905–944

What is Sex?
Kuṇḍalinī is the Sex-Force 148–149
Polarities Male and Female 920–921
Polarities within the Human Aura (graph) 921
Sexuality and the Life-force 912
Sex Natural and Divine 926–927
The Human Bipolarity 472–477
The Sexless Soul 920
To Understand Sex 917

Sex and Love
Heart Union and Sexual Union 1140
Sexual energy can be tamed by the Buddhic 1290
Sexual love 913
Sex is not Love 46, 153
The Energies of Sex and Love 912

Sexual Ignorance
Mistranslation of the term Brahmacarya 566–567
Natural Sexual Dynamism 918
Religion's warped view of sex 570
Sexual energy and poltergeist phenomena 314–315
Sexual repression has never helped 567
Sex without Love is Soul-destructive 929
Spiritual dimensions of sex are neglected 917
The Feminine Suppressed 910
The Work of the Devil? 910
To Understand Sex 917

Sexual Transmutation
Kuṇḍalinī and Alchemy 153
Lifting the sexual energy into the Heart 431, 455, 702
Sex on the Astral Plane 70
Tantric meditations on the Embrace 959
The Circle of Love 923
The Female Dominant 924–925
Through Sex which is Love 929
When Sex is Love 930

Sex Centre. *See also* Svādhiṣṭhāna Cakra
General description 46
Not understood by Humanity 1037
Overstimulation of the Sex Centre 152–153, 1228, 1431
Stimulation by the Aquarian energies 1708
The Circle of Love 923
The Heart and the Energy Centres 1332

Shades. *See also* astral shells
Materialization of a shade 314

Shadow. *See also* Darkness
Brothers of the Shadow 226–227
Shadowland 219

Shaikh
The Spiritual Master 829, 832

Shamanism. *See also* Psychism
and astral projection 303
A lower religion 328
Derivation of the word "shaman" 276
Roots of Modern Shamanism 276
The origin of spirit-worship 412
Uniting with animals 584
Yogic Powers and Psychism 579

Shamayīm, Shemayīn
Western words for "Heaven" 1352

Sharī'at
Stage One of the Radiant Way 830
The Divine Plan 830, 837
The First Stage of Spiritual Life 1160

Shekinah
God's Manifest Presence 131
Holiness to the Lord 1393
Meditations in the Heart Centre 1297
Names of the Being of Light 417
The Hasidim 648–649
The Light of Nirvāṇa 102
The Mother of the World 147
The Virgin Mother 671

Shells. *See* astral shells

Shem, Shemā
The Divine Name 1352

Shemayā
Western words for "Heaven" 1352

Sheol
The Underworld 6, 60

Sherārā
Truth (as used by Jesus) 1341

Shikantaza
To sit fully aware 800–801

Siddha
Definition 394
Mysterious Knowledge of the Siddhas 1310–1311
The Siddhas perceive the Immanent and Transcendent aspects of God 1129

Siddhi. *See also* Miracles, Powers
26 The Yoga of Miraculous Powers 577–606
Definition 156, 277, 578
Yoga-Siddhi-Śakti: the Energy of the Goddess 1487

Sikhism
Esoteric History of the Piscean Religions 833

Sila
Steps to the Experience of Zen 813

Silence. *See also* Stillness, Meditational Practices
Be Tranquil 987
Clouds of Unknowing 704–705
Cultivate Silence of the Mind 1239
Mauna: She who dwells in Silence 1578
Silence and Activity 1446
Silence, Solitude, Peace 1386
Silence Seals 1034
Stages of Silence 1444
Stillness before Battle 1095
Tao is Silent 779
The Attitude for Yoga 558
The Law of Mystic Experience 508–509
The Path of Hearing 553
The Seven Stages of Sūfī Silence 901
The Silence of the Deep 1355
The Silence of the Warrior 1008
The Silent Work, or Work in Silence 981
The Silent State 1554
The Suspending of the Mind 1208–1209
To Experience Heaven 82
Understanding your Work in Silence 1024
Via Negativa: the Passive Path 1465
Zen Silence 790–793

Silver Cord. *See also* Sūtrātma
A lower reflection of Sūtrātma 1645
Broken at death 401
Exists during the Incarnation Process 414

Sin
Hamartia: missing the mark 683
Have mercy on me, a sinner? 707
Jesus was without "sin" 668
The sin of separatism 264
The Sin of the Mindless 176

Sirr
Dimensions of the Heart (Arabic) 847

Sitā
A Name of Lalitā, the Goddess 1572

Sitting
Just Sitting 1018
Shikantaza: to sit fully aware 800–801
Zazen: Zen Sitting 798

Śiva. *See also* Brahmā-Viṣṇu-Śiva
Derivation 113
Detailed meanings 1321
Mahāvākya Practice 1477
Śivā: a Name of Lalitā, the Goddess 1573
Śiva Bīja 1551
Śiva-Śakti 1521

Śivagranthi
Knots of Consciousness 445
The knot at the Head Cakras 497, 1424

Śiva-Netra. *See also* Eye of Śiva
Definition and description 292–293
The Path of Seeing 552

Śiva-Śakti
Dimensions of the Cosmic Fire (graph) 137
Śrī-Vidyā embodies Śiva and Śakti 1521
Universal Sexual Bliss 133

Śiva Yoga
Śiva Yoga of the Liṅga Purāṇa 561

Śivōhaṁ, Śivo'haṁ
I am the Self 239
Keys to the Heart 1323
Mahāvākya Practice 1474
Śiva-Śakti 1521

Sixth State
Bhāgavata-Avasthā: the State of Glory 501

Smṛtī
Guard your Heart 1328
Remembering God in the Heart Centre 723

Smṛti
Traditional teachings 532

Śoḍaṣī
A Name of Lalitā, the Goddess 1560
The Śoḍaṣī Energy 1527
The Śoḍaṣī-Mantra 1526, 1531

Sohaṁ, So'haṁ. *See also* Haṁsa
Breathing in and out of the Heart 461
Gāyatrī (Sun) Breathing 1553
Mahāvākya Practice 1472
Pure Consciousness in the Heart 447
Rest in the Great Breath 1654–1655
Three Kinds of Breathing Meditation 1220
Three Meditations in the Heart 1292

Solar Angels
Normally dwell in the Causal Worlds 275
The Mānasaputras 216

Solar Logoi
Children of the Cosmic Creators 190
Destined by the Stars? 260–261
Solar-Systemic and Cosmic Evil 217
The Cosmic Creator-Gods 162–163
The Doctrine of the Logoi 116
The Elohīm 120
The Manifested-God 1589

Solar Logos. *See also* Sun, Sūrya, Savitā
66 The Mystery of the Sun 1585–1600
67 The Gāyatrī-Mantra 1601–1642
69 Salutations to the Sun 1657–1676
Dimensions of the Solar Logos in Cosmic Space 1591
Incarnations of the Sun 1593
Bodies of our Solar Logos 95, 122–126, 761
Solar-Systemic and Cosmic Evil 217
The Constitution of God-Immanent 122–126
The Constitution of the Solar Logos (graph) 124
The Field of Activity of our Solar Logos 1588
The Heart of the Solar Logos 1327
The Solar Constitution 1587
The Solar Dharma 163
Who is "I AM"? 1418

Solar Plexus Centre. *See also* Maṇipūra Cakra
Dangers of lower solar-plexus emotions 427
General description 47
Humanity is suffering from maladjusted solar plexus 1712

Japanese Zen focuses in the solar plexus (Hara) 798
Overstimulation of the Solar Plexus Centre 1431
Saṁyama upon the Solar Plexus Centre 586
Solar Plexus Breathing 1220
The Heart and the Energy Centres 1332
The medium for psychic telepathy 347
The opposite pole to the Third-Eye Centre 797
The seat of astral consciousness 429

Solar System. *See* Solar Logos

Solitude. *See also* Silence
Alone with God 700
A positive spiritual quality 1185
Being Alone with the Absolute 502
Being alone with yourself 768
How to have a Peaceful Mind in a Troubled World 1244
Silence, Solitude, Peace 1386
Solitude and Loneliness 1170–1171
The Practice of Silence 1443–1447
The Universal Heart Practice 846
To bring about Tranquillity 1229
You are Alone on this Way 939

Soma
Christian Hesychast definition 746
The Human Constitution (Greek) 39

Somā
Drug to induce astral projection 304

Son. *See also* Trinity
Dimensions of the Cosmic Fire (graph) 137
Mythical Concepts of God 104–105
The Christian Trinity 113
The Kingdom of God (graph) 123
The Many Mansions (graph) 611
The Threefold Logos 662

Sons of God
Jesus: the only Son of God? 669
Manifestation of the Sons of God 180
Planetary Evil 214

Sons of Mind. *See* Mānasaputras

Son of Man
Crowned with Glory 197
Jesus Christ, Son of Man 668

Sophia
Christian Hesychast definition 740
Greek Mystery School definition 733
The Boundless Feminine Intelligence 146
The Eternal Feminine 469
Western words for "Wisdom" 1354
What is Wisdom? 1685

Sōtēr
A Gnostic name for Jesus 661
Definition 664
Sōtērios: definition 129

Soul. *See* Human Soul, Spiritual Soul

Sound. *See also* Vibration, Mantra, Divine Name, Logos
47 The Primordial Sound Language 1025–1076
God's Cosmic Symphony 1649
Planetary Disturbance 1697
Sounds experienced through Kuṇḍalinī 156
Sun-Sounds 201, 1543
The Action of the Primordial Sound (graph) 165
The Creative and Destructive Power of Sound 201
The four stages of Sound 1524, 1577
The Liberating and Transforming Power of Sound 1024
The Logos: the Word of God 114–115
The Sounds of Nāda 1651
Vāk: the Divine Speech 118
Vibration and Mantra 1518–1519

Sounding-Light. *See* Logos, Word, Divine Name

Space. *See also* Ākāśa
Ākāśa Bīja 1546
Dimensions of the Solar Logos in Cosmic Space 1591
Every form is a Form of God 1313
Hṛdaya-Ākāśa: the Heart Space 1280
Tantric meditations on Space 947
The "emptiness" of Space is an illusion 1589
The Form of God is Space 109
The One Space 13
The Planes exist within the same Space 1590
The Space Element 26–28
The Western mystical understanding of "Heaven" 1352
Walls of Time and Space (graph) 21
Worlds within Worlds 886

Spanda. *See also* Vibration
Niṣspanda: no-vibration 1243
Vibration and Mantra 1518–1519

Sparkling Stone
The Jewel in the Lotus 1322
The Mystery within the Heart 1315

Speaking in tongues
General description 312–313

Spēculum Justīciae
The Mirror of Justice 1511

Speech
Misuse of the Creative Energy 48
Speech and Telepathy 348–349
The control of your speech 1237
Vāk: the Divine Speech 118

Spirit. *See also* Ātman, Paramātman, Holy Spirit
Baptism by Fire and the Spirit 627, 718, 1348
Degeneration of the word "Spirit" 319
Living Matter 134–135
Meanings in the ancient sacred languages 1341
Terms for "Spirit" in ancient languages 1343
The Descent of the Spirit (graph) 51

Spirits
Degeneration of the word "Spirit" 319
Test the spirits 336
The origin of spirit-worship 412
The Spirit-Helpers 369
Who are the Infesting Spirits? 310

Spirit-body
Incorrect term for the astral body 59

Spirit-guides
and the Astral Subplanes 64–67, 69
Beyond Spirit-Guides 336
Black Magic attracts negative spirits 371
Invited and uninvited spirit-guides 310–311
The Awakening Guides 409
The Changing Faces of the Spirit-Guides 332–333
The Coming of the Spirit-Guides 281
The Spirit-Helpers 369–371
Who are the "Spirit-Guides"? 334–335
Who are the Infesting Spirits? 310

Spirit-possession
Channelling is contagious 341
Involuntary Possession 310–311
In White Magic there is no possession 370–371
Magic: White and Black 364
Possessed Mediums 309
Psychic Disruption of groups 1155
The Evil of Criticism 1156–1157
To avoid astral interference during meditation 1186
Who are the Infesting Spirits? 310

Spirit-Spark-Atom
The Fire of Love 1255
The Imperishable Seed in the Heart 926–927
The Jewel in the Heart 1298
The Mystery within the Heart 1315
The Perennial Source of Love 438
The Universal Christ in the Heart 440

Spiritualist Movement
Roots of Modern Mediumship 318

Spirituality
Introduction III: The New Spirituality 1103–1114
Duty and Spirituality 1641
Male and Female Systems of Spirituality (graph) 1112
Piscean Spirituality and New Age Spirituality 1706
Religion and Spirituality 754
Spirituality and Renunciation 806
Spirituality Past and Future 1104
Spiritual Life and Material Life 1118
The Way of the Spirit 381
Three Schools of Spirituality 1121
Trapped Spirits 1240

Spiritual Hierarchy
72 In Service to the Spiritual Hierarchy 1719–1730
Brotherhoods of Light and Darkness 228
Ekklesia: the called-out ones 688
Hierarchies of Life (graph) 1721
Jesus: the Fire of Love 1725
Let Thy Will Be Done 1720
Manifestation in the New Age 282
Members of the Hierarchy do not spook 309
Pseudo-hierarchies on the Astral Plane 66
Pure Devotion: Initiation Mantram 1724

Saṅgha: the Spiritual Hierarchy 394
Telepathic communion with the Hierarchy 353
The Brotherhood of Light (graph) 395
The Buddha and the Christ 1722–1723
The Christ-Hierarchy and Śamballa 396
The Function of the Spiritual Hierarchy 1720
The Hierarchical Mantrams 1726–1727
The Invisible Government 980–981

Spiritual Kingdom. *See also* Spiritual Hierarchy
The Sevenfold Earth-Evolution 169

Spiritual Masters. *See also* Spiritual Teachers, Guru, Hierophant
"Ascended Masters" invented by channellers 332
Do not "follow" a Master outside yourself 1229
Female Buddhas 1110
Humility of the Great Ones 337
Masters and Mediums 326–327
The Enlightened 1702
The Guru and the Hierophant 1148
The Perfected Ones 377
The Sūfī Master 832
The Zen Master 782
The Zen Master according to Lao Tzu 780–781
To commune with genuine Masters 353

Spiritual Path
49 The Aquarian Way 1117–1144
50 The Aquarian Group-Consciousness 1145–1172

What is the Spiritual Path?
Avoid the Errors of East and West 1122–1123
Beyond Natural Evolution 1312
Beyond the Veils 894
Clarify your Objective 423
Cosmic Renewal 1452
Evolution, the Plan, the Path 1688–1692
From Personal to Cosmic Life 1428
God-Consciousness is the Wholeness of Life 504–505
In Search of Reality 1174
Learn to Die before you Die 420–421
Paths to Devāchan 81
Penetrating into the Kingdom 1707
Piscean Spirituality and New Age Spirituality 1706
Regain what you have Lost 381
Spirituality Past and Future 1104
Summary of the Process (Metanoia) 1468
The Great Way 605
The Holy Path 1285
The Lighted Way 1394–1395
The Path of Light 89
The Path to Discipleship 1149
The Science of Cosmic Consciousness 1124–1125
The Spiritual Path and psychism 319–320
The Ultimate Reality is the Meaning of Life 526–527
The Way of the Spirit 381
The Way to Higher Consciousness 329
To be taught Wisdom 353
To Manifest the Kingdom of God 1716
To speed up our mechanisms 102
Understand your Predicament 892–893
Vertical Evolution and the Path 174

Aspects of the Path
Bhakti Yoga: Divine Union by Devotion 1128
Hṛdaya-Mārga: the Threefold Way of the Heart 1236
Heart Knowing 1286
Jñāna Yoga: Right Knowledge or Realization 1124, 1236
Karma Yoga: Divine Union by Action 1132–1133
Male and Female Systems of Spirituality (graph) 1112
Paths of Spiritual Evolution 1693
Paths to the Transcendent and Immanent God 1120
Rāja Yoga: Divine Union by Meditation 1126–1127
Sūrya-Sādhanā: Sun-Worship 1604
The Dynamic Way and Passive Way 1347, 1465
The Path of Hearing 553
The Path of Mantra and the Goddess 1490
The Path of Seeing 552
The Path of Tantra 942–943
The Sevenfold Practice (Buddhi Yoga) 1698
The Three "Spiritual" Types 377
The Three Gates to God 151
The Two Paths: Knowledge and Mysticism 55, 1112
The Universal Heart Practice 846
The Warrior Path 1002–1003
The Way of the Mind 1238–1239
To Worship the Sun 1586
Types of Conscious Immortality 390–391

Stages of the Path

Development of the Seven States of Consciousness 496
Development of the Spiritual Warrior 971
Experiencing the Awakening Heart 463–465
Hierarchies of Life (graph) 1721
Signs of Progress in the Heart 1289
Signs of the awakening Kuṇḍalinī 154–156
Stages on the Path 1136–1137
Stages on the Way of Holiness 1336–1339
Steps on the Meditational Path 1196–1198
The First Circle of Life 1422
The Four Stages of Spiritual Life (Arabic) 1160–1161
The Journey of the Heart (Sūfī) 855–857
The Second Circle of Life 1438
The Seven Centres of Force in the Human Species 1385
The Seven States of Consciousness 494–496
The Stages of the Work 1385
The Third Circle of Life 1448
The three degrees of Self-Realization 1448
The Three Stages of Yoga 528–529
The Unfoldment of the Light (Christian) 718–721

General Instruction on the Path

Awaken First the Heart 428
A Summary of the Practice 1237
Being and Becoming 1415
Cultivate the Positive 1365
Duty and Spirituality 1641
Entering the Lost Kingdom 1176–1177
Going Back to the Marketplace 1172
How to Become a Buddha or a Christ 1723
Integrity and Perfection 1005
Let the Light Shine 1307
Look for the Light 1395
On Love and Meditation 1140–1143
Persevering to the End until Final Liberation 1101
Practice for Wisdom 1700–1701
Right Practice 1696–1697
Sādhanā: the Spiritual Life 1153
The Active and Passive Way (Warrior) 1011
The Future 1709
The Importance of the Heart in Approaching God 432–433
The New Age and You 1708
The New and Eternal Way 516
The Path (Metanoia) 1465–1467
The Path to Immortality 430–431
The Path to Wisdom 1702–1704
The Vision of your own Eternity 1144
To Approach the Goddess 1513
To Realize the Presence of God 1398
To Rediscover Buddhi 90
Uniting Head and Heart 1130–1131
You Alone are Responsible 258

Hindrances on the Path. *See also* obstacles, opposition, overstimulation, dangers

Causes of Group Disruption 1154–1155
Common Obstacles on the Path of Meditation 1205
Crises on the Path 1162–1165
Dangers of awakening the Kuṇḍalinī 157–158
Diseases caused by walking upon the Path 1168
Emotional Problems 1429–1431
Karma and your Spiritual Development 255
Karmic Adjustment 1379
Let Go of the Past 1241
Notes on the Spiritual Path in the New Age 1166–1167
Obstacles to Higher Consciousness 1424
Obstacles to Union with the Soul 556–557
The Testing of the Soul 1158

Traditional Paths. *See also* Yoga, Christianity, Zen, Sūfīsm

Introduction II: By Whichever Path 511–516
Balance in Spiritual Life 505
Christian Mysticism 450–451
Devotion to Kṛṣṇa 449
Life as a Zen Monk 806
Origins of Zen 752
Paths of Spiritual Evolution 1693
Search out your Heart 437
Śiva Yoga of the Liṅga Purāṇa 561
Spirituality Past and Future 1104
Tao: the Supreme Way 776–778
Techniques for the Expansion of the Heart 461
The Catholic Mystical Path 1129
The Christian Heart-Path 632
The Noble Eightfold Path of the Buddha 815
The Radiant Way (Sūfī) 830–832
The Ten Mahāyāna Precepts 814
The Thread of the Heart 844

The Way of the Radiant Heart 452–455
Three Schools of Spirituality 1121
Yoga-Mārga: the Path to Union 520
Yoga by Eight Steps 560

Spiritual Psychology
58 The Psychology of Consciousness 1363–1398
59 Time and Eternity: Action and Destiny 1399–1410
60 Metanoia: the Renaissance of the Mind 1411–1468
61 Mahāvākya: Great Truth Statements 1469–1480

What is Spiritual Psychology?
Concerned with inner transformations 380
From Personal to Cosmic Life 1428
How do you Know who You really Are? 1387
Personal Transformation vs mediumship 322
Psychology Ancient and Modern 1364
Spiritual Healing 1379
The Experience of the Transcendent 1378
The Lighted Way 1394–1395
The Presence of God 1396–1397
Transformational Psychology 1367
Western Psychology vs Spiritual Psychology 494

Human Psychology
All Hail to the Brain! 1368
Consciousness (aphorisms) 1370–1371
Desire-Streams 1377
Emotional Problems 1429–1431
Formless Consciousness 1373
Happiness Exists Within 1381
Illumined-Mind Consciousness 1427
Mind and Body 1374–1375
Mind and Thought 1376
Obstacles to Higher Consciousness 1424
Reactive-Emotional Consciousness 1426
Temporary Relief 1427
The Basic Enlightened State 1372
The Kingdom is at Hand 1453
The Seven Centres of Force in the Human Species 1385
The State of Unity of the Psyche 1383
The Three Identifications 1369
What is Consciousness? 1368–1369
Who is "I AM"? 1418
Your personal sense of self is a mystery 1388

Psychology Practice
Activating I AM: the Secret Name of God 1419
Attach Yourself to Being 1433
Bīja-Mantra and Psychology 1552
God, the Healer of Broken Hearts 1432
How to deal with Crisis situations in your Life 1435
Look for the Light 1395
Mahāvākya Practice (Great Truth Statements) 1470–1479
Meditation on the Divine Names 1454–1462
Silence, Solitude, Peace 1386
The Practice of Silence 1443–1447
The Silent Watcher Meditation 1388
The Work of Meditation 1440–1442
The Work of Metanoia 1414
To Realize the Presence of God 1398

The Psychology Path
Action (Karma) 1402–1406
Cultivate Knowledge 1366
Cultivate the Positive 1365
Destiny (Dharma) 1407–1409
Karmic Adjustment 1379
Know Thyself 1389
Oneness and Love 1450–1451
Past, Present and Future 1400–1401
Self-Worth 1382
The First Circle of Life 1422–1423
The Laws of Group Psychology 1384
The Principle of Choice 1380–1381
The Second Circle of Life 1438–1439
The Stages of the Work 1385
The Third Circle of Life 1448–1449
To Love God and the World 1392–1393
You Are the World 1390–1391

Spiritual Soul. *See also* Buddhi, Ātma-Buddhi
Buddhi: the second aspect of the Individuality 34
The Energy of Love 912
Union with the Spiritual Soul brings Freedom 251
What is Intuition? 328
Wisdom and Understanding 439

Spiritual Teachers. *See also* Spiritual Masters, Guru
A World Teacher 1728
"Channelling" the Soul 325
Descent of the Teachers 370
Incur the anger of the priestcraft 368
Living Guidance 339
Look out for the One 1004
Not all "religious" are enlightened 253
Relational Consciousness 906–907
Revelation is Continuous 1710
Teachers during the Vedic days of India 1118
The Approach to Truth 1152
The Aquarian Teachers 1147
The Guru 389
The Laws of Group Psychology 1384
The Sacrifice of the Teachers 1150–1151
The Teachers continually have to restate the Truth 368
The True Teachers 1694–1695
The Warrior, the Sage, the Ruler 972–973
Where are your Wisemen? 387

Spiritual Triad. *See* Triad

Spiritual Warrior. *See* Warrior

Spiritus. *See also* Spirit
Degeneration of the word "Spirit" 319
Equivalent words in other languages 130
Spirit 1343
Spiritus-Sanctus: Spirit-Holy 1344

Spleen Centre
and astral phenomena 47
Responsible for Vital Force in the body 1375
Spleen transfers life-force to the body 50
The medium for instinctual telepathy 346

Spontaneous human combustion
Description and explanation 316

Śraddhā
The Six Mental Qualifications 1149
To Succeed in your Quest 1330

Śramana
Source of the word "shaman" 276

Sraosha
What is the Name? 1259

Śrī
A description of the Goddess 1488
A Name of Lalitā, the Goddess 1559
Potent Vibrations: Bīja-Mantra 1548

Śrīṁ
Potent Vibrations: Bīja-Mantra 1548
Śrīṁkārī: a Name of Lalitā, the Goddess 1564
The Seed-Sound for Lakṣmī 1489
The Śrī-Vidyā-Mantras 1531–1537

Śrī Jagadambā
The Mother of the World 1498–1499

Śrī-Mahā-Rājñī
A Name of Lalitā, the Goddess 1559

Śrī-Mātā
A Name of Lalitā, the Goddess 1559

Śrī-Vidyā. *See also* Goddess
64 Śrī-Vidyā: the Holy Science 1515–1554
A Name of Lalitā, the Goddess 1560
Holy Knowledge 1517
Śiva-Śakti 1521
The Living Form of the Goddess in the Light 1522–1523
The Śrī-Vidyā-Mantra 1530
The Śrī-Vidyā-Vajra-Mantra 1531
The True Feminine 1516
The Wisdom of the Goddess 1525
Vibration and Mantra 1518–1519

Śruti
Definition 532
The scriptures were heard in deep meditation 1216

Stars. *See* Solar Logoi

Star Wars
"May the Force be with you" 132

Stella Matutīna
The Pure White Light in the Third-Eye 1511

Sterge
Terms of Love 914

Sthūla-Loka
The gross world 1707

Sthūla-Śarīra. *See also* physical body
The Personality Complex 36–37

Stigmata
Wounds of Love 699

Stillness. *See also* Silence
Action and Stillness: the Supreme Way 1083
Be Still and Know 638–639
From Action into Stillness, from Stillness into Action 1016
Guarding your Heart by Stillness 1328
Mental quiescence is required for meditation 1202
Peace of Heart 1595
Stillness before Battle 1095
To Develop Perfect Stillness 700
When the Mind is Still 768

Stone of the Wise
The Mystery within the Heart 1315

Stress
Crisis and Revelation 1711
Emotional Problems 1429–1431
Fear and Stress (Metanoia) 1434
Karmic Adjustment 1379
The Double Stress of Meditational Life 1181

Strī
An Energy-Form of the Goddess 1489
A Name of Lalitā, the Goddess 1567
Potent Vibrations: Bīja-Mantra 1548
The Strī-Mantra 1538

Strīṁ
Potent Vibrations: Bīja-Mantra 1548
The Seed-Sound for Strī 1489

Subconscious mind
A source of mediumistic communications 331
Beyond Phantasia 686–687
Desire-Streams 1377
Planetary Subconscious Mind 58
Realms of the One Mind 492–493
Subconscious Forces 236–237
Subconscious mediums 309
Subconscious Renewal 1236
The astral body is the subconscious mind 58, 236
The Personality Complex 36–37
The Power of Suggestion 237
Universal Subconscious Mind 58, 492

Subjective mind. *See* subconscious mind

Subplanes
Human Perception on the Subplanes (graph) 507
Planes and Subplanes 14
Seven Conditions in One Astral World 61
The Astral Subplanes 62–67
The Seven Subplanes of the Astral Plane (graph) 67
The Seven Subplanes of the Buddhic Plane (graph) 90
The Seven Subplanes of the Mental Plane (graph) 75
The Seven Subplanes of the Nirvāṇic Plane (graph) 99
The Seven Subplanes of the Physical Plane (graph) 16

Succubus
and poltergeist phenomena 315

Suchness
Bhūtatathatā 86
One's Original Nature 85
Prajñā 769

Śuddha
Śuddhā Bīja 1547
Śuddha-Caitanya: Pure Consciousness 1208, 1373
Śuddha-Deham: Perfected physical bodies 1310
Śuddha-Manas: Pure Mind 1208–1209
Śuddha-Mānasā: a Name of Lalitā, the Goddess 1565

Śūdra
The Servant Class 378

Suffering
Animal Suffering 222
Disease and Karma 1169
From Darkness into Light 982–983
Life need not be suffering at all 1119
Return to Primeval Happiness 1179
The Law of Action 992–993
The Mind-Created Devil 218
The Sufferings of Man 223
The Universal Intelligence 232
To bring an end to suffering 636
Why Life is Suffering 263

Sufflation
Mystical States of the Medieval Catholic Mystics 698

Sūfīsm
39 The Sūfī 827–842
40 The Sūfī Heart 843–862
41 Sūfī Prayer 863–884
42 Sūfī Mind 885–902
What is Sūfīsm?
A Sūfī is... 840–841
Esoteric History of the Piscean Religions 833
From Pisces to Aquarius 837
Mystics of Islām 828–829
Mystics of Pisces and Aquarius 836
Sūfī: definition 828
Sūfī: definition and description 513
The Influence of the Seven Rays 834–835
The One God of All 869
The Sūfī God 838
Sūfī Cosmology
Beyond the Veils 894
The Human Constitution (Arabic) 892
Understand your Predicament 892–893
Worlds of the Sūfī 886–889
Worlds of the Sūfī (graph) 890
Sūfī Psychology
Dimensions of the Mind 891
Murāqabaī: Sūfī Meditation 901
Taming the Mind 899
The Five Stages of Certainty (Arabic) 895
The Ordinary Mind 896
The Sūfī View of Mental Disorders 900
The Seven Stages of Sūfī Silence 901
The Sūfī Heart-Path
Dimensions of the Heart 847
Nūr: the Light of God 847
Qalb: the Sūfī Heart 848
Search out your Heart 437
Tauḥīd: the Divine Unity 852
The Ancient Heart-Path 845
The Four Stages of Spiritual Life (Arabic) 1160–1161
The Journey of the Heart 855–857
The Lover of God 853
The Muslim Deification Process 1191
The One and Only 839
The Purification of the Heart 849
The Radiant Way 830–832
The Revelation of God 854
The Thread of the Heart 844
The Truth in the Heart 851
The Universal Heart Practice 846
Sūfī Practice
Breathing God 870–871
El Allāh Hū: The Arabic I AM 1459
Let the Sunshine in 872
Linking the Head with the Heart 897
Meditation on the Exalted Name of God 871
Some Arabic Prayers to the Deity 850–851
Sūfī Mantras for Meditation 874–877
The 99 Arabic Divine Names of God 878–884
The Beautiful Names (Arabic) 1264–1265
The Dance of Life 873
The Mantram of Unification in the Heart Centre 866–868
The Rose of Divine Love 858–861
The Voice of God 864–865
Transformation of the Ordinary Mind 898–899

Suggestion
The Power of Suggestion 237

Suicide
Death-experience of the suicide and the murdered 404–405

Sukhāvatī
The place of happiness 76

Sūkṣma-Loka
The Suble Worlds 1707

Sūkṣma-Śarīra. *See also* astral body
The Personality Complex 36–37

Sulṭān-ul-Azkār
The King of Prayers 864

Summer Land
The lower heavens 65

Sun. *See also* Solar Logos
66 The Mystery of the Sun 1585–1600
67 The Gāyatrī-Mantra 1601–1642. *See* Gāyatrī
68 Works of Silence 1643–1656
69 Salutations to the Sun 1657–1676
The Nature of the Sun
Children of the Sun 1590
Dimensions of the Solar Logos in Cosmic Space 1591
God's Cosmic Symphony 1649
Hṛdaya-Cakra: the Heart Centre 1616
Incarnations of the Sun 1593
Our Sun is a gigantic Knot of Power 1625
The Activity of the Divine Heart 1675
The Constitution of God-Immanent 122–126
The Field of Activity of our Solar Logos 1588
The Heart of the Solar Logos 1327
The Manifested-God 1589
The Solar and Human Heart 1592
The Solar Constitution 1587
The Universal Creator-God 1588
The Word, Logos, Voice, Name 1646–1648
To Worship the Sun 1586
The Light of the Sun
Rules of Light 1597
The Light of the World 1596
The Self-Generating Light 1594
The Shining Lights 1595
The Sun Path
Duty and Spirituality 1641
Sūrya-Sādhanā: Sun-Worship 1604
There are three Suns within you 1691
The Eternal 1644
The Sun incarnated in a Perfected Spiritual Warrior 1629
The World Priest 1619
To Worship the Sun 1586
Viśva Yoga: Cosmic Union 1604
Warriors of the Sun 1618
Sun Practice
Awareness Meditation 1656
Cosmic Tuning-In: the 'I' Sound 1652
Hear the Sound within the Silence 1651
How to Meditate on the Sun 1606–1607
Meditation on the Sūtrātma 1645
Preliminary Meditation on the Sun 1605
Remember the Presence 1653
Rest in the Great Breath 1654–1655
Saṁyama upon the Sun and Moon 585
See the Light of the Logos 1650
The Savitā-Mantra 1602
The Shaft of Light from the Sun 1635
Sun Mantras
Brahma-Gāyatrī-Mantra 1638
Divine Name Solar Vibrations 1598
Gāyatrī: the Basic Hymn 1603
More Mantras to Sūrya, the Sun 1658–1674
Solar Meditation in the Cakras (graph) 1640
Sūrya-Ahaṁ: I am the Sun 1327
The Gāyatrī-Mantra (variations) 1608–1637
The Healing Sun Mantra 1599

Sundarī
The Child-Goddess Mantra 1532

Śūnyatā. *See also* Void, Formlessness
Buddhic Consciousness 85
Divine Unknowing 705
Formless conditions of existence 760
Meditating on the Void 801
Śūnya, Śūnyatā: variations of meaning 503
Śūnyatā: the Void 503
The Fullness of the Void 23

Superconscious Mind. *See also* Pure Consciousness, Mystical Consciousness, Buddhi, Buddhi-Manas, Prajñā
"Channelling" the Soul 325
Realms of the One Mind 492–493
The Experience of Illumination 816–817
What is Intuition? 328
Working consciously in the Superconscious State 582

Supernatural
Beyond physical Nature 357

Sura. *See also* Solar Angels
A-Sura: "Not a Solar Angel". 211
Divine Hierarchies 1659

Surat-Śabda-Yoga
Putting your attention on the Sound 1212

Surrender. *See also* Sacrifice
How to deal with Crisis situations in your Life 1435
Īśvara-Praṇidhāna: Devotion to God 548, 564, 569
Surrender to the Holy Breath 1341
Surrender to the Limitless 935
Surrender to the Self 87
The Law of Surrender or Sacrifice 1138
Via Negativa: the Passive Path 1465

Sūrya. *See also* Sun, Solar Logos
66 The Mystery of the Sun 1585–1600
Definition 1602, 1658
Sūrya-Ahaṁ: I am the Sun 1327
Sūrya Bīja 1551
Sūrya-Maṇḍala: the Circle of the Sun 1586
Sūrya-Maṇḍalā: a Name of Lalitā, the Goddess 1563
Sūrya-Mantra. *See* Gāyatrī
Sūrya-Nārāyaṇa: the Sun-Spirit 1608
Sūrya-Śabda: the Creative Speech of the Sun 201
Sūrya-Sādhanā: Sun-Worship 1604
Sūrya-Vaṁśa-Kṣatriya: Warriors of the Sun 1602, 1618
Sūrya Yoga 1641

Suṣumna
Definition 151
Influence of Bīja-Mantra 1523
The one Current of Life 723
The Path upward to Heavenly Regions 1332

Suṣūpti-Avasthā
The dreamless-sleep state 494–496

Suṣūpti Yoga
The Yoga of the Dream State 299

Sūtra
Definition 532
The Yoga Sūtras 532–533

Sūtrātma
Also called the Silver Cord 401
Definition and illustration 181–182
Description and meditation 1645
The triple Thread of the Self 491

Suvah-Loka. *See also* Mental Plane
and the Goal of Yoga 521
Elementary Attributes 29
Dimensions of the Solar Logos in Cosmic Space 1591
Svaḥ, Suvaḥ, Suvaha, Svaha: definition 1610

Svacitta
Your self-mind creates your world 251

Svādhiṣṭhāna Cakra. *See also* Sex Centre
General description 46
The Heart and the Energy Centres 1332

Svādhyāya
Definition 535, 564
The fourth Rule of Aṣṭāṅga Yoga 569

Svāhā
Potent Vibrations: Bīja-Mantra 1551
Svāhā, Svāhā-Devī: Names of Lalitā 1580
The difference between Svaha and Svāhā 1617

Svapnā-Avasthā. *See also* subconscious mind
Svapnā-Avasthā Siddhi: dream-state power 600
The dreaming state 494–496

Svarga-Loka
The Heaven World 76

Svarṇa-Deham
The Golden Body 1310

Svarūpa
Definition 536
Svarūpa Siddhi 579

Svastika
Definition and explanation 179
Svastika Bīja 1544
Svastika-Śakti: the Energy of the Goddess 1486

Svatantrayaśakti
Your Self-Creative Power 1519

Svāyaṁbhū
Definition 151
Svāyaṁbhū Liṅga: a Gate to God 151
Your own Self-Nature 1208

Sylphs
The Elementals 195

Symbol
Some Symbols relating to the Path (graph) 1131
Symbols of the Cosmic Elements 360, 362
Symbols of the Kuṇḍalinī Fire 132
Symbols of the Religions (graph) 515
Symbols of the Seven Major Cakras (graph) 45
The Sign of Man 41

Synesis
Gnostic Christian definition 738

Syzygie
Gnostic Christian definition 736

T

Taciturnas
The Silent Ones 1355

Tala
Negative vibration 62

Ṭalabān
The Seekers after God 836

Ṭālib
The first stage of the Journey of the Heart 855

Tamas
That which produces Darkness 1693
The force of passivity 1406
The Guṇas 139–140

Tanhā. *See also* Triśnā
The craving for physical existence 239
The desire to be born in a physical body 251
True Death is Freedom from Tanhā 424

Tanmātra
Attributes of the Elements 28–29

Tantra
43 The Circle of Love 905–944
44 The One-Hundred-and-Twelve 945–966

What is Tantra?
Natural Law 919
Relational Consciousness 906–907
Tantra: definition 906
Tantra is for the Living 909
Tantra Mind 933
Tantra Yoga: brief description 157–158
The Path of Tantra 942–943
The Path of Zen or Tantra 1121
The Way of Feminine Consciousness 944
The Way of Love 911
Zen originated as a method of Tantra 752

The Goal of Tantra
Freedom is Boundless Love 932
Sex Natural and Divine 926–927
The Meaning of Love 931
The Original Calm 965
The Path of Tantra 942–943
To Reach Unqualified Existence 911

Human Polarities. *See also* Polarity
Falling in Love 922
Polarities Male and Female 920–921
Polarities within the Human Aura (graph) 921
The Circle of Love 923
The Female Dominant 924–925
The Feminine Heart 925
The Feminine Suppressed 910
The Sexless Soul 920

Relationship. *See also* Relationship
Live and Let Live 940
Love Lost 936–937
Mother, Father and Baby 938–939
Relational Consciousness 906
Tantra is for the Living 909
The Healing Power of Touch 919
The Tragedy of Human Relationships 936
You are Alone on this Way 939
You can only Love Now 941
Warrior Jesus 908

Sex and Love. *See also* Sex, Love
Cultivate the Fires of Love 928–929
Natural Attraction 918
Natural Sexual Dynamism 918
Sexuality and the Life-Force 912
Sex Natural and Divine 926–927
Terms of Love 914
The Energies of Sex and Love 912
The Many Hues of Love 913–916
Divine Love in the Head 916
Emotional Love 914
Heart Love 915
Mental Love 915
Sexual Love 913
The Meaning of Love 931
Through Sex which is Love 929
To Understand Sex 917
When Sex is Love 930

Tantra Practice
Cultivate the Fires of Love 928–929
Tantra Mind 933–935
The 112 Methods of Instant Enlightenment 946–966
The Circle of Love 923
The Female Dominant 924
When Sex is Love 930

Tao. *See also* One Mind, Cosmic Mind, Logos
36 The Eternal Tao 771–784
Become more Yin to receive Tao 477
Chinese description of the Feminine Principle 1207
Chinese term for Nirvāṇa 96
Cosmic Sensitivity 1009
Tao: the Great I AM 774
Tao: the Great Mother 146
Tao: the Supreme Way 776–778
Tao: the Universal Mind 775
Tao cannot be found in books or scriptures 773
Tao is Silent 779
Tao Teh: Silence and Action 1446
The manifest and unmanifest Godhead 1446
The One God of All Religions 110
What is Tao? 772–773
Yin, Yang, Tao 476–477

Tapah-Loka. *See also* Paranirvāṇa
and the Goal of Yoga 521
Dimensions of the Solar Logos in Cosmic Space 1591
Elementary Attributes 29

Tapas
and miraculous powers 578, 581
Definition 535, 564
Tapas, Tapasya, Tapaḥ: definition 569
Tapas: Spiritual Purification 571
The third Rule of Aṣṭāṅga Yoga 568–569

Tārā
An Energy-Form of the Goddess 1489
A Name of Lalitā, the Goddess 1573
Tārā Bīja 1542

Ṭarīqat
Stage Two of the Radiant Way 831
The Path 830, 837
The Second Stage of Spiritual Life 1160–1161

Tarot
A brief history 362
Keys of the Mind (Keys 0, 1, 2) 492–493
Tarot Key 1: The Magician 362
Tarot Key 13: Death 398
Tarot Key 5: The Hierophant 558

Tat
Definition 84–86, 1610
From the Unconditioned cometh forth all that is 1589
Mahāvākya Practice 1474–1475
Suchness or Thatness 763
The Transcendental Godhead 112

Tathāgatā
Derivation and definition 776
Mahāvākya Practice 1477

Tattva
Attributes of the Elements 28–29

Tau
Definition 146
The ancient Egyptian word for Tao 1446

Tauḥīd
The Divine Unity 852
The God-State 1257

Teachers. *See* Spiritual Teachers, Spiritual Masters, Guru

Teilhard de Chardin
The adherers to God 239
The Divine Milieu 12

Teishō
Zen definition 807

Tejas
Tejas Bīja 1550
The Fire Element 26–28
The Radiant One 1539

Telekinesis
Saṁyama and Parapsychology 582

Telepathy
16 Telepathy 345–353
Communicating by Light 351
Heart-to-heart and Soul-telepathy 347
Impressions from the Mental Plane 80
Impressions from the Soul 350
Instinctual Telepathy 346
Invoking the Invisible Helpers 370–371
Levels of Communication (summary) 351
Mental Telepathy 347
Mental Telepathy and Psychism 352
Mental telepathy is not mediumship 322
Mind to Mind (overview) 346–347
Psychic Telepathy 347
Telepatheia: definition 80, 346
Telepathic Communion is a State of Love 350
Telepathy on the Astral Plane after death 70
The Universal Language 348–349
The workings of the Inner Feminine 1010
Thought and Energy 349
To be taught Wisdom 353
Types of Telepathy (graph) 346
Used by H.P. Blavatsky and Alice Bailey 338

Televangelism
There is nothing of Christianity in it 682

Temple
The Temple Not Made By Hands 369
The Temple of God 639
The Temple of the Goddess 1492

Temptations. *See* tests

Terra
Western words for "Earth" 1351

Tests. *See also* obstacles
Crucifixion is the Test of the Spirit 721
Temptations of Jesus 308
Tested by God and the Devil? 685
The Testing of the Soul 1158
The tests of Earth, Water, Fire and Air 306
The Tests of the Elements 1159

Tetrakti. *See also* Personality, Quaternary
Definition 34, 736

Tettei
Zen definition 807

Thatness. *See also* Suchness
Bhūtatathatā 86
One's Original Nature 85
Prajñā 769

That Of Which Nought Can Be Said
The Transcendental Godhead 112, 126

Theology
Mystical Theology 706–707
Theologia, Theologian: definitions 625, 740
Theologia: Greek Mystery School definition 734

Theophainesthai
Christian Hesychast definition 740

Theophania
An appearance of God 1270

Theoria
Christian Hesychast definition 744
Stages of Interior Prayer 694

Theos
Christian Hesychast definition 740
Greek Mystery School definition 734
Meditation on Theos (God) 714

Theosis. *See also* Apotheosis
Christian Hesychast definition 695, 740
Stages of Interior Prayer 695
The objective of Eastern Christianity 650

Theosophia
Buddhic Consciousness 87
Christian Hesychast definition 740
Greek Mystery School definition 734
Theosophos: Christian Hesychast definition 740

Theosophy
Theosophical writers were not mediums 338

Theotokos
Christian Hesychast definition 740

Therapy. *See also* healing
Future Therapy 372

Third-Eye Centre. *See also* Ājñā Cakra
Divine Love in the Head 916
General description 49
Look for the Light 1395
Meditation in the Third-Eye 1224–1225
Mental love 915
Receiver of the Light of the Soul 350
Saṁyama in the Third-Eye Centre 587
The Heart and the Energy Centres 1332
The organ of true clairvoyance 293
The Third-Eye is a door, and also a window 793

Third death. *See also* Four Deaths
A Path to Devāchan 81
Death on the Astral Plane 399, 420

Thought. *See also* Mind
Action and Destiny (Metanoia) 1420–1421
Conditioned Thinking 1084
Energy follows thought 349
Energy Materializes 363
Go on renouncing thinking 763
Mental telepathy 347
Mind and Body 1374–1375
Mind and Thought 1376
Polarities Male and Female 920–921
Powers of Consciousness 374–375
Reflective Meditation 1184
There are two kinds of thinking 1414
The Evil of Criticism 1156–1157
The Power of Thought 232
The Thought of Enlightenment 767
Thinking and Being 233
Thought and the Magical Process 360–361
Thought creates even in the Astral World 246
True Thought 79

Thoughtforms
Existing on the lower Mental Plane 75
Hallucinations in the Afterlife 408–409
National Thoughtforms 385
Prevent experience of the Heaven Worlds 82
Thoughts are things 75, 79

Three Worlds
Change is the Absolute Law in the Three Worlds 405
From Bondage to Liberation (graph) 422
Saṁsāra: Wandering in the Three Worlds 421–422
The Soul is caught up in the Three Worlds 1422
The Three Worlds 887
The Three Worlds are but the One Mind 765
The Three Worlds of Becoming 1415
The Triple Cross of the Hierophant 558
Tripurā 1556

Throat Centre. *See also* Viśuddha Cakra
An entry point for the Soul 1194
General description 48
Overstimulation of the Throat Centre 1431
Saṁyama upon the Throat Centre 586
The Centre of Creativity 428
The Heart and the Energy Centres 1332
Transmitting station for mental telepathy 347

Thrones
Christian Classification of the Hierarchies 192

Tikkun
The Hasidim 648

Time
59 Time and Eternity: Action and Destiny 1399–1410
Athā: She who is the Eternal Now 1579
Atīta, Atha, Anāgata: Past, Present, Future 583
A construct of the brain and lower mind 596, 1241
Change is the Absolute Law 405
Eternal Heavens and Hells? 68
Knowledge of the Past and the Future 583
Let Go of the Past 1241

Past, Present and Future 1400–1401
Prophecy and Destiny 294–297
Some Esoteric Teachings on Time 22
The Kingdom is at Hand 1453
The Principle of Choice 1380–1381
The Sense of Time 22–23, 68
Time is not a dimension 270, 596
Walls of Time and Space (graph) 21

Tiphareth
The Kabbalistic Tree of Life 358–359

Tirisis Kardias
Vigilance in the Heart 632

Titan
A Great One 210
The war of the Titans 271

Titikṣa
The Six Mental Qualifications 1149

Torah
Dharma: the Law 245
The Law 648
Your Fate is Before your Eyes 246

Touch
The Healing Power of Touch 919

Tradition
Introduction II: By Whichever Path 511–516
Blind Tradition (Zen) 808
Can be a handicap for Mankind 379
Conditioned Thinking 1084
Religion and Spirituality 754
Traditionis: definition 379
Tradition kills the Living Presence 707
True Thought 79
Unnecessary Practices 1111

Trāṁ
Potent Vibrations: Bīja-Mantra 1551

Tranquillity. *See also* Silence, Peace
Be Tranquil 987
Cultivate Silence of the Mind 1239
Skill in Action 989
To see the Light and hear the Inner Sound 1595
Tranquil Mind 1503

Transcendental Consciousness. *See also* Mystical Consciousness, Pure Consciousness, Buddhi
Action in the Transcendent 1080
Buddhic Consciousness 86
The Experience of the Transcendent 1378
Turīya: Pure Consciousness 498

Transcendental Meditation
Maharishi and Transcendental Meditation 1182–1183

Transfiguration
The Illumination of the Head by the Light 721

Transformational Psychology. *See also* Spiritual Psychology
The task of Transformational Psychology 1367

Transpersonal Psychology. *See also* Psychology, Spiritual Psychology
Psychology and the New Age Religion 1105–1107
The proper field of study for psychology 291
Transpersonalis: definition 1105

Transverberation
Wounds of Love 699

Tratakam
Fixing the gaze inwardly 1224

Tree of Life. *See also* Kabbalah
The Hasidim 648
The Planes and the Kabbalistic Tree of Life (graph) 359
Wisdom and Understanding 439

Tretā Yuga
The Period of the Mahāmanvantara 168

Triad. *See also* Individuality
Definition 34, 736
Qualities of the Spiritual Warrior 970
The Threefold Structure of Man (graph) 33
The Triad reflected in the Human Soul (graph) 35
The Warrior, the Sage, the Ruler 972–973

Tribalism
Nationalism and Tribalism 385
Separatism and the Law of Love 386

Triguṇā
A Name of Lalitā, the Goddess 1575

Trīṁ
Potent Vibrations: Bīja-Mantra 1550

Trimūrti. *See also* Brahmā-Viṣṇu-Śiva, Trinity
Definition 35, 113
Dimensions of the Cosmic Fire (graph) 137
Reflected in the Human Soul 35
The Kingdom of God (graph) 123
The Three-Faced God 113

Trinity. *See also* Trimūrti
Āuṁ, Ōṁ, Nāda 550–551
Christian Divine Names 1266
Cosmic Renewal 1452
Dimensions of the Cosmic Fire (graph) 137
God has three Persons or Aspects 1649
Mythical Concepts of God 104–105
The Christian Trinity 113
The Holy Trinity 1342
The Holy Trinity and Jesus 94
The Holy Trinity is found in the Heart 435
The Kingdom of God (graph) 123
The Many Mansions (graph) 611
The Mystery of the Trinity 265
The Threefold Logos 662
The Three Forces of the Warrior 996–997
The triple Thread of the Self 491

Triple cross
Symbol of the office of the Hierophant 558

Tripurāsundarī
Lalitā: the Ultimate Goddess 1556
The Vibration of Hrīṁ 1528, 1547

Triśnā. *See also* Tanhā
The desire for embodiment 251

Truth
Satyam (Satya): Truthfulness 566
Sherārā (Aramaic) 1341
The Approach to Truth 1152
The Discovery of Truth (Buddhi) 85
The Truth in the Heart 851
The Truth shall make you Free 682–683
Truth and Mythology 7
Truth is a Living Presence 1174
Truth is eternally the same 516
Truth is Universal 378
Twilight of the Christian Truth 652–653

Turīya
Buddhic Consciousness 86
Steps on the Meditational Path 1196
The awakened Crown Centre 50
The First Stage of Yoga 528
Turīya: the Fourth State 498–499
Turyā Bīja 1551

Turīya-Avasthā
Formless Consciousness 1373
The Fourth State 494–496

Turīyātīta-Avasthā
Beyond the Fourth State 495–496
The Fifth State 500

Turyātman
Seen in the Heart 446

Twofold Lives
The Second Manifest Hierarchy 191

Tyāga
Steps on the Spiritual Path 561

Tzaddikīm
Definition and description 512
Tzadik: the Guru or spiritual model 648–649

Tzaphkiel
Hebrew Angelic Names Meditation 1462

U

'Ubūdiyat
Stage Seven of the Radiant Way 832

Udāna
An aspect of the fivefold Life-force 589

UFOs. *See also* Vimānas
and illusionary spirit-guides 333
Intervention and Interference 285
Many Biblical stories are UFO stories 282
Miracles performed by UFO people 335
The Enduring Vimānas 284
UFOs are not necessarily physical 284
Vimāna People and Human Destiny 283

Umā
A Name of Lalitā, the Goddess 1575

Understanding
Turīya: Pure Consciousness 498
Wisdom and Understanding 439

Underworld
Concepts of lower Astral World 6
The Underworld (terminology) 60

Undines
The Elementals 195

Union
Being Alone with the Absolute 502
Be Still and Know 638–639
Degrees of Union with the Holy Breath 1349
God in the Heart 634–635
Heart Love 915
Heart Union and Sexual Union 1140
Mystical Union 846
The first stage of Union with God 501
The God-State 1257
The Path of Union 1339
The second stage of Union with God 502
Viśva Yoga: Cosmic Union 1604

Unity. *See also* One Mind
5 Buddhi: The Realm of Unities 83–92
Beyond War 1098
Mind-Only 974–975
Oneness and Love 1450
Oneness and Love (Metanoia) 1451
Surpassing your own Limitations 983
Tao: the Universal Mind 775
Tauḥīd: the Divine Unity 852
The Christ in the Heart 441–442
The Divine Unity Mantra 1359
The Eternal is One 512–514
The Fields of Life (the Great Breath) 1165
The Hasidim 648–649
The Omnipresent God 1108–1109
The One 1686–1687
The One and Only 839
The One God of All 869
The One God of All Religions 110
The One God over All 432
The One in Trinity, Trinity in One 1342
The One Transcendental Reality 515
The Path of Non-Duality 762
The Source of Unity 433
The Spiritual Regeneration of the world 991
The Spiritual Warrior 455
The State of Unity of the Psyche 1383
The Unity-Field of Being (graph) 1009
To Love God and the World 1392–1393
You Are the World 1390–1391
Zen is acting from the State of Unity 756

Universal Consciousness. *See also* Cosmic Consciousness, God-Consciousness
As expressed by Jesus 721
The Soul manifesting through the Crown Centre 1194

Universal Mind. *See* One Mind, Cosmic Mind, Mahat, Tao

Universal Self. *See* Ātman, Paramātman

Unmana, Unmani
Chinnamastā: the Headless Goddess 1581
The thought-less state 1174

Upaniṣad
Definition 532
How to apply the Upaniṣadic Mantras 1214
The Eastern Heart 448
The scriptures were heard in deep meditation 1216
The Upaniṣadic Mantrams 546–547
The Upaniṣads (brief introduction) 545

Uparati
The Six Mental Qualifications 1149

Upāsanā-Mūrti
Spiritual discipline, form or image 1269

Uriel
Hebrew Angelic Names Meditation 1462
Hebrew Divine Words for Healing 1456

Utkrāntiḥ Siddhi
The power of levitation 590

V

Vadhū
The Vadhū-Mantra 1538
Vadhū Bīja 1548

Vāgīśvarī
A Name of Lalitā, the Goddess 1577

Vāhan
A means of transportation in these worlds 533

Vaikharī
The Mātangī-Mantra 1535
Vaikharīvāk: physical sound 1577

Vairāgya
Divine Indifference or Dispassion 1330
Qualifications for Discipleship 1149

Vaiśya
The Trading Class (caste) 378

Vāk
Stages of descent of the Divine-Voice 1577
The Action of the Primordial Sound (graph) 165
The Path of Mantra and the Goddess 1490
Vāg-Bhāva Bīja 1550
Vāk: the Divine Speech 118
Vākya: Divine Speech, Divine Reason 1470

Valhalla
The lower heavens 65

Vāṁ
Potent Vibrations: Bīja-Mantra 1544

Vānaprastha
Periods of Life in Vedic India 907

Vareṇyaṁ
Definition 1610

Varṇa
Definition 378
The letters of Śrī-Vidyā 1523

Vas
Grail: the symbol for Spiritual Regeneration 1511

Vāsanā. *See also* Saṁskāra
Held by the World Mother 1502
Known in the state of Saṁyama 583
Saṁskāra and Vāsanā 251
To Achieve Liberation 1177
Vāsanā-Kṣaya: subconscious renewal 1236
Your karmic disposition 1330

Vaśinī
The Mistress, the Ruler of all things 1537

Vasiṣṭha
Yoga Vasiṣṭha: "the Most Excellent Yoga" 525

Vaśitva
The General Powers 581

Vasudeva
The Indwelling God 1288

Vāyu
The Air Element 26
The fivefold Life-force 589
Vāyu Bīja 1546

Veda
Definition 532
Veda Bīja 1542

Vegetable Kingdom
The Sevenfold Earth-Evolution 169

Vengeance
Jewish understanding of Karma 648
Old Testament concepts of God 104
The law of the jungle 993
The old karmic pattern 1139

Venus
The Eternal Feminine 469

Verbal prayer
The Stages of Prayer 1253

Verbum
The Cosmic Christ 662–663

Via Positiva, Via Negativa
The Twofold Way 1465

Vibhūti. *See also* Siddhi, Powers, Miracles
Definition 277
Divine Graces and Gifts 578

Vibration. *See also* Sound, Mantra, Divine Name, Logos
All forms are constructed by Sound-Vibration 1648
Divine Name Solar Vibrations 1598
God's Cosmic Symphony 1649
Heaven is Interconnectedness of Vibration 1352
Mind-Waves 1239
Niṣspanda: no-vibration 1243
Ōṁ Śrī: the Holy Vibration 1520
Sound-Vibrations of the Śrī-Vidyā Mantra 1528
Spiritual Evolution is movement into higher vibration 1413
Śrī-Vidyā is the Science of Vibrations 1525
The Ancient Primordial Language of Sound-Vibrations 1026–1027
The Creative and Destructive Power of Sound 201
The Creative Power of the Primordial Language of Sound 1075
The Logos: the Word of God 114–115
The Planes are Vibrations of the Solar Light 1594
The Vibrations you register are your "reality" 1520
The Word, Logos, Voice, Name 1646–1648
Vāk: the Divine Speech 118
Vibration and Mantra 1518–1519
Worlds within Worlds 886
Your bodies must be raised in vibration 571

Victim-consciousness
Let Go of the Past 1241
The Principle of Choice 1380–1381
Victim-consciousness is unnecessary 1401

Videhā-Mukti
Definition 1237
Without-the-body Liberation 503

Vidyā
Vidyā-Śakti: the Energy of the Goddess 1487
What is Wisdom? 1685

Vigyāna Bhairava Tantra
The One-Hundred-and-Twelve 946–966

Vihāyasa Siddhi
Powers of Divine Descent 599

Vijñānamāyākośa
Coverings over the Self 38

Vikaraṇā Bhāva Siddhi
The power of bodiless perception 598

Vimāna. *See also* UFOs
The Enduring Vimānas 284
Vimāna: a vehicle controlled by the mind 283
Vimāna-Vidyā: definition 272
Vimāna People and Human Destiny 283
Vimānika: the science of building airships 284

Vimarśa
Experienced at highest stages of Yoga 526

Violence
Ahiṁsā: non-violence 566
Death-experience of the suicide and the murdered 404–405
The Hell Condition 406–407
The Masculinization of Children 478–479
The Warrior seeks Peace not War 986
Violence and War: effects on children 486

Vipassana
The Pali word for Insight or Intuitive Vision 1221

Vipaśyanā
Definition 30
Definition and description 1221
Mindfulness in the Head 452
Vipaśyanā Yoga: Internal Observation 1222–1223

Virgin Goddess
Historical examples 105
The True Feminine 1516
The Virgin and the Mother 144
The Virgin Mother 671

Virgin Mary. *See also* Mary, Our Lady
and the mythical Divine Family 105
Names of the Being of Light 417
The Birth of the Light in the Heart 718
The Immaculate Heart of Mary, Our Lady 1513
The Primordial Mother Sea 144
The Virgin Mother confused with the mother of Jesus 671
Virgo Marīa: the Virgin Mary 1512
Virgo Potens: Virgin All-Powerful 1511

Virtue. *See also* Righteousness
Aphorisms of the Spiritual Warrior 1079–1099
Beyond Heaven 1234
Fight Evil with Good 993
Integrity and Perfection 1005

Objectives of Magic 363
Qualities of the Spiritual Warrior 970
Śat-Sampatti: the Six Virtues 1149
Sila: virtuous conduct 813
Spontaneous Benevolence 985
Ṭarīqat: the beginning of the Mystic Path 831
The Feminine Virtues 468–469
The need to practise the virtues 563
The Seven Qualities to enter Paradise 813
The Ten Mahāyāna Precepts 814
The Warrior of the Light 984
The Warrior seeks Peace not War 986
Virtue and the afterlife 411
Virtus: definition 411, 666

Virtues (Hierarchy)
Christian Classification of the Hierarchies 192

Vīrya
Definition 411

Vision. *See* Seeing, Perception

Viṣṇu. *See also* Brahmā-Viṣṇu-Śiva
A Name for the Sun-God 1608
Derivation 113
Viṣṇu Bīja 1544

Viṣṇugranthi. *See also* Hṛdayagranthi
Knots of Consciousness 445

Viṣṇu-Mūrti
The Personal God present in your Heart 1291

Visualization. *See* Seeing

Viśuddha Cakra. *See also* Throat Centre
General description 48
The Heart and the Energy Centres 1332
Viśuddha: definition 48

Viśvakarman
The Universal Creator-God 1588

Viśva-Rūpa
The Body of God (Cosmic-Form) 1129, 1327

Viśva Yoga
Uniting with the Solar Logos 1604

Vitae Patrum
Records of Early Christianity 642–643

Vital body. *See* etheric-physical body

Vivasvata
A Name for the Solar Logos 1658, 1665

Viveka
Qualifications for Discipleship 1149

Vivekajam Jñānam
Exalted Consciousness 592, 596

Voice. *See also* Logos, Divine Name, Śabda, Nāda
Ākāśa-Vāṇī: the Voice of Heaven 590
The Melodious Voice of Quan Yin 1509
The Living-Voice is Śabda-Brahman 1615
The Voice of God 864–865
The Word, Logos, Voice, Name 1646–1648
Vāk: the Divine Speech 118

Voices in the ear
Involuntary possession 310–311

Void. *See also* Formlessness, Emptiness, Śūnyatā
Created out of the Void 51
Meditating on the Void 801
Stand in the Void 1091
Śūnyatā: the Void 503
The Fullness of the Void 23

Voodoo
Animation of astral shells 81
A form of Black Magic 364
Black Magic descended from Atlantis 274
Yogic Powers and Psychism 579

Vowels
47 The Primordial Sound Language 1025–1076
Cosmic Tuning-In: the "I" Sound 1652
Hebrew Vowels were kept secret 1457
Personality Integration Chart (graph) 1333
The Vowels 1030–1040
The Vowels in the Heart 1303

Vṛndāvana
The Paradise Condition of the Heart 448–449

Vṛtti
Definition 536, 538, 1242

Vyāna
An aspect of the fivefold Life-force 589

W

Wakeful mind. *See* lower mind, Kāma-Manas

Wāqif
The charitable workers 836

War
Beyond War 1098
Religious wars 834, 838
Resulting from the Aquarian energies 1708
Scenes of Battle 1158
Stillness before Battle 1095
The Righteous Fight 1092
The Warrior seeks Peace not War 986
True War 985
Violence and War: effects on children 486
Wars in Heaven 210–211, 271

Warrior
45 The Spiritual Warrior 969–1000
46 Warrior Training 1001–1024
47 The Primordial Sound Language 1025–1076
48 The Warrior Code 1077–1102

What is the Spiritual Warrior?
Beyond War 1098
Qualities of the Spiritual Warrior 970
The Law of your Being 976
The Warrior, the Sage, the Ruler 972–973
The Warrior of the Light 984
The Warrior seeks Peace not War 986
True War 985
Warriors of the Sun 1618
Warrior Jesus 908
Who can sing praises for the Noble Warrior? 1102

Warrior Knowledge
Conditioned Thinking 1084
Light 978–979
Mind-Only 974–975
Mind in Body 988
Reincarnation and Freedom 998
The Four Degrees of Knowledge 1003
The Invisible Government 980
The Law of Action 992–993
The Significance of Warrior Greetings 1023
The Three Forces of the Warrior 996–997
The Unity-Field of Being (graph) 1009
What is Initiation? 1007

The Warrior Path
Action and Stillness: the Supreme Way 1083
Action and the Spiritual Warrior 994
Between the Two Extremes, Find the Middle Point 1100
Be Tranquil 987
Cosmic Sensitivity 1009
Development of the Spiritual Warrior 971
Family and Duty 998–999
Fight Evil with Good 993
From Darkness into Light 982–983
Integrity and Perfection 1005
Is there a Plan in your Life? 1000
Look out for the One 1004
Monks and Disciples 991
No Anger, No Enemies 986
Overactive Mind 990
Persevering to the End until Final Liberation 1101
Primordial Balance 995
Skill in Action 989
Surpassing your own Limitations 983
The Active and Passive Way 1011
The Code of the Spiritual Warrior 1101
The Righteous Fight 1092
The Structure of the Warrior School 1006–1007
The Warrior Code: a Guide for Living 1078
The Warrior Path 1002–1003
To Enter the Way of the Warrior 1004
What do you Seek out of Life? 975

Warrior Practice. *See also* Primordial Sound Language
Acting from the Centre: Spontaneous Benevolence 985
Action in the Transcendent 1080
Aphorisms of the Spiritual Warrior 1079–1099
Connecting to the Silent Source of Creation 1008
Facing the Evil Mind 1087
From Action into Stillness, from Stillness into Action 1016
Getting in Touch with your Inner Feminine 1010–1011
How to find Peace and Joy through Meditation 1013
Meditation and the Joy of Living 1012–1013
Meditation in Action 1019

Mindfulness: the Warrior Within 1017
Open-Eyes Meditations for the Warrior 1018
Resting in the No-Mind State of the Absolute 1014–1015
Stand in the Void 1091
Stillness before Battle 1095
The "No-Mind" 990
The Power of Yielding 1088
The Practice of Grounding 1005
The Silence of the Warrior 1008
To bring about Unity and avoid separation 455
Understanding your Work in Silence 1024
Warrior Breathing 1020–1022
Warrior Breathing Techniques to Develop Internal Strength 1022
Warrior Calming Breathings 1021

Wāṣif
Those who praise God continually 836

Watcher. *See also* Witness, Draṣṭā
The Silent Watcher Meditation 1388
The Watcher 1212

Water
Mountains, Clouds and Water 783
The Water Element 26
Varuṇa Bīja 1544
Waters of Life 593
Waters of Space (Nārāyaṇa) 167

Wesak festival
The Triumph of the Buddha 1722

White Magic. *See* magic

Wijd
Illumination of the Heart 857

Will, Will-power. *See also* Free Will
Dangers of the Way of the Will 428–429
Qualities of the Spiritual Warrior 970
Ray 1: Will, Power 56
The first aspect of the Sūtrātma 491
The first stream of Spiritual Energy 972–973
The Three Forces of the Warrior 996–997

Wisdom
70 Buddhi Yoga: Liberation by Wisdom 1679–1704
Belief and Experience 676–677
Buddha gave Mankind Wisdom 1270
Buddhi: the Ocean of Wisdom 84
Faith and Wisdom 849
How do you acquire Wisdom? 1696
Practice for Wisdom 1700–1701
Qualities of the Spiritual Warrior 970
Ray 2: Love, Wisdom 56
Sophia: the Wisdom Mind 146
Symbolized by the Serpent or Dragon 142
The Essence of Wisdom 1680–1684
The Hall of Wisdom 1149
The Love of Wisdom 1694
The Path to Wisdom 1702–1704
The Soul-Power 1305
The Three Forces of the Warrior 996–997
The Wisdom Language 1760
The Wisdom of the Goddess 1525
To be taught Wisdom 353
Western words for "Wisdom" 1354
What does it mean to search for Wisdom? 387
What is Wisdom? 1685
Wisdom: the Light Path 1354
Wisdom and Understanding 439

Wisdom-Mind. *See* Buddhi-Manas, Mind of Light, Prajñā

Witchcraft. *See also* Psychism, Magic
Dangers of Black Witchcraft 371
Yogic Powers and Psychism 579

Witness. *See also* Watcher, Draṣṭā
Draṣṭā: the Seer 542
Sākṣī: the Witness 1212
The Fourth State 499
Vipaśyanā: Internal Observation 1221–1223

Womb
The Golden Womb (graph) 42

Women. *See also* Feminine Principle
Discrimination by Piscean religions 384
Female Buddhas 1110
Future Masters of Tantra 944
Suppressed by caste system 378
The Female Dominant 924–925
The Feminine Heart 925
The Feminine Suppressed 910

Word. *See also* Logos, Divine Name
Āuṁ, Ōṁ, Nāda 550–551
God's Cosmic Symphony 1649
Manifests through the Avatāras 664
Meditation on the Sacred Word 1216–1217
Mistranslated as the Bible 663
Tantric meditations on the Word 951–952
The Action of the Primordial Sound (graph) 165
The Cosmic Christ 662–663
The Creative Power of the Primordial Language of Sound 1075
The Descent of the Word (graph) 118
The Heart is the door to the Word of God 438
The Logos: the Word of God 114–115
The three stages of manifestation of the Word 1353
The Universal Christ 440
The Voice of God (Sūfī) 864–865
The Word, Logos, Voice, Name 1646–1648
The Word (Metanoia) 1455
What is the Name? 1259

Work
Zen Work 810

Worldly consciousness
Art and the Follies of Man 470
In Bondage to the Mind 238
Liberation from Worldly Consciousness 1233
Protagonists of Ignorance 382–383
Separatism and the Law of Love 386
Some Human Evils 384–385
The Breakdown of Family 473
The Education System 480
The Masculinization of Children 478–479
The Ordinary Mind 896–897
The Way of the World 380
Types of Humanity 376
Where are your Wisemen? 387
Zen and the World 758–759

World Mother. *See also* Goddess, Kuṇḍalinī
8 Kuṇḍalinī and the Goddess 141–158
21 The Call of the World Mother 467–488
63 The Heart of the Divine Mother 1491–1514
Madonna and Child (graph) 469
Madonna: the Mother Principle 470
Śrī Jagadambā: the Mother of the World 1498–1499
The Breath of the Divine Mother 142
The Divine Bipolarity 471
The Feminine Virtues 468–469
The Mother of the World 147
The Virgin and the Mother 144
The World Mother of Compassionate Heart 145

Worry
Overstimulated Throat Centre 1431

Worship
Idol-Worship 655
Seged (Aramaic) 1341
The Magic of Ritual Worship 366–371
To Worship Jesus... 680
To Worship the Divine Incarnations 1270–1272
To Worship the Sun 1586
Worship only the Divine Self 1226

Wu
Terms of Awakening 766
Wu-Hsin: no-mind 763

Wu-Wei
Action in stillness or not-doing 1133
Nirvāṇa is Wu-Wei 100
The Not-Doing of the Eternal 766

Wuqūf-Qalbī
Awareness of the Heart 848

Y

Yahweh, Yahveh. *See also* IHVH, Yehovah
Christian Meditation on the Holy Breath 1346
Pronunciation of IHVH 1460
The Vowels in the Heart 1303

Yajña
Antar-Yajña: Inner Worship 1129
Definition 30
Heart Action 1331
On the Wings of Devotion 1129
Ritual Magic 366
Yajña Bīja 1551

Yāṁ
Potent Vibrations: Bīja-Mantra 1546

Yama
Definition 562, 563
Stage One of Aṣṭāṅga Yoga 566–567

Yang. *See* Yin and Yang

Yantra
Activities of Yoga-Mārga 520
Definition 1571
Meditation with a Seed 1186

Yaqīn
The Five Stages of Certainty (Arabic) 895
The Light of Certainty 848

Yehovah. *See also* IHVH, Yahweh
Derivation and pronunciation 106
Jehovah Aloah Va Daath: the Christ in the Heart 441
Pronunciation of IHVH 1460
The "jealous" God 104
The Eternal One confused with a tribal god 106
Translated as "the Lord" 121, 474, 1460

Yekhidah
The Hebrew I AM 1458

Yeshua, Yeheshua
Hebrew Divine Words for Healing 1456
Jesus: the Fire of Love 1725
Jesus Christ, Son of Man 668
Meditations in the Heart Centre 1294
Names of the Great Master Jesus 661
The Evolution of Christian Prayer 713
The Gnostic Teachings 1108
The Jesus Mantra and the Sacred Heart Initiation 1356
The Only Son of God? 669
To Call upon Jesus 679
Variations of the Name of Jesus 1356
Yeheshuah: the Christ-Child-Light in the Heart 718–719
Yeshua: the Secret Hebrew Name 1276–1277
Yeshua is you, the Human Soul 443

Yeheshuvah
The Rose of Love and the Cross of Light 1357

Yesod
The Kabbalistic Tree of Life 358–359

Yielding
The Power of Yielding 1088

Yin and Yang
Mountains, Clouds and Water 783
The Zen Master according to Lao Tzu 780–781
Yin, Yang, Tao 476–477

Yoga
23 The Goal of Yoga 519–530
24 Gems from Patañjali's Yoga Sūtras 531–558
25 Aṣṭāṅga Yoga 559–576
26 The Yoga of Miraculous Powers 577–606
70 Buddhi Yoga: Liberation by Wisdom 1679–1704
What is Yoga?
Know Yourself 604
Samādhi: the Goal of Yoga 574–575
The Goal of Yoga (graph) 521
The Great Way (conclusion) 605
The School of Yoga seeks to escape 1121
The Three Stages of Yoga 528
The Ultimate Reality is the Meaning of Life 526–527
The Upaniṣads 545
Yoga: definition 30, 180, 520
Yoga-Vidyā: definition 523
Yoga and Religion 527
Yoga-Mārga: the Path of Union 520
You don't lose yourself in Yoga 381

Aspects of Yoga

Bhakti Yoga: Divine Union by Devotion 1128
Haṭha Yoga and Rāja Yoga 524–525
Jñāna Yoga: the Path of Mental Effort and Knowledge 1124
Karma Yoga: Divine Union by Action 1132–1133
Kriyā Yoga: Union through Action 535
Rāja Yoga: Divine Union by Meditation 1126–1127
Suṣūpti Yoga: Yoga of the Dream State 276, 299
The Activities of Yoga-Mārga 520
The Dividing of Yoga 522–523
The Science of Cosmic Consciousness 1124
Viśva Yoga: Cosmic Union 1604
Yoga Vasiṣṭha: the Most Excellent Yoga 525

Yoga Practice

Āuṁ, Ōṁ, Nāda 550–551
Building the Bridge of Light 554–555
Modern Yoga Practice 576
The Art of Alignment 1202
The Attitude for Yoga 558
The Esoteric Mantram 551
The Path of Hearing 553
The Path of Seeing 552
The Upaniṣadic Mantrams 546–547
To Attain the State of Yoga 530
To meditate on the Sūtras 549
Yoga Bīja 1549
Yoga in Cosmic Consciousness 1125

Aṣṭāṅga Yoga 559–576

Beyond Āsana and Prāṇāyāma 573
Brahmacarya misconceived 567
Modern Yoga Practice 576
Pāda II Sūtra 29 562
Pāda II Sūtra 30 563
Pāda II Sūtra 31 565
Pāda II Sūtra 32 564
Samādhi: the Goal of Yoga 574–575
Śauca: Purity 570
Śiva Yoga of the Liṅga Purāṇa 561
Stage One of Aṣṭāṅga Yoga (Yama) 566–567
Stage Three of Aṣṭāṅga Yoga (Yoga) 572
Stage Two of Aṣṭāṅga Yoga (Niyama) 568–569
Tapas: Spiritual Purification 571
Yoga by Eight Steps (introduction) 560

The Yoga of Miraculous Powers 577–606

Categories of Powers 579
Cosmic Powers 602–603
Further Powers 598
Knowledge of Past Lives 601
Pāda III Sūtras 16-56 (Saṁyama on…) 583–597
Pāda IV Sūtra 1 578
Powers by Drugs? 578
Powers of Divine Descent 599
Powers of the Dream State 600
Saṁyama 582
Saṁyama and Parapsychology 582
Seek not Powers 581
The General Powers 580–581
To Taste the Elixir of Life 593
Yogic Powers and Psychism 579

Patañjali's Yoga Sūtras 531–558

Pāda I Sūtra 2 536
Pāda I Sūtra 3 536–537
Pāda I Sūtra 4 538–539
Pāda I Sūtra 23 548
Pāda I Sūtra 27 549
Pāda I Sūtra 30 556–557
Pāda II Sūtra 1 535
Pāda II Sūtra 20 542–543
Pāda II Sūtra 21 544
Pāda II Sūtra 29 562
Pāda II Sūtra 30 563
Pāda II Sūtra 31 565
Pāda II Sūtra 32 564
Pāda III Sūtras 16–56 583–597
Pāda IV Sūtra 1 578
Pāda IV Sūtra 17 540
Pāda IV Sūtra 18 541
The Sage Patañjali 534
The Yoga Sūtras (overview) 532–533
To meditate on the Sūtras 549

Buddhi Yoga 1679–1704
Evolution, the Plan, the Path 1688–1692
Practice for Wisdom 1700–1701
Right Practice 1696–1697
The Enlightened 1702
The Essence of Wisdom 1680–1684
The Great Mantram of Buddhi Yoga 1682
The Love of Wisdom 1694
The One 1686–1687
The Path to Wisdom 1702–1704
The Secret of Meditation 1698
The Sevenfold Practice 1698
The True Teachers 1694–1695
To Experience Spiritual Ecstasy 1683
What is Wisdom? 1685

Yoga-Agni-Mayam-Śarīram
A transformed physical body 1310

Yogeśvara
Lords of Yoga 1129

Yogī, Yoginī
Avoid the Errors of East and West 1122–1123
Is Renunciation Necessary? 1119
Non-Action Misinterpreted 1120
One who has attained Nirvāṇic Consciousness 102
The Knowers and the Yogīs 377
The Yoginī-Mantra 1538
Yoga by Eight Steps 560
Yogī, Yogin, Yoginī: definition 523
Yogī: definition 513

Yoni
Yoni Bīja 1550

Yuga
Definition 168

Z

Zazen
Definition 807
General description 809
Zen Sitting 798

Zen
35 The Spirit of Zen 751–770
36 The Eternal Tao 771–784
37 Zen Meditation 785–804
38 The Path of Zen 805–824

What is Zen?
A "Godless" Religion? 754–755
A Summary of Zen 820–823
Christian Mysticism and Zen 630
Christian Zen 765
Derivation of the word "Zen" 752, 807
False Zen 756–757
Origins of Zen 752
The Path of Non-Duality 762
The Path of Zen or Tantra 1121
What is Zen? 753
Zen and the World 758–759
Zen is not Psychism 757

The Goal of Zen
Enlightenment 766
Satori: the Experience of Illumination 816–817
Terms of Awakening 766
The Goal of Zen 760
The Goal of Zen (graph) 761
The Great Wisdom of the Other Shore 769
Your Original Face 87
When the Mind is Still 768

Tao: the One Mind
Messengers of the One Mind 764
No-Mind and the One Mind 763
Tao: the Great I AM 774
Tao: the Supreme Way 776–778
Tao: the Universal Mind 775
Tao is Silent 779
What is Tao? 772–773

The Zen Path
Blind Tradition 808
Kyōsaku: the "big stick" 809
Life as a Zen Monk 806
Return to Duty 812
Rules for a Modern Zen Retreat 811
Sesshin: the Zen spiritual intensive 808
Tantra is the Zen of relationship 909
The Four Vows of the Bodhisattva 814
The Japanese Zen Retreat (terminology) 807–809
The Noble Eightfold Path of the Buddha 815
The Seven Qualities to enter Paradise 813
The Steps to the Experience of Zen (Sanskrit) 813
The Ten Mahāyāna Precepts 814
The Way of the Zen Masters 818

The Zen Master. *See also* Guru, Spiritual Masters
The Enlightenment of Teh Shan 770
The Governor and the Bird Nest 815
The Masters on Meditation 804
The Way of the Zen Masters 818–819
The Zen Master 782
The Zen Master according to Lao Tzu 780–781
Two modern Zen Masters 782
Zenji: a Zen Master 807

Zen Practice
Action Zen 802
A Summary of Zen Meditation 802–803
Balanced Practice 810
Meditating on Kōans and Hua-Tous 796–797
Meditating on the Void 801
Mindfulness of Breathing 794
Mountains, Clouds and Water 783
Quietly Seeing 786
Salutation to the Buddha 795
Sayings of Lao Tzu on Zen Meditation 799
Shikantaza 800–801
The Attitude of Zen 786
The Masters on Meditation 804
The Thought of Enlightenment 767
When the Mind is Still 768
Zazen: Zen Sitting 798, 809
Zen Listening 787–793
Zen Silence 790–793

Zendō
Zen definition 807

Zikr
Prayer in the Heart 846
The repetition of a prayer 868

Zodiac
Precessional Age and Zodiacal Age 725
Zodiacal History 833
Zodiakos: definition 279

Zoe
Gnostic Christian definition 737

Zōhar
Definition 118

Zombie
Astral shells 81

Zuhd
The sixth stage of the Journey of the Heart 856

∞

APPENDIX D

The Foundation for Higher Learning

A New Age Spiritual School

In this School you have to understand the true nature of things

For the past three thousand years or so, both in the East and in the West, the Spiritual Path has been described as suitable only for those who have "renounced" the world, such as a celibate or a monk (BRAHMACĀRĪ), or a celibate ascetic (ŚRAMANA), or one who dwelled alone in silence in a forest, never speaking (MUNI), or one who has given up or suppressed all desires for physical life (SANNYĀSĪ), or a homeless wanderer with no fixed abode of any sort (SĀDHU), or one who was completely dead to Physical Plane existence (AVADHŪTA). They all had one thing in common: they hated the physical body and the Physical World (which to them was evil or just a colossal nuisance and trouble), and they thought that domestic life, family, children, work, duties to be performed in the world, were opposing the Salvation Process. This is in the past. Think about it, recognize it, for there are still people who live in the past and teach this.

Another misconception was that if you were born a woman you were decidedly unlucky and Salvation for you in this life was practically impossible; you had to wait for a life when you were incarnated into a male body. All of this is of the past and is profoundly untrue. You, as a Living Soul in the Kingdom of Souls, are neither male nor female, but belong to the species of Man, Mankind, Humankind, as distinct from the DEVAS or Angelkind, or the SURA, the Gods.

In this School you have to *understand* a lot of things. You have to understand the true nature of things, not just blindly follow a past tradition. A vast Teaching has been given for this purpose which does not simply imitate some past tradition or follow some past rules, regulations and doctrines. What you have been given is the Living Truth as it is *Now*. Can you comprehend this? Can you appreciate it?

Spirituality Past and Future 1104
Piscean and New Age Spirituality 1706
The Feminine Suppressed 910
The Sexless Soul 920
Female Buddhas 1110
The Mystery Schools and Āśramas 1148

Our mission in the world is to teach the Spiritual Principles, the Divine Laws of Life, to Mankind. Herein lies our group-purpose. We must help to show the Way as it is emerging in this coming New Age—not how it was in the past, but what is required *Now*. This School is here to help *disseminate* this new Teaching, this new way of understanding the Eternal Truth about God, Man and the Universe, to those Souls on this planet who are *ready* for the Spiritual Journey.

Our task is the Spiritual Regeneration of the world 991

In this School, *you* are responsible for your development. You are responsible for studying the Teaching and then *applying* it in your life, in your *present circumstances.* You do not have to leave the world or "renounce" the world. You have to live *in* the world but not be *of* the world (that is, not be worldly). Nobody is going to chase after you or hurry you up. You must discipline *yourself.*

Our School is for *mature* Spiritual Seekers, not for the curious, the bored or the worldly-minded, or those who want to do the Path as a spare-time hobby. Nor is it for psychics, mediums, channellers, or so-called clairvoyants and clairaudients (euphemistically called "sensitives", "intuitives", "mystics", "light-workers", and so forth in the New Age scene). These are *not* true Visionaries, Intuitives or Mystics (with Buddhic Consciousness). These are people possessing a little bit of astral development, that is all.

In this School nobody will tell you how to run your personality life

You are a Living Soul, forever dwelling in the Formless Worlds, who has incarnated temporarily in your present personality. In this School, therefore, nobody will tell you how to run your personality life—whether you should get married or not, whether you should have children or not, whether you should be in a relationship or not, whether you should work or not, or whether you should have a responsible position in life. *You* must decide these things yourself, intelligently, carefully considered and according to your Karma—the past burdens you carry with you in this life.

In the past, the Spiritual Schools, Gurus and Teachers completely interfered with your personality life; you were told continually what to do and what not to do. Today, in this School, you are considered to be an adult (spiritually) who is self-responsible, who recognizes the Vision or Goal and is able to work seriously towards it. And if you make mistakes, then you calmly fix them up, for nobody is perfect on the personality level. Only the Soul within you is Pure Light.

When you join this School, you do so with *freedom*, as your *inner choice*, because *intuitively* you feel that it is right for you, that it has the right Message. It is one's *Soul* that is guided to this School.

Do the Work yourself 1153
Rely on your Inner Self 1226
Channelling or Soul-Wisdom? 327
The Aquarian Teachers 1147
The True Teachers 1694

Mission Statement of the Foundation for Higher Learning

1

To teach the *Oneness of Life*, from the tiniest atom and particle to a vegetable, an animal, a human being, an angel, a Planetary Logos, a Solar Logos, and a vast Galactic Lord. All are One and are part of the One, the Boundless Self, the Everlasting Godhead, the Immeasurable Reality, the Boundless Immutable Being, the Universal Consciousness, the Infinite Mind.

Mind-Only 974
The One 1686

2

To teach the reality of an *unconscious evolution* (the Force of Nature) and the Path of *Conscious Evolution* which begins when an entity has reached sufficient Intelligence for self-determination and self-effort towards Higher States of Consciousness.

Vertical Evolution and the Path 174
Evolution, the Plan, the Path 1688

3

To teach the existence of a *Superhuman Evolution*, the Kingdom of God, consisting of those of the Angelic and Human Kingdoms who have completed their Conscious Evolution and have moved *above* the status of Man and Angel, and who now form the *Spiritual Hierarchy* of our planet and solar system, functioning mainly in invisible realms, on the formless levels of Being.

This Hierarchy is *not* the channelled "masters", "angels" and "spirit-guides" of the channellers and mediums (even if they use the names of the real Masters of the real Spiritual Hierarchy). Nor should this Spiritual Hierarchy of the invisible realms of our planet and solar system be confused with the ordinary, discarnate humans or the ordinary, native Angelic Kingdoms inhabiting those realms. These Human Masters and Angel Adepts are as far above the "normal" man and woman in Evolution and Consciousness as a human is above an animal, or as an angel is above a tree.

The Invisible Government 980
Saṅgha: the Spiritual Hierarchy 394
The Function of the Spiritual Hierarchy 1720
The Creative Hierarchies 187

4

To utilize the *English Language* as the general medium for communicating the Teachings, as English has been used by the Spiritual Hierarchy since 1875 to give out the Esoteric and Spiritual Doctrines. While other languages (such as French, German, Dutch or Russian) can be used when teaching, the original Message is in English.

5

To teach and apply the *Sanskrit Language* (SAṀSKṚTA: consecrated, polished) for the definition of spiritual states, conditions or realities, as the most advanced language on this planet for Spiritual Understanding, supported by Hebrew, Arabic, Latin and Greek. Each of these languages is used also for chanting and creating specific types of spiritual vibrations.

God's Writing 1761
The Two Applications of Mantra 1219

Our Sacred Music and Language

Within the Foundation for Higher Learning we have hundreds of Initiatory Mantrams and Mantra-chants in Sanskrit, Hebrew, Arabic, Latin and Greek. These are considered to be Sacred Languages.

- Latin has *Earth*-power.
- Chinese has *Water*-power.
- Hebrew and Arabic have *Fire*-power.
- Greek has *Air*-power.
- Sanskrit has *Light*-power.

The important point is that *none* of our Initiatory Mantrams or sacred chants have anything to do with the past. The Mantrams for Initiation I have renewed, enlivened with the new Energies of the Now. They are *not* connected vibrationally with any past religion, sect, cult or tradition. This is important: they do not carry any old energies with them.

The procedure for creating new chants is that first I give the Mantras to the musicians, then during retreats the new chants are created and I check them for their *mantric effect*. That is, the music has to match the MANTRA-ŚAKTI. Because it is done *now,* none of our sacred chants carry the old energies with them.

There will be a *new* Sacred Language in the future, but the time has not yet come for its manifestation.

The Cosmic Elements 26
Language of the Gods 200
The Wisdom Language 1760

6

To teach the *Art of Meditation* as the natural Way for the unfoldment of the Human Plant (Man), as an absolute necessity in Spiritual Life, and only those true forms of meditation which will spiritualize Man. This has nothing to do with forms of meditation for "relaxation" or "personal development", or for more success in this world, or for name, fame or worldly power. Such will only tie you further into SAṀSĀRA, the Wheel of Birth and Death in this world, or Reincarnation.

The Science of Meditation 1173
Meditation Practice 1201

7

The old Schools and systems of Spirituality were divided into:

- Heart: devotion, feeling, emotion.
- Head: intellectualism, thought, consciousness.
- Action: service, selfless helpfulness.

In the past, these Schools or types of Spirituality were clearly divided and you did one or the other. Today, in this School, you live and practise *all three* of them. You cultivate *Universal Love* (Heart), *Enlightened Understanding* (Head) and *Selfless Service* to the Teacher, the Group, the larger Human Family, and your own family if that is your karmic lot.

The Threefold Way 1236
Heart Knowing 1286

8

Members of our School should understand *Group Work* and *Group-Consciousness* and refrain from criticism and destructive attitudes of mind towards the Teacher and other group members, to lessen their burden of life rather than increase it.

If you are given a position of *responsibility* in our School (such as teaching, administration, music or core-group) you fulfil that Duty (DHARMA) cheerfully and happily, to the best of your abilities. You might not realize that such positions are an *extreme privilege* and not a burden; through them your Soul can help to create a better world for all Mankind. You are a small cog in a large wheel, but all large wheels depend on the small cogs.

Group Work 1146
What is True Service? 1714
The Evil of Criticism 1156
To Become a True Renunciate 257

9

Our School is *non-political, non-tribal, non-nationalistic.* Politics, tribalism and nationalism have divided Mankind for thousands of years, causing wars, conflict and exploitation. While there are differences in human traits, characteristics, habit-patterns and evolutionary attainments, Mankind on this planet is one Family. The best policy is that which benefits the most. Similarly, we don't encourage *fanatical, fundamentalist religious beliefs*, as they are the major cause of conflicts, wars, persecutions and sufferings. They are based on out-of-control emotions rather than the Light of Wisdom and the Power of Love. The ultimate Goal is the application of the Universal Love of the Christ-Consciousness for the benefit of all the Children of Man.

Nationalism and Tribalism 385
Religion and Politics 513
Christ-Consciousness 443

10

Our School is continually progressing; therefore, *you must be able to change.* The Ultimate Truth never changes—it cannot—but the way it is presented, taught and released into the Human Consciousness must necessarily change as the planet moves forward in Time and Space and Consciousness. That which has been considered highly esoteric or secret in the past is not necessarily so today, for increasingly larger numbers of people in the world are ready for the serious Spiritual Path. The Soul of Humanity is slowly maturing and, for those who are ready, the Teaching must go out.

The New and Eternal Way 516
Revelation is Continuous 1710

11

Our Spiritual School works along the *Second Ray* line, the Energy of Love and Wisdom, which is the Energy used by the Christ (Love) and the Buddha (Wisdom). This Love-Wisdom Ray is not to be confused with ordinary human "love" and ordinary worldly "knowledge". Our subsidiary Ray is the Sixth Ray, the Ray of the Spiritual Warrior, the Devotee and the Mystic. The Second Ray is Universal, all-embracing, while the Sixth Ray typifies intense individual effort.

The Seven Rays 54
The Buddha and the Christ 1722
To Become a Jīvanmukta in this Lifetime 259

12

The Sevenfold Earth-Evolution 169
The Christ-Hierarchy and Śamballa 396

We endeavour, on this Earth, to materialize the Ideals and Vision of the Spiritual Hierarchy, the Plan for our Humanity on this Earth for its rightful progress as a Kingdom of Nature, sharing in the All-Life. We understand our need to cooperate with the Angelic Kingdom and to be responsible guardians of the Animal and Vegetable Kingdoms. Life is One; its forms of expression are innumerable.

13

Quan Yin: the Mother of Compassion 1507
The Immaculate Heart of Our Lady 1513

We also have a strong link with the feminine aspect of Nature, with the Feminine Consciousness. The feminine side of Nature is best expressed by the two great Feminine AVATĀRAS: Quan Yin of China and Our Lady, Mary, the Mother of Jesus, of ancient Israel. The Goddess, the true Feminine Consciousness of Divine Nature, is:

Self-sacrificing, tender, gentle.

Loving, forgiving, all-embracing, uniting.

Full of Grace, Beauty, Radiance.

Sensitive to Life and all its forms and manifestations.

Nurturing, caring, mothering.

Transforming, inspiring, uplifting.

May She guide us always!